Second Edition

A
WORLD OF
IDEAS

ESSENTIAL READINGS
FOR COLLEGE WRITERS

EDITED BY
LEE A. JACOBUS
University of Connecticut

A Bedford Book
ST. MARTIN'S PRESS · NEW YORK

Library of Congress Catalog Card Number: 85-61296
Manufactured in the United States of America
9 8 7 6 5
f e d c b a
For information, write St. Martin's Press, Inc.,
175 Fifth Avenue, New York, N.Y. 10010
Editorial Offices: Bedford Books of St. Martin's Press,
29 Commonwealth Avenue, Boston, MA 02116

ISBN: 0-312-89221-7

Typography and design: Anna Post
Portraits: Anatoly Dverin and Lyrl C. Ahern
Cover: François Bonvin, Still Life, 1876. National Gallery, London

ACKNOWLEDGMENTS

Aristotle. "Poetics: Comedy and Epic and Tragedy." From Poetics, translated by Gerald F. Else. Copyright © 1967 by the University of Michigan.
Used by permission of the University of Michigan Press.

Acknowledgments and copyrights continue at the back of the book on
page 703, which constitutes an extension of the copyright page.

A
WORLD OF
IDEAS

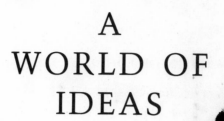

ESSENTIAL READINGS
FOR COLLEGE WRITERS

ALSO WRITTEN OR EDITED BY LEE A. JACOBUS

Improving College Reading, 1967, 1972, 1978, 1983
Aesthetics and the Arts, 1968
Issues and Response, 1968, 1972
Developing College Reading, 1970, 1979
Seventeen from Everywhere: Short Stories from around the World, 1971
Poems in Context (with William Moynihan), 1974
John Cleveland: A Critical Study, 1975
The Humanities through the Arts (with F. David Martin), 1975, 1978, 1982
The Sentence Book, 1976, 1980
The Paragraph and Essay Book, 1977
Sudden Apprehension: Aspects of Knowledge in Paradise Lost, 1976
Longman Anthology of American Drama, 1982
Humanities: The Evolution of Values, 1986
Writing as Thinking, (forthcoming)

PREFACE

When I describe this book to friends, I often say that it includes selections from Plato, Machiavelli, Jefferson, Stanton, Thoreau, Martin Luther King, Malthus, Veblen, Freud, Jung, Horney, Darwin, and nobody less important. Although that is a mild exaggeration, it is very close to the truth. When the first edition was published, I expected that the choice of selections in this book would appeal to only a small minority of people who, like me, think of the first composition course as a chance to introduce the significant ideas of our culture. But soon I found that there was a ground swell of excitement over the thought that freshmen could have in their hands a volume which gathered together a great many thinkers of the first rank from most of the disciplines students would encounter in their college education.

The selections in this volume are all of the highest quality. Each was chosen for its importance, for its range of thought, and for its capacity to sustain discussion and stimulate good writing. Unlike many freshman anthologies, this one does not offer two pages of Bacon, four pages of Thomas Kuhn, and a page-and-a-half of Aristotle. Instead, every writer is represented by as complete a selection as is practicable, averaging something close to fifteen pages. Developing a serious idea takes time. Most students respect the fact that the further they read in the work of an important thinker, the better their grasp of its ideas is.

New in This Edition

A second edition always offers a chance to improve on things. As the acknowledgments below indicate, I had the help and suggestions of almost one hundred fifty users of the book. Invariably, they expressed the hope that I would not let the second edition become more trendy, including current "in" writers. I never intended to do so, but I felt the book had some shortcomings that could be remedied. For one thing, I regretted that more women had not been included in the first edition, and for that reason you will see that the number of selections by women has been doubled, including exceptional pieces by Elizabeth Cady Stanton, Karen Horney, Simone Weil, Virginia Woolf, and Susan Sontag. For another thing, the previous edition did not contain essays on business or economics, and since the ideas of thinkers such as Adam Smith, Thomas Malthus, Thorstein Veblen, John Maynard Keynes, and Kenneth Galbraith affect each of us in our daily life, it was important that I have a chance to include them.

There is a total of thirty-three essays in this edition; the first edition had twenty-eight. A new part, Ideas in the World of Economics, is added to the previous five parts, which include Ideas in the World of Politics, Ideas in the World of Psychology, Ideas in the World of Science, Ideas in the World of Philosophy, and Ideas in the World of the Arts. Eighteen of the essays in this edition are new, and one, Darwin's "Natural Selection," appears from the first edition rather than the fifth edition of *On the Origin of Species*. The advantage is that we see Darwin's first statements of his theories, unblunted by his cautious responses to later critics.

A Text for Writers

Because this is a text for writers, I have provided a number of useful aids to help students grasp the authors' thought and to help them develop their own ideas for their writing. A general introduction called Writing About Ideas discusses the strategies of the careful reader and points the way to developing material to be used in a student's own essays. This part also introduces some rudimentary concepts of rhetoric and describes some of the rhetorical skills of the authors. There is also a sample essay, with a clear discussion of how it was created.

Introductions for Each Selection. Every selection is preceded by a detailed introduction to the life and work of the author as well as a discussion of the selection's primary ideas. The most interesting rhetorical achievements of the selection are identified and discussed with an eye toward helping the student discover how rhetorical techniques can achieve specific effects. These essays all offer useful models for writing: Douglass offers a model for the narrative, Machiavelli and Darwin the example, Bacon the use of enumeration, Wald the analysis of cause and effect. They are the kinds of models which beginning writers find useful: models of thought and models of structure—in other words, the materials of invention and arrangement. My experience is that the third stage of rhetoric, style, must wait, as Milton implied, until greater maturity of judgment.

Suggestions for Discussion and Writing. At the end of each essay is a group of discussion questions designed to be useful outside the classroom. They focus on key issues, key ideas. But they can also stimulate a general discussion. Following them are suggestions for writing which help the student practice some of the rhetorical strategies used in the selection. These suggestions range from very personal, subjective responses to essays that involve research.

Suggestions for Further Reading. At the end of the book, every selection has a list of publications for further reading and research. This is particularly helpful to the student who finds the primary selection involving enough to wish to continue in more depth. The point of the collection is to provide every reasonable assistance to students who wish to deepen their understanding of an author's work.

Instructor's Manual. I have also prepared an extensive instructor's manual with further background on the selections, examples from my own classroom responses to the author, and more suggestions for classroom discussion and student writing. A sentence outline for each selection was carefully prepared by Carol Verburg. These outlines are useful because some of the pieces need going over more than once. A sentence outline can offer good guidance for the cautious student. The idea came from Darwin's own phrase outlines preceding each chapter of his demanding book.

Acknowledgments

This edition is especially indebted to those at Bedford Books of St. Martin's Press who lavished a great deal of care and attention on every detail: Charles Christensen, Joan Feinberg, Elizabeth Schaaf, Chris Rutigliano, Frank Kirk, and Nancy Lyman. I also want to thank Anatoly Dverin and Lyrl Ahern for their wonderful portraits, which have added a special human touch to the book. I also want to thank the students—quite a few of them—who wrote me directly about their experience reading the first edition. Among those instructors who have approached me at conferences was one who taught at a small two-year college in Texas. He told me that his students had been working with the book for a semester and had not yet grown restless or bored: he wanted to know why. My answer is that students respect quality.

Among the professors who respect quality and who were immensely generous in their criticism and praise, the following all provided me with detailed recommendations for making this edition even better than the first. I hope they feel that their efforts were worthwhile. These people are Victoria Aarons, Trinity University; Stephen E. Alford, Nova College; Le Roy E. Annis, University of Puget Sound; Vern Bailey, Carleton College; Craig Barrow, University of Tennessee, Chattanooga; Stephen Bauer, College of New Rochelle; Adrian Beaudoin, Florida Junior College; Helle Bering-Jensen, Tufts University; Boyd U. Berry, Virginia Commonwealth University; Thomas N. Biuso, Colby-Sawyer College; C. S. Blinderman, Clark University; Don Blount, University of Southern Carolina, Aiken; Carol A. Bock, University of Minnesota, Duluth; Jennifer Bradley, UCLA; William K. Buckley, Indiana University Northwest; Neal H. Burns, University of Massachusetts; Margaret N. Butler, Millersville University; William K. Carpenter, Fort Hays State University; Michael Cass, Mercer University; Miriam Cheiken, Nassau Community College; Wilma Clark, University of Wisconsin, Eau Claire; Michael Clarke, Loyola University; Robert W. Cochran, University of Vermont, Burlington; Alfred Cohn, New College of Hofstra; David D. Cooper, University of California, Santa Barbara; Douglas E. Crowell, Texas Tech University; Nancy Daggett, Aims Community College; Carole Kiler Dareski, Keene State College; Elmore J. DeGrange, Southern University, New Orleans; L. Dessner, University of Toledo; Robert Di Chiara, Nassau Community College; John A. R. Dick, University of Texas, El Paso; Marya M. Dubose, Augusta College; Maurice DuQuesnay, University of Southwestern Louisiana; James M. Eldred, University of Illinois, Champaign-Urbana; Judith H. Elmusa, Suffolk University; Audrey Ellwood, Merritt College; Richard Fabrizio, Pace University; J. M. Fenwick, Anne Arundel Community College; Elinor C. Flewellen, Santa Barbara City College; Arend Flick, University of California, Santa Barbara; Jane Follis, Indiana State University, Evansville; Milton P. Foster, Eastern Michigan University; Robert H. Garner, Southern University, New Orleans; Arthur Wayne Glowka, Georgia College; Robert Golden, Rochester Institute of Technology; Ellen Goldner, Brandeis University; George Goodin, SIU; Douglas E. Grohne, Western Illinois University; L. M. Grow, Broward Community College; Rachel Hadas, Rutgers University; James Hafley, St. John's University; Virginia S. Hale, University of Hartford; Michael L. Hall, Centenary College; Evelyn Haller, Doane College; V. B. Halpert, Fairleigh Dickinson University; Judith Hayn, Washburn University; Gary Heinzel, Austin Community College; Jack Hibbard, St. Cloud State University; James E. Hicks, St. Louis University; Gail Houston, UCLA; D. Howard, Mesa College; John Hulsman, Rider College; Ann Hurley, Skidmore College; Vernon Hyles, University of Arkansas; David Ihrman, State University of New York, Binghamton; Ellwood Johnson, Western Washington University; James H. Jones, Northern Michigan University; James Kastely, University of Hawaii, Manoa; Jane Kaufman, University of Akron; Cletus Keating, University of Denver; Jill Averil Keen, University of Wisconsin, Plattesville; Elizabeth Keyser, University of California, Santa Barbara; Kathleen E. Kier, Queens College; James R. Kinzey, Virginia Commonwealth University; Earl D. Kirk, Baker University; Marcelline Krafchick, California State University; Jeanne Krochalis, Pennsylvania State University; John Lamb, Lewis University; William Lenehan, University of Wisconsin; Madelon Lief, Lawrence University; Howard Lord, New College of Hofstra University; Carmine Luisi, Brooklyn College; Raymond Mackenzie, Mankato State University; William T. Maraldo, Texas Lutheran College; Charles Marr, Edinboro University; Nathalie Marshall-Nadel, Nova University; Stephen Mattson, University of California, Santa Barbara; Mary McCord, University of Texas, San Antonio; Jessie McCune, Indiana State; Daniel C. Melnick, Cleveland State University; Kathleen Meyer, North Dakota State University; Terry L. Meyers, College of William and Mary; Lloyd Michaels, Allegheny College; Dennis Moore, University of Iowa, Iowa City; Michael Morrison, UCLA; Jerome J. Notkin, Hofstra University; Leslie Palmer, North Texas State University; James Robert Payne, New Mexico State University; Kathy Phillips, University of Hawaii, Honolulu; James Plath, University of Wisconsin, Milwaukee; Cheryl E. Pridgeon, Florida Atlantic University and College of Boca Raton; Richard K. Priebe, Virginia Commonwealth University; Richard Publow, Illinois Valley Community College; Marc L. Ratner, California State University, Hayward; Richard Reid, Grand Rapids Junior College; J. A. W. Rembert, The Citadel, Charleston; Anne B. Rogers, Centenary College; Dale H. Ross, Iowa State University; John

Rothfork, New Mexico Institute of Mining and Technology; Shirley Samuels, University of California, Berkeley; Keith W. Schlegel, Frostburg State College; Judith Schnee, Bentley College; James E. Schonewise, University of Notre Dame; Philip A. Schreffler, St. Louis Community College, Meramec; Linda G. Schulze, Rutgers University; Elizabeth S. Scott, University of Richmond; Steven R. Serafin, Long Island University; Kathleen Shaw, Modesto Junior College; Gay Sibley, University of Hawaii, Manoa; Carl Singleton, Fort Hays State University; Hassell B. Sledd, Slippery Rock University; Robert A. Smart, Bradford College; Harvey Solganick, Eastfield College; Dorothy Sterpka, University of Connecticut, Hartford; Matthew R. Stewart, Virginia Polytechnic Institute and State University; J. Michael Stitt, University of Nevada, Las Vegas; Richard Stracke, Augusta College; Joyce Suellentrop, Kansas Newman College; Tom T. Tashiro, City College/CUNY; William N. Tingle, University of California, Santa Barbara; Charles P. R. Tisdale, University of North Carolina; Patricia Tobin, Rutgers University; John R. Valone, Sacramento City College; Luise van Keuren, Juniata College; Jane R. Walpole, Piedmont Virginia Community College; Lynn Waterhouse, Trenton State College; Barbara M. Williams, Slippery Rock University; John S. Williams, University of the Pacific, Stockton; Allison Wilson, Jackson State University; William A. Wilson, San Jose State University; William C. Woods, Longwood College; Nancy Yacher, Washburn University; Sally Young, University of Tennessee, Chattanooga; and R. Zwieg, Queens College.

CONTENTS

———⚮———

PART TWO
IDEAS IN THE
WORLD OF ECONOMICS
–191–

PART FIVE

IDEAS IN THE
WORLD OF PHILOSOPHY
–493–

A
WORLD OF
IDEAS

—————◦❧◦—————

ESSENTIAL READINGS
FOR COLLEGE WRITERS

WRITING ABOUT IDEAS

An Introduction to Rhetoric

THE AUTHORS whose selections are presented in this book have one important credential: they have changed the way people think. And that means that they have changed the things people do. Reading their work puts us in touch with our intellectual heritage: part of the excitement of reading these writers is finding the sources of ideas that we have taken for granted. That process helps us decide just what we think is true and why. When Martin Luther King, Jr., wrote his "Letter from Birmingham Jail" to the pastors who seemed opposed to his ideas, one of his purposes was to help them understand what he was doing. If they disagreed with him, he wished to see them articulate their disagreements. If, as he contended, they were in basic agreement with him because of their mutual religious commitment, he demanded that they acknowledge their ideas and come forward to help him. He believed that taking a position on important ideas would produce correspondingly appropriate action. And he was right. Those who agreed with him helped to continue the most important civil rights movement our nation has seen since slavery ended in the 1860s. King's letter dramatically demonstrates that ideas can produce action—which is one obvious reason why education must center on ideas.

The selections in this book were chosen from among the most important works of each author. The six categories from which they were chosen are central to our contemporary concerns and include politics, economics, science, philosophy, psychology, and the arts. Ancients and moderns appear side by side, and every name represents a world of learning and thought.

READING FOR IDEAS

As well as being a rewarding activity in itself, reading for ideas is the first stage of preparation for writing about ideas. The minds represented in the writings in this collection extend their influence through time and beyond national frontiers to help unite us in a community of learning and awareness. But to read these essays well and to derive from them the rewards that can be ours, we must approach them with care and deliberation. We have several goals in mind when reading each essay.

To identify the most important ideas: Look for and comprehend the argument and establish the main points of the essay.

To find points that can be useful in our own essay: Identify the issues with which we can argue and those with which we can agree.

To keep track of our own observations: Note what the essay says and what responses it stimulates in us.

Annotating a Text

Annotations are notes you make as you read. In a sense, they are a dialogue between you and the writer. Though they can take many forms, they usually are underlinings (highlighting) and comments in the margins—which is why this book has generous margins. Learning how to annotate a text sometimes means overcoming reluctance to write in a book. Be daring. Write in your text. Remember that by doing so you will make your own job of writing essays easier and a more natural outcome of your reading.

Imagine as you read that you are writing a commentary on the text and keeping track of what the author is saying. My own approach is to underline key phrases, sometimes in different colors, depending on how important I think they are. Sometimes I write the general subject of a paragraph or a page in the margin at the top to remind me of what the author is focusing on. One of my purposes is to mark up what I am reading sufficiently so that when I review it, I can quickly recall what has been said.

Annotation keeps track both of what the author says and of what our responses are. No one can reduce annotation to a formula—we all do it differently—but it is not a passive act. Reading with a pencil or a pen in hand should become second nature. Without annotations, you often have to reread entire sections of an essay in order to remember the gist of an argument that may once have been clear and understandable but that, after a time lapse, has become part of the fabric of the prose and thus is "invisible." Annotation is the conquest of the invisible; it provides a quick view of the main points that are there.

Some things to aim for in annotation:

Read with a pen or a pencil.

Underline key sentences—for example, definitions and statements of purpose.

Underline key words that appear often.

Note the topic of paragraphs in the margins.

Ask questions in the margins.

Make notes in the margins to remind you to work up ideas later.

Mark passages you might want to quote in your essay.

Keep track of points with which you disagree.

Some sample annotations follow, using the first essay in the book, Niccolò Machiavelli's "The Qualities of the Prince." It is a Renaissance text in translation, which makes it challenging to work with. My annotations appear in the form of underlinings and marginal comments and questions. Only the first few paragraphs appear here, but the entire essay is annotated in my copy of the book.

A Prince's Duty Concerning Military Matters

A prince, therefore, must not have any other object nor any other thought, nor must he take anything as his profession but war, its institutions, and its discipline; because that is the only profession which befits one who commands; and it is of such importance that not only does it maintain those who were born princes, but many times it enables men of private station to rise to that position; and, on the other hand, it is evident that when princes have given more thought to personal luxuries than to arms, they have lost their state. And the first way to lose it is to neglect this art;

[marginal annotation: The prince's profession should be war.]

Examples

and the way to acquire it is to be well versed in this art.

Francesco Sforza became Duke of Milan from being a private citizen because he was armed; his sons, since they avoided the inconveniences of arms, became private citizens after having been dukes. For, among the other bad effects it causes, being disarmed

Being disarmed makes you despised. Is this true?

makes you despised; this is one of those infamies a prince should guard himself against, as will be treated below: for between an armed and an unarmed man there is no comparison whatsoever, and it is not reasonable for an armed man to obey an unarmed man willingly, nor that an unarmed man should be safe among armed servants; since, when the former is suspicious and the latter are contemptuous, it is impossible for them to work well together. And therefore, a prince who does not understand military matters, besides the other misfortunes already noted, cannot be esteemed by his own soldiers, nor can he trust them.

He must, therefore, never raise his thought from this exercise of war, and in peacetime he must train himself more than in time of war; this can be done in

Training action/mind

two ways: one by action, the other by the mind. And as far as actions are concerned, besides keeping his soldiers well disciplined and trained, he must always be out hunting, and must accustom his body to hardships in this manner; and he must also learn the na-

Knowledge of terrain

ture of the terrain, and know how mountains slope, how valleys open, how plains lie, and understand the nature of rivers and swamps; and he should devote much attention to such activities. Such knowledge is

Two benefits

useful in two ways: first, one learns to know one's own country and can better understand how to defend it; second, with the knowledge and experience of the terrain, one can easily comprehend the characteristics of any other terrain that it is necessary to explore for the first time; for the hills, valleys, plains, rivers, and swamps of Tuscany, for instance, have certain similarities to those of other provinces; so that by knowing the lay of the land in one province one can easily understand it in others. And a prince who lacks this ability lacks the most important quality in a leader; because this skill teaches you to find the enemy, choose a campsite, lead troops, organize them for battle, and besiege towns to your own advantage.

[There follow the examples of Philopoemon, who was always observing terrain for its military usefulness, and a recommendation that princes read histories and learn from them. Three paragraphs are omitted.]

On Those Things for Which Men, and Particularly Princes, Are Praised or Blamed

Now there remains to be examined what should be the methods and procedures of a prince in dealing with his subjects and friends. And because I know that many have written about this, I am afraid that by writing about it again I shall be thought of as presumptuous, since in discussing this material I depart radically from the procedures of others. But since my intention is to write something useful for anyone who understands it, it seemed more suitable to me to search after the effectual truth of the matter rather than its imagined one. And many writers have imagined for themselves republics and principalities that have never been seen nor known to exist in reality; for there is such a gap between how one lives and how one ought to live that anyone who abandons what is done for what ought to be done learns his ruin rather than his preservation: for a man who wishes to make a vocation of being good at all times will come to ruin among so many who are not good. Hence it is necessary for a prince who wishes to maintain his position to learn how not to be good, and to use this knowledge or not to use it according to necessity.

Leaving aside, therefore, the imagined things concerning a prince, and taking into account those that are true, I say that all men, when they are spoken of, and particularly princes, since they are placed on a higher level, are judged by some of these qualities which bring them either blame or praise. And this is why one is considered generous, another miserly (to

[margin handwritten notes:]
Those who are good at all times come to ruin among those who are not good.

Prince must learn not to be good.

Note the prince's reputation

use a Tuscan word, since "avaricious" in our language is still used to mean one who wishes to acquire by means of theft; we call "miserly" one who excessively avoids using what he has); one is considered a giver, the other rapacious; one cruel, another merciful; one treacherous, another faithful; one effeminate and cowardly, another bold and courageous; one humane, another haughty; one trustworthy, another cunning; one harsh, another lenient; one serious, another frivolous; one religious, another unbelieving; and the like. And I know that everyone will admit that it would be a very praiseworthy thing to find in a prince, of the qualities mentioned above, those that are held to be good, but since it is neither possible to have them nor to observe them all completely, because human nature does not permit it, a prince must be prudent enough to know how to escape the bad reputation of those vices that would lose the state for him, and must protect himself from those that will not lose it for him, if this is possible; but if he cannot, he need not concern himself unduly if he ignores these less serious vices. And, moreover, he need not worry about incurring the bad reputation of those vices without which it would be difficult to hold his state; since, carefully taking everything into account, one will discover that something which appears to be a virtue, if pursued, will end in his destruction; while some other thing which seems to be a vice, if pursued, will result in his safety and his well-being.

Prince must avoid reputation for the worst vices.

Some vices may be needed to hold the state. True? Some virtues may end in destruction.

My annotations presume several things. One is that I have read the introductory material to Machiavelli's selection and that I understand that the term "prince" means any ruler. Thus, in modern times the prince is the equivalent of a president, a prime minister, a chairman—anyone who is a national leader. Another presumption is that, as the introduction tells us, Machiavelli has a reputation for being a cynic. That is to say, he advises his prince to do whatever is needed in order to keep power—even if what is needed is immoral. The final presumption is that I have read the entire essay and that this represents only a sample of my annotations.

Keeping these presumptions in mind, let us look at the annotations and underlinings and see what they tell us about what Machiavelli has said:

A prince's profession ought to be war, meaning that the prince should be an active military man.

Princes lose their power when they do not pay enough attention to military matters.

Being disarmed makes you despised.

The prince should always be in training.

Studying terrain gives the prince knowledge of that terrain and others like it.

Machiavelli says that he differs radically from others in talking about the methods and procedures of the prince because he says what is true, not what ought to be true.

Those who are always good will come to ruin among those who are not good.

To remain in power, the prince must learn how not to be good.

The prince has to be careful of his reputation and must therefore avoid the worst vices.

But some vices may be necessary to hold on to power.

Some virtues may end in destruction.

This is a bald way of putting Machiavelli's thoughts, but it shows how annotation can help clarify what he has written. We can see that there are two important ideas presented in these paragraphs. The first is that the prince must be a military person, which we can interpret in light of Machiavelli's situation in Renaissance Italy (discussed in the selection introduction). In his day Italy was a group of rival city-states, and France, an increasingly strong national monarchy, was invading them. Machiavelli dreamed of a strong prince (he had Cesare Borgia in mind) who could fight off the French and save Italy. So he emphasized military might because he wrote in an age in which war was a constant threat.

Machiavelli anticipates the counterarguments of pacificists—those who advocate avoiding violence and war—when he tells us that those who are unarmed are despised: he gives us examples of those who lost their position as princes because they avoided being armed. It is clear that he expects these examples to be completely persuasive.

The second idea, rather more difficult and perhaps more interesting, has to do with Machiavelli's analysis of morality. Elsewhere in the selection he says that it is always nice for a prince to be virtuous. But he also says that being in power is more important than being virtuous. He admits that vices are not generally good and that the worst vices will damage the prince's reputation. On the other hand, Machiavelli says that there are some "less serious vices. And, moreover, he need not worry about incurring the bad reputation of those vices without which it would be difficult to hold his [the prince's] state." In the same spirit, he tells us that there are some virtues that might lead to the destruction of the prince.

WRITING ABOUT IDEAS

Writing about ideas performs several functions. First, it helps make our thinking available to others for examination. Naturally, the writers whose works are presented in this book benefited from the reactions of their first readers and sometimes revised their work considerably as a result of criticism. Writing about ideas also helps us to refine what we think—even without outside criticism. Writing is a self-instructional experience. We learn by writing in part because writing clarifies our thinking. When we think silently, we construct phrases and reflect upon them. When we speak, we utter those phrases, but we also sort them out so that our audience has a more tidy version of our thought. But spoken thought is difficult to sustain, since we cannot review what we said an hour earlier in order to revise it. Writing has the advantage of permitting us to extend our ideas, to work them completely through, and to revise thoroughly in light of later discoveries. It is by writing that we truly get control over our ideas.

Generating Topics for Writing

The selections in this volume are filled with high-level discussions of important ideas. They contain innumerable stimuli for our own reactions and our own writing. But reading the works of great thinkers can be chastening. Sometimes we feel that they have said it all and that there is no room for our own thought. This is never really true; it only appears, for a short while, to be true. The suggestions that follow can help you get started writing in response to the ideas of an important thinker.

The Technique of the Question. One of the most reliable ways to start is to ask a question and then to answer it. In many ways, that is what the writers in this book have done again and again. Karen Horney asked whether what Freud said about female psychology was true. She thought not. John Maynard Keynes asked himself what the economic prospects were for his grandchildren and proceeded to answer the question as best he could. George Wald, in "The Origin of Life," is essentially attempting to answer a question that has probably struck all of us: How did life begin? John Kenneth Galbraith asked questions about why poverty still existed in a prosperous economy. B. F. Skinner's "What Is Man?" poses questions about our deeper motivations. Even Aristotle asked himself what constituted tragedy. Such questioning is at the center of all inquiry.

As a writer stimulated by other thinkers, you can use the same technique. All the annotations that we gathered above can easily be turned into questions. Any of the following questions, based on the annotations and our brief summary of the passage, could be the basis of an essay.

Should a leader be armed?

Is it true that an unarmed leader is despised?

Will those leaders who are always good come to ruin among those who are not good?

To remain in power, must a leader learn how not to be good?

One technique is to structure an essay around the answer to such a question. Another is to develop a series of questions and to answer each of them in various parts of an essay. Yet another technique is to use the question indirectly—by answering it, but not obviously. Virginia Woolf, in "A Letter to a Young Poet," is actually responding to his question about whether there is any future in writing poetry. She does not come out and say, "Here is my answer." Instead, she explores the circumstances of modern poetry and, in the process, offers her answer to his question. You can do the same kind of thing.

Many kinds of questions can be asked of a passage even as brief as the sample from Machiavelli. For one thing, we can limit ourselves to our annotations and go no further. But we can also reflect on the larger issues and ask a series of questions that would constitute a fuller inquiry. Out of that inquiry we can also generate ideas for our own writing.

Two important ideas were isolated in our annotations. The first was that the prince must devote himself to war. In modern times, this implies that a president or other national leader must put matters of defense first—that all a leader's knowledge, training, and concerns must revolve around warfare. Taking that idea in general, we can develop other questions that, stimulated by Machiavelli's selection, can be used to generate essays.

Which modern leaders would Machiavelli approve?

Would Machiavelli approve of our current president?

Do military personnel make the best leaders?

Should our president have a military background?

Could a modern state survive with no army or military weapons?

What kind of a nation would we be if we did not stockpile nuclear weapons?

These questions derive from the first idea that we isolated in our annotations. The next group of questions comes from the second idea, the issue of whether a leader can afford to be moral.

Which virtues might cause a leader to lose power?

Is Machiavelli being cynical about morality, or is he being realistic (as he claims he is)? (We might also ask if Machiavelli uses the word "realistic" as a synonym for "cynical.")

Do most American leaders behave morally?

Do most leaders believe that they should behave morally?

Should our leaders be moral all the time?

Which vices can we permit our leaders to have?

Are there any vices we want our leaders to have?

Which world leaders behave most morally? Are they the ones we most respect?

Could a modern government govern well or at all if it were to behave morally in the face of immoral adversaries?

One of the reasons for reading Machiavelli is to help us confront large and serious questions. One of the reasons for writing about these ideas is to help clarify our own positions on such important issues.

Using Suggestions for Writing. Every selection in this book is followed by a number of questions and a number of writing assignments. The questions are designed to help clarify the most important issues raised in the piece. Unlike the questions derived from annotation, their purpose is to stimulate a classroom discussion so that you can benefit from hearing others' thoughts on these issues. Naturally, subjects for essays can arise from such discussion, but the discussion is most important for refining and focusing your ideas. The writing assignments, on the other hand, are explicitly meant to provide a useful starting point for producing an essay of 700 to 1,000 words.

A sample suggestion for writing about Machiavelli follows:

> Machiavelli advises the prince to study history and reflect on the actions of great men. Would you support such advice? Machiavelli mentions a number of great leaders in his essay. Which leaders would you recommend a prince should study? Do you think Machiavelli would agree?

Like most of the suggestions for writing, this one could be worked with in any one of several ways. It can be broken down into three parts. The first is the question of whether it is useful to study, as Machiavelli does, the performance of past leaders. If you agree, then the second part of the question asks you to name some leaders whose behavior you would recommend studying. If you do not agree, you can point to the performance of some past leaders and explain why their study would be pointless today. Finally, the third part of the question asks whether you think Machiavelli would agree with your choices.

To deal successfully with this suggestion for writing, you could begin by giving your reasons for recommending that a political leader study "the actions of great men." George Santayana once said, "Those who cannot remember the past are condemned to repeat it." That is, we study history in order not to have to live it over again. If you believe that a study of the past is important, the first part of an essay can answer the question of why such study could make a politician more successful.

The second part of the suggestion focuses on examples. In the sample from Machiavelli above, we omitted the examples, but in the complete essay they are very important for bringing Machiavelli's point home. Few things can convince as completely as examples, so the first thing to do is to choose several leaders to work with. If you have studied a world leader, such as Indira Gandhi, Winston Churchill, Franklin Delano Roosevelt, or Joseph Stalin, you could use that figure as one of your examples. If you have not done so, then the most appropriate procedure is to use the research library and—in the sections on history and politics—find books or articles on one or two leaders and read them with an eye to establishing their usefulness for your argument. The central question you would seek to answer is how a specific world leader could benefit from studying the behavior and conduct of a modern leader.

The third part of the suggestion for writing—whether Machiavelli would agree with you—is very speculative. It invites you to look through the selection to find quotes or comments that indicate probable agreement or disagreement on Machiavelli's part. You can base your argument only on what Machiavelli says or implies, and this means that you will have to reread his essay to find evidence that will support your view.

In a sense, this part of the suggestion establishes a procedure for working with the writing assignments. Once you have clarified the parts of the assignment and have some useful questions to guide you, and once you have determined what research, if any, is necessary, the next step will be to reread the selection with an eye to finding the most appropriate information to help you in writing your own essay. One of the most important activities in learning how to write from these selections is rereading. It is one of the most important ways in which reading about significant ideas differs from reading for entertainment. Important ideas demand reflection and reconsideration. Rereading provides both.

SOME USEFUL RHETORICAL TECHNIQUES

Every one of the selections, whether by Francis Bacon or Susan Sontag, Frederick Douglass or B. F. Skinner, is marked by the use of specific rhetorical techniques that help the author communicate complex ideas. Some of the more important rhetorical achievements are identified in the introduction to each selection so that you can observe them and possibly learn how to use them in your own writing.

"Rhetoric" is a general term used to discuss special writing techniques. For example, one of the interesting rhetorical techniques Machiavelli uses is that of illustration by example, usually to prove his points. Francis Bacon uses the technique of enumeration—partitioning his essay into four sections. Enumeration is especially useful when one wishes to be very clear or when one wishes to cover a subject point by point, using each point to accumulate more authority in the discussion. Paul Tillich uses this technique when he cites six qualities of a symbol as he discusses the relationship of the symbol to religious faith. Martin Luther King, Jr., uses the technique of allusion, reminding his readers in the clergy that St. Paul also wrote similar letters to try to help early Christians better understand the nature of their faith. By alluding to the Bible and St. Paul, King effectively reminded his audience that they were all serving God.

A great many more rhetorical techniques are present in these readings, and you will have a chance to look at them more closely as you read the individual selections. Some of the techniques are relatively easy to use because many of us already use them naturally. We study them to become aware of their value and to help remind us to use them. After all, without using rhetorical techniques it is impossible to communicate the significance of even the most important ideas. Many of the authors in this book would surely admit that the effect of their ideas actually depends upon the way they are expressed, which is a way of saying that they depend upon the rhetorical methods used to express them.

Methods of Development

Most of the more specific rhetorical methods can wait for discussion in the introductions to the individual selections. But several represent exceptionally useful general techniques. These are methods of development. They represent approaches to working up material; that is, developing ideas that contribute to the fullness and completeness of an essay. You may think of them as techniques that can be applied to any idea in almost any situation. They can enlarge upon the idea, clarify it, express it, and demonstrate its truth or effectiveness. Sometimes a technique may be direct, sometimes indirect. Sometimes it will call attention to itself; sometimes it will work behind the scenes. Sometimes it will be used alone, sometimes in conjunction with other methods. The most important techniques will be explained and then illustrated with examples from the selections in the book.

Development by Definition. Definition is essential for two purposes: the first is to make certain that you have a clear grasp of your concepts; the second is to make certain that you communicate a clear understanding to your reader. Many of the selections are devoted almost entirely to the act of definition. For example, in *The Nature of Beauty*, George Santayana begins his essay with a sentence that announces what a definition in the field of art must accomplish.

> It would be easy to find a definition of beauty that should give in a few words a telling paraphrase of the word. We know on excellent authority that beauty is truth, that it is the expression of the ideal, the symbol of devine perfection, and the sensible manifestation of the good.

> A litany of these titles of honor might easily be compiled, and repeated in praise of our divinity. Such phrases stimulate thought and give us a momentary pleasure, but they hardly bring any permanent enlightenment. A definition that should really define must be nothing less than the exposition of the origin, place, and elements of beauty as an object of human experience. We must learn from it, as far as possible, why, when, and how beauty appears, what conditions an object must fulfill to be beautiful, what elements of our nature make us sensible of beauty, and what the relation is between the constitution of the object and the excitement of our susceptibility. Nothing less will really define beauty or make us understand what esthetic appreciation is. The definition of beauty in this sense will be the task of this whole book, a task that can be only very imperfectly accomplished within its limits. (para. 1)

Santayana indicates the way in which the act of definition can give shape to an entire book. The selection that appears in this book is limited to only one aspect of definition, but in it Santayana reminds us that the act of definition is essential to establish understanding. By defining something, we always come closer to understanding it.

For you, when writing on significant ideas, the job is not to write a book but an essay. But even within an essay we can think of how the act of definition can help us. Were we to write an essay on the annotated selection from Machiavelli we might want to define a number of key ideas. For example, if we suspect that Machiavelli might be cynical in suggesting that his prince would not hold power for long if he were to act morally, we would need to define what it means to be cynical. We might also need to define "moral behavior" in political terms. When we argue any point, it is very important to spend time defining key ideas.

Martin Luther King, Jr., in "Letter from Birmingham Jail," takes time to establish some key definitions so that he can speak forcefully to his audience:

> Let us consider a more concrete example of just and unjust laws. An unjust law is a code that a numerical or power majority group compels a minority group to obey but does not make binding on itself. This is a *difference* made legal. By the same token, a just law is a code that a majority compels a minority to follow and that it is willing to follow itself. This is *sameness* made legal. (para. 17)

This is an adequate definition as far as it goes, but most serious ideas need more extensive definition than this passage gives us. And King does go further, providing what Machiavelli does in his essay: examples and explanations. Every full definition will profit from the extension of understanding that an explanation and example will provide. Consider this paragraph from King:

> Let me give another explanation. A law is unjust if it is inflicted on a minority that, as a result of being denied the right to vote, had no part in enacting or devising the law. Who can say that the legislature of Alabama which set up that state's segregation laws was democratically elected? Throughout Alabama all sorts of devious methods are used to prevent Negroes from becoming registered voters, and there are some counties in which, even though Negroes constitute a majority of the population, not a single Negro is registered. Can any law enacted under such circumstances be considered democratically structured? (para. 18)

King makes us aware of the fact that definition is complex and capable of great subtlety. It is an approach that can be used to develop a paragraph or an essay. Since some of the suggestions for writing that follow the selections ask you to use definition as a means of writing about ideas, some of the following tips should be kept in mind:

Definition can be used to develop a paragraph, a section, or an entire essay.

It considers questions of function, purpose, circumstance, origin, and implications for different groups.

Explanations and examples make all definitions more complete and effective.

Development by Comparison. Comparison is a natural operation of the mind. We rarely talk for long about any topic without resorting to a comparison with something else. We are always fascinated with comparisons between ourselves and others, and we realize that we come to know ourselves better as a result of such comparisons. Machiavelli compares the armed with the unarmed prince and shows us, by means of examples, the results of being unarmed.

Thomas Kuhn, in "The Essential Tension: Tradition and Innovation in Scientific Research," deals with two approaches to doing science. One is the rather romantic, renegade theory which suggests that great findings were made by those who sought their own course; who could not fit themselves into the patterns of things as they were; and who, because of their individuality, found dramatic solutions to sticky problems. Kuhn calls such people divergent thinkers. Then there are the traditionalists who find it comfortable to accept current thinking and to work within established patterns. Surprisingly, when Kuhn compares the two, he finds that it is the latter scientists who make the real breakthroughs. He comes to the conclusion that science thrives best when there is a tension between the two approaches. Look at how Kuhn sets up his comparison:

> I do not at all doubt that this description of "divergent thinking" and the concomitant search for those able to do it are entirely proper. Some divergence characterizes all scientific work, and gigantic divergences lie at the core of the most significant episodes in scientific development. But both my own experience in scientific research and my reading of the history of sciences lead me to wonder whether flexibility and open-mindedness have not been too exclusively emphasized as the characteristics requisite for basic research. I shall therefore suggest below that something like "convergent thinking" is just as essential to scientific advance as is divergent. Since these two modes of thought are inevitably in conflict, it will follow that the ability to support a tension that can occasionally become almost unbearable is one of the prime requisites for the very best sort of scientific research. (para. 3)

Kuhn has not only made the comparison between these two ways of thinking central to his discussion but has also shown that their opposition produces a necessary condition for progress in science. The tension between these modes of thought is expressed in the title of his essay, and the essay naturally goes on to clarify the differences and the similarities between them.

Comparison usually includes the following:

A definition of two or more elements to be compared.

Definition may be by example, explanation, description, or any combination of these.

Discussion of the qualities the elements have in common.

Discussion of the qualities the elements have in distinction from one another.

A clear reason for making the comparison.

Development by Example. Examples make abstract ideas concrete. When Virginia Woolf discusses the state of modern poetry, she does not continue for long before she begins to quote lines and cite specific examples. When she does so, she is able to make what she has to say vital and relevant. When Machiavelli talks about looking at history to learn political lessons, he actually cites specific cases and brings them to the attention of his audience, the prince. Every selection in this book offers examples as a way of convincing us of the truth of a proposition or as a way of deepening our understanding of a statement.

In some selections, such as Charles Darwin's discussion of natural selection, the argument hinges entirely on examples, and we find Darwin citing one example after another. Stephen Jay Gould shows how a particular example, that of the ichneumon fly, causes certain philosophical difficulties to theologians studying biology, and therefore to anyone who wishes to look closely at nature. The problem with the ichneumon is that it attacks caterpillars, which have earned sympathy from people, whereas the ichneumon is ugly and seems evil. As he tells us, one result is that we dislike the parasite and approve of its victim. But there is another side to this, a second theme.

> The second theme, ruthless efficiency of the parasites, leads to the opposite conclusion—grudging admiration for the victors. We learn of their skills in capturing dangerous hosts often many times larger than themselves. Caterpillars may be easy game, but the psammocharid wasps prefer spiders. They must insert their ovipositors in a safe and precise spot. Some leave a paralyzed spider in its own burrow. *Planiceps hirsutus*, for example, parasitizes a California trapdoor spider. It searches for spider tubes on sand dunes, then digs into nearby sand to disturb the spider's home and drive it out. When the spider emerges, the wasp attacks, paralyzes its victim, drags it back into its own tube, shuts and fastens the trapdoor, and deposits a single egg upon the spider's abdomen. Other psammocharids will drag a heavy spider back to a previously prepared cluster of clay or mud cells. Some amputate a spider's legs to make the passage easier. Others fly back over water, skimming a buoyant spider along the surface. (para. 13)

Examples need to be chosen carefully because the burden, not only of proof but of explanation and clarity, often depends on them. The sample suggestion given earlier for writing on Machiavelli's essay obviously implies the use of carefully chosen examples when it asks who among world leaders Machiavelli might have approved. For that reason, when doing research for an essay, it is very important to be sure that the example or examples you settle on really suit your purposes.

Examples can be used in several ways. One is to do as Darwin does and present a large number of examples that force one to a given conclusion. This is a somewhat indirect method and is sometimes time-consuming. However, the very weight of numerous examples will be unusually effective. A second method, such as Machiavelli's, can also be effective. One makes a statement that is controversial or questionable and that can be tested by example. If you provide the right example, then your audience must draw a reasonable conclusion.

When using examples, keep these points in mind:

Choose a few strong examples that support your point.

Be concrete and specific, naming names, citing events, giving details where necessary.

Develop each example as fully as possible, being sure to point out its relevance to your position.

Development by Analysis of Cause and Effect. People usually express an interest in causes. If something happens, we often ask what causes it, as if understanding the cause or causes could somehow help us accept the results. Yet dealing with cause and effect is rather subtle. In the case of definition, comparison, and examples, we can point to something specific and feel that the connections between it and our main points are reasonable. In the case of cause and effect, we must recognize that the cause of something has to be reasoned out. After an event has already occurred, it may only be possible to offer a hypothesis of a theory for its cause. In the same sense, if no effect has yet been obtained, it may only be possible to speculate on what it will be if a given plan of action is followed. In both cases, reasoning and imagination must be employed to establish the relationship of cause and effect.

And, subtle though this method of development is, it is quite natural to our general way of thinking. We can see the method in action in the following portion of paragraph 11 of the selection from Frederick Douglass's autobiography:

> I was quite disappointed at the general appearance of things in New Bedford. The impression which I had received respecting the character and condition of the people of the north, I found to be singularly erroneous. I had very strangely supposed, while in slavery, that few of the comforts, and scarcely any of the luxuries, of life were enjoyed at the north, compared with what were enjoyed by the slaveholders of the south. I probably came to this conclusion from the fact that northern people owned no slaves. I supposed that they were about upon a level with the non-slaveholding population of the south. I knew *they* were exceedingly poor, and I had been accustomed to regard their poverty as the necessary consequences of their being non-slaveholders. I had somehow imbibed the opinion that, in the absence of slaves, there could be no wealth, and very little refinement.

Douglass's conclusions were drawn from an analysis based on his experience in the South: people with slaves had wealth; those without had none. The cause (possessing slaves) naturally led in his mind to the effect (being wealthy). Notice that Douglass is pointing out that his initial conclusion was wrong. We should all be warned that the use of cause and effect must be conducted with real attention to the terms and situations we write about. It is easy to be wrong about causes and effects. Their relationship must be worked on thoughtfully.

As has been indicated, in "The Essential Tension" Thomas Kuhn examines the question of creativity in the sciences. He knows that his audience assumes that independent thinking—"divergent thinking"—is essential to making creative discoveries in science. But Kuhn demonstrates through careful argument—examining numerous instances of cause and effect—that it is most often traditional thinking that produces discoveries. His whole essay is built around the relationship of traditional thought and divergent thought in science. He uses as well the methods of definition and comparison, demonstrating that writers use a battery of methods of development in order to make their thinking full and convincing.

Everywhere in this collection authors rely on cause and effect to develop their thoughts. Thomas Jefferson establishes the relationship between the abuses of the English and the need for America to sever its colonial ties. Elizabeth Cady Stanton does the same in the Seneca Falls address when she explains the indignities suffered by women. George Wald's "The Origin of Life" is a detailed examination of the means—the causes—that could have produced the effect of life. John Kenneth Galbraith is concerned with the causes of poverty, which he feels is an anomaly in modern society. Henry David Thoreau establishes what causes demand the effect of civil disobedience. Even Simone Weil's "Spiritual Autobiography" is an examination of the causes of her becoming a Christian mystic.

The power of the rhetorical method of development through cause and effect is such that you will find it in every section of this book, in the work of virtually every author. Some suggestions to keep in mind when using it to develop your own thinking are:

Clearly establish in your own mind the cause and the effect you wish to discuss.

Develop a good line of reasoning that will demonstrate the relationship between the cause and the effect.

Be sure that the cause-effect relationship is real and not merely apparent.

Development by Analysis of Circumstances. Everything we want to discuss exists as certain circumstances. Traditionally, the discussion of circumstances has had two parts. The first is an examination of what is possible or impossible in a given situation. Whenever you are trying to convince your audience that a specific course of action should be taken, it is helpful to show that, given the circumstances, no other course is possible. On the other hand, people may intend to follow a specific course of action because none other seems possible. If you disagree with that course of action, you may have to demonstrate that another is indeed possible.

The second part of this method of development is the analysis of what has been done in the past. If something has been done in the past, then it may be possible to do it again in the future. Therefore, it is often true that a historical survey of a situation is a form of examination of circumstances.

This method guides George Wald throughout his inquiry into the origin of life. His argument centers on the concept of spontaneous generation of life on earth. His first statement is that such an explanation for the origin of life appears to be impossible. In order to prepare us for his argument he launches into an elaborate discussion of the meaning of "impossible" (see paragraph 17 and the immediately following paragraphs). Wald establishes that within the bounds of a human lifetime, the spontaneous generation of life appears impossible, but when dealing with eons of time, the phenomenon appears to become almost inevitable. Wald's is perhaps the most elaborate and theoretical discussion of possibility in this volume.

Machiavelli is also interested in the question of possibility, since he is trying to encourage his ideal prince to follow a prescribed pattern of behavior. As he constantly reminds us, if the prince does not do so it is possible that he will be deposed or killed. Taken as a whole, "The Qualities of the Prince" is a recitation of the circumstances that are necessary to guarantee success in politics. Machiavelli establishes this in a single paragraph.

> Therefore, it is not necessary for a prince to have all of the above-mentioned qualities, but it is very necessary for him to appear to have them. Furthermore, I shall be so bold as to assert this: that having them and practicing them at all times is harmful; and appearing to have them is useful; for instance, to seem merciful, faithful, humane, forthright, religious, and to be so; but his mind should be disposed in such a way that should it become necessary not to be so, he will be able and know how to change to the contrary. And it is essential to understand this: that a prince, and especially a new prince, cannot observe all those things by which men are considered good, for in order to maintain the state he is often obliged to act against his promise, against charity, against humanity, and against religion. And therefore, it is necessary that he have a mind ready to turn itself according to the way the winds of Fortune and the changeability of affairs require him; and, as I said above, as long as it is possible, he should not stray from the good, but

he should know how to enter into evil when necessity commands.
(para. 23)

This is the essential Machiavelli, the Machiavelli who is often
thought of as a cynic. He advises his prince to be virtuous but says
that it is not always possible to be so. Therefore, the prince must learn
how not to be good when "necessity commands." The circumstances,
he tells us, always determine whether it is possible to be virtuous. The
most charitable reading of this passage can only conclude that his advice is amoral.

Many of the essays in this collection rely on an analysis of circumstances. Frederick Douglass examines the circumstances of slavery and
freedom. Thomas Jefferson and Elizabeth Cady Stanton construct their
works around the device of listing one circumstance after another to
show why they must declare their independence.

When Jean Jacques Rousseau begins his selection with "Man is
born free, and everywhere he is in chains," he begins an examination
of the circumstances that have led to that fact. He examines the past—
even alluding to social structures of prehistory in an effort to establish
the origins of society. By doing so, he hopes to cast light on the present
and to explain his sad opening salvo.

When using the method of examination of circumstances to develop an idea, keep in mind the following tips:

Clarify the question of possibility and impossibility.

Review past circumstances so that future ones can be determined.

Suggest a course of action based on an analysis of possibility and
past circumstances.

Establish the present circumstances, listing them if necessary. Be
detailed; concentrate on facts.

Development by Analysis of Quotations. Not every essay in this collection refers to or quotes other writers, but a good many of them do.
And often they point to writers who are held in esteem by their audience. Sometimes the authors do not quote directly but allude to texts
that support their views. This is what Martin Luther King, Jr., does
when he reminds his audience of certain important passages in the
Bible. Similarly, Simone Weil alludes to events in the life of St. Francis. She also refers to the Indian poem, the *Bhagavad-Gita,* to Homer's *Iliad,* and to other works. But she does not quote them at length
in order to comment on them.

Virginia Woolf, however, is careful to quote modern poets in order to cast some light on the conditions of modern poetry. In the course of her letter she alludes to dozens of important writers—all of whom she presumes her poet would have known and read. But when she quotes a few lines of modern poetry, she pauses to comment on them (para. 6). She does not analyze the lines themselves. Instead, she analyzes her reactions and compares them to what she suspects the poet imagined they would be. She says:

> "I feel a jar. I feel a shock. I feel as if I had stubbed my toe on the corner of the wardrobe. Am I then, I go on to ask, shocked, prudishly and conventionally, by the words themselves? I think not. The shock is literally a shock. The poet as I guess has strained himself to include an emotion that is not domesticated and acclimatized to poetry; the effort has thrown him off his balance; he rights himself, as I am sure I shall find if I turn the page, by a violent recourse to the poetical—he invokes the moon or the nightingale."

Woolf is being slightly amusing here, particularly in her description of what the "poetical" might be. But she is also interested in her own feelings and why she has had them in response to the poetry.

In your own writing you will find plenty of opportunity to cite passages from an author whose ideas have engaged your attention. In writing an essay in response to Machiavelli, B. F. Skinner, Susan Sontag, or any of the authors in the book, you may find yourself quoting and commenting in some detail on specific lines or passages. This is especially true if you find yourself in disagreement with a point. Your first job, then, is to establish what you disagree with—and usually it helps to quote, which is essentially a way of producing evidence.

The uses of quotation can be rich and various. The most obvious technique is to place a large chunk of quotation into the discussion, setting it off much as I have done above and will do again below. But there are other ways. For example, B. F. Skinner, in "What Is Man?" sometimes invokes a flurry of quotes as a means of explaining. Examine the following paragraph for its gathering of relevant comments from writers whose primary fame comes from their concerns for humanistic values.

> The picture which emerges from a scientific analysis *is* not of a body with a person inside, but of a body which *is* a person in the sense that it displays a complex repertoire of behavior. The picture is, of course, unfamiliar. The man thus portrayed is a stranger, and from the traditional point of view he may not seem to be a man at all. "For at least one hundred years," said Joseph Wood Krutch, "we have been prejudiced in every theory, including economic determinism, mechanistic behaviorism, and relativism, that reduces the stature of man until he

ceases to be man at all in any sense that the humanists of an earlier generation would recognize." Matson has argued that "the empirical behavioral scientist . . . denies, if only by implication, that a unique being, called Man, exists." "What is now under attack," said Maslow, "is the 'being' of man." C. S. Lewis put it quite bluntly: Man is being abolished. (para. 34)

Skinner has almost no time to comment on these quotes. There are a great many of them in one paragraph—for some people's taste, too many. But each of the quotes amasses an argument. Skinner includes them because he is arguing against them, and he wants us to feel that he recognizes the seriousness of his argument and the weight of opinion that is against him. In this sense, the paragraph is successful. Skinner is the first to admit that he must account for the opinions of such worthies as Krutch, Maslow, and Lewis if he is to convince us that his new view of the nature of man is accurate.

Skinner comments on these quotes (and indirectly on many more as well) in subsequent paragraphs. He is arguing for a new view of man throughout the essay, and by quoting judiciously he can accommodate many positions that he well knows are opposed to his.

When you use quotations some pointers to remember are:

Quote accurately and do not distort the context of the original source.

Choose quotations that are most representative of your author.

Unless the quotation is absolutely self-evident in importance, offer your own clarifying comments and analysis.

Make your audience understand why you chose to quote your author: establish clearly the function of the quote.

Finally, it must be admitted that only a few important points concerning the rhetorical methods used by the authors in this book have been discussed here. Rhetoric is a complex art that needs fuller study. But the points raised above are important because they are illustrated in many of the texts you will read, and by watching them at work you can begin to learn to use them yourself. By using them you will be able to achieve in your writing the fullness and purposiveness that mark mature prose.

A SAMPLE ESSAY

The following sample essay is based on the first several paragraphs of Machiavelli's "The Qualities of the Prince" that were annotated above. The essay is based on the annotations and the questions that were developed from them:

Should a leader be armed?

Is it true that an unarmed leader is despised?

Will those leaders who are always good come to ruin among those who are not good?

To remain in power, must a leader learn how not to be good?

Not all these questions are dealt with in the essay, but they serve as a starting point and a focus. The methods of development that are discussed above form the primary rhetorical techniques of the essay. Marginal notes identify each method as it is used simply to show in detail its effectiveness. The sample essay does two things simultaneously: it attempts to clarify the meaning of Machiavelli's advice, and then it attempts to apply that advice to a contemporary circumstance. Naturally, the essay could have chosen to discuss only the Renaissance situation that Machiavelli described, but to do so would have required unusual knowledge of that period. The assumption in this sample essay is simply that the questions prompted by the annotations serve as the basis of the discussion.

The Qualities of the President

Intro-duction   Machiavelli's essay, "The Qualities of the Prince," has a number of very worrisome points. The ones that worry me most have to do with the question of whether it is reasonable to expect a leader to behave virtuously. I think this is connected to the question of whether the leader should be armed. Machiavelli emphasizes that the prince must be armed or else face the possibility that someone will take over the government. When I think about how that advice applies to modern times, particularly in terms of how our president should behave, I find Machiavelli's position very different from my own.

Circum-stance   First, I want to discuss the question of being armed. That is where Machiavelli starts, and it is an important concern. In Machiavelli's time, the late fifteenth and early sixteenth centuries, it was common for men to walk in the streets of Florence wearing a rapier for protection. The possibility of robbery or even attack by rival political groups was great in those days. Even if he had a bodyguard, it was still important for a prince to know how to fight and to be able to defend himself. Machiavelli seems to be talking only about self-defense when he recommends that the prince be armed. In our time, sadly, it too is important to think about protecting the president and other leaders.

Examples   In recent years there have been many assassination attempts on world leaders, and our president, John F. Kennedy, was killed in Dallas in 1963. His brother Robert was killed when he was campaigning for the presidency in 1968. Also in 1968 Martin Luther King, Jr., was killed in Memphis because of his beliefs in racial equality. In the 1980s Pope John Paul II was shot by a would-be assassin, as was President Ronald Reagan. They both lived, but Indira Gandhi, the leader of India, was shot and killed in 1984. This is a frightening record. Probably even Machiavelli would have been appalled. But would his solution--being armed-- have helped? I do not think so.

Cause/ effect   For one thing, I cannot believe that if the pope had a gun he would have shot his would-be assassin, Ali Acga. The thought of it is almost silly. Martin Luther King, Jr., who constantly preached the value of nonviolence, logically could not have shot at an assailant. How could John F. Kennedy have returned fire at a sniper? Robert Kennedy had bodyguards, and both President Reagan and Indira Gandhi were protected by armed guards. The presence of arms obviously does not produce the desired effect: security. The only thing that can produce that is to reduce the visibility of a leader. The president could speak on television or, when he must appear in public, use a bulletproof screen. The opportunities for would-be assassins can be reduced. But the thought of an American president carrying arms is unacceptable.

Com-parison

The question of whether a president should be armed is to some extent symbolic. Our president stands for America, and if he were to appear in press conferences or state meetings wearing a gun, he would give a symbolic message to the world: look out, we're dangerous. Cuba's Fidel Castro usually appears in a military uniform with a gun, and when he spoke at the United Nations, he was the first, and I think the only, world leader to wear a pistol there. I have seen pictures of Benito Mussolini and Adolf Hitler appearing in public in military uniform, but never in a business suit. The same is true of Libyan leader Muammar al-Qaddafi. Today when a president or a head of state is armed there is often reason to worry. The current leaders of Russia usually wear suits, but Joseph Stalin always wore a military uniform. His rule in Russia was marked by the extermination of whole groups of people and the imprisonment of many more. We do not want an armed president.

Use of quotes

also

Com-parison

Yet, Machiavelli plainly says, "among the other bad effects it causes, being disarmed makes you despised . . . for between an armed and an unarmed man there is no comparison whatsoever" (para. 2). The problem with this statement is that it is more relevant to the sixteenth century than the twentieth. In our time the threat of assassination is so great that being armed would be no sure protection, as we have seen in the case of the assassination of President Sadat of Egypt, winner of the Nobel Peace Prize. On the other hand, the pope, like Martin Luther King, Jr., would never have appeared with a weapon, and yet it can hardly be said they were despised. If anything, the world's respect for them is enormous. President Reagan also commands the world's respect, as does Margaret Thatcher, prime minister of

Great Britain. Yet neither would ever think of being armed. If what Machiavelli said was true in the early 1500s, it is pretty clear that it is not true today.

Defini-tion

All this basically translates into a question of whether a leader should be virtuous. I suppose the definition of **virtuous** would differ with different people, but I think of it as holding a moral philosophy that you try to live by. No one is ever completely virtuous, but I think a president ought to try to be so. That means the president ought to tell the truth, since that is one of the basic virtues. The cardinal virtues—which were the same in Machiavelli's time as in ours—are justice, prudence, fortitude, and temperance. In a president, the virtue of justice is absolutely a must, or else what America stands for is lost. We definitely want our president to be prudent, to use good judgment, particularly in this nuclear age, when acts of imprudence could get us blown up. Fortitude, the ability to stand up for what is right, is a must for our president. Temperance is also important; we do not want a drunk for a president, nor do we want anyone with excessive bad habits.

Conclu-sion

It seems to me that a president who was armed or who emphasized arms in the way Machiavelli appears to mean would be threatening injustice (the way Stalin did) and implying intemperance, like many armed world leaders. When I consider this issue, I cannot think of any vice that our president ought to possess at any time. Injustice, imprudence, cowardice, and intemperance are, for me, unacceptable. Maybe Machiavelli was thinking of deception and lying as necessary evils, but they are a form of injustice, and no competent president—no president who was truly virtuous—would need them. Prudence and fortitude are the two virtues most essential for diplomacy. The president who has those virtues will govern well and uphold our basic values.

The range of this essay is not great, but it does express a viewpoint that is focused and coherent. This is a brief essay, about 1,000 words. It illustrates each of the methods of development discussed in the text and shows how it helps further the argument. The writer takes issue with an aspect of Machiavelli and presents an argument based on personal opinion, but it is bolstered by reference to example and to an analysis of current political conditions as they compare with those of Machiavelli's time. A longer essay could have gone more deeply into any of the issues raised in any single paragraph, and it could have studied more closely the views of a specific president, such as Ronald Reagan, who opposed stricter gun control laws even after he had been shot.

The range of the selections in this volume is great. They represent a considerable breadth and constitute a significant introduction to thought in many areas. They are especially useful for stimulating our own thought and ideas. Obviously, there are no absolute rules for how to do this. But observing how serious writers work and how they apply rhetorical methods in their writing is one of the ways to begin our own development as writers. The suggestions for essays following each selection provide guides that can be useful for learning from these writers, who encourage our learning and reward our study.

PART ONE

IDEAS IN THE
WORLD
OF POLITICS

———❦———

Niccolò Machiavelli ··· *Jean Jacques Rousseau*
Thomas Jefferson ··· *Karl Marx*
Frederick Douglass ··· *Henry David Thoreau*
Elizabeth Cady Stanton
Martin Luther King, Jr.

INTRODUCTION

THE EIGHT SELECTIONS in this part cover a wide range of ideas concerning politics from the Renaissance to the present. Niccolò Machiavelli, Jean Jacques Rousseau, and Karl Marx are still among the most influential theorists of political and social thought. Both Elizabeth Cady Stanton and Frederick Douglass act as a nation's conscience with respect to those who would oppress others. Three men from three centuries—Thomas Jefferson, Henry David Thoreau, and Martin Luther King, Jr.—remind us that obedience to the laws of a government that legally oppresses its people has moral limits. Their bringing into question the problems that citizens can confront in the face of laws which are patently unjust places them in the forefront of the fight for broad political rights.

The authors of these works conceived and wrote them in an effort to explain controversial positions and to convince others to join them in their efforts to produce change. Jefferson's rhetoric is directed at those who would know why the United States felt it necessary to break from its parent nation by force. *The Communist Manifesto* was written to arouse members of the working class and to explain clearly what Communists stood for and why their critics misunderstood them and their cause.

Rousseau examines the basic theories that underlie all states and the concept of the state, whereas Machiavelli's rhetorical approach to the exercise of political power concentrates on practice. The practicality stressed in *The Prince* has guided politicians since the sixteenth century. Frederick Douglass reveals the awakening of the free mind, the joy that accompanies liberty. His story of achieving his freedom from slavery is powerful and moving; rhetorically, its appeal to our emotions helps to convince us of the rightness of his illegal act.

Elizabeth Cady Stanton relies on the rhetorical device of parody in her "Declaration of Sentiments and Resolutions." It was modeled directly on Thomas Jefferson's Declaration of Independence and serves as a reminder that it spoke only of men's independence, not that of women. Her demands are no less reasonable than Jefferson's, and it is a source of embarrassment that she has to redress such an omission after so long. Thoreau's "Civil Disobedience" is also a conscience-rousing piece. It aims at reminding us that we are the citizens of the nation and that we ought make our own will known. Thoreau stresses that there is a price for doing what is right but that all honest citizens must pay it.

In our own time, Martin Luther King, Jr., reminds us that freedom cannot be taken for granted by anyone. He also reminds his fellow clergymen that they cannot affirm adherence to a Christianity or a Judaism that ignores the basic rights of any people: they cannot profess religion while ignoring injustice. The connection between religion and politics was a powerful one long before the first persecutions of the Christians by the Romans. King is quick to make historical links with the early church a basic feature of his argument. To answer his critics, King constructed a carefully planned logical analysis of each complaint rendered against him. Logic has its place in rhetoric, particularly as a tool of analysis. And King's "Letter from Birmingham Jail" gives us a good sense of how logic can be used in modern writing.

One fascinating point to bear in mind is that the writers of these selections were engaged in intense political struggles even as they wrote. Douglass feared that he could be returned to slavery; Thoreau had spent roughly a day in a local jail for refusing to pay a poll tax; Elizabeth Cady Stanton was a force in the beginning of the women's movement in the United States, as was Jefferson in the beginning of the American Revolution. None of these essays is abstract or academic. Machiavelli feared that the city-states of Italy would become dominated by strong foreign nations. Hence, *The Prince* provided a model of the kind of strength and political understanding leaders needed to ward off foreign control.

It would almost appear that great ideas in politics can emerge only in times of stress and fear. Martin Luther King, Jr., wrote with astonishing eloquence—from prison. Like Thoreau, he knew that one had to be willing to pay a price to act according to his conscience, and he paid dearly. His letter is a model of rhetorical balance and structure—and of rhetorical skill.

We must remember that none of these works would be worth reading if their authors did not have the rhetorical skill necessary to move their audiences. The works exhibit a wide range of approaches and effects. Their authors relied on the models of other writers, as we see not only in the case of Elizabeth Cady Stanton but also in that of Martin Luther King, Jr., who reminded his audience of clergymen of the letters that St. Paul had written—also from prison.

Further, we might keep in mind that none of the central ideas presented in the selections was original with the writer. And each writer was well aware of the fact. The power that inheres in these essays comes not so much from the originality of the ideas but from an appropriate and convincing combination of style, energy, and commitment on the part of the writers. They convince us that what they are saying is of immense importance and that they feel strongly the emotions that are related to, and aroused by, the ideas they present. It is the depth of their commitment to these ideas, their capacity to involve us in the ideas, and the rhetorical conviction by which they present them that compel us to respond as we do.

NICCOLÒ MACHIAVELLI

The Qualities of the Prince

NICCOLÒ MACHIAVELLI (1469–1527) was an aristocrat whose fortunes wavered according to the shifts in power in Florence. Renaissance Italy was a collection of powerful city-states which were sometimes volatile and unstable. When Florence's famed Medici princes were returned to power in 1512 after eighteen years of banishment, Machiavelli did not fare well. He was suspected of crimes against the state and imprisoned. Even though he was not guilty, he had to learn to support himself as a writer instead of continuing his career in civil service.

His works often contrast two forces: luck (one's fortune) and character (one's virtues). His own character outlasted his bad luck in regard to the Medicis, and he was returned to a position of responsibility. The Prince (1513), his most celebrated work, was a general treatise on the qualities the prince (i.e., a ruler) must have to maintain his power. In a more particular way, it was directed at the Medicis to encourage them to save Italy from the predatory incursions of France and Spain, whose troops were nibbling at the crumbling Italian principalities and who would, in time, control much of Italy.

From *The Prince*. Translated by Peter Bondanella and Mark Musa.

The chapters presented here contain the core of the philosophy Machiavelli became famous for. His instructions to the prince are curiously devoid of any high-sounding moralizing or any encouragement to be good as a matter of principle. Machiavelli recommends a very practical course of action for the prince: secure power; secure it by practical, simple, and effective means. It may be that Machiavelli fully expects that the prince will use his power for good ends—certainly he does not recommend tyranny. But he also supports questionable means that will achieve the final end of becoming and remaining the prince. Machiavelli believes that there is a conflict between the ends and the means used to achieve them, and he certainly does not fret over the possible problems that may accompany the use of "unpleasant" means, such as punishment of upstarts, and in general the use of repression, imprisonment, and torture.

Machiavelli's view of human nature has come under criticism for its cynicism. He suggests that a perfectly good person would not last long in any high office because that person would have to compete with the mass of people, who, he says, are basically bad. Machiavelli constantly tells us that he is describing the world as it really is, not as it should be. He implies that if the prince operated as if the world were as it ought to be, he would not last very long. Perhaps Machiavelli is correct, but people have long resented the way he approves of cunning, deceit, and outright lying as means of staying in power.

MACHIAVELLI'S RHETORIC

This selection is impressive for its brevity. Each chapter is terse and economical. Machiavelli announces his primary point clearly; he usually refers to a historical precedent (or several) to support his point; then he explains why his position is the best one by appealing to both common sense and historical experience. In those cases in which he suspects the reader will not share his view wholeheartedly, he suggests an alternate argument, then explains why it is wrong. This is a very forceful way of presenting one's views. It gives the appearance of fairness and thoroughness—and, as we learn from reading Machiavelli, he is very much concerned with appearances. His method also gives his work fullness, a quality which makes us forget how brief it really is.

One of his rhetorical methods is to discuss opposites, including both sides of an issue. From the first he makes a number of oppositions—*the art of war and the art of life, liberality and stinginess, cruelty and clemency, the fox and the lion. The method is simplicity itself, but it is important because it employs one of the basic techniques of rhetoric—the strategy of comparison (see page 15), in which we perform one of the mind's favorite tasks, comparison and contrast. We may not have much to say about a subject, but somehow we can always think of something to say about how it relates to something else.*

The aphorism is another of Machiavelli's rhetorical weapons. The aphorism is a saying—or a sentence that sounds like a saying—which has been accepted as true. Familiar examples are "A penny saved is a penny earned" and "There is no fool like an old fool." Machiavelli tells us: To be feared is much safer than to be loved; any man who tries to be good all the time is bound to come to ruin among the great number who are not good.

Such definite statements have several important qualities. One is that they are pithy—they seem to say a great deal in a few words. Another is that they appear to contain a great deal of wisdom, in part because they are delivered with such certainty, and in part because they sound like other aphorisms which we accept as true. Finally, because they sound like aphorisms, we tend to accept them much more readily than perhaps we should. Use of language which has the appearance of truth is much more likely to be accepted as conveying truth than any other use of language. This may be why the speeches of contemporary politicians (modern versions of the prince) are often sprinkled with such expressions. Machiavelli's rhetorical technique is still reliable, still effective, and still worth studying.

———— ‹∞›· ————

The Qualities of the Prince

A Prince's Duty Concerning Military Matters

A prince, therefore, must not have any other object nor any other   1
thought, nor must he take anything as his profession but war, its institutions, and its discipline; because that is the only profession which
befits one who commands; and it is of such importance that not only

does it maintain those who were born princes, but many times it enables men of private station to rise to that position; and, on the other hand, it is evident that when princes have given more thought to personal luxuries than to arms, they have lost their state. And the first way to lose it is to neglect this art; and the way to acquire it is to be well versed in this art.

Francesco Sforza[1] became Duke of Milan from being a private citizen because he was armed; his sons, since they avoided the inconveniences of arms, became private citizens after having been dukes. For, among the other bad effects it causes, being disarmed makes you despised; this is one of those infamies a prince should guard himself against, as will be treated below: for between an armed and an unarmed man there is no comparison whatsoever, and it is not reasonable for an armed man to obey an unarmed man willingly, nor that an unarmed man should be safe among armed servants; since, when the former is suspicious and the latter are contemptuous, it is impossible for them to work well together. And therefore, a prince who does not understand military matters, besides the other misfortunes already noted, cannot be esteemed by his own soldiers, nor can he trust them.

He must, therefore, never raise his thought from this exercise of war, and in peacetime he must train himself more than in time of war; this can be done in two ways: one by action, the other by the mind. And as far as actions are concerned, besides keeping his soldiers well disciplined and trained, he must always be out hunting, and must accustom his body to hardships in this manner; and he must also learn the nature of the terrain, and know how mountains slope, how valleys open, how plains lie, and understand the nature of rivers and swamps; and he should devote much attention to such activities. Such knowledge is useful in two ways: first, one learns to know one's own country and can better understand how to defend it; second, with the knowledge and experience of the terrain, one can easily comprehend the characteristics of any other terrain that it is necessary to explore for the first time; for the hills, valleys, plains, rivers, and swamps of Tuscany,[2] for instance, have certain similarities to those of other provinces; so that by knowing the lay of the land in one province one can

---

[1]*Francesco Sforza (1401–1466)* Became duke of Milan in 1450. He was, like most of Machiavelli's examples, a skilled diplomat and soldier. His court was a model of Renaissance scholarship and gentility.

[2]*Tuscany* Florence is in the region known as Tuscany, which is noted for its beautiful hills.

easily understand it in others. And a prince who lacks this ability lacks the most important quality in a leader; because this skill teaches you to find the enemy, choose a campsite, lead troops, organize them for battle, and besiege towns to your own advantage.

Philopoemon, Prince of the Achaeans,[3] among the other praises given to him by writers, is praised because in peacetime he thought of nothing except the means of waging war; and when he was out in the country with his friends, he often stopped and reasoned with them: "If the enemy were on that hilltop and we were here with our army, which of the two of us would have the advantage? How could we attack them without breaking formation? If we wanted to retreat, how could we do this? If they were to retreat, how could we pursue them?" And he proposed to them, as they rode along, all the contingencies that can occur in an army; he heard their opinions, expressed his own, and backed it up with arguments; so that, because of these continuous deliberations, when leading his troops no unforeseen incident could arise for which he did not have the remedy.

But as for the exercise of the mind, the prince must read histories and in them study the deeds of great men; he must see how they conducted themselves in wars; he must examine the reasons for their victories and for their defeats in order to avoid the latter and to imitate the former; and above all else he must do as some distinguished man before him has done, who elected to imitate someone who had been praised and honored before him, and always keep in mind his deeds and actions; just as it is reported that Alexander the Great imitated Achilles; Caesar, Alexander; Scipio, Cyrus.[4] And anyone who reads the life of Cyrus written by Xenophon then realizes how important in the life of Scipio that imitation was to his glory and how much, in purity, goodness, humanity, and generosity, Scipio conformed to those characteristics of Cyrus that Xenophon had written about.

---

[3]***Philopoemon (253–184 B.C.), Prince of the Achaeans*** Philopoemon, from the city-state of Megalopolis, was a Greek general noted for skillful diplomacy. He led the Achaeans, a group of Greek states that formed the Achaean League, in several important expeditions, notably against Sparta. His cruelty in putting down a Spartan uprising caused him to be reprimanded by his superiors.

[4]***Cyrus (d. 529 B.C.)*** Persian emperor. Cyrus and the other figures featured in this sentence—Alexander the Great (356–323 B.C.); Achilles, hero of Homer's *Iliad*; Julius Caesar (102–44 B.C.); and Scipio Africanus, legendary Roman general—are all examples of politicians who were also great military geniuses. Xenophon (434?–?355 B.C.) was one of the earliest Greek historians; he chronicled the lives and military exploits of Cyrus and his son Darius.

Such methods as these a wise prince must follow, and never in   6
peaceful times must he be idle; but he must turn them diligently to
his advantage in order to be able to profit from them in times of adversity, so that, when Fortune changes, she will find him prepared to
withstand such times.

On Those Things for Which Men,
and Particularly Princes,
Are Praised or Blamed

Now there remains to be examined what should be the methods   7
and procedures of a prince in dealing with his subjects and friends.
And because I know that many have written about this, I am afraid
that by writing about it again I shall be thought of as presumptuous,
since in discussing this material I depart radically from the procedures
of others. But since my intention is to write something useful for anyone who understands it, it seemed more suitable to me to search after
the effectual truth of the matter rather than its imagined one. And
many writers have imagined for themselves republics and principalities that have never been seen nor known to exist in reality; for there
is such a gap between how one lives and how one ought to live that
anyone who abandons what is done for what ought to be done learns
his ruin rather than his preservation: for a man who wishes to make a
vocation of being good at all times will come to ruin among so many
who are not good. Hence it is necessary for a prince who wishes to
maintain his position to learn how not to be good, and to use this
knowledge or not to use it according to necessity.

Leaving aside, therefore, the imagined things concerning a prince,   8
and taking into account those that are true, I say that all men, when
they are spoken of, and particularly princes, since they are placed on a
higher level, are judged by some of these qualities which bring them
either blame or praise. And this is why one is considered generous,
another miserly (to use a Tuscan word, since "avaricious" in our language is still used to mean one who wishes to acquire by means of
theft; we call "miserly" one who excessively avoids using what he
has); one is considered a giver, the other rapacious; one cruel, another
merciful; one treacherous, another faithful; one effeminate and cowardly, another bold and courageous; one humane, another haughty; one
lascivious, another chaste; one trustworthy, another cunning; one
harsh, another lenient; one serious, another frivolous; one religious,
another unbelieving; and the like. And I know that everyone will ad-

mit that it would be a very praiseworthy thing to find in a prince, of the qualities mentioned above, those that are held to be good; but since it is neither possible to have them nor to observe them all completely, because human nature does not permit it, a prince must be prudent enough to know how to escape the bad reputation of those vices that would lose the state for him, and must protect himself from those that will not lose it for him, if this is possible; but if he cannot, he need not concern himself unduly if he ignores these less serious vices. And, moreover, he need not worry about incurring the bad reputation of those vices without which it would be difficult to hold his state; since, carefully taking everything into account, one will discover that something which appears to be a virtue, if pursued, will end in his destruction; while some other thing which seems to be a vice, if pursued, will result in his safety and his well-being.

On Generosity and Miserliness

Beginning, therefore, with the first of the above-mentioned quali- 9 ties, I say that it would be good to be considered generous; nevertheless, generosity used in such a manner as to give you a reputation for it will harm you; because if it is employed virtuously and as one should employ it, it will not be recognized and you will not avoid the reproach of its opposite. And so, if a prince wants to maintain his reputation for generosity among men, it is necessary for him not to neglect any possible means of lavish display; in so doing such a prince will always use up all his resources and he will be obliged, eventually, if he wishes to maintain his reputation for generosity, to burden the people with excessive taxes and to do everything possible to raise funds. This will begin to make him hateful to his subjects, and, becoming impoverished, he will not be much esteemed by anyone; so that, as a consequence of his generosity, having offended many and rewarded few, he will feel the effects of any slight unrest and will be ruined at the first sign of danger; recognizing this and wishing to alter his policies, he immediately runs the risk of being reproached as a miser.

A prince, therefore, unable to use this virtue of generosity in a 10 manner which will not harm himself if he is known for it, should, if he is wise, not worry about being called a miser; for with time he will come to be considered more generous once it is evident that, as a result of his parsimony, his income is sufficient, he can defend himself from anyone who makes war against him, and he can undertake enterprises without overburdening his people, so that he comes to be generous with all those from whom he takes nothing, who are countless, and miserly with all those to whom he gives nothing, who are few. In our times we have not seen great deeds accomplished except by those who were considered miserly; all others were done away with. Pope Julius II,[5] although he made use of his reputation for generosity in order to gain the papacy, then decided not to maintain it in order to be able to wage war; the present King of France[6] has waged many wars without imposing extra taxes on his subjects, only because his habitual parsimony has provided for the additional expenditures; the present King of Spain,[7] if he had been considered generous, would not have engaged in nor won so many campaigns.

Therefore, in order not to have to rob his subjects, to be able to defend himself, not to become poor and contemptible, and not to be forced to become rapacious, a prince must consider it of little importance if he incurs the name of miser, for this is one of those vices that permits him to rule. And if someone were to say: Caesar with his generosity came to rule the empire, and many others, because they were generous and known to be so, achieved very high positions; I reply: you are either already a prince or you are on the way to becoming one; in the first instance such generosity is damaging; in the second it is very necessary to be thought generous. And Caesar was one of those who wanted to gain the principality of Rome; but if, after obtaining this, he had lived and had not moderated his expenditures, he would have destroyed that empire. And if someone were to reply: there have existed many princes who have accomplished great deeds with their armies who have been reputed to be generous; I answer you: a prince either spends his own money and that of his subjects or that of others; in the first case he must be economical; in the second he must not restrain any part of his generosity. And for that prince who goes out with his soldiers and lives by looting, sacking, and ransoms, who controls the property of others, such generosity is necessary; otherwise he would not be followed by his troops. And with what does not belong to you or to your subjects you can be a more liberal giver, as were Cyrus, Caesar, and Alexander; for spending the wealth of oth-

11

---

[5]*Pope Julius II (1443–1513)* Giuliano della Rovere, pope from 1503 to 1513. Like many of the popes of the day, Julius II was also a diplomat and a general.

[6]*present King of France* Louis XII (1462–1515). He entered Italy on a successful military campaign in 1494.

[7]*present King of Spain* Ferdinand V (1452–1516). A studied politician; he and Queen Isabella (1451–1504) financed Christopher Columbus's voyage to the New World in 1492.

ers does not lessen your reputation but adds to it; only the spending of your own is what harms you. And there is nothing that uses itself up faster than generosity, for as you employ it you lose the means of employing it, and you become either poor or despised or, in order to escape poverty, rapacious and hated. And above all other things a prince must guard himself against being despised and hated; and generosity leads you to both one and the other. So it is wiser to live with the reputation of a miser, which produces reproach without hatred, than to be forced to incur the reputation of rapacity, which produces reproach along with hatred, because you want to be considered as generous.

On Cruelty and Mercy and Whether It Is Better to be Loved Than to be Feared or the Contrary

Proceeding to the other qualities mentioned above, I say that every prince must desire to be considered merciful and not cruel; nevertheless, he must take care not to misuse this mercy. Cesare Borgia[8] was considered cruel; nonetheless, his cruelty had brought order to Romagna,[9] united it, restored it to peace and obedience. If we examine this carefully, we shall see that he was more merciful than the Florentine people, who, in order to avoid being considered cruel, allowed the destruction of Pistoia.[10] Therefore, a prince must not worry about the reproach of cruelty when it is a matter of keeping his subjects united and loyal; for with a very few examples of cruelty he will be more compassionate than those who, out of excessive mercy, permit disorders to continue, from which arise murders and plundering; for these usually harm the community at large, while the executions that come from the prince harm one individual in particular. And the new prince, above all other princes, cannot escape the reputation of being called cruel, since new states are full of dangers. And Virgil, through Dido,

12

---

[8]*Cesare Borgia (1476–1507)* He was known for his brutality and lack of scruples, not to mention his exceptionally good luck. He was a firm ruler, son of Pope Alexander VI.

[9]*Romagna* Region northwest of Tuscany; includes the towns of Bologna, Ferrara, Ravenna, and Rimini. Borgia united it as his base of power in 1501.

[10]*Pistoia* A town near Florence, disturbed by a civil war in 1501 which could have been averted by strong repressive measures.

states: "My difficult condition and the newness of my rule make me act in such a manner, and to set guards over my land on all sides."[11]

Nevertheless, a prince must be cautious in believing and in acting, 13 nor should he be afraid of his own shadow; and he should proceed in such a manner, tempered by prudence and humanity, so that too much trust may not render him imprudent nor too much distrust render him intolerable.

From this arises an argument: whether it is better to be loved than 14 to be feared, or the contrary. I reply that one should like to be both one and the other; but since it is difficult to join them together, it is much safer to be feared than to be loved when one of the two must be lacking. For one can generally say this about men: that they are ungrateful, fickle, simulators and deceivers, avoiders of danger, greedy for gain; and while you work for their good they are completely yours, offering you their blood, their property, their lives, and their sons, as I said earlier, when danger is far away; but when it comes nearer to you they turn away. And that prince who bases his power entirely on their words, finding himself stripped of other preparations, comes to ruin; for friendships that are acquired by a price and not by greatness and nobility of character are purchased but are not owned, and at the proper moment they cannot be spent. And men are less hesitant about harming someone who makes himself loved than one who makes himself feared because love is held together by a chain of obligation which, since men are a sorry lot, is broken on every occasion in which their own self-interest is concerned; but fear is held together by a dread of punishment which will never abandon you.

A prince must nevertheless make himself feared in such a manner 15 that he will avoid hatred, even if he does not acquire love; since to be feared and not to be hated can very well be combined; and this will always be so when he keeps his hands off the property and the women of his citizens and his subjects. And if he must take someone's life, he should do so when there is proper justification and manifest cause; but, above all, he should avoid the property of others; for men forget more quickly the death of their father than the loss of their patrimony. Moreover, the reasons for seizing their property are never lacking; and he who begins to live by stealing always finds a reason for taking what belongs to others; on the contrary, reasons for taking a life are rarer and disappear sooner.

---

[11]The quotation is from the *Aeneid* (II. 563–564), the greatest Latin epic poem, written by Virgil (70–19 B.C.). Dido in the poem is a woman general who rules Carthage.

But when the prince is with his armies and has under his command 16
a multitude of troops, then it is absolutely necessary that he not worry
about being considered cruel; for without that reputation he will never
keep an army united or prepared for any combat. Among the praiseworthy deeds of Hannibal[12] is counted this: that, having a very large
army, made up of all kinds of men, which he commanded in foreign
lands, there never arose the slightest dissention, neither among themselves nor against their prince, both during his good and his bad fortune. This could not have arisen from anything other than his inhuman cruelty, which, along with his many other abilities, made him
always respected and terrifying in the eyes of his soldiers; and without
that, to attain the same effect, his other abilities would not have sufficed. And the writers of history, having considered this matter very
little, on the one hand admire these deeds of his and on the other
condemn the main cause of them.

And that it be true that his other abilities would not have been 17
sufficient can be seen from the example of Scipio, a most extraordinary
man not only in his time but in all recorded history, whose armies in
Spain rebelled against him; this came about from nothing other than
his excessive compassion, which gave to his soldiers more liberty than
military discipline allowed. For this he was censured in the senate by
Fabius Maximus,[13] who called him the corruptor of the Roman militia.
The Locrians,[14] having been ruined by one of Scipio's officers, were not
avenged by him, nor was the arrogance of that officer corrected, all
because of his tolerant nature; so that someone in the senate who tried
to apologize for him said that there were many men who knew how
not to err better than they knew how to correct errors. Such a nature
would have, in time, damaged Scipio's fame and glory if he had maintained it during the empire; but, living under the control of the senate,
this harmful characteristic of his not only concealed itself but brought
him fame.

I conclude, therefore, returning to the problem of being feared and 18
loved, that since men love at their own pleasure and fear at the pleasure of the prince, a wise prince should build his foundation upon that

---

[12]***Hannibal (247–183 B.C.)*** An amazingly inventive military tactician who led
the Carthaginian armies against Rome for more than fifteen years. He crossed the Alps
from Gaul in order to surprise Rome. He was noted for use of the ambush and for "inhuman cruelty."

[13]***Fabius Maximus (?–203 B.C.)*** Roman general who fought Hannibal. He was jealous
of the younger Roman general Scipio.

[14]***Locrians*** Inhabitants of Locri, an Italian town settled by the Greeks in 683 B.C.

which belongs to him, not upon that which belongs to others: he must strive only to avoid hatred, as has been said.

How a Prince Should Keep His Word

How praiseworthy it is for a prince to keep his word and to live by 19 integrity and not by deceit everyone knows; nevertheless, one sees from the experience of our times that the princes who have accomplished great deeds are those who have cared little for keeping their promises and who have known how to manipulate the minds of men by shrewdness; and in the end they have surpassed those who laid their foundations upon honesty.

You must, therefore, know that there are two means of fighting: 20 one according to the laws, the other with force; the first way is proper to man, the second to beasts; but because the first, in many cases, is not sufficient, it becomes necessary to have recourse to the second. Therefore, a prince must know how to use wisely the natures of the beast and the man. This policy was taught to princes allegorically by the ancient writers, who described how Achilles and many other ancient princes were given to Chiron[15] the Centaur to be raised and taught under his discipline. This can only mean that, having a half-beast and half-man as a teacher, a prince must know how to employ the nature of the one and the other; and the one without the other cannot endure.

Since, then, a prince must know how to make good use of the 21 nature of the beast, he should choose from among the beasts the fox and the lion; for the lion cannot defend itself from traps and the fox cannot protect itself from wolves. It is therefore necessary to be a fox in order to recognize the traps and a lion in order to frighten the wolves. Those who play only the part of the lion do not understand matters. A wise ruler, therefore, cannot and should not keep his word when such an observance of faith would be to his disadvantage and when the reasons which made him promise are removed. And if men were all good, this rule would not be good; but since men are a sorry lot and will not keep their promises to you, you likewise need not keep yours to them. A prince never lacks legitimate reasons to break his promises. Of this one could cite an endless number of modern ex-

---

[15]**Chiron**   A mythical figure, a centaur (half man, half horse). Unlike most centaurs, he was wise and benevolent; he was also a legendary physician.

amples to show how many pacts, how many promises have been made null and void because of the infidelity of princes; and he who has known best how to use the fox has come to a better end. But it is necessary to know how to disguise this nature well and to be a great hypocrite and a liar: and men are so simpleminded and so controlled by their present necessities that one who deceives will always find another who will allow himself to be deceived.

I do not wish to remain silent about one of these recent instances. 22 Alexander VI[16] did nothing else, he thought about nothing else, except to deceive men, and he always found the occasion to do this. And there never was a man who had more forcefulness in his oaths, who affirmed a thing with more promises, and who honored his word less; nevertheless, his tricks always succeeded perfectly since he was well acquainted with this aspect of the world.

Therefore, it is not necessary for a prince to have all of the above- 23 mentioned qualities, but it is very necessary for him to appear to have them. Furthermore, I shall be so bold as to assert this: that having them and practicing them at all times is harmful; and appearing to have them is useful; for instance, to seem merciful, faithful, humane, forthright, religious, and to be so; but his mind should be disposed in such a way that should it become necessary not to be so, he will be able and know how to change to the contrary. And it is essential to understand this: that a prince, and especially a new prince, cannot observe all those things by which men are considered good, for in order to maintain the state he is often obliged to act against his promise, against charity, against humanity, and against religion. And therefore, it is necessary that he have a mind ready to turn itself according to the way the winds of Fortune and the changeability of affairs require him; and, as I said above, as long as it is possible, he should not stray from the good, but he should know how to enter into evil when necessity commands.

A prince, therefore, must be very careful never to let anything slip 24 from his lips which is not full of the five qualities mentioned above: he should appear, upon seeing and hearing him, to be all mercy, all faithfulness, all integrity, all kindness, all religion. And there is nothing more necessary than to seem to possess this last quality. And men in general judge more by their eyes than their hands; for everyone can see but few can feel. Everyone sees what you seem to be, few perceive

---

[16]***Alexander VI (1431–1503)*** Roderigo Borgia, pope from 1492 to 1503. He was Cesare Borgia's father and a corrupt but immensely powerful pope.

what you are, and those few do not dare to contradict the opinion of the many who have the majesty of the state to defend them; and in the actions of all men, and especially of princes, where there is no impartial arbiter, one must consider the final result.[17] Let a prince therefore act to seize and to maintain the state; his methods will always be judged honorable and will be praised by all; for ordinary people are always deceived by appearances and by the outcome of a thing; and in the world there is nothing but ordinary people; and there is no room for the few, while the many have a place to lean on. A certain prince[18] of the present day, whom I shall refrain from naming, preaches nothing but peace and faith, and to both one and the other he is entirely opposed; and both, if he had put them into practice, would have cost him many times over either his reputation or his state.

On Avoiding Being Despised and Hated

But since, concerning the qualities mentioned above, I have spoken about the most important, I should like to discuss the others briefly in this general manner: that the prince, as was noted above, should think about avoiding those things which make him hated and despised; and when he has avoided this, he will have carried out his duties and will find no danger whatsoever in other vices. As I have said, what makes him hated above all else is being rapacious and a usurper of the property and the women of his subjects; he must refrain from this; and in most cases, so long as you do not deprive them of either their property or their honor, the majority of men live happily; and you have only to deal with the ambition of a few, who can be restrained without difficulty and by many means. What makes him despised is being considered changeable, frivolous, effeminate, cowardly, irresolute; from these qualities a prince must guard himself as if from a reef, and he must strive to make everyone recognize in his actions greatness, spirit, dignity, and strength; and concerning the private affairs of his subjects, he must insist that his decision be irrevocable; and he should maintain himself in such a way that no man could imagine that he can deceive or cheat him.

That prince who projects such an opinion of himself is greatly esteemed; and it is difficult to conspire against a man with such a repu-

---

[17]The Italian original, *si guarda al fine*, has often been mistranslated as "the ends justify the means," something Machiavelli never wrote. [Translators' note]

[18]**A certain prince** Probably King Ferdinand V of Spain (1452–1516).

tation and difficult to attack him, provided that he is understood to be of great merit and revered by his subjects. For a prince must have two fears: one, internal, concerning his subjects; the other, external, concerning foreign powers. From the latter he can defend himself by his good troops and friends; and he will always have good friends if he has good troops; and internal affairs will always be stable when external affairs are stable, provided that they are not already disturbed by a conspiracy; and even if external conditions change, if he is properly organized and lives as I have said and does not lose control of himself, he will always be able to withstand every attack, just as I said that Nabis the Spartan[19] did. But concerning his subjects, when external affairs do not change, he has to fear that they may conspire secretly: the prince secures himself from this by avoiding being hated or despised and by keeping the people satisfied with him; this is a necessary matter, as was treated above at length. And one of the most powerful remedies a prince has against conspiracies is not to be hated by the masses; for a man who plans a conspiracy always believes that he will satisfy the people by killing the prince; but when he thinks he might anger them, he cannot work up the courage to undertake such a deed; for the problems on the side of the conspirators are countless. And experience demonstrates that conspiracies have been many but few have been concluded successfully; for anyone who conspires cannot be alone, nor can he find companions except from amongst those whom he believes to be dissatisfied; and as soon as you have uncovered your intent to one dissatisfied man, you give him the means to make himself happy, since he can have everything he desires by uncovering the plot; so much is this so that, seeing a sure gain on the one hand and one doubtful and full of danger on the other, if he is to maintain faith with you he has to be either an unusually good friend or a completely determined enemy of the prince. And to treat the matter briefly, I say that on the part of the conspirator there is nothing but fear, jealousy, and the thought of punishment that terrifies him; but on the part of the prince there is the majesty of the principality, the laws, the defenses of friends and the state to protect him; so that, with the good will of the people added to all these things, it is impossible for anyone to be so rash as to plot against him. For, where usually a conspirator has to be afraid before he executes his evil deed, in this case he must be afraid, having the people as an enemy, even after the crime is performed, nor can he hope to find any refuge because of this.

---

[19]***Nabis the Spartan (fl. 220 B.C.)*** A Greek tyrant routed by Philopoemon and the Achaean League.

One could cite countless examples on this subject; but I want to 27
satisfy myself with only one which occurred during the time of our
fathers. Messer Annibale Bentivogli, prince of Bologna and grandfather
of the present Messer Annibale, was murdered by the Canneschi[20]
family, who conspired against him; he left behind no heir except Messer Giovanni,[21] then only a baby. As soon as this murder occurred, the
people rose up and killed all the Canneschi. This came about because
of the good will that the house of the Bentivogli enjoyed in those days;
this good will was so great that with Annibale dead, and there being
no one of that family left in the city who could rule Bologna, the Bolo-
gnese people, having heard that in Florence there was one of the Bentivogli blood who was believed until that time to be the son of a black-
smith, went to Florence to find him, and they gave him the control of
that city; it was ruled by him until Messer Giovanni became of age to
rule.

I conclude, therefore, that a prince must be little concerned with 28
conspiracies when the people are well disposed toward him; but when
the populace is hostile and regards him with hatred, he must fear
everything and everyone. And well-organized states and wise princes
have, with great diligence, taken care not to anger the nobles and to
satisfy the common people and keep them contented; for this is one
of the most important concerns that a prince has.

---

[20]*Canneschi* Prominent family in Bologna.

[21]*Giovanni Bentivogli (1443–1508)* Former tyrant of Bologna. In sequence he was
a conspirator against, then a conspirator with Cesare Borgia.

QUESTIONS

1. The usual criticism of Machiavelli is that he advises his prince to be unscrupulous. Does this seem to be the case in this excerpt?
2. Is Machiavelli correct when he asserts that the great number of people are
not good? Does our government assume that to be true, too?
3. Politicians—especially heads of state—are the contemporary counterparts
of the prince. Should successful heads of state show skill in war to the
same extent Machiavelli's prince does?
4. Clarify the advice Machiavelli gives concerning liberality and stinginess.
Is this still good advice?
5. Are modern politicians likely to succeed by following all or most of
Machiavelli's recommendations?

WRITING ASSIGNMENTS

1. In speaking of the prince's military duties, Machiavelli says, "being disarmed makes you despised." Take a stand on this issue. If possible, choose an example or instance to strengthen your argument. Is it possible that in modern society being defenseless is an advantage?

2. One of Machiavelli's most controversial statements is: "A man who wishes to make a vocation of being good at all times will come to ruin among so many who are not good." Defend or attack this view. As much as possible, use personal experiences to bolster your opinion.

3. Find evidence within this excerpt to demonstrate that Machiavelli's attitude toward human nature is accurate. Remember that the usual criticism of Machiavelli is that he is cynical—that he thinks the worst of people rather than the best. Find quotations from the excerpt that would support either or both of these views; then use them in an essay, with analysis, to clarify just what Machiavelli's views on human nature are.

4. By referring to current events and current leaders—either local, national, or international—decide whether or not Machiavelli's advice to the prince would be useful to the modern politician. Consider the question of whether the advice is completely useless, completely reliable, or whether its value depends upon specific conditions. Establish first exactly what the advice is; show how it is applicable or inapplicable for specific politicians; then critique its general usefulness.

5. Probably the chief ethical issue raised by *The Prince* is the question of whether or not the ends justify the means that need to be used to achieve them. Write an essay in which you take a stand on this question. Begin by defining the issue: What does the phrase "the ends justify the means" actually mean? What are the difficulties in accepting the fact that unworthy means may achieve worthy ends? If possible, use some historical or personal examples that will give your argument substance. Carefully analyze Machiavelli's references to circumstances in which questionable means have been (or should have been) used to achieve worthy ends. Is it possible for a politician to concern himself only with ends and ignore the means entirely?

JEAN JACQUES ROUSSEAU

The Origin of Civil Society

JEAN JACQUES ROUSSEAU (1712–1778) was the son of a watch-maker and grew to be a man of letters, with a wide variety of accomplishments. Among other works, he wrote a novel, Emile; an opera, The Village Soothsayer; and an autobiography, The Confessions. The Social Contract, published in 1762, became a bible of the French Revolution. When Rousseau died, his body was given a place of honor in the Pantheon in Paris.

The Social Contract is notable for the way in which it establishes the relationship among the members of a body politic. By emphasizing the fact that each member of a society forfeits a certain amount of personal freedom for the greater good of the whole, and by emphasizing that the sovereign has immense responsibilities to the people, Rousseau conceived the structure of government in a novel way. Today we think of that way as basically democratic, since Rousseau constantly talks about certain types of equality which he expects to find in a well-ordered society. Equality before the law is probably the most important element of that society.

Equality before the law, a concept which we approve today, was

---

From *The Social Contract*. Translated by Gerard Hopkins.

a very revolutionary view for 1762. It implied that people who were born aristocrats would be equal before the law with those who were born commoners; it implied the same thing for the wealthy property holder and the pauper. Neither of these conditions obtained in any nation of the time, although Rousseau saw some hope for such equality in the achievements of English law. Rousseau is careful not to say more than was possible considering the times, but he implies that the body politic should be a commonwealth in which property would be much more widely distributed than it was in contemporary France.

He takes an interesting stance in proposing a time which he calls the natural state when men were not joined in social orders. Eventually they surrendered that natural state for a civil state; because there was a general willingness to subordinate individual rights, government came into being. The novelty of this idea for Rousseau's day was his emphasis on government as a product of the act of the people's will rather than as a product of the force of the sovereign. It introduced, as well, the concept of the responsibility of the sovereign to govern well, a concept the French monarch Louis XV (1710–1774) was not quick to accept or understand.

ROUSSEAU'S RHETORIC

Little of what Rousseau says here is original. His way of putting his points and of organizing and clarifying them is what makes the work effective. One important technique he uses is that of analogy. His most impressive use is the analogy of the family to the state. The technique of analogy always implies comparing a very familiar thing—the family—with something less familiar—the state. Then, Rousseau looks for the similarities between the two, such as the children as the people and the father as the sovereign. Such analogies can be enlightening or dangerous, depending on how far one is willing to push them.

The main rhetorical device Rousseau uses is analysis, particularly analysis of a logical type. He proposes a statement which seems, on the surface, to be reasonable; then he analyzes it part by part until he proves to the reader that it is either to be accepted or rejected. He is conspicuous in this application of logic in his section "Of Slavery," in which he proves that slavery is not defensible on any ground, including the widely held ground that prisoners of war may legitimately be made into slaves because they owe their lives to their captors.

During his passages of analysis, Rousseau occasionally pauses to *provide definitions of terms or circumstances or concepts. It is usually during the process of defining that Rousseau clarifies his argument so that the truth can be recognized. The technique is both simple and effective and is therefore important for us to examine, since we may use it as easily as he does.*

The reference to other authorities, the strategy of testimony, is sometimes overdone by writers of this period. But Rousseau depends on only a few authorities, notably Hugo Grotius, the Dutch legal authority, and Thomas Hobbes, the English social philosopher. They are most prominent in the early pages of the selection, and they provide only a few basic points that are indispensable for the argument. Again, this rhetorical strategy is easy for most of us to use, and its effectiveness cannot be underestimated.

Finally, it should be pointed out that Rousseau is in the habit of posing a considerable number of rhetorical questions. He says, "Man is born free, and everywhere he is in chains. Many a man believes himself to be the master of others who is, no less than they, a slave. How did this change take place? I do not know. What can make it legitimate?" He tells us that for the second question he may have a few answers. The technique of posing serious questions and then attempting to answer them is effective because the clarity of the question-and-answer structure is immediately apparent to the reader. Naturally, the technique can be overworked, but a careful balancing of question and answer can help provide a clarity that might otherwise be missing.

Paradox, a rhetorical device designed to capture a reader's attention and to provoke serious thought, is one of Rousseau's strengths. Being born free, but being everywhere now in chains is one of the most arresting paradoxes in literature. It is so strong that it provokes us to share Rousseau's seriousness in searching out the reasons—even to the point of examining the birth of society itself.

The Origin of Civil Society

Note

It is my wish to inquire whether it be possible, within the civil 1
order, to discover a legitimate and stable basis of Government. This
I shall do by considering human beings as they are and laws as they
might be. I shall attempt, throughout my investigations, to maintain
a constant connection between what right permits and interest de-
mands, in order that no separation may be made between justice and
utility. I intend to begin without first proving the importance of my
subject. Am I, it will be asked, either prince or legislator that I take
it upon me to write of politics? My answer is—No; and it is for that
very reason that I have chosen politics as the matter of my book.
Were I either the one or the other I should not waste my time in
laying down what has to be done. I should do it, or else hold my
peace.

I was born into a free state and am a member of its sovereign 2
body. My influence on public affairs may be small, but because I
have a right to exercise my vote, it is my duty to learn their nature,
and it has been for me a matter of constant delight, while meditating
on problems of Government in general, to find ever fresh reasons for
regarding with true affection the way in which these things are or-
dered in my native land.

The Subject of the First Book

Man is born free, and everywhere he is in chains. Many a man 3
believes himself to be the master of others who is, no less than they,
a slave. How did this change take place? I do not know. What can
make it legitimate? To this question I hope to be able to furnish an
answer.

Were I considering only force and the effects of force, I should say: 4
"So long as a People is constrained to obey, and does, in fact, obey, it
does well. So soon as it can shake off its yoke, and succeeds in doing
so, it does better. The fact that it has recovered its liberty by virtue of

that same right by which it was stolen, means either that it is entitled to resume it, or that its theft by others was, in the first place, without justification." But the social order is a sacred right which serves as a foundation for all other rights. This right, however, since it comes not by nature, must have been built upon conventions. To discover what these conventions are is the matter of our inquiry. But, before proceeding further, I must establish the truth of what I have so far advanced.

Of Primitive Societies

The oldest form of society—and the only natural one—is the fam- 5
ily. Children remain bound to their father for only just so long as they feel the need of him for their self-preservation. Once that need ceases the natural bond is dissolved. From then on, the children, freed from the obedience which they formerly owed, and the father, cleared of his debt of responsibility to them, return to a condition of equal independence. If the bond remain operative it is no longer something imposed by nature, but has become a matter of deliberate choice. The family is a family still, but by reason of convention only.

This shared liberty is a consequence of man's nature. Its first law 6
is that of self-preservation: its first concern is for what it owes itself. As soon as a man attains the age of reason he becomes his own master, because he alone can judge of what will best assure his continued existence.

We may, therefore, if we will, regard the family as the basic model 7
of all political associations. The ruler is the father writ large: the people are, by analogy, his children, and all, ruler and people alike, alienate their freedom only so far as it is to their advantage to do so. The only difference is that, whereas in the family the father's love for his children is sufficient reward to him for the care he has lavished on them, in the State, the pleasure of commanding others takes its place, since the ruler is not in a relation of love to his people.

Grotius[1] denies that political power is ever exercised in the inter- 8
ests of the governed, and quotes the institution of slavery in support of his contention. His invariable method of arguing is to derive Right from Fact. It might be possible to adopt a more logical system of reasoning, but none which would be more favorable to tyrants.

---

[1]*Hugo Grotius (1583–1645)* A Dutch lawyer who spent some time in exile in Paris. His fame as a child prodigy was considerable; his book on the laws of war *(De jure belli)* was widely known in Europe.

According to Grotius, therefore, it is doubtful whether the term 9 "human race" belongs to only a few hundred men, or whether those few hundred men belong to the human race. From the evidence of his book it seems clear that he holds by the first of these alternatives, and on this point Hobbes[2] is in agreement with him. If this is so, then humanity is divided into herds of livestock, each with its "guardian" who watches over his charges only that he may ultimately devour them.

Just as the shepherd is superior in kind to his sheep, so, too, the 10 shepherds of men, or, in other words, their rulers, are superior in kind to their peoples. This, according to Philo,[3] was the argument advanced by Caligula,[4] the Emperor, who drew from the analogy the perfectly true conclusion that either Kings are Gods or their subjects brute beasts.

The reasoning of Caligula, of Hobbes, and of Grotius is fundamen- 11 tally the same. Far earlier, Aristotle, too, had maintained that men are not by nature equal, but that some are born to be slaves, others to be masters.

Aristotle[5] was right: but he mistook the effect for the cause. Noth- 12 ing is more certain than that a man born into a condition of slavery is a slave by nature. A slave in fetters loses everything—even the desire to be freed from them. He grows to love his slavery, as the companions of Ulysses grew to love their state of brutish transformation.[6]

If some men are by nature slaves, the reason is that they have been 13 made slaves *against* nature. Force made the first slaves: cowardice has perpetuated the species.

I have made no mention of King Adam or of the Emperor Noah, 14

---

[2]*Thomas Hobbes (1588–1679)* Known as a materialist philosopher who did not credit divine influence in politics. An Englishman, he became famous for *Leviathan,* a study of politics that treated the state as if it were a monster (leviathan) with a life of its own.

[3]*Philo (fl. c. 10 B.C.)* A Jew who had absorbed Greek culture and who wrote widely on many subjects. His studies on Mosaic Law were considered important.

[4]*Caligula (12–41 A.D.)* Roman emperor of uncertain sanity. He loved his sister Drusilla so much that he had her deified when she died. A military commander, he was assassinated by an officer.

[5]*Aristotle (384–322 B.C.)* A student of Plato; his philosophical method became the dominant intellectual force in Western thought.

[6]*state of brutish transformation* This sentence refers to the Circe episode in Homer's *Odyssey* (X–XII). Circe was a sorceress who, by means of drugs, enchanted men and turned them into swine. Ulysses (Latin name of Odysseus), king of Ithaca, is the central figure of the *Odyssey.*

the father of three great Monarchs[7] who divided up the universe between them, as did the children of Saturn,[8] whom some have been tempted to identify with them. I trust that I may be given credit for my moderation, since, being descended in a direct line from one of these Princes, and quite possibly belonging to the elder branch, I may, for all I know, were my claims supported in law, be even now the legitimate Sovereign of the Human Race.[9] However that may be, all will concur in the view that Adam was King of the World, as was Robinson Crusoe of his island, only so long as he was its only inhabitant, and that the great advantage of empire held on such terms was that the Monarch, firmly seated on his throne, had no need to fear rebellions, conspiracy, or war.

Of the Right of the Strongest

However strong a man, he is never strong enough to remain master 15 always, unless he transform his Might into Right, and Obedience into Duty. Hence we have come to speak of the Right of the Strongest, a right which, seemingly assumed in irony, has, in fact, become established in principle. But the meaning of the phrase has never been adequately explained. Strength is a physical attribute, and I fail to see how any moral sanction can attach to its effects. To yield to the strong is an act of necessity, not of will. At most it is the result of a dictate of prudence. How, then, can it become a duty?

Let us assume for a moment that some such Right does really exist. 16 The only deduction from this premise is inexplicable gibberish. For to admit that Might makes Right is to reverse the process of effect and cause. The mighty man who defeats his rival becomes heir to his Right. So soon as we can disobey with impunity, disobedience becomes legitimate. And, since the Mightiest is always right, it merely remains for us to become possessed of Might. But what validity can there be in a Right which ceases to exist when Might changes hands? If a man be constrained by Might to obey, what need has he to obey

---

[7]*the father of three great Monarchs* Adam in the Bible (Genesis 1:1–2:4) fathered Cain, Abel, and Seth. Noah's sons, Shem, Ham, and Japhet, repopulated the world after the Flood (Genesis 6:11–9:19).

[8]*children of Saturn* Saturn is a mythic god associated with the golden age of Rome. The reference to children is obscure, since Picus was his only son.

[9]*Sovereign of the Human Race* Rousseau is being ironic, of course; like the rest of us, he is descended from Adam.

by Duty? And if he is not constrained to obey, there is no further obligation on him to do so. It follows, therefore, that the word Right adds nothing to the idea of Might. It becomes, in this connection, completely meaningless.

Obey the Powers that be. If that means Yield to Force, the precept   17
is admirable but redundant. My reply to those who advance it is that no case will ever be found of its violation. All power comes from God. Certainly, but so do all ailments. Are we to conclude from such an argument that we are never to call in the doctor? If I am waylaid by a footpad at the corner of a wood, I am constrained by force to give him my purse. But if I can manage to keep it from him, is it my duty to hand it over? His pistol is also a symbol of Power. It must, then, be admitted that Might does not create Right, and that no man is under an obligation to obey any but the legitimate powers of the State. And so I continually come back to the question I first asked.

Of Slavery

Since no man has natural authority over his fellows, and since   18
Might can produce no Right, the only foundation left for legitimate authority in human societies is Agreement.

If a private citizen, says Grotius, can alienate his liberty and make   19
himself another man's slave, why should not a whole people do the same, and subject themselves to the will of a King? The argument contains a number of ambiguous words which stand in need of explanation. But let us confine our attention to one only—*alienate*. To alienate means to give or to sell. Now a man who becomes the slave of another does not give himself. He sells himself in return for bare subsistence, if for nothing more. But why should a whole people sell themselves? So far from furnishing subsistence to his subjects, a King draws his own from them, and from them alone. According to Rabelais,[10] it takes a lot to keep a King. Do we, then, maintain that a subject surrenders his person on condition that his property be taken too? It is difficult to see what he will have left.

It will be said that the despot guarantees civil peace to his subjects.   20
So be it. But how are they the gainers if the wars to which his ambition may expose them, his insatiable greed, and the vexatious demands of his Ministers cause them more loss than would any outbreak of

---

[10]***François Rabelais (1490–1553)*** French writer, author of *Gargantua* and *Pantagruel,* satires on politics and religion.

internal dissension? How do they benefit if that very condition of civil peace be one of the causes of their wretchedness? One can live peacefully enough in a dungeon, but such peace will hardly, of itself, ensure one's happiness. The Greeks imprisoned in the cave of Cyclops[11] lived peacefully while awaiting their turn to be devoured.

To say that a man gives himself for nothing is to commit oneself to an absurd and inconceivable statement. Such an act of surrender is illegitimate, null, and void by the mere fact that he who makes it is not in his right mind. To say the same thing of a whole People is tantamount to admitting that the People in question are a nation of imbeciles. Imbecility does not produce Right.   21

Even if a man can alienate himself, he cannot alienate his children. They are born free, their liberty belongs to them, and no one but themselves has a right to dispose of it. Before they have attained the age of reason their father may make, on their behalf, certain rules with a view to ensuring their preservation and well-being. But any such limitation of their freedom of choice must be regarded as neither irrevocable nor unconditional, for to alienate another's liberty is contrary to the natural order, and is an abuse of the father's rights. It follows that an arbitrary government can be legitimate only on condition that each successive generation of subjects is free either to accept or to reject it, and if this is so, then the government will no longer be arbitrary.   22

When a man renounces his liberty he renounces his essential manhood, his rights, and even his duty as a human being. There is no compensation possible for such complete renunciation. It is incompatible with man's nature, and to deprive him of his free will is to deprive his actions of all moral sanction. The convention, in short, which sets up on one side an absolute authority, and on the other an obligation to obey without question, is vain and meaningless. Is it not obvious that where we can demand everything we owe nothing? Where there is no mutual obligation, no interchange of duties, it must, surely, be clear that the actions of the commanded cease to have any moral value? For how can it be maintained that my slave has any "right" against me when everything that he has is my property? His right being *my* right, it is absurd to speak of it as ever operating to my disadvantage.   23

Grotius, and those who think like him, have found in the fact of war another justification for the so-called "right" of slavery. They ar-   24

---

[11]*cave of Cyclops* The cyclops is a one-eyed giant cannibal whose cave is the scene of one of Odysseus's triumphs in Homer's *Odyssey*.

gue that since the victor has a *right* to kill his defeated enemy, the latter may, if he so wish, ransom his life at the expense of his liberty, and that this compact is the more legitimate in that it benefits both parties.

But it is evident that this alleged *right* of a man to kill his enemies 25 is not in any way a derivative of the state of war, if only because men, in their primitive condition of independence, are not bound to one another by any relationship sufficiently stable to produce a state either of war or of peace. They are not *naturally* enemies. It is the link between *things* rather than between *men* that constitutes war, and since a state of war cannot originate in simple personal relations, but only in relations between things, private hostility between man and man cannot obtain either in a state of nature where there is no generally accepted system of private property, or in a state of society where law is the supreme authority.

Single combats, duels, personal encounters are incidents which do 26 not constitute a "state" of anything. As to those private wars which were authorized by the Ordinances of King Louis IX[12] and suspended by the Peace of God, they were merely an abuse of Feudalism—that most absurd of all systems of government, so contrary was it to the principles of Natural Right and of all good polity.

War, therefore, is something that occurs not between man and 27 man, but between States. The individuals who become involved in it are enemies only by accident. They fight not as men or even as citizens, but as soldiers: not as members of this or that national group, but as its defenders. A State can have as its enemies only other States, not men at all, seeing that there can be no true relationship between things of a different nature.

This principle is in harmony with that of all periods, and with the 28 constant practice of every civilized society. A declaration of war is a warning, not so much to Governments as to their subjects. The foreigner—whether king, private person, or nation as a whole—who steals, murders, or holds in durance the subjects of another country without first declaring war on that country's Prince, acts not as an enemy but as a brigand. Even when war has been joined, the just Prince, though he may seize all public property in enemy territory, yet respects the property and possessions of individuals, and, in so doing,

---

[12]*King Louis IX (1214–1270)* King of France, also called St. Louis. He was looked upon as an ideal monarch.

shows his concern for those rights on which his own laws are based. The object of war being the destruction of the enemy State, a commander has a perfect right to kill its defenders so long as their arms are in their hands: but once they have laid them down and have submitted, they cease to be enemies, or instruments employed by an enemy, and revert to the condition of men, pure and simple, over whose lives no one can any longer exercise a rightful claim. Sometimes it is possible to destroy a State without killing any of its subjects, and nothing in war can be claimed as a right save what may be necessary for the accomplishment of the victor's end. These principles are not those of Grotius, nor are they based on the authority of poets, but derive from the Nature of Things, and are founded upon Reason.

The Right of Conquest finds its sole sanction in the Law of the 29 Strongest. If war does not give to the victor the right to massacre his defeated enemies, he cannot base upon a nonexistent right any claim to the further one of enslaving them. We have the right to kill our enemies only when we cannot enslave them. It follows, therefore, that the right to enslave cannot be deduced from the right to kill, and that we are guilty of enforcing an iniquitous exchange if we make a vanquished foeman purchase with his liberty that life over which we have no right. Is it not obvious that once we begin basing the right of life and death on the right to enslave, and the right to enslave on the right of life and death, we are caught in a vicious circle? Even if we assume the existence of this terrible right to kill all and sundry, I still maintain that a man enslaved, or a People conquered, in war is under no obligation to obey beyond the point at which force ceases to be operative. If the victor spares the life of his defeated opponent in return for an equivalent, he cannot be said to have shown him mercy. In either case he destroys him, but in the latter case he derives value from his act, while in the former he gains nothing. His authority, however, rests on no basis but that of force. There is still a state of war between the two men, and it conditions the whole relationship in which they stand to one another. The enjoyment of the Rights of War presupposes that there has been no treaty of Peace. Conqueror and conquered have, to be sure, entered into a compact, but such a compact, far from liquidating the state of war, assumes its continuance.

Thus, in whatever way we look at the matter, the "Right" to en- 30 slave has no existence, not only because it is without legal validity, but because the very term is absurd and meaningless. The words *Slavery* and *Right* are contradictory and mutually exclusive. Whether we be considering the relation of one man to another man, or of an individual to a whole People, it is equally idiotic to say—"You and I have made a compact which represents nothing but loss to you and gain to me. I shall observe it so long as it pleases me to do so—and so shall you, until I cease to find it convenient."

That We Must Always Go Back to an Original Compact

Even were I to grant all that I have so far refuted, the champions of 31 despotism would not be one whit the better off. There will always be a vast difference between subduing a mob and governing a social group. No matter how many isolated individuals may submit to the enforced control of a single conqueror, the resulting relationship will ever be that of Master and Slave, never of People and Ruler. The body of men so controlled may be an agglomeration; it is not an association. It implies neither public welfare nor a body politic. An individual may conquer half the world, but he is still only an individual. His interests, wholly different from those of his subjects, are private to himself. When he dies his empire is left scattered and disintegrated. He is like an oak which crumbles and collapses in ashes so soon as the fire consumes it.

"A People," says Grotius, "may give themselves to a king." His 32 argument implies that the said People were already a People before this act of surrender. The very act of gift was that of a political group and presupposed public deliberation. Before, therefore, we consider the act by which a People chooses their king, it were well if we considered the act by which a People is constituted as such. For it necessarily precedes the other, and is the true foundation on which all Societies rest.

Had there been no original compact, why, unless the choice were 33 unanimous, should the minority ever have agreed to accept the decision of the majority? What right have the hundred who desire a master to vote for the ten who do not? The institution of the franchise is, in itself, a form of compact, and assumes that, at least once in its operation, complete unanimity existed.

Of the Social Pact

I assume, for the sake of argument, that a point was reached in the 34 history of mankind when the obstacles to continuing in a state of Nature were stronger than the forces which each individual could employ to the end of continuing in it. The original state of Nature, therefore, could no longer endure, and the human race would have perished had it not changed its manner of existence.

Now, since men can by no means engender new powers, but can 35 only unite and control those of which they are already possessed, there is no way in which they can maintain themselves save by coming together and pooling their strength in a way that will enable them to withstand any resistance exerted upon them from without. They must develop some sort of central direction and learn to act in concert.

Such a concentration of powers can be brought about only as the 36 consequence of an agreement reached between individuals. But the self-preservation of each single man derives primarily from his own strength and from his own freedom. How, then, can he limit these without, at the same time, doing himself an injury and neglecting that care which it is his duty to devote to his own concerns? This difficulty, in so far as it is relevant to my subject, can be expressed as follows:

"Some form of association must be found as a result of which the 37 whole strength of the community will be enlisted for the protection of the person and property of each constituent member, in such a way that each, when united to his fellows, renders obedience to his own will, and remains as free as he was before." That is the basic problem of which the Social Contract provides the solution.

The clauses of this Contract are determined by the Act of Associa- 38 tion in such a way that the least modification must render them null and void. Even though they may never have been formally enunciated, they must be everywhere the same, and everywhere tacitly admitted and recognized. So completely must this be the case that, should the social compact be violated, each associated individual would at once resume all the rights which once were his, and regain his natural liberty, by the mere fact of losing the agreed liberty for which he renounced it.

It must be clearly understood that the clauses in question can be 39 reduced, in the last analysis, to one only, to wit, the complete alienation by each associate member to the community of *all his rights*. For, in the first place, since each has made surrender of himself without reservation, the resultant conditions are the same for all: and, because they are the same for all, it is in the interest of none to make them onerous to his fellows.

Furthermore, this alienation having been made unreservedly, the 40 union of individuals is as perfect as it well can be, none of the associated members having any claim against the community. For should there be any rights left to individuals, and no common authority be empowered to pronounce as between them and the public, then each, being in some things his own judge, would soon claim to be so in all. Were that so, a state of Nature would still remain in being, the conditions of association becoming either despotic or ineffective.

In short, whoso gives himself to all gives himself to none. And, 41 since there is no member of the social group over whom we do not acquire precisely the same rights as those over ourselves which we have surrendered to him, it follows that we gain the exact equivalent of what we lose, as well as an added power to conserve what we already have.

If, then, we take from the social pact everything which is not essential to it, we shall find it to be reduced to the following terms: "each of us contributes to the group his person and the powers which he wields as a person under the supreme direction of the general will, and we receive into the body politic each individual as forming an indivisible part of the whole."

As soon as the act of association becomes a reality, it substitutes 43 for the person of each of the contracting parties a moral and collective body made up of as many members as the constituting assembly has votes, which body receives from this very act of constitution its unity, its dispersed *self*, and its will. The public person thus formed by the union of individuals was known in the old days as a *City*, but now as the *Republic* or *Body Politic*. This, when it fulfils a passive role, is known by its members as *The State*, when an active one, as *The Sovereign People*, and, in contrast to other similar bodies, as a *Power*. In respect of the constituent associates, it enjoys the collective name of *The People*, the individuals who compose it being known as *Citizens* in so far as they share in the sovereign authority, as *Subjects* in so far as they owe obedience to the laws of the State. But these different terms frequently overlap, and are used indiscriminately one for the other. It is enough that we should realize the difference between them when they are employed in a precise sense.

Of the Sovereign

It is clear from the above formula that the act of association implies a mutual undertaking between the body politic and its constituent members. Each individual comprising the former contracts, so to speak, with himself and has a twofold function. As a member of the

sovereign people he owes a duty to each of his neighb
Citizen, to the sovereign people as a whole. But we can
that maxim of Civil Law according to which no man can
undertaking entered into with himself, because there is a great difference between a man's duty to himself and to a whole of which he
forms a part.

Here it should be pointed out that a public decision which can en- 45
join obedience on all subjects to their Sovereign, by reason of the double aspect under which each is seen, cannot, on the contrary, bind the
sovereign in his dealings with himself. Consequently, it is against the
nature of the body politic that the sovereign should impose upon himself a law which he cannot infringe. For, since he can regard himself
under one aspect only, he is in the position of an individual entering
into a contract with himself. Whence it follows that there is not, nor
can be, any fundamental law which is obligatory for the whole body
of the People, not even the social contract itself. This does not mean
that the body politic is unable to enter into engagements with some
other Power, provided always that such engagements do not derogate
from the nature of the Contract; for the relation of the body politic to
a foreign Power is that of a simple individual.

But the body politic, or Sovereign, in that it derives its being sim- 46
ply and solely from the sanctity of the said Contract, can never bind
itself, even in its relations with a foreign Power, by any decision which
might derogate from the validity of the original act. It may not, for
instance, alienate any portion of itself, nor make submission to any
other sovereign. To violate the act by reason of which it exists would
be tantamount to destroying itself, and that which is nothing can produce nothing.

As soon as a mob has become united into a body politic, any attack 47
upon one of its members is an attack upon itself. Still more important is
the fact that, should any offense be committed against the body politic as
a whole, the effect must be felt by each of its members. Both duty and interest, therefore, oblige the two contracting parties to render one another
mutual assistance. The same individuals should seek to unite under this
double aspect all the advantages which flow from it.

Now, the Sovereign People, having no existence outside that of the 48
individuals who compose it, has, and can have, no interest at variance
with theirs. Consequently, the sovereign power need give no guarantee
to its subjects, since it is impossible that the body should wish to
injure all its members, nor, as we shall see later, can it injure any
single individual. The Sovereign, by merely existing, is always what it
should be.

But the same does not hold true of the relation of subject to sover- 49
eign. In spite of common interest, there can be no guarantee that the
subject will observe his duty to the sovereign unless means are found
to ensure his loyalty.

Each individual, indeed, may, as a man, exercise a will at variance 50
with, or different from, that general will to which, as citizen, he contributes. His personal interest may dictate a line of action quite other
than that demanded by the interest of all. The fact that his own existence as an individual has an absolute value, and that he is, by nature,
an independent being, may lead him to conclude that what he owes to
the common cause is something that he renders of his own free will;
and he may decide that by leaving the debt unpaid he does less harm
to his fellows than he would to himself should he make the necessary
surrender. Regarding the moral entity constituting the State as a rational abstraction because it is not a man, he might enjoy his rights as
a citizen without, at the same time, fulfilling his duties as a subject,
and the resultant injustice might grow until it brought ruin upon the
whole body politic.

In order, then, that the social compact may not be but a vain for- 51
mula, it must contain, though unexpressed, the single undertaking
which can alone give force to the whole, namely, that whoever shall
refuse to obey the general will must be constrained by the whole body
of his fellow citizens to do so: which is no more than to say that it
may be necessary to compel a man to be free—freedom being that condition which, by giving each citizen to his country, guarantees him
from all personal dependence and is the foundation upon which the
whole political machine rests, and supplies the power which works it.
Only the recognition by the individual of the rights of the community
can give legal force to undertakings entered into between citizens,
which, otherwise, would become absurd, tyrannical, and exposed to
vast abuses.

Of the Civil State

The passage from the state of nature to the civil state produces a 52
truly remarkable change in the individual. It substitutes justice for instinct in his behavior, and gives to his actions a moral basis which
formerly was lacking. Only when the voice of duty replaces physical
impulse and when right replaces the cravings of appetite does the man
who, till then, was concerned solely with himself, realize that he is
under compulsion to obey quite different principles, and that he must

now consult his reason and not merely respond to the promptings of desire. Although he may find himself deprived of many advantages which were his in a state of nature, he will recognize that he has gained others which are of far greater value. By dint of being exercised, his faculties will develop, his ideas take on a wider scope, his sentiments become ennobled, and his whole soul be so elevated, that, but for the fact that misuse of the new conditions still, at times, degrades him to a point below that from which he has emerged, he would unceasingly bless the day which freed him for ever from his ancient state, and turned him from a limited and stupid animal into an intelligent being and a Man.

Let us reduce all this to terms which can be easily compared. What 53 a man loses as a result of the Social Contract is his natural liberty and his unqualified right to lay hands on all that tempts him, provided only that he can compass its possession. What he gains is civil liberty and the ownership of what belongs to him. That we may labor under no illusion concerning these compensations, it is well that we distinguish between natural liberty which the individual enjoys so long as he is strong enough to maintain it, and civil liberty which is curtailed by the general will. Between possessions which derive from physical strength and the right of the first-comer, and ownership which can be based only on a positive title.

To the benefits conferred by the status of citizenship might be 54 added that of Moral Freedom, which alone makes a man his own master. For to be subject to appetite is to be a slave, while to obey the laws laid down by society is to be free. But I have already said enough on this point, and am not concerned here with the philosophical meaning of the word *liberty*.

Of Real Property

Each individual member of the Community gives himself to it at 55 the moment of its formation. What he gives is the whole man as he then is, with all his qualities of strength and power, and everything of which he stands possessed. Not that, as a result of this act of gift, such possessions, by changing hands and becoming the property of the Sovereign, change their nature. Just as the resources of strength upon which the City can draw are incomparably greater than those at the disposition of any single individual, so, too, is public possession when backed by a greater power. It is made more irrevocable, though not, so far, at least, as regards foreigners, more legitimate. For the State, by reason of the Social Contract which, within it, is the basis of all Rights, is the master of all its members' goods, though, in its dealings with other Powers, it is so only by virtue of its rights as first occupier, which come to it from the individuals who make it up.

The Right of "first occupancy," though more real than the "Right 56 of the strongest," becomes a genuine right only after the right of property has been established. All men have a natural right to what is necessary to them. But the positive act which establishes a man's claim to any particular item of property limits him to that and excludes him from all others. His share having been determined, he must confine himself to that, and no longer has any claim on the property of the community. That is why the right of "first occupancy," however weak it be in a state of nature, is guaranteed to every man enjoying the status of citizen. In so far as he benefits from this right, he withholds his claim, not so much from what is another's, as from what is not specifically his.

In order that the right of "first occupancy" may be legalized, the 57 following conditions must be present. (1) There must be no one already living on the land in question. (2) A man must occupy only so much of it as is necessary for his subsistence. (3) He must take possession of it, not by empty ceremony, but by virtue of his intention to work and to cultivate it, for that, in the absence of legal title, alone constitutes a claim which will be respected by others.

In effect, by according the right of "first occupancy" to a man's 58 needs and to his will to work, are we not stretching it as far as it will go? Should not some limits be set to this right? Has a man only to set foot on land belonging to the community to justify his claim to be its master? Just because he is strong enough, at one particular moment, to keep others off, can he demand that they shall never return? How can a man or a People take possession of vast territories, thereby excluding the rest of the world from their enjoyment, save by an act of criminal usurpation, since, as the result of such an act, the rest of humanity is deprived of the amenities of dwelling and subsistence which nature has provided for their common enjoyment? When Nuñez Balboa,[13] landing upon a strip of coast, claimed the Southern Sea and the whole of South America as the property of the crown of Castille, was he thereby justified in dispossessing its former inhabitants, and in excluding from it all the other princes of the earth? Grant that, and there will be no end to such vain ceremonies. It would be open to His

---

[13]*Nuñez Balboa (1475–1519)* Spanish explorer who discovered the Pacific Ocean.

Catholic Majesty[14] to claim from his Council Chamber possession of
the whole Universe, only excepting those portions of it already in the
ownership of other princes.

One can understand how the lands of individuals, separate but con- 59
tiguous, become public territory, and how the right of sovereignty, extending from men to the land they occupy, becomes at one real and
personal—a fact which makes their owners more than ever dependent,
and turns their very strength into a guarantee of their fidelity. This is
an advantage which does not seem to have been considered by the
monarchs of the ancient world, who, claiming to be no more than
kings of the Persians, the Scythians, the Macedonians, seem to have
regarded themselves rather as the rulers of men than as the masters of
countries. Those of our day are cleverer, for they style themselves
kings of France, of Spain, of England, and so forth. Thus, by controlling
the land, they can be very sure of controlling its inhabitants.

The strange thing about this act of alienation is that, far from de- 60
priving its members of their property by accepting its surrender, the
Community actually establishes their claim to its legitimate ownership, and changes what was formerly mere usurpation into a right, by
virtue of which they may enjoy possession. As owners they are Trust-
ees for the Commonwealth. Their rights are respected by their fellow
citizens and are maintained by the united strength of the community
against any outside attack. From ceding their property to the State—
and thus, to themselves—they derive nothing but advantage, since
they have, so to speak, acquired all that they have surrendered. This
paradox is easily explained once we realize the distinction between the
rights exercised by the Sovereign and by the Owner over the same
piece of property, as will be seen later.

It may so happen that a number of men begin to group themselves 61
into a community before ever they own property at all, and that only
later, when they have got possession of land sufficient to maintain
them all, do they either enjoy it in common or parcel it between themselves in equal lots or in accordance with such scale of proportion as
may be established by the sovereign. However this acquisition be
made, the right exercised by each individual over his own particular
share must always be subordinated to the overriding claim of the
Community as such. Otherwise there would be no strength in the social bond, nor any real power in the exercise of sovereignty.

---

[14]***His Catholic Majesty*** A reference to the king of Spain, probably Ferdinand II of
Aragon (1452–1516).

I will conclude this chapter, and the present Book, with a remark 62 which should serve as basis for every social system: that, so far from destroying natural equality, the primitive compact substitutes for it a moral and legal equality which compensates for all those physical inequalities from which men suffer. However unequal they may be in bodily strength or in intellectual gifts, they become equal in the eyes of the law, and as a result of the compact into which they have entered.

QUESTIONS

1. Rousseau says that the oldest and only natural form of society is the family. Is this true? Are there any other natural forms of society evident to you?
2. What is the meaning of the phrase "might makes right"?
3. Is political power ever exercised in the interest of the governed?
4. Rousseau describes a "body politic." What does he mean by the term? What does he mean by "Commonwealth" when he describes the social order by that term?
5. Rousseau emphasizes natural, moral, and legal equality. What does each kind of equality imply?

WRITING ASSIGNMENTS

1. The famous opening lines—"Man is born free, and everywhere he is in chains. Many a man believes himself to be the master of others who is, no less than they, a slave"—were greeted with extraordinary enthusiasm in Rousseau's time. Is it possible to apply these lines to the condition of people you know in your own community? In the nation at large? In what senses do people make slaves of themselves today? In what senses are they made slaves by others?
2. Define the difference between one's duty to oneself and one's duty to the whole of which one forms a part. Assume that the individual is yourself and that the "whole" is your social structure (locally, nationally, on campus). Define each kind of duty, referring as much as possible to specific acts or responsibilities; then establish the differences and the ways in which they may come into conflict with one another.
3. One of the most controversial statements in this extract is: "All men have a natural right to what is necessary to them." Examine this statement carefully. What things or circumstances are necessary to people? Be specific and inclusive. Does Rousseau indicate what is necessary and what is not? Take a stand on whether or not Rousseau is correct in his statement.

If he is correct, who should provide the necessities to those who cannot provide for themselves? Does Rousseau take into account those who cannot provide for themselves? Should the necessities be provided for those who will not (as opposed to cannot) provide for themselves? If society will not provide necessities, does the individual have the right of revolution? What rights does the individual have?

4. Consider in some detail the appropriateness of the analogy between the family and the state. Is Rousseau correct in making the analogy in the first place? To what extent does he feel it is a reasonable comparison? By analyzing the details of the family as you know it, establish what the similarities and the differences are between the family and the government. Which responsibilities in one situation carry over to the other? In what sense may it be said that learning to live in a family is preparation for learning to live in a social state?

5. Rousseau contrasts natural liberty with civil liberty. Natural liberty is possible in a state of nature; civil liberty is possible in a civil state. Define each kind of liberty carefully, using a number of examples. What will the differences be between life in a state of nature and life in a civil state? Which state is preferable? What are the reasons for your views? Point to Rousseau's own arguments (he prefers the civil state) and analyze them carefully to support your views. Look for opportunities to use analogy in treating this issue.

THOMAS JEFFERSON

The Declaration of Independence

THOMAS JEFFERSON *(1743–1826), an exceptionally accomplished and well-educated man, is probably best known for writing the Declaration of Independence, a work composed under the eyes of Benjamin Franklin, John Adams, and the Continental Congress, which spent two and a half days going over every word. The substance of the document was developed in committee, but Jefferson, because of the grace of his style, was chosen to do the actual writing. The result is one of the most memorable statements in American history.*

Jefferson had a long and distinguished career. He received a classical education and went on to become a lawyer. By the time he took a seat in the House of Burgesses, which governed Virginia, that colony was already on a course toward revolution. His "A Summary View of the Rights of British America" (1774) first brought him to the attention of those who were agitating for independence.

Jefferson's services to Virginia were considerable. In addition to serving in the House of Burgesses, he became governor (1779) and founded the University of Virginia (1809). Many details of the design of the university's buildings reflect Jefferson's considerable skill as an architect. His one book, Notes on Virginia *(1782), is sometimes personal, sometimes public, sometimes scientific, sometimes haphazard. He discusses slavery, racial differences, the effects of the envi-*

ronment on people, and some of his own feelings about revolution while describing his home state, its geography and its people.

Jefferson's services to the nation include being the first secretary of state (1789–1797), second vice-president (1797–1801), and third president (1801–1809). During his presidency he negotiated the Louisiana Purchase, buying 800,000 square miles of land west of the Mississippi from France for only $15 million. He was sympathetic to the efforts of the French to throw off their monarchy, but when Napoleon extended French influence into the rest of Europe by waging war, Jefferson was careful to keep the United States neutral.

Jefferson was a well-educated eighteenth-century gentleman. His training in the classics and his wide reading in modern authors helped him become a gifted stylist. His work has balance and eloquence as well as clarity. The Declaration of Independence says little that was not familiar or widely understood at the time, but what it does say, it says in a fashion that is memorable.

JEFFERSON'S RHETORIC

Jefferson is notable for a number of interesting techniques. One is the periodic sentence, which was very typical of the age. The first sentence of the Declaration is periodic, which means that it is long and carefully balanced, and the main point comes at the end. Such sentences are not popular today, although an occasional periodic sentence can be powerful in contemporary prose. That first sentence says (in paraphrase): When one nation must sever its relations with a parent nation . . . and stand as an independent nation itself . . . the causes ought to be explained. The entire paragraph is taken up by this one sentence. Moreover, the main body of the Declaration is devoted to listing the "causes," so we see that the most important element of the sentence comes at the end.

The periodic sentence demands certain qualities of balance and parallelism which all good writers ought to pay attention to. The first sentence in paragraph 2 demonstrates both qualities. The balance is achieved by making each part of the sentence about the same length. The parallelism is achieved by using certain key linking words in repetition (they are in roman type in the analysis below). Note how the "truths" mentioned in the first clause are enumerated in the succession of noun clauses beginning with "that"; "Rights" are enumerated in the final clause.

We hold these truths to be self-evident,
    that all men are created equal,
    that they are endowed by their Creator with certain
        unalienable Rights,
    that among these are Life, Liberty and the pursuit of Happiness.

Parallelism is one of the greatest stylistic techniques available to a writer sensitive to rhetoric. It is a natural technique—many untrained writers and speakers develop it on their own.

One result of using parallelism is that one tends to employ the very useful device of enumeration, or the list. Many writers use this technique very effectively by establishing from the first that: "There are three important issues I wish to address. . . ."; and then numbering them: "First, I want to say. . . . Secondly. . . ," and so on. Naturally, as with any technique, this can become tiresome. Used judiciously, it is exceptionally authoritative and powerful. Jefferson devotes paragraphs 3–29 to enumerating the "causes" he mentioned in paragraph 1. Each one constitutes a separate paragraph; thus, each has separate weight and importance. Each begins with "He" or "For" and is therefore in parallel structure. The technique is called anaphora, repetition of the same words at the beginning of successive lines. Jefferson's use of anaphora here is one of the best-known and most effective in all literature. The "He" referred to is England's King George III (1738–1820), who is never mentioned by name. It is not a personality Congress is opposed to; it is the sovereign of a nation which is oppressing the United States and a tyrant who is not dignified by being named. The "For" introduces grievous acts the king has given his assent for; these are offenses against the colonies.

None of the causes is developed in any detail. We do not have specific information about what trade was cut off by the British, what taxes were imposed without consent, how King George waged war or abdicated government in the colonies. Presumably, Jefferson's audience knew the details. What he did, in listing in twenty-seven paragraphs all the causes, was to point out how many there were. And all are so serious that one alone could cause a revolution. The effect of this enumeration is to illustrate the patience of the colonies up to this point. Jefferson is telling the world that the colonies have finally lost patience, as a result of the causes he lists. The Declaration of Independence projects the careful meditations and decisions of exceptionally calm, patient, and—above all—reasonable people. The periodicity of the sentences and the balance of their parallelism underscore thoughtfulness, grace, learning, and ultimately wisdom.

The Declaration of Independence

In Congress, July 4, 1776

The Unanimous Declaration of the Thirteen United States of America

When in the Course of human events, it becomes necessary for one 1
people to dissolve the political bands which have connected them with
another, and to assume among the Powers of the earth, the separate
and equal station to which the Laws of Nature and of Nature's God
entitle them, a decent respect to the opinions of mankind requires that
they should declare the causes which impel them to the separation.

We hold these truths to be self-evident, that all men are created 2
equal, that they are endowed by their Creator with certain unalienable
Rights, that among these are Life, Liberty and the pursuit of Happiness. That to secure these rights, Governments are instituted among
Men, deriving their just powers from the consent of the governed. That
whenever any Form of Government becomes destructive of these ends,
it is the Right of the People to alter or to abolish it, and to institute a
new Government, laying its foundation on such principles and organizing its powers in such form, as to them shall seem most likely to
effect their Safety and Happiness. Prudence, indeed, will dictate that
Governments long established should not be changed for light and
transient causes; and accordingly all experience hath shown, that mankind are more disposed to suffer, while evils are sufferable, than to
right themselves by abolishing the forms to which they are accustomed. But when a long train of abuses and usurpations, pursuing invariably the same Object evinces a design to reduce them under absolute Despotism, it is their right, it is their duty, to throw off such
Government, and to provide new Guards for their future security.—
Such has been the patient sufferance of these Colonies; and such is
now the necessity which constrains them to alter their former Systems
of Government. The history of the present King of Great Britain is a
history of repeated injuries and usurpations, all having in direct object
the establishment of an absolute Tyranny over these States. To prove
this, let Facts be submitted to a candid world.

He has refused his Assent to Laws, the most wholesome and nec- 3
essary for the public good.

He has forbidden his Governors to pass Laws of immediate and 4
pressing importance, unless suspended in their operation till his Assent should be obtained; and when so suspended, he has utterly neglected to attend to them.

He has refused to pass other laws for the accommodation of large 5
districts of people, unless those people would relinquish the right of
Representation in the Legislature, a right inestimable to them and formidable to tyrants only.

He has called together legislative bodies at places unusual, uncom- 6
fortable, and distant from the depository of their Public Records, for
the sole purpose of fatiguing them into compliance with his measures.

He has dissolved Representative Houses repeatedly, for opposing 7
with manly firmness his invasions on the rights of the people.

He has refused for a long time, after such dissolutions, to cause 8
others to be elected; whereby the Legislative Powers, incapable of Annihilation, have returned to the People at large for their exercise; the
State remaining in the mean time exposed to all the dangers of invasion from without, and convulsions within.

He has endeavoured to prevent the population of these States;[1] for 9
that purpose obstructing the Laws for Naturalization of Foreigners; refusing to pass others to encourage their migration hither, and raising
the conditions of new Appropriations of Lands.

He has obstructed the Administration of Justice, by refusing his 10
Assent to Laws for establishing Judiciary Powers.

He has made Judges dependent on his Will alone, for the tenure of 11
their offices, and the amount and payment of their salaries.

He has erected a multitude of New Offices, and sent hither swarms 12
of Officers to harass our People, and eat out their substance.

He has kept among us, in times of peace, Standing Armies without 13
the Consent of our legislature.

He has affected to render the Military independent of and superior 14
to the Civil Power.

He has combined with others to subject us to a jurisdiction foreign 15
to our constitution, and unacknowledged by our laws; giving his Assent to their acts of pretended Legislation:

For quartering large bodies of armed troops among us: 16

---

[1]***prevent the population of these States*** This meant limiting emigration to the Colonies, thus controlling their growth.

For protecting them, by a mock Trial, from Punishment for any 17
Murders which they should commit on the Inhabitants of these States:

For cutting off our Trade with all parts of the world: 18

For imposing taxes on us without our Consent: 19

For depriving us in many cases, of the benefits of Trial by Jury: 20

For transporting us beyond Seas to be tried for pretended offences: 21

For abolishing the free System of English Laws in a neighbouring 22
Province, establishing therein an Arbitrary government, and enlarging
its Boundaries so as to render it at once an example and fit instrument
for introducing the same absolute rule into these Colonies:

For taking away our Charters, abolishing our most valuable Laws, 23
and altering fundamentally the Forms of our Governments:

For suspending our own Legislatures, and declaring themselves in- 24
vested with Power to legislate for us in all cases whatsoever.

He has abdicated Government here, by declaring us out of his Pro- 25
tection and waging War against us.

He has plundered our seas, ravaged our Coasts, burnt our towns, 26
and destroyed the lives of our people.

He is at this time transporting large armies of foreign mercenaries 27
to compleat the works of death, desolation and tyranny, already begun
with circumstances of Cruelty & perfidy scarcely paralleled in the
most barbarous ages, and totally unworthy the Head of a civilized nation.

He has constrained our fellow Citizens taken Captive on the High 28
Seas to bear Arms against their Country, to become the executioners
of their friends and Brethren, or to fall themselves by their Hands.

He has excited domestic insurrections amongst us, and has endeav- 29
oured to bring on the inhabitants of our frontiers, the merciless Indian
Savages, whose Known rule of warfare, is an undistinguished destruction of all ages, sexes and conditions.

In every stage of these Oppressions We have Petitioned for Redress 30
in the most humble terms: Our repeated Petitions have been answered
only by repeated injury. A Prince, whose character is thus marked by
every act which may define a Tyrant, is unfit to be the ruler of a free
People.

Nor have We been wanting in attention to our British brethren. We 31
have warned them from time to time of attempts by their legislature
to extend an unwarrantable jurisdiction over us. We have reminded
them of the circumstances of our emigration and settlement here. We
have appealed to their native justice and magnanimity, and we have
conjured them by the ties of our common kindred to disavow these
usurpations, which, would inevitably interrupt our connections and

correspondence. They too have been deaf to the voice of justice and of consanguinity. We must, therefore, acquiesce in the necessity, which denounces our Separation, and hold them, as we hold the rest of mankind, Enemies in War, in Peace Friends.

We, therefore, the Representatives of the united States of America, in General Congress, Assembled, appealing to the Supreme Judge of the world for the rectitude of our intentions, do, in the Name, and by Authority of the good People of these Colonies, solemnly publish and declare, That these United Colonies are, and of Right ought to be Free and Independent States, that they are Absolved from all Allegiance to the British Crown, and that all political connection between them and the State of Great Britain, is and ought to be totally dissolved; and that as Free and Independent States, they have full Power to levy War, conclude Peace, contract Alliances, establish Commerce, and to do all other Acts and Things which Independent States may of right do. And for the support of this Declaration, with a firm reliance on the Protection of Divine Providence, we mutually pledge to each other our Lives, our Fortunes and our sacred Honor.

32

QUESTIONS

1. What are the laws of nature Jefferson refers to in paragraph 1? Is there evidence to indicate he had read Rousseau?
2. What do you think Jefferson feels is the function of government (para. 2)?
3. Find at least two examples of the periodic sentence in the Declaration.
4. Find at least one use of parallel structure in the Declaration. What key terms are repeated as a means of guaranteeing that structure?
5. Which of the causes listed in paragraphs 3–29 are the most serious? Is any one of them trivial? Is any one serious enough to cause a revolution?
6. Find the most graceful sentence in the entire Declaration. Where is it placed in the Declaration? Do you think it was put there consciously, as a means of attracting attention?

WRITING ASSIGNMENTS

1. Jefferson states that the unalienable rights of a citizen are "Life, Liberty and the pursuit of Happiness." Do you think these are indeed unalienable rights? In the course of answering this question—using careful parallelism of any sort you like—be certain that you define what each of these terms really means. Define them for yourself, for our time.
2. Write an essay with at least three periodic sentences (and underline them)

in which you discuss what you feel the function of government should be. You may want to establish first what you think Jefferson's conception of the function of government is, then compare or contrast it with your own.

3. Write a critique of Jefferson's style. What are the qualities you most value in it? Analyze a few words, expressions, sentences, or paragraphs for their stylistic achievement. Do you like or dislike his style?

4. Jefferson envisioned a government that made it possible for its citizens to have the rights of life, liberty, and the pursuit of happiness. Has Jefferson's revolutionary vision been achieved in America? Begin with a definition of your key terms: "life," "liberty," and "the pursuit of happiness." Then, taking each in turn and using any examples available—drawn from current events, your own experience, your general background in American history—take a clear and well-argued stand on whether our nation has achieved Jefferson's goal.

5. Slavery was legal in America in 1776, and Jefferson reluctantly owned slaves. He had a plan to grant gradual emancipation to the slaves, but it was never presented to Congress because he realized that Congress would never approve it. Jefferson and Franklin financed a plan to buy slaves and return them to Africa, where they founded the nation of Liberia. To what degree does the practice of slavery by the people who wrote it invalidate the Declaration of Independence? Does it invalidate it at all? Take a stand on these questions and defend it. You may wish to read the relevant chapters on Jefferson and slavery in Merrill D. Peterson's *Thomas Jefferson and the New Nation* (1970).

6. The Declaration of Independence establishes the right of the Colonies to mount a revolution against the British government. According to Jefferson, when can a government be abolished by a people? Be sure to use the technique of enumeration in qualifying the causes or conditions, in modern terms, and in reference to our own government, which would make you feel it necessary to abolish a government. As you do so, be certain to define very carefully what it means to abolish a government.

KARL MARX

The Communist Manifesto

KARL MARX (1818–1883) was born in Germany to Jewish parents
who converted to Lutheranism. A very scholarly man, Marx studied
literature and philosophy, ultimately earning a doctorate in philosophy at the University of Jena. He was denied a university position and
was forced to begin making a livelihood from journalism.

Soon after beginning his journalistic career, Marx came into conflict with Prussian authorities because of his radical social views,
and after a period of exile in Paris he was forced to live in Brussels.
After several more forced moves, Marx found his way to London,
where he finally settled in absolute poverty. His friend Friedrich Engels (1820–1895) contributed money to prevent his and his family's
starvation, and Marx wrote the books for which he is famous while
at the same time writing for and editing newspapers. His contributions to the New York Daily Herald number over three hundred items
between the years 1852 and 1862.

Marx is best known for his theories of socialism, best expressed
in The Communist Manifesto (1848)—which, like much of his im-

---

Translated by Samuel Moore. Part III of The Communist Manifesto, "Socialist and
Communist Literature," is omitted here.

portant work, was written with Engels's help—and in Das Kapital
(Capital), *published in 1867. In his own lifetime he was not well
known, nor were his ideas widely debated. Yet he was part of an
ongoing movement composed mainly of intellectuals. Vladimir Lenin
(1870–1924) was a disciple whose triumph in the Russian Revolution
of 1917 catapulted Marx to the forefront of world thought. Since 1917
Marx's thinking has been scrupulously analyzed, debated, and argued. Capitalist thinkers have found him illogical and uninformed,
whereas Communist thinkers have found him a prophet and keen analyst of social structures.*

*In England, Marx's studies concentrated on economics. His
thought centered on the concept of an ongoing class struggle between
those who owned property—the bourgeois—and those who owned
nothing but whose work produced wealth—the proletariat. Marx was
concerned with the forces of history, and his view of history was that
it is progressive and, to an extent, inevitable. This view is very prominent in* The Communist Manifesto, *particularly in his review of the
overthrow of feudal forms of government by the bourgeoisie. He
thought that it was inevitable that the bourgeoisie and the proletariat
would engage in a class struggle from which the proletariat would
emerge victorious. In essence, Marx took a materialist position. He
denied the providence of God in the affairs of man and defended the
view that economic institutions evolve naturally and that, in their
evolution, they control the social order. Thus, communism was an
inevitable part of the process, and in the* Manifesto *he was concerned
to clarify the reasons why it was inevitable.*

MARX'S RHETORIC

*The selection included here omits one section, the least important
for the modern reader. The first section has a relatively simple rhetorical structure that depends upon comparison. The title, "Bourgeois
and Proletarians," tells us right away that the section will clarify the
nature of each class and then go on to make some comparisons and
contrasts. The concepts as such were by no means as widely discussed or thought about in 1848 as they are today, so Marx is careful
to define his terms. At the same time, he establishes his theories regarding history by making further comparisons with class struggles in
earlier ages.*

Marx's style is simple and direct. He moves steadily from point to point, establishing his views on the nature of classes, on the nature of bourgeois society, on the questions of industrialism and its effects upon modern society. He considers questions of wealth, worth, nationality, production, agriculture, and machinery. Each point is dealt with in turn, usually in its own paragraph.

The organization of the next section, "Proletarians and Communists" (paras. 60–133), is not, despite its title, comparative in nature. Rather, with the proletariat defined as the class of the future, Marx tries to show that the Communist cause is the proletarian cause. In the process, Marx uses a fascinating rhetorical strategy. He assumes that he is addressed by an antagonist—presumably a bourgeois or a proletarian who is in sympathy with the bourgeois. He then proceeds to deal with each popular complaint against communism. He shows that it is not a party separate from other workers' parties (para. 61). He clarifies the question of abolition of existing property relations (paras. 68–93). He emphasizes the antagonism of capital and wage labor (para. 76); he discusses the disappearance of culture (para. 94); he clarifies the question of the family (para. 98) and of the exploitation of children (para. 101). The new system of public education is brought up (para. 102). The touchy issue of the "community of women" is raised (paras. 102–110), as well as the charge that Communists want to abolish nations (para. 111). Religion is brushed aside (para. 116), and when he is done with the complaints he gives us a rhetorical signal: "But let us have done with the bourgeois objections to Communism" (para. 126).

The rest of the second section contains a brief summary, and then Marx presents his ten-point program (para. 131). The structure is simple, direct, and effective. In the process of answering the charges against communism, Marx is able to clarify exactly what it is and what it promises. By contrast with his earlier arguments, the ten points of his Communist program seem clear, easy, and (again by contrast) almost acceptable. While the style is not dashing (despite a few memorable lines), the rhetorical structure is extraordinarily effective for the purposes at hand.

In the last section (paras. 135–146), in which Marx compares the Communists with other reform groups such as those agitating for redistribution of land and other agrarian reforms, he indicates that the Communists are everywhere fighting alongside existing groups for the rights of people who are oppressed by their societies. As Marx says, "In short, the Communists everywhere support every revolutionary movement against the existing social and political order of things." Nothing could be a more plain and direct declaration of sympathies.

The Communist Manifesto

A specter is haunting Europe—the specter of Communism. All the
Powers of old Europe have entered into a holy alliance to exorcise this
specter; Pope and Czar, Metternich[1] and Guizot,[2] French Radicals[3] and
German police-spies.

1

Where is the party in opposition that has not been decried as communistic by its opponents in power? Where the Opposition that has
not hurled back the branding reproach of Communism against the
more advanced opposition parties, as well as against its reactionary
adversaries?

2

Two things result from this fact.

3

I. Communism is already acknowledged by all European Powers to
be itself a Power.

4

II. It is high time that Communists should openly, in the face of
the whole world, publish their views, their aims, their tendencies, and
meet this nursery tale of the specter of Communism with a Manifesto
of the party itself.

5

To this end, Communists of various nationalities have assembled
in London and sketched the following Manifesto, to be published in
the English, French, German, Italian, Flemish and Danish languages.

6

Bourgeois and Proletarians[4]

The history of all hitherto existing society is the history of class
struggles.

7

---

[1]**Prince Klemens von Metternich (1773–1859)** An Austrian diplomat who had a
hand in establishing the peace after the final defeat in 1814 of Napoleon (1769–1821);
Metternich was highly influential in the crucial Vienna peace congress (1815).

[2]**François Pierre Guizot (1787–1874)** Conservative French statesman, author,
and philosopher. Like Metternich, he was opposed to communism.

[3]**French Radicals** Actually middle-class liberals who wanted a return to a republic
in 1848 after the eighteen-year reign of Louis Philippe (1773–1850), the "citizen king."

[4]By bourgeoisie is meant the class of modern Capitalists, owners of the means of
social production and employers of wage labor. By proletariat, the class of modern wage
laborers who, having no means of production of their own, are reduced to selling their
labor-power in order to live. [Marx's note]

Freeman and slave, patrician and plebeian, lord and serf, guild-mas-   8
ter and journeyman, in a word, oppressor and oppressed, stood in constant opposition to one another, carried on uninterrupted, now hidden,
now open fight, a fight that each time ended, either in a revolutionary
re-constitution of society at large, or in the common ruin of the con-
tending classes.

In the earlier epochs of history we find almost everywhere a com-   9
plicated arrangement of society into various orders, a manifold grada-
tion of social rank. In ancient Rome we have patricians, knights, ple-
beians, slaves; in the Middle Ages, feudal lords, vassals, guild-masters,
journeymen, apprentices, serfs; in almost all of these classes, again,
subordinate gradations.

The modern bourgeois society that has sprouted from the ruins of   10
feudal society, has not done away with class antagonisms. It has but
established new classes, new conditions of oppression, new forms of
struggle in place of the old ones.

Our epoch, the epoch of the bourgeoisie, possesses, however, this   11
distinctive feature; it has simplified the class antagonisms. Society as
a whole is more and more splitting up into two great hostile camps,
into two great classes directly facing each other: Bourgeoisie and Proletariat.

From the serfs of the Middle Ages sprang the chartered burghers of   12
the earliest towns. From these burgesses the first elements of the bourgeoisie were developed.

The discovery of America, the rounding of the Cape,[5] opened up   13
fresh ground for the rising bourgeoisie. The East Indian and Chinese
markets, the colonization of America, trade with the colonies, the increase in the means of exchange and in commodities generally, gave
to commerce, to navigation, to industry, an impulse never before
known, and thereby, to the revolutionary element in the tottering feudal society, a rapid development.

The feudal system of industry, under which industrial production   14
was monopolized by closed guilds, now no longer sufficed for the
growing wants of the new market. The manufacturing system took its
place. The guild-masters were pushed on one side by the manufacturing middle-class: division of labor between the different corporate
guilds vanished in the face of division of labor in each single workshop.

---

[5]*the Cape* The Cape of Good Hope, at the southern tip of Africa. This was a main sea
route for trade with India and the Orient. Europe profited immensely from the opening
up of these new markets in the sixteenth century.

Meantime the markets kept ever growing, the demand ever rising.   15
Even manufacture no longer sufficed. Thereupon, steam and machinery revolutionized industrial production. The place of manufacture was taken by the giant, Modern Industry, the place of the industrial middle-class, by industrial millionaires, the leaders of whole industrial armies, the modern bourgeois.

Modern industry has established the world market, for which the   16
discovery of America paved the way. This market has given an immense development to commerce, to navigation, to communication by land. This development has, in its turn, reacted on the extension of industry; and in proportion as industry, commerce, navigation, railways extended, in the same proportion the bourgeoisie developed, increased its capital, and pushed into the background every class handed down from the Middle Ages.

We see, therefore, how the modern bourgeoisie is itself the product   17
of a long course of development, of a series of revolutions in the modes of production and of exchange.

Each step in the development of the bourgeoisie was accompanied   18
by a corresponding political advance of that class. An oppressed class under the sway of the feudal nobility, an armed and self-governing association in the medieval commune,[6] here independent urban republic (as in Italy and Germany), there taxable "third estate"[7] of the monarchy (as in France), afterwards, in the period of manufacture proper, serving either the semi-feudal or the absolute monarchy as a counterpoise against nobility, and, in fact, corner stone of the great monarchies in general, the bourgeoisie has at last, since the establishment of Modern Industry and of the world-market, conquered for itself, in the modern representative State, exclusive political sway. The executive of the modern State is but a committee for managing the common affairs of the whole bourgeoisie.

The bourgeoisie, historically, has played a most revolutionary part.   19

The bourgeoisie, wherever it has got the upper hand, has put an   20
end to all feudal, patriarchal, idyllic relations. It has pitilessly torn asunder the motley feudal ties that bound man to his "natural superiors," and has left no other nexus between man and man than naked self-interest, than callous "cash payment." It has drowned the most

---

[6]*the medieval commune*   Refers to the growth in the eleventh century of towns whose economy was highly regulated by mutual interest and agreement.

[7]*"third estate"*   The aristocracy was the first estate, the clergy the second estate, and the bourgeoisie the third estate.

heavenly ecstasies of religious fervor,[8] of chivalrous enthusiasm, of Philistine sentimentalism, in the icy water of egotistical calculation. It has resolved personal worth into exchange value, and in place of the numberless indefeasible chartered freedoms, has set up that single, unconscionable freedom—Free Trade. In one word, for exploitation, veiled by religious and political illusions, it has substituted naked, shameless, direct, brutal exploitation.

The bourgeoisie has stripped of its halo every occupation hitherto honored and looked up to with reverent awe. It has converted the physician, the lawyer, the priest, the poet, the man of science, into its paid wage laborers.   21

The bourgeoisie has torn away from the family its sentimental veil, and has reduced the family relation to a mere money relation.   22

The bourgeoisie has disclosed how it came to pass that the brutal display of vigor in the Middle Ages, which reactionists so much admire, found its fitting complement in the most slothful indolence. It has been the first to show what man's activity can bring about. It has accomplished wonders far surpassing Egyptian pyramids, Roman aqueducts and Gothic cathedrals; it has conducted expeditions that put in the shade all former Exoduses of nations and crusades.   23

The bourgeoisie cannot exist without constantly revolutionizing the instruments of production, and thereby the relations of production, and with them the whole relations of society. Conservation of the old modes of production in unaltered form was, on the contrary, the first condition of existence for all earlier industrial classes. Constant revolutionizing of production, uninterrupted disturbance of all social conditions, everlasting uncertainty and agitation distinguish the bourgeois epoch from all earlier ones. All fixed, fast frozen relations, with their train of ancient and venerable prejudices and opinions, are swept away, all new formed ones become antiquated before they can ossify. All that is solid melts into the air, all that is holy is profaned, and man is at last compelled to face with sober senses, his real conditions of life, and his relations with his kind.   24

[8]*religious fervor* This and other terms in this sentence contain a compressed historical observation. "Religious fervor" refers to the Middle Ages; "chivalrous enthusiasm" refers to the rise of the secular state and to the military power of knights; "Philistine sentimentalism" refers to the development of popular arts and literature in the sixteenth, seventeenth, and eighteenth centuries. The word "Philistine" meant those who were generally uncultured, that is, the general public. "Sentimentalism" was a code word for the encouragement of emotional response rather than rational thought.

The need of a constantly expanding market for its products chases   25
the bourgeoisie over the whole surface of the globe. It must nestle
everywhere, settle everywhere, establish connections everywhere.

The bourgeoisie has through its exploitation of the world-market   26
given a cosmopolitan character to production and consumption in
every country. To the great chagrin of reactionists, it has drawn from
under the feet of industry the national ground on which it stood. All
old-established national industries have been destroyed or are daily
being destroyed. They are dislodged by new industries, whose introduction becomes a life and death question for all civilized nations, by
industries that no longer work up indigenous raw material, but raw
material drawn from the remotest zones; industries whose products
are consumed, not only at home, but in every quarter of the globe. In
place of the old wants, satisfied by the productions of the country, we
find new wants, requiring for their satisfaction the products of distant
lands and climes. In place of the old local and national seclusion and
self-sufficiency, we have intercourse in every direction, universal interdependence of nations. And as in material, so also in intellectual
production. The intellectual creations of individual nations become
common property. National onesidedness and narrowmindedness become more and more impossible, and from the numerous national and
local literatures there arises a world-literature.

The bourgeoisie, by the rapid improvement of all instruments of   27
production, by the immensely facilitated means of communication,
draws all, even the most barbarian nations into civilization. The cheap
prices of its commodities are the heavy artillery with which it batters
down all Chinese walls, with which it forces the barbarians' intensely
obstinate hatred of foreigners to capitulate. It compels all nations, on
pain of extinction, to adopt the bourgeois mode of production; it compels them to introduce what it calls civilization into their midst, i.e.,
to become bourgeois themselves. In a word, it creates a world after its
own image.

The bourgeoisie has subjected the country to the rule of the towns.   28
It has created enormous cities, has greatly increased the urban population as compared with the rural and has thus rescued a considerable
part of the population from the idiocy of rural life. Just as it has made
the country dependent on the towns, so it has made barbarian and
semi-barbarian countries dependent on civilized ones, nations of peasants on nations of bourgeois, the East on the West.

The bourgeoisie keeps more and more doing away with the scat-   29
tered state of the population, of the means of production, and of property. It has agglomerated population, centralized means of production,

and has concentrated property in a few hands. The necessary consequence of this was political centralization. Independent, or but loosely connected provinces, with separate interests, laws, governments, and systems of taxation, became lumped together in one nation, with one government, one code of laws, one national class interest, one frontier and one customs tariff.

The bourgeoisie, during its rule of scarce one hundred years, has 30 created more massive and more colossal productive forces than have all preceding generations together. Subjection of Nature's forces to man, machinery, application of chemistry to industry and agriculture, steam-navigation, railways, electric telegraphs, clearing of whole continents for cultivation, canalization of rivers, whole populations conjured out of the ground—what earlier century had even a presentiment that such productive forces slumbered in the lap of social labor?

We see then: the means of production and of exchange on whose 31 foundation the bourgeoisie built itself up, were generated in feudal society. At a certain stage in the development of these means of production and of exchange, the conditions under which feudal society produced and exchanged, the feudal organization of agriculture and manufacturing industry, in one word, the feudal relations of property became no longer compatible with the already developed productive forces; they became so many fetters. They had to burst asunder; they were burst asunder.

Into their place stepped free competition, accompanied by a social 32 and political constitution adapted to it, and by the economical and political sway of the bourgeois class.

A similar movement is going on before our own eyes. Modern bour- 33 geois society with its relations of production, of exchange and of property, a society that has conjured up such gigantic means of production and of exchange, is like the sorcerer, who is no longer able to control the powers of the nether world whom he has called up by his spells. For many a decade past, the history of industry and commerce is but the history of the revolt of modern productive forces against modern conditions of production, against the property relations that are the conditions for the existence of the bourgeoisie and of its rule. It is enough to mention the commercial crises that by their periodical return put on its trial, each time more threateningly, the existence of the entire bourgeois society. In these crises a great part not only of the existing products, but also of the previously created productive forces, are periodically destroyed. In these crises there breaks out an epidemic that, in all earlier epochs, would have seemed an absurdity—the epidemic of overproduction. Society suddenly finds itself put back into a state of momentary barbarism; it appears as if a famine, a universal war of devastation, had cut off the supply of every means of subsistence; industry and commerce seem to be destroyed; and why? Because there is too much civilization, too much means of subsistence, too much industry, too much commerce. The productive forces at the disposal of society no longer tend to further the development of the conditions of the bourgeois property; on the contrary, they have become too powerful for these conditions by which they are fettered, and as soon as they overcome these fetters they bring disorder into the whole of bourgeois society, endanger the existence of bourgeois property. The conditions of bourgeois society are too narrow to comprise the wealth created by them. And how does the bourgeoisie get over these crises? On the one hand by enforced destruction of a mass of productive forces; on the other, by the conquest of new markets, and by the more thorough exploitation of the old ones. That is to say, by paving the way for more extensive and more destructive crises, and by diminishing the means whereby crises are prevented.

The weapons with which the bourgeoisie felled feudalism to the ground are now turned against the bourgeoisie itself. 34

But not only has the bourgeoisie forged the weapons that bring death to itself; it has also called into existence the men who are to wield those weapons—the modern working class—the proletarians. 35

In proportion as the bourgeoisie, i.e., capital, is developed, in the same proportion is the proletariat, the modern working class, developed, a class of laborers who live only so long as they find work, and who find work only so long as their labor increases capital. These laborers, who must sell themselves piecemeal, are a commodity, like every other article of commerce, and are consequently exposed to all the vicissitudes of competition, to all the fluctuations of the market. 36

Owing to the extensive use of machinery and to division of labor, the work of the proletarians has lost all individual character, and, consequently, all charm for the workman. He becomes an appendage of the machine, and it is only the most simple, most monotonous and most easily acquired knack that is required of him. Hence, the cost of production of a workman is restricted almost entirely to the means of subsistence that he requires for his maintenance, and for the propagation of his race. But the price of a commodity, and also of labor, is equal to its cost of production. In proportion, therefore, as the repulsiveness of the work increases the wage decreases. Nay more, in proportion as the use of machinery and division of labor increases, in the same proportion the burden of toil increases, whether by prolongation 37 of the working hours, by increase of the work enacted in a given time, or by increased speed of the machinery, etc.

Modern industry has converted the little workshop of the patriar- 38 chal master into the great factory of the industrial capitalist. Masses of laborers, crowded into factories, are organized like soldiers. As privates of the industrial army they are placed under the command of a perfect hierarchy of officers and sergeants. Not only are they the slaves of the bourgeois class and of the bourgeois state, they are daily and hourly enslaved by the machine, by the overlooker, and, above all, by the individual bourgeois manufacturer himself. The more openly this despotism proclaims gain to be its end and aim, the more petty, the more hateful and the more embittering it is.

The less the skill and exertion or strength implied in manual labor, 39 in other words, the more modern industry becomes developed, the more is the labor of men superseded by that of women. Differences of age and sex have no longer any distinctive social validity for the working class. All are instruments of labor, more or less expensive to use, according to their age and sex.

No sooner is the exploitation of the laborer by the manufacturer, 40 so far at an end, that he receives his wages in cash, than he is set upon by the other portions of the bourgeoisie, the landlord, the shopkeeper, the pawnbroker, etc.

The lower strata of the middle class—the small trades-people, 41 shopkeepers and retired tradesmen generally, the handicraftsmen and peasants—all these sink gradually into the proletariat, partly because their diminutive capital does not suffice for the scale on which Modern Industry is carried on, and is swamped in the competition with the large capitalists, partly because their specialized skill is rendered worthless by new methods of production. Thus the proletariat is recruited from all classes of the population.

The proletariat goes through various stages of development. With 42 its birth begins its struggle with the bourgeoisie. At first the contest is carried on by individual laborers, then by the workpeople of a factory, then by the operatives of one trade, in one locality, against the individual bourgeois who directly exploits them. They direct their attacks not against the bourgeois conditions of production, but against the instruments of production themselves; they destroy imported wares that compete with their labor, they smash to pieces machinery, they set factories ablaze, they seek to restore by force the vanished status of the workman of the Middle Ages.

At this stage the laborers still form an incoherent mass scattered 43 over the whole country, and broken up by their mutual competition. If anywhere they unite to form more compact bodies, this is not yet the consequence of their own active union, but of the union of the bourgeoisie, which class, in order to attain its own political ends, is compelled to set the whole proletariat in motion, and is moreover yet, for a time, able to do so. At this stage, therefore, the proletarians do not fight their enemies, but the enemies of their enemies, the remnants of absolute monarchy, the landowners, the non-industrial bourgeois, the petty bourgeoisie. Thus the whole historical movement is concentrated in the hands of the bourgeoisie, every victory so obtained is a victory for the bourgeoisie.

But with the development of industry the proletariat not only increases in number; it becomes concentrated in greater masses, its strength grows and it feels that strength more. The various interests and conditions of life within the ranks of the proletariat are more and more equalized, in proportion as machinery obliterates all distinctions of labor, and nearly everywhere reduces wages to the same low level. The growing competition among the bourgeois, and the resulting commercial crisis, make the wages of the workers even more fluctuating. The unceasing improvement of machinery, ever more rapidly developing, makes their livelihood more and more precarious; the collisions between individual workmen and individual bourgeois take more and more the character of collisions between two classes. Thereupon the workers begin to form combinations (Trades' Unions)[9] against the bourgeois; they club together in order to keep up the rate of wages; they found permanent associations in order to make provision beforehand for these occasional revolts. Here and there the contest breaks out into riots. 44

Now and then the workers are victorious, but only for a time. The real fruit of their battle lies not in the immediate result but in the ever-expanding union of workers. This union is helped on by the improved means of communication that are created by modern industry, and that places the workers of different localities in contact with one another. It was just this contact that was needed to centralize the numerous local struggles, all of the same character, into one national struggle between classes. But every class struggle is a political struggle. And that union, to attain which the burghers of the Middle Ages with 45

---

[9]*combinations (Trades' Unions)* The labor movement was only beginning in 1848. It consisted of Trades' Unions that started as social clubs but soon began agitating for labor reform. They represented an important step in the growth of socialism in Europe.

their miserable highways, required centuries, the modern proletarians, thanks to railways, achieve in a few years.

This organization of the proletarians into a class, and consequently into a political party, is continually being upset again by the competition between the workers themselves. But it ever rises up again, stronger, firmer, mightier. It compels legislative recognition of particular interests of the workers by taking advantage of the divisions among the bourgeoisie itself. Thus the ten hours' bill in England[10] was carried. **46**

Altogether collisions between the classes of the old society further, in many ways, the course of development of the proletariat. The bourgeoisie finds itself involved in a constant battle. At first with the aristocracy; later on, with those portions of the bourgeoisie itself whose interests have become antagonistic to the progress of industry; at all times, with the bourgeoisie of foreign countries. In all these battles it sees itself compelled to appeal to the proletariat, to ask for its help, and thus, to drag it into the political arena. The bourgeoisie itself, therefore, supplies the proletariat with its own elements of political and general education; in other words, it furnishes the proletariat with weapons for fighting the bourgeoisie. **47**

Further, as we have already seen, entire sections of the ruling classes are, by the advance of industry, precipitated into the proletariat, or are at least threatened in their conditions of existence. These also supply the proletariat with fresh elements of enlightenment and progress. **48**

Finally, in times when the class-struggle nears the decisive hour, the process of dissolution going on within the ruling class—in fact, within the whole range of an old society—assumes such a violent, glaring character that a small section of the ruling class cuts itself adrift and joins the revolutionary class, the class that holds the future in its hands. Just as, therefore, at an earlier period, a section of the nobility went over to the bourgeoisie, so now a portion of the bourgeoisie goes over to the proletariat, and in particular, a portion of the bourgeois ideologists, who have raised themselves to the level of comprehending theoretically the historical movements as a whole. **49**

Of all the classes that stand face to face with the bourgeoisie today the proletariat alone is a really revolutionary class. The other classes **50**

---

[10]***the ten hours' bill in England*** This bill (1847) was an important innovation in labor reform. It limited the working day to only ten hours; at the time it was common for some people to work sixteen hours in a day. The bill's passage was a result of political division, not of benevolence on the part of the managers.

decay and finally disappear in the face of modern industry; the proletariat is its special and essential product.

The lower middle class, the small manufacturer, the shopkeeper, 51
the artisan, the peasant, all these fight against the bourgeoisie, to save
from extinction their existence as fractions of the middle class. They
are therefore not revolutionary, but conservative. Nay, more; they are
reactionary, for they try to roll back the wheel of history. If by chance
they are revolutionary, they are so only in view of their impending
transfer into the proletariat; they thus defend not their present, but
their future interests; they desert their own standpoint to place themselves at that of the proletariat.

The "dangerous class," the social scum, that passively rotting mass 52
thrown off by the lowest layers of old society, may, here and there, be
swept into the movement by a proletarian revolution; its conditions of
life, however, prepare it far more for the part of a bribed tool of reactionary intrigue.

In the conditions of the proletariat, those of the old society at large 53
are already virtually swamped. The proletarian is without property; his
relation to his wife and children has no longer anything in common
with the bourgeois family relations; modern industrial labor, modern
subjection to capital, the same in England as in France, in America as
in Germany, has stripped him of every trace of national character.
Law, morality, religion, are to him so many bourgeois prejudices, behind which lurk in ambush just as many bourgeois interests.

All the preceding classes that got the upper hand sought to fortify 54
their already acquired status by subjecting society at large to their conditions of appropriation. The proletarians cannot become masters of
the productive forces of society, except by abolishing their own previous mode of appropriation, and thereby also every other previous
mode of appropriation. They have nothing of their own to secure and
to fortify; their mission is to destroy all previous securities for and
insurances of individual property.

All previous historical movements were movements of minorities, 55
or in the interest of minorities. The proletarian movement is the self-
conscious, independent movement of the immense majority. The proletariat, the lowest stratum of our present society, cannot stir, cannot
raise itself up without the whole superincumbent strata of official society being sprung into the air.

Though not in substance, yet in form, the struggle of the proletariat 56
with the bourgeoisie is at first a national struggle. The proletariat of
each country must, of course, first of all settle matters with its own
bourgeoisie.

In depicting the most general phases of the development of the pro- 57
letariat, we traced the more or less veiled civil war, raging within existing society, up to the point where that war breaks out into open
revolution, and where the violent overthrow of the bourgeoisie, lays
the foundations for the sway of the proletariat.

Hitherto every form of society has been based, as we have already 58
seen, on the antagonism of oppressing and oppressed classes. But in
order to oppress a class, certain conditions must be assured to it under
which it can, at least, continue its slavish existence. The serf, in the
period of serfdom, raised himself to membership in the commune, just
as the petty bourgeois, under the yoke of feudal absolutism, managed
to develop into a bourgeois. The modern laborer, on the contrary, instead of rising with the progress of industry, sinks deeper and deeper
below the conditions of existence of his own class. He becomes a pauper, and pauperism develops more rapidly than population and wealth.
And here it becomes evident that the bourgeoisie is unfit any longer
to be the ruling class in society, and to impose its conditions of existence upon society as an over-riding law. It is unfit to rule, because it
is incompetent to assure an existence to its slave within his slavery,
because it cannot help letting him sink into such a state that it has to
feed him, instead of being fed by him. Society can no longer live under
this bourgeoisie; in other words, its existence is no longer compatible
with society.

The essential condition for the existence, and for the sway of the 59
bourgeois class, is the formation and augmentation of capital; the
condition for capital is wage labor. Wage labor rests exclusively on
competition between the laborers. The advance of industry, whose involuntary promoter is the bourgeoisie, replaces the isolation of the laborers, due to competition, by their involuntary combination, due to
association. The development of Modern Industry, therefore, cuts from
under its feet the very foundation on which the bourgeoisie produces
and appropriates products. What the bourgeoisie therefore produces,
above all, are its own grave diggers. Its fall and the victory of the proletariat are equally inevitable.

Proletarians and Communists

In what relation do the Communists stand to the proletarians as a 60
whole?

The Communists do not form a separate party opposed to other 61
working class parties.

They have no interests separate and apart from those of the prole- 62
tariat as a whole.

They do not set up any sectarian principles of their own, by which 63
to shape and mold the proletarian movement.

The Communists are distinguished from the other working class 64
parties by this only: 1. In the national struggles of the proletarians of
the different countries, they point out and bring to the front the common interests of the entire proletariat, independently of all nationality.
2. In the various stages of development which the struggle of the working class against the bourgeoisie has to pass through, they always and
everywhere represent the interests of the movement as a whole.

The Communists, therefore, are on the one hand practically the 65
most advanced and resolute section of the working class parties of
every country, that section which pushes forward all others; on the
other hand, theoretically, they have over the great mass of the proletariat the advantage of clearly understanding the line of march, the
conditions, and the ultimate general results of the proletarian movement.

The immediate aim of the Communists is the same as that of all 66
the other proletarian parties: formation of the proletariat into a class,
overthrow of the bourgeois of supremacy, conquest of political power
by the proletariat.

The theoretical conclusions of the Communists are in no way 67
based on ideas or principles that have been invented or discovered by
this or that would-be universal reformer.

They merely express, in general terms, actual relations springing 68
from an existing class struggle, from a historical movement going on
under our very eyes. The abolition of existing property relations is not
at all a distinctive feature of Communism.

All property relations in the past have continually been subject to 69
historical change consequent upon the change in historical conditions.

The French Revolution, for example, abolished feudal property in 70
favor of bourgeois property.

The distinguishing feature of Communism is not the abolition of 71
property generally, but the abolition of bourgeois property. But modern
bourgeois private property is the final and most complete expression
of the system of producing and appropriating products, that is based
on class antagonism, on the exploitation of the many by the few.

In this sense, the theory of the Communists may be summed up in 72
the single sentence: Abolition of private property.

We Communists have been reproached with the desire of abolish- 73 ing the right of personally acquiring property as the fruit of a man's own labor, which property is alleged to be the groundwork of all personal freedom, activity and independence.

Hard won, self-acquired, self-earned property! Do you mean the 74
property of the petty artisan and of the small peasant, a form of property that preceded the bourgeois form? There is no need to abolish that; the development of industry has to a great extent already destroyed it, and is still destroying it daily.

Or do you mean modern bourgeois private property? 75

But does wage labor create any property for the laborer? Not a bit. 76
It creates capital, i.e., that kind of property which exploits wage labor, and which cannot increase except upon condition of getting a new supply of wage labor for fresh exploitation. Property, in its present form, is based on the antagonism of capital and wage labor. Let us examine both sides of this antagonism.

To be a capitalist is to have not only a purely personal, but a social 77
status in production. Capital is a collective product, and only by the united action of many members, nay, in the last resort, only by the united action of all members of society, can it be set in motion.

Capital is therefore not a personal, it is a social power. 78

When, therefore, capital is converted into common property, into 79
the property of all members of society, personal property is not thereby transformed into social property. It is only the social character of the property that is changed. It loses its class character.

Let us now take wage labor. 80

The average price of wage labor is the minimum wage, i.e., that 81
quantum of the means of subsistence which is absolutely requisite to keep the laborer in bare existence as a laborer. What, therefore, the wage laborer appropriates by means of his labor, merely suffices to prolong and reproduce a bare existence. We by no means intend to abolish this personal appropriation of the products of labor, an appropriation that is made for the maintenance and reproduction of human life, and that leaves no surplus wherewith to command the labor of others. All that we want to do away with is the miserable character of this appropriation, under which the laborer lives merely to increase capital and is allowed to live only in so far as the interests of the ruling class require it.

In bourgeois society, living labor is but a means to increase accu- 82
mulated labor. In Communist society accumulated labor is but a means to widen, to enrich, to promote the existence of the laborer.

In bourgeois society, therefore, the past dominates the present; in 83

Communist society the present dominates the past. In bourgeois society, capital is independent and has individuality, while the living person is dependent and has no individuality.

And the abolition of this state of things is called by the bourgeois   84
abolition of individuality and freedom! And rightly so. The abolition of bourgeois individuality, bourgeois independence and bourgeois freedom is undoubtedly aimed at.

By freedom is meant, under the present bourgeois conditions of   85
production, free trade, free selling and buying.

But if selling and buying disappears, free selling and buying disap-   86
pears also. This talk about free selling and buying, and all the other "brave words" of our bourgeoisie about freedom in general have a meaning, if any, only in contrast with restricted selling and buying, with the fettered traders of the Middle Ages, but have no meaning when opposed to the Communistic abolition of buying and selling, of the bourgeois conditions of production, and of the bourgeoisie itself.

You are horrified at our intending to do away with private property.   87
But in your existing society private property is already done away with for nine-tenths of the population; its existence for the few is solely due to its non-existence in the hands of those nine-tenths. You reproach us, therefore, with intending to do away with a form of property, the necessary condition for whose existence is the non-existence of any property for the immense majority of society.

In one word, you reproach us with intending to do away with your   88
property. Precisely so: that is just what we intend.

From the moment when labor can no longer be converted into capi-   89
tal, money, or rent, into a social power capable of being monopolized, i.e., from the moment when individual property can no longer be transformed into bourgeois property, into capital, from that moment, you say, individuality vanishes.

You must, therefore, confess that by "individual" you mean no   90
other person than the bourgeois, than the middle-class owner of property. This person must, indeed, be swept out of the way and made impossible.

Communism deprives no man of the power to appropriate the prod-   91
ucts of society: all that it does is to deprive him of the power to subjugate the labor of others by means of such appropriation.

It has been objected that upon the abolition of private property all   92
work will cease and universal laziness will overtake us.

According to this, bourgeois society ought long ago to have gone to   93
the dogs through sheer idleness; for those of its members who work acquire nothing, and those who acquire anything do not work. The

whole of this objection is but another expression of the tautology: that there can no longer be any wage labor when there is no longer any capital.

All objections urged against the Communistic mode of producing 94 and appropriating material products have, in the same way, been urged against the Communistic modes of producing and appropriating intellectual products. Just as, to the bourgeois, the disappearance of class property is the disappearance of production itself, so the disappearance of class culture is to him identical with the disappearance of all culture.

That culture, the loss of which he laments, is, for the enormous 95 majority, a mere training to act as a machine.

But don't wrangle with us so long as you apply, to our intended 96 abolition of bourgeois property, the standard of your bourgeois notions of freedom, culture, law, etc. Your very ideas are but the outgrowth of the conditions of your bourgeois production and bourgeois property, just as your jurisprudence is but the will of your class made into a law for all, a will whose essential character and direction are determined by the economical conditions of existence of your class.

The selfish misconception that induces you to transform into eter- 97 nal laws of nature and of reason the social forms springing from your present mode of production and form of property—historical relations that rise and disappear in the progress of production—this misconception you share with every ruling class that has preceded you. What you see clearly in the case of ancient property, what you admit in the case of feudal property, you are of course forbidden to admit in the case of your own bourgeois form of property.

Abolition of the family! Even the most radical flare up at this in- 98 famous proposal of the Communists.

On what foundation is the present family, the bourgeois family, 99 based? On capital, on private gain. In its completely developed form this family exists only among the bourgeoisie. But this state of things finds its complement in the practical absence of the family among the proletarians, and in public prostitution.

The bourgeois family will vanish as a matter of course when 100 its complement vanishes, and both will vanish with the vanishing of capital.

Do you charge us with wanting to stop the exploitation of children 101 by their parents? To this crime we plead guilty.

But, you will say, we destroy the most hallowed of relations when 102 we replace home education by social.

And your education! Is not that also social, and determined by the 103 social conditions under which you educate; by the intervention, direct or indirect, of society by means of schools, etc.? The Communists have not invented the intervention of society in education; they do but seek to alter the character of that intervention, and to rescue education from the influence of the ruling class.

The bourgeois clap-trap about the family and education, about the 104
hallowed correlation of parent and child, become all the more disgusting, the more, by the action of Modern Industry, all family ties among the proletarians are torn asunder and their children transformed into simple articles of commerce and instruments of labor.

But you Communists would introduce community of women, 105
screams the whole bourgeoisie chorus.

The bourgeois sees in his wife a mere instrument of production. He 106
hears that the instruments of production are to be exploited in common, and, naturally, can come to no other conclusion, than that the lot of being common to all will likewise fall to the women.

He has not even a suspicion that the real point aimed at is to do 107
away with the status of women as mere instruments of production.

For the rest, nothing is more ridiculous than the virtuous indigna- 108
tion of our bourgeois at the community of women which, they pretend, is to be openly and officially establishd by the Communists. The Communists have no need to introduce community of women; it has existed almost from time immemorial.

Our bourgeois, not content with having the wives and daughters of 109
their proletarians at their disposal, not to speak of common prostitutes, take the greatest pleasure in seducing each others' wives.

Bourgeois marriage is in reality a system of wives in common, and 110
thus, at the most, what the Communists might possibly be reproached with, is that they desire to introduce, in substitution for a hypocritically concealed, an openly legalized community of women. For the rest, it is self-evident that the abolition of the present system of production must bring with it the abolition of the community of women springing from that system, i.e., of prostitution both public and private.

The Communists are further reproached with desiring to abolish 111
countries and nationalities.

The working men have no country. We cannot take from them 112
what they don't possess. Since the proletariat must first of all acquire political supremacy, must rise to be the leading class of the nation, must constitute itself the nation, it is, so far, itself national, though not in the bourgeois sense of the word.

National differences and antagonisms between peoples are daily 113 more and more vanishing, owing to the development of the bourgeoisie, to freedom of commerce, to the world-market, to uniformity in the mode of production and in the conditions of life corresponding thereto.

The supremacy of the proletariat will cause them to vanish still faster. United action, of the leading civilized countries at least, is one of the first conditions for the emancipation of the proletariat. 114

In proportion as the exploitation of one individual by another is put an end to, the exploitation of one nation by another will also be put an end to. In proportion as the antagonism between classes within the nation vanishes, the hostility of one nation to another will come to an end. 115

The charges against Communism made from a religious, a philosophical, and generally, from an ideological standpoint, are not deserving of serious examination. 116

Does it require deep intuition to comprehend that man's ideas, views and conceptions, in one word, man's consciousness, changes with every change in the conditions of his material existence, in his social relations and in his social life? 117

What else does the history of ideas prove than that intellectual production changes in character in proportion as material production is changed? The ruling ideas of each age have ever been the ideas of its ruling class. 118

When people speak of ideas that revolutionize society they do but express the fact that within the old society the elements of a new one have been created, and that the dissolution of the old ideas keeps even pace with the dissolution of the old conditions of existence. 119

When the ancient world was in its last throes the ancient religions were overcome by Christianity. When Christian ideas succumbed in the 18th century to rationalist ideas, feudal society fought its death-battle with the then revolutionary bourgeoisie. The ideas of religious liberty and freedom of conscience merely gave expression to the sway of free competition within the domain of knowledge. 120

"Undoubtedly," it will be said, "religious, moral, philosophical and judicial ideas have been modified in the course of historical development. But religion, morality, philosophy, political science, and law, constantly survived this change. 121

"There are, besides, eternal truths, such as Freedom, Justice, etc., that are common to all states of society. But Communism abolishes eternal truths, it abolishes all religion and all morality, instead of constituting them on a new basis; it therefore acts in contradiction to all past historical experience." 122

What does this accusation reduce itself to? The history of all past 123
society has consisted in the development of class antagonisms, antagonisms that assumed different forms at different epochs.

But whatever form they may have taken, one fact is common to all 124
past ages, viz., the exploitation of one part of society by the other. No
wonder, then, that the social consciousness of past ages, despite all the
multiplicity and variety it displays, moves within certain common
forms, or general ideas, which cannot completely vanish except with
the total disappearance of class antagonisms.

The Communist revolution is the most radical rupture with tradi- 125
tional property relations; no wonder that its development involves the
most radical rupture with traditional ideas.

But let us have done with the bourgeois objections to Communism. 126

We have seen above that the first step in the revolution by the 127
working class is to raise the proletariat to the position of ruling class,
to win the battle of democracy.

The proletariat will use its political supremacy to wrest, by de- 128
grees, all capital from the bourgeoisie, to centralize all instruments of
production in the hands of the State, i.e., of the proletariat organized
as a ruling class; and to increase the total productive forces as rapidly
as possible.

Of course, in the beginning, this cannot be effected except by 129
means of despotic inroads on the rights of property, and on the conditions of bourgeois production; by means of measures, therefore, which
appear economically insufficient and untenable, but which in the
course of the movement outstrip themselves, necessitate further inroads upon the old social order, and are unavoidable as a means of
entirely revolutionizing the mode of production.

These measures will of course be different in different countries. 130

Nevertheless in the most advanced countries the following will be 131
pretty generally applicable:

1. Abolition of property in land and application of all rents of land to 132
   public purposes.
2. A heavy progressive or graduated income tax.
3. Abolition of all right of inheritance.
4. Confiscation of the property of all emigrants and rebels.
5. Centralization of credit in the hands of the State, by means of a
   national bank with State capital and an exclusive monopoly.
6. Centralization of the means of communication and transport in
   the hands of the State.
7. Extension of factories and instruments of production owned by the

State; the bringing into cultivation of waste lands, and the improvement of the soil generally in accordance with a common plan.

8. Equal liability of all to labor. Establishment of industrial armies, especially for agriculture.
9. Combination of agriculture with manufacturing industries; gradual abolition of the distinction between town and country by a more equable distribution of the population over the country.
10. Free education for all children in public schools. Abolition of children's factory labor in its present form. Combination of education with industrial production, etc., etc.

When, in the course of development, class distinctions have disappeared, and all production has been concentrated in the hands of a vast association of the whole nation, the public power will lose its political character. Political power, properly so called, is merely the organized power of one class for oppressing another. If the proletariat during its contest with the bourgeoisie is compelled, by the force of circumstances, to organize itself as a class, if, by means of a revolution, it makes itself the ruling class, and, as such, sweeps away by force the old conditions of production, then it will, along with these conditions, have swept away the conditions for the existence of class antagonism, and of classes generally, and will thereby have abolished its own supremacy as a class. 133

In place of the old bourgeois society, with its classes and class antagonisms, we shall have an association in which the free development of each is the condition for the free development of all. . . . 134

Position of the Communists
in Relation to the Various Existing
Opposition Parties

[The preceding section] has made clear the relations of the Communists to the existing working class parties, such as the Chartists in England and the Agrarian Reforms[11] in America. 135

---

[11]***Agrarian Reforms*** Agrarian reform was a very important issue in America after the Revolution. The Chartists were a radical English group established in 1838; they demanded reforms in land and labor. They were among the more violent revolutionaries of the day. Agrarian reform, redistribution of the land, was slow to come, and the issue often sparked violence between social classes.

The Communists fight for the attainment of the immediate aims, 136
for the enforcement of the momentary interests of the working class;
but in the movement of the present they also represent and take care
of the future of that movement. In France the Communists ally themselves with the Social-Democrats[12] against the conservative and radical bourgeoisie, reserving, however, the right to take up a critical position in regard to phrases and illusions traditionally handed down
from the great Revolution.

In Switzerland they support the Radicals,[13] without losing sight of 137
the fact that this party consists of antagonistic elements, partly of
Democratic Socialists, in the French sense, partly of radical bourgeois.

In Poland they support the party that insists on an agrarian revo- 138
lution, as the prime condition for national emancipation, that party
which fomented the insurrection of Cracow in 1846.[14]

In Germany they fight with the bourgeoisie whenever it acts in a 139
revolutionary way, against the absolute monarchy, the feudal squirear-
chy, and the petty bourgeoisie.

But they never cease for a single instant to instill into the working 140
class the clearest possible recognition of the hostile antagonism between bourgeoisie and proletariat, in order that the German workers
may straightway use, as so many weapons against the bourgeoisie, the
social and political conditions that the bourgeoisie must necessarily
introduce along with its supremacy, and in order that, after the fall of
the reactionary classes in Germany, the fight against the bourgeoisie
itself may immediately begin.

The Communists turn their attention chiefly to Germany, because 141
that country is on the eve of a bourgeois revolution,[15] that is bound to
be carried out under more advanced conditions of European civilization, and with a more developed proletariat, than that of England was

---

[12]*Social-Democrats*   In France in the 1840s, a group who proposed the ideal of labor
reform through the establishment of workshops supplied with government capital.

[13]*Radicals*   By 1848, European Radicals, taking their name from the violent revolutionaries of the French Revolution (1789–1799), were a nonviolent group content to wait
for change.

[14]*the insurrection of Cracow in 1846*   Cracow was an independent city in 1846.
The insurrection was designed to join Cracow with Poland and to further large-scale social reforms.

[15]*on the eve of a bourgeois revolution*   Ferdinand Lassalle (1825–1864) developed
the German labor movement and was in basic agreement with Marx, who was nevertheless convinced that Lassalle's approach was wrong. The environment in Germany seemed
appropriate for revolution, in part because of its fragmented political structure and in part
because no major revolutions had yet occurred there.

in the seventeenth and of France in the eighteenth century, and because the bourgeois revolution in Germany will be but the prelude to an immediately following proletarian revolution.

In short, the Communists everywhere support every revolutionary 142
movement against the existing social and political order of things.

In all these movements they bring to the front, as the leading ques- 143
tion in each, the property question, no matter what its degree of development at the time.

Finally, they labor everywhere for the union and agreement of the 144
democratic parties of all countries.

The Communists disdain to conceal their views and aims. They 145
openly declare that their ends can be attained only by the forcible
overthrow of all existing social conditions. Let the ruling classes
tremble at a Communistic revolution. The proletarians have nothing
to lose but their chains. They have a world to win.

Working men of all countries, unite! 146

QUESTIONS

1. Begin by establishing your understanding of the terms "bourgeois" and "proletarian." Is the distinction Marx makes clear? Are such terms applicable to American society today? Do you feel that you can be properly associated with one or the other of these groups?
2. Marx makes the concept of social class fundamental to his theories. Can "social class" be easily defined? Are there social classes evident in our society? Are they engaged in a struggle of the sort Marx assumes?
3. What are Marx's views about the value of work in the society he describes?
4. Marx says that every class struggle is a political struggle. Is this true?
5. Examine the first part and total up the number of paragraphs devoted to the bourgeois and to the proletariat. Which class gets more paragraphs? Why?
6. Is the modern proletariat a revolutionary class?
7. Is Marx's analysis of history clear? Try to summarize his views on the progress of history.

WRITING ASSIGNMENTS

1. Defend or attack Marx's statement: "The executive of the modern State is but a committee for managing the common affairs of the whole bourgeoisie." Is this generally true? Take three "affairs of the whole bourgeoisie" and test each one in turn.

2. Examine Marx's statements regarding women. Refer especially to paragraphs 39, 98, 105, and 110. Does he give evidence that his views are in conflict with his general society? After you have a list of his statements, see if you can establish exactly what he is recommending. Do you approve of his recommendations?

3. Marx's program of ten points is listed in paragraph 132. Using the technique that Marx himself uses—taking each point in its turn, clarifying the problems with the point, and finally deciding for or against the point—evaluate his program. Which points do you feel are most beneficial to society? Which are detrimental to society? What is your overall view of the general worth of the program? Do you think it would be possible to put such a program into effect?

4. All Marx's views are predicated on the present nature of property ownership and the changes that communism will institute. He says such things as, a rupture with property relations "involves the most radical rupture with traditional ideas" (para. 125). And he discusses in depth his proposal for the rupture of property relations (paras. 68–93). Clarify the traditional property relations—what can be owned and by whom—and then contrast with that the proposals Marx makes. Establish your own views as you go along, taking issue or expressing agreement (with your reasons) with Marx as you do so. What kinds of property relations do you see around you? What kinds are most desirable for a healthy society? Does Marx get you worried?

FREDERICK DOUGLASS

─────⊸⊶─────

From
The Narrative of
the Life of Frederick Douglass,
an American Slave

*F*REDERICK DOUGLASS *(1817–1895) was born into slavery in Mary-land; he died not only a free man but a man who commanded the re-spect of his country, his government, and hosts of supporters. His owner's wife, Mrs. Auld, was a northerner and did not know about the slaveholders' practice of forbidding slaves to learn to read and write. This was a lucky accident, indeed: Mrs. Auld taught Douglass enough so that he could begin his own education—and escape to freedom.*

The selection presented here describes how Douglass gained his victory. In his description—the Narrative *was published in 1845—Douglass was careful to avoid mentioning details that would likely have hurt other slaves' chances of gaining their freedom. Douglass used the papers of a freed black sailor to impersonate him, and so he was able to sail from Baltimore to New York, where he gained his freedom. His method was dangerous but simple. He lived first in New York, then settled in New Bedford, Massachusetts.*

The rest of the Narrative *is filled with stories about his growing up as a slave. He had little connection with his family. His mother, Har-riet Bailey, was not able to be close with him, nor was he ever to know who his father was. He records not only the beatings he wit-nessed as a slave but also the conditions under which he lived and the struggles he felt within himself to be a free man. He, himself, survived brutal beatings and torture by a professional slave "breaker."*

This section of the **Narrative** is fascinating for its revelation of the observations of a freed slave concerning the world he entered. His concerns for work, economy, and justice are everywhere apparent in these pages. When they were published—apparently as a result of encouragement by Harvard students who had heard his powerful oratory—these pages made him one of the most sought-after speakers in the North. He became a lecturer for the Massachusetts Antislavery League. Yet, as a fugitive slave, he lived in constant fear of being kidnapped and returned to slavery.

After publication of an early version of his life, to avoid capture he spent a few years in England, then returned to the United States and became the editor of the **North Star**, an abolitionist paper in Rochester, New York. One of his chief concerns was for the welfare of the slaves who managed to secure their freedom. When John Brown invited him to participate in the raid at Harpers Ferry, Virginia, Douglass was famous throughout the North. He refused Brown's invitation because he believed that such an act would not benefit the antislavery cause. When the Civil War began, Douglass managed to get Lincoln's ear. Originally there were no plans to free the slaves, but Douglass helped convince Lincoln that it would help the war effort to free them, and in 1863 Lincoln delivered the Emancipation Proclamation.

The years after the war and Lincoln's death were not good for freed slaves. Terrorist groups in both the North and the South worked to keep them from enjoying freedom, and programs which might have been effective in training black ex-slaves were never fully instituted. During this time Douglass worked in various capacities for the government, both as an ambassador to foreign countries and as an official in Washington, D.C. He was the first black American to become a national figure and to have powerful influence with the government.

DOUGLASS'S RHETORIC

Douglass was essentially a self-taught man. He is said to have been a commanding speaker who could move people to agree with his views. His speeches were often full and somewhat high-flown in the fashion of the day. This excerpt from the **Narrative**, *however, is remarkable for having none of the characteristics of the overdone rhet-*

oric we find in the writing of the time. Instead, it is surprisingly direct, simple, and clear. The use of the first person is as simple as one could wish it to be, and yet the feelings that are projected are genuine and moving.

The structure Douglass employs in the Narrative is one of the most basic in all rhetoric: the chronological narrative. He begins his story at a given point in time, explaining what happened at that moment. He then progresses to the next sequence of events, always pushing the narrative closer to the present time. He even includes some key dates, so that one can measure the progress of the narrative. The structure is one that we all recognize and feel comfortable with. There are no interruptions such as flashbacks or ruminations on what might have been. Rather, after his introductory two paragraphs, he tells what happened as it happened.

Douglass's style is a bit formal by modern standards. His sentences are somewhat long, although they are carefully balanced by an occasional very brief sentence. His paragraphs are in general very long, indeed. He tends to take a given subject and work it out thoroughly before dropping it, and to begin a new subject in the next paragraph. Yet even now, 140 years later, the style appears easy and direct. No modern reader will have difficulty responding to what Frederick Douglass has to say. His views on justice, on liberty, and on the relationship between economy and government are as accessible now as they were when they were originally written.

From
The Narrative of the Life of Frederick Douglass, an American Slave

I now come to that part of my life during which I planned, and finally succeeded in making, my escape from slavery. But before narrating any of the peculiar circumstances, I deem it proper to make known my intention not to state all the facts connected with the transaction. My reasons for pursuing this course may be understood from the following: First, were I to give a minute statement of all the facts, it is not only possible, but quite probable, that others would thereby be involved in the most embarrassing difficulties. Secondly, such a statement would most undoubtedly induce greater vigilance on the part of slaveholders than has existed heretofore among them; which would, of course be the means of guarding a door whereby some dear brother bondman might escape his galling chains. I deeply regret the necessity that impels me to suppress any thing of importance connected with my experience in slavery. It would afford me great pleasure indeed, as well as materially add to the interest of my narrative, were I at liberty to gratify a curiosity, which I know exists in the minds of many, by an accurate statement of all the facts pertaining to my most fortunate escape. But I must deprive myself of this pleasure, and the curious of the gratification which such a statement would afford. I would allow myself to suffer under the greatest imputations which evil-minded men might suggest, rather than exculpate myself,[1] and thereby run the hazard of closing the slightest avenue by which a brother slave might clear himself of the chains and fetters of slavery.

I have never approved of the very public manner in which some of our western friends have conducted what they call the *underground railroad*,[2] but which, I think, by their open declarations, has been made most emphatically the *upperground railroad*. I honor those good men and women for their noble daring, and applaud them for willingly subjecting themselves to bloody persecution, by openly avowing their participation in the escape of slaves. I, however, can see very little good resulting from such a course, either to themselves or the slaves escaping; while, upon the other hand, I see and feel assured that those open declarations are a positive evil to the slaves remaining, who are seeking to escape. They do nothing towards enlightening the slave, whilst they do much towards enlightening the master. They stimulate him to greater watchfulness, and enhance his power to capture his slave. We owe something to the slaves south of the line as well as to those north of it; and in aiding the latter on their way to freedom, we should be careful to do nothing which would be likely to hinder the former from escaping from slavery. I would keep the merciless slave-

---

[1]*exculpate myself* This is a mild bit of irony; Douglass means that if he revealed his method of escape he would be innocent of the charge of not telling the whole truth.

[2]*underground railroad* An organization of "safe houses" to help escaped slaves find their way to freedom in Canada. The Fugitive Slave Act (1850) made the work of this abolitionist group a crime.

holder profoundly ignorant of the means of flight adopted by the slave. I would leave him to imagine himself surrounded by myriads of invisible tormentors, ever ready to snatch from his infernal grasp his trembling prey. Let him be left to feel his way in the dark; let darkness commensurate with his crime hover over him; and let him feel that at every step he takes, in pursuit of the flying bondman, he is running the frightful risk of having his hot brains dashed out by an invisible agency. Let us render the tyrant no aid; let us not hold the light by which he can trace the footprints of our flying brother. But enough of this. I will now proceed to the statement of those facts, connected with my escape, for which I am alone responsible, and for which no one can be made to suffer but myself.

In the early part of the year 1838, I became quite restless. I could   3
see no reason why I should, at the end of each week, pour the reward of my toil into the purse of my master. When I carried to him my weekly wages, he would, after counting the money, look me in the face with a robber-like fierceness, and ask, "Is this all?" He was satisfied with nothing less than the last cent. He would, however, when I made him six dollars, sometimes give me six cents, to encourage me. It had the opposite effect. I regarded it as a sort of admission of my right to the whole. The fact that he gave me any part of my wages was proof, to my mind, that he believed me entitled to the whole of them. I always felt worse for having received any thing; for I feared that the giving me a few cents would ease his conscience, and make him feel himself to be a pretty honorable sort of robber. My discontent grew upon me. I was ever on the look-out for means of escape; and, finding no direct means, I determined to try to hire my time, with a view of getting money with which to make my escape. In the spring of 1838, when Master Thomas[3] came to Baltimore to purchase his spring goods, I got an opportunity, and applied to him to allow me to hire my time. He unhesitatingly refused my request, and told me this was another stratagem by which to escape.[4] He told me I could go nowhere but that he could get me; and that, in the event of my running away, he should spare no pains in his efforts to catch me. He exhorted me to content myself, and be obedient. He told me, if I would be happy, I must lay out no plans for the future. He said, if I behaved myself properly, he would take care of me. Indeed, he advised me to complete thought-

---

[3]***Master Thomas***   Thomas Lloyd, his owner, had lent Douglass to Hugh Auld of Baltimore. Auld's wife, a northerner, taught Douglass to read and write.

[4]***another stratagem by which to escape***   He had escaped once before and was captured by a professional slave "breaker."

lessness of the future, and taught me to depend solely upon him for happiness. He seemed to see fully the pressing necessity of setting aside my intellectual nature, in order to contentment in slavery. But in spite of him, and even in spite of myself, I continued to think, and to think about the injustice of my enslavement, and the means of escape.

About two months after this, I applied to Master Hugh for the privilege of hiring my time. He was not acquainted with the fact that I had applied to Master Thomas, and had been refused. He too, at first, seemed disposed to refuse; but, after some reflection, he granted me the privilege, and proposed the following term: I was to be allowed all my time, make all contracts with those for whom I worked, and find my own employment; and, in return for this liberty, I was to pay him three dollars at the end of each week; find myself in[5] calking tools, and in board and clothing. My board was two dollars and a half per week. This, with the wear and tear of clothing and calking tools, made my regular expenses about six dollars per week. This amount I was compelled to make up, or relinquish the privilege of hiring my time. Rain or shine, work or no work, at the end of each week the money must be forthcoming, or I must give up my privilege. This arrangement, it will be perceived, was decidedly in my master's favor. It relieved him of all need of looking after me. His money was sure. He received all the benefits of slaveholding without its evils; while I endured all the evils of a slave, and suffered all the care and anxiety of a freeman. I found it a hard bargain. But, hard as it was, I thought it better than the old mode of getting along. It was a step towards freedom to be allowed to bear the responsibilities of a freeman, and I was determined to hold on upon it. I bent myself to the work of making money. I was ready to work at night as well as day, and by the most untiring perseverance and industry, I made enough to meet my expenses, and lay up a little money every week. I went on thus from May till August. Master Hugh then refused to allow me to hire my time longer. The ground for his refusal was a failure on my part, one Saturday night, to pay him for my week's time. This failure was occasioned by my attending a camp meeting about ten miles from Baltimore. During the week, I had entered into an engagement with a number of young friends to start from Baltimore to the camp ground early Saturday evening; and being detained by my employer, I was unable to

4

---

[5]*find myself in* Douglass means to provide himself with the means to equip himself with his tools and to pay for his board and clothing.

get down to Master Hugh's without disappointing the company. I knew that Master Hugh was in no special need of the money that night. I therefore decided to go to camp meeting, and upon my return pay him the three dollars. I staid at the camp meeting one day longer than I intended when I left. But as soon as I returned, I called upon him to pay him what he considered his due. I found him very angry; he could scarce restrain his wrath. He said he had a great mind to give me a severe whipping. He wished to know how I dared go out of the city without asking his permission. I told him I hired my time, and while I paid him the price which he asked for it, I did not know that I was bound to ask him when and where I should go. This reply troubled him; and, after reflecting a few moments, he turned to me, and said I should hire my time no longer; that the next thing he should know of, I would be running away. Upon the same plea, he told me to bring my tools and clothing home forthwith. I did so; but instead of seeking work, as I had been accustomed to do previously to hiring my time, I spent the whole week without the performance of a single stroke of work. I did this in retaliation. Saturday night, he called upon me as usual for my week's wages. I told him I had no wages; I had done no work that week. Here we were upon the point of coming to blows. He raved, and swore his determination to get hold of me. I did not allow myself a single word; but was resolved, if he laid the weight of his hand upon me, it should be blow for blow. He did not strike me, but told me that he would find me in constant employment in future. I thought the matter over during the next day, Sunday, and finally resolved upon the third day of September, as the day upon which I would make a second attempt to secure my freedom. I now had three weeks during which to prepare for my journey. Early on Monday morning, before Master Hugh had time to make any engagement for me, I went out and got employment of Mr. Butler, at his ship-yard near the drawbridge, upon what is called the City Block, thus making it unnecessary for him to seek employment for me. At the end of the week, I brought him between eight and nine dollars. He seemed very well pleased, and asked me why I did not do the same the week before. He little knew what my plans were. My object in working steadily was to remove any suspicion he might entertain of my intent to run away; and in this I succeeded admirably. I suppose he thought I was never better satisfied with my condition than at the very time during which I was planning my escape. The second week passed, and again I carried him my full wages; and so well pleased was he, that he gave me twenty-five cents (quite a large sum for a slaveholder to give a slave) and bade me to make a good use of it. I told him I would.

Things went on without very smoothly indeed, but within there   5
was trouble. It is impossible for me to describe my feelings as the time
of my contemplated start drew near. I had a number of warm-hearted
friends in Baltimore—friends that I loved almost as I did my life—and
the thought of being separated from them forever was painful beyond
expression. It is my opinion that thousands would escape from slavery,
who now remain, but for the strong cords of affection that bind them
to their friends. The thought of leaving my friends was decidedly the
most painful thought with which I had to contend. The love of them
was my tender point, and shook my decision more than all things else.
Besides the pain of separation, the dread and apprehension of a failure
exceeded what I had experienced at my first attempt. The appalling
defeat I then sustained returned to torment me. I felt assured that, if I
failed in this attempt, my case would be a hopeless one—it would seal
my fate as a slave forever. I could not hope to get off with any thing
less than the severest punishment, and being placed beyond the means
of escape. It required no very vivid imagination to depict the most
frightful scenes through which I should have to pass, in case I failed.
The wretchedness of slavery, and the blessedness of freedom, were perpetually before me. It was life and death with me. But I remained firm,
and, according to my resolution, on the third day of September, 1838,
I left my chains, and succeeded in reaching New York without the
slightest interruption of any kind. How I did so—what means I
adopted—what direction I travelled, and by what mode of conveyance—I must leave unexplained, for the reasons before mentioned.

I have been frequently asked how I felt when I found myself in a   6
free State. I have never been able to answer the question with any
satisfaction to myself. It was a moment of the highest excitement I
ever experienced. I suppose I felt as one may imagine the unarmed
mariner to feel when he is rescued by a friendly man-of-war from the
pursuit of a pirate. In writing to a dear friend, immediately after my
arrival at New York, I said I felt like one who had escaped a den of
hungry lions. This state of mind, however, very soon subsided; and I
was again seized with a feeling of great insecurity and loneliness. I was
yet liable to be taken back, and subjected to all the tortures of slavery.
This in itself was enough to damp the ardor of my enthusiasm. But
the loneliness overcame me. There I was in the midst of thousands,
and yet a perfect stranger; without home and without friends, in the
midst of thousands of my own brethren—children of a common Father, and yet I dared not to unfold to any one of them my sad condition. I was afraid to speak to any one for fear of speaking to the wrong
one, and thereby falling into the hands of money-loving kidnappers,

whose business it was to lie in wait for the panting fugitive, as the ferocious beasts of the forest lie in wait for their prey. The motto which I adopted when I started from slavery was this—"Trust no man!" I saw in every white man an enemy, and in almost every colored man cause for distrust. It was a most painful situation; and, to understand it, one must needs experience it, or imagine himself in similar circumstances. Let him be a fugitive slave in a strange land— a land given up to be the hunting-ground for slaveholders—whose inhabitants are legalized kidnappers—where he is every moment subjected to the terrible liability of being seized upon by his fellow-men, as the hideous crocodile seizes upon his prey!—I say, let him place himself in my situation—without home or friends—without money or credit—wanting shelter, and no one to give it—wanting bread, and no money to buy it—and at the same time let him feel that he is pursued by merciless men-hunters, and in total darkness as to what to do, where to go, or where to stay—perfectly helpless both as to the means of defense and means of escape—in the midst of plenty, yet suffering the terrible gnawings of hunger—in the midst of houses, yet having no home—among fellow-men, yet feeling as if in the midst of wild beasts, whose greediness to swallow up the trembling and half-famished fugitive is only equalled by that with which the monsters of the deep swallow up the helpless fish upon which they subsist—I say, let him be placed in this most trying situation—the situation in which I was placed—then, and not till then, will he fully appreciate the hardships of, and know how to sympathize with, the toil-worn and whip-scarred fugitive slave.

Thank Heaven, I remained but a short time in this distressed situation. I was relieved from it by the humane hand of Mr. David Ruggles, whose vigilance, kindness, and perseverance, I shall never forget. I am glad of an opportunity to express, as far as words can, the love and gratitude I bear him. Mr. Ruggles is now afflicted with blindness, and is himself in need of the same kind offices which he was once so forward in the performance of toward others. I had been in New York but a few days, when Mr. Ruggles sought me out, and very kindly took me to his boarding-house at the corner of Church and Lespenard Streets. Mr. Ruggles was then very deeply engaged in the memorable *Darg* case,[6] as well as attending to a number of other fugitive slaves, devising ways and means for their successful escape; and, though watched

7

---

[6]**Darg case** Mr. Ruggles tried to help a fugitive slave named Darg escape authorities who were compelled to return him to his owners.

and hemmed in on almost every side, he seemed to be more than a match for his enemies.

Very soon after I went to Mr. Ruggles, he wished to know of me 8 where I wanted to go; as he deemed it unsafe for me to remain in New York. I told him I was a calker, and should like to go where I could get work. I thought of going to Canada; but he decided against it, and in favor of my going to New Bedford, thinking I should be able to get work there at my trade. At this time, Anna,[7] my intended wife, came on; for I wrote to her immediately after my arrival at New York (notwithstanding my homeless, houseless, and helpless condition) informing her of my successful flight, and wishing her to come on forthwith. In a few days after her arrival, Mr. Ruggles called in the Rev. J. W. C. Pennington, who, in the presence of Mr. Ruggles, Mrs. Michaels, and two or three others, performed the marriage ceremony, and gave us a certificate, of which the following is an exact copy:

> THIS may certify, that I joined together in holy matrimony Frederick Johnson[8] and Anna Murray, as man and wife, in the presence of Mr. David Ruggles and Mrs. Michaels.
>
> JAMES W. C. PENNINGTON.
> *New York, Sept. 15, 1838.*

Upon receiving this certificate, and a five-dollar bill from Mr. Ruggles, I shouldered one part of our baggage, and Anna took up the other, and we set out forthwith to take passage on board of the steamboat John W. Richmond for Newport, on our way to New Bedford. Mr. Ruggles gave me a letter to a Mr. Shaw in Newport, and told me, in case my money did not serve me to New Bedford, to stop in Newport and obtain further assistance; but upon our arrival at Newport, we were so anxious to get to a place of safety, that, notwithstanding we lacked the necessary money to pay our fare, we decided to take seats in the stage, and promise to pay when we got to New Bedford. We were encouraged to do this by two excellent gentlemen, residents of New Bedford, whose names I afterward ascertained to be Joseph Ricketson and William C. Taber. They seemed at once to understand our circumstances, and gave us such assurance of their friendliness as put us fully at ease in their presence. It was good indeed to meet with such friends, at such a time. Upon reaching New Bedford, we were directed to the house of Mr. Nathan Johnson, by whom we were kindly received, and hospitably provided for. Both Mr. and Mrs. Johnson took a deep and lively

---

[7]She was free. [Douglass's note]
[8]I had changed my name from Frederick *Bailey* to that of *Johnson.* [Douglass's note]

interest in our welfare. They proved themselves quite worthy of the name of abolitionists. When the stage-driver found us unable to pay our fare, he held on upon our baggage as security for the debt. I had but to mention the fact to Mr. Johnson, and he forthwith advanced the money.

We now began to feel a degree of safety, and to prepare ourselves 10 for the duties and responsibilities of a life of freedom. On the morning after our arrival at New Bedford, while at the breakfast-table, the question arose as to what name I should be called by. The name given me by my mother was, "Frederick Augustus Washington Bailey." I, however, had dispensed with the two middle names long before I left Maryland so that I was generally known by the name of "Frederick Bailey." I started from Baltimore bearing the name of "Stanley." When I got to New York, I again changed my name to "Frederick Johnson," and thought that would be the last change. But when I got to New Bedford, I found it necessary again to change my name. The reason of this necessity was, that there were so many Johnsons in New Bedford, it was already quite difficult to distinguish between them. I gave Mr. Johnson the privilege of choosing me a name, but told him he must not take from me the name of "Frederick." I must hold on to that, to preserve a sense of my identity. Mr. Johnson had just been reading the "Lady of the Lake,"[9] and at once suggested that my name be "Douglass." From that time until now I have been called "Frederick Douglass"; and as I am more widely known by that name than by either of the others, I shall continue to use it as my own.

I was quite disappointed at the general appearance of things in New 11 Bedford. The impression which I had received respecting the character and condition of the people of the north, I found to be singularly erroneous. I had very strangely supposed, while in slavery, that few of the comforts, and scarcely any of the luxuries, of life were enjoyed at the north, compared with what were enjoyed by the slaveholders of the south. I probably came to this conclusion from the fact that northern people owned no slaves. I supposed that they were about upon a level with the non-slaveholding population of the south. I knew *they* were exceedingly poor, and I had been accustomed to regard their poverty as the necessary consequence of their being non-slaveholders. I had somehow imbibed the opinion that, in the absence of slaves, there could be no wealth, and very little refinement. And upon coming to the north,

---

[9]***"Lady of the Lake"*** A long narrative poem by Sir Walter Scott (1771–1832), published in 1810. The fugitive Lord James Douglas is a primary character.

I expected to meet with a rough, hard-handed, and uncultivated population, living in the most Spartan-like simplicity, knowing nothing of the ease, luxury, pomp, and grandeur of southern slaveholders. Such being my conjectures, any one acquainted with the appearance of New Bedford may very readily infer how palpably I must have seen my mistake.

In the afternoon of the day when I reached New Bedford, I visited 12 the wharves, to take a view of the shipping. Here I found myself surrounded with the strongest proofs of wealth. Lying at the wharves, and riding in the stream, I saw many ships of the finest model, in the best order, and of the largest size. Upon the right and left, I was walled in by granite warehouses of the widest dimensions, stowed to their utmost capacity with the necessaries and comforts of life. Added to this, almost every body seemed to be at work, but noiselessly so, compared with what I had been accustomed to in Baltimore. There were no loud songs heard from those engaged in loading and unloading ships. I heard no deep oaths or horrid curses on the laborer. I saw no whipping of men; but all seemed to go smoothly on. Every man appeared to understand his work, and went at it with a sober, yet cheerful earnestness, which betokened the deep interest which he felt in what he was doing, as well as a sense of his own dignity as a man. To me this looked exceedingly strange. From the wharves I strolled around and over the town, gazing with wonder and admiration at the splendid churches, beautiful dwellings, and finely-cultivated gardens; evincing an amount of wealth, comfort, taste, and refinement, such as I had never seen in any part of slaveholding Maryland.

Every thing looked clean, new and beautiful. I saw few or no dilapi- 13 dated houses, with poverty-stricken inmates; no half-naked children and barefooted women, such as I had been accustomed to see in Hillsborough, Easton, St. Michael's, and Baltimore. The people looked more able, stronger, healthier, and happier, than those of Maryland. I was for once made glad by a view of extreme wealth, without being saddened by seeing extreme poverty. But the most astonishing as well as the most interesting thing to me was the condition of the colored people, a great many of whom, like myself, had escaped thither as a refuge from the hunters of men. I found many, who had not been seven years out of their chains, living in finer houses, and evidently enjoying more of the comforts of life, than the average of slaveholders in Maryland. I will venture to assert that my friend Mr. Nathan Johnson (of whom I can say with a grateful heart, "I was hungry, and he gave me meat; I was thirsty, and he gave me drink; I was a stranger, and he took me in"] lived in a neater house; dined at a better table; took, paid for, and read, more newspapers; better understood the moral, religious, and political character of the nation—than nine tenths of the slaveholders in Talbot county, Maryland. Yet Mr. Johnson was a working man. His hands were hardened by toil, and not his alone, but those also of Mrs. Johnson. I found the colored people much more spirited than I had supposed they would be. I found among them a determination to protect each other from the blood-thirsty kidnapper, at all hazards. Soon after my arrival, I was told of a circumstance which illustrated their spirit. A colored man and a fugitive slave were on unfriendly terms. The former was heard to threaten the latter with informing his master of his whereabouts. Straightway a meeting was called among the colored people, under the stereotyped[10] notice, "Business of importance!" The betrayer was invited to attend. The people came at the appointed hour, and organized the meeting by appointing a very religious old gentleman as president, who, I believe, made a prayer, after which he addressed the meeting as follows: *"Friends, we have got him here, and I would recommend that you young men just take him outside the door, and kill him!"* With this, a number of them bolted at him; but they were intercepted by some more timid than themselves, and the betrayer escaped their vengeance, and has not been seen in New Bedford since. I believe there have been no more such threats, and should there be hereafter, I doubt not that death would be the consequence.

I found employment, the third day after my arrival, in stowing a 14 sloop with a load of oil. It was new, dirty, and hard work for me; but I went at it with a glad heart and a willing hand. I was now my own master. It was a happy moment, the rapture of which can be understood only by those who have been slaves. It was the first work, the reward of which was to be entirely my own. There was no Master Hugh standing ready, the moment I earned the money, to rob me of it. I worked that day with a pleasure I had never before experienced. I was at work for myself and newly-married wife. It was to me the starting-point of a new existence. When I got through with that job, I went in pursuit of a job of calking; but such was the strength of prejudice against color, among the white calkers, that they refused to work with me, and of course I could get no employment.[11] Finding my trade of

---

[10]*stereotyped* He means printed. Stereotyping is one of several methods of printing and is used to print both newspapers and books.

[11]I am told that colored persons can now get employment at calking in New Bedford—a result of anti-slavery effort. [Douglass's note]

no immediate benefit, I threw off my calking habiliments, and prepared myself to do any kind of work I could get to do. Mr. Johnson kindly let me have his wood-horse and saw, and I very soon found myself a plenty of work. There was no work too hard—none too dirty. I was ready to saw wood, shovel coal, carry the hod, sweep the chimney, or roll oil casks—all of which I did for nearly three years in New Bedford, before I became known to the anti-slavery world.

In about four months after I went to New Bedford, there came a 15 young man to me, and inquired if I did not wish to take the "Liberator."[12] I told him I did; but, just having made my escape from slavery, I remarked that I was unable to pay for it then. I, however, finally became a subscriber to it. The paper came, and I read it from week to week with such feelings as it would be quite idle for me to attempt to describe. The paper became my meat and my drink. My soul was set all on fire. Its sympathy for my brethren in bonds—its scathing denunciations of slaveholders—its faithful exposures of slavery—and its powerful attacks upon the upholders of the institution—sent a thrill of joy through my soul, such as I had never felt before!

I had not long been a reader of the "Liberator," before I got a pretty 16 correct idea of the principles, measures and spirit of the anti-slavery reform. I took right hold of the cause. I could do but little; but what I could, I did with a joyful heart, and never felt happier than when in an anti-slavery meeting. I seldom had much to say at the meetings, because what I wanted to say was said so much better by others. But, while attending an anti-slavery convention at Nantucket, on the 11th of August, 1841, I felt strongly moved to speak, and was at the same time much urged to do so by Mr. William C. Coffin, a gentleman who had heard me speak in the colored people's meeting at New Bedford. It was a severe cross, and I took it up reluctantly. The truth was, I felt myself a slave, and the idea of speaking to white people weighed me down. I spoke but a few moments, when I felt a degree of freedom, and said what I desired with considerable ease. From that time until now, I have been engaged in pleading the cause of my brethren—with what success, and with what devotion, I leave those acquainted with my labors to decide.

---

[12]*the "Liberator"*   The celebrated abolitionist newspaper edited by William Lloyd Garrison (1805–1879).

QUESTIONS

1. If you find Douglass's story engrossing, try to explain what it is about his rhetorical approach to his subject that makes it so. If you find it dull, explain why. What aspects of Douglass's style are effective? What aspects are not effective?
2. What is the significance of Douglass's concerns with the future, as expressed in paragraph 3? Can you see a psychological validity in the slave-owner's insistence on his forgetting the future entirely? Does that idea have implications for your own life?
3. What did it mean for Douglass to hire himself out? Does the practice surprise you?
4. How much freedom did Douglass have as a slave? What was the nature of that freedom?
5. Find three passages that best reveal racial awareness on the part of Douglass or others mentioned in the narrative.
6. Why was Douglass fearful of being kidnapped?

WRITING ASSIGNMENTS

1. Establish what you feel is the real importance of the "six-cents episode" in paragraph 3. Consider its implications for the value of work, the meaning of money, the relationship between slave and slaveowner, and any other related issue you feel it brings into play. How effective is this episode for revealing the most serious issues that concern Douglass?
2. In paragraph 10, Douglass discusses his name changes and alludes to the issue of his own identity. Using that passage as a starting point, take a stand on the issue of whether or not a person's name is closely connected—or connected at all—with that person's sense of his or her identity. What does Douglass reveal about his own sense of identity? Can you detect any changes he reveals in his sense of himself when he was a slave compared with when he was free?
3. Tell a story in the first person of any injustice you feel has been done to you. Use Douglass's technique of chronological narrative; his clear description of scenes; and his reference to, and description of, people and the inclusion of their names. As much as possible use his approach to tell your story.
4. In paragraph 6, Douglass says firmly that once he had gained his freedom he was determined to be wary of strangers and careful not to be kidnapped by those who would get a reward for his return. To that end he declares that he will "Trust no man!" Examine this selecion carefully and, by referring to relevant events and useful quotes, decide whether or not he held to this advice. If you feel that he did not do so, why would he include

his statement? Do you think that Douglass reveals himself to be a trusting man at heart? If so (or if not), what does that mean? What is Douglass's deepest feeling about the goodness or the badness of mankind?

5. When he goes to New Bedford, Massachusetts, he reveals a considerable degree of surprise. In paragraph 11 and several following paragraphs, he gives us his reaction and his thinking. He actually is giving forth an economic theory regarding slaveholding and the production (or maintenance) of wealth. Establish carefully just what surprises him, what conclusions he had drawn while in the South, and what new conclusions he must draw in New Bedford. What genuine conclusions do you feel must be drawn as a result of his observations? What is the economic consequence of slavery for southern society (not just for southern slaveholders)? Use the selection to gather quotations and references that will make your conclusions clearer and more forceful. Consider, too, Douglass's observations on the way blacks and whites lived and worked in New Bedford. At this time, incidentally, New Bedford was a thriving whaling town with a considerable industry and numerous economic opportunities.

HENRY DAVID THOREAU

Civil Disobedience

HENRY DAVID THOREAU *(1817–1862) began keeping a journal when he left Harvard in 1837. The journal was preserved and published, and it shows us the seriousness, determination, and elevation of moral values which is characteristic of all his great work. He is best known for* **Walden** *(1854), a record of his having left the warm congeniality of Concord, Massachusetts, and the home of his close friend, Ralph Waldo Emerson (1803–1882), for the comparative "wilds" of Walden Pond where he built a cabin, planted a garden, and lived simply.* **Walden** *tells us of the deadening influence of ownership and extols the vitality and spiritual uplift that comes from living close to nature. It also shows us that civilization's comforts sometimes rob a person of his independence, his integrity, and even his conscience.*

Thoreau and Emerson were prominent among the group of writers and thinkers who were styled the Transcendentalists. They believed that there was something which transcended the limits of sensory experience; in other words, something that transcended materialism. Their philosophy was based on the works of Immanuel Kant (1724–1804), the German idealist philosopher, Samuel Taylor Coleridge (1772–1834), the English poet; and Johann Wolfgang von Goethe (1749–1832), the German dramatist and thinker. These writers praised human intuition and the capacity to see beyond the limits of common experience.

Their philosophical idealism carried over into the plainer social concerns of the day, expressing themselves in works such as Walden and "Civil Disobedience," which was published in 1849 with the title "Resistance to Civil Government," a year after publication of The Communist Manifesto. Although Thoreau all but denies his idealism in "Civil Disobedience," it is obvious that after having spent a night in the Concord jail, he had realized he could not quietly accept his government's behavior in regard to slavery. He had begun to feel not only that it was appropriate but that it was imperative to disobey unjust laws.

In Thoreau's time the most flagrantly unjust laws were those which supported slavery. The Transcendentalists were strongly opposed to slavery and spoke out against it. Abolitionists in Massachusetts actively harbored escaped slaves and helped them move to Canada and freedom. The Fugitive Slave Act, enacted in 1850, a year after "Civil Disobedience" was published, made Thoreau a criminal because he refused to comply with Massachusetts civil authorities when in 1851 they began to return escaped slaves to the South as the law required.

"Civil Disobedience" has been much more influential in the twentieth century than it was in the nineteenth. Mohandas Gandhi (1869–1948) claimed that while he was editor of an Indian newspaper in South Africa, it helped to inspire his theories of nonviolent resistance. Gandhi eventually brought the British Empire to heel by means of these theories and won independence for India. In the 1960s, Martin Luther King, Jr., applied the same theories in the fight for racial equality in the United States. Thoreau's essay was once again of great import during the latter days of the Vietnam War, when many young men avoided being drafted because they believed that the war was unjust.

"Civil Disobedience" was written after the Walden experience, which began on July 4, 1845, and ended in the summer of 1847, when Thoreau quietly returned to Emerson's home. He also returned to "civilization" and discovered that his refusal to pay the Massachusetts poll tax—not a tax on voting but a "per head" tax imposed on all citizens to help support the Mexican War—landed him in the Concord jail. He spent just one day and one night there—his aunt paid the tax for him—but the experience was so extraordinary that he began examining it in his journal.

THOREAU'S RHETORIC

Thoreau's habit of writing in his journal lasted throughout his life, and though he intended to become a poet after college, he was soon convinced that one of the few ways he could hope to earn a living was by writing. However, he made more money from lecturing on the lyceum circuit. The lyceum was a New England institution in most towns. It resembled a kind of adult education program featuring important speakers such as the very successful Emerson and foreign lecturers. The fees were very reasonable, and in the absence of other popular entertainment, the lyceum was a popular proving ground for speakers interested in promoting their ideas.

Thus, "Civil Disobedience" went through three stages of development. First, its beginnings were rough-hewn in the journal, where the main ideas appear, and where experiments in phrasing begin. Thoreau was a constant reviser. In February 1848, "Civil Disobedience" was first delivered as a lecture at the Concord Lyceum. It urged people of conscience to actively resist a government that acted badly. When it was finally written down for publication in **Aesthetic Papers***, a proper intellectual journal edited by Elizabeth Peabody (1804–1894), the sister-in-law of another important New England writer, Nathaniel Hawthorne (1804–1864), it was refined again, and certain important details were added.*

"Civil Disobedience" bears many of the hallmarks of the spoken lecture. For one thing, it is written in the first person and addresses an audience that Thoreau expects will share many of his sentiments but certainly not all his conclusions. His message is to some extent anarchistic, virtually denying government any authority or respect. Political conservatives generally take his opening quote, "That government is best which governs least," as a rallying cry to help reduce the interference of government in everyday affairs. Such conservatives usually mean by this a reduction in the government's capacity to tax wealth for unpopular causes. Communists, too, see the essay as offering support for their cause. But, in actuality, Thoreau is quite simply opposed to any government that is not totally just, totally moral, and totally respectful of the individual.

The easiness of the pace of the essay also derives from its original form as a speech. Even such locutions as "But, to speak practically and as a citizen" (para. 3), obviously connect the essay with its origins. We can imagine that Thoreau himself was able to impart emphasis where it was demanded in the speech—although it is often said that he was certainly not an overwhelming orator. In fact, short and somewhat homely, he was an unprepossessing figure. Therefore, he was careful to be sure that the writing did the work that, for some speakers, might have been done by means of gesture and theatrics.

Thoreau's language is marked by clarity. He speaks directly to every issue, giving his own position and recommending the position he feels his audience should accept as reasonable and moral people. One impressive achievement in this selection is Thoreau's capacity to shape memorable statements, virtually aphoristic statements, which have become "quotable" generations later, beginning with his own quotation from the words of John L. O'Sullivan: "That government is best which governs least." Thoreau calls it a motto, as if one could put it on the great seal of a government, or as if it should go on a coin. It contains an interesting rhetorical flourish, impressing itself on our memory through the device of repetition: repeating "govern" and almost rhyming "best" with "least."

His most memorable statements show considerable attention to the rhetorical qualities of balance, repetition, and pattern. "The only obligation which I have a right to assume is to do at any time what I think right" (para. 4) uses the word "right" in two senses: first as a matter of personal volition; second, as a matter of moral rectitude. One's rights, in other words, become the opportunity to do right. "For it matters not how small the beginning may seem to be: what is once well done is done forever" (para. 21) also relies on repetition for its effect as well as on the balancing of the concept of a beginning with its capacity to reach out into the future. The use of the rhetorical device of chiasmus, a crisscross relationship between key words, marks "Under a government which imprisons any unjustly, the true place for a just man is also a prison" (para. 22). We see the pattern in:

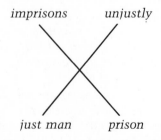

Such attention to phrasing is typical of speakers, whose expressions must catch the attention of listeners and stick in their minds. They

*do not have the advantage of referring to a text, so the text must stay
with them.*

*Thoreau relies also on analogy, comparing men with machines,
people with plants, even the citizen with states considering secession
from the Union. His analogies are effective and must thus be examined in some detail. He relies, too, on the analysis of circumstance
throughout the essay, carefully examining the actions of government
to demonstrate their qualities and their results.*

*His questions include comments on politics (para 1); on the Bible
(para. 23); on Confucius (para. 24); and finally on his contemporary,
Daniel Webster (1782–1852) (para. 41), demonstrating a wide range
of influence but avoiding the pedantic tone that can come from using
quotations too liberally or from producing them from obscure sources.
Taken all in all, this essay is simple, direct, and uncluttered. Its
influence has been in part a result of the clarity and grace which characterize Thoreau's writing at its best.*

Civil Disobedience

I heartily accept the motto—"That government is best which gov- 1
erns least",[1] and I should like to see it acted up to more rapidly and
systematically. Carried out, it finally amounts to this, which also I
believe—"That government is best which governs not at all"; and
when men are prepared for it, that will be the kind of government
which they will have. Government is at best but an expedient; but
most governments are usually, and all governments are sometimes,
inexpedient. The objections which have been brought against a standing army, and they are many and weighty, and deserve to prevail, may
also at last be brought against a standing government. The standing
army is only an arm of the standing government. The government itself, which is only the mode which the people have chosen to execute

---

[1]. . . ***governs least*** John L. O'Sullivan (1813–1895) wrote in the *United States
Magazine and Democratic Review* (1837) that "all government is evil, and the parents of
evil. . . . The best government is that which governs least." Thomas Jefferson wrote,
"That government is best which governs the least, because its people discipline themselves."

their will, is equally liable to be abused and perverted before the people can act through it. Witness the present Mexican war,[2] the work of comparatively a few individuals using the standing government as their tool; for in the outset the people would not have consented to this measure.

This American government—what is it but a tradition, a recent 2 one, endeavoring to transmit itself unimpaired to posterity but each instant losing some of its integrity? It has not the vitality and force of a single living man; for a single man can bend it to his will. It is a sort of wooden gun to the people themselves. But it is not the less necessary for this; for the people must have some complicated machinery or other, and hear its din, to satisfy that idea of government which they have. Governments show thus how successfully men can be imposed on, even impose on themselves, for their own advantage. It is excellent, we must all allow. Yet this government never of itself furthered any enterprise but by the alacrity with which it got out of its way. *It* does not keep the country free. *It* does not settle the West. *It* does not educate. The character inherent in the American people has done all that has been accomplished; and it would have done somewhat more if the government had not sometimes got in its way. For government is an expedient by which men would fain succeed in letting one another alone; and, as has been said, when it is most expedient the governed are most let alone by it. Trade and commerce, if they were not made of India-rubber, would never manage to bounce over the obstacles which legislators are continually putting in their way; and, if one were to judge these men wholly by the effects of their actions and not partly by their intentions, they would deserve to be classed and punished with those mischievous persons who put obstructions on the railroads.

But to speak practically and as a citizen, unlike those who call 3 themselves no-government men, I ask for, not at once no government, but *at once* a better government. Let every man make known what kind of government would command his respect, and that will be one step toward obtaining it.

After all, the practical reason why, when the power is once in the 4 hands of the people, a majority are permitted, and for a long period continue, to rule is not because they are most likely to be in the right,

---

[2]***The present Mexican War (1846–1848)*** The war was extremely unpopular in New England because it was an act of a bullying government anxious to grab land from a weaker nation. The United States had annexed Texas in 1845, precipitating a welcome retaliation from Mexico.

nor because this seems fairest to the minority but because they are physically the strongest. But a government in which the majority rule in all cases cannot be based on justice, even as far as men understand it. Can there not be a government in which majorities do not virtually decide right and wrong but conscience?—in which majorities decide only those questions to which the rule of expediency is applicable? Must the citizen ever for a moment, or in the least degree, resign his conscience to the legislator? Why has every man a conscience then? I think that we should be men first and subjects afterward. It is not desirable to cultivate a respect for the law, so much as for the right. The only obligation which I have a right to assume is to do at any time what I think right. It is truly enough said that a corporation has no conscience; but a corporation of conscientious men is a corporation *with* a conscience. Law never made men a whit more just; and, by means of their respect for it, even the well-disposed are daily made the agents of injustice. A common and natural result of an undue respect for law is that you may see a file of soldiers, colonel, captain, corporal, privates, powder-monkeys,[3] and all, marching in admirable order over hill and dale to the wars, against their wills, ay, against their common sense and consciences, which makes it very steep marching indeed and produces a palpitation of the heart. They have no doubt that it is a damnable business in which they are concerned; they are all peaceably inclined. Now, what are they? Men at all? or small movable forts and magazines at the service of some unscrupulous man in power? Visit the Navy-Yard,[4] and behold a marine, such a man as an American government can make, or such as it can make a man with its black arts— a mere shadow and reminiscence of humanity, a man laid out alive and standing, and already, as one may say, buried under arms with funeral accompaniments, though it may be—

> Not a drum was heard, not a funeral note,
> As his corse to the rampart we hurried;
> Not a soldier discharged his farewell shot
> O'er the grave where our hero we buried.[5]

The mass of men serve the state thus, not as men mainly, but as machines, with their bodies. They are the standing army, and the mi-

---

[3]*powder-monkeys*   The boys who delivered gunpowder to cannons.
[4]*Navy-Yard*   This is apparently the United States Naval yard at Boston.
[5]These lines are from "Burial of Sir John Moore at Corunna" (1817) by the Irish poet Charles Wolfe (1791–1823).

litia, jailers, constables, posse comitatus,[6] &c. In most cases there is no free exercise whatever of the judgment or of the moral sense; but they put themselves on a level with wood and earth and stones; and wooden men can perhaps be manufactured that will serve the purpose as well. Such command no more respect than men of straw or a lump of dirt. They have the same sort of worth only as horses and dogs. Yet such as these even are commonly esteemed good citizens. Others—as most legislators, politicians, lawyers, ministers, and office-holders— serve the state chiefly with their heads; and, as they rarely make any moral distinctions, they are as likely to serve the Devil, without *intending* it, as God. A very few, as heroes, patriots, martyrs, reformers in the great sense, and *men*, serve the state with their consciences also and so necessarily resist it for the most part; and they are commonly treated as enemies by it. A wise man will only be useful as a man and will not submit to be "clay" and "stop a hole to keep the wind away," but leave that office to his dust at least:

> I am too high-born to be propertied,
> To be a secondary at control,
> Or useful serving-man and instrument
> To any sovereign state throughout the world.[7]

He who gives himself entirely to his fellow-men appears to them useless and selfish; but he who gives himself partially to them is pronounced a benefactor and philanthropist.   6

How does it become a man to behave toward this American government today? I answer, that he cannot without disgrace be associated with it. I cannot for an instant recognize that political organization as *my* government which is the *slave's* government also.   7

All men recognize the right of revolution; that is, the right to refuse allegiance to, and to resist the government when its tyranny or its inefficiency are great and unendurable. But almost all say that such is not the case now. But such was the case, they think, in the Revolution of '75. If one were to tell me that this was a bad government because it taxed certain foreign commodities brought to its ports, it is most probable that I should not make an ado about it, for I can do without them. All machines have their friction; and possibly this does enough   8

---

[6] *posse comitatus* Literally, the power of the county; it means a law-enforcement group made up of ordinary citizens.

[7] *"clay," "stop a hole. . . wind away," I am too high born. . . .* These lines are from Shakespeare; the first is from *Hamlet*, V.i.236–7. The verse is from *King John*, V.ii.79–82.

good to counterbalance the evil. At any rate, it is a great evil to make a stir about it. But when the friction comes to have its machine, and oppression and robbery are organized, I say let us not have such a machine any longer. In other words, when a sixth of the population of a nation which has undertaken to be the refuge of liberty are slaves, and a whole country is unjustly overrun and conquered by a foreign army and subjected to military law, I think that it is not too soon for honest men to rebel and revolutionize. What makes this duty the more urgent is the fact that the country so overrun is not our own, but ours is the invading army.

Paley,[8] a common authority with many on moral questions, in his 9 chapter on the "Duty of Submission to Civil Government," resolves all civil obligation into expediency; and he proceeds to say, "that so long as the interest of the whole society requires it, that is, so long as the established government cannot be resisted or charged without public inconveniency, it is the will of God that the established government be obeyed, and no longer. . . . This principle being admitted, the justice of every particular case of resistance is reduced to a computation of the quantity of the danger and grievance on the one side, and of the probability and expense of redressing it on the other." Of this, he says, every man shall judge for himself. But Paley appears never to have contemplated those cases to which the rule of expediency does not apply, in which a people, as well as an individual, must do justice, cost what it may. If I have unjustly wrested a plank from a drowning man, I must restore it to him though I drown myself. This, according to Paley, would be inconvenient. But he that would save his life, in such a case, shall lose it. This people must cease to hold slaves and to make war on Mexico, though it cost them their existence as a people.

In their practice, nations agree with Paley; but does anyone think 10 that Massachusetts does exactly what is right at the present crisis?

> A drab of state, a cloth-o'-silver slut,
> To have her train borne up, and her soul trail in the dirt.[9]

Practically speaking, the opponents to a reform in Massachusetts are

---

[8]**William Paley (1743–1805)** An English theologian who lectured widely on moral philosophy. Paley is famous for *A View of the Evidences of Christianity* (1794). "Duty of Submission to Civil Government Explained" is Chapter 3 of Book 6 of *The Principles of Moral and Political Philosophy* (1785).

[9]**A drab. . . .** From Cyril Tournour (1575?–1626) *Revenger's Tragedy* (1605), IV.iv.70–72. "Drab" is an obsolete term for a prostitute. Thoreau quotes the lines to imply that Massachusetts is a "painted lady" with a defiled soul.

not a hundred thousand politicians at the South but a hundred thousand merchants and farmers here, who are more interested in commerce and agriculture than they are in humanity, and are not prepared to do justice to the slave and to Mexico, *cost what it may.* I quarrel not with far-off foes but with those who, near at home, co-operate with, and do the bidding of, those far away, and without whom the latter would be harmless. We are accustomed to say that the mass of men are unprepared; but improvement is slow because the few are not materially wiser or better than the many. It is not so important that many should be as good as you as that there be some absolute goodness somewhere; for that will leaven the whole lump. There are thousands who are *in opinion* opposed to slavery and to the war who yet in effect do nothing to put an end to them; who, esteeming themselves children of Washington and Franklin, sit down with their hands in their pockets and say that they know not what to do, and do nothing; who even postpone the question of freedom to the question of free trade, and quietly read the prices-current along with the latest advices from Mexico after dinner and, it may be, fall asleep over them both. What is the price-current of an honest man and patriot today? They hesitate and they regret and sometimes they petition; but they do nothing in earnest and with effect. They will wait, well disposed, for others to remedy the evil, that they may no longer have it to regret. At most, they give only a cheap vote, and a feeble countenance and God-speed, to the right, as it goes by them. There are nine hundred and ninety-nine patrons of virtue to one virtuous man. But it is easier to deal with the real possessor of a thing than with the temporary guardian of it.

All voting is a sort of gaming, like checkers or backgammon, with a slight moral tinge to it, a playing with right and wrong, with moral questions; and betting naturally accompanies it. The character of the voters is not staked. I cast my vote, perchance, as I think right; but I am not vitally concerned that that right should prevail. I am willing to leave it to the majority. Its obligation, therefore, never exceeds that of expediency. Even voting *for the right* is *doing* nothing for it. It is only expressing to men feebly your desire that it should prevail. A wise man will not leave the right to the mercy of chance, nor wish it to prevail through the power of the majority. There is but little virtue in the action of masses of men. When the majority shall at length vote for the abolition of slavery, it will be because they are indifferent to slavery, or because there is but little slavery left to be abolished by their vote. *They* will then be the only slaves. Only *his* vote can hasten the abolition of slavery who asserts his own freedom by his vote.

I hear of a convention to be held at Baltimore,[10] or elsewhere, for   12
the selection of a candidate for the Presidency, made up chiefly of editors, and men who are politicians by profession; but I think, what is
it to any independent, intelligent, and respectable man what decision
they may come to? Shall we not have the advantage of his wisdom and
honesty nevertheless? Can we not count upon some independent
votes? Are there not many individuals in the country who do not attend conventions? But no: I find that the responsible man, so called,
has immediately drifted from his position, and despairs of his country
when his country has more reason to despair of him. He forthwith
adopts one of the candidates thus selected as the only *available* one,
thus proving that he is himself *available* for any purposes of the dem-
agogue. His vote is of no more worth than that of any unprincipled
foreigner or hireling native who may have been bought. O for a man
who is a *man* and, as my neighbor says has a bone in his back which
you cannot pass your hand through! Our statistics are at fault: the
population has been returned too large. How many *men* are there to a
square thousand miles in this country? Hardly one. Does not America
offer any inducement for men to settle here? The American has dwin-
dled into an Odd Fellow[11]—one who may be known by the development of his organ of gregariousness and a manifest lack of intellect
and cheerful self-reliance; whose first and chief concern, on coming
into the world, is to see that the Almshouses are in good repair; and,
before yet he has lawfully donned the virile garb, to collect a fund for
the support of the widows and orphans that may be; who, in short,
ventures to live only by the aid of the Mutual Insurance Company,
which has promised to bury him decently.

It is not a man's duty, as a matter of course, to devote himself to   13
the eradication of any, even the most enormous wrong; he may still
properly have other concerns to engage him; but it is his duty, at least,
to wash his hands of it and, if he gives it no thought longer, not to
give it practically his support. If I devote myself to other pursuits and
contemplations, I must first see, at least, that I do not pursue them
sitting upon another man's shoulders. I must get off him first, that he
may pursue his contemplations too. See what gross inconsistency is
tolerated. I have heard some of my townsmen say, "I should like to

---

[10]***Baltimore***   In 1848 the political environment was particularly intense; it was a
seedbed for theoreticians of the Confederacy, which was only beginning to be contemplated seriously.

[11]***Odd Fellow***   The Independent Order of Odd Fellows, a fraternal and benevolent
secret society, was introduced to the United States in 1821, and Baltimore was its headquarters.

have them order me out to help put down an insurrection of the slaves, or to march to Mexico—see if I would go"; and yet these very men have each directly by their allegiance and so indirectly, at least, by their money, furnished a substitute. The soldier is applauded who refuses to serve in an unjust war by those who do not refuse to sustain the unjust government which makes the war; is applauded by those whose own act and authority he disregards and sets at naught; as if the State were penitent to that degree that it hired one to scourge it while it sinned, but not to that degree that it left off sinning for a moment. Thus, under the name of Order and Civil Government, we are all made at last to pay homage to and support our own meanness. After the first blush of sin comes its indifference; and from immoral it becomes, as it were, *un*moral, and not quite unnecessary to that life which we have made.

The broadest and most prevalent error requires the most disinter- 14
ested virtue to sustain it. The slight reproach to which the virtue of patriotism is commonly liable, the noble are most likely to incur. Those who, while they disapprove of the character and measures of a government, yield to it their allegiance and support, are undoubtedly its most conscientious supporters, and so frequently the most serious obstacles to reform. Some are petitioning the State to dissolve the Union, to disregard the requisitions of the President. Why do they not dissolve it themselves—the union between themselves and the State— and refuse to pay their quota into its treasury? Do not they stand in the same relation to the State that the State does to the Union? And have not the same reasons prevented the State from resisting the Union which have prevented them from resisting the State?

How can a man be satisfied to entertain an opinion merely, and 15
enjoy *it*? Is there any enjoyment in it if his opinion is that he is aggrieved? If you are cheated out of a single dollar by your neighbor, you do not rest satisfied with knowing that you are cheated, or with saying that you are cheated, or even with petitioning him to pay you your due; but you take effectual steps at once to obtain the full amount and see that you are never cheated again. Action from principle, the perception and the performance of right, changes things and relations; it is essentially revolutionary and does not consist wholly with anything which was. It not only divides states and churches, it divides families; ay, it divides the *individual*, separating the diabolical in him from the divine.

Unjust laws exist: shall we be content to obey them, or shall we 16
endeavor to amend them and obey them until we have succeeded, or shall we transgress them at once? Men generally, under such a govern-

ment as this, think that they ought to wait until they have persuaded the majority to alter them. They think that if they should resist the remedy would be worse than the evil. *It* makes it worse. Why is it not more apt to anticipate and provide for reform? Why does it not cherish its wise minority? Why does it cry and resist before it is hurt? Why does it not encourage its citizens to be on the alert to point out its faults and *do* better than it would have them? Why does it always crucify Christ and excommunicate Copernicus and Luther[12] and pronounce Washington and Franklin rebels?

One would think that a deliberate and practical denial of its authority was the only offence never contemplated by government; else why has it not assigned its definite, its suitable and proportionate penalty? If a man who has no property refuses but once to earn nine shillings for the State, he is put in prison for a period unlimited by any law that I know, and determined only by the discretion of those who placed him there; but if he should steal ninety times nine shillings from the State, he is soon permitted to go at large again. 17

If the injustice is part of the necessary friction of the machine of government, let it go, let it go: perchance it will wear smooth—certainly the machine will wear out. If the injustice has a spring or a pulley or a rope or a crank exclusively for itself, then perhaps you may consider whether the remedy will not be worse than the evil; but if it is of such a nature that it requires you to be the agent of injustice to another, then I say break the law. Let your life be a counter friction to stop the machine. What I have to do is to see, at any rate, that I do not lend myself to the wrong which I condemn. 18

As for adopting the ways which the State has provided for remedying the evil, I know not of such ways. They take too much time, and a man's life will be gone. I have other affairs to attend to. I came into this world, not chiefly to make this a good place to live in, but to live in it, be it good or bad. A man has not everything to do, but something; and because he cannot do *everything*, it is not necessary that he should do *something* wrong. It is not my business to be petitioning the Governor or the Legislature any more than it is theirs to petition me; and if they should not hear my petition what should I do then? But in this case the State has provided no way: its very Constitution is the evil. This may seem to be harsh and stubborn and unconcillia- 19

---

[12]***Nicolaus Copernicus (1473–1543) and Martin Luther (1483–1546)*** Copernicus revolutionized astronomy and the way humankind perceives the universe; Luther was a religious revolutionary who began the Reformation and created the first Protestant faith.

tory; but it is to treat with the utmost kindness and consideration the only spirit that can appreciate or deserves it. So is all change for the better, like birth and death, which convulse the body.

I do not hesitate to say that those who call themselves Abolition- 20 ists should at once effectually withdraw their support, both in person and property, from the government of Massachusetts, and not wait till they constitute a majority of one before they suffer the right to prevail through them. I think that it is enough if they have God on their side, without waiting for that other one. Moreover, any man more right than his neighbors constitutes a majority of one already.

I meet this American government or its representative, the State 21 government, directly and face to face once a year—no more—in the person of its tax-gatherer; this is the only mode in which a man situated as I am necessarily meets it; and it then says distinctly, Recognize me; and the simplest, the most effectual and, in the present posture of affairs, the indispensablest mode of treating with it on this head, of expressing your little satisfaction with and love for it, is to deny it then. My civil neighbor, the tax-gatherer, is the very man I have to deal with—for it is, after all, with men and not with parchment that I quarrel—and he has voluntarily chosen to be an agent of the government. How shall he ever know well what he is and does as an officer of the government, or as a man, until he is obliged to consider whether he shall treat me, his neighbor, for whom he has respect, as a neighbor and well-disposed man, or as a maniac and disturber of the peace, and see if he can get over this obstruction to his neighborliness without a ruder and more impetuous thought or speech corresponding with his action. I know this well, that if one thousand, if one hundred, if ten men whom I could name—if ten *honest* men only—ay, if *one* HONEST man in this State of Massachusetts, *ceasing to hold slaves*, were actually to withdraw from this copartnership and be locked up in the county jail therefor, it would be the abolition of slavery in America. For it matters not how small the beginning may seem to be: what is once well done is done forever. But we love better to talk about it: that we say is our mission. Reform keeps many scores of newspapers in its service but not one man. If my esteemed neighbor,[13] the State's ambassador, who will devote his days to the settlement of the question of human rights in the Council Chamber, instead of being threatened

---

[13]*esteemed neighbor* Thoreau refers to Samuel Hoar (1778–1856), a Massachusetts senator, who went to South Carolina to protest that state's practice of seizing black seamen from Massachusetts ships and enslaving them. South Carolina threatened Hoar and drove him out of the state. He did not secure the justice he demanded.

with the prisons of Carolina, were to sit down the prisoner of Massachusetts, that State which is so anxious to foist the sin of slavery upon her sister—though at present she can discover only an act of inhospitality to be the ground of a quarrel with her—the Legislature would not wholly waive the subject the following winter.

Under a government which imprisons any unjustly, the true place 22 for a just man is also a prison. The proper place today, the only place which Massachusetts has provided for her freer and less desponding spirits is in her prisons, to be put out and locked out of the State by her own act, as they have already put themselves out by their principles. It is there that the fugitive slave and the Mexican prisoner on parole and the Indian come to plead the wrongs of his race should find them; on that separate but more free and honorable ground where the State places those who are not *with* her but *against* her—the only house in a slave State in which a free man can abide with honor. If any think that their influence would be lost there, and their voices no longer afflict the ear of the State, that they would not be as an enemy within its walls, they do not know by how much truth is stronger than error, nor how much more eloquently and effectively he can combat injustice who has experienced a little in his own person. Cast your whole vote, not a strip of paper merely, but your whole influence. A minority is powerless while it conforms to the majority; it is not even a minority then; but it is irresistible when it clogs by its whole weight. If the alternative is to keep all just men in prison or give up war and slavery, the State will not hesitate which to choose. If a thousand men were not to pay their tax-bills this year, that would not be a violent bloody measure, as it would be to pay them, and enable the State to commit violence and shed innocent blood. This is, in fact, the definition of a peaceable revolution, if any such is possible. If the tax-gatherer or any other public officer asks me, as one has done, "But what shall I do?" my answer is, "If you really wish to do anything, resign your office." When the subject has refused allegiance and the officer has resigned his office, then the revolution is accomplished. But even suppose blood should flow. Is there not a sort of blood shed when the conscience is wounded? Through this wound a man's real manhood and immortality flow out, and he bleeds to an everlasting death. I see this blood flowing now.

I have contemplated the imprisonment of the offender rather than 23 the seizure of his goods—though both will serve the same purpose—because they who assert the purest right, and consequently are most dangerous to a corrupt State, commonly have not spent much time in accumulating property. To such the State renders comparatively small service, and a slight tax is wont to appear exorbitant, particularly if they are obliged to earn it by special labor with their hands. If there were one who lived wholly without the use of money, the State itself would hesitate to demand it of him. But the rich man—not to make any invidious comparison—is always sold to the institution which makes him rich. Absolutely speaking, the more money, the less virtue; for money comes between a man and his objects and obtains them for him; and it was certainly no great virtue to obtain it. It puts to rest many questions which he would otherwise be taxed to answer; while the only new question which it puts is the hard but superfluous one, how to spend it. Thus his moral ground is taken from under his feet. The opportunities of living are diminished in proportion as what are called the "means" are increased. The best thing a man can do for his culture when he is rich is to endeavor to carry out those schemes which he entertained when he was poor. Christ answered the Herodians[14] according to their condition. "Show me the tribute-money," said he—and one took a penny out of his pocket—if you use money which has the image of Caesar on it, and which he has made current and valuable, that is, *if you are men of the State* and gladly enjoy the advantages of Caesar's government, then pay him back some of his own when he demands it; "Render therefore to Caesar that which is Caesar's, and to God those things which are God's"—leaving them no wiser than before as to which was which; for they did not wish to know.

When I converse with the freest of my neighbors, I perceive that 24 whatever they may say about the magnitude and seriousness of the question, and their regard for the public tranquillity, the long and the short of the matter is that they cannot spare the protection of the existing government, and they dread the consequences to their property and families of disobedience to it. For my own part, I should not like to think that I ever rely on the protection of the State. But if I deny the authority of the State when it presents its tax-bill, it will soon take and waste all my property and so harass me and my children without end. This is hard. This makes it impossible for a man to live honestly, and at the same time comfortably, in outward respects. It will not be worth the while to accumulate property; that would be sure to go again. You must hire or squat somewhere and raise but a small crop and eat that soon. You must live within yourself and depend upon yourself always tucked up and ready for a start, and not have many

---

[14]***Herodians*** Followers of King Herod who were opposed to Jesus Christ (see Matthew 22:16).

affairs. A man may grow rich in Turkey even, if he will be in all respects a good subject of the Turkish government. Confucius[15] said: "If a state is governed by the principles of reason, poverty and misery are subjects of shame; if a state is not governed by the principles of reason, riches and honors are the subjects of shame." No; until I want the protection of Massachusetts to be extended to me in some distant Southern port, where my liberty is endangered, or until I am bent solely on building up an estate at home by peaceful enterprise, I can afford to refuse allegiance to Massachusetts and her right to my property and life. It costs me less in every sense to incur the penalty of disobedience to the State than it would to obey. I should feel as if I were worth less in that case.

Some years ago the State met me in behalf of the Church and com- 25
manded me to pay a certain sum toward the support of a clergyman whose preaching my father attended, but never I myself. "Pay," it said, "or be locked up in the jail." I declined to pay. But, unfortunately, another man saw fit to pay it. I did not see why the schoolmaster should be taxed to support the priest, and not the priest the schoolmaster; for I was not the State's schoolmaster, but I supported myself by voluntary subscription. I did not see why the lyceum should not present its tax-bill and have the State to back its demand, as well as the Church. However, at the request of the selectmen, I condescended to make some such statement as this in writing:—"Know all men by these presents, that I, Henry Thoreau, do not wish to be regarded as a member of any incorporated society which I have not joined." This I gave to the town clerk; and he has it. The State, having thus learned that I did not wish to be regarded as a member of that church, has never made a like demand on me since; though it said that it must adhere to its original presumption that time. If I had known how to name them, I should then have signed off in detail from all the societies which I never signed on to; but I did not know where to find a complete list.

I have paid no poll-tax[16] for six years. I was put into a jail once on 26
this account, for one night; and, as I stood considering the walls of solid stone, two or three feet thick, the door of wood and iron, a foot thick, and the iron grating which strained the light, I could not help

---

[15]*Confucius (550 or 551–479 B.C.)* The most important Chinese religious leader. His *Analects* (collection) treated not only religious but moral and political matters as well.

[16]*poll-tax* A tax levied on every citizen living in a given area; poll means "head," so it is a tax per head. It was about $2 and was used to support the Mexican war.

being struck with the foolishness of that institution which treated me as if I were mere flesh and blood and bones, to be locked up. I wondered that it should have concluded at length that this was the best use it could put me to and had never thought to avail itself of my services in some way. I saw that if there was a wall of stone between me and my townsmen, there was a still more difficult one to climb or break through before they could get to be as free as I was. I did not for a moment feel confined, and the walls seemed a great waste of stone and mortar. I felt as if I alone of all my townsmen had paid my tax. They plainly did not know how to treat me but behaved like persons who are underbred. In every threat and in every compliment there was a blunder; for they thought that my chief desire was to stand the other side of that stone wall. I could not but smile to see how industriously they locked the door on my meditations, which followed them out again without let or hindrance, and *they* were really all that was dangerous. As they could not reach me, they had resolved to punish my body; just as boys, if they cannot come at some person against whom they have a spite, will abuse his dog. I saw that the State was half-witted, that it was timid as a lone woman with her silver spoons, and that it did not know its friends from its foes, and I lost all my remaining respect for it and pitied it.

Thus the State never intentionally confronts a man's sense, intel- 27 lectual or moral, but only his body, his senses. It is not armed with superior wit or honesty but with superior physical strength. I was not born to be forced. I will breathe after my own fashion. Let us see who is the strongest. What force has a multitude? They only can force me who obey a higher law than I. They force me to become like themselves. I do not hear of *men* being *forced* to live this way or that by masses of men. What sort of life were that to live? When I meet a government which says to me, "Your money or your life," why should I be in haste to give it my money? It may be in a great strait and not know what to do: I cannot help that. It must help itself; do as I do. It is not worth the while to snivel about it. I am not responsible for the successful working of the machinery of society. I am not the son of the engineer. I perceive that, when an acorn and a chestnut fall side by side, the one does not remain inert to make way for the other, but both obey their own laws and spring and grow and flourish as best they can till one, perchance, overshadows and destroys the other. If a plant cannot live according to its nature, it dies; and so a man.

The night in prison was novel and interesting enough. The prison- 28 ers in their shirt-sleeves were enjoying a chat and the evening air in the doorway when I entered. But the jailer said, "Come, boys, it is time to lock up"; and so they dispersed, and I heard the sound of their steps returning into the hollow apartments. My room-mate was introduced to me by the jailer as "a first-rate fellow and a clever man." When the door was locked, he showed me where to hang my hat and how he managed matters there. The rooms were whitewashed once a month; and this one, at least, was the whitest, most simply furnished, and probably the neatest apartment in the town. He naturally wanted to know where I came from and what brought me there; and when I had told him, I asked him in my turn how he came there, presuming him to be an honest man, of course; and, as the world goes, I believe he was. "Why," said he, "they accuse me of burning a barn; but I never did it." As near as I could discover, he had probably gone to bed in a barn when drunk and smoked his pipe there; and so a barn burnt. He had the reputation of being a clever man, had been there some three months waiting for his trial to come on, and would have to wait as much longer; but he was quite domesticated and contented, since he got his board for nothing and thought that he was well treated.

He occupied one window, and I the other; and I saw that if one 29 stayed there long, his principal business would be to look out the window. I had soon read all the tracts that were left there and examined where former prisoners had broken out and where a grate had been sawed off and heard the history of the various occupants of that room; for I found that even here there was a history and a gossip which never circulated beyond the walls of the jail. Probably this is the only house in the town where verses are composed, which afterward printed in a circular form but not published. I was shown quite a long list of verses which were composed by some young men who had been detected in an attempt to escape, who avenged themselves by signing them.

I pumped my fellow-prisoner as dry as I could, for fear I should 30 never see him again; but at length he showed me which was my bed and left me to blow out the lamp.

It was like travelling into a far country, such as I had never ex- 31 pected to behold, to lie there for one night. It seemed to me that I never had heard the town-clock strike before, nor the evening sounds of the village; for we slept with the windows open, which were inside the grating. It was to see my native village in the light of the Middle Ages, and our Concord was turned into a Rhine stream, and visions of knights and castles passed before me. They were the voices of old burghers that I heard in the streets. I was an involuntary spectator and auditor of whatever was done and said in the kitchen of the adjacent village-inn—a wholly new and rare experience to me. It was a closer view of my native town. I was fairly inside of it. I never had seen its institutions before. This is one of its peculiar institutions; for it is a shire town.[17] I began to comprehend what its inhabitants were about.

In the morning our breakfasts were put through the hole in the 32 door, in small oblong-square tin pans, made to fit, and holding a pint of chocolate, with brown bread and an iron spoon. When they called for the vessels again, I was green enough to return what bread I had left; but my comrade seized it and said that I should lay that up for lunch or dinner. Soon after he was let out to work at haying in a neighboring field, whither he went every day, and would not be back till noon; so he bade me good-day, saying that he doubted if he should see me again.

When I came out of prison—for someone interfered and paid that 33 tax—I did not perceive that great changes had taken place on the common, such as he observed who went in a youth and emerged a tottering and gray-headed man; and yet a change had to my eyes come over the scene—the town and State and country—greater than any that mere time could effect. I saw yet more distinctly the State in which I lived. I saw to what extent the people among whom I lived could be trusted as good neighbors and friends; that their friendship was for summer weather only; that they did not greatly propose to do right; that they were a distinct race from me by their prejudices and superstitions, as the Chinamen and Malays are; that, in their sacrifices to humanity, they ran no risks, not even to their property; that, after all, they were not so noble but they treated the thief as he had treated them and hoped, by a certain outward observance and a few prayers, and by walking in a particular straight though useless path from time to time, to save their souls. This may be to judge my neighbors harshly; for I believe that many of them are not aware that they have such an institution as the jail in their village.

It was formerly the custom in our village, when a poor debtor came 34 out of jail, for his acquaintances to salute him, looking through their fingers, which were crossed to represent the grating of a jail window, "How do ye do?" My neighbors did not thus salute me but first looked at me and then at one another as if I had returned from a long journey. I was put into jail as I was going to the shoemaker's to get a shoe which was mended. When I was let out the next morning I proceeded to finish my errand, and having put on my mended shoe, joined a

---

[17]***shire town*** A county seat, which means the town would have a court, county offices, and jails.

huckleberry party who were impatient to put themselves under my conduct; and in half an hour—for the horse was soon tackled—was in the midst of a huckleberry field on one of our highest hills two miles off, and then the State was nowhere to be seen.

This is the whole history of "My Prisons." 35

I have never declined paying the highway tax, because I am as de- 36 sirous of being a good neighbor as I am of being a bad subject; and as for supporting schools I am doing my part to educate my fellow countrymen now. It is for no particular item in the tax-bill that I refuse to pay it. I simply wish to refuse allegiance to the State, to withdraw and stand aloof from it effectually. I do not care to trace the course of my dollar, if I could, till it buys a man or a musket to shoot one with— the dollar is innocent—but I am concerned to trace the effects of my allegiance. In fact, I quietly declare war with the State, after my fashion, though I will still make what use and get what advantage of her I can, as is usual in such cases.

If others pay the tax which is demanded of me from a sympathy 37 with the State, they do but what they have already done in their own case, or rather they abet injustice to a greater extent than the State requires. If they pay the tax from a mistaken interest in the individual taxed, to save his property, or prevent his going to jail, it is because they have not considered wisely how far they let their private feelings interfere with the public good.

This, then, is my position at present. But one cannot be too much 38 on his guard in such a case, lest his action be biassed by obstinacy or an undue regard for the opinions of men. Let him see that he does only what belongs to himself and to the hour.

I think sometimes, Why, this people mean well; they are only ig- 39 norant; they would do better if they knew how: why give your neighbors this pain to treat you as they are not inclined to? But I think again, this is no reason why I should do as they do or permit others to suffer much greater pain of a different kind. Again, I sometimes say to myself, When many millions of men, without heat, without ill will, without personal feeling of any kind, demand of you a few shillings only, without the possibility, such is their constitution, of retracting or altering their present demand, and without the possibility, on your side, of appeal to any other millions, why expose yourself to this overwhelming brute force? You do not resist cold and hunger, the winds and the waves, thus obstinately; you quietly submit to a thousand similar necessities. You do not put your head into the fire. But just in proportion as I regard this as not wholly a brute force but partly a human force, and consider that I have relations to those millions as to so many millions of men, and not of mere brute or inanimate things, I see that appeal is possible, first and instantaneously, from them to the Maker of them, and secondly, from them to themselves. But if I put my head deliberately into the fire, there is no appeal to fire or to the Maker of fire, and I have only myself to blame. If I could convince myself that I have any right to be satisfied with men as they are, and to treat them accordingly, and not according, in some respects, to my requisitions and expectations of what they and I ought to be, then, like a good Mussulman[18] and fatalist, I should endeavor to be satisfied with things as they are and say it is the will of God. And, above all, there is this difference between resisting this and a purely brute or natural force, that I can resist this with some effect; but I cannot expect, like Orpheus,[19] to change the nature of the rocks and trees and beasts.

I do not wish to quarrel with any man or nation. I do not wish to   40
split hairs, to make fine distinctions, or set myself up as better than my neighbors. I seek rather, I may say, even an excuse for conforming to the laws of the land. I am but too ready to conform to them. Indeed, I have reason to suspect myself on this head; and each year, as the tax-gatherer comes round, I find myself disposed to review the acts and position of the general and State governments, and the spirit of the people, to discover a pretext for conformity.

> We must affect our country as our par-
>   ents;
> And if at any time we alienate
> Our love or industry from doing it honor,
> We must respect effects and teach the
>   soul
> Matter of conscience and religion,
> And not desire of rule or benefit.[20]

I believe that the State will soon be able to take all my work of this sort out of my hands, and then I shall be no better a patriot than my fellow-countrymen. Seen from a lower point of view, the Constitution, with all its faults, is very good; the law and the courts are very respect-

---

[18]***Mussulman***   Muslim; a follower of the religion of Islam.

[19]***Orpheus***   In Greek mythology Orpheus was a poet whose songs were so plaintive that they affected animals, trees, and even stones.

[20]***We must affect. . . .***   From George Peele (1558?–1597?) *The Battle of Alcazar* (acted 1588–89; printed 1594), II.ii. Thoreau added these lines in a later printing of the essay. They emphasize the fact that one is disobedient to the state as one is to a parent— with love, affection, and from a cause of conscience. Disobedience is not taken lightly.

able; even this State and this American government are, in many respects, very admirable and rare things, to be thankful for, such as a great many have described them; but seen from a point of view a little higher, they are what I have described them; seen from a higher still, and the highest, who shall say what they are, or that they are worth looking at or thinking of at all?

However, the government does not concern me much, and I shall 41 bestow the fewest possible thoughts on it. It is not many moments that I live under a government, even in this world. If a man is thought-free, fancy-free, imagination-free, that which *is not* never for a long time appearing *to be* to him, unwise rulers or reformers cannot fatally interrupt him.

I know that most men think differently from myself; but those 42 whose lives are by profession devoted to the study of these or kindred subjects content me as little as any. Statesmen and legislators, standing so completely within the institution, never distinctly and nakedly behold it. They speak of moving society but have no resting-place without it. They may be men of a certain experience and discrimination and have no doubt invented ingenious and even useful systems, for which we sincerely thank them; but all their wit and usefulness lie within certain not very wide limits. They are wont to forget that the world is not governed by policy and expediency. Webster[21] never goes behind government and so cannot speak with authority about it. His words are wisdom to those legislators who contemplate no essential reform in the existing government; but for thinkers, and those who legislate for all time, he never once glances at the subject. I know of those whose serene and wise speculations on this theme would soon reveal the limits of his mind's range and hospitality. Yet, compared with the cheap professions of most reformers, and the still cheaper wisdom and eloquence of politicians in general, his are almost the only sensible and valuable words, and we thank Heaven for him. Comparatively, he is always strong, original, and, above all, practical. Still his quality is not wisdom but prudence. The lawyer's truth is not Truth but consistency, or a consistent expediency. Truth is always in harmony with herself and is not concerned chiefly to reveal the justice that may consist with wrong-doing. He well deserves to be called, as he has been called, the Defender of the Constitution. There are really no blows to be given by him but defensive ones. He is not a leader but

---

[21]***Daniel Webster (1782–1852)*** One of the most brilliant orators of his time. He was secretary of state from 1841 to 1843, which is why Thoreau thinks he cannot be a satisfactory critic of government.

a follower. His leaders are the men of '87.[22] "I have never made an effort," he says, "and never propose to make an effort; I have never countenanced an effort, and never mean to countenance an effort, to disturb the arrangement as originally made, by which the various States came into the Union." Still thinking of the sanction which the Constitution gives to slavery, he says, "Because it was a part of the original compact—let it stand." Notwithstanding his special acuteness and ability, he is unable to take a fact out of its merely political relations and behold it as it lies absolutely to be disposed of by the intellect—what, for instance, it behooves a man to do here in America to-day with regard to slavery but ventures, or is driven, to make some such desperate answer as the following, while professing to speak absolutely, and as a private man—from which what new and singular code of social duties might be inferred? "The manner," says he, "in which the governments of those States where slavery exists are to regulate it, is for their own consideration, under their responsibility to their constituents, to the general laws of propriety, humanity, and justice, and to God. Associations formed elsewhere, springing from a feeling of humanity, or any other cause, have nothing whatever to do with it. They have never received any encouragement from me, and they never will."[23]

They who know of no purer sources of truth, who have traced up 43 its stream no higher, stand, and wisely stand, by the Bible and the Constitution, and drink at it there with reverence and humility; but they who behold where it comes trickling into this lake or that pool gird up their loins once more and continue their pilgrimage toward its fountain-head.

No man with a genius for legislation has appeared in America. 44 They are rare in the history of the world. There are orators, politicians, and eloquent men by the thousand; but the speaker has not yet opened his mouth to speak who is capable of settling the much-vexed questions of the day. We love eloquence for its own sake and not for any truth which it may utter or any heroism it may inspire. Our legislators have not yet learned the comparative value of free-trade and of freedom, of union, and of rectitude, to a nation. They have no genius or talent for comparatively humble questions of taxation and finance, commerce and manufacturers and agriculture. If we were left solely to the wordy wit of legislators in Congress for our guidance, uncorrected by the seasonable experience and the effectual complaints of the peo-

---

[22]**men of '87** The men who framed the Constitution in 1787.
[23]These extracts have been inserted since the Lecture was read. [Thoreau's note]

ple, America would not long retain her rank among the nations. For eighteen hundred years, though perchance I have no right to say it, the New Testament has been written; yet where is the legislator who has wisdom and practical talent enough to avail himself of the light which it sheds on the science of legislation?

The authority of government, even such as I am willing to submit 45 to—for I will cheerfully obey those who know and can do better than I, and in many things even those who neither know nor can do so well—is still an impure one: to be strictly just, it must have the sanction and consent of the governed. It can have no pure right over my person and property but what I concede to it. The progress from an absolute to a limited monarchy, from a limited monarchy to a democracy, is a progress toward a true respect for the individual. Even the Chinese philosopher[24] was wise enough to regard the individual as the basis of the empire. Is a democracy such as we know it the last improvement possible in government? Is it not possible to take a step further towards recognizing and organizing the rights of man? There will never be a really free and enlightened State until the State comes to recognize the individual as a higher and independent power, from which all its own power and authority are derived, and treats him accordingly. I please myself with imagining a State at last which can afford to be just to all men and to treat the individual with respect as a neighbor; which even would not think it inconsistent with its own repose if a few were to live aloof from it, not meddling with it, nor embraced by it, who fulfilled all the duties of neighbors and fellowmen. A State which bore this kind of fruit and suffered it to drop off as fast as it ripened would prepare the way for a still more perfect and glorious State, which also I have imagined but not yet anywhere seen.

---

[24]***Chinese philosopher*** Thoreau means Confucius.

QUESTIONS

1. How would you characterize the tone of Thoreau's address? Is he chastising his audience? Is he praising it? What opinion do you think he has of his audience?
2. How well does Thoreau use irony? Choose an example and comment on its effectiveness. (One example is in para. 25.)
3. What do you think Thoreau's views are on the relationship of a majority and a minority in the eyes of government?
4. What kind of person does Thoreau seem to be? Can you tell much about

his personality? Do you think you would have enjoyed knowing him? If you could meet him, what would you talk about with him?

5. Are Thoreau's concepts of justice clear?

WRITING ASSIGNMENTS

1. Find the quotations that best describe government. Once you have examined them carefully, write an essay that establishes the kind of government Thoreau seems to be referring to. Be sure to include the values of the government Thoreau refers to, the way it sees its obligations to the governed, and the way it treats matters of justice and moral issues. Describe Thoreau's idea of what the American government of his time was in enough detail so that someone who has not read the essay would have a clear sense of Thoreau's view of its nature.

2. Compare the government of Thoreau's day with that of our own. How much alike are the two governments? What specific qualities do the governments have in common? What qualities differ? Do you believe that the United States government has improved since Thoreau's time? Has it improved enough so that Thoreau might want to retract some of the things he says?

3. According to Thoreau, what should the role of conscience be in government? What do you feel Thoreau means by "conscience"? Is it possible for a government to act out of conscience? If a government did act out of conscience, how would it act? Does our government act out of conscience? Does any government that you know about act out of conscience?

4. Thoreau says: "Unjust laws exist: shall we be content to obey them, or shall we endeavor to amend them and obey them until we have succeeded, or shall we transgress them at once?" (para. 16). Answer Thoreau's question in an essay that focuses on issues that are of significance to you; be as practical and cautious as you feel you should be and provide your own answer to this question, not what you feel Thoreau's answer might be. What forms would Thoreau's disobedience be likely to take? What would the limits of his actions be?

5. Establish clearly what being in jail taught Thoreau. What was life in jail like? Why did it have the effect it had on him? Is it unreasonable for Thoreau to have reacted so strongly to being in a local jail for only a single day?

6. How would Thoreau's ideal state compare with those that might be imagined by Machiavelli, Jefferson, Marx, or King? Establish the similarities you feel might show up in each vision of an ideal government, but be sure that you clearly establish what you think Thoreau's ideal would be.

ELIZABETH CADY STANTON

Declaration of Sentiments and Resolutions

*E*LIZABETH CADY STANTON (1815–1902) *was exceptionally intelligent, and because her lawyer father was willing to indulge her gifts, she was provided the best education a woman in her time in America could expect. Born and raised in Johnstown, New York, she was one of six children, five girls and one boy, Eleazar, in whom all the hopes of the family rested. When Eleazar died after graduating from college, Elizabeth strove to replace him in the admiration of her father. She studied Greek so successfully that she was admitted as the only female in the local secondary school where she demonstrated her abilities, which on the whole were superior to those of the boys with whom she studied.*

Nonetheless, she did not win the esteem she hoped for. Her father, while he loved and cared for her, continually told her he wished she had been born a boy. In Johnstown, as elsewhere, women had few rights and rather low expectations. The question of education was a case in point: it was a profound exception for Elizabeth Cady to go to school with boys or even to study what they studied. She had no hopes of following in their paths since all the professions they

---

From the *History of Woman Suffrage.*

aimed for were closed to women. This fact was painfully brought home to her when she finished secondary school. All the boys she studied with went on to Union College in Schenectady, but she was barred from attending the all-male institution. Instead, she attended a much inferior Troy Female Seminary, run by a pioneer of American education, Emma Willard (1787–1870).

Troy was as good a school as any woman in America could attend; yet it emphasized a great many traditional womanly pursuits and emphasized the principles of Calvinism that Elizabeth Cady came to believe were at the root of the problem women had in American society. In the 1830s women did not have the vote; if they were married, they could not own property; and they could not sue for divorce no matter how ugly their marital situation. A husband expected a dowry from his wife, and he could spend it exactly as he wished; on gambling, carousing, or speculating. Not until 1848, the year of the Seneca Falls Convention, did New York pass laws designed to change this situation.

Elizabeth Cady married when she was twenty-four. Her husband, Henry Stanton, was a prominent abolitionist and journalist. He had little money, and the match was not entirely blessed by Elizabeth's father. In characteristic fashion, she had the word "obey" struck from the marriage vows; and thus she had trouble finding a preacher who would adhere to her wishes. And, preferring never to be known as Mrs. Stanton, she was always addressed as Elizabeth Cady Stanton.

Early on, their life was settled in Boston, where Elizabeth found considerable intellectual companionship and stimulation. Good servants made her household tasks minimal. But soon Henry Stanton's health demanded that they move to Seneca Falls, New York, where there were few servants of any caliber, and where there were few people of intellectual independence to stimulate her. Her lot in life became much like that of any housewife, and she could not abide it.

After a discussion at tea with a number of like-minded women, she proposed a woman's convention to discuss their situation. On July 14, 1848 (a year celebrated for revolutions in every major capital of Europe), the following notice appeared in the Seneca County Courier, *a semiweekly journal:*

SENECA FALLS CONVENTION

WOMAN'S RIGHTS CONVENTION.—A Convention to discuss the social, civil, and religious condition and rights of woman, will be held in the Wesleyan Chapel, at Seneca Falls, N.Y., on Wednesday and Thursday, the 19th and 20th of July, current; commencing at 10 o'clock A.M. *During the first day the meeting will be exclusively for women, who are earnestly invited to attend. The public generally are invited to be present on the second day, when Lucretia Mott, of Philadelphia, and other ladies and gentlemen, will address the convention.*

On the appointed day, less than a week after the notice, carriages and other vehicles tied up the streets around the Wesleyan chapel with a large number of interested people. The first shock was that the chapel was locked, and the first order of business was for a man to climb through an open window to unlock the doors. The chapel was filled immediately but not only with women. Many men were present, including Frederick Douglass, and the women decided that since they were already there, the men could stay.

The convention was a significant success, establishing a pattern that has been repeated frequently since. Elizabeth Cady Stanton, in her "Declaration," figured as a radical in the assembly, proposing unheard-of reforms, such as granting women the vote, which most of the moderates in the assembly could not agree on. For a while, the assembly wished to omit the question of the vote, but Elizabeth, by presenting it as her first statement in the "Declaration," made it clear that without the right to vote on legislation and legislators, women would never be able to change the status quo. Eventually, with the help of Douglass and others, the convention accepted her position, and the women's movement in America was under way.

STANTON'S RHETORIC

Because the Seneca Falls Declaration is modeled directly on Jefferson's Declaration of Independence, we cannot get a good idea of what Stanton's rhetorical gifts were. However, by relying on Jefferson, she exercised a powerful wit (for which her other writing is well known) by reminding her audience that when the Declaration of Independence was uttered, no thought was given to half its potential audience—women. Thus, the Seneca Falls Declaration is a parody, and it is especially effective in the way it parodies its model so closely.

The same periodic sentences, parallelism, and balance are used and largely to the same effect. She employed the same profusion of one-paragraph utterances and exactly the same opening for each of them. Stanton played a marvelous trick, however. In place of the tyrannical foreign King George—Jefferson's "He"—she has put the tyrant man. Because of the power of her model, her "Declaration" gathers strength and ironically undercuts the model.

The most interesting aspect of Stanton's rhetorical structure has to do with the order in which she includes the abuses and wrongs that she asks to be made right. She begins with the vote, just as Jefferson began with the law. Both are essential to the entire argument, and both are the key to change. Whereas Jefferson demands an entirely new government, Elizabeth Cady Stanton ends by demanding the "equal participation" of women with men in the government they have already won.

----···⟨∞⟩····----

Declaration of Sentiments and Resolutions

Adopted by the Seneca Falls Convention, July 19–20, 1848

When, in the course of human events, it becomes necessary for one 1 portion of the family of man to assume among the people of the earth a position different from that which they have hitherto occupied, but one to which the laws of nature and of nature's God entitle them, a decent respect to the opinions of mankind requires that they should declare the causes that impel them to such a course.

We hold these truths to be self-evident: that all men and women 2 are created equal; that they are endowed by their Creator with certain inalienable rights; that among these are life, liberty, and the pursuit of happiness; that to secure these rights governments are instituted, deriving their just powers from the consent of the governed. Whenever any form of government becomes destructive of these ends, it is the right of those who suffer from it to refuse allegiance to it, and to insist upon the institution of a new government, laying its foundation on such principles, and organizing its powers in such form, as to them shall seem most likely to effect their safety and happiness. Prudence, indeed, will dictate that governments long established should not be changed for light and transient causes; and accordingly all experience hath shown that mankind are more disposed to suffer, while evils are sufferable, than to right themselves by abolishing the forms to which they were accustomed. But when a long train of abuses and usurpations, pursuing invariably the same object, evinces a design to reduce them under absolute despotism, it is their duty to throw off such government, and to provide new guards for their future security. Such has been the patient sufferance of the women under this government, and such is now the necessity which constrains them to demand the equal station to which they are entitled.

The history of mankind is a history of repeated injuries and usurpations on the part of man toward woman, having in direct object the establishment of an absolute tyranny over her. To prove this, let facts be submitted to a candid world.   3

He has never permitted her to exercise her inalienable right to the elective franchise.   4

He has compelled her to submit to laws, in the formation of which she had no voice.   5

He has withheld from her rights which are given to the most ignorant and degraded men—both natives and foreigners.   6

Having deprived her of this first right of a citizen, the elective franchise, thereby leaving her without representation in the halls of legislation, he has oppressed her on all sides.   7

He has made her, if married, in the eye of the law, civilly dead.   8

He has taken from her all right in property, even to the wages she earns.   9

He has made her, morally, an irresponsible being, as she can commit many crimes with impunity, provided they be done in the presence of her husband. In the covenant of marriage, she is compelled to promise obedience to her husband, he becoming to all intents and purposes, her master—the law giving him power to deprive her of her liberty, and to administer chastisement.   10

He has so framed the laws of divorce, as to what shall be the proper causes, and in case of separation, to whom the guardianship of the children shall be given, as to be wholly regardless of the happiness of women—the law, in all cases, going upon a false supposition of the supremacy of man, and giving all power into his hands.   11

After depriving her of all rights as a married woman, if single, and the owner of property, he has taxed her to support a government which recognizes her only when her property can be made profitable to it.   12

He has monopolized nearly all the profitable employments, and from those she is permitted to follow, she receives but a scanty remuneration. He closes against her all the avenues to wealth and dis-   13 tinction which he considers most honorable to himself. As a teacher of theology, medicine, or law, she is not known.

He has denied her the facilities for obtaining a thorough education, 14 all colleges being closed against her.

He allows her in Church, as well as State, but a subordinate posi- 15 tion, claiming Apostolic authority for her exclusion from the ministry, and, with some exceptions, from any public participation in the affairs of the Church.

He has created a false public sentiment by giving to the world a 16 different code of morals for men and women, by which moral delinquencies which exclude women from society, are not only tolerated, but deemed of little account in man.

He has usurped the prerogative of Jehovah himself, claiming it as 17 his right to assign for her a sphere of action, when that belongs to her conscience and to her God.

He has endeavored, in every way that he could, to destroy her con- 18 fidence in her own powers, to lessen her self-respect, and to make her willing to lead a dependent and abject life.

Now, in view of this entire disfranchisement of one-half the people 19 of this country, their social and religious degradation—in view of the unjust laws above mentioned, and because women do feel themselves aggrieved, oppressed, and fraudulently deprived of their most sacred rights, we insist that they have immediate admission to all the rights and privileges which belong to them as citizens of the United States.

In entering upon the great work before us, we anticipate no small 20 amount of misconception, misrepresentation, and ridicule; but we shall use every instrumentality within our power to effect our object. We shall employ agents, circulate tracts, petition the State and National legislatures, and endeavor to enlist the pulpit and the press in our behalf. We hope this Convention will be followed by a series of Conventions embracing every part of the country.

[The following resolutions were discussed by Lucretia Mott, Thomas and Mary Ann McClintock, Amy Post, Catharine A. F. Stebbins, and others, and were adopted:]

WHEREAS, The great precept of nature is conceded to be, that "man 21 shall pursue his own true and substantial happiness." Blackstone[1] in

---

[1]*Sir William Blackstone (1723–1780)* The most influential of English scholars of the law. His *Commentaries of the Laws of England* (4 vols., 1765–1769) form the basis of the study of law in England.

his Commentaries remarks, that this law of Nature being coeval[2] with mankind, and dictated by God himself, is of course superior in obligation to any other. It is binding over all the globe, in all countries and at all times; no human laws are of any validity if contrary to this, and such of them as are valid, derive all their force, and all their validity, and all their authority, mediately and immediately, from this original; therefore,

Resolved, That such laws as conflict, in any way, with the true and substantial happiness of woman, are contrary to the great precept of nature and of no validity, for this is "superior in obligation to any other." 22

Resolved, That all laws which prevent woman from occupying such a station in society as her conscience shall dictate, or which place her in a position inferior to that of man, are contrary to the great precept of nature, and therefore of no force or authority. 23

Resolved, That woman is man's equal—was intended to be so by the Creator, and the highest good of the race demands that she should be recognized as such. 24

Resolved, That the women of this country ought to be enlightened in regard to the laws under which they live, that they may no longer publish their degradation by declaring themselves satisfied with their present position, nor their ignorance, by asserting that they have all the rights they want. 25

Resolved, That inasmuch as man, while claiming for himself intellectual superiority, does accord to woman moral superiority, it is pre-eminently his duty to encourage her to speak and teach, as she has an opportunity, in all religious assemblies. 26

Resolved, That the same amount of virtue, delicacy, and refinement of behavior that is required of woman in the social state, should also be required of man, and the same transgressions should be visited with equal severity on both man and woman. 27

Resolved, That the objection of indelicacy and impropriety, which is so often brought against woman when she addresses a public audience, comes with a very ill-grace from those who encourage, by their attendance, her appearance on the stage, in the concert, or in feats of the circus. 28

Resolved, That woman has too long rested satisfied in the circumscribed limits which corrupt customs and a perverted application of the Scriptures have marked out for her, and that it is time she should move in the enlarged sphere which her great Creator has assigned her. 29

---

[2]*coeval* Existing simultaneously.

Resolved, That it is the duty of the women of this country to se- 30
cure to themselves their sacred right to the elective franchise.

Resolved, That the equality of human rights results necessarily 31
from the fact of the identity of the race in capabilities and responsibilities.

Resolved, therefore, That, being invested by the Creator with the 32
same capabilities, and the same consciousness of responsibility for
their exercise, it is demonstrably the right and duty of woman, equally
with man, to promote every righteous cause by every righteous means;
and especially in regard to the great subjects of morals and religion, it
is self-evidently her right to participate with her brother in teaching
them, both in private and in public, by writing and by speaking, by
any instrumentalities proper to be used, and in any assemblies proper
to be held; and this being a self-evident truth growing out of the di-
vinely implanted principles of human nature, any custom or authority
adverse to it, whether modern or wearing the hoary sanction of antiquity,
is to be regarded as a self-evident falsehood, and at war with mankind.

[At the last session Lucretia Mott[3] offered and spoke to the follow- 33
ing resolution:]

Resolved, That the speedy success of our cause depends upon the 34
zealous and untiring efforts of both men and women, for the overthrow
of the monopoly of the pulpit, and for the securing to woman an equal
participation with men in the various trades, professions, and commerce.

---

[3]***Lucretia Mott (1793–1880)*** One of the founders of the 1848 convention at which
these resolutions were presented. She is one of the earliest and most important of the
feminists who struggled to proclaim their rights. She was also a prominent abolitionist.

QUESTIONS

1. Stanton begins her "Declaration" with a diatribe against the government.
   To what extent is the government responsible for the wrongs she complains about?
2. Exactly what is Stanton complaining about? What are the wrongs that
   have been done? Do they seem important to you?
3. How much of the effect of the selection depends upon the parody of the
   Declaration of Independence?
4. Which of the individual declarations is the most important? Which is the
   least important?

5. Is any of the declarations serious enough to warrant starting a revolution?
6. Why do you think the suggestion that women deserve the vote was so hard to put across at the convention?

WRITING ASSIGNMENTS

1. Make a careful comparison between the "Declaration" and Jefferson's Declaration of Independence. What are the similarities? What are the differences? Why would Stanton's "Declaration" be particularly more distinguished because it is a parody of such a document? What weaknesses might be implied because of the close resemblance?

2. Write an essay that is essentially a declaration in the same style Stanton uses. Choose a cause carefully and follow the same pattern that Stanton follows in the selection. Establish the appropriate relationship between government and the cause that you are interested in defending or promoting.

3. To what extent is it useful to petition a government to redress the centuries of wrongs done to women? Is it the government's fault that women were treated so badly? Is the government able to have a significant effect on helping to change the unpleasant circumstances of women? Is it appropriate or inappropriate for Stanton to attack government in her search for equality?

4. The Declaration of Independence was aimed at justifying a war. Is the question of war anywhere implied in Stanton's address? If war is not the question, what is? Is there any substitute for war in Stanton's essay?

5. Read down the list of declarations and resolutions that Stanton enumerates. Have all of these issues been dealt with in our times? Would such a declaration as this still be appropriate, or has the women's movement accomplished all its goals?

6. Examine the issues treated in paragraph 16, concerning "a different code of morals" for men and women. Explain exactly what Stanton meant by that expression and consider the question of how different things are today from what they were in Stanton's day.

MARTIN LUTHER KING, Jr.

Letter from Birmingham Jail

MARTIN LUTHER KING, JR. (1929–1968) was the most influential leader for black civil rights in America for a little more than fifteen years. He was an ordained minister with a doctorate in theology from Boston University. He worked primarily in the South, where he worked steadily to overthrow laws that promoted segregation and to increase the number of black voters registered in southern communities.

The period from 1958 to 1968 was the most active in American history for demonstrations and activities that resulted in opening up opportunities for black Americans. Many laws existed prohibiting blacks from sitting in certain sections of buses, from using facilities such as water fountains in bus stations, and from sitting at luncheon counters with whites. Such laws—patently unfair and insulting, not to mention unconstitutional—were not challenged by local authorities. Martin Luther King, Jr., who had become famous for supporting a program to integrate buses in Montgomery, Alabama, was asked by the Southern Christian Leadership Conference to assist in the fight for civil rights in Birmingham, Alabama, where the SCLC meeting was to be held.

King was arrested as the result of a program of sit-ins at luncheon counters and wrote the letter printed here to a number of Christian *ministers who had criticized his position. King had been arrested before and would be arrested again—resembling Thoreau somewhat in his attitude toward laws that did not constitute moral justice.*

Eventually, the causes King had promoted were victorious. His efforts helped not only to change attitudes in the South but also to spur legislation that has benefited Americans all over the country. His views concerning nonviolence were spread throughout the world and were the basis of his successful efforts to change the character of life in America. By the early 1960s he had become a world-famous man, a man who stood for human rights and human dignity virtually everywhere. He won the Nobel Peace Prize in 1964.

King himself was nonviolent, but his program left both King and his followers open to the threat of violence. The sit-ins and voter registration programs spurred countless acts of violence, bombings, threats, and murders on the part of the white community. His life was often threatened, his home bombed, his followers harassed. He was assassinated at the Lorraine Motel in Memphis, Tennessee, on April 4, 1968. But before he died he saw—largely through his own efforts, influence, and example—the face of America change.

KING'S RHETORIC

The most obvious rhetorical tradition King assumes in this important work is that of the books of the Bible which were originally letters, such as Paul's Epistle to the Ephesians and his several letters to the Corinthians. Many of Paul's letters were written while he was in prison in Rome. In each of those instances, Paul was establishing a moral position which was far in advance of that of the citizens who received the letters, and at the same time Paul was doing the most important work of the early Christian Church: spreading the Word to those who wished to be Christians but who needed clarification and encouragement.

It is not clear that the churchmen who received the letter fully understood the rhetorical tradition King assumed—but since they were men who preached from the Bible they certainly should have understood. The general public, which is less acquainted or concerned with the Bible, may have needed some reminding, and the text itself alludes to the mission of Paul and to his communications to his people. King assumes this rhetorical tradition, not only because it is effective, but because it connects him with the deepest

aspect of his calling: spreading the gospel of Christ. Brotherhood was
his message.

King's tone is one of utmost patience with his critics. He seems
bent on winning them over to his point of view, just as he seems
confident that—because they are, like him, clergymen—their good-
will should help them see the justice of his views.

His method is that of careful reasoning, centering on the substance of their criticism, particularly focusing on their complaints
that his actions were "unwise and untimely." Each of those charges
is taken in turn, with a careful analysis of the arguments against his
position; then follows a statement, in the clearest possible terms, of
his own views and why he feels they are worth adhering to. The "Letter from Birmingham Jail" is a model of careful and reasonable analysis of a very complex situation. It succeeds largely because it remains concrete, treating one issue carefully after another, refusing to
be caught up in passion or posturing. King remains grounded in logic.
He is convinced that his statement of his views will convince his audience.

Letter from
Birmingham Jail

April 16, 1963

MY DEAR FELLOW CLERGYMEN:[1]

While confined here in the Birmingham city jail, I came across your 1
recent statement calling my present activities "unwise and untimely."

---

[1]This response to a published statement by eight fellow clergymen from Alabama
(Bishop C. C. J. Carpenter, Bishop Joseph A. Durick, Rabbi Hilton L. Grafman, Bishop
Paul Hardin, Bishop Holan B. Harmon, the Reverend George M. Murray, the Reverend
Edward V. Ramage and the Reverend Earl Stallings) was composed under somewhat con-
stricting circumstances. Begun on the margins of the newspaper in which the statement
appeared while I was in jail, the letter was continued on scraps of writing paper supplied
by a friendly Negro trusty, and concluded on a pad my attorneys were eventually permitted to leave me. Although the text remains in substance unaltered, I have indulged in the
author's prerogative of polishing it for publication. [King's note]

Seldom do I pause to answer criticism of my work and ideas. If I sought to answer all the criticisms that cross my desk, my secretaries would have little time for anything other than such correspondence in the course of the day, and I would have no time for constructive work. But since I feel that you are men of genuine good will and that your criticisms are sincerely set forth, I want to try to answer your statement in what I hope will be patient and reasonable terms.

I think I should indicate why I am here in Birmingham, since you   2
have been influenced by the view which argues against "outsiders coming in." I have the honor of serving as president of the Southern Christian Leadership Conference, an organization operating in every southern state, with headquarters in Atlanta, Georgia. We have some eighty-five affiliated organizations across the South, and one of them is the Alabama Christian Movement for Human Rights. Frequently we share staff, educational, and financial resources with our affiliates. Several months ago the affiliate here in Birmingham asked us to be on call to engage in a nonviolent direct-action program if such were deemed necessary. We readily consented, and when the hour came we lived up to our promise. So I, along with several members of my staff, am here because I was invited here. I am here because I have organizational ties here.

But more basically, I am in Birmingham because injustice is here.   3
Just as the prophets of the eighth century B.C. left their villages and carried their "thus saith the Lord" far beyond the boundaries of their home towns, and just as the Apostle Paul left his village of Tarsus[2] and carried the gospel of Jesus Christ to the far corners of the Greco-Roman world, so am I compelled to carry the gospel of freedom beyond my own home town. Like Paul, I must constantly respond to the Macedonian call for aid.[3]

Moreover, I am cognizant of the interrelatedness of all communi-   4
ties and states. I cannot sit idly by in Atlanta and not be concerned about what happens in Birmingham. Injustice anywhere is a threat to justice everywhere. We are caught in an inescapable network of mutuality, tied in a single garment of destiny. Whatever affects one directly, affects all indirectly. Never again can we afford to live with the

---

[2]*village of Tarsus*   Birthplace of St. Paul (?–67A.D.), in Asia Minor, present-day Turkey, close to Syria.

[3]*the Macedonian call for aid*   The citizens of Philippi, in Macedonia (northern Greece) were among the staunchest Christians. Paul went to their aid frequently; he also had to resolve occasional bitter disputes within the Christian community there (see Philippians 2:2–14).

narrow, provincial, "outside agitator" idea. Anyone who lives inside the United States can never be considered an outsider anywhere within its bounds.

You deplore the demonstrations taking place in Birmingham. But your statement, I am sorry to say, fails to express a similar concern for the conditions that brought about the demonstrations. I am sure that none of you would want to rest content with the superficial kind of social analysis that deals merely with effects and does not grapple with underlying causes. It is unfortunate that demonstrations are taking place in Birmingham, but it is even more unfortunate that the city's white power structure left the Negro community with no alternative.

In any nonviolent campaign there are four basic steps: collection of the facts to determine whether injustices exist; negotiation; self-purification; and direct action. We have gone through all these steps in Birmingham. There can be no gainsaying the fact that racial injustice engulfs this community. Birmingham is probably the most thoroughly segregated city in the United States. Its ugly record of brutality is widely known. Negroes have experienced grossly unjust treatment in the courts. There have been more unsolved bombings of Negro homes and churches in Birmingham than in any other city in the nation. These are the hard brutal facts of the case. On the basis of these conditions, Negro leaders sought to negotiate with the city fathers. But the latter consistently refused to engage in good-faith negotiation.

Then, last September, came the opportunity to talk with leaders of Birmingham's economic community. In the course of the negotiations, certain promises were made by the merchants—for example, to remove the stores' humiliating racial signs. On the basis of these promises, the Reverend Fred Shuttlesworth and the leaders of the Alabama Christian Movement for Human Rights agreed to a moratorium on all demonstrations. As the weeks and months went by, we realized that we were the victims of a broken promise. A few signs, briefly removed, returned; the others remained.

As in so many past experiences, our hopes had been blasted, and the shadow of deep disappointment settled upon us. We had no alternative except to prepare for direct action, whereby we would present our very bodies as a means of laying our case before the conscience of the local and the national community. Mindful of the difficulties involved, we decided to undertake a process of self-purification. We began a series of workshops on nonviolence, and we repeatedly asked ourselves: "Are you able to accept blows without retaliating?" "Are you able to endure the ordeal of jail?" We decided to schedule our direct-action program for the Easter season, realizing that except for

Christmas, this is the main shopping period of the year. Knowing that a strong economic-withdrawal program would be the by-product of direct action, we felt that this would be the best time to bring pressure to bear on the merchants for the needed change.

Then it occurred to us that Birmingham's mayoral election was 9 coming up in March, and we speedily decided to postpone action until after election day. When we discovered that the Commissioner of Public Safety, Eugene "Bull" Connor, had piled up enough votes to be in the run-off, we decided again to postpone action until the day after the run-off so that the demonstrations could not be used to cloud the issues. Like many others, we waited to see Mr. Connor defeated, and to this end we endured postponement after postponement. Having aided in this community need, we felt that our direct-action program could be delayed no longer.

You may well ask, "Why direct action? Why sit-ins, marches, and 10 so forth? Isn't negotiation a better path?" You are quite right in calling for negotiation. Indeed, this is the very purpose of direct action. Nonviolent direct action seeks to create such a crisis and foster such a tension that a community which has constantly refused to negotiate is forced to confront the issue. It seeks so to dramatize the issue that it can no longer be ignored. My citing the creation of tension as part of the work of the nonviolent resister may sound rather shocking. But I must confess that I am not afraid of the word "tension." I have earnestly opposed violent tension, but there is a type of constructive, nonviolent tension which is necessary for growth. Just as Socrates[4] felt that it was necessary to create a tension in the mind so that individuals could rise from the bondage of myths and half truths to the unfettered realm of creative analysis and objective appraisal, so must we see the need for nonviolent gadflies to create the kind of tension in society that will help men rise from the dark depths of prejudice and racism to the majestic heights of understanding and brotherhood.

The purpose of our direct-action program is to create a situation so 11 crisis-packed that it will inevitably open the door to negotiation. I therefore concur with you in your call for negotiation. Too long has our beloved Southland been bogged down in a tragic effort to live in monologue rather than dialogue.

---

[4]*Socrates (470?–399 B.C.)* The tension in the mind King refers to is created by the question-answer technique known as the Socratic method. By posing questions in the beginning of the paragraph, King shows his willingness to share Socrates' rhetorical techniques. Socrates was imprisoned and killed for his civil disobedience (see paragraph 21). He was the greatest of Greek philosophers.

One of the basic points in your statement is that the action that I   12
and my associates have taken in Birmingham is untimely. Some have
asked: "Why didn't you give the new city administration time to act?"
The only answer that I can give to this query is that the new Birmingham administration must be prodded about as much as the outgoing
one, before it will act. We are sadly mistaken if we feel that the election of Albert Boutwell as mayor will bring the millennium[5] to Birmingham. While Mr. Boutwell is a much more gentle person than Mr.
Connor, they are both segregationists, dedicated to maintenance of the
status quo. I have hoped that Mr. Boutwell will be reasonable enough
to see the futility of massive resistance to desegregation. But he will
not see this without pressure from devotees of civil rights. My friends,
I must say to you that we have not made a single gain in civil rights
without determined legal and nonviolent pressure. Lamentably, it is
an historical fact that privileged groups seldom give up their privileges
voluntarily. Individuals may see the moral light and voluntarily give
up their unjust posture; but, as Reinhold Niebuhr[6] has reminded us,
groups tend to be more immoral than individuals.

We know through painful experience that freedom is never volun-   13
tarily given by the oppressor; it must be demanded by the oppressed.
Frankly, I have yet to engage in a direct-action campaign that was
"well timed" in the view of those who have not suffered unduly from
the disease of segregation. For years now I have heard the word "Wait!"
It rings in the ear of every Negro with piercing familiarity. This "Wait"
has almost always meant "Never." We must come to see, with one of
our distinguished jurists, that "justice too long delayed is justice denied."[7]

We have waited for more than 340 years for our constitutional and   14
God-given rights. The nations of Asia and Africa are moving with jet-
like speed toward gaining political independence, but we still creep at
horse-and-buggy pace toward gaining a cup of coffee at a lunch

---

[5]*the millennium* A reference to Revelation 20, according to which the Second
Coming of Christ will be followed by 1,000 years of peace, when the devil will be inca-
pacitated. After this will come a final battle between good and evil, followed by the Last
Judgment.

[6]*Reinhold Niebuhr (1892–1971)* Protestant American philosopher who urged
church members to put their beliefs into action against social injustice. He urged Protestantism to develop and practice a code of social ethics, and wrote in *Moral Man and
Immoral Society* (1932) of the point King mentions here.

[7]*"justice too long delayed is justice denied"* Chief Justice Earl Warren's expression in 1954 was adapted from English writer Walter Savage Landor's phrase, "Justice
delayed is justice denied."

counter. Perhaps it is easy for those who have never felt the stinging darts of segregation to say, "Wait." But when you have seen vicious mobs lynch your mothers and fathers at will and drown your sisters and brothers at whim; when you have seen hate-filled policemen curse, kick, and even kill your black brothers and sisters; when you see the vast majority of your twenty million Negro brothers smothering in an airtight cage of poverty in the midst of an affluent society; when you suddenly find your tongue twisted and your speech stammering as you seek to explain to your six-year-old daughter why she can't go to the public amusement park that has just been advertised on television, and see tears welling up in her eyes when she is told that Funtown is closed to colored children, and see ominous clouds of inferiority beginning to form in her little mental sky, and see her beginning to distort her personality by developing an unconscious bitterness toward white people; when you have to concoct an answer for a five-year-old son who is asking, "Daddy, why do white people treat colored people so mean?"; when you take a cross-country drive and find it necessary to sleep night after night in the uncomfortable corners of your automobile because no motel will accept you; when you are humiliated day in and day out by nagging signs reading "white" and "colored"; when your first name becomes "nigger," your middle name becomes "boy" (however old you are) and your last name becomes "John," and your wife and mother are never given the respected title "Mrs."; when you are harried by day and haunted by night by the fact that you are a Negro, living constantly at tiptoe stance, never quite knowing what to expect next, and are plagued with inner fears and outer resentments; when you are forever fighting a degenerating sense of "nobodiness"—then you will understand why we find it difficult to wait. There comes a time when the cup of endurance runs over, and men are no longer willing to be plunged into the abyss of despair. I hope, sirs, you can understand our legitimate and unavoidable impatience.

You express a great deal of anxiety over our willingness to break 15 laws. This is certainly a legitimate concern. Since we so diligently urge people to obey the Supreme Court's decision of 1954 outlawing segregation in the public schools, at first glance it may seem rather paradoxical for us consciously to break laws. One may well ask: "How can you advocate breaking some laws and obeying others?" The answer lies in the fact that there are two types of laws: just and unjust. I would be the first to advocate obeying just laws. One has not only a legal but a moral responsibility to obey just laws. Conversely, one has a moral responsibility to disobey unjust laws. I would agree with St. Augustine[8] that "an unjust law is no law at all."

Now, what is the difference between the two? How does one determine whether a law is just or unjust? A just law is a man-made code that squares with the moral law or the law of God. An unjust law is a code that is out of harmony with the moral law. To put it in the terms of St. Thomas Aquinas:[9] An unjust law is a human law that is not rooted in eternal law and natural law. Any law that uplifts human personality is just. Any law that degrades human personality is unjust. All segregation statutes are unjust because segregation distorts the soul and damages the personality. It gives the segregator a false sense of superiority and the segregated a false sense of inferiority. Segregation, to use the terminology of the Jewish philosopher Martin Buber,[10] substitutes an "I-it" relationship for an "I-thou" relationship and ends up relegating persons to the status of things. Hence segregation is not only politically, economically, and sociologically unsound, it is morally wrong and sinful. Paul Tillich[11] has said that sin is separation. Is not segregation an existential expression of man's tragic separation, his awful estrangement, his terrible sinfulness? Thus it is that I can urge men to obey the 1954 decision of the Supreme Court, for it is morally right; and I can urge them to disobey segregation ordinances, for they are morally wrong.   16

Let us consider a more concrete example of just and unjust laws. An unjust law is a code that a numerical or power majority group compels a minority group to obey but does not make binding on itself. This is *difference* made legal. By the same token, a just law is a code that a majority compels a minority to follow and that it is willing to follow itself. This is *sameness* made legal.   17

Let me give another explanation. A law is unjust if it is inflicted   18

---

[8]*St. Augustine (354–430)* Early bishop of the Christian church; great church authority who deeply influenced the spirit of Christianity for many centuries.

[9]*St. Thomas Aquinas (1225–1274)* The greatest of the medieval Christian philosophers and one of the greatest church authorities.

[10]*Martin Buber (1878–1965)* Jewish theologian; *I and Thou* (1923) is his most famous book.

[11]*Paul Tillich (1886–1965)* An important twentieth-century Protestant theologian who held that Christianity was reasonable and effective in modern life. Tillich saw sin as an expression of man's separation from God, from himself, and from his fellow man. King sees the separation of the races as a further manifestation of man's sinfulness. Tillich, who was himself driven out of Germany by the Nazis, stresses the need for activism and the importance of action in determining moral vitality, just as does King.

on a minority that, as a result of being denied the right to vote, had no part in enacting or devising the law. Who can say that the legislature of Alabama which set up that state's segregation laws was democratically elected? Throughout Alabama all sorts of devious methods are used to prevent Negroes from becoming registered voters, and there are some counties in which, even though Negroes constitute a majority of the population, not a single Negro is registered. Can any law enacted under such circumstances be considered democratically structured?

Sometimes a law is just on its face and unjust in its application. 19 For instance, I have been arrested on a charge of parading without a permit. Now, there is nothing wrong in having an ordinance which requires a permit for a parade. But such an ordinance becomes unjust when it is used to maintain segregation and to deny citizens the First Amendment privilege of peaceful assembly and protest.

I hope you are able to see the distinction I am trying to point out. 20 In no sense do I advocate evading or defying the law, as would the rabid segregationist. That would lead to anarchy. One who breaks an unjust law must do so openly, lovingly, and with a willingness to accept the penalty. I submit that an individual who breaks a law that conscience tells him is unjust, and who willingly accepts the penalty of imprisonment in order to arouse the conscience of the community over its injustice, is in reality expressing the highest respect for law.

Of course, there is nothing new about this kind of civil disobedi- 21 ence. It was evidenced sublimely in the refusal of Shadrach, Meshach, and Abednego to obey the laws of Nebuchadnezzar,[12] on the ground that a higher moral law was at stake. It was practiced superbly by the early Christians, who were willing to face hungry lions and the excruciating pain of chopping blocks rather than submit to certain unjust laws of the Roman Empire. To a degree, academic freedom is a reality today because Socrates practiced civil disobedience. In our own nation, the Boston Tea Party represented a massive act of civil disobedience.

We should never forget that everything Adolf Hitler did in Ger- 22 many was "legal" and everything the Hungarian freedom fighters[13] did in Hungary was "illegal." It was "illegal" to aid and comfort a Jew in

---

[12]***Nebuchadnezzar (c. 630–562 B.C.)*** Chaldean king who twice attacked Jerusalem. He ordered Shadrach, Meshach, and Abedniego to worship a golden image. They refused, were cast into a roaring furnace, and were saved by God (see Daniel 1:7–3:30).

[13]***Hungarian freedom fighters*** The Hungarians rose in revolt against Soviet rule in 1956. Russian tanks put down the uprising with great force that shocked the world. Many freedom fighters died, and many others escaped to the West.

Hitler's Germany. Even so, I am sure that, had I lived in Germany at the time, I would have aided and comforted my Jewish brothers. If today I lived in a Communist country where certain principles dear to the Christian faith are suppressed, I would openly advocate disobeying that country's antireligious laws.

I must make two honest confessions to you, my Christian and Jewish brothers. First, I must confess that over the past few years I have been gravely disappointed with the white moderate. I have almost reached the regrettable conclusion that the Negro's great stumbling block in his stride toward freedom is not the White Citizen's Counciler[14] or the Ku Klux Klanner, but the white moderate, who is more devoted to "order" than to justice; who prefers a negative peace which is the absence of tension to a positive peace which is the presence of justice; who constantly says, "I agree with you in the goal you seek, but I cannot agree with your methods of direct action"; who paternalistically believes he can set the timetable for another man's freedom; who lives by a mythical concept of time and who constantly advises the Negro to wait for a "more convenient season." Shallow understanding from people of good will is more frustrating than absolute misunderstanding from people of ill will. Lukewarm acceptance is much more bewildering than outright rejection. 23

I had hoped that the white moderate would understand that law and order exist for the purpose of establishing justice and that when they fail in this purpose they become the dangerously structured dams that block the flow of social progress. I had hoped that the white moderate would understand that the present tension in the South is a necessary phase of the transition from an obnoxious negative peace, in which the Negro passively accepted his unjust plight, to a substantive and positive peace, in which all men will respect the dignity and worth of human personality. Actually, we who engage in nonviolent direct action are not the creators of tension. We merely bring to the surface the hidden tension that is already alive. We bring it out in the open, where it can be seen and dealt with. Like a boil that can never be cured so long as it is covered up but must be opened with all its ugliness to the natural medicines of air and light, injustice must be exposed, with all the tension its exposure creates, to the light of human conscience and the air of national opinion, before it can be cured. 24

In your statement you assert that our actions, even though peace- 25

---

[14]**White Citizen's Counciler** White Citizen's Councils organized in Southern states in 1954 to fight school desegregation as ordered by the Supreme Court in May 1954. The councils were not as secret or violent as the Klan; they were also ineffective.

ful, must be condemned because they precipitate violence. But is this a logical assertion? Isn't this like condemning a robbed man because his possession of money precipitated the evil act of robbery? Isn't this like condemning Socrates because his unswerving commitment to truth and his philosophical inquiries precipitated the act by the misguided populace in which they made him drink hemlock? Isn't this like condemning Jesus because his unique God-consciousness and never-ceasing devotion to God's will precipitated the evil act of crucifixion? We must come to see that, as the federal courts have consistently affirmed, it is wrong to urge an individual to cease his efforts to gain his basic constitutional rights because the quest may precipitate violence. Society must protect the robbed and punish the robber.

I had also hoped that the white moderate would reject the myth   26 concerning time in relation to the struggle for freedom. I have just received a letter from a white brother in Texas. He writes: "All Christians know that the colored people will receive equal rights eventually, but it is possible that you are in too great a religious hurry. It has taken Christianity almost two thousand years to accomplish what it has. The teachings of Christ take time to come to earth." Such an attitude stems from a tragic misconception of time, from the strangely irrational notion that there is something in the very flow of time that will inevitably cure all ills. Actually, time itself is neutral; it can be used either destructively or constructively. More and more I feel that the people of ill will have used time much more effectively than have the people of good will. We will have to repent in this generation not merely for the hateful words and actions of the bad people, but for the appalling silence of the good people. Human progress never rolls in on wheels of inevitability; it comes through the tireless efforts of men willing to be co-workers with God, and without this hard work, time itself becomes an ally of the forces of social stagnation. We must use time creatively, in the knowledge that the time is always ripe to do right. Now is the time to make real the promise of democracy and transform our pending national elegy into a creative psalm of brotherhood. Now is the time to lift our national policy from the quicksand of racial injustice to the solid rock of human dignity.

You speak of our activity in Birmingham as extreme. At first I was   27 rather disappointed that fellow clergymen would see my nonviolent efforts as those of an extremist. I began thinking about the fact that I stand in the middle of two opposing forces in the Negro community. One is a force of complacency, made up in part of Negroes who, as a result of long years of oppression, are so drained of self-respect and a sense of "somebodiness" that they have adjusted to segregation; and in part of a few middle-class Negroes who, because of a degree of academic and economic security and because in some ways they profit by segregation, have become insensitive to the problems of the masses. The other force is one of bitterness and hatred, and it comes perilously close to advocating violence. It is expressed in the various black nationalist groups that are springing up across the nation, the largest and best known being Elijah Muhammad's Muslim movement.[15] Nourished by the Negro's frustration over the continued existence of racial discrimination, this movement is made up of people who have lost faith in America, who have absolutely repudiated Christianity, and who have concluded that the white man is an incorrigible "devil."

I have tried to stand between these two forces, saying that we need 28 emulate neither the "do-nothingism" of the complacent nor the hatred and despair of the black nationalist. For there is the more excellent way of love and nonviolent protest. I am grateful to God that, through the influence of the Negro church, the way of nonviolence became an integral part of our struggle.

If this philosophy had not emerged, by now many streets of the 29 South would, I am convinced, be flowing with blood. And I am further convinced that if our white brothers dismiss as "rabble-rousers" and "outside agitators" those of us who employ nonviolent direct action, and if they refuse to support our nonviolent efforts, millions of Negroes will, out of frustration and despair, seek solace and security in black nationalist ideologies—a development that would inevitably lead to a frightening racial nightmare.[16]

Oppressed people cannot remain oppressed forever. The yearning 30 for freedom eventually manifests itself, and that is what has happened to the American Negro. Something within has reminded him of his birthright of freedom, and something without has reminded him that it can be gained. Consciously or unconsciously, he has been caught up by the *Zeitgeist*,[17] and with his black brothers of Africa and his brown and yellow brothers of Asia, South America, and the Caribbean, the

---

[15]***Elijah Muhammad's Muslim movement*** The Black Muslim movement, which began in the 1920s but flourished in the 1960s under its leader, Elijah Muhammad (1897–1975). Among notable figures who became Black Muslims were the poet Imamu Amiri Baraka (b. 1934), the world championship prizefighter Muhammad Ali (b. 1942), and the controversial reformer and religious leader Malcolm X (1925–1965). King saw their rejection of white society (and consequently brotherhood) as a threat.

[16]***a frightening racial nightmare*** The black uprisings of the 1960s in all major American cities, and the conditions that led to them, were indeed a racial nightmare. King's prophecy was quick to come true.

[17]***Zeitgeist*** German word for the intellectual, moral, and cultural spirit of the times.

United States Negro is moving with a sense of great urgency toward the promised land of racial justice. If one recognizes this vital urge that has engulfed the Negro community, one should readily understand why public demonstrations are taking place. The Negro has many pent-up resentments and latent frustrations, and he must release them. So let him march; let him make prayer pilgrimages to the city hall; let him go on freedom rides[18]—and try to understand why he must do so. If his repressed emotions are not released in nonviolent ways, they will seek expression through violence; this is not a threat but a fact of history. So I have not said to my people, "Get rid of your discontent." Rather, I have tried to say that this normal and healthy discontent can be channeled into the creative outlet of nonviolent direct action. And now this approach is being termed extremist.

But though I was initially disappointed at being categorized as an 31
extremist, as I continued to think about the matter I gradually gained a measure of satisfaction from the label. Was not Jesus an extremist for love: "Love your enemies, bless them that curse you, do good to them that hate you, and pray for them which despitefully use you, and persecute you." Was not Amos an extremist for justice: "Let justice roll down like waters and righteousness like an ever-flowing stream." Was not Paul an extremist for the Christian gospel: "I bear in my body the marks of the Lord Jesus." Was not Martin Luther an extremist: "Here I stand; I cannot do otherwise, so help me God." And John Bunyan: "I will stay in jail to the end of my days before I make a butchery of my conscience." And Abraham Lincoln: "This nation cannot survive half slave and half free." And Thomas Jefferson:[19] "We hold these truths to be self-evident, that all men are created equal. . . ." So the question is not whether we will be extremists, but what kind of extremists we will be. Will we be extremists for hate or for love? Will we be extremists for the preservation of injustice or for the extension of justice? In that dramatic scene on Calvary's hill three men were

---

[18]*freedom rides* In 1961 the Congress of Racial Equality (CORE) organized rides of whites and blacks to test segregation in southern buses and bus terminals with interstate passengers. More than 600 federal marshalls were needed to protect the riders, most of whom were arrested.

[19]*Amos, Old Testament prophet (8th century B.C.); Paul (?–67 A.D.); Martin Luther (1483–1546); John Bunyan (1628–1688); Abraham Lincoln (1809–1865); and Thomas Jefferson (1743–1826)* These figures are all noted for religious, moral, or political innovations that changed the world. Amos was a prophet who favored social justice; Paul argued against Roman law; Luther began the Reformation of the Christian Church; Bunyan was imprisoned for preaching the gospel according to his own understanding; Jefferson drafted the Declaration of Independence.

crucified. We must never forget that all three were crucified for the same crime—the crime of extremism. Two were extremists for immorality, and thus fell below their environment. The other, Jesus Christ, was an extremist for love, truth, and goodness, and thereby rose above his environment. Perhaps the South, the nation, and the world are in dire need of creative extremists.

I had hoped that the white moderate would see this need. Perhaps 32 I was too optimistic; perhaps I expected too much. I suppose I should have realized that few members of the oppressor race can understand the deep groans and passionate yearnings of the oppressed race, and still fewer have the vision to see that injustice must be rooted out by strong, persistent, and determined action. I am thankful, however, that some of our white brothers in the South have grasped the meaning of this social revolution and committed themselves to it. They are still all too few in quantity, but they are big in quality. Some—such as Ralph McGill, Lillian Smith, Harry Golden, James McBride Dabbs, Ann Braden, and Sarah Patton Boyle—have written about our struggle[20] in eloquent and prophetic terms. Others have marched with us down nameless streets of the South. They have languished in filthy, roach-infested jails, suffering the abuse and brutality of policemen who view them as "dirty nigger-lovers." Unlike so many of their moderate brothers and sisters, they have recognized the urgency of the moment and sensed the need for powerful "action" antidotes to combat the disease of segregation.

Let me take note of my other major disappointment. I have been 33 so greatly disappointed with the white church and its leadership. Of course, there are some notable exceptions. I am not unmindful of the fact that each of you has taken some significant stands on this issue. I commend you, Reverend Stallings, for your Christian stand on this past Sunday, in welcoming Negroes to your worship service on a non-segregated basis. I commend the Catholic leaders of this state for integrating Spring Hill College several years ago.

But despite these notable exceptions, I must honestly reiterate that 34 I have been disappointed with the church. I do not say this as one of those negative critics who can always find something wrong with the church. I say this as a minister of the gospel, who loves the church; who was nurtured in its bosom; who has been sustained by its spiri-

---

[20]**written about our struggle** These are all prominent southern writers who expressed their feelings regarding segregation in the South. Some of them, like Smith and Golden, wrote very popular books with a wide influence. Some, like McGill and Smith, were severely rebuked by white southerners.

tual blessings and who will remain true to it as long as the cord of life shall lengthen.

When I was suddenly catapulted into the leadership of the bus pro-   35
test in Montgomery, Alabama, a few years ago, I felt we would be supported by the white church. I felt that the white ministers, priests, and rabbis of the South would be among our strongest allies. Instead, some have been outright opponents, refusing to understand the freedom movement and misrepresenting its leaders; all too many others have been more cautious than courageous and have remained silent behind the anesthetizing security of stained-glass windows.

In spite of my shattered dreams, I came to Birmingham with the   36
hope that the white religious leadership of this community would see the justice of our cause and, with deep moral concern, would serve as the channel through which our just grievances could reach the power structure. I had hoped that each of you would understand. But again I have been disappointed. . . .

There was a time when the church was very powerful—in the time   37
when the early Christians rejoiced at being deemed worthy to suffer for what they believed. In those days the church was not merely a thermometer that recorded the ideas and principles of popular opinion; it was a thermostat that transformed the mores of society. Whenever the early Christians entered a town, the people in power became disturbed and immediately sought to convict the Christians for being "disturbers of the peace" and "outside agitators." But the Christians pressed on, in the conviction that they were "a colony of heaven," called to obey God rather than man. Small in number, they were big in commitment. They were too God intoxicated to be "astronomically intimidated." By their effort and example they brought an end to such ancient evils as infanticide and gladiatorial contests.

Things are different now. So often the contemporary church is a   38
weak, ineffectual voice with an uncertain sound. So often it is an arch-defender of the status quo. Far from being disturbed by the presence of the church, the power structure of the average community is consoled by the church's silent—and often even vocal—sanction of things as they are.

But the judgment of God is upon the church as never before. If   39
today's church does not recapture the sacrificial spirit of the early church, it will lose its authenticity, forfeit the loyalty of millions, and be dismissed as an irrelevant social club with no meaning for the twentieth century. Every day I meet young people whose disappointment with the church has turned into outright disgust.

Perhaps I have once again been too optimistic. Is organized religion   40 too inextricably bound to the status quo to save our nation and the world? Perhaps I must turn my faith to the inner spiritual church, the church within the church, as the true *ekklesia*[21] and the hope of the world. But again I am thankful to God that some noble souls from the ranks of organized religion have broken loose from the paralyzing chains of conformity and joined us as active partners in the struggle for freedom. They have left their secure congregations and walked the streets of Albany, Georgia, with us. They have gone down the highways of the South on torturous rides for freedom. Yes, they have gone to jail with us. Some have been dismissed from their churches, have lost the support of their bishops and fellow ministers. But they have acted in the faith that right defeated is stronger than evil triumphant. Their witness has been the spiritual salt that has preserved the true meaning of the gospel in these troubled times. They have carved a tunnel of hope through the dark mountain of disappointment.

I hope the church as a whole will meet the challenge of this deci- 41
sive hour. But even if the church does not come to the aid of justice, I have no despair about the future. I have no fear about the outcome of our struggle in Birmingham, even if our motives are at present misunderstood. We will reach the goal of freedom in Birmingham and all over the nation, because the goal of America is freedom. Abused and scorned though we may be, our destiny is tied up with America's destiny. Before the pilgrims landed at Plymouth, we were here. Before the pen of Jefferson etched the majestic words of the Declaration of Independence across the pages of history, we were here. For more than two centuries our forebears labored in this country without wages; they made cotton king; they built the homes of their masters while suffering gross injustice and shameful humiliation—and yet out of a bottomless vitality they continued to thrive and develop. If the inexpressible cruelties of slavery could not stop us, the opposition we now face will surely fail. We will win our freedom because the sacred heritage of our nation and the eternal will of God are embodied in our echoing demands.

Before closing I feel impelled to mention one other point in your 42
statement that has troubled me profoundly. You warmly commended the Birmingham police force for keeping "order" and "preventing violence." I doubt that you would have so warmly commended the police force if you had seen its dogs sinking their teeth into unarmed, non-

---

[21]**ekklesia** Greek word for church; it means not just the institution but the spirit of the church.

violent Negroes. I doubt that you would so quickly commend the policemen if you were to observe their ugly and inhumane treatment of Negroes here in the city jail; if you were to watch them push and curse old Negro women and young Negro girls; if you were to see them slap and kick old Negro men and young boys; if you were to observe them, as they did on two occasions, refuse to give us food because we wanted to sing our grace together. I cannot join you in your praise of the Birmingham police department.

It is true that the police have exercised a degree of discipline in 43
handling the demonstrators. In this sense they have conducted themselves rather "nonviolently" in public. But for what purpose? To preserve the evil system of segregation. Over the past few years I have consistently preached that nonviolence demands that the means we use must be as pure as the ends we seek. I have tried to make clear that it is wrong to use immoral means to attain moral ends. But now I must affirm that it is just as wrong, or perhaps even more so, to use moral means to preserve immoral ends. Perhaps Mr. Connor and his policemen have been rather nonviolent in public, as was Chief Pritchett in Albany, Georgia, but they have used the moral means of nonviolence to maintain the immoral end of racial injustice. As T. S. Eliot[22] has said, "The last temptation is the greatest treason: To do the right deed for the wrong reason."

I wish you had commended the Negro sit-inners and demonstrators 44
of Birmingham for their sublime courage, their willingness to suffer, and their amazing discipline in the midst of great provocation. One day the South will recognize its real heroes. They will be the James Merediths,[23] with the noble sense of purpose that enables them to face jeering and hostile mobs, and with the agonizing loneliness that characterizes the life of the pioneer. They will be old, oppressed, battered

---

[22]***Thomas Stearns Eliot (1888–1965)*** One of the first great twentieth-century poets writing in English. Eliot was born in the United States but in 1927 became a British citizen and a member of the Church of England. Many of his poems focused on religious and moral themes. These lines are from Eliot's play *Murder in the Cathedral*, about Saint Thomas à Becket (1118–1170), the archbishop of Canterbury, who was martyred for his opposition to King Henry II.

[23]***the James Merediths*** James Meredith (b. 1933) was the first black to become a student at the University of Mississippi. His admission in 1961 created the first important confrontation between federal and state authorities, when Governor Ross Barnett personally blocked Meredith's entry to the university. Meredith graduated in 1963 and went on to study law at Columbia University.

Negro women, symbolized in a seventy-two-year-old woman in Montgomery, Alabama, who rose up with a sense of dignity and with her people decided not to ride segregated buses, and who responded with ungrammatical profundity to one who inquired about her weariness: "My feets is tired, but my soul is at rest." They will be the young high school and college students, the young ministers of the gospel and a host of their elders, courageously and nonviolently sitting in at lunch counters and willingly going to jail for conscience' sake. One day the South will know that when these disinherited children of God sat down at lunch counters, they were in reality standing up for what is best in the American dream and for the most sacred values in our Judaeo-Christian heritage, thereby bringing our nation back to those great wells of democracy which were dug deep by the founding fathers in their formulation of the Constitution and the Declaration of Independence.

Never before have I written so long a letter. I'm afraid it is much 45 too long to take your precious time. I can assure you that it would have been much shorter if I had been writing from a comfortable desk, but what else can one do when he is alone in a narrow jail cell, other than write long letters, think long thoughts, and pray long prayers?

If I have said anything in this letter that overstates the truth and 46 indicates an unreasonable impatience, I beg you to forgive me. If I have said anything that understates the truth and indicates my having a patience that allows me to settle for anything less than brotherhood, I beg God to forgive me.

I hope this letter finds you strong in the faith. I also hope that 47 circumstances will soon make it possible for me to meet each of you, not as an integrationist or a civil rights leader but as a fellow clergyman and a Christian brother. Let us all hope that the dark clouds of racial prejudice will soon pass away and the deep fog of misunderstanding will be lifted from our fear-drenched communities, and in some not too distant tomorrow the radiant stars of love and brotherhood will shine over our great nation with all their scintillating beauty.

> Yours in the cause of
> Peace and Brotherhood,
> MARTIN LUTHER KING, JR.

QUESTIONS

1. What is the definition of "nonviolent direct action"? In what areas of human life is it best directed? Is politics its best area of application? What are the four steps in a nonviolent campaign?
2. Is King optimistic about the future of race relations in America? What evidence in the letter points in the direction of optimism or pessimism?
3. Which paragraphs in the letter are the most persuasive? Why? Did any part of the letter actually change your thinking on an important issue? Which part? Why was your thinking changed?
4. If you had to select the best-written paragraph in the essay, which would it be? Why?
5. King cites "tension" in paragraph 10 and elsewhere as a beneficial force. Is it beneficial? What kind of tension does he mean?
6. Was King an extremist (paras. 30–31)?

WRITING ASSIGNMENTS

1. In paragraph 43 King says, "I have consistently preached that nonviolence demands that the means we use must be as pure as the ends we seek." What, exactly, does he mean by this? Define the ends he seeks; define the means he approves. Do you agree with him on this point? If you have read the selection from Machiavelli, could you contrast their respective views? Which view seems more reasonable to you?
2. Write a brief letter protesting an injustice that you feel may not be entirely understood by people you respect. Clarify the nature of the injustice, the reasons that people will hold to an unjust view, and the reasons why your views should be accepted. Consult King's letter and consciously use his techniques.
3. The first part of the letter is a defense of King's having come to Birmingham as a Christian to help his fellows gain their rights. He challenges the view that he is an outsider, using such expressions as "network of mutuality" and "garment of destiny." How effective is the argument that he raises? Are you convinced by it? Examine the letter for expressions such as those just quoted that justify King's intervention on behalf of his brothers and sisters. If the logic of his position holds, what other social areas could be justifiably "intervened" into? In what area of life might you endeavor to exert your own views on behalf of mankind? Would you expect your endeavors to be welcomed? Are there any areas in which you might consider it wrong to intervene?
4. In paragraphs 15–22, King discusses two kinds of laws, those which are morally right and those which are morally wrong. Analyze his argument carefully, establishing what you feel his views are. For King, which laws are morally right? Name several such laws that you know about. Which

laws are morally wrong, according to King? Name some laws, if possible, that you have personal knowledge of. Take a stand on one or two current laws that you feel are morally wrong. Be sure to be fair in describing the laws. Establish their nature and then explain why they are morally wrong. Would you feel justified in breaking these laws? Would you feel prepared, as King was, to pay the penalties demanded of one who breaks the law?

5. Make a comparison of King's letter with sections of Paul's letters to the faithful in the New Testament. Either choose a single letter, such as the Epistle to the Romans, or select passages from Romans, the two letters to the Corinthians, the Galatians, the Ephesians, the Thessalonians, or the Philippians. What positions have Paul and King held in common or in distinction concerning brotherly love, the mission of Christ, the mission of the church, concern for the law, and the duties of the faithful? Inventory the New Testament and the letter carefully for concrete evidence of similar or contrary positions.

PART TWO

IDEAS IN THE
WORLD
OF ECONOMICS

———◆———

Adam Smith ··· *Thomas Robert Malthus*
Thorstein Veblen ··· *John Maynard Keynes*
John Kenneth Galbraith

INTRODUCTION

OFTEN THE WORLDS of economics and politics interrelate, as, for example, they do in Karl Marx's *Communist Manifesto*. Economics, however, is a study of its own, as can be perceived from the selections in this part. The range of selections covers the eighteenth through the twentieth century. Adam Smith and Thomas Malthus, both eighteenth-century thinkers, were inspired by that century's enthusiastic faith in the power of rational thought to solve all problems. We might say that economics is a product of the eighteenth century—although such a statement would certainly provoke debate. In any case, the basis of modern thinking in economics was established in that century, and we still look back to Adam Smith, not only for terminology but also for concepts and theory.

In "Of the Accumulation of Capital, or of Productive and Unproductive Labor," Adam Smith focuses our attention on one of the most persistent ideas in economics: that the well-being of any nation is connected with its output of goods. Productivity, in other words, is the key to achieving wealth. Smith's great book, *An Inquiry into the Nature and Causes of the Wealth of Nations* (1776), was among the most influential eighteenth-century works. Both our nation's preoccupation with gross national product and the shape and structure of our consumer-oriented economy derive from the concepts Smith articulated. His view that the self-seeking of ambitious business persons—their drive to attain wealth and distinction—would in the long run benefit the entire population through increasing the wealth of the nation is a view that is current in America.

Smith was therefore extremely interested in the relationship of labor and wealth. He was less concerned with the question of who should possess the wealth that labor produced—this was Marx's concern in *Das Kapital* (3 vols., 1867–1894). Rather, after having conceived the view that wealth was connected with products and the increase of products, Smith set about to determine what kinds of labor were most productive. His conclusions were that those people who ended their workday with a physical product that could be sold at a profit were productive. Those who did not—such as entertainers, thinkers, service-oriented workers—were not productive. He recognized, as do we, that such "nonproductive" laborers are valuable to a society, and he is quick to remind us of that fact. But he is also determined to make us realize who it is that produces and maintains a nation's wealth.

Thomas Robert Malthus, famous for his theories on population and its effects on a nation's wealth, begins "Population and Wealth" by showing a concern for the laboring poor. He reminds us that the welfare of a nation can best be measured according to the contentment of members of that class. He demonstrates, however, that the increase in the wealth of a nation does not necessarily translate into an increase in the comfort of the laboring poor. Using Adam Smith's economic theories, he demonstrates why this is so. Thus, Malthus is remarkable for his concern for the poor, and he reminds us of their condition with the conviction of someone who has been a close observer of them.

Malthus's views are somewhat pessimistic in *An Essay on the Principle of Population* (1798; rev. ed. 1803), although the selection presented here is balanced. His ideas about population appeared so reasonable in their time that they seemed to sound a fatal note. He explained that unchecked population growth would outstrip the land's capacity to feed people, leading to widespread famine and disorder. Modern industrial nations, however, seem to have brought population growth under control. Today, therefore, his theories are most frequently invoked when talking about Third World problems, especially hunger.

Thorstein Veblen, a crusty, difficult man, reflects some of the pessimism of those nineteenth-century thinkers who began to question the powerful surge of middle-class materialism that manifested itself in enormous wealth and smug self-satisfaction around the turn of the century. *The Theory of the Leisure Class* (1899) is a careful analysis of nineteenth-century wealth and the uses of its power. Huge fortunes had been amassed by comparatively few people, and the social order had been distorted by this wealth. Veblen was disturbed by the materialism of the culture and by the sacrifice of intellectual values to business interests and profits. We know, as a matter of hindsight, that the materialism Veblen condemned was a contributing factor to the devastation of the two world wars, in which struggles for economic and political domination almost demolished Europe.

John Maynard Keynes is probably the best known twentieth-century economist. An instructor at Cambridge University for many years, his most important early work involved an accurate and farsighted analysis of the economics of recovery after World War I. During the period of the Depression, when his essay "Economic Possibilities for Our Grandchildren" was published, his most important sphere of influence was not Great Britain but the United States, which adopted his theories, including recommendations to boost public spending, to loosen credit restrictions, and to promote a freer economic environment that could profit from expansion and growth. Keynes's theories are based on production and consumption and remain important today as the basis of modern capitalism. Keynes held that permitting ambitious business people to pursue their goals of wealth, the entire community would benefit. His views, despite revisionist trends in recent years, are still central to our economic policies in the West. They are, as we can see from his essay, essentially optimistic in attitude.

The final selection, by John Kenneth Galbraith, dates from the middle of the twentieth century and sounds a note that none of the earlier thinkers treated—the question of poverty. It is not that the earlier writers were unaware that poverty existed; after all, each mentions it in passing. Rather, it is that these writers' approach to economics was concerned with the accumulation and preservation of wealth. Galbraith, in his study of the economics of contemporary America, also focuses on wealth; the title of his most famous book is *The Affluent Society* (1958). He is, however, interested in pointing toward something greater than the issue of getting and spending, something more important than affluence per se. His concern is with the wise allocation of the wealth that American society has produced. His fears that selfishness and waste will dominate the affluent society have led him to write about some of the most important social issues related to economics: poverty and its effects. If Adam Smith is correct in seeing wealth as the appropriate subject matter of economics, then Galbraith is pointing to a negative quality, the opposite of wealth, as also being worthy of close examination.

Most of these economic theorists agree that a healthy economy can relieve the misery and suffering of a population. Most agree that wealth and plenty are preferable to impoverishment and want. But some are also concerned with the effects of materialism and greed on the spiritual life of a nation. Veblen sees a society in which spiritual values are withering; Galbraith sees a society with enormous power to bring about positive social change, the capacity to make positive moral decisions. But Galbraith, for all his optimism, reminds us that we have made very little progress in an area of economics that has been a focus of thought and action for a generation.

ADAM SMITH

Of the Accumulation of Capital, or of Productive and Unproductive Labor

ADAM SMITH (1723–1790) *wrote in a way that is striking in its modernity. We read his work with a sense that it has affected our lives and that it will continue to do so. Smith was born in Kirkcaldy, on the east coast of Scotland. He attended Glasgow University and took a degree from Oxford, after which he gave a series of lectures on rhetoric in his hometown. They were successful lectures and resulted in his appointment as professor of logic at Glasgow in 1751. A year later he moved to a professorship in moral philosophy that had been vacated by Thomas Craggie, one of his former teachers. Smith's early reputation was entirely dependent on his work in moral philosophy.*

Smith's classic and best-known book is An Inquiry into the Nature and Causes of the Wealth of Nations *(1776), an examination of the economic system of the modern nation which had reached, as England had, the commercial level of progress. Smith had established a number of levels, from the hunter-gatherer culture to the modern commercial culture, which he treated as stages through which a nation had to pass on its way to becoming modern. In this sense, he was something of an evolutionist in economics.*

From *An Inquiry into the Wealth of Nations.*

Wealth of Nations *is quite different in both tone and concept from his earlier success,* Theory of Moral Sentiments *(1759), which postulated a social order based, at least in part, on altruism; that is, on individuals aiding one another. On the contrary,* Wealth of Nations *asserts that the best economic results are obtained in an environment in which individuals work for their own interests and their own gain. The result of this kind of effort, Smith assures us, is the general improvement of a society. His theory is simply that the industry of the individual will benefit everyone in the nation by producing more wealth. His view is that the greater the wealth of the nation becomes, the better the lot of every individual in the nation will be.*

"Of the Accumulation of Capital" establishes an important part of Smith's views about the relationship of capital to the well-being of a nation. There is no question that Smith is an ardent capitalist who feels an almost messianic need to spread its doctrine. He maintained throughout his life that Wealth of Nations *was one with his writings on moral and social issues and that his lifework, if complete, would demonstrate that his views included the basic elements of any society. Smith frequently refers to moral issues even in this selection. Often, his concern is to demonstrate that there is a moral overtone to the actions of all participants of an economy.*

The distinction that he draws between productive and unproductive labor is striking in part because a reader assumes that the distinction implies the difference between valuable and useless labor. But this is not so. Among those whose labor is unproductive are the armies and navies of the world as well as its lawyers, opera singers, and its teachers (although he does not designate them). All such people certainly are valuable for a society. They do not produce a product that can be resold at a profit, however. Everything they are valued for ceases when they cease laboring; nothing tangible is left behind to be passed on to someone else. The laborer making mousetraps knows that after a day's work there will be x number of mousetraps that can be "consumed" by customers who need them.

Wealth is produced by productive labor. If with the nonessential income from that labor one wishes to engage a singer, or other unproductive laborer, why, that is fine. To spend all one's disposable income on such things, however, is to risk impoverishment because the stock of capital is not being replenished but depleted.

Smith demonstrates that the wealthiest nations are those which take care to have their stock of capital increased rather than diminished. He compares the prodigal man (who wastes his resources on nonproductive labor) with the frugal man (who adds to his store of capital). Smith's judgment of these men is harsh: "every prodigal appears to be a public enemy and every frugal man a public benefactor" (para. 25).

His analysis of economic circumstances in his own time was aided by research in the field. He traveled on the Continent from 1764 to 1766 as a private tutor to the duke of Buccleuch, and thus his references to French towns and their economic character have the weight of observation to give them substance. He is naturally chauvinistic about England. He implies that his own time is much more industrious than those that preceded his and also implies that the wealth of England is greater than that of other European nations.

Smith is particularly disturbed by waste and dissipation. He regards them as moral issues because he believes that the individual either improves or degrades society through frugal or prodigal behavior. As he says, "Parsimony, and not industry, is the immediate cause of the increase of capital" (para. 16). By being parsimonious—saving even in face of the temptation to spend—one increases his store of capital; only in that way can capital be retained.

The extent to which Smith is suspicious of governments further demonstrates his commitment to the individual. In a sense, we can credit Smith with an abundance of optimism, since he believed that self-interest, a natural quality of virtually everyone, would in the long run prove a boon to society. He also believed that individuals did not necessarily benefit from government, particularly since government spent almost all its funds on unproductive labor: maintaining an army and navy and hordes of civil servants who produced nothing that could be resold at a profit. His most optimistic note is sounded when he admits that most governments are wasteful and contribute little to the wealth of a nation but that in England the individual's drive to better himself financially is so great that there is no danger of the government's having a permanently negative effect on the economy.

SMITH'S RHETORIC

This selection is a tightly reasoned work that offers an expanded definition and comparison of productive and unproductive labor. The points that Smith has to make are neither easily grasped nor obvious, so it is important for him to proceed slowly, using examples where possible, but depending primarily on the logical predictions which arise from the careful definition of terms.

He bases his economic theories on the assumption that consumable goods are the basic items which affect the wealth of the nation. He goes so far as to say that the amount of money which can circulate in a nation is directly connected with the quantity of consumable goods available for sale. When we think about the weekly review our news media give us of the gross national product, we realize that Smith's theories are not far from the ones that govern our own economy. Yet in this essay we see that his energies are given over to demonstrating the validity of his arguments. His method is close reasoning.

Because he is a competent rhetorician, his argument tends to rely on dialectical oppositions, almost in the manner of Karl Marx. He constantly dichotomizes in order to prove his points. He begins with the dialectic of productive and unproductive labor, moves on to the dialectic of capital and revenue, and continues with the dialectic of the frugal and the prodigal. It is a powerful technique that has one advantage for Smith: it establishes the categories of the argument so forcefully that it is all but impossible for us to see beyond them so as to break out of the limits of the argument.

In the manner of the eighteenth century, Smith's prose is clear, balanced, and marked by careful use of parallelism. In this sense, he has some of the qualities we find in Thomas Jefferson's prose. As a result of the balance and parallelism, many of the most important statements Smith makes are memorable, quotable, almost aphoristic. In paragraph 1 we find this statement: "A man grows rich by employing a multitude of manufacturers: he grows poor by maintaining a multitude of menial servants." Two independent clauses, one on the subject of growing rich, the other on the subject of growing poor, are paralleled with one another, balanced almost perfectly in their structure.

Smith knows precisely what he is doing in his stylistic choices, and his awareness of the value of the aphorism is clear from his own quote: "It is better, says the proverb, to play for nothing than to work for nothing" (para. 12). Many statements in this essay are similarly quotable, which intensifies the rhetorical power of the essay. There is a weight—a sententiousness—in these sentences that gives us the impression that they are, indeed, as powerful in their meaning and persuasiveness as they seem to be. Their very structure and nature makes us eager to accept them as being true.

Of the Accumulation of Capital, or of Productive and Unproductive Labor

There is one sort of labor which adds to the value of the subject 1
upon which it is bestowed: there is another which has no such effect. The former, as it produces a value, may be called productive;
the latter, unproductive labor. Thus the labor of a manufacturer
adds, generally, to the value of the materials which he works upon,
that of his own maintenance, and of his master's profit. The labor of
a menial servant, on the contrary, adds to the value of nothing.
Though the manufacturer has his wages advanced to him by his master, he, in reality, costs him no expense, the value of those wages being
generally restored, together with a profit, in the improved value of the
subject upon which his labor is bestowed. But the maintenance of a
menial servant never is restored. A man grows rich by employing a
multitude of manufacturers: he grows poor by maintaining a multitude of menial servants. The labor of the latter, however, has its value,
and deserves its reward as well as that of the former. But the labor of
the manufacturer fixes and realizes itself in some particular subject or
vendible commodity, which lasts for some time at least after that labor is past. It is, as it were, a certain quantity of labor stocked and
stored up to be employed, if necessary, upon some other occasion.
That subject, or what is the same thing, the price of that subject, can
afterwards, if necessary, put into motion a quantity of labor equal to
that which had originally produced it. The labor of the menial servant,
on the contrary, does not fix or realize itself in any particular subject
or vendible commodity. His services generally perish in the very instant of their performance and seldom leave any trace or value behind
them for which an equal quantity of service could afterwards be procured.

The labor of some of the most respectable orders in the society is, 2
like that of menial servants, unproductive of any value and does not
fix or realize itself in any permanent subject, or vendible commodity,
which endures after that labor is past and for which an equal quantity
of labor could afterwards be procured. The sovereign, for example,

with all the officers both of justice and war who serve under him, the whole army and navy, are unproductive laborers. They are the servants of the public and are maintained by a part of the annual produce of the industry of other people. Their service, how honorable, how useful, or how necessary soever, produces nothing for which an equal quantity of service can afterwards be procured. The protection, security, and defence of the commonwealth, the effect of their labor this year, will not purchase its protection, security, and defence for the year to come. In the same class must be ranked, some both of the gravest and most important, and some of the most frivolous professions: churchmen, lawyers, physicians, men of letters of all kinds; players, buffoons, musicians, opera-singers, opera-dancers, &c. The labor of the meanest of these has a certain value, regulated by the very same principles which regulate that of every sort of labor; and that of the noblest and most useful produces nothing which could afterwards purchase or procure an equal quantity of labor. Like the declamation of the actor, the harangue of the orator, or the tune of the musician, the work of all of them perishes in the very instant of its production.

Both productive and unproductive laborers, and those who do not 3 labor at all, are all equally maintained by the annual produce of the land and labor of the country. This produce, how great soever, can never be infinite, but must have certain limits. According, therefore, as a smaller or greater proportion of it is in any one year employed in maintaining unproductive hands, the more in the one case and the less in the other will remain for the productive, and the next year's produce will be greater or smaller accordingly; the whole annual produce, if we except the spontaneous productions of the earth, being the effect of productive labor. Though the whole annual produce of the land and labor of every country is, no doubt, ultimately destined for supplying the consumption of its inhabitants and for procuring a revenue to them; yet when it first comes either from the ground, or from the hands of the productive laborers, it naturally divides itself into two parts. One of them, and frequently the largest, is, in the first place, destined for replacing a capital, or for renewing the provisions, materials, and finished work, which had been withdrawn from a capital; the other for constituting a revenue either to the owner of this capital, as the profit of his stock; or to some other person, as the rent of his land. Thus, of the produce of land, one part replaces the capital of the farmer; the other pays his profit and the rent of the landlord; and thus constitutes a revenue both to the owner of this capital, as the profits of his stock; and to some other person, as the rent of his land. Of the produce of a great manufactory, in the same manner, one part, and that always the largest, replaces the capital of the undertaker of the work; the other pays his profit, and thus constitutes a revenue to the owner of this capital.

That part of the annual produce of the land and labor of any coun- 4 try which replaces a capital never is immediately employed to maintain any but productive hands. It pays the wages of productive labor only. That which is immediately destined for constituting a revenue either as profit or as rent may maintain indifferently either productive or unproductive hands.

Whatever part of his stock a man employs as a capital he always 5 expects is to be replaced to him with a profit. He employs it, therefore, in maintaining productive hands only; and after having served in the function of a capital to him, it constitutes a revenue to them. Whenever he employs any part of it in maintaining unproductive hands of any kind, that part is, from that moment, withdrawn from his capital and placed in his stock reserved for immediate consumption.

Unproductive laborers, and those who do not labor at all, are all 6 maintained by revenue; either, first, by that part of the annual produce which is originally destined for constituting a revenue to some particular persons, either as the rent of land or as the profits of stock; or, secondly, by that part which, though originally destined for replacing a capital and for maintaining productive laborers only, yet when it comes into their hands, whatever part of it is over and above their necessary subsistence, may be employed in maintaining indifferently either productive or unproductive hands. Thus, not only the great landlord or the rich merchant but even the common workman, if his wages are considerable, may maintain a menial servant; or he may sometimes go to a play or a puppet-show, and so contribute his share towards maintaining one set of unproductive laborers; or he may pay some taxes, and thus help to maintain another set, more honorable and useful, indeed, but equally unproductive. No part of the annual produce, however, which had been originally destined to replace a capital, is ever directed towards maintaining unproductive hands, till after it has put into motion its full complement of productive labor, or all that it could put into motion in the way in which it was employed. The workman must have earned his wages by work done before he can employ any part of them in this manner. That part too is generally but a small one. It is his spare revenue only, of which productive laborers have seldom a great deal. They generally have some, however; and in the payment of taxes the greatness of their number may compensate, in some measure, the smallness of their contribution. The rent of land and the profits of stock are everywhere, therefore, the principal sources from which unproductive hands derive their subsistence. These are the two sorts of revenue of which the owners have generally most to spare. They might both maintain indifferently either productive or unproductive hands. They seem, however, to have some predilection for the latter. The expense of a great lord feeds generally more idle than industrious people. The rich merchant, though with his capital he maintains industrious people only, yet by his expense, that is, by the employment of his revenue, he feeds commonly the very same sort as the great lord.

The proportion, therefore, between the productive and unproductive hands depends very much in every country upon the proportion between that part of the annual produce, which, as soon as it comes either from the ground or from the hands of the productive laborers, is destined for replacing a capital, and that which is destined for constituting a revenue, either as rent or as profit. This proportion is very different in rich from what it is in poor countries. 7

Thus, at present, in the opulent countries of Europe, a very large, frequently the largest portion of the produce of the land, is destined for replacing the capital of the rich and independent farmer; the other for paying his profits, and the rent of the landlord. But anciently, during the prevalence of the feudal government, a very small portion of the produce was sufficient to replace the capital employed in cultivation. It consisted commonly in a few wretched cattle, maintained altogether by the spontaneous produce of uncultivated land, and which might, therefore, be considered as a part of that spontaneous produce. It generally too belonged to the landlord and was by him advanced to the occupiers of the land. All the rest of the produce properly belonged to him too, either as rent for his land or as profit upon this paltry capital. The occupiers of land were generally bondmen, whose persons and effects were equally his property. Those who were not bondmen were tenants at will, and though the rent which they paid was often nominally little more than a quit-rent,[1] it really amounted to the whole produce of the land. Their lord could at all times command their labor in peace and their service in war. Though they lived at a distance from his house, they were equally dependent upon him as his retainers who lived in it. 8

But the whole produce of the land undoubtedly belongs to him who can dispose of the labor and service of all those whom it maintains. In the present state of Europe, the share of the landlord seldom exceeds a 9

---

[1]**quit-rent** Rent paid in place of services owed the feudal landlord.

third, sometimes not a fourth part of the whole produce of the land. The rent of land, however, in all the improved parts of the country has been tripled and quadrupled since those ancient times; and this third or fourth part of the annual produce is, it seems, three or four times greater than the whole had been before. In the progress of improvement, rent, though it increases in proportion to the extent, diminishes in proportion to the produce of the land.

In the opulent countries of Europe, great capitals are at present employed in trade and manufactures. In the ancient state, the little trade that was stirring, and the few homely and coarse manufactures that were carried on required but very small capitals. These, however, must have yielded very large profits. The rate of interest was nowhere less than ten percent, and their profits must have been sufficient to afford this great interest. At present the rate of interest, in the improved parts of Europe, is nowhere higher than six percent and in some of the most improved it is so low as four, three, and two percent. Though that part of the revenue of the inhabitants which is derived from the profits of stock is always much greater in rich than in poor countries, it is because the stock is much greater: in proportion to the stock the profits are generally much less.

That part of the annual produce, therefore, which, as soon as it comes either from the ground, or from the hands of the productive laborers, is destined for replacing a capital, is not only much greater in rich than in poor countries but bears a much greater proportion to that which is immediately destined for constituting a revenue either as rent or as profit. The funds destined for the maintenance of productive labor are not only much greater in the former than in the latter but bear a much greater proportion to those which, though they may be employed to maintain either productive or unproductive hands, have generally a predilection for the latter.

The proportion between those different funds necessarily determines in every country the general character of the inhabitants as to industry or idleness. We are more industrious than our forefathers; because in the present times the funds destined for the maintenance of industry are much greater in proportion to those which are likely to be employed in the maintenance of idleness than they were two or three centuries ago. Our ancestors were idle for want of a sufficient encouragement to industry. It is better, says the proverb, to play for nothing than to work for nothing. In mercantile and manufacturing towns, where the inferior ranks of people are chiefly maintained by the employment of capital, they are in general industrious, sober, and thriving; as in many English and in most Dutch towns. In those towns

which are principally supported by the constant or occasional residence of a court,[2] and in which the inferior ranks of people are chiefly
maintained by the spending of revenue, they are in general idle, dis-
solute, and poor; as at Rome, Versailles, Compiegne, and Fontainbleau.
If you except Rouen and Bourdeaux, there is little trade or industry in
any of the parliament towns of France;[3] and the inferior ranks of people, being chiefly maintained by the expense of the members of the
courts of justice,[4] and of those who come to plead before them, are in
general idle and poor. The great trade of Rouen and Bourdeaux seems
to be altogether the effect of their situation. Rouen is necessarily the
entrepôt[5] of almost all the goods which are brought either from foreign
countries or from the maritime provinces of France, for the consumption of the great city of Paris. Bourdeaux is in the same manner the
entrepôt of the wines which grow upon the banks of the Garonne and
of the rivers which run into it, one of the richest wine countries in the
world, and which seems to produce the wine fittest for exportation, or
best suited to the taste of foreign nations. Such advantageous situations necessarily attract a great capital by the great employment
which they afford it; and the employment of this capital is the cause
of the industry of those two cities. In the other parliament towns of
France, very little more capital seems to be employed than what is
necessary for supplying their own consumption; that is, little more
than the smallest capital which can be employed in them. The same
thing may be said of Paris, Madrid, and Vienna. Of those three cities,
Paris is by far the most industrious: but Paris itself is the principal
market of all the manufactures established at Paris, and its own consumption is the principal object of all the trade which it carries on.
London, Lisbon, and Copenhagen are, perhaps, the only three cities in
Europe which are both the constant residence of a court, and can at
the same time be considered as trading cities, or as cities which trade
not only for their own consumption but for that of other cities and
countries. The situation of all the three is extremely advantageous and
naturally fits them to be the entrepôts of a great part of the goods

---

[2]*a court* European nations were generally ruled from a royal court. Smith is disdain-
ful of them because of their insistence on show and their inevitable wastefulness.

[3]*parliament towns of France* Each province had a parliament of its own centered in
a specific town. These regional parliaments were dissolved after the French Revolution.
Smith's point is that government produces nothing and is an expense to be borne rather
than a profit to be shared.

[4]*courts of justice* An ironic reference to part of the machinery of parliament; the
curiae regiae, or king's courts, were an example of the unusual expense of government.

[5]*entrepôt* A trade or marketing center; also, a warehousing area.

destined for the consumption of distant places. In a city where a great revenue is spent, to employ with advantage a capital for any other purpose than for supplying the consumption of that city is probably more difficult than in one in which the inferior ranks of people have no other maintenance but what they derive from the employment of such a capital. The idleness of the greater part of the people who are maintained by the expense of revenue corrupts, it is probable, the industry of those who ought to be maintained by the employment of capital, and renders it less advantageous to employ a capital there than in other places. There was little trade or industry in Edinburgh before the Union.[6] When the Scotch parliament was no longer to be assembled in it, when it ceased to be the necessary residence of the principal nobility and gentry of Scotland, it became a city of some trade and industry. It still continues, however, to be the residence of the principal courts of justice in Scotland, of the boards of customs and excise, &c. A considerable revenue, therefore, still continues to be spent in it. In trade and industry it is much inferior to Glasgow, of which the inhabitants are chiefly maintained by the employment of capital. The inhabitants of a large village, it has sometimes been observed, after having made considerable progress in manufactures, have become idle and poor in consequence of a great lord's having taken up his residence in their neighborhood.

The proportion between capital and revenue, therefore, seems everywhere to regulate the proportion between industry and idleness. Wherever capital predominates, industry prevails; wherever revenue, idleness. Every increase or diminution of capital, therefore, naturally tends to increase or diminish the real quantity of industry, the number of productive hands, and consequently, the exchangeable value of the annual produce of the land and labor of the country, the real wealth and revenue of all its inhabitants. 13

Capitals are increased by parsimony and diminished by prodigality and misconduct. 14

Whatever a person saves from his revenue he adds to his capital and either employs it himself in maintaining an additional number of productive hands or enables some other person to do so by lending it to him for an interest, that is, for a share of the profits. As the capital of an individual can be increased only by what he saves from his annual revenue or his annual gains, so the capital of a society, which is 15

---

[6]***the Union*** The political joining together of Scotland with England as one nation in 1707.

the same with that of all the individuals who compose it, can be increased only in the same manner.

Parsimony, and not industry, is the immediate cause of the increase of capital. Industry, indeed, provides the subject which parsimony accumulates. But whatever industry might acquire, if parsimony did not save and store up, the capital would never be the greater. 16

Parsimony, by increasing the fund which is destined for the maintenance of productive hands, tends to increase the number of those hands whose labor adds to the value of the subject upon which it is bestowed. It tends therefore to increase the exchangeable value of the annual produce of the land and labor of the country. It puts into motion an additional quantity of industry, which gives an additional value to the annual produce. 17

What is annually saved is as regularly consumed as what is annually spent, and nearly in the same time too; but it is consumed by a different set of people. That portion of his revenue which a rich man annually spends is in most cases consumed by idle guests and menial servants who leave nothing behind them in return for their consumption. That portion which he annually saves, as for the sake of the profit it is immediately employed as a capital, is consumed in the same manner, and nearly in the same time too, but by a different set of people, by laborers, manufacturers, and artificers, who re-produce with a profit the value of their annual consumption. His revenue, we shall suppose, is paid him in money. Had he spent the whole, the food, clothing, and lodging, which the whole could have purchased, would have been distributed among the former set of people. By saving a part of it, as that part is for the sake of the profit immediately employed as a capital either by himself or by some other person, the food, clothing, and lodging, which may be purchased with it, are necessarily reserved for the latter. The consumption is the same, but the consumers are different. 18

By what a frugal man annually saves, he not only affords maintenance to an additional number of productive hands, for that or the ensuing year, but, like the founder of a public workhouse, he establishes as it were a perpetual fund for the maintenance of an equal number in all times to come. The perpetual allotment and destination of this fund, indeed, is not always guarded by any positive law, by any trust-right or deed of mortmain.[7] It is always guarded, however, by a very powerful principle, the plain and evident interest of every individual to whom any share of it shall ever belong. No part of it can ever 19

---

[7]***deed of mortmain*** A transfer of monies to a charitable organization.

afterwards be employed to maintain any but productive hands without an evident loss to the person who thus perverts it from its proper destination.

The prodigal perverts it in this manner. By not confining his ex- 20
pense within his income, he encroaches upon his capital. Like him who perverts the revenues of some pious foundation to profane purposes, he pays the wages of idleness with those funds which the frugality of his forefathers had, as it were, consecrated to the maintenance of industry. By diminishing the funds destined for the employment of productive labor, he necessarily diminishes, so far as it depends upon him, the quantity of that labor which adds a value to the subject upon which it is bestowed, and, consequently, the value of the annual produce of the land and labor of the whole country, the real wealth and revenue of its inhabitants. If the prodigality of some was not compensated by the frugality of others, the conduct of every prodigal, by feeding the idle with the bread of the industrious, tends not only to beggar himself but to impoverish his country.

Though the expense of the prodigal should be altogether in home- 21
made, and no part of it in foreign commodities, its effect upon the productive funds of the society would still be the same. Every year there would still be a certain quantity of food and clothing which ought to have maintained productive, employed in maintaining unproductive hands. Every year, therefore, there would still be some diminution in what would otherwise have been the value of the annual produce of the land and labor of the country.

This expense, it may be said indeed, not being in foreign goods, and 22
not occasioning any exportation of gold and silver, the same quantity of money would remain in the country as before. But if the quantity of food and clothing, which were thus consumed by unproductive, had been distributed among productive hands, they would have re-produced, together with a profit, the full value of their consumption. The same quantity of money would in this case equally have remained in the country, and there would besides have been a reproduction of an equal value of consumable goods. There would have been two values instead of one.

The same quantity of money, besides, cannot long remain in any 23
country in which the value of the annual produce diminishes. The sole use of money is to circulate consumable goods. By means of it, provisions, materials, and finished work are bought and sold and distributed to their proper consumers. The quantity of money, therefore, which can be annually employed in any country, must be determined by the value of the consumable goods annually circulated within it. These

must consist either in the immediate produce of the land and labor of the country itself or in something which had been purchased with some part of that produce. Their value, therefore, must diminish as the value of that produce diminishes, and along with it the quantity of money which can be employed in circulating them. But the money which by this annual diminution of produce is annually thrown out of domestic circulation will not be allowed to lie idle. The interest of whoever possesses it requires that it should be employed. But having no employment at home it will, in spite of all laws and prohibitions, be sent abroad, and employed in purchasing consumable goods which may be of some use at home. Its annual exportation will in this manner continue for some time to add something to the annual consumption of the country beyond the value of its own annual produce. What in the days of its prosperity had been saved from that annual produce, and employed in purchasing gold and silver, will contribute for some little time to support its consumption in adversity. The exportation of gold and silver is, in this case, not the cause but the effect of its declension, and may even, for some little time, alleviate the misery of that declension.

The quantity of money, on the contrary, must in every country 24 naturally increase as the value of the annual produce increases. The value of the consumable goods annually circulated within the society being greater, will require a greater quantity of money to circulate them. A part of the increased produce, therefore, will naturally be employed in purchasing, wherever it is to be had, the additional quantity of gold and silver necessary for circulating the rest. The increase of those metals will in this case be the effect, not the cause, of the public prosperity. Gold and silver are purchased everywhere in the same manner. The food, clothing, and lodging, the revenue and maintenance of all those whose labor or stock is employed in bringing them from the mine to the market, is the price paid for them in Peru as well as in England. The country which has this price to pay will never be long without the quantity of those metals which it has occasion for; and no country will ever long retain a quantity which it has no occasion for.

Whatever, therefore, we may imagine the real wealth and revenue 25 of a country to consist in, whether in the value of the annual produce of its land and labor, as plain reason seems to dictate; or in the quantity of the precious metals which circulate within it, as vulgar prejudices suppose; in either view of the matter, every prodigal appears to be a public enemy and every frugal man a public benefactor.

The effects of misconduct are often the same as those of prodigal- 26 ity. Every injudicious and unsuccessful project in agriculture, mines, fisheries, trade, or manufactures tends in the same manner to diminish the funds destined for the maintenance of productive labor. In every such project, though the capital is consumed by productive hands only, yet, as by the injudicious manner in which they are employed, they do not reproduce the full value of their consumption, there must always be some diminution in what would otherwise have been the productive funds of the society.

It can seldom happen, indeed, that the circumstances of a great 27 nation can be much affected either by the prodigality or misconduct of individuals; the profusion or imprudence of some being always more than compensated by the frugality and good conduct of others.

With regard to profusion, the principle which prompts to expense 28 is the passion for present enjoyment; which, though sometimes violent and very difficult to be restrained, is in general only momentary and occasional. But the principle which prompts to save is the desire of bettering our condition, a desire which, though generally calm and dispassionate, comes with us from the womb and never leaves us till we go into the grave. In the whole interval which separates those two moments, there is scarce perhaps a single instant in which any man is so perfectly and completely satisfied with his situation as to be without any wish of alteration or improvement of any kind. An augmentation of fortune is the means by which the greater part of men propose and wish to better their condition. It is the means the most vulgar and the most obvious; and the most likely way of augmenting their fortune is to save and accumulate some part of what they acquire, either regularly and annually, or upon some extraordinary occasions. Though the principle of expense, therefore, prevails in almost all men upon some occasions, and in some men upon almost all occasions, yet in the greater part of men, taking the whole course of their life at an average, the principle of frugality seems not only to predominate but to predominate very greatly.

With regard to misconduct, the number of prudent and successful 29 undertakings is everywhere much greater than that of injudicious and unsuccessful ones. After all our complaints of the frequency of bankruptcies, the unhappy men who fall into this misfortune make but a very small part of the whole number engaged in trade and all other sorts of business; not much more perhaps than one in a thousand. Bankruptcy is perhaps the greatest and most humiliating calamity which can befall an innocent man. The greater part of men, therefore, care sufficiently careful to avoid it. Some, indeed, do not avoid it; as some do not avoid the gallows.

Great nations are never impoverished by private, though they 30 sometimes are by public prodigality and misconduct. The whole, or almost the whole public revenue, is in most countries employed in maintaining unproductive hands. Such are the people who compose a numerous and splendid court, a great eccleciastical establishment, great fleets and armies, who in time of peace produce nothing and in time of war acquire nothing which can compensate the expense of maintaining them, even while the war lasts. Such people, as they themselves produce nothing, are all maintained by the produce of other men's labor. When multiplied, therefore, to an unnecessary number, they may in a particular year consume so great a share of this produce as not to leave a sufficiency for maintaining the productive laborers, who should reproduce it next year. The next year's produce, therefore, will be less than that of the foregoing, and if the same disorder should continue, that of the third year will be still less than that of the second. Those unproductive hands, who should be maintained by a part only of the spare revenue of the people, may consume so great a share of their whole revenue, and thereby oblige so great a number to encroach upon their capitals, upon the funds destined for the maintenance of productive labor, that all the frugality and good conduct of individuals may not be able to compensate the waste and degradation of produce occasioned by this violent and forced encroachment.

This frugality and good conduct, however, is upon most occasions, 31 it appears from experience, sufficient to compensate, not only the private prodigality and misconduct of individuals, but the public extravagance of government. The uniform, constant, and uninterrupted effort of every man to better his condition, the principle from which the public and national, as well as private opulence is originally derived, is frequently powerful enough to maintain the natural progress of things toward improvement, in spite both of the extravagance of government and of the greatest errors of administration. Like the unknown principle of animal life, it frequently restores health and vigor to the constitution, in spite, not only of the disease, but of the absurd prescriptions of the doctor.

The annual produce of the land and labor of any nation can be in- 32 creased in its value by no other means but by increasing either the number of its productive laborers or the productive powers of those laborers who had before been employed. The number of its productive laborers, it is evident, can never be much increased, but in consequence of an increase of capital, or of the funds destined for maintaining them. The productive powers of the same number of laborers cannot be increased, but in consequence either of some addition and improvement to those machines and instruments which facilitate and abridge labor; or of a more proper division and distribution of employment. In either case an additional capital is almost always required. It is by means of an additional capital only that the undertaker of any work can either provide his workmen with better machinery or make a more proper distribution of employment among them. When the work to be done consists of a number of parts, to keep every man constantly employed in one way requires a much greater capital than where every man is occasionally employed in every different part of the work. When we compare, therefore, the state of a nation at two different periods and find that the annual produce of its land and labor is evidently greater at the latter than at the former, that its lands are better cultivated, its manufactures more numerous and more flourishing, and its trade more extensive, we may be assured that its capital must have increased during the interval between those two periods and that more must have been added to it by the good conduct of some than had been taken from it either by the private misconduct of others or by the public extravagance of government. But we shall find this to have been the case of almost all nations, in all tolerably quiet and peaceable times, even of those who have not enjoyed the most prudent and parsimonious governments. To form a right judgment of it, indeed, we must compare the state of the country at periods somewhat distant from one another. The progress is frequently so gradual that, at near periods, the improvement is not only not sensible but from the declension either of certain branches of industry, or of certain districts of the country, things which sometimes happen though the country in general be in great prosperity, there frequently arises a suspicion that the riches and industry of the whole are decaying.

The annual produce of the land and labor of England, for example, is certainly much greater than it was a little more than a century ago, at the restoration of Charles II.[8] Though at present few people, I believe, doubt of this, yet during this period five years have seldom passed away in which some book or pamphlet has not been published, written too with such abilities as to gain some authority with the public, and pretending to demonstrate that the wealth of the nation was fast declining, that the country was depopulated, agriculture neglected, manufactures decaying, and trade undone. Nor have these publications been all party pamphlets, the wretched offspring of falsehood and ven-

33

---

[8]***restoration of Charles II (1630–1685)*** King of England from 1660 to 1685. The Restoration of the Stuart Crown in 1660 was the cause for much jubilation among English citizenry.

ality. Many of them have been written by very candid and very intelligent people who wrote nothing but what they believed and for no other reason but because they believed it.

The annual produce of the land and labor of England again was [34] certainly much greater at the restoration than we can suppose it to have been about an hundred years before, at the accession of Elizabeth.[9] At this period, too, we have all reason to believe, the country was much more advanced in improvement than it had been about a century before, towards the close of the dissensions between the houses of York and Lancaster.[10] Even then it was probably in a better condition than it had been at the Norman conquest,[11] and at the Norman conquest than during the confusion of the Saxon Heptarchy.[12] Even at this early period it was certainly a more improved country than at the invasion of Julius Caesar,[13] when its inhabitants were nearly in the same state with the savages in North America.

In each of those periods, however, there was not only much private [35] and public profusion, many expensive and unnecessary wars, great perversion of the annual produce from maintaining productive to maintain unproductive hands; but sometimes, in the confusion of civil discord, such absolute waste and destruction of stock as might be supposed not only to retard, as it certainly did, the natural accumulation of riches, but to have left the country at the end of the period, poorer than at the beginning. Thus, in the happiest and most fortunate period of them all, that which has passed since the restoration, how many disorders and misfortunes have occurred which, could they have been foreseen, not only the impoverishment, but the total ruin of the country would have been expected from them? The fire and the plague of

---

[9]*the accession of Elizabeth* Elizabeth was crowned queen in 1558; she died in 1603.

[10]*dissensions* A reference to the War of the Roses between the houses of Lancaster and York, 1455–1485.

[11]*the Norman conquest* The conquest of Britain by the Norman French beginning in 1066.

[12]*Saxon Heptarchy (A.D. 400–500)* Seven Saxon kingdoms of Northumbria, Mercia, East Anglia, Essex, Kent, Sussex, and Wessex. The heptarchy was a period of stability in England but also one of rivalry between kings.

[13]*Julius Caesar* His invasion dates from 57–50 B.C. At that time the Celts were described as savage; they fought the Roman legions naked and used terrifying war cries that sometimes caused the Romans to drop their weapons and run.

London,[14] the two Dutch wars,[15] the disorders of the revolution,[16] the war in Ireland,[17] the four expensive French wars of 1688, 1702, 1742, and 1756, together with the two rebellions of 1715 and 1745.[18] In the course of the four French wars the nation has contracted more than a hundred and forty-five millions of debt, over and above all the other extraordinary annual expense which they occasioned so that the whole cannot be computed at less than two hundred millions. So great a share of the annual produce of the land and labor of the country has, since the revolution, been employed upon different occasions, in maintaining an extraordinary number of unproductive hands. But had not those wars given this particular direction to so large a capital, the greater part of it would naturally have been employed in maintaining productive hands, whose labor would have replaced, with a profit, the whole value of their consumption. The value of the annual produce of the land and labor of the country would have been considerably increased by it every year, and every year's increase would have augmented still more that of the following year. More houses would have been built, more lands would have been improved, and those which had been improved before would have been better cultivated, more manufactures would have been established, and those which had been established before would have been more extended; and to what height the real wealth and revenue of the country might, by this time, have been raised it is not perhaps very easy even to imagine.

---

[14]***The fire and the plague of London*** Two great domestic disasters: in 1664–65 the plague killed some 75,000 inhabitants; in 1666, the fire burned September 2–5 and destroyed four-fifths of the City of London.

[15]***Dutch wars*** Several wars were fought to establish a balance of power in seventeenth-century Europe. The first war was 1652–54 and the second 1672–74. England allied with France and with German principalities to draw up a treaty with the Dutch Republic, which was an important commercial and military power in that period.

[16]***the revolution*** Smith may be referring to the English Civil War (1642–49) or to the "bloodless revolution" of 1688.

[17]***the war in Ireland*** There were many wars in Ireland. Smith may be referring to the most recent full-scale war, which began during the English Civil War in 1642 against King Charles I, but which continued in earnest against Charles's successor, Oliver Cromwell, in 1652.

[18]***the two rebellions of 1715 and 1745*** These were Jacobite rebellions, which hoped to place a Catholic Stuart monarch on the throne in place of the Protestant Hanoverian or Georgian kings. The rebellion of 1745–1756 ended with Charles Stuart (Bonnie Prince Charlie) wandering a fugitive in Scotland, but making of himself a romantic hero much admired by writers of historical romances.

But though the profusion of government must, undoubtedly, have 36 retarded the natural progress of England towards wealth and improvement, it has not been able to stop it. The annual produce of its land and labor is, undoubtedly, much greater at present than it was either at the restoration or at the revolution. The capital, therefore, annually employed in cultivating this land and in maintaining this labor, must likewise be much greater. In the midst of all the extractions of government, this capital has been silently and gradually accumulated by the private frugality and good conduct of individuals, by their universal, continual, and uninterrupted effort to better their own condition. It is this effort, protected by law and allowed by liberty to exert itself in the manner that is most advantageous, which has maintained the progress of England towards opulence and improvement in almost all former times and which, it is to be hoped, will do so in all future times. England, however, as it has never been blessed with a very parsimonious government, so parsimony has at no time been the characteristic virtue of its inhabitants. It is the highest impertinence and presumption, therefore, in kings and ministers to pretend to watch over the economy of private people, and to restrain their expense, either by sumptuary laws[19] or by prohibiting the importation of foreign luxuries. They are themselves always, and without any exception, the greatest spendthrifts in the society. Let them look well after their own expense, and they may safely trust private people with theirs. If their own extravagance does not ruin the state, that of their subjects never will.

As frugality increases, and prodigality diminishes the public capi- 37 tal, so the conduct of those whose expense just equals their revenue, without either accumulating or encroaching, neither increases nor diminishes it. Some modes of expense, however, seem to contribute more to the growth of public opulence than others.

The revenue of an individual may be spent either in things which 38 are consumed immediately, and in which one day's expense can neither alleviate nor support that of another; or it may be spent in things more durable, which can therefore be accumulated, and in which every day's expense may, as he chooses, either alleviate or support and heighten the effect of that of the following day. A man of fortune, for example, may either spend his revenue in a profuse and sumptuous table and in maintaining a great number of menial servants and a multitude of dogs and horses; or contenting himself with a frugal table and few attendants, he may lay out the greater part of it in adorning his

---

[19]**sumptuary laws**   Laws restricting the manufacture or sale of items deemed wasteful or extravagant.

house or his country villa, in useful or ornamental buildings, in useful or ornamental furniture, in collecting books, statues, pictures; or in things more frivolous, jewels, baubles, ingenious trinkets of different kinds; or, what is most trifling of all, in amassing a great wardrobe of fine clothes, like the favorite and minister of a great prince who died a few years ago. Were two men of equal fortune to spend their revenue, the one chiefly in the one way, the other in the other, the magnificence of the person whose expense had been chiefly in durable commodities would be continually increasing, every day's expense contributing something to support and heighten the effect of that of the public. To reduce very much the number of his servants, to reform his table from great profusion to great frugality, to lay down his equipage after he has once set it up are changes which cannot escape the observation of his neighbors and which are supposed to imply some acknowledgment of preceding bad conduct. Few, therefore, of those who have once been so unfortunate as to launch out too far into this sort of expense have afterwards the courage to reform till ruin and bankruptcy oblige them. But if a person has, at any time, been at too great an expense in building, in furniture, in books or pictures, no imprudence can be inferred from his changing his conduct. These are things in which further expense is frequently rendered unnecessary by former expense; and when a person stops short, he appears to do so, not because he has exceeded his fortune, but because he has satisfied his fancy.

The expense, besides, that is laid out in durable commodities gives maintenance, commonly, to a greater number of people than that which is employed in the most profuse hospitality. Of two or three hundredweight[20] of provisions, which may sometimes be served up at a great festival, one-half, perhaps, is thrown to the dunghill, and there is always a great deal wasted and abused. But if the expense of this entertainment had been employed in setting to work masons, carpenters, upholsterers, mechanics, &c. a quantity of provisions of equal value would have been distributed among a still greater number of people, who would have bought them in penny-worths and pound weights,[21] and not have lost or thrown away a single ounce of them. In the one way, besides, this expense maintains productive, in the

39

---

[20]**hundredweight**   A quantity of goods weighing a hundred pounds (it now weighs 110 pounds).

[21]**penny-worths and pound weights**   These are smaller quantities of goods than the hundredweight. The point is that less waste occurs when products are sold or used in smaller quantities.

other unproductive hands. In the one way, therefore, it increases, in the other, it does not increase, the exchangeable value of the annual produce of the land and labor of the country.

I would not, however, by all this be understood to mean that the one species of expense always betokens a more liberal or generous spirit than the other. When a man of fortune spends his revenue chiefly in hospitality, he shares the greater part of it with his friends and companions; but when he employs it in purchasing such durable commodities, he often spends the whole upon his own person and gives nothing to anybody without an equivalent. The latter species of expense, therefore, especially when directed towards frivolous objects, the little ornaments of dress and furniture, jewels, trinkets, gewgaws, frequently indicates, not only a trifling, but a base and selfish disposition. All that I mean is that the one sort of expense, as it always occasions some accumulation of valuable commodities, as it is more favorable to private frugality and, consequently, to the increase of the public capital, and as it maintains productive rather than unproductive hands, conduces more than the other to the growth of public opulence.

40

QUESTIONS

1. Establish as precisely as possible the distinction between productive and unproductive labor. In addition to those occupations mentioned in the selection, what other kinds of labor would fit these categories?
2. Is Smith's theory of productive and unproductive labor reasonable? Is it convincing?
3. Clarify Smith's distinctions between capital and revenue as discussed in paragraphs 13–16. Are these distinctions significant for our economy?
4. Examine Smith's statement, "Parsimony, and not industry, is the immediate cause of the increase of capital" (para. 16). Do you think he is correct in his judgment? What reasons does he give that support this statement.
5. What does Smith mean when he explains who should benefit from the wealth of the land: "But the whole produce of the land undoubtedly belongs to him who can dispose of the labor and service of all those whom it maintains" (para. 9). Do you agree with this view?

WRITING ASSIGNMENTS

1. In a short essay, explain what you feel are Smith's most important points about the general nature of economics. Determine what makes them im-

portant and comment on the extent to which you feel the points he makes are relevant to our economy. Consider his concerns for labor and for ownership of land and manufacturing facilities and his attitudes toward capital and revenue.

2. Discuss the position Smith takes on money. Beginning with paragraph 23, he comments extensively on the nature and use of money, saying, among other things: "The sole use of money is to circulate consumable goods." Do you think this is true? Before you attempt to defend or attack Smith's view, spend some time clarifying exactly what it is. Then examine it in enough detail so that you can take a reasonable position on the question.

3. Take a stand on the issue that is basic to Smith's position: that pursuing one's self-interest will, in the long run, produce a happier society. He discusses this idea in part in paragraph 28, where he says: "An augmentation of fortune is the means by which the greater part of men propose and wish to better their condition." Define the key elements of this statement and try to decide how his argument illustrates its truth. Then take a stand on Smith's position. Have things changed sufficiently enough since Smith's time so that this view is no longer valid? Or are economic conditions in our time similar enough to those of Smith's day so that these views can be accepted as still valid?

4. Smith is very harsh on government. His government was a parliamentary monarchy; that is, an elective body guided by a prime minister chosen by the king. It is different in character from a democratic assembly such as those in many modern nations, but does that fact mean that his judgment about the waste of government is any less true? In paragraph 30 he says, "The whole, or almost the whole public revenue, is in most countries employed in maintaining unproductive hands." He cites the maintenance of the church, of the armies, and of the people at court (meaning attendants at the courts of kings and queens). What is the consequence of a government's maintaining so many idle hands? Why do governments do so? Must they? Does Smith's judgment apply today?

5. The comparison between the prodigal man and the frugal man is, in part, an effort to demonstrate the means by which societies become wealthy. Comment on the comparison: establish clearly what Smith is saying and then go on to analyze his view. Is he correct in assuming that the prodigal man can ruin a society and that the frugal man is responsible for building it? Do these kinds of people exist today, and should we be careful to reward the frugal people so that they affect our society more positively?

6. What do you think Smith would make of our modern welfare system? Write a section of five to ten paragraphs, which you feel could be inserted into this essay, expressing Smith's hypothetical views. Try to imitate his style but most of all try to present what you think his theoretical position would be. Do you think he would have other solutions to our welfare problems? What do you believe he would think the result of our welfare programs would be? Would he consider people on welfare to be prodigal or frugal?

THOMAS ROBERT MALTHUS

Population and Wealth

THOMAS ROBERT MALTHUS (1766–1834) lived in England during the Age of Reason in the eighteenth century and the romantic period in the early decades of the nineteenth century. On the one hand, he absorbed the view that all things were explainable, that even such a concept as population in relation to economics would eventually yield to rational thought if one could clearly conceive it and proceed, by observation and example, to clarify its nature. On the other hand, as an heir to romantic movement, he can be seen, especially in this chapter from **An Essay on the Principle of Population** (1798; rev. ed. 1803) as moved by romantic views of the dignity of mankind and the value of the common man. Malthus's concern with the happiness of the laboring poor in this selection is not totally characteristic of his thinking, but it does give an insight into the social forces that were at work in his time, and it demonstrates his willingness to embrace the most positive views of the worth of people (which is perhaps ironic to say of a man who was known primarily for his pessimism).

The earliest versions of this essay on population were worked out while he was pastor of a church in Surrey in 1797. He had taken a

---

From *An Essay on the Principle of Population.*

degree at Jesus College, Cambridge University, and had accepted holy orders, a not-uncommon course for scholarly men in eighteenth-century England; however, once his book was published in expanded form in 1803, he came to the notice of the East India Company, an influential British commercial and political organization. He was asked to become a professor at its college in Haileybury shortly after he married in 1805. He accepted and remained there for the rest of his life. The essence of his theory of population was viewed as pessimistic: he believed that the increase in population would, if unchecked, outstrip the capacity of the land to provide subsistence for the nation's population.

As he explained in his early chapters, the force of the sexual drive is such that few restraints could affect it. He declared that population increases geometrically, whereas the food supply can increase only arithmetically, making it a certainty that sooner or later famine would strike even England. Analysts have pointed out that although his argument was extremely persuasive, it proved wrong. For one thing, his view on the relationship of the geometric and arithmetic increases turns out to have no validity in reality. Malthus had no means of demonstrating the validity of his claim other than his belief that it was so. Therefore, all the reasoning he did based on this premise naturally led to an erroneous conclusion.

Until he added an interesting ingredient to his views on population growth, he increased the gloom of Europe's pessimistic thinkers. The ingredient was moral restraint in the form of late marriage and sexual abstinence prior to marriage. Without this moral restraint, the future appeared totally dim; with it—since it was at least possible if unlikely—the future of mankind could be brighter. When his work was first published without mention of this restraint, he seemed to be an unrelenting pessimist. For example, he discarded the value of any mechanical form of birth control on the grounds that it would make people even more slothful than they already were. He thought that people are naturally lazy and that they will not work unless threatened by starvation. Mechanical means of birth control would reduce the population by such an extent that starvation would never be a threat, and therefore people would be totally lazy and probably totally miserable as a result.

Malthus's views were not original, although the strength of his prose convinced his contemporaries of their originality. Those who were students of economics saw his theories as pointing to the inevitable. In the late nineteenth century, when it was clear that his theories were not proving to be true, he remained only an empty prophet *of doom. Malthus could not have foreseen the incredible increase in agricultural yield brought about by scientific farming and by the impact of gasoline-powered farm machinery. He also could not have foreseen the impact in the second half of the twentieth century of inexpensive means of birth control. Therefore, economists in the modern industrial world worry far less about a Malthusian population explosion than they did in Malthus's time.*

Malthus's name is most evoked today in connection with Third World nations, in which religious and social pressures have kept the population rate so high that it has strained the capacity of local agriculture to produce adequate supplies of food. In the late 1980s the world has seen this most dramatically in the African nations suffering from repeated drought. Conservative estimates indicate that 142 million Africans will be directly affected by hunger, that 34 million will risk starvation, and that perhaps close to 10 million will risk death from disease. Malthus's theories are often cited with respect to such an environment. Moreover, even though his theories are based on inaccurate information, the obvious connection between the size of population and the capacity of a land to feed it will have more impact in underdeveloped nations such as Sudan or Ethiopia than in highly technologized agricultural-industrial nations such as Canada, which, with a small population and great landmass, exports colossal amounts of grain to much of the world.

"Population and Wealth" was written with a clear eye toward responding to Adam Smith's Wealth of Nations. *Malthus saw, as did relatively few people in his time, that any theory of economics that was to be of value would have to include the impact of population on wealth. Otherwise, it would have little practical value. In the selection Malthus sets out to clarify the relationship of the wealth of nations to the well-being of labor. The novelty of his approach consists in part in his concern for the laboring poor. And it may be that the most novel and most important insight of this chapter (chapter 16 in his book) is his certainty that the health of a nation should be measured by the health and happiness of the laboring poor, which, as he points out, constitute its most numerous class.*

MALTHUS'S RHETORIC

This is a persuasive essay intending to show that Adam Smith is in "probable error" when he says that increasing the stock and revenue of a nation will increase the funds for the maintenance of labor.

Smith's terms, which Malthus uses in this essay, mean simply that the wealth (stock and revenue) of a nation can increase or decrease. Smith feels that as it increases the "funds for maintenance of labor"— that is, the money which labor will earn or be apportioned—will go directly to labor. In other words, people at the lowest level will benefit from the increase in the wealth of the nation. Malthus denied this to be so and set about trying to demonstrate the truth of his position.

The methods Malthus uses to argue his point do not center on examples and statistical analyses, as a modern economist might approach the problem. Instead, he relies on logical analysis. His argument is that because in England the move was away from agricultural employment and toward factory employment, even though the factory produces new goods, their price will rise simply because the cost of farm goods will rise. Therefore, the higher wages that factory workers earn will buy less food. The laborer, in Malthus's view, could never really benefit from the increased revenue and stock of the nation. Even postulating, as he does, better farming techniques, the gap between the price of farm products and the income of the laborer is certain to widen.

Even worse, he points out that since the poor laborers now work in factories—which were much worse than he admits in this essay— their health will suffer. They will be worse off than before, even if the nation grows wealthy. In paragraph 1 Malthus uses a careful definition of the happiness of man; it depends on two things: "health and the command of the necessaries and conveniences of life." His argument is such that if we accept his definition, we will follow the logic of his argument and ultimately accept it.

The most important rhetorical techniques he uses are not stylistic, there is very little grace or felicity of expression. The prose is clear and balanced, and careful attention has been paid to employing the simplest, most direct means of expression. His is a plain style that, in comparison with some noted "stylists" of his time, is welcome. Yet his attention is not primarily to style but to logic. The reader's greatest reward will come from examining the way in which he establishes a premise, awaits our acceptance of it, then adds a further premise and draws his conclusion.

Consider, as an example, the logic of paragraph 4. Malthus is willing to admit that even with labor moving away from agriculture, food prices might not rise dramatically or even at all. Improved farming can control that. The demand for factory labor will increase the laborer's salary. If the laborer earns more, however, then the prices of the objects he manufactures will also rise. If this happens, the la-

borer will obviously show no actual increase in wealth. Therefore,
since the laborer is no longer in the healthy atmosphere of the farm,
there is a net loss. The laborer has no more disposable income than
before, while the unhealthy confines of the factory will cause ill
health—which strikes at the first ingredient of happiness.

Malthus's writing is filled with such logical passages. Observing
them closely can help us see why he was thought to be such a pow-
erful writer in his own time. It can also help us understand better the
contribution of logic to rhetorical strength in an essay.

Population and Wealth

The professed object of Dr. Adam Smith's[1] inquiry is the nature   1
and causes of the wealth of nations. There is another inquiry, however,
perhaps still more interesting, which he occasionally mixes with it; I
mean an inquiry into the causes which affect the happiness of nations,
or the happiness and comfort of the lower orders of society, which is
the most numerous class in every nation. I am sufficiently aware of
the near connection of these two subjects, and that the causes which
tend to increase the wealth of a State tend also, generally speaking, to
increase the happiness of the lower classes of the people. But perhaps
Dr. Adam Smith has considered these two inquiries as still more
nearly connected than they really are; at least he has not stopped to
take notice of those instances where the wealth of a society may increase (according to his definition of wealth) without having any tendency to increase the comforts of the laboring part of it. I do not mean
to enter into a philosophical discussion of what constitutes the proper
happiness of man; but shall merely consider two universally acknowledged ingredients, health and the command of the necessaries and conveniences of life.

Little or no doubt can exist that the comforts of the laboring poor   2
depend upon the increase of the funds destined for the maintenance of
labor; and will be very exactly in proportion to the rapidity of this

---

[1]*Adam Smith (1723–1790)* The reference is to *Wealth of Nations.* See the previous selection.

increase. The demand for labor which such increase would occasion, by creating a competition in the market, must necessarily raise the value of labor; and, till the additional number of hands required were reared, the increased funds would be distributed to the same number of persons as before the increase, and therefore every laborer would live comparatively at his ease. But perhaps Dr. Adam Smith errs in representing every increase of the revenue or stock of a society as an increase of these funds. Such surplus stock or revenue will, indeed, always be considered by the individual possessing it as an additional fund from which he may maintain more labor: but it will not be a real and effectual fund for the maintenance of an additional number of laborers unless the whole, or at least a great part of this increase of the stock or revenue of the society, be convertible into a proportional quantity of provisions; and it will not be so convertible where the increase has arisen merely from the produce of labor and not from the produce of land. A distinction will in this case occur between the number of hands which the stock of the society could employ and the number which its territory can maintain.

To explain myself by an instance. Dr. Adam Smith defines the wealth of a nation to consist in the annual produce of its land and labor. This definition evidently includes manufactured produce as well as the produce of the land. Now supposing a nation, for a course of years, was to add what it saved from its yearly revenue to its manufacturing capital solely, and not to its capital employed upon land, it is evident that it might grow richer according to the above definition, without a power of supporting a greater number of laborers and therefore without an increase in the real funds for the maintenance of labor. There would, notwithstanding, be a demand for labor from the power which each manufacturer would possess, or at least think he possessed, of extending his old stock in trade or of setting up fresh works. This demand would of course raise the price of labor; but if the yearly stock of provisions in the country was not increasing, this rise would soon turn out to be merely nominal, as the price of provisions must necessarily rise with it. The demand for manufacturing laborers might, indeed, entice many from agriculture and thus tend to diminish the annual produce of the land; but we will suppose any effect of this kind to be compensated by improvements in the instruments of agriculture and the quantity of provisions therefore to remain the same. Improvements in manufacturing machinery would cause the annual produce of the labor of the country to be upon the whole greatly increased. The wealth therefore of the country would be increasing annually, according to the definition, and might not perhaps be increasing very slowly.

The question is whether wealth increasing in this way has any ten- 4
dency to better the condition of the laboring poor. It is a self-evident
proposition that any general rise in the price of labor, the stock of
provisions remaining the same, can only be a nominal rise, as it must
very shortly be followed by a proportional rise in provisions. The increase in the price of labor therefore, which we have supposed, would
have little or no effect in giving the laboring poor a greater command
over the necessaries and conveniences of life. In this respect they
would be nearly in the same state as before. In one other respect they
would be in a worse state. A greater proportion of them would be employed in manufactures and fewer, consequently, in agriculture. And
this exchange of professions will be allowed, I think, by all to be very
unfavorable in respect of health, one essential ingredient of happiness,
besides the greater uncertainty of manufacturing labor arising from the
capricious taste of man, the accidents of war, and other causes.

It may be said, perhaps, that such an instance as I have supposed 5
could not occur because the rise in the price of provisions would immediately turn some additional capital into the channel of agriculture.
But this is an event which may take place very slowly, as it should be
remarked, that a rise in the price of labor had preceded the rise of
provisions and would, therefore, impede the good effects upon agriculture which the increased value of the produce of the land might otherwise have occasioned.

It might also be said that the additional capital of the nation would 6
enable it to import provisions sufficient for the maintenance of those
whom its stock could employ. A small country with a large navy and
great inland accommodations for carriage, such as Holland, may indeed import and distribute an effectual quantity of provisions; but the
price of provisions must be very high to make such an importation
and distribution answer in large countries less advantageously circum-
stanced in this respect.

An instance, accurately such as I have supposed, may not perhaps 7
ever have occurred; but I have little doubt that instances nearly ap-
proximating to it may be found without any very laborious search.
Indeed I am strongly inclined to think that England herself, since the
revolution,[2] affords a very striking elucidation of the argument in
question.

---

[2]***the revolution*** The English revolution began in 1642 and may be said to have ended
when King Charles I was beheaded in 1649. The revolution was a struggle between parliament and the king; the economic issues were centered on the rising power of the mercantile middle classes and the declining power of the landed aristocracy.

The commerce of this country, internal as well as external, has 8
certainly been rapidly advancing during the last century. The exchangeable value in the market of Europe of the annual produce of its
land and labor has, without doubt, increased very considerably. But
upon examination it will be found that the increase has been chiefly
in the produce of labor and not in the produce of land; and therefore,
though the wealth of the nation has been advancing with a quick pace,
the effectual funds for the maintenance of labor have been increasing
very slowly; and the result is such as might be expected. The increasing wealth of the nation has had little or no tendency to better the
condition of the laboring poor. They have not, I believe, a greater
command of the necessaries and conveniences of life; and a much
greater proportion of them than at the period of the revolution is employed in manufactures and crowded together in close and unwholesome rooms.

Could we believe the statement of Dr. Price[3] that the population 9
of England has decreased since the revolution, it would even appear
that the effectual funds for the maintenance of labor had been declining during the progress of wealth in other respects. For I conceive that
it may be laid down as a general rule that if the effectual funds for the
maintenance of labor are increasing, that is, if the territory can maintain, as well as the stock employ, a greater number of laborers, this
additional number will quickly spring up even in spite of such wars as
Dr. Price enumerates. And consequently if the population of any country has been stationary or declining, we may safely infer that, however
it may have advanced in manufacturing wealth, its effectual funds for
the maintenance of labor cannot have increased.

It is difficult, however, to conceive that the population[4] of England 10
has been declining since the revolution; though every testimony con-
curs to prove that its increase, if it has increased, has been very slow.
In the controversy which the question has occasioned Dr. Price undoubtedly appears to be much more completely master of his subject
and to possess more accurate information than his opponents. Judging
simply from this controversy, I think one should say that Dr. Price's

---

[3]***Dr. Richard Price (1723–1791)*** A philosopher whose writings on government
finance were popular in his time. He wrote *An Appeal to the Public on the Subject of
the National Debt* (1772; rev. ed. 1774). He also wrote on the American Revolution and
was instructive in the colonies' decision to go to war.

[4]***the population*** Ironically, Malthus had virtually no reliable data on matters of population. In 1700 the population of England was 5.5 million; in 1801 it was 8.9 million.
Population was obviously not declining since the revolution.

point is nearer being proved than Mr. Howlett's.[5] Truth probably lies between the two statements, but this supposition makes the increase of population since the revolution to have been very slow in comparison with the increase of wealth.

That the produce of the land has been decreasing, or even that it 11 has been absolutely stationary during the last century, few will be disposed to believe. The inclosure of commons and waste lands[6] certainly tends to increase the food of the country; but it has been asserted with confidence that the inclosure of common fields has frequently had a contrary effect and that large tracts of land, which formerly produced great quantities of corn, by being converted into pasture both employ fewer hands and feed fewer mouths than before their inclosure. It is, indeed, an acknowledged truth that pasture land produces a smaller quantity of human subsistence than corn land[7] of the same natural fertility; and could it be clearly ascertained that from the increased demand for butchers meat of the best quality, and its increased price in consequence, a greater quantity of good land has annually been employed in grazing, the diminution of human subsistence which this circumstance would occasion might have counterbalanced the advantages derived from the inclosure of waste lands and the general improvements in husbandry.

It scarcely need be remarked that the high price of butchers meat 12 at present, and its low price formerly, were not caused by the scarcity in the one case or the plenty in the other but by the different expense sustained at the different periods in preparing cattle for the market. It is, however, possible that there might have been more cattle a hundred years ago in the country than at present; but no doubt can be entertained that there is much more meat of a superior quality brought to market at present than ever there was. When the price of butchers meat was very low, cattle were reared chiefly upon waste lands; and except for some of the principal markets were probably killed with but little other fatting. The veal that is sold so cheap in some distant counties at present bears little other resemblance than the name to that

---

[5]***John Howlett (1731–1804)*** A severe critic of Dr. Price in "An Examination of Dr. Price's Essay on the Population of England and Wales" (1781). He wrote influential essays on statistics and the condition of people in England.

[6]***commons and waste lands*** Lands formerly used in common for the pasturage of livestock of a village; they were enclosed during this period. They were used by landowners to pasture their own livestock, and the result was that the poor suffered great hardship, while the strains of cattle improved.

[7]***corn land*** Land that supports the basic grain of the area, such as wheat, rye, or rice.

which is bought in London. Formerly, the price of butchers meat would not pay for rearing, and scarcely for feeding cattle on land that would answer in tillage; but the present price will not only pay for fatting cattle on the very best land but will even allow of the rearing many on land that would bear good crops of corn. The same number of cattle, or even the same weight of cattle at the different periods when killed, will have consumed (if I may be allowed the expression) very different quantities of human subsistence. A fatted beast may in some respects be considered, in the language of the French economists, as an unproductive laborer: he has added nothing to the value of the raw produce that he has consumed. The present system of grazing undoubtedly tends more than the former system to diminish the quantity of human subsistence in the country in proportion to the general fertility of the land.

I would not by any means be understood to say that the former 13 system either could, or ought, to have continued. The increasing price of butchers meat is a natural and inevitable consequnce of the general progress of cultivation; but I cannot help thinking that the present great demand for butchers meat of the best quality, and the quantity of good land that is in consequence annually employed to produce it, together with the great number of horses at present kept for pleasure, are the chief causes that have prevented the quantity of human food in the country from keeping pace with the generally increased fertility of the soil; and a change of custom in these respects would, I have little doubt, have a very sensible effect on the quantity of subsistence in the country and consequently on its population.

The employment of much of the most fertile land in grazing, the 14 improvements in agricultural instruments, the increase of large farms, and particularly the diminution of the number of cottages throughout the kingdom all concur to prove that there are not probably so many persons employed in agricultural labor now as at the period of the revolution. Whatever increase of population, therefore, has taken place must be employed almost wholly in manufactures; and it is well known that the failure of some of these manufactures merely from the caprice of fashion, such as the adoption of muslins instead of silks, or of shoe-strings and covered buttons instead of buckles and metal buttons, combined with the restraints in the market of labor arising from corporation and parish laws,[8] have frequently driven thousands on charity for support. The great increase of the poor rates[9] is, indeed, of

---

[8]*corporation and parish laws* Local laws that place a burden on local industry.
[9]*poor rates* Property taxes, sometimes used to support the poor.

itself a strong evidence that the poor have not a greater command of the necessaries and conveniences of life; and if to the consideration that their condition in this respect is rather worse than better be added the circumstance that a much greater proportion of them is employed in large manufactories unfavorable both to health and virtue, it must be acknowledged that the increase of wealth of late years has had no tendency to increase the happiness of the laboring poor.

That every increase of the stock or revenue of a nation cannot be   15 considered as an increase of the real funds for the maintenance of labor and, therefore, cannot have the same good effect upon the condition of the poor, will appear in a strong light if the argument be applied to China.

Dr. Adam Smith observes that China has probably long been as   16 rich as the nature of her laws and institutions will admit; but that with other laws and institutions, and if foreign commerce were had in honor, she might still be much richer. The question is, would such an increase of wealth be an increase of the real funds for the maintenance of labor and consequently tend to place the lower classes of people in China in a state of greater plenty?

It is evident that if trade and foreign commerce were held in great   17 honor in China; from the plenty of laborers and the cheapness of labor she might work up manufactures for foreign sale to an immense amount. It is equally evident that from the great bulk of provisions, and the amazing extent of her inland territory, she could not in return import such a quantity as would be any sensible addition to the annual stock of subsistence in the country. Her immense amount of manufactures, therefore, she would exchange, chiefly, for luxuries collected from all parts of the world. At present, it appears that no labor whatever is spared in the production of food. The country is rather over peopled in proportion to what its stock can employ, and labor is therefore so abundant that no pains are taken to abridge it. The consequence of this is, probably, the greatest production of food that the soil can possibly afford: for it will be generally observed that processes for abridging labor, though they may enable a farmer to bring a certain quantity of grain cheaper to market, tend rather to diminish than increase the whole produce; and in agriculture, therefore, may in some respects be considered rather as private than public advantages. An immense capital could not be employed in China in preparing manufactures for foreign trade without taking off so many laborers from agriculture as to alter this state of things and in some degree to diminish the produce of the country. The demand for manufacturing laborers would naturally raise the price of labor; but as the quantity of subsistence would not be increased, the price of provisions would keep pace with it; or even more than keep pace with it if the quantity of provisions were really decreasing. The country would be evidently advancing in wealth: the exchangeable value of the annual produce of its land and labor would be annually augmented; yet the real funds for the maintenance of labor would be stationary or even declining; and consequently the increasing wealth of the nation would rather tend to depress than to raise the condition of the poor. With regard to the command over the necessaries and comforts of life, they would be in the same or rather worse state than before; and a great part of them would have exchanged the healthy labors of agriculture for the unhealthy occupations of manufacturing industry.

The argument perhaps appears clearer when applied to China because it is generally allowed that the wealth of China has been long stationary. With regard to any other country it might be always a matter of dispute at which of the two periods, compared, wealth was increasing the fastest; as it is upon the rapidity of the increase of wealth at any particular period that Dr. Adam Smith says the condition of the poor depends. It is evident, however, that two nations might increase, exactly with the same rapidity, in the exchangeable value of the annual produce of their land and labor; yet if one had applied itself chiefly to agriculture, and the other chiefly to commerce, the funds for the maintenance of labor, and consequently the effect of the increase of wealth in each nation, would be extremely different. In that which had applied itself chiefly to agriculture, the poor would live in great plenty, and population would rapidly increase. In that which had applied itself chiefly to commerce, the poor would be comparatively but little benefited, and consequently population would increase slowly.

18

QUESTIONS

1. What seem to be the social circumstances of Malthus's England? How would you imagine the conditions of labor to be at the time of his writing (about 1800)?
2. Look up the enclosure laws in a history of England. How clear was Malthus's awareness of the social changes that these laws produced?
3. Establish the requirements Malthus set for the happiness of man. Precisely what do his terms mean?
4. Is the analysis of the relationship of wealth and population optimistic or pessimistic? Explain why you would defend one view rather than the other.

5. What are the strengths of Malthus's prose style? Which passage do you find especially difficult? Which do you find especially clear?

WRITING ASSIGNMENTS

1. Write a brief essay that clarifies the main points in Malthus's argument. Which parts of his argument are most important? Which are most persuasive? In the course of determining what his views are, offer your own commentary on your sense of their pertinence to economic affairs today.
2. The question Malthus addresses himself to in this selection concerns the question of whether a nation's increased wealth will have a direct benefit on the laboring poor. In today's American economy, the poor are generally on welfare rather than laboring. Write an essay that analyzes our current situation (as far as you are aware of it) and that treats the question of whether the poor in a modern industrialized nation will benefit from the increased wealth of that nation. What factors that Malthus raises are still valid? Which new factors can you add to the argument?
3. Malthus says that the increased wealth of England was the result of labor's increased productivity, not of the increased productivity of the land (para 8). Indeed, he points out that, with more land used for grazing cattle, there had actually been a decrease in the productivity of human food from the land. Write an essay that defends the view that in the case of increases in laborers' productivity, there should be greater income for laborers. Take into account, however, the fact that the increases in productivity may be the result of decisions made by managers, who do none of the labor of production, and by owners, whose capital investments make the laborers' jobs possible in the first place. Which of these three groups deserves the greatest share in the new wealth produced?
4. In paragraph 14, Malthus talks about the possible failures of manufactures. The laborer who dedicates a lifetime to manufacture takes enormous risks, Malthus says, just in the changes in fashions or production that may put him or her out of work. What risks do laborers take in our society in the security of their jobs? Are the questions of stylishness the same today—or of the same importance—as they were in Malthus's day? What are the issues that the laborer ought to be aware of in devoting a lifetime to manufacture?
5. Write a commentary on the argument, beginning with paragraph 15, that compares China with England. The basic view is that China is overpopulated and that the result is a devaluing of labor. There are many hands to do the work, and therefore labor is cheap. What can we learn from this example about the supply of labor and its value? Is labor susceptible to the laws of supply and demand?

THORSTEIN VEBLEN

Pecuniary Emulation

THORSTEIN VEBLEN (1857–1929) is one of America's most power-fully original thinkers in the areas of economics, business, and soci-ology. A product of the Scandinavian settlements of the Midwest, he was educated at Carleton College in Northfield, Minnesota, and was awarded the Ph.D. in philosophy at Yale University. One of the inter-esting ironies of his career is that, brilliant though he was, he did not immediately proceed to an academic appointment. He languished for seven years on the farm in Minnesota, reading—a fate similar to that of the great English poet John Milton, who spent a period of time on his father's estate before moving into a worldly career.

The reasons for Veblen's having been ignored by the academic world seem to have centered on his difficult personality and on his extremely unpopular views of the direction of the American economy and of the nation's overall social structure. He was profoundly critical of the dominance of business interests over the interests of social bet-terment. He castigated the nation for its slavish worship of the canons of consumption. The passage included here is from his most famous book, **The Theory of the Leisure Class** (1899), in which he develops

---

From The Theory of the Leisure Class. The Portable Veblen.

a fascinating view of America as a culture that delights in abundance, waste, and conspicuous consumption. Conspicuous consumption is economic showing off. As a modern slogan puts it approvingly, "If you've got it, flaunt it."

Veblen felt that "flaunting it" was central to the American way of life, especially the way of life the leisure class that the American economics of abundance had produced. He condemned conspicuous consumption as fundamentally wasteful and as risking an ultimate financial collapse and a terrible fate for those who were poor. Interestingly, Veblen died in the year in which the spiraling economy, inflated by waves of selfish enthusiasm and reckless speculation, crashed so resoundingly that much of the nation was plunged into a decade of poverty.

It is no wonder that such a telling critic should at first have been kept from the rewards of academic life: he was too savage a gadfly to be tolerated. Yet he eventually succeeded. He taught at the University of Chicago after graduate studies in economics at Cornell. He taught at the New School for Social Research in New York City and at Stanford University in California for a short time as well. But the sad fact is that he was never a popular teacher: he begrudged his students their grades, usually marking them all C. He was a classroom mumbler, a monotone dryasdust. Yet, he had one of the most sparkling minds of his generation. Those students who persisted and got through the dull classroom periods were rewarded with experience so intense that later many of them wrote remarkable memoirs.

Among his many publications, virtually all are of more interest now than they were while he was alive. His greatest fame was posthumous. It was after his death that his views began to be appreciated as those of a farseeing economics savant. One of his books, The Higher Learning in America (1918), is a biting attack on the willingness of America's universities to be dominated by capitalist businesses. The subservience of the universities to the demands of profits resulted in the universities' goals of producing passive, malleable, and acceptable workers for the needs of business and industry. Veblen would much rather have had the universities forsake the world of business and concentrate on the goals of thorough education, even if it produced graduates who were not likely to be comfortable in the then repressive structure of American business. His book is obviously as relevant today as ever, and his views are certainly as unpopular as they were in his own time.

His "Pecuniary Emulation" discusses the question of the development of the urge to accumulate wealth. In Veblen's America, huge fortunes had been amassed by innumerable American tycoons, among them the group often known as robber barons, those who defied most common ethical principles of decency and fairness in order to make themselves almost unbelievably wealthy. Veblen saw these men as predatory and was led to compare their behavior with the predatory beasts of the wilderness. This, in turn, led him to the analogy with Darwinian evolution and the "survival of the fittest."

Veblen's study includes ideas of evolutionary progress in economics. Interestingly, Marx too had such views. Yet Veblen did not have Marx's purposes of recommending communism as the final stage of evolution of the modern state. Rather, he wanted to show that the question of ownership is susceptible to analysis in evolutionary terms. That is, if one examined its beginnings, he or she would be able to understand in depth the drive (clearly evident in his own time) of people to accumulate far more wealth and goods than they could ever use.

Like many of his expressions, the term "pecuniary emulation" becomes clear as we progress through the selection. People live in a social milieu; their behavior is understood and measured in terms of their neighbors. They emulate each other in their own social sphere; and when they indulge in pecuniary emulation, they are indulging in amassing money in order to be like their neighbors. As he says, "The currently accepted legitimate end of effort becomes the achievement of a favorable comparison with other men; and therefore the repugnance to futility to a good extent coalesces with the incentive of emulation" (para. 19). In other words, the desire for achievement and the fear of failure (repugnance to futility) derive largely from the emulation of others who have been successful and the need to compare oneself with them. As he says in the same paragraph: "Among the motives which lead men to accumulate wealth, the primacy, both in scope and intensity, therefore, continues to belong to this motive of pecuniary emulation."

The section analyzes the sociological implications of a drive toward wealth, resting primarily on a comparison of contemporary practices with those of the earliest forms of society. Veblen traces the development of the concept of individual property, distinguishes ownership from simple appropriation (something like owning a river rather than simply using it), and attempts an analysis of the need to accumulate more than can be consumed. Such accumulation is, after all, what wealth is. For Veblen it therefore represents an unusual and curious fact. His analysis is as pertinent for us as it was for his contemporaries at the end of the century.

VEBLEN'S RHETORIC

Several qualities of his writing set Veblen apart from some of the other writers in this book. For one thing, he argues a position based upon an entirely hypothetical construct: the primitive societies from which we developed. He hypothesizes an evolutionary development from a barbarian culture, as he puts it, to the current industrial model. In this, he is not unlike Adam Smith and Thomas Malthus. But his analysis is detailed and his argument follows conclusively from his postulation.

Another uncommon quality is the use of unusual terminology that does not become clear until one is relatively deep into the essay. Thus, "pecuniary emulation" is an opaque expression until one begins to sort out the terminology near the end of the essay. The same is true of the term "invidious comparison," which usually implies simply a comparison that casts the thing compared in a dark light. "Invidious" means "obnoxious or repugnant." But Veblen is using the term simply to suggest a profound difference. A man of wealth becomes wealthy in order to create an "invidious comparison" with neighbors: the wealthy man make himself very different from his neighbor.

Finally, Veblen reveals a bit of crustiness—and probably some of the qualities that made him an unpopular teacher—in his delight in complex words. His use of language is not so brilliant as to cast him into the company of Matthew Arnold and William Hazlitt, to name two who influenced him; but he is certainly compelling and demanding. His views are of great moment; he demands that we rise to his level, and he refuses to lower himself to ours. The result of this rhetorical approach to style is to set him apart, to make him appear more difficult than he is, and ultimately to reward us with a view of an interesting mind commanding an unusual vocabulary for the purposes of making us sit up and take notice. Veblen rewards our efforts with the product of insights that actually change our way of thinking about social issues and about the drive toward accumulation that we call the need for creating wealth.

Pecuniary Emulation

In the sequence of cultural evolution the emergence of a leisure 1
class coincides with the beginning of ownership. This is necessarily
the case, for these two institutions result from the same set of economic forces. In the inchoate phase[1] of their development they are but
different aspects of the same general facts of social structure.

It is as elements of social structure—conventional facts—that lei- 2
sure and ownership are matters of interest for the purpose in hand. An
habitual neglect of work does not constitute a leisure class; neither
does the mechanical fact of use and consumption constitute ownership. The present inquiry, therefore, is not concerned with the beginning of indolence, nor with the beginning of the appropriation of useful articles to individual consumption. The point in question is the
origin and nature of a conventional leisure class on the one hand and
the beginnings of individual ownership as a conventional right or equitable claim on the other hand.

The early differentiation out of which the distinction between a 3
leisure and a working class arises is a division maintained between
men's and women's work in the lower stages of barbarism. Likewise
the earliest form of ownership is an ownership of the women by the
able-bodied men of the community. The facts may be expressed in
more general terms, and truer to the import of the barbarian theory of
life, by saying that it is an ownership of the woman by the man.

There was undoubtedly some appropriation of useful articles before 4
the custom of appropriating women arose. The usages of existing archaic communities in which there is no ownership of women is warrant for such a view. In all communities the members, both male and
female, habitually appropriate to their individual use a variety of useful things; but these useful things are not thought of as owned by the
person who appropriates and consumes them. The habitual appropriation and consumption of certain slight personal effects goes on without raising the question of ownership; that is to say, the question of a
conventional, equitable claim to extraneous things.

The ownership of women begins in the lower barbarian stages of 5

---

[1]*inchoate phase* The early, languageless phase, before things are codified, set up, and explained.

239

culture, apparently with the seizure of female captives. The original reason for the seizure and appropriation of women seems to have been their usefulness as trophies. The practice of seizing women from the enemy as trophies gave rise to a form of ownership-marriage, resulting in a household with a male head. This was followed by an extension of slavery to other captives and inferiors, besides women, and by an extension of ownership-marriage to other women than those seized from the enemy. The outcome of emulation under the circumstances of a predatory life, therefore, has been on the one hand a form of marriage resting on coercion, and on the other hand the custom of ownership. The two institutions are not distinguishable in the initial phase of their development; both arise from the desire of the successful men to put their prowess in evidence by exhibiting some durable result of their exploits. Both also minister to that propensity for mastery which pervades all predatory communities. From the ownership of women the concept of ownership extends itself to include the products of their industry, and so there arises the ownership of things as well as of persons.

In this way a consistent system of property in goods is gradually 6 installed. And although in the latest stages of the development, the serviceability of goods for consumption has come to be the most obtrusive element of their value, still, wealth has by no means yet lost its utility as an honorific evidence of the owner's prepotence.[2]

Wherever the institution of private property is found, even in a 7 slightly developed form, the economic process bears the character of a struggle between men for the possession of goods. It has been customary in economic theory, and especially among those economists who adhere with least faltering to the body of modernized classical doctrines, to construe this struggle for wealth as being substantially a struggle for subsistence. Such is, no doubt, its character in large part during the earlier and less efficient phases of industry. Such is also its character in all cases where the "niggardliness of nature" is so strict as to afford but a scanty livelihood to the community in return for strenuous and unremitting application to the business of getting the means of subsistence. But in all progressing communities an advance is presently made beyond this early stage of technological development. Industrial efficiency is presently carried to such a pitch as to afford something appreciably more than a bare livelihood to those engaged in the industrial process. It has not been unusual for economic theory to

---

[2]***prepotence*** Superior power.

speak of the further struggle for wealth on this new industrial basis as a competition for an increase of the comforts of life—primarily for an increase of the physical comforts which the consumption of goods affords.

The end of acquisition and accumulation is conventionally held to 8 be the consumption of the goods accumulated—whether it is consumption directly by the owner of the goods or by the household attached to him and for this purpose identified with him in theory. This is at least felt to be the economically legitimate end of acquisition, which alone it is incumbent on the theory to take account of. Such consumption may of course be conceived to serve the consumer's physical wants—his physical comfort—or his so-called higher wants—spiritual, aesthetic, intellectual, or what not; the latter class of wants being served indirectly by an expenditure of goods, after the fashion familiar to all economic readers.

But it is only when taken in a sense far removed from its naïve 9 meaning that consumption of goods can be said to afford the incentive from which accumulation invariably proceeds. The motive that lies at the root of ownership is emulation; and the same motive of emulation continues active in the further development of the institution to which it has given rise and in the development of all those features of the social structure which this institution of ownership touches. The possession of wealth confers honor; it is an invidious distinction. Nothing equally cogent can be said for the consumption of goods, nor for any other conceivable incentive to acquisition, and especially not for any incentive to the accumulation of wealth.

It is of course not to be overlooked that in a community where 10 nearly all goods are private property the necessity of earning a livelihood is a powerful and ever-present incentive for the poorer members of the community. The need of subsistence and of an increase of physical comfort may for a time be the dominant motive of acquisition for those classes who are habitually employed at manual labor, whose subsistence is on a precarious footing, who possess little and ordinarily accumulate little; but it will appear in the course of the discussion that even in the case of these impecunious classes the predominance of the motive of physical want is not so decided as has sometimes been assumed. On the other hand, so far as regards those members and classes of the community who are chiefly concerned in the accumulation of wealth, the incentive of subsistence or of physical comfort never plays a considerable part. Ownership began and grew into a human institution on grounds unrelated to the subsistence minimum. The dominant incentive was from the outset the invidious distinction attaching to wealth, and, save temporarily and by exception, no other motive has usurped the primacy at any later stage of the development.

Property set out with being booty held as trophies of the successful 11 raid. So long as the group had departed but little from the primitive communal organization, and so long as it still stood in close contact with other hostile groups, the utility of things or persons owned lay chiefly in an invidious comparison between their possessor and the enemy from whom they were taken. The habit of distinguishing between the interests of the individual and those of the group to which he belongs is apparently a later growth. Invidious comparison between the possessor of the honorific booty and his less successful neighbors within the group was no doubt present early as an element of the utility of the things possessed, though this was not at the outset the chief element of their value. The man's prowess was still primarily the group's prowess, and the possessor of the booty felt himself to be primarily the keeper of the honor of his group. This appreciation of exploit from the communal point of view is met with also at later stages of social growth, especially as regards the laurels of war.[3]

But so soon as the custom of individual ownership begins to gain 12 consistency, the point of view taken in making the invidious comparison on which private property rests will begin to change. Indeed, the one change is but the reflex of the other. The initial phase of ownership, the phase of acquisition by naïve seizure and conversion, begins to pass into the subsequent stage of an incipient organization of industry on the basis of private property (in slaves); the horde develops into a more or less self-sufficing industrial community; possessions then come to be valued not so much as evidence of successful foray, but rather as evidence of the prepotence of the possessor of these goods over other individuals within the community. The invidious comparison now becomes primarily a comparison of the owner with the other members of the group. Property is still of the nature of trophy, but, with the cultural advance, it becomes more and more a trophy of successes scored in the game of ownership carried on between the members of the group under the quasi-peaceable methods of nomadic life.

Gradually, as industrial activity further displaces predatory activity 13 in the community's everyday life and in men's habits of thought, accumulated property more and more replaces trophies of predatory exploit as the conventional exponent of prepotence and success. With

---

[3]*laurels of war*   The term is mildly ironic and refers to the honors or prizes of war. Veblen means a man's military exploits are especially significant in society.

the growth of settled industry, therefore, the possession of wealth gains in relative importance and effectiveness as a customary basis of repute and esteem. Not that esteem ceases to be awarded on the basis of other, more direct evidence of prowess; not that successful predatory aggression or warlike exploit ceases to call out the approval and admiration of the crowd, or to stir the envy of the less successful competitors; but the opportunities for gaining distinction by means of this direct manifestation of superior force grow less available both in scope and frequency. At the same time opportunities for industrial aggression, and for the accumulation of property by the quasi-peaceable methods of nomadic industry, increase in scope and availability. And it is even more to the point that property now becomes the most easily recognized evidence of a reputable degree of success as distinguished from heroic or signal achievement. It therefore becomes the conventional basis of esteem. Its possession in some amount becomes necessary in order to attain any reputable standing in the community. It becomes indispensable to accumulate, to acquire property, in order to retain one's good name. When accumulated goods have in this way once become the accepted badge of efficiency, the possession of wealth presently assumes the character of an independent and definitive basis of esteem. The possession of goods, whether acquired aggressively by one's own exertion or passively by transmission through inheritance from others, becomes a conventional basis of reputability. The possession of wealth, which was at the outset valued simply as an evidence of efficiency, becomes, in popular apprehension, itself a meritorious act. Wealth is now itself intrinsically honorable and confers honor on its possessor. By a further refinement, wealth acquired passively by transmission from ancestors or other antecedents presently becomes even more honorific than wealth acquired by the possessor's own effort; but this distinction belongs at a later stage in the evolution of the pecuniary culture and will be spoken of in its place.

Prowess and exploit may still remain the basis of award of the highest popular esteem, although the possession of wealth has become the basis of commonplace reputability and of a blameless social standing. The predatory instinct and the consequent approbation of predatory efficiency are deeply ingrained in the habits of thought of those peoples who have passed under the discipline of a protracted predatory culture. According to popular award, the highest honors within human reach may, even yet, be those gained by an unfolding of extraordinary predatory efficiency in war, or by a quasi-predatory efficiency in statecraft; but for the purposes of a commonplace decent standing in the community these means of repute have been replaced by the acquisition and accumulation of goods. In order to stand well in the eyes of the community, it is necessary to come up to a certain, somewhat indefinite, conventional standard of wealth; just as in the earlier predatory stage it is necessary for the barbarian man to come up to the tribe's standard of physical endurance, cunning, and skill at arms. A certain standard of wealth in the one case, and of prowess in the other, is a necessary condition of reputability, and anything in excess of this normal amount is meritorious.

Those members of the community who fall short of this, some- 15 what indefinite, normal degree of prowess or of property suffer in the esteem of their fellow-men; and consequently they suffer also in their own esteem, since the usual basis of self-respect is the respect accorded by one's neighbors. Only individuals with an aberrant temperment can in the long run retain their self-esteem in the face of the disesteem of their fellows. Apparent exceptions to the rule are met with, especially among people with strong religious convictions. But these apparent exceptions are scarcely real exceptions, since such persons commonly fall back on the putative approbation[4] of some supernatural witness of their deeds.

So soon as the possession of property becomes the basis of popular 16 esteem, therefore, it becomes also a requisite to that complacency which we call self-respect. In any community where goods are held in severalty[5] it is necessary, in order to his own peace of mind, that an individual should possess as large a portion of goods as others with whom he is accustomed to class himself; and it is extremely gratifying to possess something more than others. But as fast as a person makes new acquisitions, and becomes accustomed to the resulting new standard of wealth, the new standard forthwith ceases to afford appreciably greater satisfaction than the earlier standard did. The tendency in any case is constantly to make the present pecuniary standard the point of departure for a fresh increase of wealth; and this in turn gives rise to a new standard of sufficiency and a new pecuniary classification of one's self as compared with one's neighbors. So far as concerns the present question, the end sought by accumulation is to rank high in comparison with the rest of the community in point of pecuniary strength. So long as the comparison is distinctly unfavorable to himself, the normal, average individual will live in chronic dissatisfaction with his present lot; and when he has reached what may be called the

---

[4]*putative approbation* Supposed approval.
[5]*held in severalty* Goods that are owned by individuals, not shared with others.

normal pecuniary standard of the community, or of his class in the community, this chronic dissatisfaction will give place to a restless straining to place a wider and ever-widening pecuniary interval between himself and this average standard. The invidious comparison can never become so favorable to the individual making it that he would not gladly rate himself still higher relatively to his competitors in the struggle for pecuniary reputability.

In the nature of the case, the desire for wealth can scarcely be satiated in any individual instance, and evidently a satiation of the average or general desire for wealth is out of the question. However widely, or equally, or "fairly," it may be distributed, no general increase of the community's wealth can make any approach to satiating this need, the ground of which is the desire of everyone to excel everyone else in the accumulation of goods. If, as is sometimes assumed, the incentive to accumulation were the want of subsistence or of physical comfort, then the aggregate economic wants of a community might conceivably be satisfied at some point in the advance of industrial efficiency; but since the struggle is substantially a race for reputability on the basis of an invidious comparison, no approach to a definitive attainment is possible. 17

What has just been said must not be taken to mean that there are no other incentives to acquisition and accumulation than this desire to excel in pecuniary standing and so gain the esteem and envy of one's fellow-men. The desire for added comfort and security from want is present as a motive at every stage of the process of accumulation in a modern industrial community; although the standard of sufficiency in these respects is in turn greatly affected by the habit of pecuniary emulation. To a great extent this emulation shapes the methods and selects the objects of expenditure for personal comfort and decent livelihood. 18

Besides this, the power conferred by wealth also affords a motive to accumulation. That propensity for purposeful activity and that repugnance to all futility of effort which belong to man by virtue of his character as an agent do not desert him when he emerges from the naïve communal culture where the dominant note of life is the unanalyzed and undifferentiated solidarity of the individual with the group with which his life is bound up. When he enters upon the predatory stage, where self-seeking in the narrower sense becomes the dominant note, this propensity goes with him still, as the pervasive trait that shapes his scheme of life. The propensity for achievement and the repugnance to futility remain the underlying economic motive. The propensity changes only in the form of its expression and in the proxi- 19 mate objects to which it directs the man's activity. Under the régime of individual ownership the most available means of visibly achieving a purpose is that afforded by the acquisition and accumulation of goods; and as the self-regarding antithesis between man and man[6] reaches fuller consciousness, the propensity for achievement—the instinct of workmanship—tends more and more to shape itself into a straining to excel others in pecuniary achievement. Relative success, tested by an invidious pecuniary comparison with other men, becomes the conventional end of action. The currently accepted legitimate end of effort becomes the achievement of a favorable comparison with other men; and therefore the repugnance to futility to a good extent coalesces with the incentive of emulation. It acts to accentuate the struggle for pecuniary reputability by visiting with a sharper disapproval all shortcoming and all evidence of shortcoming in point of pecuniary success. Purposeful effort comes to mean, primarily, effort directed to or resulting in a more creditable showing of accumulated wealth. Among the motives which lead men to accumulate wealth, the primacy, both in scope and intensity, therefore, continues to belong to this motive of pecuniary emulation.

In making use of the term "invidious," it may perhaps be unnecessary to remark, there is no intention to extol or depreciate, or to commend or deplore any of the phenomena which the word is used to characterize. The term is used in a technical sense as describing a comparison of persons with a view to rating and grading them in respect of relative worth or value—in an aesthetic or moral sense—and so awarding and defining the relative degrees of complacency with which they may legitimately be contemplated by themselves and by others. An invidious comparison is a process of valuation of persons in respect of worth. 20

---

[6]*antithesis between man and man*   Vying or competition between men.

QUESTIONS

1. What is your interpretation of the term "pecuniary emulation"? What makes the term difficult to understand at first? Does Veblen achieve any advantage because of its complexity?
2. Veblen assumes that humanity has experienced a cultural evolution. Explain what he means by this and try to decide if he is right.

3. Veblen often refers to the leisure class. What do you think he means by this term? Do you think there were many people who fit into this class? Do you think they were aware they were members of it?

4. At the end of this selection, Veblen says he is not judging but simply describing the facts. Does the essay bear this out?

5. What are Veblen's most valid criticisms of modern industrial economies? Are they any less valid for today's economy than they seem to have been for his?

WRITING ASSIGNMENTS

1. In paragraph 6, Veblen says, "wealth has by no means yet lost its utility as an honorific evidence of the owner's prepotence." This was said of the culture of America in 1899. Is it any less true today? What signs do you see of the fact that wealth seems to impart a sense of potency or power to the wealthy? In what ways do the wealthy most use their power or potency?

2. In the early part of the essay, Veblen speculates about a barbarian way of life in which people appropriated objects, such as tools, but did not conceive of ownership until male warriors carried off women prisoners as booty. They then owned the women and regarded them as trophies. Examine Veblen's reasoning on this point by explaining what his theories are and then by considering the evidence or reasons on which he bases his views. Is his theory convincing? Once you have determined what his theory is, offer your own views on the subject. How do you think mankind first began to develop the concept of ownership?

3. What would society be like today if the concept of individual ownership had never developed? What might have developed instead? Write an essay that describes a hypothetical society in which nothing could be owned by an individual and in which no individual would ever wish to own anything. Would such a society be possible? Would it be better or worse than the kind of society we have today? Would you want to live in it? Do you know of any such society in either the past or the present?

4. One of Veblen's basic assumptions is that our economic system evolved from early stages to the stage it has now reached. Examine this view by establishing what you think these stages are and then hypothesize about what the next stage of economic and social evolution is likely to be for our "postindustrial" phase of development. What will our economic and social system be like in the next stage? How long do you think it will take to reach it?

5. In paragraph 13, Veblen says that, in the latest stages of industrial society, "the possession of wealth . . . becomes . . . itself a meritorious act. Wealth is now itself intrinsically honorable and confers honor on its pos-

sessor. By a further refinement, wealth acquired passively by transmission from ancestors or other antecedents presently becomes even more honorific than wealth acquired by the possessor's own effort." To what extent is Veblen correct in his evaluation? Is it true that inherited wealth imparts greater honor than wealth that is acquired through labor? Remember that we sometimes call people who have made their own fortune the nouveau riche and that the term is never meant as a compliment. Why do people use such a term for those who have acquired wealth? Why is inherited wealth thought to be so much more honorific than acquired wealth? Do you think that wealth should be honorific at all?

6. Veblen says, "A certain standard of wealth in the one case, and of prowess in the other, is a necessary condition of reputability, and anything in excess of this normal amount is meritorious" (para. 14). What is this standard in our society? He admits that it is "somewhat indefinite" (para. 15), but is it possible to discuss it well enough so that others can understand that it does indeed exist? What signs give evidence of it? In paragraph 15 he also says that when men fall in the esteem of others by not reaching the indefinite level, they also fall in self-esteem. Moreover, "the usual basis of self-respect is the respect accorded by one's neighbors." Examine these points and show, by example and description, the extent to which Veblen is correct in describing the society you know.

JOHN MAYNARD KEYNES

———◦∞◦———

Economic Possibilities for Our Grandchildren

JOHN MAYNARD KEYNES (1883–1946) became one of the most influential economists in modern times after his extraordinary analyses of economic decisions following World War I. He advised his own government, Great Britain, between the two world wars and during and after World War II. His advice to the United States government was responsible for policies that helped to restore economic prosperity in Europe.

His first famous book, The Economic Consequences of the Peace *(1919), was written after he left his official position with the government in Britain during negotiations leading to the Treaty of Versailles. That document clarified the political and economic terms of the surrender of Germany and its allies at the end of World War I. He was outraged at the plans for demanding reparations from Germany for damages during the war, and he was especially appalled at the behavior of President Woodrow Wilson, whom he thought was both stupid and hypocritical. The publication of* The Economic Consequences of the Peace *immediately established him not only as the most original economic mind of his generation but also as a kind of prophet. He pointed out that the economic strictures imposed on Germany would produce economic collapse and social disorder. He, like many others, was fearful that Germany might become Communist—*

as Karl Marx predicted it would—as did Russia during a period of war and social upheaval.

His views were prophetic, but his analysis of the situation in Germany was not completely accurate. He felt that the Treaty of Versailles had been motivated by political and military considerations and that it had ignored the impact of economic issues. This he feared would lead to collapse, and to an extent it did. But the fact is that Britain and France had modified their demands for reparations, and the economic conditions of most Germans before the Great Depression of 1929 were not as bad as he predicted they would be.

"Economic Possibilities for Our Grandchildren" was originally presented as a talk in 1928 before the depression; it was extensively revised and was published the fall of 1930. In this selection, Keynes offers a number of interesting prophecies that are quite remarkable, given the deplorable economic conditions of the times. He understood that long-term worldwide economic progress must be based on widespread improvement of the conditions of most people in modernized nations.

He pointed out that four factors were essential to guarantee continued economic prosperity: control of population; avoidance of wars and civil dissensions; permitting science to be unimpeded in matters proper to it; and ensuring that production continue to exceed consumption at the proper rate (para. 34). One of his major contributions to United States economic policy was his view that during a depression the government must spend vast sums of money on social programs and on programs that would pump money into the economy. President Roosevelt followed his advice, which was best articulated in General Theory of Employment, Interest and Money (1936). This treatise still forms the basis of most of our theories of how capitalism works. In 1936, however, the prevailing philosophy for ending a depression was to stop government spending and wait for the system to correct itself; in this way inflation could be kept under control. Keynes reasoned that a major depression was a form of deflation; he believed, therefore, that the prevailing theory was wrong. He convinced Roosevelt, and the United States began to achieve economic recovery before Great Britain did. World War II ended the depression in part by requiring the spending of even greater amounts of government money.

Another of Keynes's views was that economic prosperity is linked to spending on the part of the average citizen. He championed easy credit—certainly one of the chief reasons for prosperity among average citizens today—and discouraged the practice of saving at the then current interest rates. *Savings could only help the economy if they were lent out for investment in industry. He was especially negative in his attitude toward hoarding gold, which, as he says in the selection, does not produce interest. It is barren, just as an economic system based on the gold standard would be. Since 1937, we have not had a gold standard. The government controls the nation's money supply, and our policies are guided by Keynesian monetarism and resultant views concerning the government's role in spending.*

Whereas Keynes advocated government spending during the depression, he was fearful that a boom economy brought about by war might lead to another collapse. His most modern recommendations were guarded concerning the government's role in spending: during a boom economy it caused inflation. Thus, it was desirable to limit spending.

In the final analysis, Keynes remained a highly optimistic economist. He perceived that economists were capable of affecting social policy and that they could make a mark on the culture. His views about money and spending were designed to help spread the wealth of a nation among the greatest number of people. He advised Great Britain on how it could finance World War II in part by taking large tax contributions from the very wealthy and keeping them in a kind of "savings" account so that the general mass of people during wartime would not have much money to spend. Doing this would prevent massive inflation. Britain followed his plans in modified form and has generally done so since.

KEYNES'S RHETORIC

The title of the essay indicates its most obvious rhetorical resource, the examination of the question of possibility. But that also implies an examination of cause and effect, and Keynes spends much of his time explaining why certain effects he predicts can be reasonably expected. One technique is presenting a compressed historical review (paras. 5–9) explaining why we can expect that population stability and the incredible technological fruits of science will make our lives more prosperous.

But Keynes was also interested in deeper issues. He asserts that by the year 2030 the most important thing for most people will not be what choices they have in their work but how they can develop the art of life so that they can use leisure time well. The rich of the 1930s, whom he jokingly called the "advance guard" of the rest of

the population, was doing a bad job of using leisure time. Keynes
hoped that future generations could deal with it in better ways.

In the largest sense, this essay is an argument. However, even
though its materials are essentially complex and technical, Keynes's
prose is simple and direct. His audiences for the first version of the
essay were small academic societies at Cambridge University, where
Keynes was long a teacher of economics. The essay was later deliv-
ered as a lecture in Madrid; after revisions, it was printed in a polit-
ical journal. Keynes's style in this piece is marked by simplicity and
directness, with the result that it is accessible to a wide range of
readers.

Economic Possibilities for Our Grandchildren

We are suffering just now from a bad attack of economic pessi- 1
mism. It is common to hear people say that the epoch of enormous
economic progress which characterized the nineteenth century is over;
that the rapid improvement in the standard of life is now going to slow
down—at any rate in Great Britain; that a decline in prosperity is more
likely than an improvement in the decade which lies ahead of us.

I believe that this is a wildly mistaken interpretation of what is 2
happening to us. We are suffering, not from the rheumatics of old age,
but from the growing-pains of over-rapid changes, from the painfulness
of readjustment between one economic period and another. The increase of technical efficiency has been taking place faster than we can
deal with the problem of labor absorption; the improvement in the
standard of life has been a little too quick; the banking and monetary
system of the world has been preventing the rate of interest from falling as fast as equilibrium requires. And even so, the waste and confusion which ensue relate to not more than 7½ percent of the national
income; we are muddling away one and sixpence in the £, have only
18s 6d,[1] when we might, if we were more sensible, have £1; yet, nevertheless, the 18s 6d mounts up to as much as the £1 would have been

---

[1]*£, s, d* English money: pound, shilling, and pence. In 1930 the pound sterling was
worth $5; there were 20 shillings in a pound and 12 pence in a shilling.

five or six years ago. We forget that in 1929 the physical output of the industry of Great Britain was greater than ever before, and that the net surplus of our foreign balance available for new foreign investment, after paying for all our imports, was greater last year than that of any other country, being indeed 50 percent greater than the corresponding surplus of the United States. Or again—if it is to be a matter of comparisons—suppose that we were to reduce our wages by a half, repudiate four-fifths of the national debt, and hoard our surplus wealth in barren gold instead of lending it at 6 percent or more, we should resemble the now much-envied France. But would it be an improvement?

The prevailing world depression, the enormous anomaly of unemployment in a world full of wants, the disastrous mistakes we have made, blind us to what is going on under the surface—to the true interpretation of the trend of things. For I predict that both of the two opposed errors of pessimism which now make so much noise in the world will be proved wrong in our own time—the pessimism of the revolutionaries who think that things are so bad that nothing can save us but violent change, and the pessimism of the reactionaries who consider the balance of our economic and social life so precarious that we must risk no experiments. 3

My purpose in this essay, however, is not to examine the present or the near future, but to disembarrass myself of short views and take wings into the future. What can we reasonably expect the level of our economic life to be a hundred years hence? What are the economic possibilities for our grandchildren? 4

From the earliest times of which we have record—back, say to two thousand years before Christ—down to the beginning of the eighteenth century, there was no very great change in the standard of life of the average man living in the civilized centers of the earth. Ups and downs certainly. Visitations of plague, famine, and war. Golden intervals. But no progressive, violent change. Some periods perhaps 50 percent better than others—at the utmost 100 percent better—in the four thousand years which ended (say) in A.D. 1700. 5

This slow rate of progress, or lack of progress, was due to two reasons—to the remarkable absence of important technical improvements and to the failure of capital to accumulate. 6

The absence of important technical inventions between the prehistoric age and comparatively modern times is truly remarkable. Almost everything which really matters and which the world possessed at the commencement of the modern age was already known to man at the dawn of history. Language, fire, the same domestic animals which we 7 have today, wheat, barley, the vine and the olive, the plough, the wheel, the oar, the sail, leather, linen and cloth, bricks and pots, gold and silver, copper, tin, and lead—and iron was added to the list before 1000 B.C.—banking, statecraft, mathematics, astronomy, and religion. There is no record of when we first possessed these things.

At some epoch before the dawn of history—perhaps even in one of 8 the comfortable intervals before the last ice age—there must have been an era of progress and invention comparable to that in which we live today. But through the greater part of recorded history there was nothing of the kind.

The modern age opened, I think, with the accumulation of capital 9 which began in the sixteenth century. I believe—for reasons with which I must not encumber the present argument—that this was initially due to the rise of prices, and the profits to which that led, which resulted from the treasure of gold and silver which Spain brought from the New World into the Old. From that time until today the power of accumulation by compound interest,[2] which seems to have been sleeping for many generations, was reborn and renewed its strength. And the power of compound interest over two hundred years is such as to stagger the imagination.

Let me give in illustration of this a sum which I have worked out. 10 The value of Great Britain's foreign investments today is estimated at about £4,000 million. This yields us an income at the rate of about 6½ percent. Half of this we bring home and enjoy; the other half, namely, 3¼ percent, we leave to accumulate abroad at compound interest. Something of this sort has now been going on for about 250 years.

For I trace the beginnings of British foreign investment to the trea- 11 sure which Drake stole from Spain in 1580. In that year he returned to England bringing with him the prodigious spoils of the *Golden Hind*.[3] Queen Elizabeth was a considerable shareholder in the syndicate which had financed the expedition. Out of her share she paid off the whole of England's foreign debt, balanced her budget, and found herself with about £40,000 in hand. This she invested in the Levant

---

[2] *compound interest* Interest that money at loan earns, including earnings on the accumulated interest.

[3] **Golden Hind** The ship Sir Francis Drake (1545?–1596) used to explore the Pacific (1572) and in which he circumnavigated the globe. He was the first Englishman to see the Pacific and to sail around the world. He also brought home Spanish booty to provide Queen Elizabeth with badly needed cash.

Company[4]—which prospered. Out of the profits of the Levant Company, the East India Company[5] was founded; and the profits of this great enterprise were the foundation of England's subsequent foreign investment. Now it happens that £40,000 accumulating at 3¼ percent compound interest approximately corresponds to the actual volume of England's foreign investments at various dates, and would actually amount today to the total of £4,000 million which I have already quoted as being what our foreign investments now are. Thus, every £1 which Drake brought home in 1580 has now become £100,000. Such is the power of compound interest!

From the sixteenth century, with a cumulative crescendo[6] after the eighteenth, the great age of science and technical inventions began, which since the beginning of the nineteenth century has been in full flood—coal, steam, electricity, petrol,[7] steel, rubber, cotton, the chemical industries, automatic machinery and the methods of mass production, wireless, printing, Newton, Darwin, and Einstein,[8] and thousands of other things and men too famous and familiar to catalogue.

What is the result? In spite of an enormous growth in the population of the world, which it has been necessary to equip with houses and machines, the average standard of life in Europe and the United States has been raised, I think, about fourfold. The growth of capital has been on a scale which is far beyond a hundredfold of what any previous age had known. And from now on we need not expect so great an increase of population.

If capital increases, say, 2 percent per annum, the capital equipment of the world will have increased by a half in twenty years, and seven and a half times in a hundred years. Think of this in terms of material things—houses, transport, and the like.

At the same time technical improvements in manufacture and transport have been proceeding at a greater rate in the last ten years

12

13

14

15

---

[4]***the Levant Company*** An English trading company set up to do business with the Middle Eastern countries.

[5]***the East India Company*** An important English trading company founded in 1600 and dissolved in 1873. It began as a commercial enterprise but ended as a political one, taking a hand in the governance of India.

[6]***crescendo*** A building up of intensity.

[7]***petrol*** Gasoline.

[8]***Isaac Newton (1642–1727), Charles Darwin (1809–1882), and Albert Einstein (1879–1955)*** Scientists whose work changed the world in the eighteenth, nineteenth, and twentieth centuries, respectively.

than ever before in history. In the United States factory output per head was 40 percent greater in 1925 than in 1919. In Europe we are held back by temporary obstacles, but even so it is safe to say that technical efficiency is increasing by more than 1 percent per annum compound. There is evidence that the revolutionary technical changes, which have so far chiefly affected industry, may soon be attacking agriculture. We may be on the eve of improvements in the efficiency of food production as great as those which have already taken place in mining, manufacture, and transport. In quite a few years—in our own lifetimes I mean—we may be able to perform all the operations of agriculture, mining, and manufacture with a quarter of the human effort to which we have been accustomed.

For the moment the very rapidity of these changes is hurting us 16 and bringing difficult problems to solve. Those countries are suffering relatively which are not in the vanguard of progress. We are being afflicted with a new disease of which some readers may not yet have heard the name, but of which they will hear a great deal in the years to come—namely, *technological unemployment*. This means unemployment due to our discovery of means of economising the use of labor outrunning the pace at which we can find new uses for labor.

But this is only a temporary phase of maladjustment. All this 17 means in the long run *that mankind is solving its economic problem.* I would predict that the standard of life in progressive countries one hundred years hence will be between four and eight times as high as it is today. There would be nothing surprising in this even in the light of our present knowledge. It would not be foolish to contemplate the possibility of a far greater progress still.

Let us, for the sake of argument, suppose that a hundred years 18 hence we are all of us, on the average, eight times better off in the economic sense than we are today. Assuredly there need be nothing here to surprise us.

Now it is true that the needs of human beings may seem to be 19 insatiable. But they fall into two classes—those needs which are absolute in the sense that we feel them whatever the situation of our fellow human beings may be, and those which are relative in the sense that we feel them only if their satisfaction lifts us above, makes us feel superior to, our fellows. Needs of the second class, those which satisfy the desire for superiority, may indeed be insatiable; for the higher the general level, the higher still are they. But this is not so true of the absolute needs—a point may soon be reached, much sooner perhaps than we all of us are aware of, when these needs are satisfied in the sense that we prefer to devote our further energies to non-economic purposes.

Now for my conclusion, which you will find, I think, to become 20
more and more startling to the imagination the longer you think about it.

I draw the conclusion that, assuming no important wars and no 21
important increase in population, the *economic problem* may be solved, or be at least within sight of solution, within a hundred years. This means that the economic problem is not—if we look into the future—*the permanent problem of the human race.*

Why, you may ask, is this so startling? It is startling because—if, 22
instead of looking into the future, we look into the past—we find that the economic problem, the struggle for subsistence, always has been hitherto the primary, most pressing problem of the human race—not only of the human race, but of the whole of the biological kingdom from the beginnings of life in its most primitive forms.

Thus we have been expressly evolved by nature—with all our im- 23
pulses and deepest instincts—for the purpose of solving the economic problem. If the economic problem is solved, mankind will be deprived of its traditional purpose.

Will this be a benefit? If one believes at all in the real values of 24
life, the prospect at least opens up the possibility of benefit. Yet I think with dread of the readjustment of the habits and instincts of the ordinary man, bred into him for countless generations, which he may be asked to discard within a few decades.

To use the language of today—must we not expect a general "ner- 25
vous breakdown"? We already have a little experience of what I mean—a nervous breakdown of the sort which is already common enough in England and the United States amongst the wives of the well-to-do classes, unfortunate women, many of them, who have been deprived by their wealth of their traditional tasks and occupations— who cannot find it sufficiently amusing, when deprived of the spur of economic necessity, to cook and clean and mend, yet are quite unable to find anything more amusing.

To those who sweat for their daily bread leisure is a longed-for 26
sweet—until they get it.

There is the traditional epitaph written for herself by the old char- 27
woman:

> Don't mourn for me, friends, don't weep for me never,
> For I'm going to do nothing for ever and ever.

This was her heaven. Like others who look forward to leisure, she conceived how nice it would be to spend her time listening-in—for there was another couplet which occurred in her poem:

> With psalms and sweet music the heavens'll be ringing,
> But I shall have nothing to do with the singing.

Yet it will only be for those who have to do with the singing that life will be tolerable—and how few of us can sing!

Thus for the first time since his creation man will be faced with his real, his permanent problem—how to use his freedom from pressing economic cares, how to occupy the leisure, which science and compound interest will have won for him, to live wisely and agreeably and well. 28

The strenuous purposeful money-makers may carry all of us along with them into the lap of economic abundance. But it will be those peoples, who can keep alive, and cultivate into a fuller perfection, the art of life itself and do not sell themselves for the means of life, who will be able to enjoy the abundance when it comes. 29

Yet there is no country and no people, I think, who can look forward to the age of leisure and of abundance without a dread. For we have been trained too long to strive and not to enjoy. It is a fearful problem for the ordinary person, with no special talents, to occupy himself, especially if he no longer has roots in the soil or in custom or in the beloved conventions of a traditional society. To judge from the behavior and the achievements of the wealthy classes today in any quarter of the world, the outlook is very depressing! For these are, so to speak, our advance guard—those who are spying out the promised land for the rest of us and pitching their camp there. For they have most of them failed disastrously, so it seems to me—those who have an independent income but no associations or duties or ties—to solve the problem which has been set them. 30

I feel sure that with a little more experience we shall use the new-found bounty of nature quite differently from the way in which the rich use it today, and will map out for ourselves a plan of life quite otherwise than theirs. 31

For many ages to come the old Adam[9] will be so strong in us that everybody will need to do *some* work if he is to be contented. We shall do more things for ourselves than is usual with the rich today, only 32

---

[9]**old Adam** The Bible, in Genesis, explains that Adam, after his fall, was condemned to earn his living by the sweat of his brow.

too glad to have small duties and tasks and routines. But beyond this, we shall endeavor to spread the bread thin on the butter—to make what work there is still to be done to be as widely shared as possible. Three-hour shifts or a fifteen-hour week may put off the problem for a great while. For three hours a day is quite enough to satisfy the old Adam in most of us!

There are changes in other spheres too which we must expect to come. When the accumulation of wealth is no longer of high social importance, there will be great changes in the code of morals. We shall be able to rid ourselves of many of the pseudo-moral principles which have hag-ridden us for two hundred years, by which we have exalted some of the most distasteful of human qualities into the position of the highest virtues. We shall be able to afford to dare to assess the money-motive at its true value. The love of money as a possession— as distinguished from the love of money as a means to the enjoyments and realities of life—will be recognised for what it is, a somewhat disgusting morbidity, one of those semi-criminal, semi-pathological propensities which one hands over with a shudder to the specialists in mental disease. All kinds of social customs and economic practices, affecting the distribution of wealth and of economic rewards and penalties, which we now maintain at all costs, however distasteful and unjust they may be in themselves, because they are tremendously useful in promoting the accumulation of capital, we shall then be free, at last, to discard.

Of course there will still be many people with intense, unsatisfied purposiveness who will blindly pursue wealth—unless they can find some plausible substitute. But the rest of us will no longer be under any obligation to applaud and encourage them. For we shall inquire more curiously than is safe today into the true character of this "purposiveness" with which in varying degrees Nature has endowed almost all of us. For purposiveness means that we are more concerned with the remote future results of our actions than with their own quality or their immediate effects on our own environment. The "purposive" man is always trying to secure a spurious and delusive immortality for his acts by pushing his interest in them forward into time. He does not love his cat, but his cat's kittens; nor, in truth, the kittens, but only the kittens' kittens, and so on forward for ever to the end of catdom. For him jam is not jam unless it is a case of jam tomorrow and never jam today. Thus by pushing his jam always forward into the future, he strives to secure for his act of boiling it an immortality.

Let me remind you of the Professor in *Sylvie and Bruno:*[10]   35

"Only the tailor, sir, with your little bill," said a meek voice outside the door.

"Ah, well, I can soon settle *his* business," the Professor said to the children, "if you'll just wait a minute. How much is it, this year, my man?" The tailor had come in while he was speaking.

"Well, it's been a-doubling so many years, you see," the tailor replied, a little gruffly, "and I think I'd like the money now. It's two thousand pound, it is!"

"Oh, that's nothing!" the Professor carelessly remarked, feeling in his pocket, as if he always carried at least *that* amount about with him. "But wouldn't you like to wait just another year and make it *four* thousand? Just think how rich you'd be! Why, you might be a *king*, if you liked!"

"I don't know as I'd care about being a king," the man said thoughtfully. "But it *dew* sound a powerful sight o' money! Well, I think I'll wait—"

"Of course you will!" said the Professor. "There's good sense in *you*, I see. Good-day to you, my man!"

"Will you ever have to pay him that four thousand pounds?" Sylvie asked as the door closed on the departing creditor.

"*Never*, my child!" the Professor replied emphatically. "He'll go on doubling it till he dies. You see, it's *always* worth while waiting another year to get twice as much money!"

.   .   .

I see us free, therefore, to return to some of the most sure and   36 certain principles of religion and traditional virtue—that avarice is a vice, that the exaction of usury is a misdemeanor, and the love of money is detestable, that those walk most truly in the paths of virtue and sane wisdom who take least thought for the morrow. We shall once more value ends above means and prefer the good to the useful. We shall honor those who can teach us how to pluck the hour and the day virtuously and well, the delightful people who are capable of taking direct enjoyment in things, the lilies of the field who toil not, neither do they spin.[11]

---

[10]**Sylvie and Bruno**   A children's book by Charles Lutwidge Dodgson (1832–1898), published in 1889. Another book, *Sylvie and Bruno Concluded*, was published in 1894. Dodgson is better known as Lewis Carroll, author of *Alice's Adventures in Wonderland* (1865).

[11]**lilies of the field**   Matthew 6:28. "Consider the lilies of the field, how they grow; they toil not, neither do they spin." Jesus implied that the faithful should pay more attention to their faith than on how they were to get on in the world. Keynes is subtly twisting the words, but he is suggesting that we should have faith in the expansion and development of the economy.

But beware! The time for all this is not yet. For at least another 37 hundred years we must pretend to ourselves and to everyone that fair is foul and foul is fair; for foul is useful and fair is not. Avarice and usury and precaution must be our gods for a little longer still. For only they can lead us out of the tunnel of economic necessity into daylight.

I look forward, therefore, in days not so very remote, to the greatest 38 change which has ever occurred in the material environment of life for human beings in the aggregate. But, of course, it will all happen gradually, not as a catastrophe. Indeed, it has already begun. The course of affairs will simply be that there will be ever larger and larger classes and groups of people from whom problems of economic necessity have been practically removed. The critical difference will be realized when this condition has become so general that the nature of one's duty to one's neighbor is changed. For it will remain reasonable to be economically purposive for others after it has ceased to be reasonable for oneself.

The *pace* at which we can reach our destination of economic bliss 39 will be governed by four things—our power to control population, our determination to avoid wars and civil dissensions, our willingness to entrust to science the direction of those matters which are properly the concern of science, and the rate of accumulation as fixed by the margin between our production and our consumption; of which the last will easily look after itself, given the first three.

Meanwhile, there will be no harm in making mild preparations for 40 our destiny, in encouraging, and experimenting in, the arts of life as well as the activities of purpose.

But, chiefly, do not let us overestimate the importance of the eco- 41 nomic problem, or sacrifice to its supposed necessities other matters of greater and more permanent significance. It should be a matter for specialists—like dentistry. If economists could manage to get themselves thought of as humble, competent people, on a level with dentists, that would be splendid!

QUESTIONS

1. What was the view of the economic future when Keynes began this essay? What is the current view today?
2. Keynes talks early about compound interest. What is it, and how does an economy benefit by taking advantage of it?
3. The slow rate of economic progress before 1700 was caused by two specific conditions. What were they?
4. What is the role of science in achieving the economic growth that Keynes believes is possible?

5. In paragraph 21 and thereafter, Keynes talks about the economic possibilities for the twenty-first century. What are they? Do they seem reasonable to you?

WRITING ASSIGNMENTS

1. Keynes issues an important injunction in paragraph 28: "to live wisely and agreeably and well." In paragraph 29 he continues: "The strenuous purposeful money-makers may carry all of us along with them into the lap of economic abundance. But it will be those peoples, who can keep alive, and cultivate into a fuller perfection, the art of life itself and do not sell themselves for the means of life, who will be able to enjoy the abundance when it comes." What do you interpret the cultivation of "the art of life itself" to be? How does one cultivate it? What are its ingredients? What aspects of your education are preparing you for it? How aware is your society of the need to cultivate the art of life? Who is doing it best? Are you planning your own life in order to achieve the "fuller perfection" that Keynes refers to?

2. Keynes states that four conditions must be met in order to guarantee the kind of economic prosperity and progress that he expects (para. 39). Clarify each one so that a potential reader will understand them and then analyze the modern situation to see whether the conditions Keynes hoped for are being met. Based on the extent to which these conditions are being attained, how bright is the prospect for the immediate future?

3. Nowhere in the essay does Keynes discuss the fate of those who are displaced by technological change; nor does he discuss what to do about people who cannot share in the production of wealth for whatever reason. The poor, in other words, are not addressed directly in the essay. He does expect the poor to benefit from the work of the money-makers, however. Is he correct? Is it possible that the following quote, from paragraph 38, is an indirect reference to welfare programs?

   The course of affairs will simply be that there will be ever larger and larger classes and groups of people from whom problems of economic necessity have been practically removed. The critical difference will be realized when this condition has become so general that the nature of one's duty to one's neighbor is changed. For it will remain reasonable to be economically purposive for others after it has ceased to be reasonable for oneself.

   Has this prediction already come true? What evidence have you to support your answer?

4. In one of his most interesting predictions, Keynes says that our age will see a great deal of technological unemployment: "We are being afflicted with a new disease of which some readers may not yet have heard the

name, but of which they will hear a great deal in the years to come—namely, *technological unemployment*. This means unemployment due to our discovery of means of economising the use of labor outrunning the pace at which we can find new uses for labor" (para. 16). In a brief essay, establish the degree to which this prediction has come true. What are the technological changes that have caused modern unemployment? Which changes seem to you to be the most important ones? Do you think that society is as optimistic about these changes as Keynes is? Do you feel optimistic? What are you doing to prepare yourself for the technological changes that are coming in the future? What is our society doing?

5. Keynes points out that those nations which are "not in the vanguard of progress" (para. 16) are suffering despite the generally positive outlook for the economic future. Which nations do you see that are not in the vanguard and that are suffering? What is the nature of their suffering? What should the nations who are in the forefront of progress do regarding the suffering nations?

JOHN KENNETH GALBRAITH

※

The Position of Poverty

JOHN KENNETH GALBRAITH (b. 1908) was born in Canada but has been an American citizen since 1937. His Canadian background was rural, and his early experiences were connected with farming in Ontario, which helps to explain his having taken his first university degree in agricultural science. It may also help to explain why, in his many books on subjects such as economics, the State Department, Indian art, and government, he has always been praised for making it simple for a layperson to understand sometimes complex concepts. Sometimes, of course, he has been criticized for oversimplifying some issues, but on the whole, he has made a brilliant success of writing with wit and up-tempo humor about issues that are basically perplexing and sometimes troubling.

Galbraith was professor of economics at Harvard University for many years. During the presidential campaigns of Adlai Stevenson in 1952 and 1956, he assisted the Democrats as a speech writer and economics adviser. He performed the same tasks for John F. Kennedy in 1960, including drafting Kennedy's inaugural address. Kennedy appointed Galbraith ambassador to India, a post that he maintained for a little over two years, including the period during which India

---

From *The Affluent Society.*

and China fought a border war. His experiences in India resulted in Ambassador's Journal: A Personal Account of the Kennedy Years *(1969). Kennedy called Galbraith his finest ambassadorial appointment, and since Kennedy's own father had been an ambassador, that constitutes significant praise.*

Galbraith's involvement with politics was somewhat unusual for an academic economist at that time. It seems to have stemmed from strongly held personal views on the social issues of his time. One of the most important contributions of his best-known and probably most significant book, The Affluent Society *(1958, rev. ed. 1976), presented his analysis of America's economic ambitions. He pointed out that at that time the welfare of the economy was entirely tied up in the measurement and growth of the gross national product. Economists and government officials concentrated on boosting output. He tried to help people see that, by itself, this goal was misdirected. The result, he said, would be a profusion of products that people really did not need and would not benefit from. It would result in creating artificial needs for things that had no ultimate value. Concentrating on bigger, more luxurious automobiles and building in a "planned obsolescence" that essentially put consumers in an economic squirrel cage seemed to him to be wasteful and ultimately destructive.*

Galbraith suggested that America concentrate on genuine needs and satisfy them immediately. He was deeply concerned about the environment and suggested that clean air was a priority that took precedence over all consumer goods. He supported development of the arts and stressed that the improvement of housing across the nation was of first importance. His effort was directed at trying to help Americans change certain basic values. He wished to help them give up the pursuit of useless consumer novelties and to substitute a program of genuine development of the society. The commitment to consumer products as the basis of the economy naturally argued against a redirection of effort toward the solution of social problems.

"The Position of Poverty" is interesting because it is among the few statements made in economics on the question of what the country can or should do about the poor. As Galbraith points out at the beginning of the selection, economists generally comment on the entire economy and, when they do, give only lip service to the problem of poverty. The result is that we do not understand poverty very well, and we are not likely to make much progress in ridding it from society.

Galbraith is exceptionally clear in his essay so that little commentary is needed to establish its importance. He is insightful in clarify-

ing two kinds of poverty: case poverty and insular poverty. Case poverty is restricted to an individual and his or her family. Alcoholism, ignorance, mental deficiency, discrimination, or specific handicaps seem to be the cause of such poverty. It is an individual, not a group disorder. Insular poverty affects a group in a given area—an "island" within the larger society. He points to poverty in Appalachia and in the slums of major cities, where most of the people in those "islands" are at or below the poverty level. Insular poverty is linked to the environment, and its causes are somehow derived from that environment.

His analysis is perceptive and influential, and while little or no progress has been made in solving the problem of poverty since 1959, he assures us that there are things that can be done to help eradicate it. He also warns that it demands the nation's will, however, and that the nation may lack the will. As he wisely pointed out, the cause of the impoverished was not likely to be a popular political issue in 1958. Because the poverty-stricken are a minority, few politicians, he reasoned, would make them a campaign issue. Actually, he was wrong. Kennedy in 1960, Lyndon Johnson in 1964, and Jimmy Carter in 1972 made programs for the poor central among their governmental concerns. Because of the war in Vietnam and other governmental policies, however, the 1960s and early 1970s were a time of staggering inflation that wiped out any of the advances the poverty-stricken had made. The extent to which this is true is observable instantly on reading the work; the income figures for 1959 seem so unbelievably low as to make us think we are reading about the last century rather than the mid-twentieth century.

GALBRAITH'S RHETORIC

The most important rhetorical achievement of the piece is its style. This is an example of the elevated plain style: a clear, direct, and basically simple approach to language that only occasionally admits a somewhat learned vocabulary—as in the use of a very few words such as "opulent," "unremunerative," and "ineluctable." The vast majority of words he uses are ordinary ones.

He breaks the essay into six carefully numbered sections. This is a way of highlighting its basic structure and subtly reminding us that he has clearly separated its elements into related groups so that he can speak directly to aspects of his subject rather than to the entire subject. Rhetoricians sometimes call this technique division, and its *effect is to impart clarity and to confer a sense of authority on the writer.*

Galbraith relies on statistical information that the reader can examine if necessary. This information is treated in the early stages of the piece as a prologue. Once such information has been given, Galbraith draws some conclusions from it, proceeding in the manner of a logician establishing premises and deriving the necessary conclusions. The subject is sober and sobering, and so is the style. The issues are complex, uncertain, and difficult, but the style is direct, confident, and essentially simple. This is the secret of the success of the book from which this selection comes. The Affluent Society *has been translated into well over a dozen languages and has been a bestseller around the globe. And despite the fact that the statistical information is outdated, it remains an influential book. Its fundamental insights are such that it is likely to be relevant to our economic circumstances for generations to come.*

The Position of Poverty

"The study of the causes of poverty," Alfred Marshall[1] observed at the turn of the century, "is the study of the causes of the degradation of a large part of mankind." He spoke of contemporary England as well as of the world beyond. A vast number of people both in town and country, he noted, had insufficient food, clothing and house-room; they were: "Overworked and undertaught, weary and careworn, without quiet and without leisure." The chance of their succor, he concluded, gave to economic studies, "their chief and their highest interest."

No contemporary economist would be likely to make such an observation about the United States. Conventional economic discourse makes obeisance to the continued existence of some poverty. "We must remember that we still have a great many poor people." In the nineteen-sixties, poverty promised, for a time, to become a subject of

1

2

---

[1]*Alfred Marshall (1842–1924)* An English economist whose *Principles of Economics* (1890) was long a standard text and is still relied on by some economists for its theories of costs, value, and distribution.

serious political concern. Then war came and the concern evaporated or was displaced. For economists of conventional mood, the reminders that the poor still exist are a useful way of allaying uneasiness about the relevance of conventional economic goals. For some people, wants must be synthesized. Hence, the importance of the goods to them is not *per se* very high. So much may be conceded. But others are far closer to physical need. And hence we must not be cavalier about the urgency of providing them with the most for the least. The sales tax may have merit for the opulent, but it still bears heavily on the poor. The poor get jobs more easily when the economy is expanding. Thus, poverty survives in economic discourse partly as a buttress to the conventional economic wisdom.

The privation of which Marshall spoke was, a half century ago, the 3 common lot at least of all who worked without special skill. As a general affliction, it was ended by increased output which, however imperfectly it may have been distributed, nevertheless accrued in substantial amount to those who worked for a living. The result was to reduce poverty from the problem of a majority to that of a minority. It ceased to be a general case and became a special case. It is this which has put the problem of poverty into its peculiar modern form.

For poverty does survive. In part, it is a physical matter; those af- 4 flicted have such limited and insufficient food, such poor clothing, such crowded, cold and dirty shelter that life is painful as well as comparatively brief. But just as it is far too tempting to say that, in matters of living standards, everything is relative, so it is wrong to rest everything on absolutes. People are poverty-stricken when their income, even if adequate for survival, falls radically behind that of the community. Then they cannot have what the larger community regards as the minimum necessary for decency; and they cannot wholly escape, therefore, the judgment of the larger community that they are indecent. They are degraded for, in the literal sense, they live outside the grades or categories which the community regards as acceptable.

Since the first edition of this book appeared, and one hopes how- 5 ever slightly as a consequence, the character and dimension of this degradation have become better understood. There have also been fulsome promises that poverty would be eliminated. The performance on these promises has been less eloquent.

The degree of privation depends on the size of the family, the place 6 of residence—it will be less with given income in rural areas than in the cities—and will, of course, be affected by changes in living costs. The Department of Health, Education and Welfare has established rough standards, appropriately graded to family size, location and changing prices, to separate the poor from the less poor and the affluent. In 1972, a non-farm family of four was deemed poor if it had an income of $4275; a couple living otherwise than on a farm was called poor if it had less than $2724 and an unattached individual if receiving less than $2109. A farm family of four was poor with less than $3639; of two with less than $2315.[2]

By these modest standards, 24.5 million households, including individuals and families, were poor in 1972 as compared with 13.4 million in 1959. Because of the increase in population, and therewith in the number of households, in these years the reduction in the number of poor households, as a proportion of all households, was rather greater—from 24 percent in 1959 to 12 percent in 1972.[3]   7

One can usually think of the foregoing deprivation as falling into   8 two broad categories. First, there is what may be called *case* poverty. This one encounters in every community, rural or urban, however prosperous that community or the times. Case poverty is the poor farm family with the junk-filled yard and the dirty children playing in the bare dirt. Or it is the gray-black hovel beside the railroad tracks. Or it is the basement dwelling in the alley.

Case poverty is commonly and properly related to some character-   9 istic of the individuals so afflicted. Nearly everyone else has mastered his environment; this proves that it is not intractable. But some quality peculiar to the individual or family involved—mental deficiency, bad health, inability to adapt to the discipline of industrial life, uncontrollable procreation, alcohol, discrimination involving a very limited minority, some educational handicap unrelated to community shortcoming, or perhaps a combination of several of these handicaps—has kept these individuals from participating in the general well-being.

Second, there is what may be called *insular* poverty—that which   10 manifests itself as an "island" of poverty. In the island, everyone or nearly everyone is poor. Here, evidently, it is not easy to explain matters by individual inadequacy. We may mark individuals down as intrinsically deficient in social performance; it is not proper or even wise so to characterize an entire community. The people of the island have been frustrated by some factor common to their environment.

Case poverty exists. It has also been useful to those who have   11 needed a formula for keeping the suffering of others from causing suffering to themselves. Since this poverty is the result of the deficien-

---

[2]*Statistical Abstract of the United States*, 1974, p. 389. [Galbraith's note]
[3]*Statistical Abstract*, p. 389. [Galbraith's note]

cies, including the moral shortcomings, of the persons concerned, it is possible to shift the responsibility to those involved. They are worthless and, as a simple manifestation of social justice, they suffer for it. Or, at a somewhat higher level of social perception and compassion, it means that the problem of poverty is sufficiently solved by private and public charity. This rescues those afflicted from the worst consequences of their inadequacy or misfortune; no larger social change or reorganization is suggested. Except as it may be insufficient in its generosity, the society is not at fault.

Insular poverty yields to no such formulas. In earlier times, when 12 agriculture and extractive industries were the dominant sources of livelihood, something could be accomplished by shifting the responsibility for low income to a poor natural endowment and thus, in effect, to God. The soil was thin and stony, other natural resources absent and hence the people were poor. And, since it is the undoubted preference of many to remain in the vicinity of the place of their birth, a homing instinct that operates for people as well as pigeons, the people remained in the poverty which heaven had decreed for them. It is an explanation that is nearly devoid of empirical application. Connecticut is very barren and stony and incomes are very high. Similarly Wyoming. West Virginia is well watered with rich mines and forests and the people are very poor. The South is much favored in soil and climate and similarly poor and the very richest parts of the South, such as the Mississippi-Yazoo Delta, have long had a well-earned reputation for the greatest deprivation. Yet so strong is the tendency to associate poverty with natural causes that even individuals of some modest intelligence will still be heard, in explanation of insular poverty, to say, "It's basically a poor country." "It's a pretty barren region."

Most modern poverty is insular in character and the islands are the 13 rural and urban slums. From the former, mainly in the South, the southern Appalachians and Puerto Rico, there has been until recent times a steady flow of migrants, some white but more black, to the latter. Grim as life is in the urban ghetto, it still offers more hope, income and interest than in the rural slum. Largely in consequence of this migration, the number of poor farm families—poor by the standards just mentioned—declined between 1959 and 1973 from 1.8 million to 295,000. The decline in the far larger number of poor non-farm households in these years was only from 6.5 million to 4.5 million.[4]

---

[4]U.S. Department of Commerce, *Current Population Reports*, "Consumer Income," Series P-60, No. 98 (Washington, D.C.: U.S. Government Printing Office, 1975). [Galbraith's note]

This is not the place to provide a detailed profile of this poverty. 14
More than half of the poor households are headed by a woman, although in total women head only 9 percent of families. Over 30 percent are black, another 10 percent are of Spanish origin. A very large
proportion of all black households (31 percent in 1973 as compared
with 8 percent of whites) fall below the poverty line. Especially on the
farms, where the young have departed for the cities, a disproportionate
number of the poor are old. More often than not, the head of the
household is not in the labor force at all.

But the more important characteristic of insular poverty is forces, 15
common to all members of the community, which restrain or prevent
participation in economic life at going rates of return. These restraints
are several. Race, which acts to locate people by their color rather than
by the proximity to employment, is obviously one. So are poor educational facilities. (And this effect is further exaggerated when the poorly
educated, endemically a drug on the labor market, are brought together
in dense clusters by the common inadequacy of the schools available
to blacks and the poor.) So is the disintegration of family life in the
slum which leaves households in the hands of women. Family life itself is in some measure a manifestation of affluence. And so, without
doubt, is the shared sense of helplessness and rejection and the resulting demoralization which is the product of the common misfortune.

The most certain thing about this poverty is that it is not remedied 16
by a general advance in income. Case poverty is not remedied because
the specific individual inadequacy precludes employment and participation in the general advance. Insular poverty is not directly alleviated
because the advance does not remove the specific frustrations of environment to which the people of these islands are subject. This is not
to say that it is without effect. If there are jobs outside the ghetto or
away from the rural slum, those who are qualified, and not otherwise
constrained, can take them and escape. If there are no such jobs, none
can escape. But it remains that advance cannot improve the position
of those who, by virtue of self or environment, cannot participate.

With the transition of the very poor from a majority to a compara- 17
tive minority position, there has been a change in their political position. Any tendency of a politician to identify himself with those of the
lowest estate usually brought the reproaches of the well-to-do. Political pandering and demagoguery were naturally suspected. But, for the
man so reproached, there was the compensating advantage of align-
ment with a large majority. Now any politician who speaks for the
very poor is speaking for a small and generally inarticulate minority.

As a result, the modern liberal politician regularly aligns himself not with the poverty-ridden members of the community but with the far more numerous people who enjoy the far more affluent income of (say) the modern trade union member or the intellectual. Ambrose Bierce, in *The Devil's Dictionary*, called poverty "a file provided for the teeth of the rats of reform."[5] It is so no longer. Reform now concerns itself with the needs of people who are relatively well-to-do—whether the comparison be with their own past or with those who are really at the bottom of the income ladder.

In consequence, a notable feature of efforts to help the very poor is   18
their absence of any very great political appeal.[6] Politicians have found it possible to be indifferent where they could not be derisory. And very few have been under a strong compulsion to support these efforts.

The concern for inequality and deprivation had vitality only so   19
long as the many suffered while a few had much. It did not survive as a decisive political issue in a time when the many had much even though others had much more. It is our misfortune that when inequality declined as an issue, the slate was not left clean. A residual and in some ways rather more hopeless problem remained.

An affluent society, that is also both compassionate and rational   20
would, no doubt, secure to all who needed it the minimum income essential for decency and comfort. The corrupting effect on the human spirit of unearned revenue has unquestionably been exaggerated as, indeed, have the character-building values of hunger and privation. To secure to each family a minimum income, as a normal function of the society, would help ensure that the misfortunes of parents, deserved or otherwise, were not visited on their children. It would help ensure that poverty was not self-perpetuating. Most of the reaction, which no doubt would be adverse, is based on obsolete attitudes. When poverty was a majority phenomenon, such action could not be afforded. A poor society, as this essay has previously shown, had to enforce the rule that the person who did not work could not eat. And possibly it was justified in the added cruelty of applying the rule to those who could not work or whose efficiency was far below par. An affluent society has no similar excuse for such rigor. It can use the forthright remedy of providing income for those without. Nothing requires such a society

---

[5]***Ambrose Bierce (1842–1914?)*** A southern American writer noted for satirical writings such as the one quoted.

[6]This was true of the Office of Economic Opportunity—the so-called poverty program—and was ultimately the reason for its effective demise. [Galbraith's note]

to be compassionate. But it no longer has a high philosophical justification for callousness.

The notion that income is a remedy for indigency has a certain 21 forthright appeal.[7] As elsewhere argued, it would also ease the problems of economic management by reducing the reliance on production as a source of income. The provision of such a basic source of income must henceforth be the first and the strategic step in the attack on poverty.

But it is only one step. In the past, we have suffered from the sup- 22 position that the only remedy for poverty lies in remedies that allow people to look after themselves—to participate in the economy. Nothing has better served the conscience of people who wished to avoid inconvenient or expensive action than an appeal, on this issue, to Calvinist precept—"The only sound way to solve the problem of poverty is to help people help themselves." But this does not mean that steps to allow participation and to keep poverty from being self-perpetuating are unimportant. On the contrary. It requires that the investment in children from families presently afflicted be as little below normal as possible. If the children of poor families have first-rate schools and school attendance is properly enforced; if the children, though badly fed at home, are well nourished at school; if the community has sound health services, and the physical well-being of the children is vigilantly watched; if there is opportunity for advanced education for those who qualify regardless of means; and if, especially in the case of urban communities, housing is ample and housing standards are enforced, the streets are clean, the laws are kept, and recreation is adequate—then there is a chance that the children of the very poor will come to maturity without inhibiting disadvantage. In the case of insular poverty, this remedy requires that the services of the community be assisted from outside. Poverty is self-perpetuating partly because the poorest communities are poorest in the services which would eliminate it. To eliminate poverty efficiently, we must, indeed, invest more than proportionately in the children of the poor community. It is there that high quality schools, strong health services, special provision for nutrition and recreation are most needed to compensate for the very low investment which families are able to make in their own offspring.

The effect of education and related investment in individuals is to 23 help them overcome the restraints that are imposed by their environ-

---

[7]As earlier noted, in the first edition, the provision of a guaranteed income was discussed but dismissed as "beyond reasonable hope." [Galbraith's note]

ment. These need also to be attacked even more directly—by giving the mobility that is associated with plentiful, good and readily available housing, by provision of comfortable, efficient and economical mass transport, by making the environment pleasant and safe, and by eliminating the special health handicaps that afflict the poor.

Nor is case poverty entirely resistant to such remedies. Much can 24 be done to treat those characteristics which cause people to reject or be rejected by the modern industrial society. Educational deficiencies can be overcome. Mental deficiencies can be treated. Physical handicaps can be remedied. The limiting factor is not a lack of knowledge of what can be done. Overwhelmingly, it is a shortage of money.

It will be clear that, to a remarkable extent, the remedy for poverty 25 leads to the same requirements as those for social balance. The restraints that confine people to the ghetto are those that result from insufficient investment in the public sector. And the means to escape from these constraints and to break their hold on subsequent generations just mentioned—better nutrition and health, better education, more and better housing, better mass transport, an environment more conducive to effective social participation—all, with rare exceptions, call for massively greater investment in the public sector. In recent years, the problems of the urban ghetto have been greatly discussed but with little resultant effect. To a certain extent, the search for deeper social explanations of its troubles has been motivated by the hope that these (together with more police) might lead to solutions that would somehow elide the problem of cost. It is an idle hope. The modern urban household is an extremely expensive thing. We have not yet taken the measure of the resources that must be allocated to its public tasks if it is to be agreeable or even tolerable. And first among the symptoms of an insufficient allocation is the teeming discontent of the modern ghetto.

A further feature of these remedies is to be observed. Their conse- 26 quence is to allow participation in the economic life of the larger community—to make people and the children of people who are now idle productive. This means that they will add to the total output of goods and services. We see once again that even by its own terms the present preoccupation with the private sector of the economy as compared with the whole spectrum of human needs is inefficient. The parallel with investment in the supply of trained and educated manpower discussed above will be apparent.

But increased output of goods is not the main point. Even to the 27 most intellectually reluctant reader, it will now be evident that enhanced productive efficiency is not the motif of this volume. The very fact that increased output offers itself as a by-product of the effort to eliminate poverty is one of the reasons. No one would be called up to write at such length on a problem so easily solved as that of increasing production. The main point lies elsewhere. Poverty—grim, degrading and ineluctable—is not remarkable in India. For few, the fate is otherwise. But in the United States, the survival of poverty is remarkable. We ignore it because we share with all societies at all times the capacity for not seeing what we do not wish to see. Anciently this has enabled the nobleman to enjoy his dinner while remaining oblivious to the beggars around his door. In our own day, it enables us to travel in comfort by Harlem and into the lush precincts of midtown Manhattan. But while our failure to notice can be explained, it cannot be excused. "Poverty," Pitt[8] exclaimed, "is no disgrace but it is damned annoying." In the contemporary United States, it is not annoying but it is a disgrace.

---

[8]***William Pitt (1759–1806)*** British prime minister from 1783 to 1801 and, briefly, again in 1804 and 1805.

QUESTIONS

1. What is the fundamental difference between the attitude Alfred Marshall held toward the poor (para. 1) and the attitude contemporary economists hold?
2. Galbraith avoids a specific definition of poverty because he says it changes from society to society. How would you define poverty as it exists in our society? What are its major indicators?
3. According to Galbraith, what is the relationship of politics to poverty?
4. What, according to this essay, seem to be the causes of poverty?
5. Clarify the distinctions Galbraith makes between case poverty and insular poverty. Are they reasonable distinctions?
6. Does Galbraith oversimplify the issues of poverty in America?
7. Galbraith first published this piece in 1958. How much has changed in our attitudes toward poverty since then? What kinds of progress seem to have been made on the question of poverty?

WRITING ASSIGNMENTS

1. In paragraph 4, Galbraith says, "People are poverty-stricken when their income, even if adequate for survival, falls radically behind that of the com-

munity. Then they cannot have what the larger community regards as the minimum necessary for decency; and they cannot wholly escape, therefore, the judgment of the larger community that they are indecent. They are degraded for, in the literal sense, they live outside the grades or categories which the community regards as acceptable." Examine what he says here and explain what he means. Is this an accurate description of poverty? Would you amend it? If so, in what ways? If you accept his description of poverty, what public policy would you recommend to deal with it? What would be the consequences of accepting Galbraith's description?

2. Galbraith points out some anomalies of poverty and place. For example, he notes that West Virginia is rich in resources but that its people have been notable for their poverty. Connecticut, on the other hand, is poor in resources, with stony, untillable land, and its people have been notable for their wealth. Some economists have also pointed out that, when the Americas were settled, South America had the gold, the lush tropics that yielded food and fruit for the asking, and that it held the promise of immense wealth. North America had a harsh climate, stubborn soil conditions, and dense forests that needed clearing. Yet North America has less poverty than does South America. Write a brief essay in which you consider whether what is said above is too simplified to be useful. If it is not, what do you think is the reason for the economic distinctions that Galbraith and others point out?

3. What personal experiences have you had with poverty? Are you familiar with examples of case poverty? If so, describe them in such a way as to help others understand them. Do you have any insight into the causes that produced the poverty? How could poor people in this category be rescued from poverty? What is their social situation in the community?

4. Examine the newspapers for the last several days and look through back issues of magazines such as *Time, Newsweek*, the *New Republic, The New Leader*, or *U.S. News and World Report*. How much attention do they pay to the question of poverty? Present a survey of the views you find and compare them with Galbraith's. How much agreement or disagreement is there? Would the level of the nation's concern with poverty please Galbraith?

5. Write a brief essay in which you delineate what you think is the current political attitude toward poverty. If possible, gather some recent statements made by politicians. Analyze them to see how closely they tally with Galbraith's concerns and views. Do any specific politicians act as spokespeople for the poor?

6. Galbraith says that the position of poverty has resulted from a dramatic change in our society, from a circumstance in which most people were poor and only a few were affluent to one in which most people are affluent and only a few are poor. Is Galbraith correct in this assessment? Interview your parents and grandparents and their friends. By this means, establish the validity of Galbraith's claim, then explain what you feel are the prob-

lems the poor face as a result of their minority status. If possible, during your interviews ask what feelings your parents and their friends have about the poverty-stricken. What feelings do you have? Are they shared by your friends?

PART THREE

IDEAS IN THE WORLD OF PSYCHOLOGY

Sigmund Freud · · · Carl Jung
Karen Horney · · · B. F. Skinner

INTRODUCTION

PSYCHOLOGY has often been described as a science in its infancy; however, it has done an immense amount of growing in the twentieth century. All the psychologists in this part are modern primarily because most of the exciting discoveries in psychology were made during their professional careers. The most important discovery is probably that of the unconscious mind, which was first discussed in the works of the American psychologist William James (1842–1910). But it was the work of Sigmund Freud around the turn of the century that most startled the world of psychology, since he began to suggest the functions of the unconscious mind as a repository of painful emotions and repressed thoughts. He also suggested means by which the unconscious mind could be apprehended—through the complex symbolic language of dreams and through free-associating during conversation with an analyst. Thus, his psychoanalytic methods are based upon the analysis of a patient's dreams and of the patient's free association while lying on a couch and talking with a doctor.

One of Freud's most controversial theories is that nervous disorders are sexual in origin. He probably most alarmed the psychological community by his theories of infantile sexuality, in which he demonstrated that even infants have sexual urges and needs. He also postulated certain theories concerning instincts that are natural to human beings. For a time, it was exceedingly controversial to suggest that humans, like other animals, had instincts. Freud, however, dared to assert that our sexual needs, as well as our need for sustenance, was instinctive and that because we all live in a regulated community, we are bound to have conflicts between our instinctual and our social needs.

What Sigmund Freud has to say in his essay on infantile sexuality seems fairly tame and perhaps even a bit obvious to us today. But it was a bombshell in its own day. People had always thought that children had no psychosexual awareness or drives until after puberty. Freud demonstrated that the sexual drive, which he had predicated as the strongest of psychic drives, was present even in the infant. His study was a pioneering effort that changed the nature of psychology entirely.

Freud's most distinguished follower was Carl Jung, who eventually broke away from Freud's influence and developed his own distinctive approach to psychology. Whereas Freud concentrated on the unique qualities of the individual's unconscious, Jung began to conceive of something quite different: a collective unconscious of the entire race. Freud believed that every individual fashioned a unique unconscious as a result of personal experiences in his or her social environment. In addition to that, Jung postulated a collective unconscious that is transmitted to everyone through heredity. It is observable in a pattern of responses to what he called archetypal situations, which are biologically and culturally applicable to people in all times and places.

Like Freud, Jung saw that myth was a rich source of insight into our psychological needs. Jung, however, went so far as to insist that myth is a repository of the collective unconscious of the race. By examining it, we can develop insights into our own psychological nature. His "The Concept of the Collective Unconscious" gives only some of his reasoning. He developed the idea much further in later work when he began to explore specific archetypal patterns that he felt pertained to all of us. The archetypes are connected with basic human situations—one of them, the mother archetype, pertains to the natural relationship we all have with our mother. Even if we did not know our own mother, we still have a psychological need to establish a healthy relationship with our concept of the mother. This explains, to an extent, the profusion of myths centering on a mother figure. The same may be said of the father and myths centering on father figures. Jung's essay on the collective unconscious is only an introduction to his ideas, but it is a remarkable and certainly a controversial one.

Karen Horney, a contemporary of both Freud and Jung, developed certain special interests when she began to respond to some of Freud's theories concerning the sexual development of women. His theory was that girls naturally developed penis envy when they realized that they lacked some anatomical features that boys possessed. Horney began to examine the evidence she gathered by relying not only on myth but also on the behavior of primitive peoples as recorded in anthropological studies. She theorized that envy was more on the part of men than of women. She asserted that men are envious of the power of women to create life out of their bodies and that as a result, they ascribe extraordinary powers to female deities.

Ultimately, Horney began to work in detail on developing coherent theories of feminine psychology, an effort that constituted the bulk of her work in Germany before she came to the United States when Hitler rose to power in the 1930s. Her work is distinctive, scholarly, and thorough. Like the work of Freud and Jung, hers too is controversial.

B. F. Skinner, quite a different kind of psychologist, is no less controversial. His theories of behavioral psychology assume that human beings are, like all animals, a product of the interaction between our psychology and our environment. Our behavior can be modified by both rewards and punishments. Moreover, he believes that in our society the price we pay for the freedom to do as we are able to do may be too great. He believes, too, that we have reached the point at which we will have to surrender much of this freedom in order to achieve greater stability and happiness. Skinner's views are not popular with traditional humanists because he professes a "scientific" view of humankind that sees us as much more closely related to animals than we have been willing to admit.

B. F. Skinner, rarely noted for his stylistic felicities, relies on the time-honored technique of the rhetorical question. The title of his essay—"What Is Man?"—is a question that the ancients struggled with. It implies that a special relationship exists between man and the animal world and between man and the divine world. Like the other authors in this part, Skinner moves to examine a certain body of evidence and then to draw conclusions that he feels may not be popular. His conclusions concerning the extent to which we are self-directed individuals are difficult for most of us to accept. The answer to the question What is man? is not at all what we might have wished.

These writers are exceptionally skillful, though their purpose is to explain, not to dazzle us. They write an expository prose that strives to be as clear as possible while also convincing us of the truth of their position. None of these writers makes an emotional appeal to us; each is careful to provide evidence and to caution us concerning the inferences we may draw from it. Each provides careful reasoning and guideposts to help us understand exactly where we are in the essay and what is implied by the points made.

SIGMUND FREUD

Infantile Sexuality

SIGMUND FREUD (1856–1939) is, in the minds of many, the father of modern psychology. He developed the psychoanalytic method, the examination of the mind using methods of dream analysis, the analysis of the unconscious through free association, and the correlation of findings with attitudes toward sexuality and sexual development. His theories changed the way people treated neurosis and most other mental disorders. Today his theories are spread all over the world.

Freud was born in Freiberg, Moravia (now in Czechoslovakia), and moved to Vienna, Austria, when he was four. He lived and worked in Vienna until he was put under house arrest by the Nazis. He was released in 1938 and moved to London. The psychoanalytic movement of the twentieth century has often been described as a Viennese movement, or at least as a movement closely tied to the prosperity of the Viennese middle-class intellectuals of the time.

As a movement, psychoanalysis shocked most of the world by postulating a superego, which establishes high standards of behavior;

From *Three Essays on the Theory of Sexuality*. Translated by A. A. Brill.

an ego, which corresponds to the apparent personality; an id, which includes the deepest primitive forces of life; and an unconscious into which thoughts and memories we cannot face are "repressed" or "sublimated." The origin of much mental illness, the theory presumes, is in the inability of the mind to find a way to sublimate—express in harmless and often creative ways—the painful thoughts which have been repressed. Dreams and unconscious actions sometimes act as "releases" or harmless expressions of these thoughts and memories.

Difficult as some of these ideas were to accept, they did not cause quite the furor of the present excerpt, from a book that was hotly debated and sometimes violently rejected: **Three Essays on the Theory of Sexuality** *(1905)*. At that time, Freud had become convinced by his work with neurotic patients that much of what disturbed them was connected with their sexuality. That led him to review the research on infantile sexuality and add to it with his own findings. It was also natural to his way of thinking to produce a theory of behavior built upon his researches.

What infuriated people so much was the suggestion that tiny children, even infants, had a sexual life. That it should also figure in the psychological health of the adult was almost as serious. Most people rejected the idea out of hand because it did not square with what they already believed or with what they felt they observed. The typical Freudian habit of seeing psychoanalytic "meaning" in otherwise innocent gestures, such as thumbsucking and bed-wetting, was brought into play in his observations on the sexuality of infants. Freud had a gift for interpretation—analysis—of apparently meaningless events. His capacity to find meaning in such events is still resented by many readers, but that is in part because they do not accept Freud's view that the psychological being—the person—makes every word, gesture, and act "meaningful" to his whole being. For Freud there are no accidents; there are psychological intentions. When we understand those intentions, we begin to understand ourselves.

Freud knew that sexuality was perhaps the most powerful force in the psyche. He knew that middle-class propriety would be revolted by having to contemplate the concepts he presents in this piece. It is doubtful that he expected the middle class to accept his views. Yet he was rightly convinced that his views were too important to be swept aside in fear that society might be offended.

FREUD'S RHETORIC

Because this treatise is not aimed at a general public, Freud is left free to address a general scientific community. He spares them no details regarding bodily functions; he adds little color to an already graceful style. His rhetorical technique is quite simple: he establishes a theory, reviews the evidence which he and others have gathered, then derives certain conclusions from his process.

One would not think of this piece as having a beginning, a middle, and a conclusion. It has rather independent sections that treat specific problems and observations. All of the sections come under the general heading of infantile sexuality, and all relate to the general theory that Freud develops: that there is a connection between infantile sexuality and mature sexuality and that it is revealed in the common amnesia—the forgetting or repressing from conscious memory—of experiences related to sexual awareness in both the infant and the hysteric patient.

If one had to give a name to his rhetorical approach, it might best be called the process of evidence and inference. In this sense, it is similar to the accepted methods of science in most fields. Evidence points to an inference, which then must be tested by analysis. We observe the process as we read Freud's work.

This method sounds very straightforward and artless. Freud's writing is generally marked by those qualities. But there is one rhetorical technique which he is the master of: the memorable phrase. For example, the term "psychoanalysis," which we take so much for granted, was invented by Freud when he was thirty-nine; it is now universally used. The term "Oedipus complex," describing the condition of wishing your same-sex parent dead so that you will be left to "marry" your opposite-sex parent, is also universal now. "Penis envy," used in this selection, is known worldwide, as is the "castration complex." Freud changed both our language and our world.

Infantile Sexuality

The Neglect of the Infantile. It is a part of popular belief about the 1
sexual instinct that it is absent in childhood and that it first appears
in the period of life known as puberty. This, though a common error,
is serious in its consequences and is chiefly due to our ignorance of
the fundamental principles of the sexual life. A comprehensive study
of the sexual manifestations of childhood would probably reveal to us
the essential features of the sexual instinct and would show us its
development and its composition from various sources.

It is quite remarkable that those writers who endeavor to explain 2
the qualities and reactions of the adult individual have given so much
more attention to the ancestral period than to the period of the individual's own existence—that is, they have attributed more influence
to heredity than to childhood. As a matter of fact, it might well be
supposed that the influence of the latter period would be easier to understand, and that it would be entitled to more consideration than heredity. To be sure, one occasionally finds in medical literature notes
on the premature sexual activities of small children, about erections
and masturbation and even reactions resembling coitus, but these are
referred to merely as exceptional occurrences, as curiosities, or as
deterring[1] examples of premature perversity. No author has, to my
knowledge, recognized the normality of the sexual instinct in childhood, and in the numerous writings on the development of the child
the chapter on "Sexual Development" is usually passed over.

Infantile Amnesia. The reason for this remarkable negligence I seek 3
partly in conventional considerations, which influence writers because
of their own bringing up, and partly to a psychic phenomenon which
thus far has remained unexplained. I refer to the peculiar amnesia
which veils from most people (not from all) the first years of their
childhood, usually the first six or eight years. So far, it has not occurred to us that this amnesia should surprise us, though we have good
reasons for it. For we are informed that during those years which have
left nothing except a few incomprehensible memory fragments, we

---

[1]*deterring* frightening.

have vividly reacted to impressions, that we have manifested human pain and pleasure and that we have expressed love, jealousy and other passions as they then affected us. Indeed, we are told that we have uttered remarks which proved to grown-ups that we possessed understanding and a budding power of judgment. Still we know nothing of all this when we become older. Why does our memory lag behind all our other psychic activities? We really have reason to believe that at no time of life are we more capable of impressions and reproductions[2] than during the years of childhood.

On the other hand we must assume, or we may convince ourselves through psychological observations on others, that the very impressions which we have forgotten have nevertheless left the deepest traces in our psychic life, and acted as determinants for our whole future development. We conclude therefore that we do not deal with a real forgetting of infantile impressions but rather with an amnesia similar to that observed in neurotics for later experiences, the nature of which consists in their being kept away from consciousness (repression). But what forces bring about this repression of the infantile impressions? He who can solve this riddle will also explain hysterical amnesia.[3]

We shall not, however, hesitate to assert that the existence of the infantile amnesia gives us a new point of comparison between the psychic states of the child and those of the psychoneurotic. We have already encountered another point of comparison when confronted by the fact that the sexuality of the psychoneurotic preserves the infantile character or has returned to it. May there not be an ultimate connection between the infantile and the hysterical amnesias?

The connection between infantile and hysterical amnesias is really more than a mere play of wit. Hysterical amnesia which serves the repression can only be explained by the fact that the individual already possesses a sum of memories which were withdrawn from conscious disposal and which by associative connection now seize that which is acted upon by the repelling forces of the repression emanating from consciousness. We may say that without infantile amnesia there would be no hysterical amnesia.

I therefore believe that the infantile amnesia which causes the individual to look upon his childhood as if it were a *prehistoric* time and

4

5

6

7

---

[2] ***reproductions*** imitations, such as mimicry.
[3] ***hysterical amnesia*** The forgetfulness induced by psychological shock; Freud sees a connection between it and the fact that we forget most of our earliest experience, even though it is of crucial importance to our growth.

conceals from him the beginning of his own sexual life—that this amnesia, is responsible for the fact that one does not usually attribute any value to the infantile period in the development of the sexual life. One single observer cannot fill the gap which has been thus produced in our knowledge. As early as 1896, I had already emphasized the significance of childhood for the origin of certain important phenomena connected with the sexual life, and since then I have not ceased to put into the foreground the importance of the infantile factor for sexuality.

The Sexual Latency Period
of Childhood and Its Interruptions

The extraordinary frequent discoveries of apparently abnormal and exceptional sexual manifestations in childhood, as well as the discovery of infantile reminiscences in neurotics, which were hitherto unconscious, allow us to sketch the following picture of the sexual behavior of childhood. It seems certain that the newborn child brings with it the germs of sexual feelings which continue to develop for some time and then succumb to a progressive suppression, which may in turn be broken through by the regular advances of the sexual development or may be checked by individual idiosyncrasies. Nothing is known concerning the laws and periodicity of this oscillating course of development. It seems, however, that the sexual life of the child mostly manifests itself in the third or fourth year in some form accessible to observation. 8

Sexual Inhibition. It is during this period of total or at least partial latency[4] that the psychic forces develop which later act as inhibitions on the sexual life, and narrow its direction like dams. These psychic forces are loathing, shame, and moral and esthetic ideal demands. We may gain the impression that the erection of these dams in the civilized child is the work of education; and surely education contributes much to it. In reality, however, this development is organically determined and can occasionally be produced without the help of education. Indeed education remains properly within its assigned domain if 9

---

[4]*latency* period when sexual interests are not evident, as before puberty.

it strictly follows the path laid out by the organic,[5] and only imprints it somewhat cleaner and deeper.

Reaction Formation and Sublimation. What are the means that ac- 10 complish these very important constructions so important for the later personal culture and normality? They are probably brought about at the cost of the infantile sexuality itself. The influx of this sexuality does not stop even in this latency period, but its energy is deflected either wholly or partially from sexual utilization and conducted to other aims. The historians of civilization seem to be unanimous in the opinion that such deflection of sexual motive powers from sexual aims to new aims, a process which merits the name of *sublimation*,[6] has furnished powerful components for all cultural accomplishments. We will, therefore, add that the same process acts in the development of every individual, and that it begins to act in the sexual latency period.

We can also venture an opinion about the mechanisms of such sub- 11 limation. The sexual feelings of these infantile years would on the one hand be unusable, since the procreating functions are postponed—this is the chief character of the latency period; on the other hand, they would as such be perverse, as they would emanate from erogenous zones and from impulses which in the individual's course of development could only evoke a feeling of displeasure. They, therefore, awaken psychic counterforces (feelings of reaction), which build up the already mentioned psychical dams of disgust, shame and morality.

The Interruptions of the Latency Period. Without deluding ourselves 12 as to the hypothetical nature and deficient clearness of our understanding regarding the infantile period of latency and delay, we will return to reality and state that such a utilization of the infantile sexuality represents an ideal bringing up from which the development of the individual usually deviates in some measure, often very considerably. A part of the sexual manifestation which has withdrawn from sublimation occasionally breaks through, or a sexual activity remains throughout the whole duration of the latency period until the rein-

---

[5]***the organic***   Freud means that the organism—the person—comes to certain understandings as a factor of growth and development. Education must respect organic growth and try not to get "out of order" with it.

[6]**sublimation**   A psychological process whereby drives, such as the sexual drive, are transformed into different expressions, such as transforming a powerful sexual drive into a drive to make money or to excel in a given field.

forced breaking through of the sexual instinct in puberty. In so far as they have paid any attention to infantile sexuality, the educators behave as if they shared our views concerning the formation of the moral defense forces at the cost of sexuality. They seem to know that sexual activity makes the child uneducable, for they consider all sexual manifestations of the child as an "evil" in the face of which little can be accomplished. We have, however, every reason for directing our attention to those phenomena so much feared by the educators, for we expect to find in them the solution of the primary structure of the sexual instinct.

The Manifestations of Infantile Sexuality

Thumbsucking. For reasons which we shall discuss later, we will take 13 as a model of the infantile sexual manifestations thumbsucking, to which the Hungarian pediatrist, Lindner, has devoted an excellent essay.

Thumbsucking, which manifests itself in the nursing baby and 14 which may be continued till maturity or throughout life, consists in a rhythmic repetition of sucking contact with the mouth (the lips), wherein the purpose of taking nourishment is excluded. A part of the lip itself, the tongue, which is another preferable skin region within reach, and even the big toe—may be taken as objects for sucking. Simultaneously, there is also a desire to grasp things, which manifests itself in a rhythmical pulling of the ear lobe and which may cause the child to grasp a part of another person (generally the ear) for the same purpose. The pleasure-sucking is connected with a full absorption of attention and leads to sleep or even to a motor reaction in the form of an orgasm. Pleasure-sucking is often combined with a rubbing contact with certain sensitive parts of the body, such as the breast and external genitals. It is by this path that many children go from thumbsucking to masturbation.

Lindner himself clearly recognized the sexual nature of this activ- 15 ity and openly emphasized it. In the nursery, thumbsucking is often treated in the same way as any other sexual "naughtiness" of the child. A very strong objection was raised against this view by many pediatrists and neurologists, which in part is certainly due to the confusion between the terms "sexual" and "genital." This contradiction raises the difficult question, which cannot be avoided, namely, in what general traits do we wish to recognize the sexual expression of the child.

I believe that the association of the manifestations into which we have gained an insight through psychoanalytic investigation justifies us in claiming thumbsucking as a sexual activity. Through thumbsucking we can study directly the essential features of infantile sexual activities.

Autoerotism. It is our duty here to devote more time to this manifestation. Let us emphasize the most striking character of this sexual activity which is, that the impulse is not directed to other persons but that the child gratifies himself on his own body; to use the happy term invented by Havelock Ellis, we will say that he is *autoerotic.*[7]

It is, moreover, clear that the action of the thumbsucking child is determined by the fact that he seeks a pleasure which he has already experienced and now remembers. Through the rhythmic sucking on a portion of the skin or mucous membrane, he finds gratification in the simplest way. It is also easy to conjecture on what occasions the child first experienced this pleasure which he now strives to renew. The first and most important activity in the child's life, the sucking from the mother's breast (or its substitute), must have acquainted him with this pleasure. We would say that the child's lips behaved like an *erogenous zone,* and that the stimulus from the warm stream of milk was really the cause of the pleasurable sensation. To be sure, the gratification of the erogenous zone was at first united with the gratification of the need for nourishment. The sexual activity leans first on one of the self-preservative functions and only later makes itself independent of it. He who sees a satiated child sink back from the mother's breast and fall asleep with reddened cheeks and blissful smile, will have to admit that this picture remains as typical of the expression of sexual gratification in later life. But the desire for repetition of sexual gratification is then separated from the desire for taking nourishment; a separation which becomes unavoidable with the appearance of teeth when the nourishment is no longer sucked but chewed. The child does not make use of a strange object for sucking but prefers his own skin, because it is more convenient, because it thus makes himself independent of the outer world which he cannot control, and because in this way he creates for himself, as it were, a second, even if an inferior, erogenous zone. This inferiority of this second region urges him later to seek the same parts, the lips of another person. ("It is a pity that I cannot kiss myself," might be attributed to him.)

16

17

---

[7]**autoerotic** English psychologist Havelock Ellis (1859–1939) used the term to refer to masturbatory behavior.

Not all children suck their thumbs. It may be assumed that it is   18
found only in children in whom the erogenous significance of the lip-
zone is constitutionally reinforced. If the latter is retained in some
children, they develop into kissing epicures with a tendency to perverse kissing, or as men, they show a strong desire for drinking and
smoking. But should repression come into play, they then show disgust for eating and evince hysterical vomiting. By virtue of the community of the lip-zone, the repression encroaches upon the instinct of
nourishment. Many of my female patients showing disturbances in
eating, such as *hysterical globus,*[8] choking sensations and vomiting
have been energetic thumbsuckers in infancy.

In thumbsucking or pleasure-sucking, we are already able to ob-   19
serve the three essential characters of an infantile sexual manifestation. It has its origin in an *anaclitic*[9] relation to a physical function
which is very important for life; it does not yet know any sexual object, that is, it is *autoerotic,* and its sexual aim is under the control of
an *erogenous zone.* Let us assume for the present that these characteristics also hold true for most of the other activities of the infantile
sexual instinct.

The Sexual Aim of
the Infantile Sexuality

Characteristic Erogenous Zones. From the example of thumbsucking,   20
we may gather a great many points useful for distinguishing an erogenous zone. It is a portion of skin or mucous membrane in which stimuli produce a feeling of pleasure of definite quality. There is no doubt
that the pleasure-producing stimuli are governed by special conditions;
as yet we do not know them. The rhythmic characters must play some
part and this strongly suggests an analogy to tickling. It does not, however, appear so certain whether the character of the pleasurable feeling
evoked by the stimulus can be designated as "peculiar," and in what
part of this peculiarity the sexual factor consists. Psychology is still
groping in the dark when it concerns matters of pleasure and pain, and
the most cautious assumption is therefore the most advisable. We may
perhaps later come upon reasons which seem to support the peculiar
quality of the sensation of pleasure.

---

[8]**hysterical globus**   abnormal reaction to putting things in the mouth.
[9]**anaclitic**   characterized by a strong emotional—but not sexual—dependence.

The erogenous quality may adhere most notably to definite regions 21 of the body. As is shown by the example of thumbsucking, there are predestined erogenous zones. But the same example also shows that any other region of skin or mucous membrane may assume the function of an erogenous zone, hence it must bring along a certain adaptability for it. The production of the sensation of pleasure therefore depends more on the quality of the stimulus than on the nature of the bodily region. The thumbsucking child looks around on his body and selects any portion of it for pleasure-sucking, and becoming accustomed to this particular part, he then prefers it. If he accidentally strikes upon a predestined region, such as breast, nipple or genitals, it naturally gets the preference. A very analogous tendency to displacement is again found in the symptomatology of hysteria. In this neurosis, the repression mostly affects the genital zones proper, and they in turn transmit their excitability to the other zones which are usually dormant in adult life, but then behave exactly like genitals. But besides this, just as in thumbsucking, any other region of the body may become endowed with the excitation of the genitals and raised to an erogenous zone. Erogenous and hysterogenous zones show the same characters.[10]

The Infantile Sexual Aim. The sexual aim of the infantile impulse 22 consists in the production of gratification through the proper excitation of this or that selected erogenous zone. To have a desire for its repetition, this gratification must have been previously experienced, and we may be sure that nature has devised definite means so as not to leave this experience of gratification to mere chance. The arrangement which has fulfilled this purpose for the lip-zone, we have already discussed; it is the simultaneous connection of this part of the body with the taking of nourishment. We shall also meet other similar mechanisms as sources of sexuality. The state of desire for repetition of gratification can be recognized through a peculiar feeling of tension which in itself is rather of a painful character, and through a *centrally-conditioned* feeling of itching or sensitiveness which is projected into the peripheral erogenous zone. The sexual aim may therefore be formulated by stating that the main object is to substitute for the projected feeling of sensitiveness in the erogenous zone that outer stimulus which removes the feeling of sensitiveness by evoking the feeling

---

[10]Further reflection and evaluation of other observations lead me to attribute the quality of erotism to all parts of the body and inner organs. [Freud's note]

of gratification. This external stimulus consists usually in a manipulation which is analogous to sucking.

It is in full accord with our physiological knowledge, if the need 23 happens to be awakened also peripherally, through an actual change in the ercgenous zone. The action is puzzling only to some extent, as one stimulus seems to want another applied to the same place for its own abrogation.

The Masturbatic
Sexual Manifestations

It is a matter of great satisfaction to know that there is nothing 24 further of great importance to learn about the sexual activity of the child, after the impulse of one erogenous zone has become comprehensible to us. The most pronounced differences are found in the action necessary for the gratification, which consists in sucking for the lip-zone, and which must be replaced by other muscular actions in the other zones, depending on their situation and nature.

The Activity of the Anal Zone. Like the lip-zone, the anal zone is, 25 through its position, adapted to produce an anaclisis of sexuality to other functions of the body. It should be assumed that the erogenous significance of this region of the body was originally very strong. Through psychoanalysis, one finds, not without surprise, the many transformations that normally take place in the sexual excitations emanating from here, and that this zone often retains for life a considerable fragment of genital irritability. The intestinal catarrhs[11] which occur quite frequently during infancy, produce sensitive irritations in this zone, and we often hear it said that intestinal catarrh at this delicate age causes "nervousness." In later neurotic diseases, they exert a definite influence on the symptomatic expression of the neurosis, placing at its disposal the whole sum of intestinal disturbances. Considering the erogenous significance of the anal zone which has been retained at least in transformation, one should not laugh at the hemorrhoidal influences to which the old medical literature attached so much weight in the explanation of neurotic states.

Children utilizing the erogenous sensitiveness of the anal zone, can 26 be recognized by their holding back of fecal masses until through ac-

---

[11]*catarrhs* inflammation of the membrane.

cumulation there result violent muscular contractions; the passage of these masses through the anus is apt to produce a marked irritation of the mucous membrane. Besides the pain, this must also produce a sensation of pleasure. One of the surest premonitions of later eccentricity or nervousness is when an infant obstinately refuses to empty his bowel when placed on the chamber by the nurse, and controls this function at his own pleasure. It naturally does not concern him that he will soil his bed; all he cares for is not to lose the subsidiary pleasure in defecating. Educators have again shown the right inkling when they designate children who withhold these functions as naughty.

The content of the bowel which acts as a stimulus to the sexually 27 sensitive surface of mucous membrane, behaves like the precursor of another organ which does not become active until after the phase of childhood. In addition, it has other important meanings to the nursling. It is evidently treated as an additional part of the body; it represents the first "donation," the disposal of which expresses the pliability while the retention of it can express the spite of the little being towards his environment. From the idea of "donation," he later derives the meaning of the "babe," which according to one of the infantile sexual theories, is supposed to be acquired through eating, and born through the bowel.

The retention of fecal masses, which is at first intentional in order 28 to utilize them, as it were, for masturbatic excitation of the anal zone, is at least one of the roots of constipation so frequent in neurotics. The whole significance of the anal zone is mirrored in the fact that there are but few neurotics who have not their special scatologic[12] customs, ceremonies, etc., which they retain with cautious secrecy.

Real masturbatic irritation of the anal zone by means of the fingers, 29 evoked through either centrally or peripherally supported itching, is not at all rare in older children.

The Activity of the Genital Zone. Among the erogenous zones of the 30 child's body, there is one which certainly does not play the first role, and which cannot be the carrier of the earliest sexual feeling, which, however, is destined for great things in later life. In both male and female, it is connected with the voiding of urine (penis, clitoris), and in the former, it is enclosed in a sack of mucous membrane, probably in order not to miss the irritations caused by the secretions which may arouse sexual excitement at an early age. The sexual activities of this

---

[12]*scatologic* pertaining to excrement, waste, or feces.

erogenous zone, which belongs to the real genitals, are the beginning of the later "normal" sexual life.

Owing to the anatomical position, the overflowing of secretions, 31 the washing and rubbing of the body, and to certain accidental excitements (the wandering of intestinal worms in the girl), it happens that the pleasurable feeling which these parts of the body are capable of producing makes itself noticeable to the child, even during the sucking age, and thus awakens a desire for repetition. When we consider the sum of all these arrangements and bear in mind that the measures for cleanliness hardly produce a different result than uncleanliness, we can scarcely ignore the fact that the infantile masturbation from which hardly anyone escapes, forms the foundation for the future primacy of this erogenous zone for sexual activity. The action of removing the stimulus and setting free the gratification consists in a rubbing contiguity with the hand or in a certain previously-formed pressure reflex, effected by the closure of the thighs. The latter procedure seems to be the more common in girls. The preference for the hand in boys already indicates what an important part of the male sexual activity will be accomplished in the future by the mastery impulse.

I can only make it clearer if I state that the infantile masturbation 32 should be divided into three phases. The first phase belongs to the nursing period, the second to the short flourishing period of sexual activity at about the fourth year, and only the third corresponds to the one which is often considered exclusively as masturbation of puberty.

Second Phase of Childhood Masturbation. Infantile masturbation 33 seems to disappear after a brief time, but it may continue uninterruptedly till puberty and thus represent the first marked deviation from that development which is desirable for civilized man. At some time during childhood after the nursing period, the sexual instinct of the genitals re-awakens and continues active for some time until it is again suppressed, or it may continue without interruption. The possible relations are very diverse and can only be elucidated through a more precise analysis of individual cases. The details, however, of this *second* infantile sexual activity leave behind the profoundest (unconscious) impressions in the person's memory; if the individual remains healthy they determine his character and if he becomes sick after puberty, they determine the symptomatology of his neurosis. In the latter case, it is found that this sexual period is forgotten and the conscious reminiscences pointing to it are displaced; I have already mentioned that I would like to connect the normal infantile amnesia with this infantile sexual activity. By psychoanalytic investigation, it is possible to bring to consciousness the forgotten material and thereby to remove a compulsion which emanates from the unconscious psychic material.

The Return of Infantile Masturbation. The sexual excitation of the 34 nursing period returns during the designated years of childhood as a centrally determined tickling sensation demanding masturbatic gratification, or as a pollution-like process which, analogous to the pollution of maturity, may attain gratification without the aid of any action. The latter case is more frequent in girls and in the second half of childhood; its determinants are not well understood, but it often, though not regularly, seems to have as a basis a period of early active masturbation. The symptomatology of this sexual manifestation is poor; the genital apparatus is still undeveloped and all signs are therefore displayed by the urinary apparatus which is, so to say, the guardian of the genital apparatus. Most of the so-called bladder disturbances of this period are of a sexual nature; whenever the *enuresis nocturna*[13] does not represent an epileptic attack, it corresponds to a pollution.

The return of the sexual activity is determined by inner and outer 35 causes, which can be conjectured from the formation of the neurotic symptoms and can be definitely revealed by psychoanalytic investigations. The internal causes will be discussed later; the accidental outer causes attain at this time a great and permanent importance. As the first outer cause, there is the influence of seduction which prematurely treats the child as a sexual object; under conditions favoring impressions, this teaches the child the gratification of the genital zones and thus, usually forces it to repeat this gratification in masturbation. Such influences can come from adults or other children. I cannot admit that I overestimated its frequency or its significance in my contributions to the etiology[14] of hysteria, though I did not know then that normal individuals may have the same experiences in their childhood, and hence placed a higher value on seductions than on the factors found in the sexual constitution and development. It is quite obvious that no seduction is necessary to awaken the sexual life of the child, that such an awakening may come on spontaneously from inner sources.

Polymorphous-Perverse Disposition. It is instructive to know that un- 36 der the influence of seduction, the child may become polymorphous-

---

[13]**enuresis nocturna**   nighttime bed-wetting.
[14]***etiology***   the source or cause of something, especially of a disease.

perverse[15] and may be misled into all sorts of transgressions. This goes to show that the child carries along the adaptation for them in his disposition. The formation of such perversions meets but slight resistance because the psychic dams against sexual transgressions, such as shame, loathing and morality—which depend on the age of the child—are not yet erected or are only in the process of formation. In this respect, the child perhaps does not behave differently from the average uncultured woman in whom the same polymorphous-perverse disposition exists. Such a woman may remain sexually normal under usual conditions, but under the guidance of a clever seducer, she will find pleasure in every perversion and will retain it as her sexual activity. The same polymorphous or infantile disposition fits the prostitute for her professional activity, still it is absolutely impossible not to recognize in the uniform disposition to all perversions, as shown by an enormous number of prostitutes and by many women who do not necessarily follow this calling, a universal and primitive human tendency.

Partial Impulses. For the rest, the influence of seduction does not aid 37 us in unravelling the original relations of the sexual instinct, but rather confuses our understanding of the same, inasmuch as it prematurely supplies the child with a sexual object at a time when the infantile sexual instinct does not yet evince any desire for it. We must admit, however, that the infantile sexual life, though mainly under the control of erogenous zones, also shows components which from the very beginning point to other persons as sexual objects. Among these, we may mention the impulses for looking, showing off, and for cruelty, which manifest themselves somewhat independently of the erogenous zones and only later enter into intimate relationship with the sexual life; but along with the erogenous sexual activity they are noticeable even in the infantile years, as separate and independent strivings. The little child is, above all, shameless, and during his early years, he evinces definite pleasure in displaying his body and especially his sex organs. A counterpart to this perverse desire, the curiosity to see other persons' genitals, probably appears first in the later years of childhood when the hindrance of the feeling of shame has already reached a certain development. Under the influence of seduction, the looking perversion may attain great importance for the sexual life of the child. Still, from my investigations of the childhood years

---

[15]*polymorphous-perverse* Freud's term for a person whose sexual expression is oral, anal, and genital rather than the usual adult expression, essentially genital.

of normal and neurotic patients, I must conclude that the impulse for looking can appear in the child as a spontaneous sexual manifestation. Small children, whose attention has once been directed to their own genitals—usually by masturbation—are wont to progress in this direction without outside interference and to develop a vivid interest in the genitals of their playmates. As the occasion for the gratification of such curiosity is generally afforded during the gratification of both excrementitious needs, such children become *voyeurs*[16] and are zealous spectators at the voiding of urine and feces of others. After this tendency has been repressed, the curiosity to see the genitals of others (one's own or those of the other sex) remains as a tormenting desire which in some neurotic cases, furnishes the strongest motive-power for the formation of symptoms.

The cruelty component of the sexual instinct develops in the child 38 with still greater independence of those sexual activities which are connected with erogenous zones. Cruelty is intimately related to the childish character, since the inhibition which restrains the mastery impulse before it causes pain to others—that is, the capacity for sympathy—develops comparatively late. As we know that a thorough psychological analysis of this impulse has not as yet been successfully done, we may assume that the feelings of cruelty emanate from the mastery impulse and appear at a period in the sexual life before the genitals have taken on their later role. This feeling then dominates a phase of the sexual life which we shall later describe as the pregenital organization. Children who are distinguished for evincing especial cruelty to animals and playmates may be justly suspected of an intensive and a premature sexual activity which emanates from the erogenous zones. But in a simultaneous prematurity of all sexual impulses, the erogenous sexual activity surely seems to be primary. The absence of the barrier of sympathy carries with it the danger that a connection formed in childhood between cruelty and the erogenous impulses will not be broken in later life.

An erogenous source of the passive impulse for cruelty (masoch- 39 ism) is found in the painful irritation of the gluteal region,[17] which is familiar to all educators since the confessions of J. J. Rousseau. This has justly caused them to demand that physical punishment, which is usually directed to this part of the body, should be withheld from all

---

[16]**voyeurs** Those who get special pleasure from looking on, especially at something secret or private.

[17]*gluteal region* The buttocks, where children are spanked. Rousseau in his *Confessions* (1782) admits a certain pleasure in corporal punishment.

children in whom the libido might be forced into collateral roads by the later demands of cultural education.

Study of Infantile
Sexual Investigation

Inquisitiveness. About the same time as the sexual life of the child 40 reaches its first rich development, from the age of three to the age of five, there appear the beginnings of that activity which are ascribed to the impulse for knowledge and investigation. The desire for knowledge can neither be reckoned among the elementary instinctive components, nor can it be altogether subsumed under sexuality. Its activity corresponds, on the one hand, to a sublimated form of acquisition, and on the other hand, the energy with which it works comes from the looking impulse. Its relation to the sexual life, however, is of particular importance, for we have learned from psychoanalysis that the inquisitiveness of children is directed to sexual problems unusually early and in an unexpectedly intensive manner; indeed, curiosity may perhaps first be awakened by sexual problems.

The Riddle of the Sphinx. It is not theoretical but practical interests, 41 which start the work of the child's investigation activity. The menace to the conditions of his existence through the actual or expected arrival of a new child, the fear of losing the care and love which is connected with this event, cause the child to become thoughtful and sagacious.[18] Corresponding with the history of this awakening, the first problem with which he occupies himself is not the question as to the difference between the sexes, but the riddle: Where do children come from? In a distorted form which can easily be unravelled, this is the same riddle which was proposed by the Theban Sphinx.[19] The fact of the two sexes is usually first accepted by the child without struggle and hesitation. It is quite natural for the male child to presuppose in all persons he knows a genital like his own, and to find it impossible to harmonize the lack of it with his conception of others.

The Castration Complex and Penis Envy. This conviction is energet- 42 ically adhered to by the boy and stubbornly defended against the con-

---

[18]*sagacious* shrewd, cunning.
[19]*Theban Sphinx* The sphinx, half man and half lion, waited outside Thebes for years, killing all who passed by and could not solve its riddle. Oedipus answered the riddle: "What walks on four legs in the morning, two legs in the day, and three legs in the evening?" The answer: man, who crawls in infancy, walks upright in his prime, and uses a cane in old age.

tradictions which soon result, and is only given up after severe internal struggles (castration complex). The substitute formations of this lost penis on the part of the woman play a great role in the formation of many perversions.[20]

The assumption of the same (male) genital in all persons is the first 43 of the remarkable and consequential infantile sexual theories. It is of little help to the child when biological science agrees with his preconceptions and recognizes the feminine clitoris as the real substitute for the penis. The little girl does not react with similar rejections when she sees the differently formed genital of the boy. She is immediately prepared to recognize it and soon becomes envious of the penis; this envy reaches its highest point in the consequentially important wish that she also should be a boy.

Birth Theories. Many people can remember distinctly how intensely 44 they interested themselves, in the prepubescent period, in the question of where children came from. The anatomical solutions at that time read very differently; the children come out of the breast or are cut out of the body, or the navel opens itself to let them out. Outside of analysis, one only seldom remembers this investigation from early childhood years, for it had long since merged into repression; its results, however, are thoroughly uniform. One gets children by eating something special (as in the fairy tale) or they are born through the bowel, like a passage. These infantile theories recall the structures in the animal kingdom, especially the *cloaca*[21] of those animals which are on a lower scale than mammals.

Sadistic Conception of the Sexual Act. If children at so tender an age 45 witness the sexual act between adults, for which an occasion is furnished by the conviction of the adults that little children cannot understand anything sexual, they cannot help conceiving the sexual act as a kind of maltreating or overpowering; that is, it impresses them in a sadistic sense. Psychoanalysis teaches us also that such an early childhood impression contributes much to the disposition for a later sadistic displacement of the sexual aim. Besides this, children also oc-

---

[20]One has the right to speak also of a castration complex in women. Male and female children form the theory that originally the woman, too, had a penis, which has been lost through castration. The conviction finally won (that the woman has no penis) often produces in the male a lasting depreciation of the other sex. [Freud's note]

[21]**cloaca** All-purpose anal opening (as in a frog). The Latin word literally means a sewer.

cupy themselves with the problem of what the sexual act consists, or, as they grasp it, of what marriage consists, and seek the solution to the mystery usually in an intimacy carried on through the functions of urination and defecation.

The Typical Failure of the Infantile Sexual Investigation. It can be   46
stated in general about infantile sexual theories that they are models of the child's own sexual constitution, and that despite their grotesque mistakes, they show more understanding of the sexual processes than is credited to their creators. Children also notice the pregnancy of their mother and know how to interpret it correctly. The stork fable is very often related before auditors who respond with a deep, but mostly mute suspicion. Inasmuch as two elements remain unknown to infantile sexual investigation, namely, the role of the fructifying semen and the existence of the female genital opening—precisely the same points in which the infantile organization is still backward—the effort of the infantile mind regularly remains fruitless and ends in a rejection, which not infrequently leaves a lasting injury to the desire for knowledge. The sexual investigation of these early childhood years is always conducted alone; it signifies the first step towards an independent orientation of the world, and causes a marked estrangement between the child and the persons of his environment who formerly enjoyed his full confidence.

QUESTIONS

1. Freud begins with the question of the neglect of the infantile, the fact that most people paid little attention to the individual child's development (paras. 1–7). Explain what he means in these first seven paragraphs.
2. Children are said to go through a period of sexual latency. Clarify Freud's views on this question.
3. What kinds of sexual instincts are described in this selection? Are they recognizably sexual? Instinctual?
4. What are erogenous zones? Consult paragraph 20 and following.
5. Referring to paragraphs 42–43, clarify what Freud means by "castration complex" and "penis envy." What is their bearing on infantile sexuality?
6. What kind of audience would have found this work interesting and provocative? What kind would have found it repulsive? What kind would have found it unbelievable? Does Freud feel he must convince an unfriendly audience?

WRITING ASSIGNMENTS

1. Freud's complaint concerning the neglect of research and investigation into infantile behavior was written in 1905. Have things changed since then? What makes you feel that there is as much, less, or more neglect now than at that time? Do you feel that most people accept Freud's views on infantile sexuality now? Do you yourself accept his views?

2. Even the general educated public of 1905 found the theories expressed in this work utterly unacceptable. They were revolted both by Freud's views and by his methods of research. What would be distressing, alarming, or revolting about this piece? What could possibly cause people to react violently to Freud's views? Are there still people who would have such a reaction?

3. Take an aspect of Freud's theories with which you disagree and present your own argument. You may resort to your own childhood memories or those of friends. Refer directly to the aspects of Freud's thinking that seem least convincing to you and explore your reasons for rejecting them.

4. In paragraph 18, Freud refers to "kissing epicures." Establish just what is meant by that term, then clarify such persons' behavior. Do such epicures exist today? What is their current behavior? Have you known any? You may wish to supplement your personal knowledge by conducting two or three interviews with people who do know them. Be sure to try to connect your information with Freud's thoughts.

5. You may wish to offer your own theories concerning infantile sexuality. If so, you may use Freud's subject headings (where relevant to your theories) and rewrite the sections using your own thinking, your own evidence, and your own theories. Choose those subject headings that you feel are most important to your ideas. Headings such as "The Sexual Latency Period of Childhood and Its Interruptions," "Sexual Inhibition," and "The Sexual Aim of the Infantile Sexuality" may be of use to you. Naturally, you may make up your own headings if you wish.

6. The concepts of the castration complex and penis envy are both quite controversial. After establishing what Freud means by the terms, examine them to find out whether they are reasonable theories of behavior or whether they are not fully tenable. Moreover, consider the effect of holding such theories on matters related to social behavior—controversies related to feminism, for instance. Gather reactions from your friends. Do their views support Freud's theories or not? Do their views matter to you?

CARL JUNG

———⟨∞⟩———

The Concept of the
Collective Unconscious

CARL GUSTAV JUNG (1875–1961) was probably the most famous disciple of Sigmund Freud. A Swiss physician, he collaborated with Freud between 1907 and 1913. His eventual break with Freud came over the concept of the collective unconscious, which is sketched in this selection. Freud simply could not agree with Jung's idea of the nature of archetypes. Jung observed that the dreams of his patients were patterned after myths and mythologies that they could have had no knowledge of. This observation led Jung to begin an intensive study of mythology that revealed a range of dreamlike symbols that he took to be expressions of psychological ingredients of the unconscious. His conclusion was that mythology was a collective repository of such symbols and that myths arose from the psychological pressures of culture.

Once armed with that view, Jung also observed that certain patterns repeated themselves in myths, and he called these patterns archetypes. These archetypes were patterns that the individual had to adapt to healthfully; otherwise, he or she would risk developing complexes which would need to be dealt with by a doctor.

Jung believed that one of the modern world's problems is that humankind has misunderstood its archetypal nature, which in this selection he clearly links with human instinct. His view, as he explains *cogently, is that archetypes arise from repeated patterns of human behavior and that they are inherited by all of us. In other words, they are not part of our individual experiential memory; rather, they are ingrained and part of a biological-cultural memory. This is a radical view, one that certainly did not square with the mainstream of scientific thinking at the time Jung proposed it. Partly because it was commonly believed that the human being was born with a tabula rasa—a clean slate, with nothing in one's brain—all such thinking was rejected outright. Recent research by the linguist Noam Chomsky, however, insists that the child is born with an inbuilt patterned adaptation for language in the brain. Such views make it easier to regard Jung's concept with an open mind.*

A principal example of the archetype that Jung uses in this essay is that of the dual birth. We know, of course, that literature is filled with the concept of rebirth—of the necessity of rebirth for maturation. There are cultures with myths centering on rebirth and myths postulating two parents. Jung points to the dual-mother motif in mythology and shows how it resides in our concept of a real mother and a godmother. It also resides in the concept of a real mother and an alma mater—a foster mother, or university, in which the individual is reborn intellectually. Many secret societies, such as fraternities and international groups like the Masons, depend on this concept for their rituals. It is an archetype we see in all societies, and as individuals, we are susceptible to it.

Another archetype Jung refers to is connected with the political realities of Europe when he wrote: the revival of pagan rituals in the ceremonies of Hitler's Germany. This essay was originally delivered as a lecture in London in October 1936, when Hitler was expanding Germany's control over Europe. The Nazis had earlier consolidated their power by means of a series of demonstrations that attracted hundreds of thousands of people. The demonstrations featured huge swastika banners, hundreds of pikes with symbols reminiscent of the Roman era, intense emotional oratory designed to whip people into an anti-Semitic frenzy, and a spectacle of lights and flags that mesmerized a nation. It was an example of mass hysteria. The archetype was the archetype of power associated with a father figure, the führer, the fire bringer, the leader.

The archetype that Jung offers as proof of his view that the collective unconscious exists is derived from Jung's observation of a patient who suffered one of the most common delusions of modern life: he thought he was the Saviour. When the patient saw the sun, he also saw a phallus, and he connected it with the wind. As Jung points out, this connection was made in ancient times and resides in the literature of the occult, which Jung treats as a source of mythic symbol. We are familiar with the cults of the sun—virtually all religions developed one. The sun is the symbol of the hero, of the male figure, or the father.

Elsewhere, Jung talks about the mother archetype, explaining that since all of us have a mother, we need to adjust our feelings and needs regarding the mother to the realities of our situation. If, for instance, one has a dominating, consuming mother instead of one who is yielding and supportive, he or she might develop a mother complex and possibly become mentally unstable as a result of it. Similarly, a young person's unreasonable expectation of the person's relationship with his or her father can indeed produce the psychotic effects Jung describes.

The archetypes are fundamental to humanity. They represent the constant patterns of life that humans experience, and their force is such that we expect to establish a healthy relationship with them. When we do, we may be happy; when we do not, we may become ill.

JUNG'S RHETORIC

Because this is a speech delivered to a group of physicians and those interested in Jung's findings in psychology, it is admirably clear. It is expository in nature. In it, Jung states exactly what the basis of his thinking is, attempting on the one hand to convince his audience that what he says is true and on the other hand to explain his theories in detail so that those who understand will comprehend their seriousness.

He begins with a careful definition, labeled as such. This is a technique that is likely to guarantee clarity, though it is not the most graceful way to begin an essay. But Jung is less concerned with being graceful—although even in translation his prose is certainly not ungainly—than he is with being understood.

The second section treats the psychological implications of the concept of the collective unconscious, linking the concept with the instincts and explaining that there is a difference between the personal unconscious, which is developed through living and experience, and the collective unconscious, which is inherited and involuntary.

The third section concerns the ways in which proof may be determined. Jung points especially to dreams and reminds us that there are many patterns of dreams that each of us shares with others. Dreams reveal the symbols of the unconscious (the unconscious, because it is wordless, communicates entirely with symbols) that correlate, he points out, with ancient myth. Further, he establishes that those recurrent patterns of symbols which seem to be archetypes must also be discovered in ancient myth to be validated as archetypes. Therefore, in one sense, examining myth is the best way to clarify the archetype and its power and thus see into the true nature of the collective unconscious.

Jung concludes with an example that came from his psychiatric practice and that he referred to several times in his writing. It was a striking moment when he saw that the delusion of his schizophrenic patient was patterned after an ancient concept. What it proved to Jung was that the patient had come to grief because of his inability to work out an amicable relationship with the father archetype.

Jung's example may not prove his argument. Indeed, Jung says he is interested in the etiology (the cause or beginning) of complexes, and it is up to us to decide whether the etiology he proposes is reasonable. Of course, as he well knows, the concept of a collective unconscious is unreasonable; but then, as he points out, so is much of the psychic content of the mind. His observations are helpful in putting us in touch with the irrational content of our minds.

—⋅⋅⋅≫∞≪⋅⋅—

The Concept of the Collective Unconscious

Probably none of my empirical concepts has met with so much   1
misunderstanding as the idea of the collective unconscious. In what follows I shall try to give (1) a definition of the concept, (2) a description of what it means for psychology, (3) an explanation of the method of proof, and (4) an example.

Definition

The collective unconscious is a part of the psyche which can be 2
negatively distinguished from a personal unconscious by the fact that
it does not, like the latter, owe its existence to personal experience
and consequently is not a personal acquisition. While the personal unconscious is made up essentially of contents which have at one time
been conscious but which have disappeared from consciousness, and
therefore have never been individually acquired, but owe their existence exclusively to heredity. Whereas the personal unconscious consists for the most part of *complexes*, the content of the collective unconscious is made up essentially of *archetypes*.

The concept of the archetype, which is an indispensable correlate 3
of the idea of the collective unconscious, indicates the existence of
definite forms in the psyche which seem to be present always and everywhere. Mythological research calls them "motifs"; in the psychology of primitives they correspond to Lévy-Bruhl's[1] concept of "représentations collectives," and in the field of comparative religion they
have been defined by Hubert and Mauss[2] as "categories of the imagination." Adolf Bastian[3] long ago called them "elementary" or "primor-
dial thoughts." From these references it should be clear enough that
my idea of the archetype—literally a pre-existent form—does not stand
alone but is something that is recognized and named in other fields of
knowledge.

My thesis, then, is as follows: In addition to our immediate con- 4
sciousness, which is of a thoroughly personal nature and which we
believe to be the only empirical psyche (even if we tack on the personal unconscious as an appendix), there exists a second psychic system of a collective, universal, and impersonal nature which is identical
in all individuals. This collective unconscious does not develop individually but is inherited. It consists of pre-existent forms, the archetypes, which can only become conscious secondarily and which give
definite form to certain psychic contents.

---

[1]***Lucien Lévy-Bruhl (1857–1939)*** French philosopher, psychologist, and ethnolo-
gist. He is especially well known for his studies of the psychology of preliterate peoples.

[2]***Henri Hubert (1872–1927) and Marcel Mauss (1872–1950)*** French anthropologists whose study of rituals of sacrifice determined that it was the ritual act of sacrifice
itself, not what was to be gained by it, that was important. The act of sacrifice was an
act of communication between the human and the divine.

[3]***Adolf Bastian (1826–1905)*** A prominent German student of anthropology
whose *The Peoples of Eastern Asia* was published in the early 1860s.

The Psychological Meaning of the Collective Unconscious

Medical psychology, growing as it did out of professional practice, insists on the *personal* nature of the psyche. By this I mean the views of Freud and Adler.[4] It is a *psychology of the person,* and its etiological or causal factors are regarded almost wholly as personal in nature. Nonetheless, even this psychology is based on certain general biological factors, for instance on the sexual instinct or on the urge for self-assertion, which are by no means merely personal peculiarities. It is forced to do this because it lays claim to being an explanatory science. Neither of these views would deny the existence of *a priori* instincts[5] common to man and animals alike, or that they have a significant influence on personal psychology. Yet instincts are impersonal, universally distributed, hereditary factors of a dynamic or motivating character, which very often fail so completely to reach consciousness that modern psychotherapy is faced with the task of helping the patient to become conscious of them. Moreover, the instincts are not vague and indefinite by nature, but are specifically formed motive forces which, long before there is any consciousness, and in spite of any degree of consciousness later on, pursue their inherent goals. Consequently they form very close analogies to the archetypes, so close, in fact, that there is good reason for supposing that the archetypes are the unconscious images of the instincts themselves, in other words, that they are *patterns of instinctual behavior.*

The hypothesis of the collective unconscious is, therefore, no more daring than to assume there are instincts. One admits readily that human activity is influenced to a high degree by instincts, quite apart from the rational motivations of the conscious mind. So if the assertion is made that our imagination, perception, and thinking are likewise influenced by inborn and universally present formal elements, it seems to me that a normally functioning intelligence can discover in this idea just as much or just as little mysticism as in the theory of instincts. Although this reproach of mysticism has frequently been levelled at my concept, I must emphasize yet again that the concept of the collective unconscious is neither a speculative nor a philosophical but an empirical matter. The question is simply this: are there or are there not unconscious, universal forms of this kind? If they exist,

---

[4]*Alfred Adler (1870–1937)* One of Freud's most important contemporaries. He was a psychiatrist and founded the Ethical Culture Society.

[5]*a priori* Inborn; causative.

then there is a region of the psyche which one can call the collective unconscious. It is true that the diagnosis of the collective unconscious is not always an easy task. It is not sufficient to point out the often obviously archetypal nature of unconscious products, for these can just as well be derived from acquisitions through language and education. Cryptomnesia[6] should also be ruled out, which it is almost impossible to do in certain cases. In spite of all these difficulties, there remain enough individual instances showing the autochthonous[7] revival of mythological motifs to put the matter beyond any reasonable doubt. But if such an unconscious exists at all, psychological explanation must take account of it and submit certain alleged personal etiologies[8] to sharper criticism.

What I mean can perhaps best be made clear by a concrete example. You have probably read Freud's discussion[9] of a certain picture by Leonardo da Vinci: St. Anne with the Virgin Mary and the Christ-child. Freud interprets this remarkable picture in terms of the fact that Leonardo himself had two mothers. This causality is personal. We shall not linger over the fact that this picture is far from unique, nor over the minor inaccuracy that St. Anne happens to be the grand-mother of Christ and not, as required by Freud's interpretation, the mother, but shall simply point out that interwoven with the apparently personal psychology there is an impersonal motif well known to us from other fields. This is the motif of the *dual mother*, an archetype to be found in many variants in the field of mythology and comparative religion and forming the basis of numerous "représentations collectives." I might mention, for instance, the motif of the *dual descent*, that is descent from human and divine parents, as in the case of Heracles, who received immortality through being unwittingly adopted by Hera.[10] What was a myth in Greece was actually a ritual in Egypt: Pharaoh was both human and divine by nature. In the birth chambers of the Egyptian temples Pharaoh's second, divine conception and birth is depicted on the walls; he is "twice-born." It is an idea that

7

---

[6]*Cryptomnesia* Literally, hidden memory or thought.

[7]*autochthonous* Pertaining to the original natives of a place; thus, Jung refers to the earliest myths of any region.

[8]*etiologies* Causes, beginnings.

[9]*Leonardo da Vinci and a Memory of His Childhood*, sec. IV, translated by Alan Tyson in Sigmund Freud, *Standard Edition of the Complete Psychological Works*, II (London, 1957). [Jung's note]

[10]*Heracles . . . Hera* Heracles (or Hercules) was the greatest of the Greek heroes, the son of Zeus and Alcmene. Hera was the wife of Zeus, who adopted Heracles after the birth of Athena.

underlies all rebirth mysteries, Christianity included. Christ himself is "twice-born": through his baptism in the Jordan he was regenerated and reborn from water and spirit. Consequently, in the Roman liturgy the font is designated the "uterus ecclesiae,"[11] and, as you can read in the Roman missal, it is called this even today, in the "benediction of the font" on Holy Saturday before Easter. Further, according to an early Christian-Gnostic[12] idea, the spirit which appeared in the form of a dove was interpreted as Sophia-Sapientia—Wisdom and the Mother of Christ. Thanks to this motif of the dual birth, children today, instead of having good and evil fairies who magically "adopt" them at birth with blessings or curses, are given sponsors—a "godfather" and a "godmother."

The idea of a second birth is found at all times and in all places. In the earliest beginnings of medicine it was a magical means of healing; in many religions it is the central mystical experience; it is the key idea in medieval, occult philosophy, and, last but not least, it is an infantile fantasy occurring in numberless children, large and small, who believe that their parents are not their real parents but merely foster-parents to whom they were handed over. Benvenuto Cellini[13] also had this idea, as he himself relates in his autobiography.   8

Now it is absolutely out of the question that all the individuals who believe in a dual descent have in reality always had two mothers, or conversely that those few who shared Leonardo's fate have infected the rest of humanity with their complex. Rather, one cannot avoid the assumption that the universal occurrence of the dual-birth motif together with the fantasy of the two mothers answers an omnipresent human need which is reflected in these motifs. If Leonardo da Vinci did in fact portray his two mothers in St. Anne and Mary—which I doubt—he nonetheless was only expressing something which countless millions of people before and after him have believed. The vulture symbol (which Freud also discusses in the work mentioned) makes this view all the more plausible. With some justification he quotes as the source of the symbol the *Hieroglyphica* of Horapollo,[14] a book   9

---

[11]*"uterus ecclesiae"*   The womb of the churches.

[12]**Christian-Gnostic**   Christian Gnostics were a sect of the early church; they were routed from the church by the second century A.D.

[13]**Benvenuto Cellini (1500–1571)**   A Renaissance artist; he is perhaps best known for his swaggering *Autobiography of Benvenuto Cellini* (begun in 1558).

[14]**Hieroglyphica of Horapollo**   Horapollo lived in the fourth century in Egypt. His *Hieroglyphica* (2 vols.) professes to translate Egyptian hieroglyphics into Greek, but there is considerable doubt about their accuracy.

much in use in Leonardo's time. There you read that vultures are female only and symbolize the mother. They conceive through the wind
(pneuma). This word took on the meaning of "spirit" chiefly under the
influence of Christianity. Even in the account of the miracle at
Pentecost[15] the pneuma still has the double meaning of wind and
spirit. This fact, in my opinion, points without doubt to Mary, who, a
virgin by nature, conceived through the pneuma, like a vulture. Furthermore, according to Horapollo, the vulture also symbolizes Athene,
who sprang, unbegotten, directly from the head of Zeus, was a virgin,
and knew only spiritual motherhood. All this is really an allusion to
Mary and the rebirth motif. There is not a shadow of evidence that
Leonardo meant anything else by his picture. Even if it is correct to
assume that he identified himself with the Christ-child, he was in all
probability representing the mythological dual-mother motif and by no
means his own personal prehistory. And what about all the other artists who painted the same theme? Surely not all of them had two
mothers?

Let us now transpose Leonardo's case to the field of the neuroses, 10
and assume that a patient with a mother complex is suffering from the
delusion that the cause of his neurosis lies in his having really had
two mothers. The personal interpretation would have to admit that he
is right—and yet it would be quite wrong. For in reality the cause of
his neurosis would lie in the reactivation of the dual-mother archetype, quite regardless of whether he had one mother or two mothers,
because, as we have seen, this archetype functions individually and
historically without any reference to the relatively rare occurrence of
dual motherhood.

In such a case, it is of course tempting to presuppose so simple and 11
personal a cause, yet the hypothesis is not only inexact but totally
false. It is admittedly difficult to understand how a dual mother motif—unknown to a physician trained only in medicine—could have so
great a determining power as to produce the effect of a traumatic condition. But if we consider the tremendous powers that lie hidden in
the mythological and religious sphere in man, the etiological significance of the archetype appears less fantastic. In numerous cases of
neurosis the cause of the disturbance lies in the very fact that the psychic life of the patient lacks the co-operation of these motive forces.

---

[15]***miracle at Pentecost*** Acts 2:4 "And suddenly there came a sound from heaven as
of a rushing mighty wind, and it filled all the house where they were sitting. And there
appeared unto them cloven tongues like as of fire, and it sat upon each of them. And they
were all filled with the Holy Ghost, and began to speak with other tongues, as the Spirit
gave them utterance."

Nevertheless a purely personalistic psychology, by reducing everything to personal causes, tries its level best to deny the existence of archetypal motifs and even seeks to destroy them by personal analysis. I consider this a rather dangerous procedure which cannot be justified medically. Today you can judge better than you could twenty years ago the nature of the forces involved. Can we not see how a whole nation is reviving an archaic symbol, yes, even archaic religious forms, and how this mass emotion is influencing and revolutionizing the life of the individual in a catastrophic manner?[16] The man of the past is alive in us today to a degree undreamt of before the war,[17] and in the last analysis what is the fate of great nations but a summation of the psychic changes in individuals?

So far as a neurosis is really only a private affair, having its roots exclusively in personal causes, archetypes play no role at all. But if it is a question of a general incompatibility or an otherwise injurious condition productive of neuroses in relatively large numbers of individuals, then we must assume the presence of constellated archetypes. Since neuroses are in most cases not just private concerns, but *social* phenomena, we must assume that archetypes are constellated in these cases too. The archetype corresponding to the situation is activated, and as a result those explosive and dangerous forces hidden in the archetype come into action, frequently with unpredictable consequences. There is no lunacy people under the domination of an archetype will not fall a prey to. If thirty years ago anyone had dared to predict that our psychological development was tending towards a revival of the medieval persecutions of the Jews,[18] that Europe would again tremble before the Roman fasces[19] and the tramp of legions, that people would once more give the Roman salute as two thousand years ago, and that instead of the Christian Cross an archaic swastika would lure onward millions of warriors ready for death—why, that man would have been hooted at as a mystical fool. And today? Surprising as it may seem, all this absurdity is a horrible reality. Private life,

12

---

[16]*catastophic manner*   Jung was writing with the rise of Hitler in the background of his thoughts.

[17]*the war*   World War I.

[18]*medieval persecutions of the Jews*   Persecution of the Jews in the Middle Ages was sporadic but frequent. The zeal built up from the Crusades; the efforts to retrieve the Holy Land from the Arabs contributed to anti-Jewish feeling.

[19]*Roman fasces*   Fasces are bundles of rods tied around an ax with the blade projecting. Roman magistrates carried them as an emblem of authority and a symbol of the strength implied in holding together. Fascism took its name from the Roman fasces.

private etiologies, and private neuroses have become almost a fiction in the world of today. The man of the past who lived in a world of archaic "représentations collectives" has risen again into very visible and painfully real life, and this not only in a few unbalanced individuals but in many millions of people.

There are as many archetypes as there are typical situations in life. 13 Endless repetition has engraved these experiences into our psychic constitution, not in the form of images filled with content, but at first only as *forms without content*, representing merely the possibility of a certain type of perception and action. When a situation occurs which corresponds to a given archetype, that archetype becomes activated and a compulsiveness appears, which, like an instinctual drive, gains its way against all reason and will, or else produces a conflict of pathological dimensions, that is to say, a neurosis.

Method of Proof

We must now turn to the question of how the existence of arche- 14 types can be proved. Since archetypes are supposed to produce certain psychic forms, we must discuss how and where one can get hold of the material demonstrating these forms. The main source, then, is *dreams*, which have the advantage of being involuntary, spontaneous products of the unconscious psyche and are therefore pure products of nature not falsified by any conscious purpose. By questioning the individual one can ascertain which of the motifs appearing in the dream are known to him. From those which are unknown to him we must naturally exclude all motifs which *might* be known to him, as for instance—to revert to the case of Leonardo—the vulture symbol. We are not sure whether Leonardo took this symbol from Horapollo or not, although it would have been perfectly possible for an educated person of that time, because in those days artists were distinguished for their wide knowledge of the humanities. Therefore, although the bird motif is an archetype par excellence, its existence in Leonardo's fantasy would still prove nothing. Consequently, we must look for motifs which could not possibly be known to the dreamer and yet behave functionally in his dream in such a manner as to coincide with the functioning of the archetype known from historical sources.

Another source for the material we need is to be found in "active 15 imagination." By this I mean a sequence of fantasies produced by deliberate concentration. I have found that the existence of unrealized, unconscious fantasies increases the frequency and intensity of dreams, and that when these fantasies are made conscious the dreams change their character and become weaker and less frequent. From this I have drawn the conclusion that dreams often contain fantasies which "want" to become conscious. The sources of dreams are often repressed instincts which have a natural tendency to influence the conscious mind. In cases of this sort, the patient is simply given the task of contemplating any one fragment of fantasy that seems significant to him—a chance idea, perhaps, or something he has become conscious of in a dream—until its context becomes visible, that is to say, the relevant associative material in which it is embedded. It is not a question of the "free association" recommended by Freud for the purpose of dream-analysis, but of elaborating the fantasy by observing the further fantasy material that adds itself to the fragment in a natural manner.

This is not the place to enter upon a technical discussion of the   16
method. Suffice it to say that the resultant sequence of fantasies relieves the unconscious and produces material rich in archetypal images and associations. Obviously, this is a method that can only be used in certain carefully selected cases. The method is not entirely without danger, because it may carry the patient too far away from reality. A warning against thoughtless application is therefore in place.

Finally, very interesting sources of archetypal material are to be   17
found in the delusions of paranoiacs, the fantasies observed in trance-states, and the dreams of early childhood, from the third to the fifth year. Such material is available in profusion, but it is valueless unless one can adduce convincing mythological parallels. It does not, of course, suffice simply to connect a dream about a snake with the mythological occurrence of snakes, for who is to guarantee that the functional meaning of the snake in the dream is the same as in the mythological setting? In order to draw a valid parallel, it is necessary to know the functional meaning of the individual symbol, and then to find out whether the apparently parallel mythological symbol has a similar context and therefore the same functional meaning. Establishing such facts not only requires lengthy and wearisome researches, but is also an ungrateful subject for demonstration. As the symbols must not be torn out of their context, one has to launch forth into exhaustive descriptions, personal as well as symbological, and this is practically impossible in the framework of a lecture. I have repeatedly tried it at the risk of sending one half of my audience to sleep.

An Example

I am choosing as an example a case which, though already pub- 18
lished, I use again because its brevity makes it peculiarly suitable for
illustration. Moreover, I can add certain remarks which were omitted
in the previous publication.

About 1906 I came across a very curious delusion in a paranoid 19
schizophrenic who had been interned for many years. The patient had
suffered since his youth and was incurable. He had been educated at a
State school and been employed as a clerk in an office. He had no
special gifts, and I myself knew nothing of mythology or archaeology
in those days, so the situation was not in any way suspect. One day I
found the patient standing at the window, wagging his head and blinking into the sun. He told me to do the same, for then I would see
something very interesting. When I asked him what he saw, he was
astonished that I could see nothing, and said: "Surely you see the sun's
penis—when I move my head to and fro, it moves too, and that is
where the wind comes from." Naturally I did not understand this
strange idea in the least, but I made a note of it. Then about four years
later, during my mythological studies, I came upon a book by the late
Albrecht Dieterich[20] the well-known philologist, which threw light on
this fantasy. The work, published in 1910, deals with a Greek papyrus
in the Bibliothèque Nationale, Paris. Dieterich believed he had discovered a Mithraic ritual[21] in one part of the text. The text is undoubtedly
a religious prescription for carrying out certain incantations in which
Mithras is named. It comes from the Alexandrian school[22] of mysticism and shows affinities with certain passages in the Leiden papyri
and the *Corpus Hermeticum.*[23] In Dieterich's text we read the following directions:

---

[20]***Albrecht Dieterich (1866–1908)*** Professor at Heidelberg whose work included
research into ancient religions.

[21]***Mithraic ritual*** Mithraism was a cult favored by the Roman legionnaires and one
of the chief competitors with early Christianity. It involved complex attitudes toward
light and the sun as well as the ritual slaughtering of a heifer during ceremonies.

[22]***Alexandrian school*** A school of philosophers that flourished in the second century A.D. in Alexandria, Egypt. The members were exceptional textual scholars whose
work with sacred writings promoted a very mystical school of religious studies. Their
mysticism implied direct contact with God.

[23]***Leiden papyri and the* Corpus Hermeticum** The writings of Hermes Trismegistes
were introduced into Europe in the fifteenth century in the translation of Giovanni Pico
della Mirandola (1463–1494). They were thought to be powerful magic treatises that in-
tersected with the teachings of Plato and of Christianity.

Draw breath from the rays, draw in three times as strongly as you can and you will feel yourself raised up and walking towards the height, and you will seem to be in the middle of the aerial region. . . . The path of the visible gods will appear through the disc of the sun, who is God my father. Likewise the so-called tube, the origin of the ministering wind. For you will see hanging down from the disc of the sun something that looks like a tube. And towards the regions westward it is as though there were an infinite east wind. But if the other wind should prevail towards the regions of the east, you will in like manner see the vision veering in that direction.

It is obviously the author's intention to enable the reader to experience the vision which he had, or which at least he believes in. The reader is to be initiated into the inner religious experience either of the author, or—what seems more likely—of one of those mystic communities of which Philo Judaeus[24] gives contemporary accounts. The fire- or sun-god here invoked is a figure which has close historical parallels, for instance with the Christ-figure of the Apocalypse.[25] It is therefore a "représentation collective," as are also the ritual actions described, such as the imitating of animal noises, etc. The vision is embedded in a religious context of a distinctly ecstatic nature and describes a kind of initiation into mystic experience of the Deity. 20

Our patient was about ten years older than I. In his megalomania, he thought he was God and Christ in one person. His attitude towards me was patronizing; he liked me probably because I was the only person with any sympathy for his abstruse ideas. His delusions were mainly religious, and when he invited me to blink into the sun like he did and waggle my head he obviously wanted to let me share his vision. He played the role of the mystic sage and I was the neophyte. He felt he was the sun-god himself, creating the wind by wagging his head to and fro. The ritual transformation into the Deity is attested by Apuleius in the Isis mysteries,[26] and moreover in the form of a Helios 21

---

[24]*Philo Judaeus (20 B.C.?–50 A.D.?)* Jewish philosopher in Alexandria, a mystic, but also an interpreter of the laws. He commented on the religious communities that flourished in Alexandria around the time of Christ.

[25]*Christ-figure of the Apocalypse* See Revelations 1:9 in which St. John sees a vision of Christ punctuated by candlesticks and stars "and his countenance was as the sun shineth in his strength."

[26]*Apuleius in the Isis mysteries* In *The Golden Ass* Apuleius (second century A.D.) tells a story of searching and confusion, explained ultimately as an initiation rite of the mysteries of Isis, a religion popular in the first several centuries after Christ. Much of what we know about initiation rituals comes from this text.

apotheosis.[27] The meaning of the "ministering wind" is probably the same as the procreative pneuma,[28] which streams from the sun-god into the soul and fructifies it. The association of sun and wind frequently occurs in ancient symbolism.

It must now be shown that this is not a purely chance coincidence   22 of two isolated cases. We must therefore show that the idea of a wind-tube connected with God or the sun exists independently of these two testimonies and that it occurs at other times and in other places. Now there are, as a matter of fact, medieval paintings that depict the fructification of Mary with a tube or hose-pipe coming down from the throne of God and passing into her body, and we can see the dove or the Christ-child flying down it. The dove represents the fructifying agent, the wind of the Holy Ghost.

Now it is quite out of the question that the patient could have had   23 any knowledge whatever of a Greek papyrus published four years later, and it is in the highest degree unlikely that his vision had anything to do with the rare medieval representations of the Conception, even if through some incredibly improbable chance he had ever seen a copy of such a painting. The patient was certified in his early twenties. He had never travelled. And there is no such picture in the public art gallery in Zurich, his native town.

I mention this case not in order to prove that the vision is an ar-   24 chetype but only to show you my method of procedure in the simplest possible form. If we had only such cases, the task of investigation would be relatively easy, but in reality the proof is much more complicated. First of all, certain symbols have to be isolated clearly enough to be recognizable as typical phenomena, not just matters of chance. This is done by examining a series of dreams, say a few hundred, for typical figures, and by observing their development in the series. The same method can be applied to the products of active imagination. In this way it is possible to establish certain continuities or modulations of one and the same figure. You can select any figure which gives the impression of being an archetype by its behavior in the series of dreams or visions. If the material at one's disposal has been well observed and is sufficiently ample, one can discover interesting facts about the variations undergone by a single type. Not only the type

---

[27]*form of a Helios apotheosis* Apotheosis is the act of becoming a god, often by being absorbed by or taken up by the sun (helios).

[28]*procreative pneuma* A wind which produces life. For the ancients, certain winds were thought capable of making women pregnant. It is a persistent and common concept.

itself but its variants too can be substantiated by evidence from comparative mythology and ethnology. I have described the method of investigation elsewhere[29] and have also furnished the necessary case material.

---

[29]*Psychology and Alchemy*, Part II. [Jung's note]

QUESTIONS

1. What does Jung mean by the unconscious? What is the unconscious part of our mind and how does it reveal itself?
2. What is the difference between the personal unconscious and the collective unconscious?
3. How does the archetype relate to the unconscious? What is an archetype?
4. How does Jung reach the conclusion that postulating a collective unconscious is no more daring than postulating the existence of instincts?
5. What is the connection between myth and our unconscious?

WRITING ASSIGNMENTS

1. Write a brief summary of the contents of this selection. Your purpose is to restate the primary ideas in the selection for someone who did not read it and did not discuss it. In other words, you are trying to present as fair and objective a summary as possible in order to communicate the basic concepts in the essay.
2. To what extent do you feel yourself aware of possessing an unconscious? Examine yourself as carefully as possible to determine if you seem to have some of the psychic qualities Jung seems to postulate for most people. If you like, ask friends whether they feel themselves aware of an unconscious. What does your research force you to conclude?
3. Choose a myth that is either Greek or Roman. Establish what its most basic pattern is and decide whether it represents an archetype. To do this, reduce it to a schematic structure, such as the journey into hell of Ulysses, Aeneas, Christ, and Dante (just to choose one pattern that does repeat itself) and see if it correlates with a basic human activity. In the case of the journey into hell, it correlates with every person's maturation: the overcoming of the fear of death and the determination to live on. If one could not overcome the fear of death, what kind of psychic damage might be done?
4. Do some dream research, either by keeping track of your own dreams or by examining the dreams of others. Write down yours and others' dreams in as simple a form as possible. Look for recurrent patterns and recurrent

symbols such as water, fire, mountains, towers, poles, caverns, wind, flying (related to the wind), journeys, and flowers. Describe the most interesting dreams you collect and then try to find a pattern to them. What elements seem to repeat themselves? How much do you think we share in common in our dreams? How many of the dreams seemed to have some kind of connection with myths?

5. One of the most carefully developed archetypes Jung discusses elsewhere is the mother archetype. He cites the Madonna as an example of this archetype as it is developed by Christianity, and he points out that in earlier civilizations, a madonnalike goddess was celebrated widely. If you wish, establish what the nature of the Madonna is to her child. Use paintings and visual representations as well as consulting the Book of Matthew in the New Testament. What is the cultural ideal (i.e., the archetype) of the mother as revealed in the Madonna? Is this ideal instinctive? Do you feel that it is an appropriate ideal for all modern women to aspire to? If a woman did not feel it appropriate, could her rejection of the archetype result in psychic damage? If so, what kind of damage?

6. What mythic figures best establish the cultural ideal of a son's relationship with a father? Is there an instinctive relationship felt on the part of either the father or the son? What qualities of modern life seem to be in conflict with that ideal? To what extent is modern life preserving the ideal? Establish the archetypal relation and then comment, using personal experience and observation, on the psychic effects of struggling against the archetypal patterns of behavior.

KAREN HORNEY

The Distrust
Between the Sexes

KAREN HORNEY (1885–1952) was a distinguished psychiatrist who developed her career somewhat independently of the influence of Sigmund Freud. In her native Germany, she taught in the Berlin Psychoanalytic Institute from the end of World War I until 1932, a year before Hitler officially came to power. She was naturally influenced by Freud's work—as was every other psychoanalyst. But she found that, brilliant as it was, it did not satisfy her on important issues regarding female sexuality.

In Germany, Horney's research was centered on questions about female psychology. The selection is part of that work, coming from her book, Feminine Psychology, (1931). She did not agree with Freud's contention that penis envy dominated the psychological behavior of women. She thought that he oversimplified female sexuality and that the truth, demonstrated through her own analysis, was vastly different. Her most significant early efforts were devoted to demonstrating the limits of Freud's contention, and in the process she was able to produce a different analysis, resulting in works of the sort presented here.

She immigrated to America in 1932, and she began writing a distinguished series of publications on neurosis. Her career in Chicago was remarkable. Not only did she found the American Institute for

Psychoanalysis (1941) and the American Journal of Psychoanalysis; *she also produced such important books as* The Neurotic Personality of Our Time *(1937);* New Ways in Psychoanalysis *(1939); and* Self-Analysis *(1942). Her work was rooted in cultural studies, and among her principal points was the fact that neuroses, including sexual problems, are caused by cultural influences and pressures that the individual simply cannot deal with. Freud thought the reverse, placing the causal force of neuroses in sexuality.*

Her studies constantly brought her back to the question of interpersonal relations, and she saw the pressures of failed relationships as resulting from, in many cases, neurotic patterns that developed in childhood. The selection focuses particularly on the relationship that individuals establish with their mother or their father. Her insistence that childhood patterns affect adult behavior is consonant with Freudianism; however, her interpretations are somewhat different. Unlike Freud, she looks toward anthropological studies of behavior to help interpret behavior of modern people in light of such studies.

Horney claims that the distrust between the sexes cannot be explained away as existing only in individuals; rather, it is a widespread fact that must arise because of psychological forces that exist in men and women. She discusses a number of cultural practices in primitive people in an effort to suggest that even without the modern cultural trappings that we feel ourselves burdened by, the two sexes suffer anxieties in their relationship. She also looks at the normal relationship of the individual in a family setting, showing that normal expectations of relations between child and parent can sometimes be frustrated and that the result can be seriously harmful.

In addition, she examines the nature of culture, reminding us that early societies were often matriarchal; that is, they were centered not on men and manly activities but on women. Her views about matriarchy are quite suggestive in psychological terms. The mystery of a woman is connected with her creative nature: she produces newborn. The envy, as she sees it, is on the part of men, who, in order to compensate for women's capacities to create life, spend their energies creating "state, religion, art, and science" (para. 14).

Horney is interesting for her frankness. She speaks directly about sexual matters and about what she sees as male anxieties. She holds that there are distinct areas of conflict between men and women, and she contends that they are psychological in origin.

HORNEY'S RHETORIC

This is an expository essay, establishing the truth of hypothesis by pointing to a range of evidence from a variety of sources. Her view is that the distrust between the sexes is the result of cultural forces that the individual is only dimly aware of. In this sense, she aligns herself with the Freudians, who constantly point to influences on the individual that are subconscious in nature and, therefore, are not part of the individual's self-awareness.

In a sense, her essay is itself an analysis of the relationship between men and women, with a look back at the history of culture. Her technique—a review of older societies—establishes that the current nature of the relationship between men and women is colored by the fact that modern society is dominated by patriarchal institutions. In ancient times, however, society may well have been matriarchal.

This selection was originally delivered as a lecture to the German Women's Medical Association in November 1930, and most of the audience was female. Consequently, the nature of the imagery, the frankness of the discourse, and the cultural focus is given to issues that would have a distinct impact on women. When we read this essay, we realize that Karen Horney is speaking with special frankness that, were she speaking to a mixed audience, she might have altered.

Her method of writing is analytical, as she tells us several times. She is searching for causes within the culture as well as within the individual, and this is the procedure used in her analysis. Her range of causal analysis is wide, including the comparative study of cultures (ethnology) as well as personal psychology. Her capacity to call on earlier writers and cultures shows an enormous scope. It also helps convince us of the seriousness of her inquiry.

———⟨∞⟩———

The Distrust
Between the Sexes

As I begin to talk to you today about some problems in the relationship between the sexes, I must ask you not to be disappointed. I will not concern myself primarily with the aspect of the problem that is most important to the physician. Only at the end will I briefly deal with the question of therapy. I am far more concerned with pointing out to you several psychological reasons for the distrust between the sexes.

The relationship between men and women is quite similar to that 2 between children and parents, in that we prefer to focus on the positive aspects of these relationships. We prefer to assume that love is the fundamentally given factor and that hostility is an accidental and avoidable occurrence. Although we are familiar with slogans such as "the battle of the sexes" and "hostility between the sexes," we must admit that they do not mean a great deal. They make us overfocus on sexual relations between men and women, which can very easily lead us to a too one-sided view. Actually, from our recollection of numerous case histories, we may conclude that love relationships are quite easily destroyed by overt or covert hostility. On the other hand we are only too ready to blame such difficulties on individual misfortune, on incompatibility of the partners, and on social or economic causes.

The individual factors, which we find causing poor relations be- 3 tween men and women, may be the pertinent ones. However, because of the great frequency, or better, the regular occurrence of disturbances in love relations, we have to ask ourselves whether the disturbances in the individual cases might not arise from a common background; whether there are common denominators for this easily and frequently arising suspiciousness between the sexes?

It is almost impossible to attempt within the framework of a brief 4 lecture to give you a complete survey of so large a field. I therefore will not even mention such factors as the origin and effects of such social institutions as marriage. I merely intend to select at random some of the factors that are psychologically understandable and pertain to the causes and effects of the hostility and tension between the sexes.

I would like to start with something very commonplace—namely, 5 that a good deal of this atmosphere of suspiciousness is understandable and even justifiable. It apparently has nothing to do with the individual partner, but rather with the intensity of the affects[1] and with the difficulty of taming them.

We know or may dimly sense, that these affects can lead to ecstasy, 6 to being beside oneself, to surrendering oneself, which means a leap into the unlimited and the boundless. This is perhaps why real passion

---

[1] *affects* Feelings, emotions, or passions.

is so rare. For like a good businessman, we are loath to put all our eggs in one basket. We are inclined to be reserved and ever ready to retreat. Be that as it may, because of our instinct for self preservation, we all have a natural fear of losing ourselves in another person. That is why what happens to love, happens to education and psychoanalysis; everybody thinks he knows all about them, but few do. One is inclined to overlook how little one gives of oneself, but one feels all the more this same deficiency in the partner, the feeling of "You never really loved me." A wife who harbors suicidal thoughts because her husband does not give her all his love, time, and interest, will not notice how much of her own hostility, hidden vindictiveness, and aggression are expressed through her attitude. She will feel only despair because of her abundant "love," while at the same time she will feel most intensely and see most clearly the lack of love in her partner. Even Strindberg[2] [who was a misogynist] defensively managed to say on occasion that he was no woman hater, but that women hated and tortured him.

Here we are not dealing with pathological phenomena at all. In pathological cases we merely see a distortion and exaggeration of a general and normal occurrence. Anybody, to a certain extent, will be inclined to overlook his own hostile impulses, but under pressure of his own guilty conscience, may project them onto the partner. This process must, of necessity, cause some overt or covert distrust of the partner's love, fidelity, sincerity, or kindness. This is the reason why I prefer to speak of distrust between the sexes and not of hatred; for in keeping with our own experience we are more familiar with the feeling of distrust. 7

A further, almost unavoidable, source of disappointment and distrust in our normal love life derives from the fact that the very intensity of our feelings of love stirs up all of our secret expectations and longings for happiness, which slumber deep inside us. All our unconscious wishes, contradictory in their nature and expanding boundlessly on all sides, are waiting here for their fulfillment. The partner is supposed to be strong, and at the same time helpless, to dominate us and be dominated by us, to be ascetic and to be sensuous. He should rape us and be tender, have time for us exclusively and also be intensely involved in creative work. As long as we assume that he could actually fulfill all these expectations, we invest him with the glitter of sexual overestimation. We take the magnitude of such overvaluation for the 8

---

[2]***August Strindberg (1849–1912)*** A Swedish playwright and novelist whose portraits of women were dark and influenced by his misogyny (hatred of women).

measure of our love, while in reality it merely expresses the magnitude of our expectations. The very nature of our claims makes their fulfillment impossible. Herein lies the origin of the disappointments with which we may cope in a more or less effective way. Under favorable circumstances we do not even have to become aware of the great number of our disappointments, just as we have not been aware of the extent of our secret expectations. Yet there remain traces of distrust in us, as in a child who discovers that his father cannot get him the stars from the sky after all.

Thus far, our reflections certainly have been neither new nor specifically analytical and have often been better formulated in the past. The analytical approach begins with the question: What special factors in human development lead to the discrepancy between expectations and fulfillment and what causes them to be of special significance in particular cases? Let us start with a general consideration. There is a basic difference between human and animal development—namely, the long period of the infant's helplessness and dependency. The paradise of childhood is most often an illusion with which adults like to deceive themselves. For the child, however, this paradise is inhabited by too many dangerous monsters. Unpleasant experiences with the opposite sex seem to be unavoidable. We need only recall the capacity that children possess, even in their very early years, for passionate and instinctive sexual desires similar to those of adults and yet different from them. Children are different in the aims of their drives, but above all, in the pristine integrity of their demands. They find it hard to express their desires directly, and where they do, they are not taken seriously. Their seriousness sometimes is looked upon as being cute, or it may be overlooked or rejected. In short, children will undergo painful and humiliating experiences of being rebuffed, being betrayed, and being told lies. They also may have to take second place to a parent or sibling, and they are threatened and intimidated when they seek, in playing with their own bodies, those pleasures that are denied them by adults. The child is relatively powerless in the face of all this. He is not able to ventilate his fury at all, or only to a minor degree, nor can he come to grips with the experience by means of intellectual comprehension. Thus, anger and aggression are pent up within him in the form of extravagant fantasies, which hardly reach the daylight of awareness, fantasies that are criminal when viewed from the standpoint of the adult, fantasies that range from taking by force and stealing, to those about killing, burning, cutting to pieces, and choking. Since the child is vaguely aware of these destructive forces within him, he feels, according to the talion law,[3] equally threatened by the adults. Here is the origin of those infantile anxieties of which no child remains entirely free. This already enables us to understand better the fear of love of which I have spoken before. Just here, in this most irrational of all areas, the old childhood fears of a threatening father or mother are reawakened, putting us instinctively on the defensive. In other words, the fear of love will always be mixed with the fear of what we might do to the other person, or what the other person might do to us. A lover in the Aru Islands,[4] for example, will never make a gift of a lock of hair to his beloved, because should an argument arise, the beloved might burn it, thus causing the partner to get sick.

I would like to sketch briefly how childhood conflicts may affect   10
the relationship to the opposite sex in later life. Let us take as an example a typical situation: The little girl who was badly hurt through some great disappointment by her father, will transform her innate instinctual wish to receive from the man, into a vindictive one of taking from him by force. Thus the foundation is laid for a direct line of development to a later attitude, according to which she will not only deny her maternal instincts, but will have only one drive, i.e., to harm the male, to exploit him, and to suck him dry. She has become a vampire. Let us assume that there is a similar transformation from the wish to receive to the wish to take away. Let us further assume that the latter wish was repressed due to anxiety from a guilty conscience; then we have here the fundamental constellation for the formation of a certain type of woman who is unable to relate to the male because she fears that every male will suspect her of wanting something from him. This really means that she is afraid that he might guess her repressed desires. Or by completely projecting onto him her repressed wishes, she will imagine that every male merely intends to exploit her, that he wants from her only sexual satisfaction, after which he will discard her. Or let us assume that a reaction formation of excessive modesty will mask the repressed drive for power. We then have the type of woman who shies away from demanding or accepting anything from her husband. Such a woman, however, due to the return of the repressed, will react with depression to the nonfulfillment of her unex-

---

[3]***talion law*** Law which demands that the criminal be given the same punishment as was suffered by the victim—an eye for an eye.
[4]***Aru Islands*** Islands in Indonesia that were especially interesting for modern anthropologists.

pressed, and often unformulated, wishes. She thus unwittingly jumps from the frying pan into the fire, as does her partner, because a depression will hit him much harder than direct aggression. Quite often the repression of aggression against the male drains all her vital energy. The woman then feels helpless to meet life. She will shift the entire responsibility for her helplessness onto the man, robbing him of the very breath of life. Here you have the type of woman who, under the guise of being helpless and childlike, dominates her man.

These are examples that demonstrate how the fundamental attitude of women toward men can be disturbed by childhood conflicts. In an attempt to simplify matters, I have stressed only one point, which, however, seems crucial to me—the disturbance in the development of motherhood. 11

I shall now proceed to trace certain traits of male psychology. I do not wish to follow individual lines of development, though it might be very instructive to observe analytically how, for instance, even men who consciously have a very positive relationship with women and hold them in high esteem as human beings, harbor deep within themselves a secret distrust of them; and how this distrust relates back to feelings toward their mothers, which they experienced in their formative years. I shall focus rather on certain typical attitudes of men toward women and how they have appeared during various eras of history and in different cultures, not only as regards sexual relationships with women, but also, and often more so, in nonsexual situations, such as in their general evaluation of women. 12

I shall select some random examples, starting with Adam and Eve. Jewish culture, as recorded in the Old Testament, is outspokenly patriarchal. This fact reflects itself in their religion, which has no maternal goddesses; in their morals and customs, which allow the husband the right to dissolve the marital bond simply by dismissing his wife. Only by being aware of this background can we recognize the male bias in two incidents of Adam's and Eve's history. First of all, woman's capacity to give birth is partly denied and partly devaluated: Eve was made of Adam's rib and a curse was put on her to bear children in sorrow. In the second place, by interpreting her tempting Adam to eat of the tree of knowledge as a sexual temptation, woman appears as the sexual temptress, who plunges man into misery. I believe that these two elements, one born out of resentment, the other out of anxiety, have damaged the relationship between the sexes from the earliest times to the present. Let us follow this up briefly. Man's fear of woman is deeply rooted in sex, as is shown by the simple fact that it is only the sexually attractive woman of whom he is afraid and who, 13 although he strongly desires her, has to be kept in bondage. Old women, on the other hand, are held in high esteem, even by cultures in which the young woman is dreaded and therefore suppressed. In some primitive cultures the old woman may have the decisive voice in the affairs of the tribe; among Asian nations also she enjoys great power and prestige. On the other hand, in primitive tribes woman is surrounded by taboos during the entire period of her sexual maturity. Women of the Arunta tribe are able to magically influence the male genitals. If they sing to a blade of grass and then point it at a man or throw it at him, he becomes ill or loses his genitals altogether. Women lure him to his doom. In a certain East African tribe, husband and wife do not sleep together, because her breath might weaken him. If a woman of a South African tribe climbs over the leg of a sleeping man, he will be unable to run; hence the general rule of sexual abstinence two to five days prior to hunting, warfare, or fishing. Even greater is the fear of menstruation, pregnancy, and childbirth. Menstruating women are surrounded by extensive taboos—a man who touches a menstruating woman will die. There is one basic thought at the bottom of all this: Woman is a mysterious being who communicates with spirits and thus has magic powers that she can use to hurt the male. He must therefore protect himself against her powers by keeping her subjugated. Thus the Miri in Bengal do not permit their women to eat the flesh of the tiger, lest they become too strong. The Watawela of East Africa keep the art of making fire a secret from their women, lest women become their rulers. The Indians of California have ceremonies to keep their women in submission; a man is disguised as a devil to intimidate the women. The Arabs of Mecca exclude women from religious festivities to prevent familiarity between women and their overlords. We find similar customs during the Middle Ages—the Cult of the Virgin[5] side by side with the burning of witches; the adoration of "pure" motherliness, completely divested of sexuality, next to the cruel destruction of the sexually seductive woman. Here again is the implication of underlying anxiety, for the witch is in communication with the devil. Nowadays, with our more humane forms of aggression, we burn women only figuratively, sometimes with undisguised hatred,

---

[5]**Cult of the Virgin** During the Counter Reformation in the later sixteenth and early seventeenth centuries, the Roman Catholic Church promoted a strong emotional attachment to the Virgin Mary, which resulted in the production of innumerable paintings and sculptures. Protestants regarded this scornfully as a revival of a cult and separate from the main stream of Christianity. Horney points out the irony of venerating the mother of God while tormenting human women by burning them at the stake.

sometimes with apparent friendliness. In any case "The Jew must burn."[6] In friendly and secret autos-da-fé,[7] many nice things are said about women, but it is just unfortunate that in her God-given natural state, she is not the equal of the male. Moebius[8] pointed out that the female brain weighs less than the male one, but the point need not be made in so crude a way. On the contrary, it can be stressed that woman is not at all inferior, only different, but that unfortunately she has fewer or none of those human or cultural qualities that man holds in such high esteem. She is said to be deeply rooted in the personal and emotional spheres, which is wonderful; but unfortunately, this makes her incapable of exercising justice and objectivity, therefore disqualifying her for positions in law and government and in the spiritual community. She is said to be at home only in the realm of eros. Spiritual matters are alien to her innermost being, and she is at odds with cultural trends. She therefore is, as Asians frankly state, a second-rate being. Woman may be industrious and useful but is, alas, incapable of productive and independent work. She is, indeed, prevented from real accomplishment by the deplorable, bloody tragedies of menstruation and childbirth. And so every man silently thanks his God, just as the pious Jew does in his prayers, that he was not created a woman.

Man's attitude toward motherhood is a large and complicated chapter. One is generally inclined to see no problem in this area. Even the misogynist is obviously willing to respect woman as a mother and to venerate her motherliness under certain conditions, as mentioned above regarding the Cult of the Virgin. In order to obtain a clearer picture, we have to distinguish between two attitudes: men's attitudes toward motherliness, as represented in its purest form in the Cult of the Virgin, and their attitude toward motherhood as such, as we encounter it in the symbolism of the ancient mother goddesses. Males will always be in favor of motherliness, as expressed in certain spiritual qualities of women, i.e., the nurturing, selfless, self-sacrificing mother; for she is the ideal embodiment of the woman who could ful-

14

---

[6]*"The Jew must burn."* This is a quote from *Nathan the Wise* by the eighteenth-century German author Gotthold Ephraim Lessing, a humanist and a spokesman for enlightenment and rationality. The expression became a colloquialism. It meant no matter how worthy and well-intentioned his acts, by virtue of being a Jew, a man was guilty. [Translator's note]

[7]*autos-da-fé* Literally, acts of faith. It was a term used to refer to the hearing at which the Holy Inquisition gave its judgment on a case of heresy, and its most common use is to refer to the burning of heretics at the stake.

[8]*Paul Julius Moebius (1853–1907)* German neurologist and student of the pathological traits of geniuses such as Rousseau, Goethe, Schopenhauer, and Nietzsche.

fill all his expectations and longings. In the ancient mother goddesses, man did not venerate motherliness in the spiritual sense, but rather motherhood in its most elemental meaning. Mother goddesses are earthy godesses, fertile like the soil. They bring forth new life and they nurture it. It was this life-creating power of woman, an elemental force, that filled man with admiration. And this is exactly the point where problems arise. For it is contrary to human nature to sustain appreciation without resentment toward capabilities that one does not possess. Thus, a man's minute share in creating new life became, for him, an immense incitement to create something new on his part. He has created values of which he might well be proud. State, religion, art, and science are essentially his creations, and our entire culture bears the masculine imprint.

However, as happens elsewhere, so it does here; even the greatest 15 satisfactions or achievements, if born out of sublimation, cannot fully make up for something for which we are not endowed by nature. Thus there has remained an obvious residue of general resentment of men against women. This resentment expresses itself, also in our times, in men's distrustful defensive maneuvers against the threat of women's invasion of their domains; hence their tendency to devalue pregnancy and childbirth and to overemphasize male genitality. This attitude does not express itself in scientific theories alone, but is also of far-reaching consequence for the entire relationship between the sexes, and for sexual morality in general. Motherhood, especially illegitimate motherhood, is very insufficiently protected by law—with the one exception of a recent attempt at improvement in Russia. Conversely, there is ample opportunity for the fulfillment of the male's sexual needs. Emphasis on irresponsible sexual indulgence, and devaluation of women to an object of purely physical needs, are further consequences of this masculine attitude.

From Bachofen's[9] investigations we know that this state of the cul- 16 tural supremacy of the male has not existed since the beginning of time, but that women once occupied a central position. This was the era of the so-called matriarchy, when law and custom were centered around the mother. Matricide was then, as Sophocles[10] showed in the *Eumenides*, the unforgivable crime, while patricide, by comparison,

---

[9]*J. J. Bachofen (1815–1887)* One of the earliest German ethnologists who proposed, in 1861, that a pattern of matriarchy—in which the female was the dominant figure in society—had existed in the earliest societies.

[10]*Sophocles (496?–406 B.C.)* A great Greek tragedian. However, Horney is probably referring to Aeschylus (525?–426 B.C.), who wrote the *Eumenides*, the play she mentions.

was a minor offense. Only in recorded historical times have men begun, with minor variations, to play the leading role in the political, economical, and judicial fields, as well as in the area of sexual morality. At present we seem to be going through a period of struggle in which women once more dare to fight for their equality. This is a phase, the duration of which we are not yet able to survey.

I do not want to be misunderstood as having implied that all disaster results from male supremacy and that relations between the sexes would improve if women were given the ascendency. However, we must ask ourselves why there should have to be any power struggle at all between the sexes. At any given time, the more powerful side will create an ideology suitable to help maintain its position and to make this position acceptable to the weaker one. In this ideology the differentness of the weaker one will be interpreted as inferiority, and it will be proven that these differences are unchangeable, basic, or God's will. It is the function of such an ideology to deny or conceal the existence of a struggle. Here is one of the answers to the question raised initially as to why we have so little awareness of the fact that there is a struggle between the sexes. It is in the interest of men to obscure this fact; and the emphasis they place on their ideologies has caused women, also, to adopt these theories. Our attempt at resolving these rationalizations and at examining these ideologies as to their fundamental driving forces, is merely a step on the road taken by Freud.[11] 17

I believe that my exposition shows more clearly the origin of resentment than the origin of dread, and I therefore want to discuss briefly the latter problem. We have seen that the male's dread of the female is directed against her as a sexual being. How is this to be understood? The clearest aspect of this dread is revealed by the Arunta tribe. They believe that the woman has the power to magically influence the male genital. This is what we mean by castration anxiety in analysis. It is an anxiety of psychogenic origin that goes back to feelings of guilt and old childhood fears. Its anatomical-psychological nucleus lies in the fact that during intercourse the male has to entrust his genitals to the female body, that he presents her with his semen and interprets this as a surrender of vital strength to the woman, similar to his experiencing the subsiding of erection after intercourse as evidence of having been weakened by the woman. Although the following idea has not been thoroughly worked through yet, it is highly probable, according to analytical and ethnological data, that the relationship to the mother is more strongly and directly associated with 18

---

[11]*Sigmund Freud (1856–1939)* See the introduction to his selection in this part.

the fear of death than the relationship to the father. We have learned to understand the longing for death as the longing for reunion with the mother. In African fairy tales it is a woman who brings death into the world. The great mother goddesses also brought death and destruction. It is as though we were possessed by the idea that the one who gives life is also capable of taking it away. There is a third aspect of the male's dread of the female that is more difficult to understand and to prove, but that can be demonstrated by observing certain recurrent phenomena in the animal world. We can see that the male is quite frequently equipped with certain specific stimulants for attracting the female, or with specific devices for seizing her during sexual union. Such arrangements would be incomprehensible if the female animal possessed equally urgent or abundant sexual needs as does the male. As a matter of fact, we see that the female rejects the male unconditionally, after fertilization has occurred. Although examples taken from the animal world may be applied to human beings only with the greatest of caution, it is permissible, in this context, to raise the following question: Is it possible that the male is sexually dependent on the female to a higher degree than the woman is on him, because in women part of the sexual energy is linked to generative processes? Could it be that men, therefore, have a vital interest in keeping women dependent on them? So much for the factors that seem to be at the root of the great power struggle between men and women, insofar as they are of a psychogenic nature and related to the male.

That many-faceted thing called love succeeds in building bridges 19 from the loneliness on this shore to the loneliness on the other one. These bridges can be of great beauty, but they are rarely built for eternity and frequently they cannot tolerate too heavy a burden without collapsing. Here is the other answer to the question posed initially of why we see love between the sexes more distinctly than we see hate— because the union of the sexes offers us the greatest possibilities for happiness. We therefore are naturally inclined to overlook how powerful are the destructive forces that continually work to destroy our chances for happiness.

We might ask in conclusion, how can analytical insights contribute 20 to diminish the distrust between the sexes? There is no uniform answer to this problem. The fear of the power of the affects and the difficulty in controlling them in a love relationship, the resulting conflict between surrender and self-preservation, between the I and the Thou[12]

---

[12]***the I and the Thou***   A reference to Martin Buber's book *I and Thou.* Buber (1878–1965), a Jewish theologian and philosopher, is associated with modern existentialism.

is an entirely comprehensible, unmitigatable, and as it were, normal phenomenon. The same thing applies in essence to our readiness for distrust, which stems from unresolved childhood conflicts. These childhood conflicts, however, can vary greatly in intensity, and will leave behind traces of variable depth. Analysis not only can help in individual cases to improve the relationship with the opposite sex, but it can also attempt to improve the psychological conditions of childhood and forestall excessive conflicts. This, of course, is our hope for the future. In the momentous struggle for power, analysis can fulfill an important function by uncovering the real motives of this struggle. This uncovering will not eliminate the motives, but it may help to create a better chance for fighting the struggle on its own ground instead of relegating it to peripheral issues.

QUESTIONS

1. Is it true that there is hostility between the sexes?
2. What are some of the most important childhood experiences that can affect adult behavior toward the opposite sex?
3. This selection was a lecture delivered in Germany in 1930. To what extent do its concerns seem to be no longer relevant? To what extent are the concerns Horney cites still relevant?
4. Do you think this essay will promote better relations between men and women?
5. What kinds of expectations do women seem to have of men? What kinds do men have of women? Do their expectations tend to contribute to hostility in specific ways? Think about Horney's description of expectations in paragraph 8.
6. How do the examples of behavior in primitive cultures contribute to an understanding of the relationship between the sexes in our culture?
7. Is Horney pessimistic or optimistic about relationships between the sexes?

WRITING ASSIGNMENTS

1. In paragraph 9, Horney says that unpleasant experiences with the opposite sex are unavoidable. Is this true? What unpleasant experiences have you had with the opposite sex? What unpleasant experiences have you observed?
2. Horney mentions that the intensity of our feelings can stir up secret longings for, and expectations of, the opposite sex (para. 8). What kinds of secret expectations do you feel each sex might have about the other in a

relationship? Why would such expectations remain secret? Does the fact of secrecy contribute to problems? Does it contribute to hostility?

3. Deep in the essay, in paragraph 14, Horney talks about the possibility of envy contributing to the hostility between the sexes. She says, "For it is contrary to human nature to sustain appreciation without resentment toward capabilities that one does not possess." Do you think she is correct? And do you think she is correct in assuming that envy may have something to do with the hostility between the sexes? Examine your own experience to see whether you recall instances of envy on your part toward a member of the opposite sex (or vice versa).

4. At one point Horney says that "Man's fear of woman is deeply rooted in sex" (para. 13). Is this true? Is woman's fear of man deeply rooted in sex? Examine this question by comparing at least two, and preferably four, magazines for their revelations concerning the psychology of men and women. Choose two men's magazines and two women's magazines. Compare their visual material, particularly photographs of members of the opposite sex. Also compare the fiction and look for signs of a specifically male or female form of fantasy. Compare the advertising to see how distinct the interests of men and women are—and try to relate these to psychological concerns.

5. Horney is very direct in her discussion of male dominance in society, saying not only that it exists but asking "could it be that men, therefore, have a vital interest in keeping women dependent on them?" (para. 18). Do you feel this is true? Conduct an interview with one man and one woman. Find out whether they feel the same or whether they feel differently about this question. Ask them if they see an effort on the part of men to keep women dependent, and then ask them what form any such dependency takes. Do their opinions agree? Where do you stand on this issue?

6. At one point, Horney discusses the question of how different men are from women. Write an essay in which you show the extent to which women are different from men. If possible, sample others' opinions and see if they feel that there are important differences. To what extent would differences between men and women contribute toward hostility?

B. F. SKINNER

What Is Man?

BURRHUS FREDERICK SKINNER *(b. 1904) is an experimental psychologist known for his theories of behaviorism. Behavioral psychology focuses on the ways animals and people behave in response to the myriad complexities of their physical and psychological environment. Skinner's thought has moved in interesting directions, particularly in dealing with the questions of freedom. To some extent, he holds, freedom is not entirely desirable in modern society. It is something that we can outgrow.*

Skinner's emphasis is on the reaction of the individual to the world in which he is placed, and to some extent Skinner sees the individual as a function of that world, as a person whose behavior is essentially created by reinforcement. Reinforcement may be aversive: punishment, such as a spanking, loss of a job, imprisonment. It may be positive: praise, a new job, greater privileges. The "contingencies of reinforcement," an expression he uses often in the present selection, can be aversive, positive, or both. Whatever form they take, they will create the personal behavior of most (if not all) individuals. In posing the question "What is man?" Skinner consciously raises

From *Beyond Freedom and Dignity.*

questions that have been addressed throughout the ages, from ancient Greek philosophers to modern theologians. In answering the question, he is trying to point the way to a new vision.

He calls his vision a scientific view of mankind. By calling it that he includes in his thinking the results of a considerable body of research into the behavior of lower animals as well as of human beings. He has studied the contingencies of reinforcement that have produced learning, which has, in turn, produced behavior of various sorts. To some extent, Skinner's scientific approach has postulated a view of the individual as not being the autonomous agent one would ordinarily assume. The "autonomous agent"—another of Skinner's key terms in this selection—feels able to do anything that free will dictates. The autonomous agent seems to be free and independent. But Skinner points out that such freedom and independence are to some extent illusions. The culture, the family, the peer group, even the prejudices and ignorances of the individual—all combine as contingencies of reinforcement not only to reduce but actually to erase the autonomy of the individual. "Autonomy," in this sense, refers to the individual, personally controlled behavior that each person (as well as each squirrel, rat, and lower animal) feels he or she has.

Naturally, Skinner's views are not wholeheartedly endorsed by most people who adhere to a more traditional view of humankind. Skinner seems heartless and, perhaps, merely scientific. Yet, Skinner's claims suggest that he is most interested in pulling aside the veil of illusion that makes us feel we are free and makes us accept the unconsciously imposed limits on freedom that most of us do. As he points out, cultures have long agreed to maintain certain fictions in order to explain something about the forces that act on people. The Greeks concerned themselves with the gods and with fate. The Christian view focuses on Jesus and God's providence. The eighteenth-century philosophers thought of the world in terms of a machine and believed that there was an ascertainable range of causes and effects that controls people's behavior. Skinner's view is different. He sees people as learning to adapt to an environment without even realizing that they do so. The invisible or unconscious aspects of this process of adaptation are the things that Skinner hopes we will begin to understand.

SKINNER'S RHETORIC

The most obvious rhetorical device Skinner uses is the rhetorical question: What is man? The rest of the essay is, quite logically, an *answer to that question. In the first sentences of the first paragraph, Skinner shifts the ground of the discussion by establishing that the question must be answered, not by looking mainly at the person, but by looking at the environment in which the person thrives. However, used to criticism of the simplified environmentalism that dominated nineteenth-century thought, he begins to clarify the entire nature of environment by examining the ways in which it begins to take over the function of direction, which had been thought to be the preserve only of the individual. He then goes on to examine traits of character, which are generally thought to reside only within the individual, and to show how they, too, are dependent upon the environment.*

Even the extent to which the world can be known is brought into question by Skinner (paras. 8–18), and the issues concerning words and the way they work to affect our sense of knowledge are clarified. From there, Skinner addresses the question of thinking, which he calls "the last stronghold of autonomous man." Thinking is something people share with other beings, as Skinner shows, and certain kinds of misunderstanding, shown to be buried in the "metaphor of storage" (paras. 23–29) in which it is assumed that a person can "possess" knowledge, his or her past, culture, even his or her character. This thinking leads to a consideration of the self (paras. 32–38) and to a rejection of low-grade views of man as a machine (paras. 39–41). In four paragraphs, Skinner discusses the question of direction and purpose in life (paras. 42–45), and then he springs an interesting trap. The chapter to that point had been clearly predicting the doom of autonomous man, with whom the reader has been led to identify. But in the beginning of paragraph 46 he says, "It is only autonomous man who has reached a dead end. Man himself may be controlled by his environment, but it is an environment which is almost wholly of his own making."

The point Skinner wishes to make in answering the question he poses is that until we realize the truth of what it means for autonomous man to be given up as a worn-out fiction, we will misunderstand our own nature. When Socrates insisted that we must know ourselves in order to function in the world, he raised the same issues Skinner has raised. But Skinner's answers to the most basic question—What is man?—are somewhat different from any we have heard before.

What Is Man?

As a science of behavior adopts the strategy of physics and biology,   1
the autonomous agent[1] to which behavior has traditionally been attributed is replaced by the environment—the environment in which the
species evolved and in which the behavior of the individual is shaped
and maintained. The vicissitudes of "environmentalism" show how
difficult it has been to make this change. That a man's behavior owes
something to antecedent events and that the environment is a more
promising point of attack than man himself has long been recognized.
As Crane Brinton observed, "a program to change things not just to
convert people" was a significant part of the English, French, and Russian revolutions.[2] It was Robert Owen,[3] according to Trevelyan, who
first "clearly grasped and taught that environment makes character and
that environment is under human control" or, as Gilbert Seldes[4]
wrote, "that man is a creature of circumstance, that if you changed the
environments of thirty little Hottentots and thirty little aristocratic
English children, the aristocrats would become Hottentots, for all
practical purposes, and the Hottentots little conservatives."

The evidence for a crude environmentalism is clear enough. People   2
are extraordinarily different in different places, and possibly just because of the places. The nomad on horseback in Outer Mongolia and
the astronaut in outer space are different people, but, as far as we
know, if they had been exchanged at birth, they would have taken each
other's place. (The expression "change places" shows how closely we

---

[1]**autonomous agent** Skinner's term for the individual who feels he is a free agent
directed by his own will and basically undirected by outside forces.

[2]**revolutions** The English "Glorious Revolution" of 1688 introduced a constitutional
monarchy; the French Revolution, 1789, created a republic (for a time); the Russian Revolution, 1917, introduced a communist government.

[3]**Robert Owen (1771–1858)** A Welsh industrialist and reformer who brought better living conditions and education to workers at his cotton mills in New Lanark, England, agitated for improved working conditions throughout England, and supported the
new labor union movement. Owen's social thought can be seen in his *A New View of
Society* (1813). In 1825 he founded a utopian community in the United States, at New
Harmony, Indiana, but it failed, and he lost most of his fortune.

[4]**. . . Gilbert Seldes** Crane Brinton, G. M. Trevelyan, and Seldes are all writers
on history, behavior, and thought.

346

identify a person's behavior with the environment in which it occurs.)
But we need to know a great deal more before that fact becomes useful.
What is it about the environment that produces a Hottentot? And
what would need to be changed to produce an English conservative
instead?

Both the enthusiasm of the environmentalist and his usually ig- 3
nominious failure are illustrated by Owen's utopian experiment at
New Harmony. A long history of environmental reform—in education,
penology, industry, and family life, not to mention government and
religion—has shown the same pattern. Environments are constructed
on the model of environments in which good behavior has been observed, but the behavior fails to appear. Two hundred years of this
kind of environmentalism has very little to show for itself, and for a
simple reason. We must know how the environment works before we
can change it to change behavior. A mere shift in emphasis from man
to environment means very little.

Let us consider some examples in which the environment takes 4
over the function and role of autonomous man. The first, often said to
involve human nature, is *aggression*. Men often act in such a way that
they harm others, and they often seem to be reinforced by signs of
damage to others. The ethologists[5] have emphasized contingencies of
survival which would contribute these features to the genetic endowment of the species, but the contingencies of reinforcement in the lifetime of the individual are also significant, since anyone who acts aggressively to harm others is likely to be reinforced in other ways—for
example, by taking possession of goods. The contingencies explain the
behavior quite apart from any state or feeling of aggression or any ini-
tiating act by autonomous man.

Another example involving a so-called "trait of character" is *indus-* 5
try. Some people are industrious in the sense that they work energeti-
cally for long periods of time, while others are lazy and idle in the
sense that they do not. "Industry" and "laziness" are among thousands
of so-called "traits." The behavior they refer to can be explained in
other ways. Some of it may be attributed to genetic idiosyncrasies (and
subject to change only through genetic measures), and the rest to environmental contingencies, which are much more important than is
usually realized. Regardless of any normal genetic endowment, an organism will range between vigorous activity and complete quiescence

---

[5]*ethologists* Those who study the formation and evolution of the human *ethos*,
that is, the moral nature or guiding principles of a human group.

depending upon the schedules on which it has been reinforced. The explanation shifts from a trait of character to an environmental history of reinforcement.

A third example, a "cognitive" activity, is *attention*. A person responds only to a small part of the stimuli impinging upon him. The traditional view is that he himself determines which stimuli are to be effective by "paying attention" to them. Some kind of inner gatekeeper is said to allow some stimuli to enter and to keep all others out. A sudden or strong stimulus may break through and "attract" attention, but the person himself seems otherwise to be in control. An analysis of the environmental circumstances reverses the relation. The kinds of stimuli which break through by "attracting attention" do so because they have been associated in the evolutionary history of the species or the personal history of the individual with important—e.g., dangerous—things. Less forceful stimuli attract attention only to the extent that they have figured in contingencies of reinforcement. We can arrange contingencies which ensure that an organism—even such a "simple" organism as a pigeon—will attend to one object and not to another, or to one property of an object, such as its color, and not to another, such as its shape. The inner gatekeeper is replaced by the contingencies to which the organism has been exposed and which select the stimuli to which it reacts.

In the traditional view a person perceives the world around him and acts upon it to make it known to him. In a sense he reaches out and grasps it. He "takes it in" and possesses it. He "knows" it in the Biblical sense in which a man knows a woman. It has even been argued that the world would not exist if no one perceived it. The action is exactly reversed in an environmental analysis. There would, of course, be no perception if there were no world to be perceived, but an existing world would not be perceived if there were no appropriate contingencies. We say that a baby perceives his mother's face and knows it. Our evidence is that the baby responds in one way to his mother's face and in other ways to other faces or other things. He makes this distinction not through some mental act of perception but because of prior contingencies. Some of these may be contingencies of survival. Physical features of a species are particularly stable parts of the environment in which a species evolves. (That is why courtship and sex and relations between parent and offspring are given such a prominent place by ethologists.) The face and facial expressions of the human mother have been associated with security, warmth, food, and other important things, during both the evolution of the species and the life of the child.

We learn to perceive in the sense that we learn to respond to things 8
in particular ways because of the contingencies of which they are a
part. We may perceive the sun, for example, simply because it is an
extremely powerful stimulus, but it has been a permanent part of the
environment of the species throughout its evolution and more specific
behavior with respect to it could have been selected by contingencies
of survival (as it has been in many other species). The sun also figures
in many current contingencies of reinforcement: we move into or out
of sunlight depending on the temperature; we wait for the sun to rise
or set to take practical action; we talk about the sun and its effects;
and we eventually study the sun with the instruments and methods of
science. Our perception of the sun depends on what we do with respect
to it. Whatever we do, and hence however we perceive it, the fact remains that it is the environment which acts upon the perceiving person, not the perceiving person who acts upon the environment.

The perceiving and knowing which arise from verbal contingencies 9
are even more obviously products of the environment. We react to an
object in many practical ways because of its color; thus, we pick and
eat red apples of a particular variety but not green. It is clear that we
can "tell the difference" between red and green, but something more
is involved when we say that we *know* that one apple is red and the
other green. It is tempting to say that knowing is a cognitive process
altogether divorced from action, but the contingencies provide a more
useful distinction. When someone asks about the color of an object
which he cannot see, and we tell him that it is red, *we* do nothing
about the object in any other way. It is the person who has questioned
us and heard our answer who makes a practical response which depends on color. Only under verbal contingencies can a speaker respond
to an isolated property to which a nonverbal response cannot be made.
A response made to the property of an object without responding to
the object in any other way is called *abstract*. Abstract thinking is the
product of a particular kind of environment, not of a cognitive faculty.

As listeners we acquire a kind of knowledge from the verbal behav- 10
ior of others which may be extremely valuable in permitting us to
avoid direct exposure to contingencies. We learn from the experience
of others by responding to what they say about contingencies. When
we are warned against doing something or are advised to do something,
there may be no point in speaking of knowledge, but when we learn
more durable kinds of warnings and advice in the form of maxims or
rules, we may be said to have a special kind of knowledge about the
contingencies to which they apply. The laws of science are descriptions of contingencies of reinforcement, and one who knows a scien-

tific law may behave effectively without being exposed to the contingencies it describes. (He will, of course, have very different feelings about the contingencies, depending on whether he is following a rule or has been directly exposed to them. Scientific knowledge is "cold," but the behavior to which it gives rise is as effective as the "warm" knowledge which comes from personal experience.)

Isaiah Berlin has referred to a particular sense of knowing, said to have been discovered by Giambattista Vico.[6] It is "the sense in which I know what it is to be poor, to fight for a cause, belong to a nation, to join or abandon a church or a party, to feel nostalgia, terror, the omnipresence of a god, to understand a gesture, a work of art, a joke, a man's character, that one is transformed or lying to oneself." These are the kinds of things one is likely to learn through direct contact with contingencies rather than from the verbal behavior of others, and special kinds of feelings are no doubt associated with them, but, even so, the knowledge is not somehow directly given. A person can know what it is to fight for a cause only after a long history during which he has learned to perceive and to know that state of affairs called fighting for a cause.

The role of the environment is particularly subtle when what is known is the knower himself. If there is no external world to initiate knowing, must we not then say that the knower himself acts first? This is, of course, the field of consciousness, or awareness, a field which a scientific analysis of behavior is often accused of ignoring. The charge is a serious one and should be taken seriously. Man is said to differ from the other animals mainly because he is "aware of his own existence." He knows what he is doing; he knows that he has had a past and will have a future; he "reflects on his own nature"; he alone follows the classical injunction "Know thyself." Any analysis of human behavior which neglected these facts would be defective indeed. And some analyses do. What is called "methodological behaviorism" limits itself to what can be publicly observed; mental processes may exist, but they are ruled out of scientific consideration by their nature. The "behavioralists" in political science and many logical positivists[7] in philosophy have followed a similar line. But self-observation can be studied, and it must be included in any reasonably complete account

11

12

---

[6]*Giovanni Battista Vico (1668–1724)* Italian philosopher whose theories of history involve cycles of repetition of behavior. Sir Isaiah Berlin (b. 1909) is a British historian of ideas and philosopher.

[7]*logical positivists* Twentieth-century thinkers who felt human knowledge was limited to only those things that could be known from observation.

of human behavior. Rather than ignore consciousness, an experimental analysis of behavior has stressed certain crucial issues. The question is not whether a man can know himself but what he knows when he does so.

The problem arises in part from the indisputable fact of privacy: a 13 small part of the universe is enclosed within a human skin. It would be foolish to deny the existence of that private world, but it is also foolish to assert that because it is private it is of a different nature from the world outside. The difference is not in the stuff of which the private world is composed, but in its accessibility. There is an exclusive intimacy about a headache, or heartache, or a silent soliloquy. The intimacy is sometimes distressing (one cannot shut one's eyes to a headache), but it need not be, and it has seemed to support the doctrine that knowing is a kind of possession.

The difficulty is that although privacy may bring the knower closer 14 to what he knows, it interferes with the process through which he comes to know anything. As we saw in [an earlier chapter], the contingencies under which a child learns to describe his feelings are necessarily defective; the verbal community cannot use the procedures with which it teaches a child to describe objects. There are, of course, natural contingencies under which we learn to respond to private stimuli, and they generate behavior of great precision; we could not jump or walk or turn a handspring if we were not being stimulated by parts of our own body. But very little awareness is associated with this kind of behavior and, in fact, we behave in these ways most of the time without being aware of the stimuli to which we are responding. We do not attribute awareness to other species which obviously use similar private stimuli. To "know" private stimuli is more than to respond to them.

The verbal community specializes in self-descriptive contingencies. It asks such questions as: What did you do yesterday? What are you doing now? What will you do tomorrow? Why did you do that? Do you really want to do that? How do you feel about that? The answers help people to adjust to each other effectively. And it is because such questions are asked that a person responds to himself and his behavior in the special way called knowing or being aware. Without the help of a verbal community all behavior would be unconscious. Consciousness is a social product. It is not only *not* the special field of autonomous man, it is *not* within range of a solitary man.

And it is not within the range of accuracy of anyone. The privacy 16 which seems to confer intimacy upon self-knowledge makes it impossible for the verbal community to maintain precise contingencies. In-

trospective vocabularies are by nature inaccurate, and that is one reason why they have varied so widely among schools of philosophy and
psychology. Even a carefully trained observer runs into trouble when
new private stimuli are studied. (Independent evidence of private stimulation—for example, through physiological measures—would make it
possible to sharpen the contingencies which generate self-observation
and would, incidentally, confirm the present interpretation. Such evidence would not, as we noted in [an earlier chapter], offer any support
for a theory which attributed human behavior to an observable inner
agent.)

Theories of psychotherapy which emphasize awareness assign a   17
role to autonomous man which is properly, and much more effectively, reserved for contingencies of reinforcement. Awareness may
help if the problem is in part a lack of awareness, and "insight" into
one's condition may help if one then takes remedial action, but awareness or insight alone is not always enough, and it may be too much.
One need not be aware of one's behavior or the conditions controlling
it in order to behave effectively—or ineffectively. On the contrary, as
the toad's inquiry of the centipede demonstrates, constant self-observation may be a handicap. The accomplished pianist would perform
badly if he were as clearly aware of his behavior as the student who is
just learning to play.

Cultures are often judged by the extent to which they encourage   18
self-observation. Some cultures are said to breed unthinking men, and
Socrates[8] has been admired for inducing men to inquire into their own
nature, but self-observation is only a preliminary to action. The extent
to which a man *should* be aware of himself depends upon the importance of self-observation for effective behavior. Self-knowledge is valuable only to the extent that it helps to meet the contingencies under
which it has arisen.

Perhaps the last stronghold of autonomous man is that complex   19
"cognitive" activity called thinking. Because it is complex, it has
yielded only slowly to explanation in terms of contingencies of reinforcement. When we say that a person *discriminates* between red and
orange, we imply that discrimination is a kind of mental act. The

---

[8]*Socrates (469?–399 B.C.)* Greek philosopher. Socrates insisted upon rigorous
self-examination no matter what the cost. He was put to death for "corrupting the youth"
of Athens, which may indicate the problems inherent in promoting individualism in certain societies.

person himself does not seem to be doing anything; he responds in different ways to red and orange stimuli, but this is the result of discrimination rather than the act. Similarly, we say that a person *generalizes*—say, from his own limited experience to the world at large—but all we see is that he responds to the world at large as he has learned to respond to his own small world. We say that a person *forms a concept or an abstraction,* but all we see is that certain kinds of contingencies of reinforcement have brought a response under the control of a single property of a stimulus. We say that a person *recalls* or *remembers* what he has seen or heard, but all we see is that the present occasion evokes a response, possibly in weakened or altered form, acquired on another occasion. We say that a person *associates* one word with another, but all we observe is that one verbal stimulus evokes the response previously made to another. Rather than suppose that it is therefore autonomous man who discriminates, generalizes, forms concepts or abstractions, recalls or remembers, and associates, we can put matters in good order simply by noting that these terms do not refer to forms of behavior.

A person may take explicit action, however, when he solves a problem. In putting a jigsaw puzzle together he may move the pieces around to improve his chances of finding a fit. In solving an equation he may transpose, clear fractions, and extract roots to improve his chances of finding a form of the equation he has already learned how to solve. The creative artist may manipulate a medium until something of interest turns up. Much of this can be done covertly, and it is then likely to be assigned to a different dimensional system, but it can always be done overtly, perhaps more slowly but also often more effectively, and with rare exceptions it must have been learned in overt form. The culture promotes thinking by constructing special contingencies. It teaches a person to make fine discriminations by making differential reinforcement more precise. It teaches techniques to be used in solving problems. It provides rules which make it unnecessary to be exposed to the contingencies from which the rules are derived, and it provides rules for finding rules. 20

Self-control, or self-management, is a special kind of problem solving which, like self-knowledge, raises all the issues associated with privacy. We have discussed some techniques in connection with aversive control in [an earlier chapter]. It is always the environment which builds the behavior with which problems are solved, even when the problems are to be found in the private world inside the skin. None of this has been investigated in a very productive way, but the inadequacy of our analysis is no reason to fall back on a miracle-working 21

mind. If our understanding of contingencies of reinforcement is not yet
sufficient to explain all kinds of thinking, we must remember that the
appeal to mind explains nothing at all.

In shifting control from autonomous man to the observable envi-   22
ronment we do not leave an empty organism. A great deal goes on
inside the skin, and physiology will eventually tell us more about it.
It will explain why behavior is indeed related to the antecedent events
of which it can be shown to be a function. The assignment is not
always correctly understood. Many physiologists regard themselves as
looking for the "physiological correlates" of mental events. Physiological research is regarded as simply a more scientific version of introspection. But physiological techniques are not, of course, designed to
detect or measure personalities, ideas, attitudes, feelings, impulses,
thoughts, or purposes. (If they were, we should have to answer a third
question in addition to those raised in [an earlier chapter]: How can a
personality, idea, feeling, or purpose affect the instruments of the
physiologist?) At the moment neither introspection nor physiology
supplies very adequate information about what is going on inside a
man as he behaves, and since they are both directed inward, they have
the same effect of diverting attention from the external environment.

Much of the misunderstanding about an inner man comes from the   23
metaphor of storage. Evolutionary and environmental histories change
an organism, but they are not stored within it. Thus, we observe that
babies suck their mothers' breasts, and we can easily imagine that a
strong tendency to do so has survival value, but much more is implied
by a "sucking instinct" regarded as something a baby possesses which
enables it to suck. The concept of "human nature" or "genetic endowment" is dangerous when taken in that sense. We are closer to human
nature in a baby than in an adult, or in a primitive culture than in an
advanced, in the sense that environmental contingencies are less likely
to have obscured the genetic endowment, and it is tempting to dramatize that endowment by implying that earlier stages have survived in
concealed form: man is a naked ape, and "the paleolithic bull which
survives in man's inner self still paws the earth whenever a threatening gesture is made on the social scene." But anatomists and physiologists will not find an ape, or a bull, or for that matter instincts. They
will find anatomical and physiological features which are the product
of an evolutionary history.

The personal history of the individual is also often said to be stored   24
within him. For "instinct" read "habit." The cigarette habit is presumably something more than the behavior said to show that a person
possesses it; but the only other information we have concerns the rein-

forcers and the schedules of reinforcement which make a person smoke a great deal. The contingencies are not stored; they have simply left a changed person.

The environment is often said to be stored in the form of memo- 25 ries: to recall something we search for a copy of it, which can then be seen as the original thing was seen. As far as we know, however, there are no copies of the environment in the individual *at any time,* even when a thing is present and being observed. The products of more complex contingencies are also said to be stored; the repertoire acquired as a person learns to speak French is called a "knowledge of French."

Traits of character, whether derived from contingencies of survival 26 or contingencies of reinforcement, are also said to be stored. A curious example occurs in Follett's *Modern American Usage:* "We say *He faced these adversities bravely,* aware without thought that the bravery is a property of the man, not of the facing; a brave act is poetic shorthand for the act of a person who shows bravery by performing it." But we call a man brave because of his acts, and he behaves bravely when environmental circumstances induce him to do so. The circumstances have changed his behavior; they have not implanted a trait or virtue.

Philosophies are also spoken of as things possessed. A man is said 27 to speak or act in certain ways because he has a particular philosophy—such as idealism, dialectical materialism, or Calvinism.[9] Terms of this kind summarize the effect of environmental conditions which it would now be hard to trace, but the conditions must have existed and should not be ignored. A person who possesses a "philosophy of freedom" is one who has been changed in certain ways by the literature of freedom.

The issue has had a curious place in theology. Does man sin be- 28 cause he is sinful, or is he sinful because he sins? Neither question points to anything very useful. To say that a man is sinful because he sins is to give an operational definition of sin. To say that he sins because he is sinful is to trace his behavior to a supposed inner trait. But whether or not a person engages in the kind of behavior called

---

[9]*idealism, dialectical materialism, or Calvinism Idealism* is the belief that reality is found in ideas rather than objects themselves; *dialectical materialism* is a Marxian belief in the conflict and resolution of powerful forces as well as a belief in material values and their reality; *Calvinism* is a strict Protestant religion which insists that people are totally depraved and only a few will be saved by the grace of God. All these philosophies have strong adherents today.

sinful depends upon circumstances which are not mentioned in either question. The sin assigned as an inner possession (the sin a person "knows") is to be found in a history of reinforcement. (The expression "God-fearing" suggests such a history, but piety, virtue, the immanence of God, a moral sense, or morality does not. As we have seen, man is not a moral animal in the sense of possessing a special trait or virtue; he has built a kind of social environment which induces him to behave in moral ways.)

These distinctions have practical implications. A recent survey of white Americans is said to have shown that "more than half blamed the inferior educational and economic status of blacks on 'something about Negroes themselves.'" The "something" was further identified as "lack of motivation," which was to be distinguished from *both* genetic and environmental factors. Significantly, motivation was said to be associated with "free will." To neglect the role of the environment in this way is to discourage any inquiry into the defective contingencies responsible for a "lack of motivation." 29

It is in the nature of an experimental analysis of human behavior that it should strip away the functions previously assigned to autonomous man and transfer them one by one to the controlling environment. The analysis leaves less and less for autonomous man to do. But what about man himself? Is there not something about a person which is more than a living body? Unless something called a self survives, how can we speak of self-knowledge or self-control? To whom is the injunction "Know thyself" addressed? 30

It is an important part of the contingencies to which a young child is exposed that his own body is the only part of his environment which remains the same *(idem)* from moment to moment and day to day. We say that he discovers his *identity* as he learns to distinguish between his body and the rest of the world. He does this long before the community teaches him to call things by name and to distinguish "me" from "it" or "you." 31

A self is a repertoire of behavior appropriate to a given set of contingencies. A substantial part of the conditions to which a person is exposed may play a dominant role, and under other conditions a person may report, "I'm not myself today," or, "I couldn't have done what you said I did, because that's not like me." The identity conferred upon a self arises from the contingencies responsible for the behavior. Two or more repertoires generated by different sets of contingencies compose two or more selves. A person possesses one repertoire appropriate to his life with his friends and another appropriate to his life 32 with his family, and a friend may find him a very different person if he sees him with his family or his family if they see him with his friends. The problem of identity arises when situations are intermingled, as when a person finds himself with both his family and his friends at the same time.

Self-knowledge and self-control imply two selves in this sense. The self-knower is almost always a product of social contingencies, but the self that is known may come from other sources. The controlling self (the conscience or superego) is of social origin, but the controlled self is more likely to be the product of genetic susceptibilities to reinforcement (the id, or the Old Adam). The controlling self generally represents the interests of others, the controlled self the interests of the individual. 33

The picture which emerges from a scientific analysis *is* not of a body with a person inside, but of a body which *is* a person in the sense that it displays a complex repertoire of behavior. The picture is, of course, unfamiliar. The man thus portrayed is a stranger, and from the traditional point of view he may not seem to be a man at all. "For at least one hundred years," said Joseph Wood Krutch,[10] "we have been prejudiced in every theory, including economic determinism, mechanistic behaviorism, and relativism, that reduces the stature of man until he ceases to be man at all in any sense that the humanists of an earlier generation would recognize." Matson has argued that "the empirical behavioral scientist . . . denies, if only by implication, that a unique being, called Man, exists." "What is now under attack," said Maslow, "is the 'being' of man." C. S. Lewis[11] put it quite bluntly: Man is being abolished. 34

There is clearly some difficulty in identifying the man to whom these expressions refer. Lewis cannot have meant the human species, for not only is it not being abolished, it is filling the earth. (As a result it may eventually abolish itself through disease, famine, pollution, or a nuclear holocaust, but that is not what Lewis meant.) Nor are individual men growing less effective or productive. We are told that what 35

---

[10]*Joseph Wood Krutch (1893–1970)* American critic and writer whose books and essays on nature were famed. His most famous book is *The Measure of Man* (1954). He also wrote *Henry David Thoreau* (1948), a highly regarded biography and appreciation.

[11]*Abraham Maslow (1908–1970) and C. S. Lewis (1898–1963)* Widely known as writers on human values. Maslow, an American psychologist, based his thinking on a hierarchy of human needs, from survival at the bottom to self-actualization at the top. Lewis, an English critic and novelist, was one of the foremost twentieth-century spokesmen for orthodox Christian belief.

is threatened is "man *qua*[12] man" or "man in his humanity," or "man as Thou not It," or "man as a person not a thing." These are not very helpful expressions, but they supply a clue. What is being abolished is autonomous man—the inner man, the homunculus,[13] the possessing demon, the man defended by the literatures of freedom and dignity.

His abolition has long been overdue. Autonomous man is a device used to explain what we cannot explain in any other way. He has been constructed from our ignorance, and as our understanding increases, the very stuff of which he is composed vanishes. Science does not de-humanize man, it de-homunculizes him, and it must do so if it is to prevent the abolition of the human species. To man *qua* man we read-ily say good riddance. Only by dispossessing him can we turn to the real causes of human behavior. Only then can we turn from the in-ferred to the observed, from the miraculous to the natural, from the inaccessible to the manipulable. 36

It is often said that in doing so we must treat the man who survives as a mere animal. "Animal" is a pejorative term, but only because "man" has been made spuriously honorific. Krutch has argued that whereas the traditional view supports Hamlet's exclamation, "How like a god!," Pavlov,[14] the behavioral scientist, emphasized "How like a dog!" But that was a step forward. A god is the archetypal pattern of an explanatory fiction, of a miracle-working mind, of the metaphysi-cal. Man is much more than a dog, but like a dog he is within range of a scientific analysis. 37

It is true that much of the experimental analysis of behavior has been concerned with lower organisms. Genetic differences are mini-mized by using special strains; environmental histories can be con-trolled, perhaps from birth; strict regimens can be maintained during long experiments; and very little of this is possible with human sub-jects. Moreover, in working with lower animals the scientist is less likely to put his own responses to the experimental conditions among his data, or to design contingencies with an eye to their effect on him rather than on the experimental organism he is studying. No one is disturbed when physiologists study respiration, reproduction, nutri-tion, or endocrine systems in animals; they do so to take advantage of very great similarities. Comparable similarities in behavior are being 38

---

[12]*qua* as.

[13]*homunculus* A tiny man; in Goethe's *Faust*, a kind of possessing spirit.

[14]*Ivan Pavlov (1849–1936)* Russian psychologist who conditioned a dog to sali-vate upon the ringing of a bell. Much behaviorist psychology is based upon his experi-ments.

discovered. There is, of course, always the danger that methods designed for the study of lower animals will emphasize only those characteristics which they have in common with men, but we cannot discover what is "essentially" human until we have investigated non-human subjects. Traditional theories of autonomous man have exaggerated species differences. Some of the complex contingencies of reinforcement now under investigation generate behavior in lower organisms which, if the subjects were human, would traditionally be said to involve higher mental processes.

Man is not made into a machine by analyzing his behavior in me- 39 chanical terms. Early theories of behavior, as we have seen, represented man as a push-pull automaton, close to the nineteenth-century notion of a machine, but progress has been made. Man is a machine in the sense that he is a complex system behaving in lawful ways, but the complexity is extraordinary. His capacity to adjust to contingencies of reinforcement will perhaps be eventually simulated by machines, but this has not yet been done, and the living system thus simulated will remain unique in other ways.

Nor is man made into a machine by inducing him to use machines. 40 Some machines call for behavior which is repetitive and monotonous, and we escape from them when we can, but others enormously extend our effectiveness in dealing with the world around us. A person may respond to very small things with the help of an electron microscope and to very large things with radiotelescopes, and in doing so he may seem quite inhuman to those who use only their unaided senses. A person may act upon the environment with the delicate precision of a micromanipulator or with the range and power of a space rocket, and his behavior may seen inhuman to those who rely only on muscular contractions. (It has been argued that the apparatus used in the operant laboratory misrepresents natural behavior because it introduces an external source of power, but men use external sources when they fly kites, sail boats, or shoot bows and arrows. They would have to abandon all but a small fraction of their achievements if they used only the power of their muscles.) People record their behavior in books and other media, and the use they make of the records may seem quite inhuman to those who can use only what they remember. People describe complex contingencies in the form of rules, and rules for manipulating rules, and they introduce them into electronic systems which "think" with a speed that seems quite inhuman to the unaided thinker. Human beings do all this with machines, and they would be less than human if they did not. What we now regard as machine-like behavior was, in fact, much commoner before the invention of these devices. The slave in the cotton field, the bookkeeper on his high stool, the student being drilled by a teacher—these were the machine-like men.

Machines replace people when they do what people have done, and 41 the social consequences may be serious. As technology advances, machines will take over more and more of the functions of men, but only up to a point. We build machines which reduce some of the aversive features of our environment (grueling labor, for example) and which produce more positive reinforcers. We build them precisely because they do so. We have no reason to build machines to be reinforced by these consequences, and to do so would be to deprive ourselves of reinforcement. If the machines man makes eventually make him wholly expendable, it will be by accident, not design.

An important role of autonomous man has been to give human 42 behavior direction, and it is often said that in dispossessing an inner agent we leave man himself without a purpose. As one writer has put it, "Since a scientific psychology must regard human behavior objectively, as determined by necessary laws, it must represent human behavior as unintentional." But "necessary laws" would have this effect only if they referred exclusively to antecedent conditions. Intention and purpose refer to selective consequences, the effects of which can be formulated in "necessary laws." Has life, in all the forms in which it exists on the surface of the earth, a purpose, and is this evidence of intentional design? The primate hand evolved *in order that* things might be more successfully manipulated, but its purpose is to be found not in a prior design but rather in the process of selection. Similarly, in operant conditioning the purpose of a skilled movement of the hand is to be found in the consequences which follow it. A pianist neither acquires nor executes the behavior of playing a scale smoothly because of a prior intention of doing so. Smoothly played scales are reinforcing for many reasons, and they select skilled movements. In neither the evolution of the human hand nor in the acquired use of the hand is any prior intention or purpose at issue.

The argument for purpose seems to be strengthened by moving 43 back into the darker recesses of mutation. Jacques Barzun[15] has argued that Darwin and Marx both neglected not only human purpose but the creative purpose responsible for the variations upon which natural se-

---

[15]*Jacques Barzun (b. 1907)* A noted American scholar; Skinner is referring to his book, *Darwin, Marx, and Wagner.*

lection plays. It may prove to be the case, as some geneticists have argued, that mutations are not entirely random, but nonrandomness is not necessarily the proof of a creative mind. Mutations will not be random when geneticists explicitly design them in order that an organism will meet specific conditions of selection more successfully, and geneticists will then seem to be playing the role of the creative Mind in pre-evolutionary theory, but the purpose they display will have to be sought in their culture, in the social environment which has induced them to make genetic changes appropriate to contingencies of survival.

There is a difference between biological and individual purpose in   44
that the latter can be felt. No one could have felt the purpose in the development of the human hand, whereas a person can in a sense feel the purpose with which he plays a smooth scale. But he does not play a smooth scale *because* he feels the purpose of doing so; what he feels is a by-product of his behavior in relation to its consequences. The relation of the human hand to the contingencies of survival under which it evolved is, of course, out of reach of personal observation; the relation of the behavior to contingencies of reinforcement which have generated it is not.

A scientific analysis of behavior dispossesses autonomous man and   45
turns the control he has been said to exert over to the environment. The individual may then seem particularly vulnerable. He is henceforth to be controlled by the world around him, and in large part by other men. Is he not then simply a victim? Certainly men have been victims, as they have been victimizers, but the word is too strong. It implies despoliation, which is by no means an essential consequence of interpersonal control. But even under benevolent control is the individual not at best a spectator who may watch what happens but is helpless to do anything about it? Is he not "at a dead end in his long struggle to control his own destiny"?

It is only autonomous man who has reached a dead end. Man him-   46
self may be controlled by his environment, but it is an environment which is almost wholly of his own making. The physical environment of most people is largely man-made. The surfaces a person walks on, the walls which shelter him, the clothing he wears, many of the foods he eats, the tools he uses, the vehicles he moves about in, most of the things he listens to and looks at are human products. The social environment is obviously man-made—it generates the language a person speaks, the customs he follows, and the behavior he exhibits with respect to the ethical, religious, governmental, economic, educational,

and psychotherapeutic institutions which control him. The evolution of a culture is in fact a kind of gigantic exercise in self-control. As the individual controls himself by manipulating the world in which he lives, so the human species has constructed an environment in which its members behave in a highly effective way. Mistakes have been made, and we have no assurance that the environment man has constructed will continue to provide gains which outstrip the losses, but man as we know him, for better or for worse, is what man has made of man.

This will not satisfy those who cry "Victim!" C. S. Lewis protested: 47 ". . . the power of man to make himself what he pleases . . . means . . . the power of some men to make other men what they please." This is inevitable in the nature of cultural evolution. The controlling *self* must be distinguished from the controlled self, even when they are both inside the same skin, and when control is exercised through the design of an external environment, the selves are, with minor exceptions, distinct. The person who unintentionally or intentionally introduces a new cultural practice is only one among possibly billions who will be affected by it. If this does not seem like an act of self-control, it is only because we have misunderstood the nature of self-control in the individual.

When a person changes his physical or social environment "inten- 48 tionally"—that is, in order to change human behavior, possibly including his own—he plays two roles: one as a controller, as the designer of a controlling culture, and another as the controlled, as the product of a culture. There is nothing inconsistent about this; it follows from the nature of the evolution of a culture, with or without intentional design.

The human species has probably not undergone much genetic 49 change in recorded time. We have only to go back a thousand generations to reach the artists of the caves of Lascaux.[16] Features which bear directly on survival (such as resistance to disease) change substantially in a thousand generations, but the child of one of the Lascaux artists transplanted to the world of today might be almost indistinguishable from a modern child. It is possible that he would learn more slowly than his modern counterpart, that he could maintain only a smaller repertoire without confusion, or that he would forget more quickly;

---

[16]*caves of Lascaux*   Lascaux is in southwest France. The caves discovered there were painted with bison, elk, and other figures some 15,000 to 20,000 years ago. Other such caves have been found in Spain and elsewhere in France.

we cannot be sure. But we can be sure that a twentieth-century child transplanted to the civilization of Lascaux would not be very different from the children he met there, for we have seen what happens when a modern child is raised in an impoverished environment.

Man has greatly changed himself as a person in the same period of 50 time by changing the world in which he lives. Something of the order of a hundred generations will cover the development of modern religious practices, and something of the same order of magnitude modern government and law. Perhaps no more than twenty generations will account for modern industrial practices, and possibly no more than four or five for education and psychotherapy. The physical and biological technologies which have increased man's sensitivity to the world around him and his power to change that world have taken no more than four or five generations.

Man has "controlled his own destiny," if that expression means 51 anything at all. The man that man has made is the product of the culture man has devised. He has emerged from two quite different processes of evolution: the biological evolution responsible for the human species and the cultural evolution carried out by that species. Both of these processes of evolution may now accelerate because they are both subject to intentional design. Men have already changed their genetic endowment by breeding selectively and by changing contingencies of survival, and they may now begin to introduce mutations directly related to survival. For a long time men have introduced new practices which serve as cultural mutations, and they have changed the conditions under which practices are selected. They may now begin to do both with a clearer eye to the consequences.

Man will presumably continue to change, but we cannot say in 52 what direction. No one could have predicted the evolution of the human species at any point in its early history, and the direction of intentional genetic design will depend upon the evolution of a culture which is itself unpredictable for similar reasons. "The limits of perfection of the human species," said Étienne Cabet[17] in Voyage en Icarie, "are as yet unknown." But, of course, there are no limits. The human species will never reach a final state of perfection before it is exterminated—"some say in fire, some in ice," and some in radiation.

---

[17]*Étienne Cabet (1788–1856)* A French communist whose Voyage en Icarie (1840) offers a plan for a utopia which Cabet in 1848 tried to put into practice. He purchased land in the Red River in Texas, then sent 1,500 settlers there. The experiment failed. He later took his "Icarians" to Nauvoo, Illinois, a former Mormon settlement, where he remained their leader until his death.

The individual occupies a place in a culture not unlike his place in 53 the species, and in early evolutionary theory that place was hotly debated. Was the species simply a type of individual, and if so, in what sense could it evolve? Darwin himself declared species "to be purely subjective inventions of the taxonomist." A species has no existence except as a collection of individuals, nor has a family, tribe, race, nation, or class. A culture has no existence apart from the behavior of the individuals who maintain its practices. It is always an individual who behaves, who acts upon the environment and is changed by the consequences of his action, and who maintains the social contingencies which *are* a culture. The individual is the carrier of both his species and his culture. Cultural practices, like genetic traits, are transmitted from individual to individual. A new practice, like a new genetic trait, appears first in an individual and tends to be transmitted if it contributes to his survival as an individual.

Yet, the individual is at best a locus in which many lines of devel- 54 opment come together in a unique set. His individuality is unquestioned. Every cell in his body is a unique genetic product, as unique as that classic mark of individuality, the fingerprint. And even within the most regimented culture every personal history is unique. No intentional culture can destroy that uniqueness, and, as we have seen, any effort to do so would be bad design. But the individual nevertheless remains merely a stage in a process which began long before he came into existence and will long outlast him. He has no ultimate responsibility for a species trait or a cultural practice, even though it was he who underwent the mutation or introduced the practice which became part of the species or culture. Even if Lamarck[18] had been right in supposing that the individual could change his genetic structure through personal effort, we should have to point to the environmental circumstances responsible for the effort, as we shall have to do when geneticists begin to change the human endowment. And when an individual engages in the intentional design of a cultural practice, we must turn to the culture which induces him to do so and supplies the art or science he uses.

One of the great problems of individualism, seldom recognized as 55 such, is death—the inescapable fate of the individual, the final assault on freedom and dignity. Death is one of those remote events which are brought to bear on behavior only with the aid of cultural practices.

---

[18]*Jean Baptiste Lamarck (1744–1829)* French scientist who thought that it was possible to inherit acquired characteristics genetically.

What we see is the death of others, as in Pascal's[19] famous metaphor: "Imagine a number of men in chains, all under sentence of death, some of whom are each day butchered in the sight of the others; those remaining see their own condition in that of their fellows, and looking at each other with grief and despair await their turn. This is an image of the human condition." Some religions have made death more important by picturing a future existence in heaven or hell, but the individualist has a special reason to fear death, engineered not by a religion but by the literatures of freedom and dignity. It is the prospect of personal annihilation. The individualist can find no solace in reflecting upon any contribution which will survive him. He has refused to act for the good of others and is therefore not reinforced by the fact that others whom he has helped will outlive him. He has refused to be concerned for the survival of his culture and is not reinforced by the fact that the culture will long survive him. In the defense of his own freedom and dignity he has denied the contributions of the past and must therefore relinquish all claim upon the future.

Science has probably never demanded a more sweeping change in a 56 traditional way of thinking about a subject, nor has there ever been a more important subject. In the traditional picture a person perceives the world around him, selects features to be perceived, discriminates among them, judges them good or bad, changes them to make them better (or, if he is careless, worse), and may be held responsible for his action and justly rewarded or punished for its consequences. In the scientific picture a person is a member of a species shaped by evolutionary contingencies of survival, displaying behavioral processes which bring him under the control of the environment in which he lives, and largely under the control of a social environment which he and millions of others like him have constructed and maintained during the evolution of a culture. The direction of the controlling relation is reversed: a person does not act upon the world, the world acts upon him.

It is difficult to accept such a change simply on intellectual 57 grounds and nearly impossible to accept its implications. The reaction of the traditionalist is usually described in terms of feelings. One of these, to which the Freudians have appealed in explaining the resistance to psychoanalysis, is wounded vanity. Freud himself expounded,

---

[19]***Blaise Pascal (1623–1662)*** French philosopher and scientist. He was generally enigmatic in his thought, particularly in his *Pensées* (1658), in which he begins to call all knowledge into doubt. Pascal was a devout Catholic, but the religious orthodoxy of his work is subject to debate.

as Ernest Jones[20] has said, "the three heavy blows which narcissism or self-love of mankind had suffered at the hands of science. The first was cosmological and was dealt by Copernicus;[21] the second was biological and was dealt by Darwin; the third was psychological and was dealt by Freud." (The blow was suffered by the belief that something at the center of man knows all that goes on within him and that an instrument called will power exercises command and control over the rest of one's personality.) But what are the signs or symptoms of wounded vanity, and how shall we explain them? What people *do* about such a scientific picture of man is call it wrong, demeaning, and dangerous, argue against it, and attack those who propose or defend it. They do so not out of wounded vanity but because the scientific formulation has destroyed accustomed reinforcers. If a person can no longer take credit or be admired for what he does, then he seems to suffer a loss of dignity or worth, and behavior previously reinforced by credit or admiration will undergo extinction. Extinction often leads to aggressive attack.

Another effect of the scientific picture has been described as a loss   58
of faith or "nerve," as a sense of doubt or powerlessness, or as discouragement, depression, or despondency. A person is said to feel that he can do nothing about his own destiny. But what he feels is a weakening of old responses which are no longer reinforced. People are indeed "powerless" when long-established verbal repertoires prove useless. For example, one historian has complained that if the deeds of men are "to be dismissed as simply the product of material and psychological conditioning," there is nothing to write about; "change must be at least partially the result of conscious mental activity."

Another effect is a kind of nostalgia. Old repertoires break through,   59
as similarities between present and past are seized upon and exaggerated. Old days are called the good old days, when the inherent dignity of man and the importance of spiritual values were recognized. Such fragments of outmoded behavior tend to be "wistful"—that is, they have the character of increasingly unsuccessful behavior.

These reactions to a scientific conception of man are certainly un-   60
fortunate. They immobilize men of good will, and anyone concerned with the future of his culture will do what he can to correct them. No

---

[20]***Ernest Jones (1879–1958)*** A follower of Freud. His book *Hamlet and Oedipus* (1949) applies Freud's theory to a literary classic, Shakespeare's *Hamlet*.
[21]***Nicolaus Copernicus (1473–1543)*** Polish astronomer who theorized that the earth revolved around the sun. His theory revolutionized astronomy and shook the foundations of Western thought.

theory changes what it is a theory about. Nothing is changed because we look at it, talk about it, or analyze it in a new way. Keats drank confusion to Newton[22] for analyzing the rainbow, but the rainbow remained as beautiful as ever and became for many even more beautiful. Man has not changed because we look at him, talk about him, and analyze him scientifically. His achievements in science, government, religion, art, and literature remain as they have always been, to be admired as one admires a storm at sea or autumn foliage or a mountain peak, quite apart from their origins and untouched by a scientific analysis. What does change is our chance of doing something about the subject of a theory. Newton's analysis of the light in a rainbow was a step in the direction of the laser.[23]

The traditional conception of man is flattering; it confers reinforc- 61 ing privileges. It is therefore easily defended and can be changed only with difficulty. It was designed to build up the individual as an instrument of countercontrol, and it did so effectively but in such a way as to limit progress. We have seen how the literatures of freedom and dignity, with their concern for autonomous man, have perpetuated the use of punishment and condoned the use of only weak nonpunitive techniques, and it is not difficult to demonstrate a connection between the unlimited right of the individual to pursue happiness and the catastrophes threatened by unchecked breeding, the unrestrained affluence which exhausts resources and pollutes the environment, and the imminence of nuclear war.

Physical and biological technologies have alleviated pestilence and 62 famine and many painful, dangerous, and exhausting features of daily life, and behavioral technology can begin to alleviate other kinds of ills. In the analysis of human behavior it is just possible that we are slightly beyond Newton's position in the analysis of light, for we are beginning to make technological applications. There are wonderful possibilities—and all the more wonderful because traditional approaches have been so ineffective. It is hard to imagine a world in which people live together without quarreling, maintain themselves

---

[22]*Sir Isaac Newton (1642–1727)* English scientist who invented differential and integral calculus and established the theory of gravity. His theories gave rise to a mechanical explanation of the universe in which all phenomena could be treated in terms of cause and effect. The English poet John Keats (1795–1821) reacted against Newton's analysis of the rainbow because he felt science was removing the romance and mystery from nature.

[23]*laser* A highly focused beam of electrons; a form of light. (The word is an acronym for *l*ight *a*mplification by *s*timulated *e*mission of *r*adiation.)

by producing the food, shelter, and clothing they need, enjoy themselves and contribute to the enjoyment of others in art, music, literature, and games, consume only a reasonable part of the resources of the world and add as little as possible to its pollution, bear no more children than can be raised decently, continue to explore the world around them and discover better ways of dealing with it, and come to know themselves accurately and, therefore, manage themselves effectively. Yet all this is possible, and even the slightest sign of progress should bring a kind of change which in traditional terms would be said to assuage wounded vanity, offset a sense of hopelessness or nostalgia, correct the impression that "we neither can nor need to do anything for ourselves," and promote a "sense of freedom and dignity" by building "a sense of confidence and worth." In other words, it should abundantly reinforce those who have been induced by their culture to work for its survival.

An experimental analysis shifts the determination of behavior from autonomous man to the environment—an environment responsible both for the evolution of the species and for the repertoire acquired by each member. Early versions of environmentalism were inadequate because they could not explain how the environment worked, and much seemed to be left for autonomous man to do. But environmental contingencies now take over functions once attributed to autonomous man, and certain questions arise. Is man then "abolished"? Certainly not as a species or as an individual achiever. It is the autonomous inner man who is abolished, and that is a step forward. But does man not then become merely a victim or passive observer of what is happening to him? He is indeed controlled by his environment, but we must remember that it is an environment largely of his own making. The evolution of a culture is a gigantic exercise in self-control. It is often said that a scientific view of man leads to wounded vanity, a sense of hopelessness, and nostalgia. But no theory changes what it is a theory about; man remains what he has always been. And a new theory may change what can be done with its subject matter. A scientific view of man offers exciting possibilities. We have not yet seen what man can make of man. 63

QUESTIONS

1. Define the key terms of the chapter: "autonomous man," "contingencies of reinforcement," "environment," "the individual." Are there other key terms that need definition?

2. Skinner has not provided much of the scientific data on which his views are based because he wishes to address a general audience, one that can profit from the results, rather than the process, of scientific research. Should he have provided more scientific data? Is his audience a general audience? Would you like more data, more experimental information?

3. What are the most important ideas set forth in this piece? How do they relate to the area of psychology?

4. What kinds of different environments does Skinner take into account in the chapter? He mentions physical and social environments in paragraph 48. Are those the only ones there are?

5. Skinner believes that his view is scientific. Is he correct?

WRITING ASSIGNMENTS

1. One of the chief issues in the selection is concerned with the nature of the self. In an essay which uses Skinner's technique of the rhetorical question, answer the following question as carefully as he answers his: What is a self? Refer to paragraphs 32–34. Try to clarify what Skinner thinks the self is and offer, as you do so, your own views.

2. Examine the selection for reference to character traits. By referring to specific quotations, and by analyzing them carefully in relation to one another, explain what Skinner means by "character traits." Is his analysis of this term reasonable? Is he convincing in suggesting that character traits may not be "permanent" or "basic" as we had thought?

3. Look around you for examples of contingencies of reinforcement. What kind of person does your environment seem to encourage you to be? What kinds of reinforcement are available in your immediate environment? Be as specific as possible in answering these questions.

4. Answer the question: Am I an autonomous agent? Use Skinner's strategy of examining first the environment in which you live, giving special attention to the contingencies of reinforcement which you are aware of. Then proceed to examine your own inner nature—insofar as that is possible—to see what that will contribute to your autonomy. Consider, as you answer this question, the issues of identity that are raised in the selection in paragraph 32 and thereafter. Does the process of answering this question help you to a better insight into your own identity?

5. Answer the question: Are my friends autonomous agents? Using Skinner's theories of contingencies of reinforcement, examine the behavior of two or three of your friends (or one in depth). Do they feel that they are free to do as they wish? Do you believe that they are aware of the limits on their freedom or of the degree to which they react to the reinforcements in their environment? To what extent is their behavior predictable by an outside observer?

6. In this selection, Skinner is basically predicting the death knell of the concept of the individual as an autonomous agent. What does he see as the alternative to this concept? Analyze closely the section of the piece beginning with paragraph 45 and ending with paragraph 55. What exactly is Skinner saying in these paragraphs? What will replace the concept of man as an autonomous agent? Is Skinner's view acceptable to you? How would you describe his vision of the future? Establish what his thinking is on the nature of the individual in the future.

PART FOUR

IDEAS IN THE WORLD OF SCIENCE

Francis Bacon · · · Charles Darwin
C. P. Snow · · · George Wald
Thomas Kuhn · · · Stephen Jay Gould

INTRODUCTION

MODERN SCIENCE seems to owe its incredible expansion to the inquiries made in the seventeenth century in Europe. To that age we owe advances in astronomy, leading to the discovery of new planets as well as to the final clarification of the earth as round rather than flat. (The ancients knew the earth was round, but medieval theologians insisted that the earth was flat.) During this century, there were many other scientific advances, among them the invention of the microscope and discoveries in biology, such as the theory of the circulation of the blood. There was progress in theory and understanding of the world in virtually every science.

Part of the credit for those discoveries goes to Sir Francis Bacon, whose early writings encouraged scientists to be both adventurous and relentless in their investigations. His pioneering efforts cleared the way for accurate thought in his age. The publication of Bacon's *Novum Organum* (1620), from which the first selection comes, was particularly important in this respect. Bacon realized that the human mind was so muddled with a variety of prejudices and illusions that it could not begin to undertake the gigantic task of reforming humankind's vision of the world until it faced and dealt with its own limitations. His four idols (illusions) are habits of thought that are so thoroughly ingrained in most people that they are not aware of them. In a series of brilliant analyses and observations, Bacon made people aware of these limitations. Even now, these limitations are at work, retarding progress in thought. Before Bacon, however, few people knew of them.

Charles Darwin, despite his credentials as a trained minister in the Church of England, caused a remarkable stir in the middle of the nineteenth century when he developed his ideas concerning evolution. In "Natural Selection," Darwin explains how alterations in species can be selected by nature for survival, just as we select desirable changes in breeds of domestic animals. Variations in a given species may appear naturally, he explains, but even more important is the fact that the fittest of the variations will soon dominate the rest. Survival, Darwin implies, is what nature is most interested in. It selects for the fittest individuals and so guarantees the fitness of the stock. Darwin's theories have caused controversy since their first statement, but scientists have carried on his work, modifying his views but demonstrating their essential correctness.

Stephen Jay Gould's "Nonmoral Nature" attempts to examine some of the theological questions that were inevitably raised by Darwin's work. He examines a number of predators, especially the remarkable ichneumon wasps, and demonstrates that they operate with an exceptional degree of efficiency in achieving a goal that people sometimes find repugnant. Since the ichneumon always wins, and its host, the caterpillar, virtually always loses, we are in the interesting situation of rooting for the underdog and assuming, somehow, that the predatory ichneumon is evil. Such thinking, Gould warns us, is irrelevant in the world of nature; it is relevant only in the world of humankind. Gould's work has reinforced the observations of Darwin, and in some of his writing he has attempted to show that, regarding theological or moral issues, there is no real conflict between Darwin's views and those of traditional religion. Gould's advice is to approach nature through science, not through a people-centered perspective.

C. P. Snow is also concerned with moral issues. As a nuclear physicist, he reminds us that the scientists who created the atomic bomb were not the people who decided how the bomb was to be used. This peculiar relationship between producer and product is typical of modern science, and it requires scientists to take a new view of their role. In Snow's youth scientists felt that their concerns were not specifically moral; but today, he believes that they must assume a role of leadership in establishing the appropriate moral uses of scientific advances. For example, he points out that scientists have an obligation, not only to help effect arms control but also to help solve the problem of world hunger, which scientists can help to achieve if they have the will to do so.

George Wald is not as concerned with the issues of morality as are Gould and Snow. Rather, he focuses on a tantalizing issue that interests us all: how life began. He believes that there are two choices: that of creation by a supernatural being and that of spontaneous generation. He examines the arguments for both sides, shows why they have been accepted or rejected in the past, then begins to construct an extraordinarily elaborate argument to show why one of these choices may be accepted. The ingenuity of his argument is such that it is, at times, dazzling.

Thomas Kuhn's essay is concerned with the education of scientists and, in a sense, brings us to Francis Bacon again. He reminds us that making scientific discoveries may not depend upon what he refers to as divergent thinking that is often prized by those who wish to be creative. Kuhn shows us that traditional thinking spawns scientific revolutions. It is a novel thought—particularly in today's age, which we sometimes think of as being a revolutionary one—but it is one that deserves attention.

The rhetorical strategies of these writers tend to the tried and true.

Each writer is under an obligation to make difficult ideas clear to the general reader. Some naturally assume that their audience is more knowledgeable than others do—some use highly technical language—but all are careful to define their terms, to use a language that is intelligible to the careful reader.

Bacon's use of enumeration—setting forth his ideas as being four in number—is a simple, direct way of guiding us through his essay. Once having told us that he will treat four issues, he proceeds to do so, one after the other. Darwin emphasizes the use of testimony, calling forth witness after witness to add to the strength of his argument. C. P. Snow examines the circumstances around the development of the atomic bomb, pointing out that the scientists involved believed that society was struggling against an ultimate terror: Nazi brutality. That belief naturally colored the scientists' moral attitudes. Thomas Kuhn's use of enumeration and verbal signposts telling what comes next is quite impressive. Stephen Jay Gould is equally impressive when he analyzes traditional views of nature and finds them rooted in the rhetorical device of metonymy, a device that expresses a part of something as if it were the whole thing. In his case, it is treating a part of nature, which is created by God, as if it were God. Thus, if the ichneumon he studies is thought of as part of God, and if we think of it as evil, we risk an impossible paradox. Metaphoric thinking, Gould explains, also involves seeing the world of the ichneumon as if it were part of the world of human beings. This is a very old intellectual dilemma—it is one of Bacon's four idols—and we see that Bacon's insights are by no means limited to the seventeenth century. They inform our own age.

FRANCIS BACON

The Four Idols

FRANCIS BACON, Lord Verulam (1561–1626), lived during some
of the most exciting times in history. Among his contemporaries
were the essayist Michel de Montaigne; the playwrights Christopher
Marlowe and William Shakespeare; the adventurer Sir Francis
Drake; and Queen Elizabeth I, in whose reign he held several high
offices. He became lord high chancellor of England in 1618, but fell
from power in 1621 through a complicated series of actions, among
which was his complicity in a bribery scheme. Yet his so-called
crimes were minor, despite the fact he paid dearly for them. His
book of Essays (1597) was exceptionally popular during his lifetime,
and when he found himself without a proper job, he devoted himself to what he declared to be his own true work, writing about philosophy and science.

His purposes in Novum Organum (The New Organon), published
in 1620, were to replace the old organon, or instrument of thought,
Aristotle's treatises on logic and thought. Despite the absolute stran-
glehold Aristotle held on sixteenth- and seventeenth-century minds
through the fact that Aristotle's texts were used everywhere in schools

From *Novum Organum*.

and colleges, Bacon thought that his logic would produce error. In Novum Organum he tried to set the stage for a new attitude toward logic and scientific inquiry. He proposed a system of reasoning usually referred to as induction. It is a quasi-scientific method involving the collecting and inventorying of a great mass of observations from nature. Once this mass of observations was gathered and organized, Bacon believed, the truth about what is observed would leap out at one.

Bacon is often credited with having invented the scientific method, but this notion is not accurate. He was on the right track with respect to collecting and observing. What he was wrong about was the result of that gathering. After all, one could watch an infinite number of apples (and oranges, too) fall to the ground without having the slightest sense of why they do so. What Bacon failed to realize— and he died before he could get close enough to scientific observation to realize it—is the creative function of the scientist as expressed in the hypothesis. The hypothesis—a shrewd guess about why something happens—is then tested by the kinds of observations Bacon approved.

Nonetheless, "The Four Idols" is a brilliant work. It does establish the requirements for the kind of observation that produces true scientific knowledge. Bacon despaired of any science in his own day, in part because no one paid any attention to the ways in which the idols strangled thought, observation, and imagination. He realized that the would-be scientist was foiled even before he began. Bacon was a farsighted man. He was correct about the failures of science in his time; and he was correct, moreover, about the fact that scientific advance would depend on sensory perception and on aids to perception, such as microscopes and telescopes. The really brilliant aspect of "The Four Idols" is the fact that Bacon focuses, not on what is observed, but on the instrument of observation, the human mind. Only when the instrument is freed of error can its observations be relied upon.

BACON'S RHETORIC

Bacon was trained during the great age of English rhetoric, and his prose (even though it is translated from Latin) shows the clarity, balance, and organization that naturally characterize the prose writing of seventeenth-century England. The most basic device Bacon uses is enumeration: stating clearly that there are four idols and implying that he will treat each one in turn.

Enumeration is one of the most common and most reliable rhetorical devices. The listener hears a speaker say, "I have only three things I want to say today. . . ." And the listener is alerted to listen for all three, while being secretly grateful that there are only three. The reader, when encountering complex material, is always happy to have such "road signs" as, "The second aspect of this question is . . . ."

"The Four Idols" begins, after a three-paragraph introduction, with a single paragraph devoted to each idol, so that we have an early definition of each idol and a sense of what to look for. Paragraphs 8–16 cover only the issues related to the Idols of the Tribe: the problems all people have simply because they are people. Paragraphs 17–22 consider the Idols of the Cave, those particular fixations individuals have because of their special backgrounds or limitations. Paragraphs 23–26 treat of the questions related to Idols of the Marketplace, particularly those that deal with the way people misuse words and abuse definitions. The remainder of the selection treats of the Idols of the Theater, which relate entirely to philosophic systems and preconceptions—all of which tend to narrow the scope of research and understanding.

Enumeration works within each of these groups of paragraphs as well. Bacon often begins a paragraph with such statements as, "There is one principal . . . distinction between different minds" (para. 19). Or he says, "The idols imposed by words on the understanding are of two kinds" (para. 24). The effect is to ensure clarity where confusion could easily reign.

As an added means of achieving clarity, Bacon sets aside a single paragraph—the last—as a summary of the main points that have been made, and in the order in which they were made.

Within any section of this selection, Bacon depends upon observation, example, and reason to make his points. When he speaks of a given idol, he defines it, gives several examples to make it clearer, discusses its effects on thought, then dismisses it as dangerous. He then goes on to the next idol. In some cases, and where appropriate, he names those who are victims of a specific idol. In each case he tries to be thorough, explanatory, and convincing.

Not only is this work a landmark in thought; it is also, because of its absolute clarity, a beacon. We can still profit from its light.

The Four Idols

The idols[1] and false notions which are now in possession of the   1
human understanding, and have taken deep root therein, not only so
beset men's minds that truth can hardly find entrance, but even after
entrance obtained, they will again in the very instauration[2] of the sciences meet and trouble us, unless men being forewarned of the danger
fortify themselves as far as may be against their assaults.

There are four classes of idols which beset men's minds. To these   2
for distinction's sake I have assigned names—calling the first class
Idols of the Tribe; the second, *Idols of the Cave;* the third, *Idols of the
Marketplace;* the fourth, *Idols of the Theater.*

The formation of ideas and axioms by true induction[3] is no doubt   3
the proper remedy to be applied for the keeping off and clearing away
of idols. To point them out, however, is of great use; for the doctrine
of idols is to the interpretation of nature what the doctrine of the re-
futation of sophisms[4] is to common logic.

The *Idols of the Tribe* have their foundation in human nature it-   4
self, and in the tribe or race of men. For it is a false assertion that the
sense of man is the measure of things. On the contrary, all perceptions
as well of the sense as of the mind are according to the measure of the
individual and not according to the measure of the universe. And the
human understanding is like a false mirror, which, receiving rays irregularly, distorts and discolors the nature of things by mingling its
own nature with it.

The *Idols of the Cave* are the idols of the individual man. For ev-   5

---

[1]*idols* By this term Bacon means phantoms or illusions (see note 21). The Greek
philosopher Democritus spoke of *eidola,* tiny representations of things that impressed
themselves on the mind.

[2]*instauration* renewal; renovation.

[3]*induction* Bacon championed induction as the method by which new knowledge
is developed. As he saw it, induction involved a patient gathering, inventorying, and categorizing of facts in the hope that a large number of them would point to the truth. As a
process of gathering evidence from which inferences are drawn, induction is contrasted
with Aristotle's method, *deduction,* according to which a theory is established and the
truth deduced. Deduction places the stress on the authority of the expert; induction
places the stress on the facts themselves.

[4]*sophisms* Apparently intelligent statements that are wrong; false wisdom.

eryone (besides the errors common to human nature in general) has a cave or den of his own, which refracts[5] and discolors the light of nature; owing either to his own proper and peculiar nature; or to his education and conversation with others; or to the reading of books, and the authority of those whom he esteems and admires; or to the differences of impressions, accordingly as they take place in a mind preoccupied and predisposed or in a mind indifferent and settled; or the like. So that the spirit of man (according as it is meted out to different individuals) is in fact a thing variable and full of perturbation,[6] and governed as it were by chance. Whence it was well observed by Heraclitus[7] that men look for sciences in their own lesser worlds, and not in the greater or common world.

There are also idols formed by the intercourse and association of men with each other, which I call *Idols of the Marketplace*, on account of the commerce and consort of men there. For it is by discourse that men associate; and words are imposed according to the apprehension of the vulgar.[8] And therefore the ill and unfit choice of words wonderfully obstructs the understanding. Nor do the definitions or explanations wherewith in some things learned men are wont[9] to guard and defend themselves, by any means set the matter right. But words plainly force and overrule the understanding, and throw all into confusion and lead men away into numberless empty controversies and idle fancies. 6

Lastly, there are idols which have immigrated into men's minds from the various dogmas of philosophies, and also from wrong laws of demonstration.[10] These I call *Idols of the Theater*; because in my judgment all the received systems[11] are but so many stage-plays, representing worlds of their own creation after an unreal and scenic fashion. Nor is it only of the systems now in vogue, or only of the ancient sects and philosophies, that I speak; for many more plays of the same kind may yet be composed and in like artificial manner set forth; seeing 7

---

[5]*refracts* deflects, bends back, alters.

[6]*perturbation* Uncertainty, disturbance. In astronomy, the motion caused by the gravity of nearby planets.

[7]*Heraclitus (535?–?475 B.C.)* Greek philosopher who believed that there was no reality except in change; all else was illusion. He also believed that fire was the basis of all the world and that everything we see is a transformation of it.

[8]*vulgar* common people.

[9]*wont* accustomed.

[10]*laws of demonstration* Bacon may be referring to Aristotle's logical system of syllogism and deduction.

[11]*received systems* official or authorized views of scientific truth.

that errors the most widely different have nevertheless causes for the most part alike. Neither again do I mean this only of entire systems, but also of many principles and axioms in science, which by tradition, credulity, and negligence, have come to be received.

But of these several kinds of idols I must speak more largely and 8 exactly, that the understanding may be duly cautioned.

The human understanding is of its own nature prone to suppose 9 the existence of more order and regularity in the world than it finds. And though there be many things in nature which are singular and unmatched, yet it devises for them parallels and conjugates and relatives[12] which do not exist. Hence the fiction that all celestial bodies move in perfect circles; spirals and dragons being (except in name) utterly rejected. Hence too the element of fire with its orb is brought in, to make up the square with the other three which the sense perceives. Hence also the ratio of density[13] of the so-called elements is arbitrarily fixed at ten to one. And so on of other dreams. And these fancies affect not dogmas only, but simple notions also.

The human understanding when it has once adopted an opinion 10 (either as being the received opinion or as being agreeable to itself) draws all things else to support and agree with it. And though there be a greater number and weight of instances to be found on the other side, yet these it either neglects and despises, or else by some distinction sets aside and rejects; in order that by this great and pernicious predetermination the authority of its former conclusions may remain inviolate. And therefore it was a good answer that was made by one who when they showed him hanging in a temple a picture of those who had paid their vows as having escaped shipwreck, and would have him say whether he did not now acknowledge the power of the gods— "Ay," asked he again, "but where are they painted that were drowned after their vows?" And such is the way of all superstition, whether in astrology, dreams, omens, divine judgments, or the like; wherein men having a delight in such vanities, mark the events where they are fulfilled, but where they fail, though this happen much oftener, neglect and pass them by. But with far more subtlety does this mischief insinuate itself into philosophy and the sciences; in which the first conclu-

---

[12]*parallels and conjugates and relatives* A reference to the habit of assuming that phenomena are regular and ordered, consisting of squares, triangles, circles, and other regular shapes.

[13]*ratio of density* The false assumption that the relationship of mass or weight to volume was ten to one. This is another example of Bacon's complaint, establishing a convenient regular "relative" or relationship.

sion colors and brings into conformity with itself all that come after, though far sounder and better. Besides, independently of that delight and vanity which I have described, it is the peculiar and perpetual error of the human intellect to be more moved and excited by affirmatives than by negatives; whereas it ought properly to hold itself indifferently disposed towards both alike. Indeed, in the establishment of any true axiom, the negative instance is the more forcible of the two.

The human understanding is moved by those things most which 11 strike and enter the mind simultaneously and suddenly, and so fill the imagination; and then it feigns and supposes all other things to be somehow, though it cannot see how, similar to those few things by which it is surrounded. But for that going to and fro to remote and heterogeneous instances, by which axioms are tried as in the fire,[14] the intellect is altogether slow and unfit, unless it be forced thereto by severe laws and overruling authority.

The human understanding is unquiet; it cannot stop or rest, and 12 still presses onward, but in vain. Therefore it is that we cannot conceive of any end or limit to the world, but always as of necessity it occurs to us that there is something beyond. Neither again can it be conceived how eternity has flowed down to the present day; for that distinction which is commonly received of infinity in time past and in time to come can by no means hold; for it would thence follow that one infinity is greater than another, and that infinity is wasting away and tending to become finite. The like subtlety arises touching the infinite divisibility of lines,[15] from the same inability of thought to stop. But this inability interferes more mischievously in the discovery of causes:[16] for although the most general principles in nature ought

---

[14]***tried as in the fire*** Trial by fire is a figure of speech representing thorough, rigorous testing even to the point of risking what is tested. An axiom is a statement of apparent truth that has not yet been put to the test of examination and investigation.

[15]***infinite divisibility of lines*** This gave rise to the paradox of Zeno, the Greek philosopher of the fifth century B.C. who showed that it was impossible to get from one point to another because one had to pass the midpoint of the line determined by the two original points, and then the midpoint of the remaining distance, and then of that remaining distance, down to an infinite number of points. By using accepted truths to "prove" an absurdity about motion, Zeno actually hoped to prove that motion itself did not exist. This is the "subtlety" or confusion Bacon says is produced by the "inability of thought to stop."

[16]***discovery of causes*** Knowledge of the world was based on four causes: efficient (who made it?); material (what is it made of?); formal (what is its shape?); and final (what is its purpose?). The scholastics concentrated their thinking on the first and last, while the "middle causes," related to matter and shape, were the proper subject matter of science because they alone yielded to observation. (See paragraph 33.)

to be held merely positive, as they are discovered, and cannot with truth be referred to a cause; nevertheless, the human understanding being unable to rest still seeks something prior in the order of nature. And then it is that in struggling towards that which is further off, it falls back upon that which is more nigh at hand; namely, on final causes: which have relation clearly to the nature of man rather than to the nature of the universe, and from this source have strangely defiled philosophy. But he is no less an unskilled and shallow philosopher who seeks causes of that which is most general, than he who in things subordinate and subaltern[17] omits to do so.

The human understanding is no dry light, but receives an infusion 13 from the will and affections;[18] whence proceed sciences which may be called "sciences as one would." For what a man had rather were true he more readily believes. Therefore he rejects difficult things from impatience of research; sober things, because they narrow hope; the deeper things of nature, from superstition; the light of experience, from arrogance and pride, lest his mind should seem to be occupied with things mean and transitory; things not commonly believed, out of deference to the opinion of the vulgar. Numberless in short are the ways, and sometimes imperceptible, in which the affections color and infect the understanding.

But by far the greatest hindrance and aberration of the human un- 14 derstanding proceeds from the dullness, incompetency, and deceptions of the senses; in that things which strike the sense outweigh things which do not immediately strike it, though they be more important. Hence it is that speculation commonly ceases where sight ceases; insomuch that of things invisible there is little or no observation. Hence all the working of the spirits[19] enclosed in tangible bodies lies hid and unobserved of men. So also all the more subtle changes of form in the parts of coarser substances (which they commonly call alteration, though it is in truth local motion through exceedingly small spaces) is in like manner unobserved. And yet unless these two things just mentioned be searched out and brought to light, nothing great can be achiev ed in nature, as far as the production of works is concerned. So again the essential nature of our common air, and of all bodies less dense than air (which are very many) is almost unknown. For the sense by itself is a thing infirm and erring; neither can instruments for en-

---

[17]*subaltern*   lower in status.
[18]*will and affections*   human free will and emotional needs and responses.
[19]*spirits*   the soul or animating force.

larging or sharpening the senses do much; but all the truer kind of
interpretation of nature is effected by instances and experiments fit
and apposite;[20] wherein the sense decides touching the experiment
only, and the experiment touching the point in nature and the thing
itself.

The human understanding is of its own nature prone to abstrac- 15
tions and gives a substance and reality to things which are fleeting.
But to resolve nature into abstractions is less to our purpose than to
dissect her into parts; as did the school of Democritus,[21] which went
further into nature than the rest. Matter rather than forms should be
the object of our attention, its configurations and changes of configuration, and simple action, and law of action or motion; for forms are
figments of the human mind, unless you will call those laws of action
forms.

Such then are the idols which I call *Idols of the Tribe;* and which 16
take their rise either from the homogeneity of the substance of the
human spirit,[22] or from its preoccupation, or from its narrowness, or
from its restless motion, or from an infusion of the affections, or from
the incompetency of the senses, or from the mode of impression.

The *Idols of the Cave* take their rise in the peculiar constitution, 17
mental or bodily, of each individual; and also in education, habit, and
accident. Of this kind there is a great number and variety; but I will
instance those the pointing out of which contains the most important
caution, and which have most effect in disturbing the clearness of the
understanding.

Men become attached to certain particular sciences and specula- 18
tions, either because they fancy themselves the authors and inventors
thereof, or because they have bestowed the greatest pains upon them
and become most habituated to them. But men of this kind, if they
betake themselves to philosophy and contemplations of a general character, distort and color them in obedience to their former fancies; a
thing especially to be noticed in Aristotle,[23] who made his natural

---

[20]*apposite* appropriate; well related.

[21]*Democritus (460?–?370 B.C.)* Greek philosopher who thought the world was
composed of atoms. Bacon felt such "dissection" to be useless because it was impractical.
Yet Democritus's concept of the *eidola,* the mind's impressions of things, may have
contributed to Bacon's idea of "the idol."

[22]*human spirit* human nature.

[23]*Aristotle (384–322 B.C.)* Greek philosopher whose *Organon* (system of logic)
dominated the thought of Bacon's time. Bacon sought to overthrow Aristotle's hold on
science and thought.

philosophy[24] a mere bondservant to his logic, thereby rendering it contentious and well nigh useless. The race of chemists[25] again out of a few experiments of the furnace have built up a fantastic philosophy, framed with reference to a few things; and Gilbert[26] also, after he had employed himself most laboriously in the study and observation of the loadstone, proceeded at once to construct an entire system in accordance with his favorite subject.

There is one principal and, as it were, radical distinction between 19 different minds, in respect of philosophy and the sciences, which is this: that some minds are stronger and apter to mark the differences of things, others to mark their resemblances. The steady and acute mind can fix its contemplations and dwell and fasten on the subtlest distinctions: the lofty and discursive mind recognizes and puts together the finest and most general resemblances. Both kinds however easily err in excess, by catching the one at gradations, the other at shadows.

There are found some minds given to an extreme admiration of 20 antiquity, others to an extreme love and appetite for novelty; but few so duly tempered that they can hold the mean, neither carping at what has been well laid down by the ancients, nor despising what is well introduced by the moderns. This however turns to the great injury of the sciences and philosophy; since these affectations of antiquity and novelty are the humors[27] of partisans rather than judgments; and truth is to be sought for not in the felicity of any age, which is an unstable thing, but in the light of nature and experience, which is eternal. These factions therefore must be abjured,[28] and care must be taken that the intellect be not hurried by them into assent.

Contemplations of nature and of bodies in their simple form break 21 up and distract the understanding, while contemplations of nature and bodies in their composition and configuration overpower and dissolve the understanding: a distinction well seen in the school of Leucippus[29]

---

[24]***natural philosophy*** The scientific study of nature in general—biology, zoology, geology, etc.

[25]***chemists*** Alchemists had developed a "fantastic philosophy" from their experimental attempts to transmute lead into gold.

[26]***William Gilbert (1540–1603)*** An English scientist who studied magnetism and codified many laws related to magnetic fields. He was particularly ridiculed by Bacon for being too narrow in his researches.

[27]***humors*** used in a medical sense to mean a distortion caused by imbalance.

[28]***abjured*** renounced, sworn off, repudiated.

[29]***Leucippus (fifth century B.C.)*** Greek philosopher; teacher of Democritus and inventor of the atomistic theory. His works survive only in fragments.

and Democritus as compared with the other philosophies. For that school is so busied with the particles that it hardly attends to the structure; while the others are so lost in admiration of the structure that they do not penetrate to the simplicity of nature. These kinds of contemplation should therefore be alternated and taken by turns; that so the understanding may be rendered at once penetrating and comprehensive, and the inconveniences above mentioned, with the idols which proceed from them, may be avoided.

Let such then be our provision and contemplative prudence for 22 keeping off and dislodging the *Idols of the Cave,* which grow for the most part either out of the predominance of a favorite subject, or out of an excessive tendency to compare or to distinguish, or out of partiality for particular ages, or out of the largeness or minuteness of the objects contemplated. And generally let every student of nature take this as a rule—that whatever his mind seizes and dwells upon with peculiar satisfaction is to be held in suspicion, and that so much the more care is to be taken in dealing with such questions to keep the understanding even and clear.

But the *Idols of the Marketplace* are the most troublesome of all: 23 idols which have crept into the understanding through the alliances of words and names. For men believe that their reason governs words; but it is also true that words react on the understanding; and this it is that has rendered philosophy and the sciences sophistical and inactive. Now words, being commonly framed and applied according to the capacity of the vulgar, follow those lines of division which are most obvious to the vulgar understanding. And whenever an understanding of greater acuteness or a more diligent observation would alter those lines to suit the true divisions of nature, words stand in the way and resist the change. Whence it comes to pass that the high and formal discussions of learned men end oftentimes in disputes about words and names; with which (according to the use and wisdom of the mathematicians) it would be more prudent to begin, and so by means of definitions reduce them to order. Yet even definitions cannot cure this evil in dealing with natural and material things; since the definitions themselves consist of words, and those words beget others: so that it is necessary to recur to individual instances, and those in due series and order; as I shall say presently when I come to the method and scheme for the formation of notions and axioms.[30]

The idols imposed by words on the understanding are of two kinds. 24

---

[30]**notions and axioms** conceptions and definitive statements of truth.

They are either names of things which do not exist (for as there are things left unnamed through lack of observation, so likewise are there names which result from fantastic suppositions and to which nothing in reality responds), or they are names of things which exist, but yet confused and ill-defined, and hastily and irregularly derived from realities. Of the former kind are Fortune, the Prime Mover, Planetary Orbits, Element of Fire, and like fictions which owe their origin to false and idle theories.[31] And this class of idols is more easily expelled, because to get rid of them it is only necessary that all theories should be steadily rejected and dismissed as obsolete.

But the other class, which springs out of a faulty and unskillful 25 abstraction, is intricate and deeply rooted. Let us take for example such a word as *humid;* and see how far the several things which the word is used to signify agree with each other; and we shall find the word *humid* to be nothing else than a mark loosely and confusedly applied to denote a variety of actions which will not bear to be reduced to any constant meaning. For it both signifies that which easily spreads itself round any other body; and that which in itself is indeterminate and cannot solidize; and that which readily yields in every direction; and that which easily divides and scatters itself; and that which easily unites and collects itself; and that which readily flows and is put in motion; and that which readily clings to another body and wets it; and that which is easily reduced to a liquid, or being solid easily melts. Accordingly when you come to apply the word—if you take it in one sense, flame is humid; if in another, air is not humid; if in another, fine dust is humid; if in another, glass is humid. So that it is easy to see that the notion is taken by abstraction only from water and common and ordinary liquids, without any due verification.

There are however in words certain degrees of distortion and error. 26 One of the least faulty kinds is that of names of substances, especially of lowest species and well-deduced (for the notion of *chalk* and of *mud* is good, of *earth* bad);[32] a more faulty kind is that of actions, as *to generate, to corrupt, to alter;* the most faulty is of qualities (except such as are the immediate objects of the sense), as *heavy, light, rare, dense,* and the like. Yet in all these cases some notions are of neces-

---

[31]*idle theories* These are things that cannot be observed and thus do not exist. Fortune is fate; the Prime Mover is God or some "first" force; the notion that planets orbited the sun was considered as "fantastic" as these others, or as the idea that everything was made up of fire and its many permutations.

[32]**earth bad** Chalk and mud were useful in manufacture; hence they were terms of approval. *Earth* is used here in the sense we use *dirt,* as in "digging in the dirt."

sity a little better than others, in proportion to the greater variety of subjects that fall within the range of the human sense.

But the *Idols of the Theater* are not innate, nor do they steal into 27 the understanding secretly, but are plainly impressed and received into the mind from the play-books of philosophical systems and the perverted rules of demonstration.[33] To attempt refutations in this case would be merely inconsistent with what I have already said: for since we agree neither upon principles nor upon demonstrations, there is no place for argument. And this is so far well, inasmuch as it leaves the honor of the ancients untouched. For they are no wise disparaged—the question between them and me being only as to the way. For as the saying is, the lame man who keeps the right road outstrips the runner who takes a wrong one. Nay, it is obvious that when a man runs the wrong way, the more active and swift he is the further he will go astray.

But the course I propose for the discovery of sciences is such as 28 leaves but little to the acuteness and strength of wits, but places all wits[34] and understandings nearly on a level. For as in the drawing of a straight line or perfect circle, much depends on the steadiness and practice of the hand, if it be done by aim of hand only, but if with the aid of rule or compass, little or nothing; so is it exactly with my plan. But though particular confutations[35] would be of no avail, yet touching the sects and general divisions of such systems I must say something; something also touching the external signs which show that they are unsound; and finally something touching the causes of such great infelicity and of such lasting and general agreement in error; that so the access to truth may be made less difficult, and the human understanding may the more willingly submit to its purgation and dismiss its idols.

Idols of the Theater, or of systems, are many, and there can be and 29 perhaps will be yet many more. For were it not that now for many ages men's minds have been busied with religion and theology; and were it not that civil governments, especially monarchies, have been averse to such novelties, even in matters speculative; so that men labor therein to the peril and harming of their fortunes—not only unrewarded, but exposed also to contempt and envy; doubtless there would

---

[33]*perverted rules of demonstration* Another complaint against Aristotle's logic as misapplied in Bacon's day.

[34]*wits* intelligence, reasoning powers.

[35]*confutations* Specific counterarguments. Bacon means that he cannot offer particular arguments against each scientific sect; thus he offers a general warning.

have arisen many other philosophical sects like to those which in great variety flourished once among the Greeks. For as on the phenomena of the heavens many hypotheses may be constructed, so likewise (and more also) many various dogmas may be set up and established on the phenomena of philosophy. And in the plays of this philosophical theater you may observe the same thing which is found in the theater of the poets, that stories invented for the stage are more compact and elegant, and more as one would wish them to be, than true stories out of history.

In general, however, there is taken for the material of philosophy 30 either a great deal out of a few things, or a very little out of many things; so that on both sides philosophy is based on too narrow a foundation of experiment and natural history, and decides on the authority of too few cases. For the rational school of philosophers[36] snatches from experience a variety of common instances, neither duly ascertained nor diligently examined and weighed, and leaves all the rest to meditation and agitation of wit.

There is also another class of philosophers,[37] who having bestowed 31 much diligent and careful labor on a few experiments, have thence made bold to educe and construct systems; wresting all other facts in a strange fashion to conformity therewith.

And there is yet a third class,[38] consisting of those who out of faith 32 and veneration mix their philosophy with theology and traditions; among whom the vanity of some has gone so far aside as to seek the origin of sciences among spirits and genii.[39] So that this parent stock of errors—this false philosophy—is of three kinds; the sophistical, the empirical, and the superstitious. . . .

But the corruption of philosophy by superstition and an admixture 33 of theology is far more widely spread, and does the greatest harm,

---

[36]*rational school of philosophers* Platonists who felt that human reason alone could discover the truth and that experiment was unnecessary. Their observation of experience produced only a "variety of common instances" from which they reasoned.

[37]*another class of philosophers* William Gilbert (1540–1603) experimented tirelessly with magnetism, from which he derived numerous odd theories. Though Gilbert was a true scientist, Bacon thought of him as limited and on the wrong track.

[38]*a third class* Pythagoras (d. 497? B.C.) was a Greek philosopher who experimented rigorously with mathematics and a tuned string. He is said to have developed the musical scale. His theory of reincarnation, or the transmigration of souls, was somehow based on his travels in India and his work with scales. The superstitious belief in the movement of souls is what Bacon complains of.

[39]*genii* Oriental demons or spirits; a slap at Pythagoras, who traveled in the Orient.

whether to entire systems or to their parts. For the human understanding is obnoxious to the influence of the imagination no less than to the influence of common notions. For the contentious and sophistical kind of philosophy ensnares the understanding; but this kind, being fanciful and tumid[40] and half poetical, misleads it more by flattery. For there is in man an ambition of the understanding, no less than of the will, especially in high and lofty spirits.

Of this kind we have among the Greeks a striking example in Pythagoras, though he united with it a coarser and more cumbrous superstition; another in Plato and his school,[41] more dangerous and subtle. It shows itself likewise in parts of other philosophies, in the introduction of abstract forms and final causes and first causes, with the omission in most cases of causes intermediate, and the like. Upon this point the greatest caution should be used. For nothing is so mischievous as the apotheosis of error; and it is a very plague of the understanding for vanity to become the object of veneration. Yet in this vanity some of the moderns have with extreme levity indulged so far as to attempt to found a system of natural philosophy on the first chapter of Genesis, on the book of Job, and other parts of the sacred writings; seeking for the dead among the living: which also makes the inhibition and repression of it the more important, because from this unwholesome mixture of things human and divine there arises not only a fantastic philosophy but also an heretical religion. Very meet it is therefore that we be sober-minded, and give to faith that only which is faith's. . . .

So much concerning the several classes of Idols, and their equipage: all of which must be renounced and put away with a fixed and solemn determination, and the understanding thoroughly freed and cleansed; the entrance into the kingdom of man, founded on the sciences, being not much other than the entrance into the kingdom of heaven, whereinto none may enter except as a little child.

---

[40]***tumid*** overblown, swollen.

[41]***Plato and his school*** Plato's religious bent was further developed by Plotinus (205–270 A.D.) in his *Enneads*. Although Plotinus was not a Christian, his Neo-Platonism was welcomed as a philosophy compatible with Christianity.

QUESTIONS

1. Which of Bacon's idols is the most difficult to understand? Do your best to define it.
2. Which of these idols do we still need to worry about? Why? What dangers does it present?
3. What does Bacon mean by saying that our senses are weak (para. 14)? Is he correct in making that statement?
4. Occasionally Bacon says something in such a way that it seems a bit like an aphorism (see the introduction to Machiavelli). Find at least one such expression in this selection. Upon examination, does the expression have as much meaning as it seems to have?
5. What kind of readers did Bacon expect for this piece? What clues does his way of communicating provide regarding the nature of his anticipated readers?

WRITING ASSIGNMENTS

1. What special background—hobbies, skills, work experience, interests, intellectual commitments—do you have that you feel are special? Name at least three specific things in which you are involved. Using Bacon's technique of enumeration, show how each can affect your examination of, say, the best way to learn; the best way to use spare time; the best way to stay healthy; the best way to entertain a boyfriend or a girlfriend (choose one of these subjects or choose your own subject).
2. Which of Bacon's idols most seriously applies to you as a person? Using enumeration, put the idols in order of importance as you see them affecting your own judgment. If you prefer, you may write about which idol you believe is most important in impeding scientific investigation today.
3. Is it true, as Bacon says in paragraph 10, that people are in general more excited by affirmation than by negation? Do we really stress the positive and deemphasize the negative in the conduct of our general affairs? Find at least three instances in which people seem to gravitate toward the positive or the negative in a series of situations in daily life. Try to establish whether or not Bacon has, in fact, described what is a habit of mind.
4. In paragraph 13, Bacon states that the "will and affections" enter into matters of thought. By this he means that our understanding of what we observe is conditioned by what we want and what we feel. Thus, when he says, "For what a man had rather were true he more readily believes," he tells us that people tend to believe what they want to believe. Test this statement by means of observation. Find out, for example, how many older people are convinced that the world is deteriorating, how many younger people feel that there is a plot on the part of older people to hold them

back, how many women feel that men consciously oppress women, and how many men feel that feminists are not as feminine as they should be. What other beliefs can you discover that seem to have their origin in what people want to believe rather than in what is true?

5. Establish the extent to which the Idols of the Marketplace are relevant to issues in modern life. In particular, study the language used in the newspapers (and important magazines) to discuss nuclear warfare. To what extent are official words (those uttered by governments) designed to obscure issues? In what sense are they misleading? Consult the discussion in paragraph 23 and following paragraphs to answer this question. In what sense do "words stand in the way and resist . . . change" in regard to debate on nuclear war. If you wish to substitute another major issue (e.g., abortion, improving secondary schools, social welfare services, taxation, prayer in the schools), feel free to do so.

6. Bacon's views on religion have always been questionable. He grew up in a very religious time, but his writings rarely discuss religion positively. In this work he talks about giving "to faith only that which is faith's." He seems to feel that scientific investigation is something quite separate from religion. Examine this work carefully to establish what you think Bacon's view on this question is. Then take a stand on the issue of the relationship between religion and science. Should science be totally independent of religious concerns? Should religious issues control scientific experimentation? What does Bacon mean when he complains about the vanity of founding "a system of natural philosophy on the first chapter of Genesis, on the book of Job, and other parts of the sacred writings" (para. 34)? "Natural philosophy" means biology, chemistry, physics, and science in general. Are Bacon's complaints justified? Would his complaints be relevant today?

CHARLES DARWIN

Natural Selection

CHARLES DARWIN *(1809–1882) was trained as a minister in the Church of England, but he was also the grandson of one of England's greatest horticulturists, Erasmus Darwin. Partly as a way of putting off taking orders in the church, and partly because of his natural curiosity and scientific enterprise, Darwin managed to find himself performing the functions of a naturalist on the H.M.S.* Beagle, *which was engaged in scientific explorations around South America during the years 1831–1836. Darwin's fascinating book,* Voyage of the Beagle *(1839), details the experiences he had and offers us some views of his self-education as a naturalist.*

His experiences on the Beagle *led him to take note of variations in species of animals he found in various separate locales, particularly between remote islands and the mainland. Varieties—his term for any visible (or invisible) differences in markings, coloration, size or*

From *On the Origin of Species by Means of Natural Selection.* This text is from the first edition, 1859. In the five subsequent editions, Darwin hedged more and more on his theory, often introducing material in defense against objections. The first edition is vigorous and direct; this edition jolted the worlds of science and religion out of their complaisance. In later editions, this chapter was titled "Natural Selection; or, Survival of the Fittest " shape of appendages, organs, or bodies—were of some peculiar use, he believed, for the animals in the environment in which he found them. He was not certain of what kind of use these varieties might be, and he did not know whether the changes that created the varieties resulted from the environment or from some chance operation of nature. Ultimately, he concluded that varieties in nature were caused by three forces: (1) natural selection, in which varieties occur spontaneously by chance but are then "selected" for because they are aids to survival; (2) direct action of the environment, in which non-adaptive varieties do not survive because of climate, food conditions, or the like; and (3) the effects of use or disuse of a variation (somewhat like the short beak of a bird in paragraph 9 in the extract). Sexual selection, which figures prominently in this work, was later thought to be less significant by Darwin.

The idea of evolution—the gradual change of species through some kind of modification of varieties—had been in the air for many years when Darwin began his work. The English scientists C.W. Wells in 1813 and Patrick Matthew in 1831 had both proposed theories of natural selection, although Darwin was unaware of their work. Alfred Russel Wallace (1823–1913), a younger English scientist, revealed in 1858 that he was about to propose the same theory of evolution as was Darwin. They joined and published their theories (in sketchy form) together, and the next year Darwin rushed his Origin of Species to press.

Darwin does not mention human beings as part of the evolutionary process in the selection. Because he was particularly concerned with the likelihood of adverse reactions on the part of theologians, he merely promised later discussion of that subject. It came in The Descent of Man (1871), the companion to On the Origin of Species.

When Darwin returned to England after completing his researches on the Beagle, he supplemented his knowledge with information gathered from breeders of pigeons, livestock, dogs, and horses. This research, it must be noted, was rather limited, involving relatively few samples, and was conducted according to comparatively unscientific practices. Yet, it corresponded with his observations of nature. The fact was that man could cause changes in species; it was Darwin's task to show that nature—through the process of natural selection—could do the same thing.

Naturally, The Descent of Man stirred up a great deal of controversy between the church and Darwin's supporters. Note since the Roman Catholic Church denied the fact that the earth went around the sun, as Galileo had proved scientifically in 1632 (and was banished *for his pains), had there been a more serious confrontation of science and religion. Darwin was ridiculed by ministers and doubted by older scientists; but he was stoutly defended by younger scientists, many of whom had arrived at conclusions similar to Darwin's. In the end, Darwin's views were accepted by the Church of England, and when he died in 1882 he was lionized and buried at Westminster Abbey in London. Only recently, controversy concerning his work has arisen again.*

D A R W I N ' S   R H E T O R I C

Darwin's writing is fluent, smooth, and stylistically sophisti-cated. Yet, his material is burdensome, detailed, and in general not appealing. Despite these drawbacks, he manages to keep the reader engaged. His rhetorical method depends entirely upon the yoking of thesis and demonstration. He uses the topic of definition frequently, but he most frequently uses the topic of testimony, as he gathers information and instances, both real and imaginary, from many dif-ferent sources.

Interestingly enough, Darwin said that he used Francis Bacon's method of induction in his researches. That means the gathering of evidence of many instances of a given phenomenon, from which the truth—or a natural law—will emerge. The fact is that Darwin did not quite follow this path. He did, as most modern scientists do, establish a hypothesis after a period of observation; then he looked for evidence that would confirm or disconfirm the hypothesis. He was careful to include examples that argued against his view, but like most scien-tists, he emphasized the importance of the positive samples.

Induction plays a part in the rhetoric of this selection in that the selection is dominated by examples. There are examples taken from the breeding of birds, from the condition of birds in nature, from domestic farm animals and their breeding; and there are many, many examples taken from botany, including the breeding of plants and the interdependence between certain insects and certain plants. Erasmus Darwin was famous for his work with plants, and it is nat-ural that such observations would play an important part in his grandson's thinking.

The process of natural selection is carefully discussed, particu-larly in paragraph 8 and thereafter. Darwin emphasizes its positive nature and its differences from selection by human breeders. The topic of comparison, which appears frequently in the selection, is most conspicuous in these paragraphs. He postulates a nature in which the fittest survive because they are best adapted for survival, but he does not dwell on the fate of those who are unfit individuals. Later writers, often misapplying his theories, were to do that.

———————————•⌘•———————————

Natural Selection

How will the struggle for existence . . . act in regard to varia- 1
tion? Can the principle of selection, which we have seen is so potent
in the hands of man, apply in nature? I think we shall see that it can
act most effectually. Let it be borne in mind in what an endless number of strange pecularities our domestic productions, and, in a lesser
degree, those under nature, vary; and how strong the hereditary tendency is. Under domestication, it may be truly said that the whole
organization becomes in some degree plastic.[1] Let it be borne in mind
how infinitely complex and close-fitting are the mutual relations of all
organic beings to each other and to their physical conditions of life.
Can it, then, be thought improbable, seeing that variations useful to
man have undoubtedly occurred, that other variations useful in some
way to each being in the great and complex battle of life, should sometimes occur in the course of thousands of generations? If such do occur, can we doubt (remembering that many more individuals are born
than can possibly survive) that individuals having any advantage, however slight, over others, would have the best chance of surviving and
or procreating their kind? On the other hand, we may feel sure that
any variation in the least degree injurious would be rigidly destroyed.
This preservation of favorable variations and the rejection of injurious
variations, I call Natural Selection. Variations neither useful nor injurious would not be affected by natural selection, and would be left a
fluctuating element, as perhaps we see in the species called polymorphic.[2]

---

[1] *plastic* Capable of being shaped and changed.
[2] *species called polymorphic* Species that have more than one form over the course
of their lives, such as butterflies.

We shall best understand the probable course of natural selection 2
by taking the case of a country undergoing some physical change, for
instance, of climate. The proportional numbers of its inhabitants
would almost immediately undergo a change, and some species might
become extinct. We may conclude, from what we have seen of the
intimate and complex manner in which the inhabitants of each country are bound together, that any change in the numerical proportions
of some of the inhabitants, independently of the change of climate
itself, would most seriously affect many of the others. If the country
were open on its borders, new forms would certainly immigrate, and
this also would seriously disturb the relations of some of the former
inhabitants. Let it be remembered how powerful the influence of a
single introduced tree or mammal has been shown to be. But in the
case of an island, or of a country partly surrounded by barriers, into
which new and better adapted forms could not freely enter, we should
then have places in the economy of nature which would assuredly be
better filled up, if some of the original inhabitants were in some manner modified; for, had the area been open to immigration, these same
places would have been seized on by intruders. In such case, every
slight modification, which in the course of ages chanced to arise, and
which in any way favored the individuals of any of the species, by
better adapting them to their altered conditions, would tend to be preserved; and natural selection would thus have free scope for the work
of improvement.

We have reason to believe . . . that a change in the conditions of 3
life, by specially acting on the reproductive system, causes or increases
variability; and in the foregoing case the conditions of life are supposed to have undergone a change, and this would manifestly be favorable to natural selection, by giving a better chance of profitable variations occurring; and unless profitable variations do occur, natural
selection can do nothing. Not that, as I believe, any extreme amount
of variability is necessary; as man can certainly produce great results
by adding up in any given direction mere individual differences, so
could Nature, but far more easily, from having incomparably longer
time at her disposal. Nor do I believe that any great physical change,
as of climate, or any unusual degree of isolation to check immigration,
is actually necessary to produce new and unoccupied places for natural
selection to fill up by modifying and improving some of the varying
inhabitants. For as all the inhabitants of each country are struggling
together with nicely balanced forces, extremely slight modifications in
the structure or habits of one inhabitant would often give it an advantage over others; and still further modifications of the same kind

would often still further increase the advantage. No country can be named in which all the native inhabitants are now so perfectly adapted to each other and to the physical conditions under which they live, that none of them could anyhow be improved; for in all countries, the natives have been so far conquered by naturalized productions, that they have allowed foreigners to take firm possession of the land. And as foreigners have thus everywhere beaten some of the natives, we may safely conclude that the natives might have been modified with advantage, so as to have better resisted such intruders.

As man can produce and certainly has produced a great result by 4 his methodical and unconscious means of selection, what may not nature effect? Man can act only on external and visible characters; nature cares nothing for appearances, except in so far as they may be useful to any being. She can act on every internal organ, on every shade of constitutional difference, on the whole machinery of life. Man selects only for his own good; Nature only for that of the being which she tends. Every selected character is fully exercised by her; and the being is placed under well-suited conditions of life. Man keeps the natives of many climates in the same country; he seldom exercises each selected character in some peculiar and fitting manner; he feeds a long and a short beaked pigeon on the same food; he does not exercise a long-backed or long-legged quadruped in any peculiar manner; he exposes sheep with long and short wool to the same climate. He does not allow the most vigorous males to struggle for the females. He does not rigidly destroy all inferior animals, but protects during each varying season, as far as lies in his power, all his productions. He often begins his selection by some half-monstrous form; or at least by some modification prominent enough to catch his eye, or to be plainly useful to him. Under nature, the slightest difference of structure or constitution may well turn the nicely balanced scale in the struggle for life, and so be preserved. How fleeting are the wishes and efforts of man! how short his time! and consequently how poor will his products be, compared with those accumulated by nature during whole geological periods. Can we wonder, then, that nature's productions should be far "truer" in character than man's productions; that they should be infinitely better adapted to the most complex conditions of life, and should plainly bear the stamp of far higher workmanship?

It may be said that natural selection is daily and hourly scrutiniz- 5 ing, throughout the world, every variation, even the slightest; rejecting that which is bad, preserving and adding up all that is good; silently and insensibly working, whenever and wherever opportunity offers, at the improvement of each organic being in relation to its organic and inorganic conditions of life. We see nothing of these slow changes in progress, until the hand of time has marked the long lapse of ages, and then so imperfect is our view into long past geological ages, that we only see that the forms of life are now different from what they formerly were.

Although natural selection can act only through and for the good 6 of each being, yet characters and structures, which we are apt to consider as of very trifling importance, may thus be acted on. When we see leaf-eating insects green, and bark-feeders mottled-grey; the alpine ptarmigan white in winter, the red-grouse the color of heather, and the black-grouse that of peaty earth, we must believe that these tints are of service to these birds and insects in preserving them from danger. Grouse, if not destroyed at some period of their lives, would increase in countless numbers; they are known to suffer largely from birds of prey; and hawks are guided by eyesight to their prey—so much so that on parts of the Continent[3] persons are warned not to keep white pigeons, as being the most liable to destruction. Hence I can see no reason to doubt that natural selection might be most effective in giving the proper color to each kind of grouse, and in keeping that color, when once acquired, true and constant. Nor ought we to think that the occasional destruction of an animal of any particular color would produce little effect; we should remember how essential it is in a flock of white sheep to destroy every lamb with the faintest trace of black. In plants, the down on the fruit and the color of the flesh are considered by botanists as characters of the most trifling importance; yet we hear from an excellent horticulturist, Downing,[4] that in the United States, smooth-skinned fruits suffer far more from a beetle, a curculio,[5] than those with down; that purple plums suffer far more from a certain disease than yellow plums; whereas another disease attacks yellow-fleshed peaches far more than those with other colored flesh. If, with all the aids of art, these slight differences make a great difference in cultivating the several varieties, assuredly, in a state of nature, where the trees would have to struggle with other trees and with a host of enemies, such differences would effectually settle which variety, whether a smooth or downy, a yellow or purple fleshed fruit, should succeed.

---

[3]**Continent** European continent; the contiguous land mass of Europe, excluding the British Isles.

[4]*Andrew Jackson Downing (1815–1852)* American horticulturist and specialist in fruit and fruit trees.

[5]**curculio** A weevil.

In looking at many small points of difference between species, 7 which, as far as our ignorance permits us to judge, seem to be quite unimportant, we must not forget that climate, food, etc., probably produce some slight and direct effect. It is, however, far more necessary to bear in mind that there are many unknown laws of correlation[6] of growth, which, when one part of the organization is modified through variation and the modifications are accumulated by natural selection for the good of the being, will cause other modifications, often of the most unexpected nature.

As we see that those variations which under domestication appear 8 at any particular period of life, tend to reappear in the offspring at the same period—for instance, in the seeds of the many varieties of our culinary and agricultural plants; in the caterpillar and cocoon stages of the varieties of the silkworm; in the eggs of poultry, and in the color of the down of their chickens; in the horns of our sheep and cattle when nearly adult—so in a state of nature, natural selection will be enabled to act on and modify organic beings at any age, by the accumulation of profitable variations at that age, and by their inheritance at a corresponding age. If it profit a plant to have its seeds more and more widely disseminated by the wind, I can see no greater difficulty in this being effected through natural selection than in the cotton-planter increasing and improving by selection the down in the pods on his cotton-trees. Natural selection may modify and adapt the larva of an insect to a score of contingencies, wholly different from those which concern the mature insect. These modifications will no doubt effect, through the laws of correlation, the structure of the adult; and probably in the case of those insects which live only for a few hours, and which never feed, a large part of their structure is merely the correlated result of successive changes in the structure of their larvae. So, conversely, modifications in the adult will probably often affect the structure of the larva; but in all cases natural selection will ensure that modifications consequent on other modifications at a different period of life, shall not be in the least degree injurious: for if they became so, they would cause the extinction of the species.

Natural selection will modify the structure of the young in relation 9 to the parent, and of the parent in relation to the young. In social animals it will adapt the structure of each individual for the benefit of the community; if each in consequence profits by the selected change.

---

[6]*laws of correlation* In certain plants and animals, one condition relates to another, as in the case of blue-eyed white cats, which are always deaf; the reasons are not clear.

What natural selection cannot do is to modify the structure of one species, without giving it any advantage, for the good of another species; and though statements to this effect may be found in works of natural history, I cannot find one case which will bear investigation. A structure used only once in an animal's whole life, if of high importance to it, might be modified to any extent by natural selection; for instance, the great jaws possessed by certain insects, and used exclusively for opening the cocoon—or the hard tip to the beak of nestling birds, used for breaking the egg. It has been asserted that of the best short-beaked tumbler-pigeons, more perish in the egg than are able to get out of it; so that fanciers[7] assist in the act of hatching. Now, if nature had to make the beak of a full-grown pigeon very short for the bird's own advantage, the process of modification would be very slow, and there would be simultaneously the most rigorous selection of the young birds within the egg, which had the most powerful and hardest beaks, for all with weak beaks would inevitably perish; or, more delicate and more easily broken shells might be selected, the thickness of the shell being known to vary like every other structure.

Sexual Selection

Inasmuch as peculiarities often appear under domestication in one sex and become hereditarily attached to that sex, the same fact probably occurs under nature, and if so, natural selection will be able to modify one sex in its functional relations to the other sex, or in relation to wholly different habits of life in the two sexes, as is sometimes the case with insects. And this leads me to say a few words on what I call Sexual Selection. This depends, not on a struggle for existence, but on a struggle between the males for possession of the females; the result is not death to the unsuccessful competitor, but few or no offspring. Sexual selection is, therefore, less rigorous than natural selection. Generally, the most vigorous males, those which are best fitted for their places in nature, will leave most progeny. But in many cases, victory will depend not on general vigor, but on having special weapons, confined to the male sex. A hornless stag or spurless cock would have a poor chance of leaving offspring. Sexual selection by always allowing the victor to breed might surely give indomitable courage, length to the spur, and strength to the wing to strike in the spurred leg, as well as the brutal cock fighter,[8] who knows well that he can

10

---

[7]*fanciers* Amateurs who raise and race pigeons.

[8]*brutal cock fighter* Cockfights were a popular spectator sport in England, especially for gamblers; but many people considered them a form of horrible brutality.

improve his breed by careful selection of the best cocks. How low in the scale of nature this law of battle descends, I know not; male alligators have been described as fighting, bellowing, and whirling round, like Indians in a wardance, for the possession of the females; male salmons have been seen fighting all day long; male stag-beetles often bear wounds from the huge mandibles[9] of other males. The war is, perhaps, severest between the males of polygamous animals,[10] and these seem oftenest provided with special weapons. The males of carnivorous animals are already well armed; though to them and to others, special means of defense may be given through means of sexual selection, as the mane to the lion, the shoulder-pad to the boar, and the hooked jaw to the male salmon; for the shield may be as important for victory as the sword or spear.

Among birds, the contest is often of a more peaceful character. All those who have attended to the subject believe that there is the severest rivalry between the males of many species to attract, by singing, the females. The rock-thrush of Guiana,[11] birds of paradise, and some others, congregate; and successive males display their gorgeous plumage and perform strange antics before the females, which standing by as spectators, at last choose the most attractive partner. Those who have closely attended to birds in confinement well know that they often take individual preferences and dislikes: thus Sir R. Heron[12] has described how one pied peacock was eminently attractive to all his hen birds. It may appear childish to attribute any effect to such apparently weak means: I cannot here enter on the details necessary to support this view; but if man can in a short time give elegant carriage and beauty to his bantams,[13] according to his standard of beauty, I can see no good reason to doubt that female birds, by selecting, during thousands of generations, the most melodious or beautiful males, according to their standard of beauty, might produce a marked effect. I strongly suspect that some well-known laws with respect to the plumage of male and female birds, in comparison with the plumage of the young, can be explained on the view of plumage having been chiefly modified by sexual selection, acting when the birds have come to the breeding

[9]*mandibles* Jaws.

[10]*polygamous animals* Animals that typically have more than one mate.

[11]*Guiana* British Guiana, on the east coast of South America.

[12]*Sir Robert Heron (1765–1854)* English politician who maintained a menagerie of animals.

[13]*bantams* Cocks bred for fighting.

age or during the breeding season; the modifications thus produced being inherited at corresponding ages or seasons, either by the males alone, or by the males and females; but I have not space here to enter on this subject.

Thus it is, as I believe, that when the males and females of any 12 animal have the same general habits of life, but differ in structure, color, or ornament, such differences have been mainly caused by sexual selection; that is, individual males have had, in successive generations, some slight advantage over other males, in their weapons, means of defense, or charms; and have transmitted these advantages to their male offspring. Yet, I would not wish to attribute all such sexual differences to this agency: for we see peculiarities arising and becoming attached to the male sex in our domestic animals (as the wattle in male carriers, horn-like protuberances in the cocks of certain fowls, etc.), which we cannot believe to be either useful to the males in battle, or attractive to the females. We see analogous cases under nature, for instance, the tuft of hair on the breast of the turkey-cock, which can hardly be either useful or ornamental to this bird; indeed, had the tuft appeared under domestication, it would have been called a monstrosity.

Illustrations of the Action of Natural Selection

In order to make it clear how, as I believe, natural selection acts, I 13 must beg permission to give one or two imaginary illustrations. Let us take the case of a wolf, which preys on various animals, securing some by craft, some by strength, and some by fleetness; and let us suppose that the fleetest prey, a deer for instance, had from any change in the country increased in numbers, or that other prey had decreased in numbers, during that season of the year when the wolf is hardest pressed for food. I can under such circumstances see no reason to doubt that the swiftest and slimmest wolves would have the best chance of surviving, and so be preserved or selected, provided always that they retained strength to master their prey at this or at some other period of the year, when they might be compelled to prey on other animals. I can see no more reason to doubt this, than that man can improve the fleetness of his greyhounds by careful and methodical selection, or by that unconscious selection which results from each man trying to keep the best dogs without any thought of modifying the breed.

Even without any change in the proportional numbers of the ani- 14
mals on which our wolf preyed, a cub might be born with an innate
tendency to pursue certain kinds of prey. Nor can this be thought very
improbable; for we often observe great differences in the natural tendencies of our domestic animals; one cat, for instance, taking to catch
rats, another mice; one cat, according to Mr. St. John,[14] bringing home
winged game, another hares or rabbits, and another hunting on marshy
ground and almost nightly catching woodcocks or snipes. The tendency to catch rats rather than mice is known to be inherited. Now, if
any slight innate change of habit or of structure benefited an individual wolf, it would have the best chance of surviving and of leaving
offspring. Some of its young would probably inherit the same habits or
structure, and by the repetition of this process, a new variety might be
formed which would either supplant or coexist with the parent-form
of wolf. Or, again, the wolves inhabiting a mountainous district, and
those frequenting the lowlands, would naturally be forced to hunt different prey; and from the continued preservation of the individuals
best fitted for the two sites, two varieties might slowly be formed.
These varieties would cross and blend where they met; but to this
subject of intercrossing we shall soon have to return. I may add, that,
according to Mr. Pierce,[15] there are two varieties of the wolf inhabiting
the Catskill Mountains in the United States, one with a light grey-
hound-like form, which pursues deer, and the other more bulky, with
shorter legs, which more frequently attacks the shepherd's flocks.

Let us now take a more complex case. Certain plants excrete a 15
sweet juice, apparently for the sake of eliminating something injurious
from their sap; this is effected by glands at the base of the stipules[16]
in some Leguminosæ, and at the back of the leaf of the common laurel.
This juice, though small in quantity, is greedily sought by insects. Let
us now suppose a little sweet juice or nectar to be excreted by the
inner bases of the petals of a flower. In this case insects in seeking the
nectar would get dusted with pollen, and would certainly often transport the pollen from one flower to the stigma of another flower. The
flowers of two distinct individuals of the same species would thus get
crossed; and the act of crossing, we have good reason to believe (as
will hereafter be more fully alluded to), would produce very vigorous

---

[14]*Charles William George St. John (1809–1856)* An English naturalist whose
book, *Wild Sports and Natural History of the Highlands,* was published in 1846 and in
a second edition in 1848.

[15]*Pierce* Unidentified.

[16]*stipules* Spines at the base of a leaf.

seedlings, which consequently would have the best chance of flourish-ing and surviving. Some of these seedlings would probably inherit the nectar-excreting power. Those individual flowers which had the largest glands or nectaries, and which excreted most nectar, would be oftenest visited by insects, and would be oftenest crossed; and so in the long-run would gain the upper hand. Those flowers, also, which had their stamens and pistils[17] placed, in relation to the size and habits of the particular insects which visited them, so as to favor in any degree the transportal of their pollen from flower to flower, would likewise be favored or selected. We might have taken the case of insects visiting flowers for the sake of collecting pollen instead of nectar; and as pollen is formed for the sole object of fertilization, its destruction appears a simple loss to the plant; yet if a little pollen were carried, at first oc-casionally and then habitually, by the pollen-devouring insects from flower to flower, and a cross thus effected, although nine-tenths of the pollen were destroyed, it might still be a great gain to the plant; and those individuals which produced more and more pollen, and had larger and larger anthers,[18] would be selected.

When our plant, by this process of the continued preservation or natural selection of more and more attractive flowers, had been ren-dered highly attractive to insects, they would, unintentionally on their part, regularly carry pollen from flower to flower; and that they can most effectually do this, I could easily show by many striking in-stances. I will give only one—not as a very striking case, but as like-wise illustrating one step in the separation of the sexes of plants, pres-ently to be alluded to. Some holly-trees bear only male flowers, which have four stamens producing rather a small quantity of pollen, and a rudimentary pistil; other holly-trees bear only female flowers; these have a full-sized pistil, and four stamens with shrivelled anthers, in which not a grain of pollen can be detected. Having found a female tree exactly sixty yards from a male tree, I put the stigmas[19] of twenty flowers, taken from different branches, under the microscope, and on all, without exception, there were pollen-grains, and on some a profu-sion of pollen. As the wind had set for several days from the female to the male tree, the pollen could not thus have been carried. The weather had been cold and boisterous, and therefore not favorable to bees; nevertheless every female flower which I examined had been ef-

16

---

[17]***stamens and pistils*** Sexual organs of plants. The male and female organs appear together in the same flower.

[18]***anthers*** An anther is that part of the stamen that contains pollen.

[19]***stigmas*** Where the plant's pollen develops.

fectually fertilized by the bees, accidentally dusted with pollen, having flown from tree to tree in search of nectar. But to return to our imaginary case: as soon as the plant had been rendered so highly attractive to insects that pollen was regularly carried from flower to flower, another process might commence. No naturalist doubts the advantage of what has been called the "physiological division of labor"; hence we may believe that it would be advantageous to a plant to produce stamens alone in one flower or on one whole plant, and pistils alone in another flower or on another plant. In plants under culture and placed under new conditions of life, sometimes the male organs and sometimes the female organs become more or less impotent; now if we suppose this to occur in ever so slight a degree under nature, then as pollen is already carried regularly from flower to flower, and as a more complete separation of the sexes of our plant would be advantageous on the principle of the division of labor, individuals with this tendency more and more increased, would be continually favored or selected, until at last a complete separation of the sexes would be effected.

Let us now turn to the nectar-feeding insects in our imaginary case: 17 we may suppose the plant of which we have been slowly increasing the nectar by continued selection, to be a common plant; and that certain insects depended in main part on its nectar for food. I could give many facts, showing how anxious bees are to save time; for instance, their habit of cutting holes and sucking the nectar at the bases of certain flowers, which they can, with a very little more trouble, enter by the mouth. Bearing such facts in mind, I can see no reason to doubt that an accidental deviation in the size and form of the body, or in the curvature and length of the proboscis,[20] etc., far too slight to be appreciated by us, might profit a bee or other insect, so that an individual so characterized would be able to obtain its food more quickly, and so have a better chance of living and leaving descendants. Its descendants would probably inherit a tendency to a similar slight deviation of structure. The tubes of the corollas[21] of the common red and incarnate clovers (Trifolium pratense and incarnatum) do not on a hasty glance appear to differ in length; yet the hive-bee can easily suck the nectar out of the incarnate clover, but not out of the common red clover, which is visited by humble-bees[22] alone; so that whole fields of the red clover offer in vain an abundant supply of precious nectar to

---

[20]*proboscis*   Snout.

[21]*corollas*   Inner set of floral petals.

[22]*humble-bees*   Bumblebees.

the hive-bee. Thus it might be a great advantage to the hive-bee to have a slightly longer or differently constructed proboscis. On the other hand, I have found by experiment that the fertility of clover greatly depends on bees visiting and moving parts of the corolla, so as to push the pollen on to the stigmatic surface. Hence, again, if humble-bees were to become rare in any country, it might be a great advantage to the red clover to have a shorter or more deeply divided tube to its corolla, so that the hive-bee could visit its flowers. Thus I can understand how a flower and a bee might slowly become, either simultaneously or one after the other, modified and adapted in the most perfect manner to each other, by the continued preservation of individuals presenting mutual and slightly favourable deviations of structure.

I am well aware that this doctrine of natural selection, exemplified 18 in the above imaginary instances, is open to the same objections which were at first urged against Sir Charles Lyell's noble views[23] on "the modern changes of the earth, as illustrative of geology"; but we now very seldom hear the action, for instance, of the coast-waves, called a trifling and insignificant cause, when applied to the excavation of gigantic valleys or to the formation of the longest lines of inland cliffs. Natural selection can act only by the preservation and accumulation of infinitesimally small inherited modifications, each profitable to the preserved being; and as modern geology has almost banished such views as the excavation of a great valley by a single diluvial[24] wave, so will natural selection, if it be a true principle, banish the belief of the continued creation of new organic beings, or of any great and sudden modification in their structure.

---

[23]*Sir Charles Lyell's noble views*   Lyell (1797–1879) was an English geologist whose landmark work, *Principles of Geology* (1830–1833), Darwin read while on the *Beagle*. The book inspired Darwin, and the two scientists became friends. Lyell was shown portions of *The Origin of Species* while Darwin was writing it.

[24]*diluvial*   Pertaining to a flood. Darwin means that geological changes, such as those which caused the Grand Canyon, were no longer thought of as being created instantly by flood (or other catastrophes), but were considered to have developed over a long period of time, as he imagines happened in the evolution of species.

QUESTIONS

1. Darwin uses the metaphor of a "battle for life" (para. 1). What is the value of this metaphor for understanding the substance of his ideas?
2. What are the differences between natural selection and selection by hu-

mans? Why would it be easier to believe in the force of one but not of the other?

3. Does Darwin assume that natural selection is a positive force?
4. Why doesn't Darwin discuss varieties and selection with reference to people in this work?
5. What kind of a reception does Darwin seem to expect for his work?
6. In later editions, Darwin used "The Survival of the Fittest" as a subtitle for this chapter. What changes might that imply? Is it a better title than simply "Natural Selection"?

WRITING ASSIGNMENTS

1. In paragraph 13, Darwin uses imaginary examples. Compare the value of his genuine examples and these imaginary ones. How effective is the use of imaginary examples in an argument? What requirements would an imaginary example have to have in order to be forceful in an argument? Do you find Darwin's imaginary examples to be strong or weak?
2. From paragraph 14 on, Darwin discusses the process of modification of a species through its beginning in the modification of an individual. Explain, insofar as you understand the concept, just how a species could be modified by a variation which would occur in just one individual. In your explanation, use Darwin's rhetorical technique of the imaginary example.
3. Write an essay which takes as its thesis statement the following sentence from paragraph 18: "Natural selection can act only by the preservation and accumulation of infinitesimally small inherited modifications, each profitable to the preserved being." Be sure to examine the work carefully to find other statements by Darwin that will give added strength, clarity, and meaning to this one. You may also employ the Darwinian device of presenting "imaginary instances" in your essay.
4. A controversy exists concerning the Darwinian theory of evolution. Explore the *Readers' Guide to Periodical Literature* for up-to-date information on the creationist-evolutionist conflict in schools. Look up either term or both to see what articles you can find. Establish the nature of the controversy and attempt to defend one side. Use your knowledge of natural selection gained from this piece. Remember, too, that Darwin was trained as a minister of the church and was very concerned about religious opinion.
5. When Darwin wrote this piece, he believed that sexual selection was of great importance in evolutionary changes in species. Assuming that this belief is true, establish the similarities between sexual selection in plants and animals with sexual selection, as you have observed it, in people. Paragraphs 10–12 discuss this issue. Darwin does not discuss people, but it is clear that physical and stylistic distinctions between the sexes have some bearing on selection. Assuming that to be true, what qualities in people (physical and mental) are likely to survive? Why?

6. In the Middle Ages and earlier the official view of the church was that the world was flat. Columbus proved that the world was round, and the church agreed not to argue with him. The official view of the church was that the sun went around the earth. When Galileo proved otherwise, he was forced to deny his observations and then he was banished. Only later, in the face of overwhelming evidence, did the church back down. Regarding Darwin, the church held that all species were created on a specially appointed day; evolution was impossible. The Church of England and the Roman Catholic Church, after some struggle, seem to have accepted Darwin's views. Why is it still difficult for some religious organizations to accept Darwin's views? In order to deal with this question, you may have to interview some people connected with a church that holds that Darwin's views are inaccurate. You may also find some religious literature attacking Darwin. If so, establish what the concern of some churches and other religious organizations may be. Make as clear an argument for such organizations' point of view as you can.

C. P. SNOW

The Moral Un-Neutrality of Science

CHARLES PERCY SNOW (1905–1980) was among a handful of men who, in the years following World War II, were able to span the gulf between the sciences and the humanities. He is singular in that he was trained as a physicist at Cambridge, receiving his Ph.D. in 1930, but became well known as a novelist. His work in science was in the field of molecular physics, and thus it is no surprise that the focus of this selection eventually moves toward questions concerning nuclear fission and the moral issues surrounding the existence of atomic weapons.

Snow was not a distinguished scientist; most of his career at Cambridge involved administrative tasks, and that activity in turn helped him play a role in governmental agencies concerned with nuclear physics. In this selection he describes himself as an ex-scientist only because he had been away from his laboratory research for such a long time. Yet his background is in a demanding intellectual field, and his qualifications to speak for science are certainly of the first order.

Snow became a novelist partly for relaxation—his first book was a mystery novel. But he soon began to write about the kinds of people he knew: scientists conducting significant research. In their lives he saw the material of high drama. He began a series of related novels in 1940—Strangers and Brothers—and included ten separate books, the last of which was published in 1968. The New Men (1954) was on the subject of research into atomic fission and its ultimate adaptation to the uses of warfare. He refers to the book obliquely in his discussion. Critics have taken Snow seriously as a novelist, and part of his interest lies in his unusual knowledge of scientists and their world; few writers since the eighteenth century have been as conversant in that field as C. P. Snow.

During the 1950s, his lecture, "The Two Cultures and the Scientific Revolution," caused an international stir. His view was that the specialized education of the modern world had created a division between humanists and scientists and that the split between them might not be reparable. Further, it was a split that had moral implications—a few of which are examined here—because the results of science were not under the control of the people who created them, and the people who created them did not have the educational or the moral background of the humanist. The question of the two cultures was debated and discussed for a dozen years. During that time university curricula in the United States and Great Britain were changed in order to help lessen the division.

In this essay, Snow confronts a simple but profoundly important question. He argues that science is not an amoral activity and that scientists should be as concerned with the moral implications of their actions as any other group might be. Because there is a division between the producers of scientific knowledge and those who put that knowledge into action, however, the moral position of the scientist is not easy to define. Scientists, for example, created the atomic bomb, but they did not decide to use it or to stockpile it. Those decisions were political ones. Because of that, the scientist is sometimes seen as morally detached from the uses to which his or her discoveries are put.

Since Snow is talking about atomic energy and atomic weaponry, however, and since the technology on which weaponry depends is clearly a product of modern science, he is eager to establish the complexity of moral involvement. The scientists who produced the bomb are "citizen soldiers"; nonetheless, they are involved in the military implications of their discoveries.

SNOW'S RHETORIC

Snow proceeds carefully and thoroughly. He begins his essay by stating that moral questions are implicit in science itself. For example, there is a connection between the creativity of the artist and the creativity of the scientist, as there is between the elegance of a work of art and that of a scientific theory or discovery. Thus, science has *an aesthetic component. Those who studied philosophy at Cambridge when Snow was there would recall that aesthetics and ethics were both part of the same branch of philosophy because both disciplines involved choices that often imply moral decision; thus, if one accepts Snow's opening argument, one also accepts his overall position.*

Snow makes some interesting claims about the question of truth and about the pursuit of knowledge. He believes that these are connected with ethics and morality. Of course, the question of truth is naturally connected with morality, but it is not so clear how knowledge becomes a moral issue. Yet, he argues cogently that it does.

One of Snow's strategies is to point out that scientists are not "inhuman"; they are not as different from the rest of us as popular culture would have us believe. He then claims that since science is a profession, scientists as a group may have even higher moral standards than do people in general. His argument is subtle: If scientists are moral, must we not, then, accept the thesis that their work is moral as well? Similarly, if scientists are like ordinary people, does not their work have the moral capacity for evil as well as for good?

Snow notes that the atomic bomb was produced at a time when it was clear that the world was involved in a great moral struggle. Hitler was obviously an evil force; if Nazi Germany had produced the bomb first, the entire world would have been in jeopardy. Thus, a weapon of such immense evil potential was produced by scientists whose intentions were morally defensible.

Snow also employs analogy. He reminds us that even though what he says is true, the scientists who produced the bomb were on a "moral escalator" and that there may come a time when they should say no. Snow examines a disturbing possibility in the latter part of the essay, explaining that it is not only possible but likely that somewhere, sometime, some of the stockpiled atomic bombs will explode. As he says, it can happen as a result of any one of a number of causes, but what the cause is matters little; the effect is what is important.

Obviously, then, Snow brings us to several conclusions. The first is that there is a moral imperative to control nuclear arms. The second is that there is an equally important moral imperative to help feed that portion of the world that is hungry and starving. It is feasible to feed the world. If it is, then it is morally essential that we do so. But, as he says, the means are there, the will is not. And will is a moral issue. His essay leaves us with the clear sense that the achievements of science exist in a moral sphere and that we must take moral action in order to make those achievements acceptable to the world.

The Moral Un-Neutrality
of Science

Scientists are the most important occupational group in the world 1
today. At this moment, what they do is of passionate concern to the
whole of human society. At this moment, the scientists have little
influence on the world effect of what they do. Yet, potentially, they
can have great influence. The rest of the world is frightened both of
what they do—that is, of the intellectual discoveries of science—and
of its effect. The rest of the world, transferring its fears, is frightened
of the scientists themselves and tends to think of them as radically
different from other men.

As an ex-scientist, if I may call myself so, I know that is nonsense. 2
I have even tried to express in fiction some kinds of scientific temper-
ament and scientific experience. I know well enough that scientists
are very much like other men. After all, we are all human, even if
some of us don't give that appearance. I think I would be prepared to
risk a generalization. The scientists I have known (and because of my
official life I have known as many as anyone in the world) have been
in certain respects at least as morally admirable as any other group of
intelligent men.

That is a sweeping statement, and I mean it only in a statistical 3
sense. But I think there is just a little in it. The moral qualities I admire in scientists are quite simple ones, but I am very suspicious of
attempts to oversubtilize moral qualities. It is nearly always a sign,
not of true sophistication, but of a specific kind of triviality. So I admire in scientists very simple virtues—like courage, truth-telling,
kindness—in which, judged by the low standards which the rest of us
manage to achieve, the scientists are not deficient. I think on the
whole the scientists make slightly better husbands and fathers than
most of us, and I admire them for it. I don't know the figures, and I
should be curious to have them sorted out, but I am prepared to bet
that the proportion of divorces among scientists is slightly but significantly less than that among other groups of similar education and
income. I do not apologize for considering that a good thing.

A close friend of mine is a very distinguished scientist. He is also 4
one of the few scientists I know who has lived what we used to call a

Bohemian life. When we were both younger, he thought he would undertake historical research to see how many great scientists had been as fond of women as he was. I think he would have felt mildly supported if he could have found a precedent. I remember his reporting to me that his researches hadn't had any luck. The really great scientists seemed to vary from a few neutral characters to a large number who were depressingly "normal." The only gleam of comfort was to be found in the life of Jerome Cardan;[1] and Cardan wasn't anything like enough to outweigh all the others.

So scientists are not much different from other men. They are certainly no worse than other men. But they do differ from other men in one thing. That is the point I started with. Whether they like it or not, what they do is of critical importance for the human race. Intellectually, it has transformed the climate of our time. Socially, it will decide whether we live or die, and how we live or die. It holds decisive powers for good and evil. *That* is the situation in which the scientists find themselves. They may not have asked for it, or may only have asked for it in part, but they cannot escape it. They think, many of the more sensitive of them, that they don't deserve to have this weight of responsibility heaved upon them. All they want to do is to get on with their work. I sympathize. But the scientists can't escape the responsibility—any more than they, or the rest of us, can escape the gravity of the moment in which we stand.

There is of course one way to contract out. It has been a favorite way for intellectual persons caught in the midst of water too rough for them.

It consists of the invention of categories—or, if you like, of the division of moral labor. That is, the scientists who want to contract out say, *we* produce the tools. *We* stop there. It is for *you*—the rest of the world, the politicians—to say how the tools are used. The tools may be used for purposes which most of us would regard as bad. If so, we are sorry. But as scientists, that is no concern of ours.

This is the doctrine of the ethical neutrality of science. I can't accept it for an instant. I don't believe any scientist of serious feeling can accept it. It is hard, some think, to find the precise statements which will prove it wrong. Yet we nearly all feel intuitively that the invention of comfortable categories is a moral trap. It is one of the easier

5

6

7

8

---

[1]*Jerome Cardan (1501–1576)* An Italian physician whose medical theories were founded on astrology. He figured out the day of his death by calculation, then starved to make his prediction come true. He was well known as a mathematician.

methods of letting the conscience rust. It is exactly what the early nineteenth-century economists, such as Ricardo,[2] did in the face of the facts of the first industrial revolution. We wonder now how men, intelligent men, can have been so morally blind. We realize how the exposure of that moral blindness gave Marxism[3] its apocalyptic force. We are now, in the middle of the scientific or second industrial revolution, in something like the same position as Ricardo. Are we going to let our consciences rust? Can we ignore that intimation we nearly all have, that scientists have a unique responsibility? Can we believe it, that science is morally neutral?

To me—it would be dishonest to pretend otherwise—there is only   9 one answer to those questions. Yet I have been brought up in the presence of the same intellectual categories as most Western scientists. It would also be dishonest to pretend that I find it easy to construct a rationale which expresses what I now believe. The best I can hope for is to fire a few sighting shots. Perhaps someone who sees more clearly than I can will come along and make a real job of it.

Let me begin with a remark which seems some way off the point.   10 Anyone who has ever worked in any science knows how much aesthetic joy he has obtained. That is, in the actual *activity* of science, in the process of making a discovery, however humble it is, one can't help feeling an awareness of beauty. The subjective experience, the aesthetic satisfaction, seems exactly the same as the satisfaction one gets from writing a poem or a novel, or composing a piece of music. I don't think anyone has succeeded in distinguishing between them. The literature of scientific discovery is full of this aesthetic joy. The very best communication of it that I know comes in G. H. Hardy's book,[4] *A Mathematician's Apology.* Graham Greene once said he

---

[2] **David Ricardo (1712–1823)**   A British economist whose work was deductive and scientific. He theorized that increasing the wages of British workers would increase the birth rate; thus, stingy mill owners had further cause to keep wages down throughout the early nineteenth century.

[3] **Marxism**   Essentially communism, the belief that labor and management are at odds and that the only solution is the communal ownership of property in which labor owns its own product. Theories of modern communism have derived from the work of Karl Marx—see the *Communist Manifesto* in Part One of this book.

[4] **G. H. Hardy's book**   Godfrey Harold Hardy (1877–1947), a British mathematician who taught at Cambridge. His best work was in pure mathematics, although one of his discoveries became useful in genetic studies in predicting the distribution of recessive genes.

thought that, along with Henry James's prefaces,[5] this was the best account of the artistic experience ever written. But one meets the same thing throughout the history of science. Bolyai's great yell of triumph[6] when he saw he could construct a self-consistent, non-Euclidean geometry; Rutherford's revelation[7] to his colleagues that he knew what the atom was like; Darwin's slow, patient, timorous certainty[8] that at last he had got there—all these are voices, different voices, of aesthetic ecstasy.

That is not the end of it. The *result* of the activity of science, the   11
actual finished piece of scientific work, has an aesthetic value in itself. The judgments passed on it by other scientists will more often than not be expressed in aesthetic terms: "That's beautiful!" or "That really is very pretty!" (as the understating English tend to say). The aesthetics of scientific constructs, like the aesthetics of works of art, are variegated. We think some of the great syntheses, like Newton's,[9] beautiful because of their classical simplicity, but we see a different kind of beauty in the relativistic extension of the wave equation or the interpretation of the structure of deoxyribonucleic acid,[10] perhaps because of the touch of unexpectedness. Scientists know their kinds of beauty when they see them. They are suspicious, and scientific history shows they have always been right to have been so, when a subject is in an "ugly" state. For example, most physicists feel in their bones that the present bizarre assembly of nuclear particles, as grotesque as a stamp collection, can't possibly be, in the long run, the last word.

---

[5]***Graham Greene . . . Henry James's prefaces*** Graham Greene (b. 1898), like Henry James (1843–1916), is an important English novelist. James's prefaces to the uniform 1914 New York Edition of his works are viewed as landmark studies of the act of literary creativity.

[6]***Bolyai's great yell of triumph*** Johann Bolyai (1802–1860) was an important Hungarian mathematician. In 1820 he began to develop a workable non-Euclidean geometry.

[7]***Rutherford's revelation*** Ernest Rutherford (1871–1937) was one of the most important British nuclear physicists; he is known for his discovery of the atomic nucleus.

[8]***Darwin's . . . certainty*** Charles Darwin (1809–1882) was very careful to build up evidence he considered irrefutable before publishing his work on evolution. His "timorous certainty" refers to his slowness in making his work known to the world. He published his work when he did only because another scientist, Alfred Russel Wallace, was about to make known similar findings.

[9]***Isaac Newton (1642–1727)*** British scientist who invented calculus and developed a workable theory of gravitation. The "great synthesis" refers to the apparently organic relationship among his theories of motion and gravity. They implied a rational order to the universal laws of physics and gave rise to theories that saw the universe as an orderly machine functioning smoothly and efficiently.

[10]***deoxyribonucleic acid*** DNA, the basic building block of the gene.

We should not restrict the aesthetic values to what we call "pure" science. Applied science has its beauties, which are, in my view, identical in nature. The magnetron[11] has been a marvellously useful device, but it was a beautiful device, not exactly apart from its utility but because it did, with such supreme economy, precisely what it was designed to do. Right down in the field of development, the aesthetic experience is as real to engineers. When they forget it, when they begin to design heavy-power equipment about twice as heavy as it needs to be, engineers are the first to know that they are lacking virtue. 12

There is no doubt, then, about the aesthetic content of science, both in the activity and the result. But aesthetics has no connection with morals, say the categorizers. I don't want to waste time on peripheral issues—but are you quite sure of that? Or is it possible that these categories are inventions to make us evade the human and social conditions in which we now exist? But let us move straight on to something else, which is right in the grain of the activity of science and which is at the same time quintessentially moral. I mean, the desire to find the truth. 13

By *truth*, I don't intend anything complicated, once again. I am using the word as a scientist uses it. We all know that the philosophical examination of the concept of empirical truth gets us into some curious complexities, but most scientists really don't care. They know that the truth, as they use the word and as the rest of us use it in the language of common speech, is what makes science work. That is good enough for them. On it rests the whole great edifice of modern science. They have a sneaking sympathy for Rutherford, who, when asked to examine the philosophical bases of science, was inclined to reply, as he did to the metaphysician Samuel Alexander[12]: "Well, what have you been talking all your life, Alexander? Just hot air! Nothing but hot air!" 14

Anyway, truth in their own straightforward sense is what the scientists are trying to find. They want to find what is *there*. Without that desire, there is no science. It is the driving force of the whole activity. It compels the scientist to have an overriding respect for truth, every stretch of the way. That is, if you're going to find what is 15

---

[11]**magnetron** An electron tube in which the flow of electrons can be controlled by a magnetic field; it is used to generate alternating currents.

[12]**Samuel Alexander (1859–1938)** An English professor of ethics who believed in evolutionary ethics. His most important book was *Moral Order and Progress* (1899).

there, you mustn't deceive yourself or anyone else. You musn't lie to yourself. At the crudest level, you mustn't fake your experiments.

Curiously enough, scientists do try to behave like that. A short 16
time ago, I wrote a novel in which the story hinged on a case of scientific fraud. But I made one of my characters, who was himself a very good scientist, say that, considering the opportunities and temptations, it is astonishing how few such cases there are. We have all heard of perhaps half a dozen open and notorious ones, which are on the record for anyone to read—ranging from the "discovery" of the L radiation to the singular episode of the Piltdown man.[13]

We have all, if we have lived any time in the scientific world, heard 17
private talk of something like another dozen cases which for various reasons are not yet public property. In some cases, we know the motives for the cheating—sometimes, but not always, sheer personal advantage, such as getting money or a job. But not always. A special kind of vanity has led more than one man into scientific faking. At a lower level of research, there are presumably some more cases. There must have been occasional Ph.D. students who scraped by with the help of a bit of fraud.

But the total number of all these men is vanishingly small by the 18
side of the total number of scientists. Incidentally, the effect on science of such frauds is also vanishingly small. Science is a self-correcting system. That is, no fraud (or honest mistake) is going to stay undetected for long. There is no need for an extrinsic scientific criticism, because criticism is inherent in the process itself. So that all that a fraud can do is waste the time of the scientists who have to clear it up.

The remarkable thing is not the handful of scientists who deviate 19
from the search for truth but the overwhelming numbers who keep to it. That is a demonstration, absolutely clear for anyone to see, of moral behavior on a very large scale.

We take it for granted. Yet it is very important. It differentiates 20
science in its widest sense (which includes scholarship) from all other intellectual activities. There is a built-in moral component right in the core of the scientific activity itself. The desire to find the truth is itself a moral impulse, or at least contains a moral impulse. The way in which a scientist tries to find the truth imposes on him a constant moral discipline. We say a scientific conclusion—such as the contra-

---

[13]***Piltdown man*** Supposedly an example of an early form of man found in England (Piltdown, Sussex) in 1911 but exposed as a hoax in 1953.

diction of parity by Lee and Yang[14]—is "true," in the limited sense of scientific truth, just as we say that it is "beautiful" according to the criteria of scientific aesthetics. We also know that to reach this conclusion took a set of actions which would have been useless without the moral motive. That is, all through the experiments of Wu[15] and her colleagues, there was the constant moral exercise of seeking and telling the truth. To scientists, who are brought up in this climate, this seems as natural as breathing. Yet it is a wonderful thing. Even if the scientific activity contained only this one moral component, that alone would be enough to let us say that it was morally un-neutral.

But is this the only moral component? All scientists would agree   21
about the beauty and the truth. In the Western world, they wouldn't agree on much more. Some will feel with me in what I am going to say. Some will not. That doesn't affect me much, except that I am worried by the growth of an attitude I think very dangerous, a kind of technological conformity disguised as cynicism. I shall say a little more about that later. As for disagreement, G. H. Hardy used to comment that a serious man ought not to waste his time stating a majority opinion—there are plenty of others to do that. That was the voice of classical scientific nonconformity. I wish that we heard it more often.

Let me cite some grounds for hope. Any of us who were working   22
in science before 1933 can remember what the atmosphere was like. It is a terrible bore when aging men speak about the charms of their youth. Yet I am going to irritate you—just as Talleyrand[16] irritated his juniors—by saying that unless one was on the scene before 1933, one hasn't known the sweetness of the scientific life. The scientific world of the twenties was as near to being a full-fledged international community as we are likely to get. Don't think I'm saying that the men involved were superhuman or free from the ordinary frailties. That wouldn't come well from me, who has spent a fraction of my writing life pointing out that scientists are, first and foremost, men. But the atmosphere of the twenties in science was filled with an air of benevolence and magnanimity which transcended the people who lived in it.

---

[14]*Tsung-Dao Lee . . . Chen Ning Yang* Nobel Prize winners for physics in 1957. See note 15.

[15]*Chien-Shiung Wu, (b. 1912)* A prominent Chinese-born physicist who taught at Columbia University and who, with Tsung-Dao Lee and Chen Ning Yang of the Institute of Advanced Studies, made important discoveries about the behavior of beta particles.

[16]*Charles Maurice de Talleyrand-Périgord (1754–1838)* An influential French statesman associated with Napoleon Bonaparte. He was a clever and powerful engineer of the Treaty of Vienna, which ended the Napoleonic Wars in 1814–15.

Anyone who ever spent a week in Cambridge or Göttingen or Co-   23
penhagen, felt it all round him. Rutherford had very human faults, but
he was a great man with abounding human generosity. For him the
world of science was a world that lived on a plane above the nation-
state, and lived there with joy. That was at least as true of those two
other great men, Niels Bohr and Franck[17] and some of that spirit
rubbed off on to the pupils round them. The same was true of the
Roman school of physics.

The personal links within this international world were very close.   24
It is worth remembering that Peter Kapitza,[18] who was a loyal Soviet
citizen, honored my country by working in Rutherford's laboratory for
many years. He became a fellow of the Royal Society, a fellow of Trinity College, Cambridge, and the founder and kingpin of the best physics club Cambridge has known. He never gave up his Soviet citizenship and is now director of the Institute of Physical Problems in
Moscow. Through him a generation of English scientists came to have
personal knowledge of their Russian colleagues. These exchanges were
then, and have remained, more valuable than all the diplomatic exchanges ever invented.

The Kapitza phenomenon couldn't take place now. I hope to live   25
to see the day when a young Kapitza can once more work for sixteen
years in Berkeley or Cambridge and then go back to an eminent place
in his own country. When that can happen, we are all right. But after
the idyllic years of world science, we passed into a tempest of history,
and, by an unfortunate coincidence, we passed into a technological
tempest too.

The discovery of atomic fission broke up the world of international   26
physics. "This has killed a beautiful subject," said Mark Oliphant,[19]
the father figure of Australian physics, in 1945, after the bombs had
dropped. In intellectual terms, he has not turned out to be right. In
spiritual and moral terms, I sometimes think he was.

A good deal of the international community of science remains in   27
other fields—in great areas of biology, for example. Many biologists are

---

[17]*Niels Bohr (1885–1962). . . James Franck (1882–1963)* Bohr was a Danish
physicist who worked on the first atomic bomb; Franck was a German physicist who
specialized in atomic structure.

[18]*Peter Kapitza (b. 1894)* Russian physicist who taught at Cambridge but was detained on a visit to Russia in 1935. He refused to work on nuclear weapons and was
placed under house arrest for six years by Stalin. He won the Nobel Prize for physics in
1978.

[19]*Mark Oliphant (b. 1901)* He was assistant director of research at the Cavendish
Laboratory in Cambridge in 1935. He eventually became governor of South Australia.

feeling the identical liberation, the identical joy at taking part in a magnanimous enterprise, that physicists felt in the twenties. It is more than likely that the moral and intellectual leadership of science will pass to biologists, and it is among them that we shall find the Einsteins,[20] Rutherfords and Bohrs of the next generation.

Physicists have had a bitterer task. With the discovery of fission, 28 and with some technical breakthroughs in electronics, physicists became, almost overnight, the most important military resource a nation-state could call on. A large number of physicists became soldiers not in uniform. So they have remained, in the advanced societies, ever since.

It is very difficult to see what else they could have done. All this 29 began in the Hitler war. Most scientists thought then that Nazism was as near absolute evil as a human society can manage. I myself thought so. I still think so, without qualification. That being so, Nazism had to be fought, and since the Nazis might make fission bombs—which we thought possible until 1944, and which was a continual nightmare if one was remotely in the know—well, then, we had to make them too. Unless one was an unlimited pacifist, there was nothing else to do. And unlimited pacifism is a position which most of us cannot sustain.

Therefore I respect, and to a large extent share, the moral attitudes 30 of those scientists who devoted themselves to making the bomb. But the trouble is, when you get on to any kind of moral escalator, to know whether you're ever going to be able to get off. When scientists became soldiers they gave up something, so imperceptibly that they didn't realize it, of the full scientific life. Not intellectually. I see no evidence that scientific work on weapons of maximum destruction has been in any intellectual respect different from other scientific work. But there is a moral difference.

It may be—scientists who are better men than I am often take this 31 attitude, and I have tried to represent it faithfully in one of my books—that this is a moral price which, in certain circumstances, has to be paid. Nevertheless, it is no good pretending that there is not a moral price. Soldiers have to obey. That is the foundation of their morality. It is not the foundation of the scientific morality. Scientists have to question and if necessary to rebel. I don't want to be misunderstood. I am no anarchist. I am not suggesting that loyalty is not a

---

[20]***Albert Einstein (1879–1955)*** The father of modern nuclear physics. His theory of relativity led to the development of the atomic bomb and other applications of nuclear power.

prime virtue. I am not saying that all rebellion is good. But I am saying that loyalty can easily turn into conformity, and that conformity can often be a cloak for the timid and self-seeking. So can obedience, carried to the limit. When you think of the long and gloomy history of man, you will find that far more, and far more hideous, crimes have been committed in the name of obedience that have ever been committed in the name of rebellion. If you doubt that, read William Shirer's *Rise and Fall of the Third Reich.*[21] The German officer corps were brought up in the most rigorous code of obedience. To themselves, no more honorable and God-fearing body of men could conceivably exist. Yet in the name of obedience, they were party to, and assisted in, the most wicked large-scale actions in the history of the world.

Scientists must not go that way. Yet the duty to question is not   32 much of a support when you are living in the middle of an organized society. I speak with feeling here. I was an official for twenty years. I went into official life at the beginning of the war, for the reasons that prompted my scientific friends to begin to make weapons. I stayed in that life until a year ago, for the same reason that made my scientific friends turn into civilian soldiers. The official's life in England is not quite so disciplined as a soldier's, but it is very nearly so. I think I know the virtues, which are very great, of the men who live that disciplined life. I also know what for me was the moral trap. I, too, had got onto an escalator. I can put the result in a sentence: I was coming to hide behind the institution; I was losing the power to say no.

Only a very bold man, when he is a member of an organized soci-   33 ety, can keep the power to say no. I tell you that, not being a very bold man, or one who finds it congenial to stand alone, away from his colleagues. We can't expect many scientists to do it. Is there any tougher ground for them to stand on? I suggest to you that there is. I believe that there is a spring of moral action in the scientific activity which is at least as strong as the search for truth. The name of this spring is *knowledge*. Scientists *know* certain things in a fashion more immediate and more certain than those who don't comprehend what science is. Unless we are abnormally weak or abnormally wicked men, this knowledge is bound to shape our actions. Most of us are timid, but to an extent, knowledge gives us guts. Perhaps it can give us guts strong enough for the jobs in hand.

I had better take the most obvious example. All physical scientists   34

---

[21]**Rise and Fall of the Third Reich**   *The Rise and Fall of the Third Reich: A History of Nazi Germany* (1960) is one of the most widely read studies of the inner workings of Nazi politics and the development of the totalitarian state.

know that it is relatively easy to make plutonium.[22] We know this, not as a journalistic fact at second hand, but as a fact in our own experience. We can work out the number of scientific and engineering personnel needed for a nation-state to equip itself with fission and fusion bombs. We *know* that, for a dozen or more states, it need only take perhaps six years, perhaps less. Even the best informed of us always exaggerate these periods.

This we know, with the certainty of—what shall I call it?—engi-   35
neering truth. We also—most of us—are familiar with statistics and the nature of odds. We know, with the certainty of statistical truth, that if enough of these weapons are made, by enough different states, some of them are going to blow up, through accident, or folly, or madness—the motives don't matter. What does matter is the nature of the statistical fact.

All this we *know*. We know it in a more direct sense than any   36
politician because it comes from our direct experience. It is part of our minds. Are we going to let it happen?

All this we *know*. It throws upon scientists a direct and personal   37
responsibility. It is not enough to say that scientists have a responsibility as citizens. They have a much greater one than that, and one different in kind. For scientists have a moral imperative to say what they know. It is going to make them unpopular in their own nation-states. It may do worse than make them unpopular. That doesn't matter. Or at least, it does matter to you and me, but it must not count in the face of the risks.

For we genuinely know the risks. We are faced with an either-or,   38
and we haven't much time. The *either* is acceptance of a restriction of nuclear armaments. This is going to begin, just as a token, with an agreement on the stopping of nuclear tests. The United States is not going to get the 99.9 percent "security" that it has been asking for. This is unobtainable, though there are other bargains that the United States could probably secure. I am not going to conceal from you that this course involves certain risks. They are quite obvious, and no honest man is going to blink them. That is the *either*. The *or* is not a risk but a certainty. It is this. There is no agreement on tests. The nuclear arms race between the United States and the U.S.S.R. not only continues but accelerates. Other countries join in. Within, at the most, six years,[23] China and several other states have a stock of nuclear bombs.

---

[22]***plutonium*** A highly radioactive element used for nuclear weapons and nuclear reactors.

[23]This was not quite right. It took slightly longer, but not much (1971). [Snow's note]

Within, at the most, ten years, some of those bombs are going off. I am saying this as responsibly as I can. *That* is the certainty. On the one side, therefore, we have a finite risk. On the other side we have a certainty of disaster. Between a risk and a certainty, a sane man does not hesitate.

It is the plain duty of scientists to explain this either-or. It is a duty which seems to me to come from the moral nature of the scientific activity itself.

The same duty, though in a much more pleasant form, arises with respect to the benevolent powers of science. For scientists know, and again with the certainty of scientific knowledge, that we possess every scientific fact we need to transform the physical life of half the world. And transform it within the span of people now living. I mean, we have all the resources to help half the world live as long as we do and eat enough. All that is missing is the will. We *know* that. Just as we know that you in the United States, and to a slightly lesser extent we in the United Kingdom, have been almost unimaginably lucky. We are sitting like people in a smart and cosy restaurant and we are eating comfortably, looking out of the window into the streets. Down on the pavement are people who are looking up at us, people who by chance have different colored skins from ours, and are rather hungry. Do you wonder that they don't like us all that much? Do you wonder that we sometimes feel ashamed of ourselves, as we look out through that plate glass?

Well, it is within our power to get started on that problem. We are morally impelled to. We all know that, if the human species does solve that one, there will be consequences which are themselves problems. For instance, the population of the world will become embarrassingly large. But that is another challenge. There are going to be challenges to our intelligence and to our moral nature as long as man remains man. After all, a challenge is not, as the word is coming to be used, an excuse for slinking off and doing nothing. A challenge is something to be picked up.

For all these reasons, I believe the world community of scientists has a final responsibility upon it—a greater responsibility than is pressing on any other body of men. I do not pretend to know how they will bear this responsibility. These may be famous last words, but I have an inextinguishable hope. For, as I have said, there is no doubt that the scientific activity is both beautiful and truthful. I cannot prove it, but I believe that, simply because scientists cannot escape their own knowledge, they also won't be able to avoid showing themselves disposed to good.

39

40

41

42

QUESTIONS

1. Do you agree with Snow's opening statement, that "Scientists are the most important occupational group in the world today"?
2. What makes scientists different from other people?
3. Snow spends a good deal of time explaining that scientists are really quite like other people. What observations lead him to this conclusion? Do you agree with him?
4. In paragraph 5, Snow says that science holds "decisive powers for good and evil." Does science really have as significant a moral quantum as Snow suggests?
5. Explain what Snow means by a "moral escalator" (para. 30; see also para. 32).
6. Snow mentions the truth quite often. What do you think he means by it, and what is its relationship to science?

WRITING ASSIGNMENTS

1. Establish the obligation that you feel is incumbent upon a scientist in the modern world. What kinds of moral standards do you think scientists should uphold? Do you believe that most scientists today actually uphold those standards? Do you feel they should? What could persuade a scientist who does not uphold such standards that he or she ought to do so?
2. Review your education in the sciences. How careful is the training of a person in the sciences in regard to the expected moral values that must be upheld? Is scientific education clear on issues of morality? Examine recent newspaper or magazine articles on scientific subjects to see if there is evidence of such a concern about moral education. What kind of education would be moral in nature?
3. Do you think that a moral component ought to be included in the education of the scientist? What form would that be likely to take in the education of a scientist at the grade school, high school, and college levels? What are the best kinds of moral education? Were you aware of any specific moral education at any level in your schooling? Be specific in your recollections and comment on the usefulness of any such education that you can remember.
4. Governments rely upon scientists for their weaponry, for their technological edge over the competition, and for their capacity to outstrip their rivals. What view do you think that our own government takes toward the moral obligation of our scientists? Do you think that our government is more concerned with our scientists' moral character than is the government of our chief political rival? How does a scientist respond morally to his or her government's demands for more and better weaponry?
5. In general, contemporary religious organizations (the churches and major

ethical organizations) strongly approve of the development of atomic weapons and of their dispersal. Is such a position on the part of religious groups a conflict of moral values? Examine the churches' positions on the dispersal of atomic weaponry by looking up articles in the *Reader's Guide to Periodical Literature* or by finding articles in recent church publications. What is the position of the church to which you belong? If you do not belong to a specific church, choose one and write to its headquarters in your area. If possible, interview a church leader. Establish what that church's position is on nuclear production and stockpiling. Is it a moral position that would satisfy Snow?

GEORGE WALD

The Origin of Life

GEORGE WALD (b. 1906) is a Nobel Prize winner in the field of physiology and medicine and was one of the most popular professors at Harvard University, where he began teaching in 1934. His primary contributions in science relate to the physiology of sight. He discovered that vitamin A is present in the retina, and this discovery led to a clearer sense of how we see and how the chemistry of the retina affects sight.

Wald's essay is a highly speculative argument that explores past theories of life's origins, considers the alternatives available to us in choosing a theory, then takes a position and follows it to its conclusion. The two theories that have been postulated are the supernatural creation of life (as in the Book of Genesis) and spontaneous generation of organic life from inorganic materials. Wald tells us that there is no third choice. It is natural that he should choose to defend the scientific view that life developed spontaneously, and his method of arguing the point is remarkable.

First, we must admit that Wald does not make the question so simple that those of us with no sense of what chemistry is or what biology implies can follow him closely. In fact, only those with a superior understanding of chemistry, biology, and physics can hope to follow him in every detail. Nonetheless, for those of us who are patient and who are willing to read on even when we do not know the difference between an enyzme and a peptide or between fermentation and photosynthesis, the point of what Wald is saying becomes clear. Those who understand the demanding complexities of the scientific circumstances Wald describes will appreciate his detail and seriousness; the rest will appreciate the extraordinary complexity of the phenomenon he is attempting to examine: life itself.

Some scientists have complained because Wald uses the word "God" frequently in his discussion of scientific fact. As Wald said in a New Yorker interview in 1966, "We live in a world of chance, yet not of accident. God gambles, but he does not cheat." This statement is particularly interesting in light of the selection because Wald does not treat seriously the biblical version of the creation. In his opening remarks he states that most cultures have a myth of the creation of life by supernatural means, and he cites the Bible as our culture's creation myth. Wald's views on God are, then, rather complex.

Once Wald has established both that spontaneous generation was a view held in the past and why it had to be discarded, he then proceeds to defend it. In one of the most remarkable sequences in any selection in this book, Wald examines the question of possibility and probability. His discussion involves low-level mathematics and a step-by-step argument showing that when time is factored into any equation concerning possibility, eventually possibility becomes probability and probability becomes inevitability.

This feature of his argument is especially powerful, since he applies the question of probability to an event that happened once: the origin of life itself. Further, since life is natural and all that is required for it is natural, Wald argues that it is natural for life to generate spontaneously. In fact, the essay ends with speculation about the possibility of life in other parts of the universe. He believes that life must proliferate throughout the universe, and because the "rules" that govern life are deep within its molecular structures, that life must be relatively uniform.

Wald is working with significant concepts. His discussion of time alone is of a magnitude that baffles the imagination. The complexity of the molecular elements of life, he demonstrates, is mind-boggling. But Wald is also convinced of his position, and he finds it a source of wonder, not alarm, that it may be true.

WALD'S RHETORIC

Wald is a brilliant speaker. His career in the 1960s and the 1970s took him to many public platforms where he spoke to enthusiastic *throngs. He maintains a sense of wonder in his approach to science, and it parallels the amazement of the layman in relation to the intricacies of scientific thought. In this essay he is speaking to a knowledgeable audience. He is not communicating with people who are illiterate in science; yet he is also not addressing those whose technical knowledge is so great that only a handful of them could understand him. His efforts are directed toward explaining a series of complex ideas in ways they can be grasped by many people.*

In rhetorical strategy, Wald relies first on the overarching question of possibility, which dominates the essay. His purpose is to demonstrate that it is possible for life to generate spontaneously on earth. He states that one must think of the conditions that existed in prehistory when, for example, there was no free oxygen in the atmosphere. We would think of that condition as lethal for organic compounds, yet he demonstrates that the converse is true: it was essential to them. He points out that the generation of life spontaneously is no longer possible because the environment has been radically altered by life itself.

The most important rhetorical device Wald uses is argument by hypothesis, supplemented occasionally by example. The lengthy discussion of the probability of life generating on earth takes up the bulk of the middle of the essay (paras. 17–28). In this section, Wald progresses from the relative simplicity of the probability of heads or tails in a coin toss to the astonishingly complex question of the probability of an event that can happen only once.

It is especially remarkable to see how Wald can take an event that seems to be extremely unlikely ever to happen and demonstrate that, by extending the ordinary time frame to the scope of cosmic time, such an event could eventually be thought of as inevitable. Wald uses a form of logic that, if we accept it, goes a long way toward helping prove his argument.

Wald's patience is matched only by his thoroughness. He treats every aspect of the question in turn. He considers each aspect thoroughly, examines it from several points of view, then works it out in detail. As we read, we learn about the achievements of past scientists and about the behavior of molecules in numerous circumstances, and then are invited to speculate about the future and the questions concerning life far beyond the boundaries of our own world. Wald produces an atmosphere of awe, an awe that becomes admiration and astonishment at the complexity of something that most of us take too lightly. While grappling with the issue of life's creation, we can hardly resist being impressed by the wonder of life itself.

The Origin of Life

About a century ago the question, How did life begin? which has interested men throughout their history, reached an impasse. Up to that time two answers had been offered: one that life had been created supernaturally, the other that it arises continually from the nonliving. The first explanation lay outside science; the second was now shown to be untenable. For a time scientists felt some discomfort in having no answer at all. Then they stopped asking the question.

Recently ways have been found again to consider the origin of life as a scientific problem—as an event within the order of nature. In part this is the result of new information. But a theory never rises of itself, however rich and secure the facts. It is an act of creation. Our present ideas in this realm were first brought together in a clear and defensible argument by the Russian biochemist A. I. Oparin in a book called *The Origin of Life*,[1] published in 1936. Much can be added now to Oparin's discussion, yet it provides the foundation upon which all of us who are interested in this subject have built.

The attempt to understand how life originated raises a wide variety of scientific questions, which lead in many and diverse directions and should end by casting light into many obscure corners. At the center of the enterprise lies the hope not only of explaining a great past event—important as that should be—but of showing that the explanation is workable. If we can indeed come to understand how a living organism arises from the nonliving, we should be able to construct one—only of the simplest description, to be sure, but still recognizably alive. This is so remote a possibility now that one scarcely dares to acknowledge it; but it is there nevertheless.

One answer to the problem of how life originated is that it was created. This is an understandable confusion of nature with technology. Men are used to making things; it is a ready thought that those things not made by men were made by a superhuman being. Most of the cultures we know contain mythical accounts of a supernatural creation of life. Our own tradition provides such an account in the open-

---

[1] *Alexander I. Oparin (1894–1980)* Russian biologist, author of *The Origin of Life*. He has defended the view that life arose from chemical matter.

ing chapters of Genesis. There we are told that beginning on the third day of the Creation, God brought forth living creatures—first plants, then fishes and birds, then land animals and finally man.

The more rational elements of society, however, tended to take a more naturalistic view of the matter. One had only to accept the evidence of one's senses to know that life arises regularly from the nonliving: worms from mud, maggots from decaying meat, mice from refuse of various kinds. This is the view that came to be called spontaneous generation. Few scientists doubted it. Aristotle, Newton, William Harvey, Descartes, van Helmont,[2] all accepted spontaneous generation without serious question. Indeed, even the theologians—witness the English Jesuit John Turberville Needham[3]—could subscribe to this view, for Genesis tells us, not that God created plants and most animals directly, but that He bade the earth and waters to bring them forth; since this directive was never rescinded, there is nothing heretical in believing that the process has continued.

But step by step, in a great controversy that spread over two centuries, this belief was whittled away until nothing remained of it. First the Italian Francesco Redi[4] showed in the seventeenth century that meat placed under a screen, so that flies cannot lay their eggs on it, never develops maggots. Then in the following century the Italian abbé Lazzaro Spallanzani[5] showed that a nutritive broth, sealed off from the air while boiling, never develops microorganisms, and hence never rots. Needham objected that by too much boiling Spallanzani had rendered the broth, and still more the air above it, incompatible with life. Spallanzani could defend his broth; when he broke the seal of his flasks, allowing new air to rush in, the broth promptly began to rot. He could find no way, however, to show that the air in the sealed flask

5

6

---

[2]**Aristotle** Wald refers to a number of important scientists from the Greek era to the present. For Aristotle see Part Six of this book; for Newton see note 9 in C. P. Snow's essay in this part; William Harvey (1578–1657) discovered the circulation of the blood; René Descartes (1596–1650) was a French philosopher interested in the way we know things; Jean Baptiste van Helmont (1580–1644), a Belgian chemist, worked with gases and discovered carbon dioxide.

[3]**John Turberville Needham (1713–1781)** An English naturalist and priest who staunchly defended the theory of spontaneous generation and attempted to offer scientific evidence supporting the theory.

[4]**Francesco Redi (1626?–1689?)** Italian naturalist and physician to the dukes of Tuscany.

[5]**Lazzaro Spallanzani (1729–1799)** Italian scientist who studied fertilization and the digestive properties of saliva.

had not been vitiated. This problem finally was solved by Louis Pasteur[6] in 1860, with a simple modification of Spallanzani's experiment. Pasteur too used a flask containing boiling broth, but instead of sealing off the neck he drew it out in a long, S-shaped curve with its end open to the air. While molecules of air could pass back and forth freely, the heavier particles of dust, bacteria and molds in the atmosphere were trapped on the walls of the curved neck and only rarely reached the broth. In such a flask the broth seldom was contaminated; usually it remained clear and sterile indefinitely.

This was only one of Pasteur's experiments. It is no easy matter to   7
deal with so deeply ingrained and commonsense a belief as that in spontaneous generation. One can ask for nothing better in such a pass than a noisy and stubborn opponent, and this Pasteur had in the naturalist Félix Pouchet,[7] whose arguments before the French Academy of Sciences drove Pasteur to more and more rigorous experiments. When he had finished, nothing remained of the belief in spontaneous generation.

We tell this story to beginning students of biology as though it   8
represents a triumph of reason over mysticism. In fact it is very nearly the opposite. The reasonable view was to believe in a single, primary act of supernatural creation. There is no third position. For this reason many scientists a century ago chose to regard the belief in spontaneous generation as a "philosophical necessity." It is a symptom of the philosophical poverty of our time that this necessity is no longer appreciated. Most modern biologists, having reviewed with satisfaction the downfall of the spontaneous generation hypothesis, yet unwilling to accept the alternative belief in special creation, are left with nothing.

I think a scientist has no choice but to approach the origin of life   9
through a hypothesis of spontaneous generation. What the controversy reviewed above showed to be untenable is only the belief that living organisms arise spontaneously under present conditions. We have now to face a somewhat different problem: how organisms may have arisen spontaneously under different conditions in some former period, granted that they do so no longer.

---

[6]***Louis Pasteur (1822–1895)*** French chemist; he "disproved" the theory of spontaneous generation and undertook studies that eventually produced the germ theory of infection. He discovered a vaccine for smallpox and instructed people to purify their milk by boiling it.

[7]***Félix-Archimede Pouchet (1800–1872)*** French physician and naturalist. Louis Pasteur attacked his theories of spontaneous evolution and of the spontaneous generation of life. He wrote *New Experiments on Spontaneous Generation* (1863).

To make an organism demands the right substances in the right 10
proportions and in the right arrangement. We do not think that anything more is needed—but that is problem enough.

The substances are water, certain salts—as it happens, those found 11
in the ocean—and carbon compounds. The latter are called *organic*
compounds because they scarcely occur except as products of living
organisms.

Organic compounds consist for the most part of four types of at- 12
oms: carbon, oxygen, nitrogen and hydrogen. These four atoms together constitute about 99 percent of living material, for hydrogen and
oxygen also form water. The organic compounds found in organisms
fall mainly into four great classes: carbohydrates, fats, proteins and
nucleic acids. . . . The fats are simplest, each consisting of three fatty
acids joined to glycerol. The starches and glycogens are made of sugar
units strung together to form long straight and branched chains. In
general only one type of sugar appears in a single starch or glycogen;
these molecules are large, but still relatively simple. The principal
function of carbohydrates and fats in the organism is to serve as fuel—
as a source of energy.

The nucleic acids introduce a further level of complexity. They are 13
very large structures, composed of aggregates of at least four types of
unit—the nucleotides—brought together in a great variety of proportions and sequences. An almost endless variety of different nucleic acids is possible, and specific differences among them are believed to be
of the highest importance. Indeed, these structures are thought by
many to be the main constituents of the genes, the bearers of hereditary constitution.

Variety and specificity, however, are most characteristic of the pro- 14
teins, which include the largest and most complex molecules known.
The units of which their structure is built are about 25 different amino
acids. These are strung together in chains hundreds to thousands of
units long, in different proportions, in all types of sequence and with
the greatest variety of branching and folding. A virtually infinite number of different proteins is possible. Organisms seem to exploit this
potentiality, for no two species of living organism, animal or plant,
possess the same proteins.

Organic molecules therefore form a large and formidable array, end- 15
less in variety and of the most bewildering complexity. One cannot
think of having organisms without them. This is precisely the trouble,
for to understand how organisms originated we must first of all explain how such complicated molecules could come into being. And
that is only the beginning. To make an organism requires not only a

tremendous variety of these substances, in adequate amounts and proper proportions, but also just the right arrangement of them. Structure here is as important as composition—and what a complication of structure! The most complex machine man has devised—say an electronic brain—is child's play compared with the simplest of living organisms. The especially trying thing is that complexity here involves such small dimensions. It is on the molecular level; it consists of a detailed fitting of molecule to molecule such as no chemist can attempt.

One has only to contemplate the magnitude of this task to concede   16
that the spontaneous generation of a living organism is impossible. Yet here we are—as a result, I believe, of spontaneous generation. It will help to digress for a moment to ask what one means by "impossible."

With every event one can associate a probability—the chance that   17
it will occur. This is always a fraction, the proportion of times the event occurs in a large number of trials. Sometimes the probability is apparent even without trial. A coin has two faces; the probability of tossing a head is therefore 1/2. A die has six faces; the probability of throwing a deuce is 1/6. When one has no means of estimating the probability beforehand, it must be determined by counting the fraction of successes in a large number of trials.

Our everyday concept of what is impossible, possible or certain de-   18
rives from our experience: the number of trials that may be encompassed within the space of a human lifetime, or at most within recorded human history. In this colloquial, practical sense I concede the spontaneous origin of life to be "impossible." It is impossible as we judge events in the scale of human experience.

We shall see that this is not a very meaningful conception. For one   19
thing, the time with which our problem is concerned is geological time, and the whole extent of human history is trivial in the balance. We shall have more to say of this later.

But even within the bounds of our own time there is a serious flaw   20
in our judgment of what is possible. It sounds impressive to say that an event has never been observed in the whole of human history. We should tend to regard such an event as at least "practically" impossible, whatever probability is assigned to it on abstract grounds. When we look a little further into such a statement, however, it proves to be almost meaningless. For men are apt to reject reports of very improbable occurrences. Persons of good judgment think it safer to distrust the alleged observer of such an event than to believe him. The result is that events which are merely very extraordinary acquire the repu-

tation of never having occurred at all. Thus the highly improbable is made to appear impossible.

To give an example: Every physicist knows that there is a very 21 small probability, which is easily computed, that the table upon which I am writing will suddenly and spontaneously rise into the air. The event requires no more than that the molecules of which the table is composed, ordinarily in random motion in all directions, should happen by chance to move in the same direction. Every physicist concedes this possibility; but try telling one that you have seen it happen. Recently I asked a friend, a Nobel laureate in physics, what he would say if I told him that. He laughed and said that he would regard it as more probable that I was mistaken than that the event had actually occurred.

We see therefore that it does not mean much to say that a very 22 improbable event has never been observed. There is a conspiracy to suppress such observations, not among scientists alone, but among all judicious persons, who have learned to be skeptical even of what they see, let alone of what they are told. If one group is more skeptical than others, it is perhaps lawyers, who have the harshest experience of the unreliability of human evidence. Least skeptical of all are the scientists, who, cautious as they are, know very well what strange things are possible.

A final aspect of our problem is very important. When we consider 23 the spontaneous origin of a living organism, this is not an event that need happen again and again. It is perhaps enough for it to happen once. The probability with which we are concerned is of a special kind; it is the probability that an event occur *at least once*. To this type of probability a fundamentally important thing happens as one increases the number of trials. However improbable the event in a single trial, it becomes increasingly probable as the trials are multiplied. Eventually the event becomes virtually inevitable. For instance, the chance that a coin will not fall head up in a single toss is 1/2. The chance that no head will appear in a series of tosses is $1/2 \times 1/2 \times 1/2 \ldots$ as many times over as the number of tosses. In 10 tosses the chance that no head will appear is therefore 1/2 multiplied by itself 10 times, or 1/1,000. Consequently the chance that a head will appear at least once in 10 tosses is 999/1,000. Ten trials have converted what started as a modest probability to a near certainty.

The same effect can be achieved with any probability, however 24 small, by multiplying sufficiently the number of trials. Consider a reasonably improbable event, the chance of which is 1/1,000. The chance that this will not occur in one trial is 999/1,000. The chance that it won't occur in 1,000 trials is 999/1,000 multiplied together 1,000 times. This fraction comes out to be 37/100. The chance that it will happen at least once in 1,000 trials is therefore one minus this number —63/100—a little better than three chances out of five. One thousand trials have transformed this from a highly improbable to a highly probable event. In 10,000 trials the chance that this event will occur at least once comes out to be 19,999/20,000. It is now almost inevitable.

It makes no important change in the argument if we assess the 25 probability that an event occur at least two, three, four or some other small number of times rather than at least once. It simply means that more trials are needed to achieve any degree of certainty we wish. Otherwise everything is the same.

In such a problem as the spontaneous origin of life we have no way 26 of assessing probabilities beforehand, or even of deciding what we mean by a trial. The origin of a living organism is undoubtedly a stepwise phenomenon, each step with its own probability and its own conditions of trial. Of one thing we can be sure, however: whatever constitutes a trial, more such trials occur the longer the interval of time.

The important point is that since the origin of life belongs in the 27 category of at-least-once phenomena, time is on its side. However improbable we regard this event, or any of the steps which it involves, given enough time it will almost certainly happen at least once. And for life as we know it, with its capacity for growth and reproduction, once may be enough.

Time is in fact the hero of the plot. The time with which we have 28 to deal is of the order of two billion years. What we regard as impossible on the basis of human experience is meaningless here. Given so much time, the "impossible" becomes possible, the possible probable, and the probable virtually certain. One has only to wait: time itself performs the miracles.

This brings the argument back to its first stage: the origin of or- 29 ganic compounds. Until a century and a quarter ago the only known source of these substances was the stuff of living organisms. Students of chemistry are usually told that when, in 1828, Friedrich Wöhler[8] synthesized the first organic compound, urea, he proved that organic compounds do not require living organisms to make them. Of course it showed nothing of the kind. Organic chemists are alive; Wöhler

---

[8]*Friedrich Wöhler (1800–1882)* He held the chair of chemistry at the University of Göttingen; he is famous for having first synthesized the organic compound urea, thus beginning the discipline of organic chemistry.

merely showed that they can make organic compounds externally as well as internally. It is still true that with almost negligible exceptions all the organic matter we know is the product of living organisms.

The almost negligible exceptions, however, are very important for our argument. It is now recognized that a constant, slow production of organic molecules occurs without the agency of living things. Certain geological phenomena yield simple organic compounds. So, for example, volcanic eruptions bring metal carbides to the surface of the earth, where they react with water vapor to yield simple compounds of carbon and hydrogen. The familiar type of such a reaction is the process used in old-style bicycle lamps in which acetylene is made by mixing iron carbide with water. 30

Recently Harold Urey,[9] Nobel laureate in chemistry, has become interested in the degree to which electrical discharges in the upper atmosphere may promote the formation of organic compounds. One of his students, S. L. Miller, performed the simple experiment of circulating a mixture of water vapor, methane (CH_4), ammonia (NH_3) and hydrogen—all gases believed to have been present in the early atmosphere of the earth—continuously for a week over an electric spark. The circulation was maintained by boiling the water in one limb of the apparatus and condensing it in the other. At the end of the week the water was analyzed by the delicate method of paper chromatography. It was found to have acquired a mixture of amino acids![10] Glycine and alanine, the simplest amino acids and the most prevalent in proteins, were definitely identified in the solution, and there were indications it contained aspartic acid and two others. The yield was surprisingly high. This amazing result changes at a stroke our ideas of the probability of the spontaneous formation of amino acids. 31

A final consideration, however, seems to me more important than all the special processes to which one might appeal for organic syntheses in inanimate nature. 32

It has already been said that to have organic molecules one ordinarily needs organisms. The synthesis of organic substances, like almost everything else that happens in organisms, is governed by the special class of proteins called enzymes—the organic catalysts which greatly accelerate chemical reactions in the body. Since an enzyme is 33

---

[9]*Harold Urey (1893–1980)* American chemist and Nobel Prize winner who helped develop the first atomic bomb.

[10]*amino acids* The basic chemical building blocks of proteins. Proteins are required for human metabolism.

not used up but is returned at the end of the process, a small amount of enzyme can promote an enormous transformation of material.

Enzymes play such a dominant role in the chemistry of life that it is exceedingly difficult to imagine the synthesis of living material without their help. This poses a dilemma, for enzymes themselves are proteins, and hence among the most complex organic components of the cell. One is asking, in effect, for an apparatus which is the unique property of cells in order to form the first cell. 34

This is not, however, an insuperable difficulty. An enzyme, after all, is only a catalyst; it can do no more than change the *rate* of a chemical reaction. It cannot make anything happen that would not have happened, though more slowly, in its absence. Every process that is catalyzed by an enzyme, and every product of such a process, would occur without the enzyme. The only difference is one of rate. 35

Once again the essence of the argument is time. What takes only a few moments in the presence of an enzyme or other catalyst may take days, months or years in its absence; but given time, the end result is the same. 36

Indeed, this great difficulty in conceiving of the spontaneous generation of organic compounds has its positive side. In a sense, organisms demonstrate to us what organic reactions and products are *possible*. We can be certain that, given time, all these things must occur. Every substance that has ever been found in an organism displays thereby the finite probability of its occurrence. Hence, given time, it should arise spontaneously. One has only to wait. 37

It will be objected at once that this is just what one cannot do. Everyone knows that these substances are highly perishable. Granted that, within long spaces of time, now a sugar molecule, now a fat, now even a protein might form spontaneously, each of these molecules should have only a transitory existence. How are they ever to accumulate; and, unless they do so, how form an organism? 38

We must turn the question around. What in our experience, is known to destroy organic compounds? Primarily two agencies: decay and the attack of oxygen. But decay is the work of living organisms, and we are talking of a time before life existed. As for oxygen, this introduces a further and fundamental section of our argument. 39

It is generally conceded at present that the early atmosphere of our planet contained virtually no free oxygen. Almost all the earth's oxygen was bound in the form of water and metal oxides. If this were not so, it would be very difficult to imagine how organic matter could accumulate over the long stretches of time that alone might make possible the spontaneous origin of life. This is a crucial point, therefore, 40 and the statement that the early atmosphere of the planet was virtually oxygen-free comes forward so opportunely as to raise a suspicion of special pleading. I have for this reason taken care to consult a number of geologists and astronomers on this point, and am relieved to find that it is well defended. I gather that there is a widespread though not universal consensus that this condition did exist. Apparently something similar was true also for another common component of our atmosphere—carbon dioxide. It is believed that most of the carbon on the earth during its early geological history existed as the element or in metal carbides and hydrocarbons; very little was combined with oxygen.

This situation is not without its irony. We tend usually to think 41
that the environment plays the tune to which the organism must dance. The environment is given; the organism's problem is to adapt to it or die. It has become apparent lately, however, that some of the most important features of the physical environment are themselves the work of living organisms. Two such features have just been named. The atmosphere of our planet seems to have contained no oxygen until organisms placed it there by the process of plant photosynthesis.[11] It is estimated that at present all the oxygen of our atmosphere is renewed by photosynthesis once in every 2,000 years, and that all the carbon dioxide passes through the process of photosynthesis once in every 300 years. In the scale of geological time, these intervals are very small indeed. We are left with the realization that all the oxygen and carbon dioxide of our planet are the products of living organisms, and have passed through living organisms over and over again.

In the early history of our planet, when there were no organisms or 42
any free oxygen, organic compounds should have been stable over very long periods. This is the crucial difference between the period before life existed and our own. If one were to specify a single reason why the spontaneous generation of living organisms was possible once and is so no longer, this is the reason.

We must still reckon, however, with another destructive force 43
which is disposed of less easily. This can be called spontaneous dissolution—the counterpart of spontaneous generation. We have noted that any process catalyzed by an enzyme can occur in time without the enzyme. The trouble is that the processes which synthesize an organic substance are reversible: any chemical reaction which an en-

---

[11]***plant photosynthesis***   The process by which plants use sunlight and chlorophyll to manufacture oxygen from carbon dioxide.

zyme may catalyze will go backward as well as forward. We have spoken as though one has only to wait to achieve synthesis of all kinds; it is truer to say that what one achieves by waiting is *equilibria* of all kinds—equilibria in which the synthesis and dissolution of substances come into balance.

In the vast majority of the processes in which we are interested the 44 point of equilibrium lies far over toward the side of dissolution. That is to say, spontaneous dissolution is much more probable, and hence proceeds much more rapidly, than spontaneous synthesis. For example, the spontaneous union, step by step, of amino acid units to form a protein has a certain small probability, and hence might occur over a long stretch of time. But the dissolution of the protein or of an intermediate product into its component amino acids is much more probable, and hence will go ever so much more rapidly. The situation we must face is that of patient Penelope waiting for Odysseus,[12] yet much worse: each night she undid the weaving of the preceding day, but here a night could readily undo the work of a year or a century.

How do present-day organisms manage to synthesize organic com- 45 pounds against the forces of dissolution? They do so by a continuous expenditure of energy. Indeed, living organisms commonly do better than oppose the forces of dissolution; they grow in spite of them. They do so, however, only at enormous expense to their surroundings. They need a constant supply of material and energy merely to maintain themselves, and much more of both to grow and reproduce. A living organism is an intricate machine for performing exactly this function. When, for want of fuel or through some internal failure in its mechanism, an organism stops actively synthesizing itself in opposition to the processes which continuously decompose it, it dies and rapidly disintegrates.

What we ask here is to synthesize organic molecules without such 46 a machine. I believe this to be the most stubborn problem that confronts us—the weakest link at present in our argument. I do not think it by any means disastrous, but it calls for phenomena and forces some of which are as yet only partly understood and some probably still to be discovered.

At present we can make only a beginning with this problem. We 47 know that it is possible on occasion to protect molecules from dissolution by precipitation or by attachment to other molecules. A wide

---

[12]***Penelope waiting for Odysseus*** In Homer's *Odyssey*, Penelope waited twenty years for her husband Odysseus to return from the Trojan War. She is a symbol of the patient, faithful wife.

variety of such precipitation and "trapping" reactions is used in modern chemistry and biochemistry to promote syntheses. Some molecules appear to acquire a degree of resistance to disintegration simply through their size. So, for example, the larger molecules composed of amino acids—polypeptides and proteins—seem to display much less tendency to disintegrate into their units than do smaller compounds of two or three amino acids.

Again, many organic molecules display still another type of integrating force—a spontaneous impulse toward structure formation. Certain types of fatty molecules—lecithins and cephalins—spin themselves out in water to form highly oriented and well-shaped structures—the so-called myelin figures. Proteins sometimes orient even in solution, and also may aggregate in the solid state in highly organized formations. Such spontaneous architectonic tendencies[13] are still largely unexplored, particularly as they may occur in complex mixtures of substances, and they involve forces the strength of which has not yet been estimated. 48

What we are saying is that possibilities exist for opposing *intra*molecular dissolution by *inter*molecular aggregations of various kinds. The equilibrium between union and disunion of the amino acids that make up a protein is all to the advantage of disunion, but the aggregation of the protein with itself or other molecules might swing the equilibrium in the opposite direction: perhaps by removing the protein from access to the water which would be required to disintegrate it or by providing some particularly stable type of molecular association. 49

In such a scheme the protein appears only as a transient intermediate, an unstable way-station, which can either fall back to a mixture of its constituent amino acids or enter into the formation of a complex structural aggregate: amino acids $\leftrightarrows$ protein $\rightarrow$ aggregate. 50

Such molecular aggregates, of various degrees of material and architectural complexity, are indispensable intermediates between molecules and organisms. We have no need to try to imagine the spontaneous formation of an organism by one grand collision of its component molecules. The whole process must be gradual. The molecules form aggregates, small and large. The aggregates add further molecules, thus growing in size and complexity. Aggregates of various kinds interact with one another to from still larger and more complex structures. In this way we imagine the ascent, not by jumps or master strokes, but gradually, piecemeal, to the first living organisms. 51

---

[13]***architectonic tendencies*** Normal patterns assumed by molecular structures—such as crystals or spirals.

Where may this have happened? It is easiest to suppose that life 52 first arose in the sea. Here were the necessary salts and the water. The latter is not only the principal component of organisms, but prior to their formation provided a medium which could dissolve molecules of the widest variety and ceaselessly mix and circulate them. It is this constant mixture and collision of organic molecules of every sort that constituted in large part the "trials" of our earlier discussion of probabilities.

The sea in fact gradually turned into a dilute broth, sterile and ox- 53 ygen-free. In this broth molecules came together in increasing number and variety, sometimes merely to collide and separate, sometimes to react with one another to produce new combinations, sometimes to aggregate into multimolecular formations of increasing size and complexity.

What brought order into such complexes? For order is as essential 54 here as composition. To form an organism, molecules must enter into intricate designs and connections; they must eventually form a self-repairing, self-constructing dynamic machine. For a time this problem of molecular arrangement seemed to present an almost insuperable obstacle in the way of imagining a spontaneous origin of life, or indeed the laboratory synthesis of a living organism. It is still a large and mysterious problem, but it no longer seems insuperable. The change in view has come about because we now realize that it is not altogether necessary to *bring* order into this situation; a great deal of order is implicit in the molecules themselves.

The epitome of molecular order is a crystal. In a perfect crystal the 55 molecules display complete regularity of position and orientation in all planes of space. At the other extreme are fluids—liquids or gases— in which the molecules are in ceaseless motion and in wholly random orientations and positions.

Lately it has become clear that very little of a living cell is truly 56 fluid. Most of it consists of molecules which have taken up various degrees of orientation with regard to one another. That is, most of the cell represents various degrees of approach to crystallinity—often, however, with very important differences from the crystals most familiar to us. Much of the cell's crystallinity involves molecules which are still in solution—so-called liquid crystals—and much of the dynamic, plastic quality of cellular structure, the capacity for constant change of shape and interchange of material, derives from this condition. Our familiar crystals, furthermore, involve only one or a very few types of molecule, while in the cell a great variety of different molecules come together in some degree of regular spacing and orientation—i.e., some degree of crystallinity. We are dealing in the cell with highly mixed crystals and near-crystals, solid and liquid. The laboratory study of this type of formation has scarcely begun. Its further exploration is of the highest importance for our problem.

In a fluid such as water the molecules are in very rapid motion. 57 Any molecules dissolved in such a medium are under a constant barrage of collisions with water molecules. This keeps small and moderately sized molecules in a constant turmoil; they are knocked about at random, colliding again and again, never holding any position or orientation for more than an instant. The larger a molecule is relative to water, the less it is disturbed by such collisions. Many protein and nucleic acid molecules are so large that even in solution their motions are very sluggish, and since they carry large numbers of electric charges distributed about their surfaces, they tend even in solution to align with respect to one another. It is so that they tend to form liquid crystals.

We have spoken above of architectonic tendencies even among 58 some of the relatively small molecules: the lecithins and cephalins. Such molecules are insoluble in water yet possess special groups which have a high affinity for water. As a result they tend to form surface layers, in which their water-seeking groups project into the water phase, while their water-repelling portions project into the air, or into an oil phase, or unite to form an oil phase. The result is that quite spontaneously such molecules, when exposed to water, take up highly oriented positions to form surface membranes, myelin figures and other quasi-crystalline structures.

Recently several particularly striking examples have been reported 59 of the spontaneous production of familiar types of biological structure by protein molecules. Cartilage and muscle offer some of the most intricate and regular patterns of structure to be found in organisms. A fiber from either type of tissue presents under the electron microscope a beautiful pattern of cross striations of various widths and densities, very regularly spaced. The proteins that form these structures can be coaxed into free solution and stirred into completely random orientation. Yet on precipitating, under proper conditions, the molecules realign with regard to one another to regenerate with extraordinary fidelity the original patterns of the tissues.

We have therefore a genuine basis for the view that the molecules 60 of our oceanic broth will not only come together spontaneously to form aggregates but in doing so will spontaneously achieve various types and degrees of order. This greatly simplifies our problem. What it means is that, given the right molecules, one does not have to do everything for them; they do a great deal for themselves.

Oparin has made the ingenious suggestion that natural selection, 61 which Darwin proposed to be the driving force of organic evolution, begins to operate at this level. He suggests that as the molecules come together to form colloidal aggregates, the latter begin to compete with one another for material. Some aggregates, by virtue of especially favorable composition or internal arrangement, acquire new molecules more rapidly than others. They eventually emerge as the dominant types. Oparin suggests further that considerations of optimal size enter at this level. A growing colloidal particle may reach a point at which it becomes unstable and breaks down into smaller particles, each of which grows and redivides. All these phenomena lie within the bounds of known processes in nonliving systems.

We suppose that all these forces and factors, and others perhaps yet 62 to be revealed, together give us eventually the first living organism. That achieved, how does the organism continue to live?

We have already noted that a living organism is a dynamic struc- 63 ture. It is the site of a continuous influx and outflow of matter and energy. This is the very sign of life, its cessation the best evidence of death. What is the primal organism to use as food, and how derive the energy it needs to maintain itself and grow?

For the primal organism, generated under the conditions we have 64 described, only one answer is possible. Having arisen in an oceanic broth of organic molecules, its only recourse is to live upon them. There is only one way of doing that in the absence of oxygen. It is called fermentation: the process by which organisms derive energy by breaking organic molecules and rearranging their parts. The most familiar example of such a process is the fermentation of sugar by yeast, which yields alcohol as one of the products. Animal cells also ferment sugar, not to alcohol but to lactic acid. These are two examples from a host of known fermentations.

The yeast fermentation has the following over-all equation: 65 $C_6H_{12}O_6 \rightarrow 2\ CO_2 + 2\ C_2H_5OH$ + energy. The result of fragmenting 180 grams of sugar into 88 grams of carbon dioxide and 92 grams of alcohol is to make available about 20,000 calories of energy for the use of the cell. The energy is all that the cell derives by this transaction; the carbon dioxide and alcohol are waste products which must be got rid of somehow if the cell is to survive.

The cell, having arisen in a broth of organic compounds accumu- 66 lated over the ages, must consume these molecules by fermentation in order to acquire the energy it needs to live, grow and reproduce. In doing so, it and its descendants are living on borrowed time. They are consuming their heritage, just as we in our time have nearly consumed our heritage of coal and oil. Eventually such a process must come to an end, and with that life also should have ended. It would have been necessary to start the entire development again.

Fortunately, however, the waste product carbon dioxide saved this 67 situation. This gas entered the ocean and the atmosphere in ever-increasing quantity. Some time before the cell exhausted the supply of organic molecules, it succeeded in inventing the process of photosynthesis. This enabled it, with the energy of sunlight, to make its own organic molecules: first sugar from carbon dioxide and water, then, with ammonia and nitrates as sources of nitrogen, the entire array of organic compounds which it requires. The sugar synthesis equation is: $6\ CO_2 + 6\ H_2O + sunlight \rightarrow C_6H_{12}O_6 + 6\ O_2$. Here 264 grams of carbon dioxide plus 108 grams of water plus about 700,000 calories of sunlight yield 180 grams of sugar and 192 grams of oxygen.

This is an enormous step forward. Living organisms no longer 68 needed to depend upon the accumulation of organic matter from past ages; they could make their own. With the energy of sunlight they could accomplish the fundamental organic syntheses that provide their substance, and by fermentation they could produce what energy they needed.

Fermentation, however, is an extraordinarily inefficient source of 69 energy. It leaves most of the energy potential of organic compounds unexploited; consequently huge amounts of organic material must be fermented to provide a modicum of energy. It produces also various poisonous waste products—alcohol, lactic acid, acetic acid, formic acid and so on. In the sea such products are readily washed away, but if organisms were ever to penetrate to the air and land, these products must prove a serious embarrassment.

One of the by-products of photosynthesis, however, is oxygen. 70 Once this was available, organisms could invent a new way to acquire energy, many times as efficient as fermentation. This is the process of cold combustion called respiration: $C_6H_{12}O_6 + O_2 \rightarrow 6\ CO_2 + 6\ H_2O + energy$. The burning of 180 grams of sugar in cellular respiration yields about 700,000 calories, as compared with the approximately 20,000 calories produced by fermentation of the same quanitity of sugar. This process of combustion extracts all the energy that can possibly be derived from the molecules which it consumes. With this process at its disposal, the cell can meet its energy requirements with a minimum expenditure of substance. It is a further advantage that the products of respiration—water and carbon dioxide—are innocuous and easily disposed of in any environment.

It is difficult to overestimate the degree to which the invention of   71
cellular respiration released the forces of living organisms. No organism that relies wholly upon fermentation has ever amounted to much. Even after the advent of photosynthesis, organisms could have led only a marginal existence. They could indeed produce their own organic materials, but only in quantities sufficient to survive. Fermentation is so profligate a way of life that photosynthesis could do little more than keep up with it. Respiration used the material of organisms with such enormously greater efficiency as for the first time to leave something over. Coupled with fermentation, photosynthesis made organisms self-sustaining; coupled with respiration, it provided a surplus. To use an economic analogy, photosynthesis brought organisms to the subsistence level; respiration provided them with capital. It is mainly this capital that they invested in the great enterprise of organic evolution.

The entry of oxygen into the atmosphere also liberated organisms   72
in another sense. The sun's radiation contains ultraviolet components which no living cell can tolerate. We are sometimes told that if this radiation were to reach the earth's surface, life must cease. That is not quite true. Water absorbs ultraviolet radiation very effectively, and one must conclude that as long as these rays penetrated in quantity to the surface of the earth, life had to remain under water. With the appearance of oxygen, however, a layer of ozone[14] formed high in the atmosphere and absorbed this radiation. Now organisms could for the first time emerge from the water and begin to populate the earth and air. Oxygen provided not only the means of obtaining adequate energy for evolution but the protective blanket of ozone which alone made possible terrestrial life.

This is really the end of our story. Yet not quite the end. Our entire   73
concern in this argument has been to bring the origin of life within the compass of natural phenomena. It is of the essence of such phenomena to be repetitive, and hence, given time, to be inevitable.

This is by far our most significant conclusion—that life, as an or-   74
derly natural event on such a planet as ours, was inevitable. The same can be said of the whole of organic evolution. All of it lies within the order of nature, and apart from details all of it was inevitable.

---

[14]*layer of ozone* Ozone is an isotope of oxygen (O_3 instead of O_2) that has risen in the atmosphere and lies in layers above the earth's air. It is essential for protecting life on earth from excessive ultraviolet radiation.

Astronomers have reason to believe that a planet such as ours—of 75
about the earth's size and temperature, and about as well lighted—is a
rare event in the universe. Indeed, filled as our story is with improbable phenomena, one of the least probable is to have had such a body
as the earth to begin with. Yet though this probability is small, the
universe is so large that it is conservatively estimated at least 100,000
planets like the earth exist in our galaxy alone. Some 100 million galaxies lie within the range of our most powerful telescopes, so that
throughout observable space we can count apparently on the existence
of at least 10 million million planets like our own.

What it means to bring the origin of life within the realm of natural 76
phenomena is to imply that in all these places life probably exists—
life as we know it. Indeed, I am convinced that there can be no way of
composing and constructing living organisms which is fundamentally
different from the one we know—though this is another argument, and
must await another occasion. Wherever life is possible, given time, it
should arise. It should then ramify into a wide array of forms, differing
in detail from those we now observe (as did earlier organisms on the
earth) yet including many which should look familiar to us—perhaps
even men.

We are not alone in the universe, and do not bear alone the whole 77
burden of life and what comes of it. Life is a cosmic event—so far as
we know the most complex state of organization that matter has
achieved in our cosmos. It has come many times, in many places—
places closed off from us by impenetrable distances, probably never to
be crossed even with a signal. As men we can attempt to understand
it, and even somewhat to control and guide its local manifestations.
On this planet that is our home, we have every reason to wish it well.
Yet should we fail, all is not lost. Our kind will try again elsewhere.

QUESTIONS

1. Explain the nature of the two alternatives for the beginning of life. Do you
agree that there is no middle ground between them?
2. In paragraph 4, Wald says that we confuse nature with technology when
we talk about the creation of life. What does he mean? What are the implications of his statement?
3. What does Wald mean by "life as we know it" (para. 76)?
4. What do molecules have to do with the origin of life?
5. Where does Wald assume life began? Why?
6. Does Wald's argument about the origin of life convince you? If so, why? If
not, why not?

WRITING ASSIGNMENTS

1. To some extent, Wald is arguing from probability. First, determine as clearly as possible what you think his argument is. Paragraphs 17–28 contain the substance of his argument. Exactly what is he trying to convince us of, and what methods does he use? Summarize his argument, then analyze its strengths and weaknesses. What aspects of his argument are the most difficult ones to establish? Which aspects surprise you the most?

2. Time is one of the most important elements in Wald's argument. What do you think he achieves by focusing so closely on time? Is it as potent an element in his argument as he believes it is? In paragraph 28 he says: "Time is in fact the hero of the plot. The time with which we have to deal is of the order of two billion years. What we regard as impossible on the basis of human experience is meaningless here. Given so much time, the 'impossible' becomes possible, the possible probable, and the probable virtually certain. One has only to wait: time itself performs the miracles." Do you agree with these studies? Why is Wald led to his conclusion?

3. Examine the way in which Wald deals with counterarguments. Does he give opposing viewpoints a fair shake? He deals with two objections. One, beginning with paragraph 32, deals with the production of organic molecules from nonorganic material. The other, beginning with paragraph 38, treats the dissolution or destruction of organic molecules. How fully does Wald represent the opposing view or objection? Can you think of counterarguments that Wald has not presented? What are the chief rhetorical strategies that Wald uses in his arguments? Are they effective?

4. Beginning with paragraph 54, Wald discusses order in nature at the molecular level. What does he say about it? What is the importance of molecular order for the origin of life? Explain the molecular difference between fluids and solids and comment on whether the natural crystallinity of solids has any bearing on the beginning of life. Would it have any bearing on the nature of life on other planets?

5. In the concluding paragraphs, Wald comments on the probability of life on other planets. He thinks it is virtually certain that there is such life. Do you agree with him? If there were life on other planets, would it be recognizable to us, as Wald suggests? Would its patterns resemble those found in life on earth? What scientific reasons do you have to support your answers to these questions?

THOMAS S. KUHN

The Essential Tension: Tradition and Innovation in Scientific Research

THOMAS KUHN (b. 1922) began as a physicist but soon switched from research to the study of the history of science. His contributions in that field have been so striking as to represent a revolution in thought. His first book, The Structure of Scientific Revolutions (1962; 1970; 3rd ed. 1982), was a landmark in the history of science. He followed that work with a book on the effects of the Copernican revolution on thought as well as a book of essays, The Essential Tension (1976), from which the selection presented here, a lecture first delivered in 1959, is taken.

Kuhn is an educator and a scholar, and has taught the history of science at Harvard University, the University of California at Berkeley, and Princeton University. He has been associated with the Institute for Advanced Study. Currently he teaches at the Massachusetts Institute of Technology (MIT). The talk which follows was delivered to a group of teachers and scholars at the University of Utah at a conference dedicated to discovering scientific talent in young people. As such, the conference was composed of people who were interested in creativity, imagination, and the intellectual problems involved with becoming a scientist.

Kuhn has an interesting concept buried deep within this talk, one that concerns the basic personality type that makes a good scientist.

This is not his focus, to be sure, nor does it directly enter into his thesis statement, but it underlies most of what he is saying. His conclusion is that the best scientist is that person who is most capable of working within the existing traditions of science. In fact, his conclusion is that in the long run such a person will be the most creative kind of scientist. Because this view is not quite what his audience expected to hear, it is buried rather than featured in his talk.

KUHN'S RHETORIC

Because Kuhn's presentation was given as a talk—and was only slightly altered for inclusion in his book—it has many of the typical rhetorical ingredients of a talk. One is the "signpost"—the statement of direction the speaker is taking. In paragraph 6 he points to time limitations which prevent him from giving a wide range of historical examples. He tells us in paragraph 7 that he will now "try briefly to epitomize the nature of education in the natural sciences." In paragraph 10 he tells us, "I shall shortly inquire about . . . ." In paragraph 18 he says, "and this is the point"; in paragraph 21, "What I have said so far. . ."; and in paragraph 26, "As first planned, my paper was to have ended at this point." All these signposts are set up to alert us to his direction, the moments of change of direction, the moments of summation, and the conclusion. Kuhn naturally refers to himself as "I," as most speakers do. Such a relaxed mode of address puts his listeners at ease and makes it simpler for him to explain what he is doing as he does it.

Kuhn also uses an age-old technique typical of a spoken address on a serious subject. He divides the talk into recognizable parts:

Introduction, in which he explains who he is and what he is going to talk about (paras. 1 and 2). His central thesis is stated at the end of paragraph 1.

Body, in which several subsections deal with separate issues:

1. A clarification of the tension between divergent and convergent thinking, with an emphasis on convergent thought (paras. 3–14). Paragraph 14 has a clear sense of a conclusion.

2. A discussion of the nature of education of scientists with an eye toward discovering what kind of personality the scientist should have (paras. 15–24), ending in another conclusion.

Conclusion, in which Kuhn adds a postscript, which is the final conclusion, summarizing his main argument (paras. 26–30).

Kuhn carefully considers theories that are contrary to his own, and while he does not use as many examples as, say, Darwin does, he offers a few key examples to help bolster his argument, as in his discussion of the wave–particle theories of light (para. 11), of science before Isaac Newton (para. 12), and his final discussion of Thomas Edison (1847–1931) in paragraph 29. All the while what he is doing is illustrating the essential tension between two kinds of thinking—the divergent thinking that his audience has already defined as necessary to creativity and the convergent thinking which he has deduced is essential to scientific progress. There must be a tension between these two kinds of thinking in the mind of the scientist who wishes to make creative discoveries. The topic of comparison is used implicitly throughout the essay.

Because his point is somewhat irregular—proposing that creativity comes directly out of the most complete commitment to tradition—Kuhn is careful to prepare his audience carefully for his conclusions. He realizes that what he is saying is a bit paradoxical, and he is cautious to make it clear that he is aware of the complexities of his position. What he wants most is to make his audience aware of the fact that looking only for examples of divergent thinking in prospective scientists is a mistake. Those whose thinking is essentially divergent in nature must accept the essential tension.

The Essential Tension: Tradition and Innovation in Scientific Research

I am grateful for the invitation to participate in this important con- 1
ference,[1] and I interpret it as evidence that students of creativity themselves possess the sensitivity to divergent approaches that they seek to
identify in others. But I am not altogether sanguine[2] about the outcome of your experiment with me. As most of you already know, I am
no psychologist, but rather an ex-physicist now working in the history
of science. Probably my concern is no less with creativity than your
own, but my goals, my techniques, and my sources of evidence are so
very different from yours that I am far from sure how much we do, or
even *should*, have to say to each other. These reservations imply no
apology: rather they hint at my central thesis. In the sciences, as I
shall suggest below, it is often better to do one's best with the tools at
hand than to pause for contemplation of divergent approaches.

If a person of my background and interests has anything relevant 2
to suggest to this conference, it will not be about your central concerns, the creative personality and its early identification. But implicit
in the numerous working papers distributed to participants in this
conference is an image of the scientific process and of the scientist;
that image almost certainly conditions many of the experiments you
try as well as the conclusions you draw; and about it the physicist-
historian may well have something to say. I shall restrict my attention
to one aspect of this image—an aspect epitomized as follows in one of
the working papers: The basic scientist "must lack prejudice to a degree where he can look at the most 'self-evident' facts or concepts
without necessarily accepting them, and, conversely, allow his imagination to play with the most unlikely possibilities.". . . In the more
technical language supplied by other working papers, . . . this aspect

---

[1]**this important conference** It was a conference on the identification of scientific
talent held at the University of Utah in 1959.
[2]**sanguine** hopeful or optimistic.

of the image recurs as an emphasis upon "divergent thinking, . . . the freedom to go off in different directions, . . . rejecting the old solution and striking out in some new direction."

I do not at all doubt that this description of "divergent thinking" and the concomitant search for those able to do it are entirely proper. Some divergence characterizes all scientific work, and gigantic divergences lie at the core of the most significant episodes in scientific development. But both my own experience in scientific research and my reading of the history of sciences lead me to wonder whether flexibility and open-mindeness have not been too exclusively emphasized as the characteristics requisite for basic research. I shall therefore suggest below that something like "convergent thinking" is just as essential to scientific advance as is divergent. Since these two modes of thought are inevitably in conflict, it will follow that the ability to support a tension that can occasionally become almost unbearable is one of the prime requisites for the very best sort of scientific research.

I am elsewhere studying these points more historically, with emphasis on the importance to scientific development of "revolutions."[3] These are episodes—exemplified in their most extreme and readily recognized form by the advent of Copernicanism, Darwinism, or Einsteinianism—in which a scientific community abandons one time-honored way of regarding the world and of pursuing science in favor of some other, usually incompatible, approach to its discipline. I have argued in the draft that the historian constantly encounters many far smaller but structurally similar revolutionary episodes and that they are central to scientific advance. Contrary to a prevalent impression, most new discoveries and theories in the sciences are not merely additions to the existing stockpile of scientific knowledge. To assimilate them the scientist must usually rearrange the intellectual and manipulative equipment he has previously relied upon, discarding some elements of his prior belief and practice while finding new significances in and new relationships between many others. Because the old must be revalued and reordered when assimilating the new, discovery and invention in the sciences are usually intrinsically revolutionary. Therefore, they do demand just that flexibility and open-mindedness that characterize, or indeed define, the divergent thinker. Let us henceforth take for granted the need for these characteristics. Unless many scientists possessed them to a marked degree, there would be no scientific revolutions and very little scientific advance.

---

[3][Thomas Kuhn,] *The Structure of Scientific Revolutions* (Chicago, 1962). [Kuhn's note]

Yet flexibility is not enough, and what remains is not obviously   5
compatible with it. Drawing from various fragments of a project still
in progress, I must now emphasize that revolutions are but one of two
complementary aspects of scientific advance. Almost none of the research undertaken by even the greatest scientists is designed to be revolutionary, and very little of it has any such effect. On the contrary,
normal research, even the best of it, is a highly convergent activity
based firmly upon a settled consensus acquired from scientific education and reinforced by subsequent life in the profession. Typically, to
be sure, this convergent or consensus-bound research ultimately results in revolution. Then, traditional techniques and beliefs are abandoned and replaced by new ones. But revolutionary shifts of a scientific tradition are relatively rare, and extended periods of convergent
research are the necessary preliminary to them. As I shall indicate below, only investigations firmly rooted in the contemporary scientific
tradition are likely to break that tradition and give rise to a new one.
That is why I speak of an "essential tension" implicit in scientific
research. To do his job the scientist must undertake a complex set of
intellectual and manipulative commitments. Yet his claim to fame, if
he has the talent and good luck to gain one, may finally rest upon his
ability to abandon this net of commitments in favor of another of his
own invention. Very often the successful scientist must simultaneously display the characteristics of the traditionalist and of the
iconoclast.[4]

The multiple historical examples upon which any full documenta-   6
tion of these points must depend are prohibited by the time limitations of the conference. But another approach will introduce you to at
least part of what I have in mind—an examination of the nature of
education in the natural sciences. One of the working papers for this
conference . . . quotes Guilford's very apt description of scientific education as follows: "[It] has emphasized abilities in the areas of con-

---

[4]Strictly speaking, it is the professional group rather than the individual scientist that
must display both these characteristics simultaneously. In a fuller account of the ground
covered in this paper that distinction between individual and group characteristics would
be basic. Here I can only note that, though recognition of the distinction weakens the
conflict or tension referred to above, it does not eliminate it. Within the group some
individuals may be more traditionalistic, others more iconoclastic, and their contributions may differ accordingly. Yet education, institutional norms, and the nature of the
job to be done will inevitably combine to insure that all group members will, to a greater
or lesser extent, be pulled in both directions. [Kuhn's note] An *iconoclast* is not traditional, but likes to break with the past, often in very dramatic ways.

vergent thinking and evaluation, often at the expense of development in the area of divergent thinking. We have attempted to teach students how to arrive at 'correct' answers that our civilization has taught us are correct. . . . Outside the arts [and I should include most of the social sciences] we have generally discouraged the development of divergent-thinking abilities, unintentionally." That characterization seems to me eminently just, but I wonder whether it is equally just to deplore the product that results. Without defending plain bad teaching, and granting that in this country the trend to convergent thinking in all education may have proceeded entirely too far, we may nevertheless recognize that a rigorous training in convergent thought has been intrinsic to the sciences almost from their origin. I suggest that they could not have achieved their present state or status without it.

Let me try briefly to epitomize the nature of education in the natural sciences, ignoring the many significant yet minor differences between the various sciences and between the approaches of different educational institutions. The single most striking feature of this education is that, to an extent totally unknown in other creative fields, it is conducted entirely through textbooks. Typically, undergraduate *and* graduate students of chemistry, physics, astronomy, geology, or biology acquire the substance of their fields from books written especially for students. Until they are ready, or very nearly ready, to commence work on their own dissertations, they are neither asked to attempt trial research projects nor exposed to the immediate products of research done by others, that is, to the professional communications that scientists write for each other. There are no collections of "readings" in the natural sciences. Nor are science students encouraged to read the historical classics of their fields—works in which they might discover other ways of regarding the problems discussed in their textbooks, but in which they would also meet problems, concepts, and standards of solution that their future professions have long since discarded and replaced.

In contrast, the various textbooks that the student does encounter display different subject matters, rather than, as in many of the social sciences, exemplifying different approaches to a single problem field. Even books that compete for adoption in a single course differ mainly in level and in pedagogic detail, not in substance or conceptual structure. Last, but most important of all, is the characteristic technique of textbook presentation. Except in their occasional introductions, science textbooks do not describe the sorts of problems that the professional may be asked to solve and the variety of techniques available for their solution. Rather, these books exhibit concrete problem solutions that the profession has come to accept as paradigms,[5] and they then ask the student, either with a pencil and paper or in the laboratory, to solve for himself problems very closely related in both method and substance to those through which the textbook or the accompanying lecture has led him. Nothing could be better calculated to produce "mental sets" or *Einstellungen*.[6] Only in their most elementary courses do other academic fields offer as much as a partial parallel.

Even the most faintly liberal educational theory must view this 9 pedagogic technique as anathema. Students, we would all agree, must begin by learning a good deal of what is already known, but we also insist that education give them vastly more. They must, we say, learn to recognize and evaluate problems to which no unequivocal solution has yet been given; they must be supplied with an arsenal of techniques for approaching these future problems; and they must learn to judge the relevance of these techniques and to evaluate the possibly partial solutions which they can provide. In many respects these attitudes toward education seem to me entirely right, and yet we must recognize two things about them. First, education in the natural sciences seems to have been totally unaffected by their existence. It remains a dogmatic initiation in a pre-established tradition that the student is not equipped to evaluate. Second, at least in the period when it was followed by a term in an apprenticeship relation, this technique of exclusive exposure to a rigid tradition has been immensely productive of the most consequential sorts of innovations.

I shall shortly inquire about the pattern of scientific practice that 10 grows out of this educational initiation and will then attempt to say why that pattern proves quite so successful. But first, an historical excursion will reinforce what has just been said and prepare the way for what is to follow. I should like to suggest that the various fields of natural science have not always been characterized by rigid education in exclusive paradigms, but that each of them acquired something like that technique at precisely the point when the field began to make rapid and systematic progress. If one asks about the origin of our contemporary knowledge of chemical composition, of earthquakes, of biological reproduction, of motion through space, or of any other subject matter known to the natural sciences, one immediately encounters a

---

[5]*paradigms*   Patterns or models of thought; the established views of the way something works or is.
[6]*Einstellungen*   outlook (German).

characteristic pattern that I shall here illustrate with a single example.

Today, physics textbooks tell us that light exhibits some properties 11 of a wave and some of a particle: both textbook problems and research problems are designed accordingly. But both this view and these textbooks are products of an early twentieth-century revolution. (One characteristic of scientific revolutions is that they call for the rewriting of science textbooks.) For more than half a century before 1900, the books employed in scientific education had been equally unequivocal in stating that light was wave motion. Under those circumstances scientists worked on somewhat different problems and often embraced rather different sorts of solutions to them. The nineteenth-century textbook tradition does not, however, mark the beginning of our subject matter. Throughout the eighteenth century and into the early nineteenth, Newton's *Opticks*[7] and the other books from which men learned science taught almost all students that light was particles, and research guided by this tradition was again different from that which succeeded it. Ignoring a variety of subsidiary changes within these three successive traditions, we may therefore say that our views derive historically from Newton's views by way of two revolutions in optical thought, each of which replaced one tradition of convergent research with another. If we make appropriate allowances for changes in the locus[8] and materials of scientific education, we may say that each of these three traditions was embodied in the sort of education by exposure to unequivocal paradigms that I briefly epitomized above. Since Newton, education and research in physical optics have normally been highly convergent.

The history of theories of light does not, however, begin with New- 12 ton. If we ask about knowledge in the field before his time, we encounter a significantly different pattern—a pattern still familiar in the arts and in some social sciences, but one which has largely disappeared in the natural sciences. From remote antiquity until the end of the seventeenth century there was no single set of paradigms for the study of physical optics. Instead, many men advanced a large number of different views about the nature of light. Some of these views found few adherents, but a number of them gave rise to continuing schools of

---

[7]*Opticks (1704)* By Sir Isaac Newton (1642–1727); one of the most important studies of light and color theory. The book began as a series of lectures in Trinity College, Cambridge. Newton developed here his theory that light was composed of tiny individual corpuscles, or particles.

[8]*locus* place.

optical thought. Although the historian can note the emergence of new points of view as well as changes in the relative popularity of older ones, there was never anything resembling consensus. As a result, a new man entering the field was inevitably exposed to a variety of conflicting viewpoints; he was forced to examine the evidence for each, and there always was good evidence. The fact that he made a choice and conducted himself accordingly could not entirely prevent his awareness of other possibilities. This earlier mode of education was obviously more suited to produce a scientist without prejudice, alert to novel phenomena, and flexible in his approach to his field. On the other hand, one can scarcely escape the impression that, during the period characterized by this more liberal educational practice, physical optics made very little progress.[9]

The preconsensus (we might here call it the divergent) phase in the development of physical optics is, I believe, duplicated in the history of all other scientific specialties, excepting only those that were born by the subdivision and recombination of pre-existing disciplines. In some fields, like mathematics and astronomy, the first firm consensus is prehistoric. In others, like dynamics, geometric optics, and parts of physiology, the paradigms that produced a first consensus date from classical antiquity. Most other natural sciences, though their problems were often discussed in antiquity, did not achieve a first consensus until after the Renaissance. In physical optics, as we have seen, the first firm consensus dates only from the end of the seventeenth century; in electricity, chemistry, and the study of heat, it dates from the eighteenth; while in geology and the nontaxonomic[10] parts of biology no very real consensus developed until after the first third of the nineteenth century. This century appears to be characterized by the emergence of a first consensus in parts of a few of the social sciences. 13

In all the fields named above, important work was done before the achievement of the maturity produced by consensus. Neither the na- 14

---

[9]The history of physical optics before Newton has recently been well described by Vasco Ronchi in *Histoire de la lumière*, trans. J. Taton (Paris, 1956). His account does justice to the element I elaborate too little above. Many fundamental contributions to physical optics were made in the two millennia before Newton's work. Consensus is not prerequisite to a sort of progress in the natural sciences, any more than it is to progress in the social sciences or the arts. It is, however, prerequisite to the sort of progress that we now generally refer to when distinguishing the natural sciences from the arts and from most social sciences. [Kuhn's note]

[10]**nontaxonomic** unrelated to the classification of plants and animals.

ture nor the timing of the first consensus in these fields can be understood without a careful examination of both the intellectual and the manipulative techniques[11] developed before the existence of unique paradigms. But the transition to maturity is not less significant because individuals practiced science before it occurred. On the contrary, history strongly suggests that, though one can practice science—as one does philosophy or art or political science—without a firm consensus, this more flexible practice will not produce the pattern of rapid consequential scientific advance to which recent centuries have accustomed us. In that pattern, development occurs from one consensus to another, and alternate approaches are not ordinarily in competition. Except under quite special conditions, the practitioner of a mature science does not pause to examine divergent modes of explanation or experimentation.

I shall shortly ask how this can be so—how a firm orientation toward an apparently unique tradition can be compatible with the practice of the disciplines most noted for the persistent production of novel ideas and techniques. But it will help first to ask what the education that so successfully transmits such a tradition leaves to be done. What can a scientist working within a deeply rooted tradition and little trained in the perception of significant alternatives hope to do in his professional career? Once again limits of time force me to drastic simplification, but the following remarks will at least suggest a position that I am sure can be documented in detail.

In pure or basic science[12]—that somewhat ephemeral category of research undertaken by men whose most immediate goal is to increase understanding rather than control of nature—the characteristic problems are almost always repetitions, with minor modifications, of problems that have been undertaken and partially resolved before. For example, much of the research undertaken within a scientific tradition is an attempt to adjust existing theory or existing observation in order to bring the two into closer and closer agreement. The constant examination of atomic and molecular spectra during the years since the birth of wave mechanics, together with the design of theoretical approximations for the prediction of complex spectra, provides one important instance of this typical sort of work. Another was provided by

---

[11]***manipulative techniques***   practical testing, as opposed to theorizing.
[12]***pure or basic science***   The distinction, pure and applied, is equivalent to the distinction between theoretical and practical science.

the remarks about the eighteenth-century development of Newtonian dynamics[13] in the paper on measurement supplied to you in advance of the conference.[14] The attempt to make existing theory and observation conform more closely is not, of course, the only standard sort of research problem in the basic sciences. The development of chemical thermodynamics[15] or the continuing attempts to unravel organic structure illustrate another type—the extension of existing theory to areas that it is expected to cover but in which it has never before been tried. In addition, to mention a third common sort of research problem, many scientists constantly collect the concrete data (e.g., atomic weights, nuclear moments[16]) required for the application and extension of existing theory.

These are normal research projects in the basic sciences, and they illustrate the sorts of work on which all scientists, even the greatest, spend most of their professional lives and on which many spend all. Clearly their pursuit is neither intended nor likely to produce fundamental discoveries or revolutionary changes in scientific theory. Only if the validity of the contemporary scientific tradition is assumed do these problems make much theoretical or any practical sense. The man who suspected the existence of a totally new type of phenomenon or who had basic doubts about the validity of existing theory would not think problems so closely modeled on textbook paradigms worth undertaking. It follows that the man who does undertake a problem of this sort—and that means all scientists at most times—aims to elucidate the scientific tradition in which he was raised rather than to change it. Furthermore, the fascination of his work lies in the difficulties of elucidation rather than in any surprises that the work is likely to produce. Under normal conditions the research scientist is not an innovator but a solver of puzzles, and the puzzles upon which he concentrates are just those which he believes can be both stated and solved within the existing scientific tradition. 17

Yet—and this is the point—the ultimate effect of this tradition-bound work has invariably been to change the tradition. Again and 18

---

[13]*Newtonian dynamics* Newton's three laws of motion are: (1) An object stays at rest until an outside force moves it. (2) The change of motion is proportional to the force that moves it. (3) To every action there is an equal and opposite reaction.

[14]A revised version appeared in *Isis* 52 (1961): 161–93. [Kuhn's note]

[15]*chemical thermodynamics* laws determining motion, usually of gases, in relation to heat.

[16]*atomic weights, nuclear moments* Atomic weight of an element is the average of its isotopes, the average number of atoms in its molecule. Nuclear moment is the axis of the molecule, its center.

again the continuing attempt to elucidate a currently received tradition has at last produced one of those shifts in fundamental theory, in problem field,[17] and in scientific standards to which I previously referred as scientific revolutions. At least for the scientific community as a whole, work within a well-defined and deeply ingrained tradition seems more productive of tradition-shattering novelties than work in which no similarly convergent standards are involved. How can this be so? I think it is because no other sort of work is nearly so well suited to isolate for continuing and concentrated attention those loci of trouble or causes of crisis upon whose recognition the most fundamental advances in basic science depend.

As I have indicated in the first of my working papers, new theories and, to an increasing extent, novel discoveries in the mature sciences are not born *de novo*.[18] On the contrary, they emerge from old theories and within a matrix[19] of old beliefs about the phenomena that the world does *and does not* contain. Ordinarily such novelties are far too esoteric and recondite[20] to be noted by the man without a great deal of scientific training. And even the man with considerable training can seldom afford simply to go out and look for them, let us say by exploring those areas in which existing data and theory have failed to produce understanding. Even in a mature science there are always far too many such areas, areas in which no existing paradigms seem obviously to apply and for whose exploration few tools and standards are available. More likely than not the scientist who ventured into them, relying merely upon his receptivity to new phenomena and his flexibility to new patterns of organization, would get nowhere at all. He would rather return his science to its preconsensus or natural history phase.

Instead, the practitioner of a mature science, from the beginning of his doctoral research, continues to work in the regions for which the paradigms derived from his education and from the research of his contemporaries seem adequate. He tries, that is, to elucidate topographical detail on a map whose main outlines are available in advance, and he hopes—if he is wise enough to recognize the nature of his field—that he will some day undertake a problem in which the anticipated does

19

20

---

[17]***problem field*** theoretical questions.
[18]**de novo** over again; from the start.
[19]***matrix*** interrelated group of, in this case, beliefs; when one changes, all are altered.
[20]***esoteric and recondite*** designed for specially trained people and difficult to understand.

not occur, a problem that goes wrong in ways suggestive of a fundamental weakness in the paradigm itself. In the mature sciences the prelude to much discovery and to all novel theory is not ignorance, but the recognition that something has gone wrong with existing knowledge and beliefs.

What I have said so far may indicate that it is sufficient for the productive scientist to adopt existing theory as a lightly held tentative hypothesis, employ it *faute de mieux*[21] in order to get a start in his research, and then abandon it as soon as it leads him to a trouble spot, a point at which something has gone wrong. But though the ability to recognize trouble when confronted by it is surely a requisite for scientific advance, trouble must not be too easily recognized. The scientist requires a thoroughgoing commitment to the tradition with which, if he is fully successful, he will break. In part this commitment is demanded by the nature of the problems the scientist normally undertakes. These, as we have seen, are usually esoteric puzzles whose challenge lies less in the information disclosed by their solutions (all but its details are often known in advance) than in the difficulties of technique to be surmounted in providing any solution at all. Problems of this sort are undertaken only by men assured that there is a solution which ingenuity can disclose, and only current theory could possibly provide assurance of that sort. That theory alone gives meaning to most of the problems of normal research. To doubt it is often to doubt that the complex technical puzzles which constitute normal research have any solutions at all. Who, for example, would have developed the elaborate mathematical techniques required for the study of the effects of interplanetary attractions upon basic Keplerian orbits[22] if he had not assumed that Newtonian dynamics, applied to the planets then known, would explain the last details of astronomical observation? But without that assurance, how would Neptune have been discovered and the list of planets changed?

In addition, there are pressing practical reasons for commitment. Every research problem confronts the scientist with anomalies[23] whose sources he cannot quite identify. His theories and observations never quite agree; successive observations never yield quite the same

21

22

---

[21]**faute de mieux**   for want of something better.

[22]***Keplerian orbits***   Johannes Kepler (1571–1630) discovered that the planets move in elliptical, not circular orbits. He recognized the gravitational pull of the sun and planets and was noted for the care and exactitude of his measurements.

[23]***anomalies***   unaccountable variations from what is expected.

results; his experiments have both theoretical and phenomenological[24] by-products which it would take another research project to unravel. Each of these anomalies or incompletely understood phenomena could conceivably be the clue to a fundamental innovation in scientific theory or technique, but the man who pauses to examine them one by one never completes his first project. Reports of effective research repeatedly imply that all but the most striking and central discrepancies could be taken care of by current theory if only there were time to take them on. The men who make these reports find most discrepancies trivial or uninteresting, an evaluation that they can ordinarily base only upon their faith in current theory. Without that faith their work would be wasteful of time and talent.

Besides, lack of commitment too often results in the scientist's undertaking problems that he has little chance of solving. Pursuit of an anomaly is fruitful only if the anomaly is more than nontrivial. Having discovered it, the scientist's first efforts and those of his profession are to do what nuclear physicists are now doing. They strive to generalize the anomaly, to discover other and more revealing manifestations of the same effect, to give it structure by examining its complex interrelationships with phenomena they still feel they understand. Very few anomalies are susceptible to this sort of treatment. To be so they must be in explicit and unequivocal conflict with some structurally central tenet of current scientific belief. Therefore, their recognition and evaluation once again depend upon a firm commitment to the contemporary scientific tradition. 23

This central role of an elaborate and often esoteric tradition is what I have principally had in mind when speaking of the essential tension in scientific research. I do not doubt that the scientist must be, at least potentially, an innovator, that he must possess mental flexibility, and that he must be prepared to recognize troubles where they exist. That much of the popular stereotype is surely correct, and it is important accordingly to search for indices of the corresponding personality characteristics. But what is no part of our stereotype and what appears to need careful integration with it is the other face of this same coin. We are, I think, more likely fully to exploit our potential scientific talent if we recognize the extent to which the basic scientist must also be a firm traditionalist, or, if I am using your vocabulary at all correctly, a convergent thinker. Most important of all, we must seek to understand 24

---

[24]*phenomenological*   related to perceptible events.

how these two superficially discordant modes of problem solving can be reconciled both within the individual and within the group.

Everything said above needs both elaboration and documentation. 25 Very likely some of it will change in the process. This paper is a report on work in progress. But, though I insist that much of it is tentative and all of it incomplete, I still hope that the paper has indicated why an educational system best described as an initiation into an unequivocal tradition should be thoroughly compatible with successful scientific work. And I hope, in addition, to have made plausible the historical thesis that no part of science has progressed very far or very rapidly before this convergent education and correspondingly convergent normal practice became possible. Finally, though it is beyond my competence to derive personality correlates from this view of scientific development, I hope to have made meaningful the view that the productive scientist must be a traditionalist who enjoys playing intricate games by pre-established rules in order to be a successful innovator who discovers new rules and new pieces with which to play them.

As first planned, my paper was to have ended at this point. But 26 work on it, against the background supplied by the working papers distributed to conference participants, has suggested the need for a postscript. Let me therefore briefly try to eliminate a likely ground of misunderstanding and simultaneously suggest a problem that urgently needs a great deal of investigation.

Everything said above was intended to apply strictly only to basic 27 science, an enterprise whose practitioners have ordinarily been relatively free to choose their own problems. Characteristically, as I have indicated, these problems have been selected in areas where paradigms were clearly applicable but where exciting puzzles remained about how to apply them and how to make nature conform to the results of the application. Clearly the inventor and applied scientist are not generally free to choose puzzles of this sort. The problems among which they may choose are likely to be largely determined by social, economic, or military circumstances external to the sciences. Often the decision to seek a cure for a virulent disease, a new source of household illumination, or an alloy able to withstand the intense heat of rocket engines must be made with little reference to the state of the relevant science. It is, I think, by no means clear that the personality characteristics requisite for pre-eminence in this more immediately practical sort of work are altogether the same as those required for a great achievement in basic science. History indicates that only a few individuals, most of whom worked in readily demarcated areas, have achieved eminence in both.

I am by no means clear where this suggestion leads us. The troublesome distinctions between basic research,[25] applied research, and invention need far more investigation. Nevertheless, it seems likely, for example, that the applied scientist, to whose problems no scientific paradigm need be fully relevant, may profit by a far broader and less rigid education than that to which the pure scientist has characteristically been exposed. Certainly there are many episodes in the history of technology in which lack of more than the most rudimentary scientific education has proved to be an immense help. This group scarcely needs to be reminded that Edison's electric light[26] was produced in the face of unanimous scientific opinion that the arc light could not be "subdivided," and there are many other episodes of this sort.

This must not suggest, however, that mere differences in education will transform the applied scientist into a basic scientist or vice versa. One could at least argue that Edison's personality, ideal for the inventor and perhaps also for the "oddball" in applied science, barred him from fundamental achievements in the basic sciences. He himself expressed great scorn for scientists and thought of them as wooly-headed people to be hired when needed. But this did not prevent his occasionally arriving at the most sweeping and irresponsible scientific theories of his own. (The pattern recurs in the early history of electrical technology: both Tesla[27] and Gramme[28] advanced absurd cosmic schemes that they thought deserved to replace the current scientific knowledge of their day.) Episodes like this reinforce an impression that the per-

---

[25]*basic research*   Research designed to establish new theories. Other types of research attempt to put basic research to some practical use.

[26]*electric light*   Thomas Alva Edison (1847–1931) did not invent the electric light, but did the applied research that made it a practical commercial product, which it became in 1882.

[27]*Nikola Tesla (1856–1943)*   Yugoslavian inventor of carbon arc lighting, in which a huge electrical charge bridges a gap with a bright flash. He also invented alternating current. In later years he claimed to be able to communicate with distant planets and to be able to split the earth like an apple.

[28]*Zenobé-Theophile Gramme (1826–1901)*   A basically untrained French scientist and inventor who worked with direct and alternating current. He held some wild and ignorant views of the power of magnetism.

sonality requisites of the pure scientist and of the inventor may be quite different, perhaps with those of the applied scientist lying somewhere between.[29]

Is there a further conclusion to be drawn from all this? One speculative thought forces itself upon me. If I read the working papers correctly, they suggest that most of you are really in search of the *inventive* personality, a sort of person who does emphasize divergent thinking but whom the United States has already produced in abundance. In the process you may be ignoring certain of the essential requisites of the basic scientist, a rather different sort of person, to whose ranks America's contributions have as yet been notoriously sparse. Since most of you are, in fact, Americans, this correlation may not be entirely coincidental.

30

---

[29]For the attitude of scientists toward the technical possibility of the incandescent light see Francis A. Jones, *Thomas Alva Edison* (New York, 1908), pp. 99–100, and Harold C. Passer, *The Electrical Manufacturers, 1875–1900* (Cambridge, Mass., 1953), pp. 82–83. For Edison's attitude toward scientists see Passer, ibid., pp. 180–81. For a sample of Edison's theorizing in realms otherwise subject to scientific treatments see Dagobert D. Runes, ed., *The Diary and Sundry Observations of Thomas Alva Edison* (New York, 1948), pp. 205–44, passim. [Kuhn's note]

QUESTIONS

1. What is divergent thinking? Give some examples from your own experience.
2. What is convergent thinking? Give some examples from your experience.
3. Assuming that Kuhn's audience was committed to the principles of divergent thinking before they heard his talk, do you feel that they would have changed their minds after hearing it? What are your reasons for thinking they would (or would not) have changed their minds?
4. Find all the signposts in the talk that explain where the argument is heading, what Kuhn is planning to do, and what he has done. How effective are these signposts for following his argument? Do you find them annoying or helpful? Are there any places where they are needed but not supplied?
5. Kuhn talks about reaching a consensus in science. What does he mean? See paragraphs 12–13.

WRITING ASSIGNMENTS

1. Kuhn is interested in the kind of personality that would be best suited to doing creative work in science. After listening to his talk, if you were a member of the audience responsible for selecting a potential scientist from a group of young people, what personality characteristics would you look for? What, in Kuhn's view, are the intellectual and personal characteristics of scientists that are most likely to ensure scientific discovery in the future?

2. Much of what Kuhn has to say about thinking relates directly to the way in which education in the sciences is conducted. The student is asked to master the basic paradigms of a branch of science—theories, models, patterns, examples—that are at hand. What are your views on the nature of scientific education? Based on your own experience, what is praiseworthy about it? What is not praiseworthy about it? Is science education much as Kuhn describes it?

3. What is it about the very nature of science that suits it best to convergent thinking? Consider the discovery of facts, laws, and principles that really work and that do not admit of much variance. Why would science resist divergent thought? What would actually constitute divergent thought in science? Why is consensus such a deterrent to divergence? *Should* it be a deterrent to divergence? What are the alternatives, if any, to such consensus?

4. In paragraph 3, Kuhn asserts that "these two modes of thought" (divergence and convergence) "are inevitably in conflict." Is this statement necessarily true? Find examples in any area of inquiry—science, politics, religion, education, or any other area that interests you—which help you decide just what the nature of the conflict (if there is one) actually is. If you find that there is no conflict, explain why there is none. If you find that there is conflict, explain why there is. Use Kuhn's rhetorical techniques of beginning with an introduction, dividing your topic in the body of the essay, and ending with a summary conclusion. Structure your essay like a talk and offer some of the same kinds of signposts that Kuhn uses.

5. If the principle of convergent thinking and the commitment to tradition and consensus were followed in education the way Kuhn says they should be followed in science, what would your educational experience have been like? Try to imagine what grade school would have been like and contrast that with what your actual experience was. Do the same thing regarding secondary school and college. Is divergent thinking more desirable or less desirable in education than in science? Is it more respected than convergent thinking? In your essay, try to give some examples from your own experience of when convergent thinking was most clearly expected of you and when divergent thinking was expected.

6. Look for examples of convergent and divergent thinking in your social life and write an essay based on your findings. Are most of your friends likely to be convergent or divergent in their thinking? Choose some specific persons and instances of their thinking. If possible, spend some time in observation of your friends (and yourself) to see which kind of thinking is more prevalent. How much tolerance do your friends have for divergent thinking? How much tolerance do older people seem to have for divergent thinking? What seem to be the most touchy issues with respect to divergent thinking? Make your essay into the shape of a talk like Kuhn's, using signposts, an introduction, a body, and a conclusion. Use the first person throughout.

STEPHEN JAY GOULD

Nonmoral Nature

STEPHEN JAY GOULD *(b. 1941) is professor of geology at Harvard University, where his field of interest centers on the special evolutionary problems related to species of Bahamaian snails. He decided to become a paleontologist when he was five years old, after his father had taken him to the American Museum of Natural History in New York City, where he first saw reconstructed dinosaurs.*

Gould has become well known for his essays on science, essays that have had the clarity needed to explain complex concepts to a general audience but that have also been informed by a superb scientific understanding. His articles for Natural History *magazine have been widely quoted and also collected in book form. His books have been praised and have won prizes. With works such as* Ever Since Darwin *(1977),* The Panda's Thumb *(1980),* The Mismeasure of Man *(1982), and* The Flamingo's Smile *(1985), Gould has constantly pointed to the significance of the work of the scientist he most frequently praises, Charles Darwin. His books have been celebrated around the world, and in 1981 Gould won a MacArthur Fellowship— a stipend of more than $38,000 a year for five years to permit him to do any work he wishes.*

"Nonmoral Nature" concerns itself with a highly controversial issue: the religious "reading" of natural events. Gould has frequently given testimony at legislative hearings in which creationists have insisted that the Bible's version of creation be taught in science courses

as scientific fact. Gould opposes this position because he views the account of the creation in Genesis as a religious, not a scientific, one. He points out that Darwin (who was trained as a minister) did not think there was conflict between his theories and religious beliefs.

Gould's primary point in this selection is that the behavior of animals in nature—with ruthless and efficient predators inflicting pain on an essentially helpless prey—has presented theologians with very exacting problems. If God is good and if creation reveals his goodness, how does one account for the suffering of nature's victims?

Gould examines in great detail certain specific issues that plagued nineteenth-century theologians. The behavior of the ichneumon wasp, an efficient wasp that plants its egg in a host caterpillar or aphid, is his special concern, since the phenomenon epitomized by the ichneumon baffled theologians. There are so many species of ichneumons that it could not be regarded as an isolated phenomenon. Part of Gould's approach is to describe the behavior of the ichneumon in detail to make it plain that the total mechanism of the predatory, parasitic animal is complex, subtle, and brilliant.

It is almost impossible to read this selection without developing a sense of respect for the predator, something that was extremely difficult, if not impossible, for nineteenth-century theologians to do. Their problem, Gould asserts, was that they anthropomorphized the behavior of these insects. That is, they thought of them in human terms. The act of predation was seen in the same light as we see the acts of human thugs who toy with their victims, or as Gould puts it, the acts of official state-hired killers whose job was, in Renaissance England, to inflict as much pain as possible on traitors before killing them. This model is a kind of lens through which the behavior of predators was interpreted and understood. The ichneumons paralyze their host and then eat it from the inside out; they take great care not to permit a victim to die until the last morsel is consumed.

Instead of an anthropocentric—human-centered—view, Gould wants us to take a scientific view as well as to see the predators' behavior in the same sympathetic manner in which we observe the victims' behavior. If we do so, he asserts, we will come to think of the ichneumon as nonmoral—of nature as nonmoral—rather than to think of its act of predation in moral terms, as if predators were instruments of evil. The concept of evil, he says, is limited to human beings. The world of nature is unconcerned with it, and if we apply morality to nature, we end up merely seeing nature as a reflection of our own beliefs and values. Instead, he wishes us to conceive of nature as he thinks it is, something apart from strictly human values.

GOULD'S RHETORIC

Gould's writing is distinguished for its clarity and directness. In this essay, he relies on the testimony of renowned authorities, establishing at once a remarkable breadth of interest and revealing considerably detailed learning about his subject. He explores a number of theories with sympathy and care, demonstrating their limits before offering his own views.

Since his field of interest is advanced biology, he runs the risk of losing the general reader. He might have oversimplified his subject in order to avoid doing this, but he does not: he does not shrink from using Latin classifications to identify his subject matter, but he defines each specialized term when he first uses it. He clarifies each opposing argument and demonstrates, in his analysis, what its limitations and potentials are.

Interestingly, instead of employing a metaphor in order to help convince us of a significant fact or critical opinion, Gould "deconstructs" a metaphor that was once in wide use. In other words, he reveals the metaphor to us; he shows us how it has affected belief and then asks us to reject the metaphor so as to see the world as it actually is. The metaphor is simple: the animal world is comparable to the human world with respect to ethical (normal) behavior. Since the behavior of animals is metaphorically like that of people, the ethical issue must be deep in the grain of nature. This view is mistaken, Gould says. Maintaining the metaphor is inviting and can be irresistible. Yet we must resist it.

Gould also makes widespread use of the rhetorical device of metonymy in which a part of something stands for the whole. Thus, the details of nature, which is God's creation, are made to reflect the entirety, which is God. Therefore, the behavior of the ichneumon comes to stand for the nature of God; and because the ichneumon's behavior is adjudged evil by those who hold to the first metaphor, there is a terrible contradiction which cannot be rationalized by theological arguments.

Gould shows us just how difficult the problem of the theologian is. Then he shows us a way out. But it is a way out that depends on our capacity to think differently from the way we may be used to doing. It may demand a change on our part, and some may not be able to achieve it.

Nonmoral Nature

When the Right Honorable and Reverend Francis Henry, earl of 1
Bridgewater,[1] died in February, 1829, he left £8,000 to support a series
of books "on the power, wisdom and goodness of God, as manifested
in the creation." William Buckland,[2] England's first official academic
geologist and later dean of Westminster, was invited to compose one
of the nine Bridgewater Treatises. In it he discussed the most pressing
problem of natural theology: If God is benevolent and the Creation
displays his "power, wisdom and goodness," then why are we surrounded with pain, suffering, and apparently senseless cruelty in the
animal world?

Buckland considered the depredation of "carnivorous races" as the 2
primary challenge to an idealized world in which the lion might dwell
with the lamb. He resolved the issue to his satisfaction by arguing that
carnivores actually increase "the aggregate of animal enjoyment" and
"diminish that of pain." The death of victims, after all, is swift and
relatively painless, victims are spared the ravages of decreptitude and
senility, and populations do not outrun their food supply to the greater
sorrow of all. God knew what he was doing when he made lions. Buckland concluded in hardly concealed rapture:

> The appointment of death by the agency of carnivora, as the ordinary
> termination of animal existence, appears therefore in its main results
> to be a dispensation of benevolence; it deducts much from the aggre-
> gate amount of the pain of universal death; it abridges, and almost an-
> nihilates, throughout the brute creation, the misery of disease, and ac-
> cidental injuries, and lingering decay; and imposes such salutary
> restraint upon excessive increase of numbers, that the supply of food
> maintains perpetually a due ratio to the demand. The result is, that the
> surface of the land and depths of the waters are ever crowded with myr-
> iads of animated beings, the pleasures of whose life are co-extensive

---

[1]*Reverend Francis Henry, earl of Bridgewater (1756–1829)* He was the eighth and
last earl of Bridgewater. He was also a naturalist and a Fellow at All Souls College, Oxford, before he became earl of Bridgewater in 1823. On his death, he left a fund to be used
for the publication of the Bridgewater Treatises, essay discussions of the moral implications of scientific research and discoveries.

[2]*William Buckland (1784–1856)* An English clergyman and also a geologist. His
essay, "Geology and Mineralogy," was a Bridgewater Treatise in 1836.

with its duration; and which throughout the little day of existence that is allotted to them, fulfill with joy the functions for which they were created.

We may find a certain amusing charm in Buckland's vision today, but such arguments did begin to address "the problem of evil" for many of Buckland's contemporaries—how could a benevolent God create such a world of carnage and bloodshed? Yet these claims could not abolish the problem of evil entirely, for nature includes many phenomena far more horrible in our eyes than simple predation. I suspect that nothing evokes greater disgust in most of us than slow destruction of a host by an internal parasite—slow ingestion, bit by bit, from the inside. In no other way can I explain why *Alien*, an uninspired, grade-C, formula horror film, should have won such a following. That single scene of Mr. Alien, popping forth as a baby parasite from the body of a human host, was both sickening and stunning. Our nineteenth-century forebears maintained similar feelings. Their greatest challenge to the concept of a benevolent deity was not simple predation—for one can admire quick and efficient butcheries, especially since we strive to construct them ourselves—but slow death by parasitic ingestion. The classic case, treated at length by all the great naturalists, involved the so-called ichneumon fly. Buckland had sidestepped the major issue.

The ichneumon fly, which provoked such concern among natural theologians, was a composite creature representing the habits of an enormous tribe. The Ichneumonoidea are a group of wasps, not flies, that include more species than all the vertebrates combined (wasps, with ants and bees, constitute the order Hymenoptera; flies, with their two wings—wasps have four—form the order Diptera). In addition, many related wasps of similar habits were often cited for the same grisly details. Thus, the famous story did not merely implicate a single aberrant species (perhaps a perverse leakage from Satan's realm), but perhaps hundreds of thousands of them—a large chunk of what could only be God's creation.

The ichneumons, like most wasps, generally live freely as adults but pass their larval life as parasites feeding on the bodies of other animals, almost invariably members of their own phylum, Arthropoda. The most common victims are caterpillars (butterfly and moth larvae), but some ichneumons prefer aphids and others attack spiders. Most hosts are parasitized as larvae, but some adults are attacked, and many tiny ichneumons inject their brood directly into the egg of their host.

The free-flying females locate an appropriate host and then convert it to a food factory for their own young. Parasitologists speak of ectoparasitism when the uninvited guest lives on the surface of its host, and endoparasitism when the parasite dwells within. Among endoparasitic ichneumons, adult females pierce the host with their ovipositor and deposit eggs within it. (The ovipositor, a thin tube extending backward from the wasp's rear end, may be many times as long as the body itself.) Usually, the host is not otherwise inconvenienced for the moment, at least until the eggs hatch and the ichneumon larvae begin their grim work of interior excavation. Among ectoparasites, however, many females lay their eggs directly upon the host's body. Since an active host would easily dislodge the egg, the ichneumon mother often simultaneously injects a toxin that paralyzes the caterpillar or other victim. The paralysis may be permanent, and the caterpillar lies, alive but immobile, with the agent of its future destruction secure on its belly. The egg hatches, the helpless caterpillar twitches, the wasp larva pierces and begins its grisly feast.

Since a dead and decaying caterpillar will do the wasp larva no 7 good, it eats in a pattern that cannot help but recall, in our inappropriate, anthropocentric interpretation, the ancient English penalty for treason—drawing and quartering, with its explicit object of extracting as much torment as possible by keeping the victim alive and sentient. As the king's executioner drew out and burned his client's entrails, so does the ichneumon larva eat fat bodies and digestive organs first, keeping the caterpillar alive by preserving intact the essential heart and central nervous system. Finally, the larva completes its work and kills its victim, leaving behind the caterpillar's empty shell. Is it any wonder that ichneumons, not snakes or lions, stood as the paramount challenge to God's benevolence during the heyday of natural theology?

As I read through the nineteenth- and twentieth-century literature 8 on ichneumons, nothing amused me more than the tension between an intellectual knowledge that wasps should not be described in human terms and a literary or emotional inability to avoid the familiar categories of epic and narrative, pain and destruction, victim and vanquisher. We seem to be caught in the mythic structures of our own cultural sagas, quite unable, even in our basic descriptions, to use any other language than the metaphors of battle and conquest. We cannot render this corner of natural history as anything but story, combining the themes of grim horror and fascination and usually ending not so much with pity for the caterpillar as with admiration for the efficiency of the ichneumon.

I detect two basic themes in most epic descriptions: the struggles 9 of prey and the ruthless efficiency of parasites. Although we acknowledge that we witness little more than automatic instinct or physiological reaction, still we describe the defenses of hosts as though they represented conscious struggles. Thus, aphids kick and caterpillars may wriggle violently as wasps attempt to insert their ovipositors. The pupa of the tortoise-shell butterfly (usually considered an inert creature silently awaiting its conversion from duckling to swan) may contort its abdominal region so sharply that attacking wasps are thrown into the air. The caterpillars of *Hapalia*, when attacked by the wasp *Apanteles machaeralis*, drop suddenly from their leaves and suspend themselves in air by a silken thread. But the wasp may run down the thread and insert its eggs nonetheless. Some hosts can encapsulate the injected egg with blood cells that aggregate and harden, thus suffocating the parasite.

J. H. Fabre,[3] the great nineteenth-century French entomologist, who remains to this day the preeminently literate natural historian of insects, made a special study of parasitic wasps and wrote with an unabashed anthropocentrism about the struggles of paralyzed victims (see his books *Insect Life* and *The Wonders of Instinct*). He describes some imperfectly paralyzed caterpillars that struggle so violently every time a parasite approaches that the wasp larvae must feed with unusual caution. They attach themselves to a silken strand from the roof of their burrow and descend upon a safe and exposed part of the caterpillar: 10

> The grub is at dinner: head downwards, it is digging into the limp belly of one of the caterpillars. . . At the least sign of danger in the heap of caterpillars, the larva retreats . . . and climbs back to the ceiling, where the swarming rabble cannot reach it. When peace is restored, it slides down [its silken cord] and returns to table, with its head over the viands and its rear upturned and ready to withdraw in case of need.

In another chapter, he describes the fate of a paralyzed cricket: 11

> One may see the cricket, bitten to the quick, vainly move its antennae and abdominal styles, open and close its empty jaws, and even move a foot, but the larva is safe and searches its vitals with impunity. What an awful nightmare for the paralyzed cricket!

Fabre even learned to feed some paralyzed victims by placing a syrup of sugar and water on their mouthparts—thus showing that they remained alive, sentient, and (by implication) grateful for any palliation of their inevitable fate. If Jesus, immobile and thirsting on the 12

---

[3]*Jean-Henri Fabre (1823–1915)* A French entomologist whose patient study of insects earned him the nickname, "the Virgil of Insects." His writings are voluminous and, at times, elegant.

cross, received only vinegar from his tormentors, Fabre at least could make an ending bittersweet.

The second theme, ruthless efficiency of the parasites, leads to the opposite conclusion—grudging admiration for the victors. We learn of their skill in capturing dangerous hosts often many times larger than themselves. Caterpillars may be easy game, but the psammocharid wasps prefer spiders. They must insert their ovipositors in a safe and precise spot. Some leave a paralyzed spider in its own burrow. *Planiceps hirsutus*, for example, parasitizes a California trapdoor spider. It searches for spider tubes on sand dunes, then digs into nearby sand to disturb the spider's home and drive it out. When the spider emerges, the wasp attacks, paralyzes its victim, drags it back into its own tube, shuts and fastens the trapdoor, and deposits a single egg upon the spider's abdomen. Other psammocharids will drag a heavy spider back to a previously prepared cluster of clay or mud cells. Some amputate a spider's legs to make the passage easier. Others fly back over water, skimming a buoyant spider along the surface. 13

Some wasps must battle with other parasites over a host's body. *Rhyssella curvipes* can detect the larvae of wood wasps deep within alder wood and drill down to its potential victims with its sharply ridged ovipositor. *Pseudorhyssa alpestris*, a related parasite, cannot drill directly into wood since its slender ovipositor bears only rudimentary cutting ridges. It locates the holes made by *Rhyssella*, inserts its ovipositor, and lays an egg on the host (already conveniently paralyzed by *Rhyssella*), right next to the egg deposited by its relative. The two eggs hatch at about the same time, but the larva of *Pseudorhyssa* has a bigger head bearing much larger mandibles. *Pseudorhyssa* seizes the smaller *Rhyssella* larva, destroys it, and proceeds to feast upon a banquet already well prepared. 14

Other praises for the efficiency of mothers invoke the themes of early, quick, and often. Many ichneumons don't even wait for their hosts to develop into larvae, but parasitize the egg directly (larval wasps may then either drain the egg itself or enter the developing host larva). Others simply move fast. *Apanteles militaris* can deposit up to seventy-two eggs in a single second. Still others are doggedly persistent. *Aphidius gomezi* females produce up to 1,500 eggs and can parasitize as many as 600 aphids in a single working day. In a bizarre twist upon "often," some wasps indulge in polyembryony, a kind of iterated supertwinning. A single egg divides into cells that aggregate into as many as 500 individuals. Since some polyembryonic wasps parasitize caterpillars much larger than themselves and may lay up to six eggs in each, as many as 3,000 larvae may develop within, and feed 15 upon, a single host. These wasps are endoparasites and do not paralyze their victims. The caterpillars writhe back and forth, not (one suspects) from pain, but merely in response to the commotion induced by thousands of wasp larvae feeding within.

The efficiency of mothers is matched by their larval offspring. I 16
have already mentioned the pattern of eating less essential parts first, thus keeping the host alive and fresh to its final and merciful dispatch. After the larva digests every edible morsel of its victim (if only to prevent later fouling of its abode by decaying tissue), it may still use the outer shell of its host. One aphid parasite cuts a hole in the belly of its victim's shell, glues the skeleton to a leaf by sticky secretions from its salivary gland, and then spins a cocoon to pupate within the aphid's shell.

In using inappropriate anthropocentric language in this romp 17
through the natural history of ichneumons, I have tried to emphasize just why these wasps became a preeminent challenge to natural theology—the antiquated doctrine that attempted to infer God's essence from the products of his creation. I have used twentieth-century examples for the most part, but all themes were known and stressed by the great nineteenth-century natural theologians. How then did they square the habits of these wasps with the goodness of God? How did they extract themselves from this dilemma of their own making?

The strategies were as varied as the practitioners; they shared only 18
the theme of special pleading for an a priori doctrine[4]—they knew that God's benevolence was lurking somewhere behind all these tales of apparent horror. Charles Lyell[5] for example, in the first edition of his epochal *Principles of Geology* (1830–1833), decided that caterpillars posed such a threat to vegetation that any natural checks upon them could only reflect well upon a creating deity, for caterpillars would destroy human agriculture "did not Providence put causes in operation to keep them in due bounds."

The Reverend William Kirby[6], rector of Barham and Britain's fore- 19

---

[4]***an a priori doctrine*** *A priori* means beforehand, and Gould refers to those who approach a scientific situation with a preestablished view in mind. He is suggesting that such an approach prevents the kind of objectivity and fairness that scientific examination is supposed to produce.

[5]***Charles Lyell (1797–1875)*** An English geologist who established the glacial layers of the Eocene (dawn of recent), Miocene (less recent), and Pliocene (more recent) epochs during his excavations of Tertiary period strata in Italy. He was influential in urging Darwin to publish his theories. His work is still respected.

[6]***The Reverend William Kirby (1759–1850)*** An English specialist in insects. He was the author of a Bridgewater Treatise, *The History, Habits, and Instincts of Animals* (2 vols., 1835).

most entomologist, chose to ignore the plight of caterpillars and focused instead upon the virtue of mother love displayed by wasps in
provisioning their young with such care.

> The great object of the female is to discover a proper nidus for her eggs.
> In search of this she is in constant motion. Is the caterpillar of a but-
> terfly or moth the appropriate food for her young? You see her alight
> upon the plants where they are most usually to be met with, run
> quickly over them, carefully examining every leaf, and, having found
> the unfortunate object of her search, insert her sting into its flesh, and
> there deposit an egg. . . . The active Ichneumon braves every danger,
> and does not desist until her courage and address have insured subsist-
> ence for one of her future progeny.

Kirby found this solicitude all the more remarkable because the 20
female wasp will never see her child and enjoy the pleasures of parent-
hood. Yet her love compels her to danger nonetheless:

> A very large proportion of them are doomed to die before their young
> come into existence. But in these the passion is not extinguished. . . .
> When you witness the solicitude with which they provide for the se-
> curity and sustenance of their future young, you can scarcely deny to
> them love for a progeny they are never destined to behold.

Kirby also put in a good word for the marauding larvae, praising 21
them for their forbearance in eating selectively to keep their caterpillar
prey alive. Would we all husband our resources with such care!

> In this strange and apparently cruel operation one circumstance is truly
> remarkable. The larva of the Ichneumon, though every day, perhaps for
> months, it gnaws the inside of the caterpillar, and though at last it has
> devoured almost every part of it except the skin and intestines, care-
> fully all this time it avoids injuring the vital organs, as if aware that its
> own existence depends on that of the insect upon which it preys! . . .
> What would be the impression which a similar instance amongst the
> race of quadrupeds would make upon us? If, for example, an animal
> . . . should be found to feed upon the inside of a dog, devouring only
> those parts not essential to life, while it cautiously left uninjured the
> heart, arteries, lungs, and intestines—should we not regard such an in-
> stance as a perfect prodigy, as an example of instinctive forebearance
> almost miraculous? [The last three quotes come from the 1856, and last
> pre-Darwinian, edition of Kirby and Spence's *Introduction to Entomol-
> ogy*.]

This tradition of attempting to read moral meaning from nature did 22
not cease with the triumph of evolutionary theory after Darwin published *On the Origin of Species* in 1859—for evolution could be read

as God's chosen method of peopling our planet, and ethical messages might still populate nature. Thus, St. George Mivart,[7] one of Darwin's most effective evolutionary critics and a devout Catholic, argued that "many amiable and excellent people" had been misled by the apparent suffering of animals for two reasons. First, however much it might hurt, "physical suffering and moral evil are simply incommensurable." Since beasts are not moral agents, their feelings cannot bear any ethical message. But secondly, lest our visceral sensitivities still be aroused, Mivart assures us that animals must feel little, if any, pain. Using a favorite racist argument of the time—that "primitive" people suffer far less than advanced and cultured people—Mivart extrapolated further down the ladder of life into a realm of very limited pain indeed: Physical suffering, he argued,

> depends greatly upon the mental condition of the sufferer. Only during consciousness does it exist, and only in the most highly organized men does it reach its acme. The author has been assured that lower races of men appear less keenly sensitive to physical suffering than do more cultivated and refined human beings. Thus only in man can there really be any intense degree of suffering, because only in him is there that intellectual recollection of past moments and that anticipation of future ones, which constitute in great part the bitterness of suffering. The momentary pang, the present pain, which beasts endure, though real enough, is yet, doubtless, not to be compared as to its intensity with the suffering which is produced in man thorugh his high prerogative of self-consciousness [from *Genesis of Species*, 1871].

It took Darwin himself to derail this ancient tradition—in that gentle way so characteristic of his radical intellectual approach to nearly everything. The ichneumons also troubled Darwin greatly and he wrote of them to Asa Gray[8] in 1860:

> I own that I cannot see as plainly as others do, and as I should wish to do, evidence of design and beneficence on all sides of us. There seems

---

[7]***St. George Mivart (1827–1900)*** English anatomist and biologist who examined the comparative anatomies of insect-eating and meat-eating animals. A convert to Roman Catholicism in 1844, his inability to reconcile religious and evolutionary theories resulted in his excommunication from the church in 1900.

[8]***Asa Gray (1810–1888)*** America's most important botanist. His works, which are still considered important, are *Structural Botany* (1879), *The Elements of Botany* (1887), *How Plants Grow* (1858), and *How Plants Behave* (1872). Gray was a serious critic of Darwin and wrote a great number of letters to him; but he was also a firm believer in Darwinian evolution. Since he was also a well-known member of an evangelical Protestant faith, he was effective in countering religious attacks on Darwin by showing that there is no conflict between Darwinism and religion.

to me too much misery in the world. I cannot persuade myself that a beneficent and omnipotent God would have designedly created the Ichneumonidae with the express intention of their feeding within the living bodies of Caterpillars, or that a cat should play with mice.

Indeed, he had written with more passion to Joseph Hooker[9] in 1856: "What a book a devil's chaplain might write on the clumsy, wasteful, blundering, low, and horribly cruel works of nature!"

This honest admission—that nature is often (by our standards) cruel and that all previous attempts to find a lurking goodness behind everything represent just so much absurd special pleading—can lead in two directions. One might retain the principle that nature holds moral messages for humans, but reverse the usual perspective and claim that morality consists in understanding the ways of nature and doing the opposite. Thomas Henry Huxley[10] advanced this argument in his famous essay on *Evolution and Ethics* (1893): 24

> The practice of that which is ethically best—what we call goodness or virtue—involves a course of conduct which, in all respects, is opposed to that which leads to success in the cosmic struggle for existence. In place of ruthless self-assertion it demands self-restraint; in place of thrusting aside, or treading down, all competitors, it requires that the individual shall not merely respect, but shall help his fellows. . . . It repudiates the gladiatorial theory of existence. . . . Laws and moral precepts are directed to the end of curbing the cosmic process.

The other argument, more radical in Darwin's day but common now, holds that nature simply is as we find it. Our failure to discern the universal good we once expected does not record our lack of insight or ingenuity but merely demonstrates that nature contains no moral messages framed in human terms. Morality is a subject for philosophers, theologians, students of the humanities, indeed for all thinking people. The answers will not be read passively from nature; they do not, and cannot, arise from the data of science. The factual 25

---

[9]*Joseph Hooker (1817–1911)* English botanist who studied flowers in exotic locations such as Tasmania, the Antarctic, New Zealand, and India. He was, along with Charles Lyell, a friend of Darwin and one of those who urged him to publish *On the Origin of Species*. He was the director of London's Kew Gardens from 1855–1885.

[10]*Thomas Henry Huxley (1825–1895)* An English naturalist who, quite independent of organizations and formal support, became one of the most important scientists of his time. He searched for a theory of evolution that was based on a rigorous examination of the facts and found, in Darwin's work, the theory that he could finally respect. He was a strong champion of Darwin.

state of the world does not teach us how we, with our powers for good and evil, should alter or preserve it in the most ethical manner.

Darwin himself tended toward this view, although he could not, as 26 a man of his time, thoroughly abandon the idea that laws of nature might reflect some higher purpose. He clearly recognized that the specific manifestations of those laws—cats playing with mice, and ichneumon larvae eating caterpillars—could not embody ethical messages, but he somehow hoped that unknown higher laws might exist "with the details, whether good or bad, left to the working out of what we may call chance."

Since ichneumons are a detail, and since natural selection is a law 27 regulating details, the answer to the ancient dilemma of why such cruelty (in our terms) exists in nature can only be that there isn't any answer—and that the framing of the question "in our terms" is thoroughly inappropriate in a natural world neither made for us nor ruled by us. It just plain happens. It is a strategy that works for ichneumons and that natural selection has programmed into their behavioral repertoire. Caterpillars are not suffering to teach us something; they have simply been outmaneuvered, for now, in the evolutionary game. Perhaps they will evolve a set of adequate defenses sometime in the future, thus sealing the fate of ichneumons. And perhaps, indeed probably, they will not.

Another Huxley, Thomas's grandson Julian,[11] spoke for this posi- 28 tion, using as an example—yes, you guessed it—the ubiquitous ichneumons:

> Natural selection, in fact, though like the mills of God in grinding slowly and grinding small, has few other attributes that a civilized religion would call divine. . . . Its products are just as likely to be aesthetically, morally, or intellectually repulsive to us as they are to be attractive. We need only think of the ugliness of *Sacculina* or a bladderworm, the stupidity of a rhinoceros or a stegosaur, the horror of a female mantis devouring its mate or a brood of ichneumon flies slowly eating out a caterpillar.

It is amusing in this context, or rather ironic since it is too serious to be amusing, that modern creationists accuse evolutionists of preaching a specific ethical doctrine called secular humanism and thereby demand equal time for their unscientific and discredited views. If nature is nonmoral, then evolution cannot teach any ethical theory at all. The

---

[11]***Thomas's grandson, Julian*** Julian Huxley (1887–1975), an English biologist and a brother of the novelist Aldous Huxley.

assumption that it can has abetted a panoply of social evils that ideo-
logues falsely read into nature from their beliefs—eugenics and (mis-
named) social Darwinism prominently among them. Not only did Darwin eschew any attempt to discover an antireligious ethic in nature,
he also expressly stated his personal bewilderment about such deep
issues as the problem of evil. Just a few sentences after invoking the
ichneumons, and in words that express both the modesty of this splendid man and the compatibility, through lack of contact, between science and true religion, Darwin wrote to Asa Gray,

> I feel most deeply that the whole subject is too profound for the human
> intellect. A dog might as well speculate on the mind of Newton. Let
> each man hope and believe what he can.

QUESTIONS

1. What is the chief theological problem presented in this essay?
2. Is this essay primarily a scientific one? What signs point to Gould's efforts
   to be scientific rather than sociologic or theologic?
3. Do people of our age feel the same sort of dilemma regarding nature as
   nineteenth-century theologians did?
4. Explain the process by which the ichneumon parasitizes its host.
5. What do you think is the most important part of Gould's argument that
   nature is nonmoral?

WRITING ASSIGNMENTS

1. In a brief essay, try to answer the question Gould examines in paragraph
   1: "Why are we surrounded with pain, suffering, and apparently senseless
   cruelty in the animal world?"
2. Is the fact of such pain, suffering, and apparently senseless cruelty a religious issue? If so, in what way is it? If not, demonstrate why.
3. In paragraph 17, Gould describes natural theology as "the antiquated doctrine that attempted to infer God's essence from the products of his creation." Is this a reasonable description of natural theology as you understand it? In the process of answering this question, clarify what a theology
   that based its claims in an observation of nature would be able to claim
   about the essence of God. What kind of religion would be possible if all
   theology were based on the behavior of natural life, including ichneumons?
4. Thomas Henry Huxley, in paragraph 24, refers to a "gladiatorial theory of
   existence." What kind of theory of existence would develop from thinking
   of nature—both animal and human—in terms of the behavior of gladia-

tors? Establish the gladiatorial theory of nature and then explain how it would alter human nature if we were to shape our lives by it.

5. Gould points out that even after having established his theory of evolution, Darwin could not "thoroughly abandon the idea that laws of nature might reflect some higher purpose" (para. 26). Assuming that you are in agreement with Darwin but that you also see the problems that Gould has presented us, clarify what the higher purpose of a nature such as Gould describes might be. Does Gould's description of the behavior of the ichneumon (or any other) predator in any way compromise the idea that nature has a higher purpose? Does Gould hold that it has a higher purpose?

6. Compare this essay with Francis Bacon's "The Four Idols." What intellectual issues does it share with Bacon's essay? Is there a common ground between them regarding science and their attitude toward religion? What is it? What might Francis Bacon have decided about the ultimate ethical issues raised by a consideration of the ichneumon? Do you think that Bacon would have held the same views about the ichneumon's predatory powers as did the nineteenth-century theologians? That is, would he have conceived of nature in ethical/moral terms?

PART FIVE

IDEAS IN THE WORLD OF PHILOSOPHY

—⟨∞⟩—

Plato · · · *John Locke*
Bertrand Russell · · · *Simone Weil*
Paul Tillich

INTRODUCTION

Philosophy has no traceable beginnings and no imaginable endings. But for most Western thinkers its roots reach down to the giants of the golden age of Athenian Greece: Socrates; his student, Plato; and Plato's student, Aristotle. Since their time, philosophy has developed innumerable schools, movements, and waves of influence. Every age has had to evolve philosophical systems to help characterize the problems of the times, put them into an intellectual perspective, and begin the clarification of thought that is essential to every reflective human being. As Socrates said, "The unexamined life is not worth living." Philosophers, by nature, are examiners of life. The result of their work is to help increase our understanding of why life is worth living and, by extension, how we can make our own lives more worthwhile.

The first selection in this part, Plato's "The Allegory of the Cave," is the premier document in ancient Greek philosophy. Its influence on later thought has been remarkable. Plato pictures us as being like people who live in a cave watching shadows on the wall before us. We think those shadows are real because we can see no other features of the real world. In fact, however, the shadows are the appearances of things, the sensory qualities—which, he holds, are all that we can ever hope to apprehend. Plato tells us that there is something behind sensory qualities, some *reality* that, because we are limited by our senses, we cannot see or even imagine. Plato insists that the *real* can exist only in a pure spiritual realm. And since, in the Platonic scheme of things, we originally came from that realm, we have a dim memory of the real—equivalent, in a sense, to John Locke's innate ideas—and we interpret our sensory experience in accordance with our memory. Thus, there is a resemblance between the spiritual ideal and the sensory experiences we have; but the resemblance is merely as close as the shadows in the cave are to the people who cast them.

John Locke, a seventeenth-century English philosopher, lived in turbulent times and found himself in a nation whose religious views shifted dramatically from Puritanism to Anglicanism to Catholicism and back to Anglicanism with astonishing rapidity. This disorientation of one of the most fundamental areas of belief tended to disorient philosophers regarding what could be known with certainty. Locke, who was a Puritan at heart, clung to human reason as a basis for discovering the truth about things, and in the manner of the Puritan, who always felt belief to be a matter of personal conscience, he insisted on the power of the individual to conceive the most important truths. An external authority was not needed.

Among modern philosophers, English Nobel Prize winner Bertrand Russell must be viewed as a major force. He is also a brilliant writer. His discussion of "A Free Man's Worship" is elegantly phrased and remarkably worded. He warns us that we must be cautious as moderns to avoid worshiping mere power, whether it takes the form of political force, money, or influence. Rather, we must look within our own natures to discover the sources of human goodness. We are alone in the universe, we must recognize our own best natures. Out of that recognition comes a source of worship that befits a modern civilization.

The French philosopher Simone Weil wrote "Spiritual Autobiography" as a letter to a priest during World War II. Her concerns, like Russell's, are with the ways in which she can establish her own faith and maintain her own integrity. Weil was born a Jew but felt herself to be essentially a Christian. Her religious beliefs were stimulated by her reading the English seventeenth-century religious poets George Herbert, Richard Crashaw, and John Donne. She felt her faith to be ecstatic and mystical—much as those poets did—and she resisted baptism into the church in part because she wanted her faith to be personal instead of institutional. She felt a deep communion with Christ, which she discusses in a philosophical way while writing to her friend, and she explains herself clearly and patiently. She is an example of a modern philosopher confronted by ideas and feelings that we associate with an earlier time. Yet, her own times were a period of such extraordinary crisis that there is no question that intense moments of soul-searching would occur in the lives of intellectuals like Weil.

The philosopher Paul Tillich, born in Germany, is more properly known as a theologian, and his "Symbols of Faith," is less personal than Weil's essay. Tillich writes not about his own beliefs but about belief itself. He believes that faith is expressed in symbols and that a proper understanding of the symbolic language of faith is essential if the meaning of faith is to be achieved. He demonstrates the problems connected with objectifying matters of faith—much in the manner of Russell in his discussion of the worship of physical phenomena like volcanoes. Tillich is interested in establishing the reality of, and maintaining faith in, the infinitude of God. He tells us that any effort to restrict God as a being occupying a specific place is an effort to make God finite like us: it is a subtle form of modern materialism.

Philosophy is the process by which we rigorously examine life. By practicing it, we make life—and our own lives—more valuable. We make life worth living because by practicing philosophy we are doing something that is unique to human beings: reflecting on our own nature. We know of nothing else in the universe that can do that. Being philosophical is both unique and essential to the human condition.

The rhetorical range of these essays is interesting, especially since most philosophers confront the problems inherent in addressing very abstract subject matter. Plato solves his problem by using an allegory to communicate his views. Locke, in contrast, relies on logical analysis and argumentation. He has confidence in reason's capacity to understand matters of philosophical debate, and his essay is a model of arriving at truth by means of argument. Russell relies on analysis, the separation of the totality of his subject into parts. He takes one element of his subject, discusses it thoroughly, then goes on to the next element. He also uses the device of the summary to remind us of what we have learned as we proceed through the essay.

One of Weil's rhetorical strategies is to appear to have none; she is writing a letter, much as Martin Luther King, Jr., did. And some of the same kinds of effects he achieves through knowing his audience well are also achieved by her. She is relaxed and direct, and she can allude to events and writers who are known to her audience. Of course, her letter, like most of what she wrote, was written with an eye to the larger audience of her readers. Thus, there is a sense of formality and completeness that we usually do not attempt in personal letters. Tillich writes in a much different tradition, that of the philosophical argument. His reasoning, like Locke's, is deliberate and detailed. He relies heavily on definition, from which he proceeds to establish the position he thinks is logically implied by his terms and his understanding of those terms.

One surprise may come from realizing that some of these philosophers employ intense imagery and creative metaphor. But doing this is one of the ways they can use to deal effectively with the abstract nature of their subject since imagery and metaphor make things more concrete. And, while being philosophical may be a very abstract experience—and the highest calling of reflective humankind—the use of strictly abstract terminology is not absolutely necessary to the process of explaining a philosophical position. The appropriate use of rhetorical strategies, in reference to both organization and style, pay rich rewards when the mode of address is philosophical.

PLATO

The Allegory of the Cave

PLATO *(428–347 B.C.) was born into an aristocratic Athenian family and educated according to the best precepts available. He eventually became a student of Socrates and later involved himself closely with Socrates' work and teaching. Plato was not only Socrates' finest student but was also the student who immortalized Socrates in his works. Most of Plato's works are philosophical essays, with Socrates as a character speaking in a dialogue with one or more students or listeners. Thus, Plato permits us the vision of Socrates written by one who knew him and listened carefully to what he said.*

The times in which Plato lived were turbulent indeed. In 404 B.C. Athens was defeated by Sparta and was governed by tyrants. Political life in Athens was dangerous. Plato felt, however, that he could effect positive change in Athenian politics until, in 384 B.C., Socrates was tried unjustly for corrupting the youth of Athens and put to death. After that, Plato withdrew from public life and devoted himself to writing and to the Academy which he founded in an olive grove in Athens. The Academy endured for almost a thousand years, which tells us how greatly Plato's thought was valued.

From *The Republic.* Translated by Benjamin Jowett.

Although it is not easy to condense Plato's views, he may be said to have held the world of sense perception as inferior to the world of ideal entities that exist only in a pure spiritual realm. These ideals, or forms, had been perceived directly by everyone before birth, and then dimly remembered here on earth. But the memory, even dim as it is, makes it possible for people to understand what is perceived by the senses despite the fact that the senses are so unreliable and perceptions are so imperfect.

This view of reality has long been important to philosophers because it gives a philosophical basis to antimaterialistic thought. It values the spirit first and frees people from the tyranny of sensory perception and sensory reward. In the case of love, Plato held that Eros leads us to a reverence for the body and its pleasures; but the thrust of his teaching is that the body is a metaphor for spiritual delights. Plato assures us that the body is only a starting point and that it can eventually lead both to spiritual fulfillment and to the appreciation of true beauty.

"The Allegory of the Cave" is, on the one hand, a discussion of politics—the Republic *is a treatise on justice and the ideal government. On the other hand, it has long stood for a kind of demonstration of the fact that if our perceptions are what we must rely upon to know the truth about the world, then we actually know very little about it. We know what we perceive, but we have no way of knowing anything beyond that.*

This allegory has been persuasive for centuries and remains at the center of thought that attempts to counter the pleasures of the sensual life. Most religions aim for spiritual refinement and praise the qualities of the soul, which lies beyond perception. Thus, it comes as no surprise that Christianity and other religions have not only praised Plato but have developed systems of thought that bear a close resemblance to his. Later refinements of his thought, usually called Neo-Platonism, have been influential even into modern times.

PLATO'S RHETORIC

Two very important rhetorical techniques are at work in the following selection. The first and more obvious—at least on one level— is the reliance on the allegory, a story in which the characters and situations are meant to resemble people and situations in another context. It is a difficult technique to use well, although we have the example of Aesop's fables in which hares and tortoises represent people and their foibles. *The advantage of the technique is that a complex and sometimes unpopular argument can be fought and won before the audience realizes that an argument is being fought. The disadvantage of the technique is that the terms of the allegory may only approximate the situation which it reflects; thus, the argument may fail to be convincing.*

Another rhetorical technique Plato uses is the dialogue. In fact, it is a hallmark of Plato's work, since most of his writings are called dialogues. The Symposium, Apology, Phaedo, Crito, Meno, *and most of the famous works are all written in dialogue form. Usually Socrates is speaking to a student or a friend about highly abstract issues. Socrates asks questions which require simple answers. Slowly, the questioning proceeds to unravel the answers to the most complex of issues.*

This use of the question-and-answer dialogue is basically the Socratic method. Socrates analyzes the answer to each question, examines the implications of those answers, then asserts the truth. The method is functional in part because Plato's theory is that people do not learn things; they remember them. That is, since people came originally from heaven, where they knew the truth, they already possess that knowledge and must recover it by means of the dialogue. Socrates' method is ideally suited to that purpose.

Beyond these techniques, however, we must look at Plato's style. It is true that he is working with very difficult ideas, but the style of the work is so clear, simple, and direct that few people would have trouble understanding what is said at any given moment. Considering the influence this work has had on world thought and the reputation Plato had earned by the time he came to write the Republic, *it is remarkable that the style is so plain and so accessible. It is significant that such a great mind can express itself with such impressive clarity. Part of that capacity is due to Plato's respect for rhetoric and its proper uses.*

The Allegory of the Cave

SOCRATES, GLAUCON. The den, the prisoners: the light at a distance;

And now, I said, let me show in a figure how far our 1 nature is enlightened or unenlightened:—Behold! human beings living in an underground den, which has a mouth open towards the light and reaching all along the den; here they have been from their childhood, and have their legs and necks chained so that they cannot move, and can only see before them, being prevented by the chains from turning round their heads. Above and behind them a fire is blazing at a distance, and between the fire and the prisoners there is a raised way; and you will see, if you look, a low wall built along the way, like the screen which marionette players have in front of them, over which they show the puppets.

I see. 2

the low wall, and the moving figures of which the shadows are seen on the opposite wall of the den.

And do you see, I said, men passing along the wall 3 carrying all sorts of vessels, and statues and figures of animals made of wood and stone and various materials, which appear over the wall? Some of them are talking, others silent.

You have shown me a strange image, and they are 4 strange prisoners.

Like ourselves, I replied; and they see only their own 5 shadows, or the shadows of one another, which the fire throws on the opposite wall of the cave?

True, he said; how could they see anything but the 6 shadows if they were never allowed to move their heads?

And of the objects which are being carried in like 7 manner they would only see the shadows?

Yes, he said. 8

And if they were able to converse with one another, 9 would they not suppose that they were naming what was actually before them?

Very true. 10

And suppose further that the prison had an echo 11 which came from the other side, would they not be sure

502

The prisoners would mistake the shadows for realities.

to fancy when one of the passers-by spoke that the voice which they heard came from the passing shadow?

No question, he replied. 12

To them, I said, the truth would be literally nothing 13 but the shadows of the images.

That is certain. 14

And now look again, and see what will naturally fol- 15 low if the prisoners are released and disabused of their error. At first, when any of them is liberated and compelled suddenly to stand up and turn his neck round and walk and look towards the light, he will suffer sharp pains; the glare will distress him, and he will be unable to see the realities of which in his former state he had seen the shadows; and then conceive some one saying to him, that what he saw before was an illusion, but that now, when he is approaching nearer to being and his eye is turned towards more real existence, he has a clearer

And when released, they would still persist in maintaining the superior truth of the shadows.

vision—what will be his reply? And you may further imagine that his instructor is pointing to the objects as they pass and requiring him to name them,—will he not be perplexed? Will he not fancy that the shadows which he formerly saw are truer than the objects which are now shown to him?

Far truer. 16

And if he is compelled to look straight at the light, 17 will he not have a pain in his eyes which will make him turn away to take refuge in the objects of vision which he can see, and which he will conceive to be in reality clearer than the things which are now being shown to him?

True, he said. 18

When dragged upwards, they would be dazzled by excess of light.

And suppose once more, that he is reluctantly 19 dragged up a steep and rugged ascent, and held fast until he is forced into the presence of the sun himself, is he not likely to be pained and irritated? When he approaches the light his eyes will be dazzled, and he will not be able to see anything at all of what are now called realities.

Not all in a moment, he said. 20

He will require to grow accustomed to the sight of 21 the upper world. And first he will see the shadows best, next the reflections of men and other objects in the water, and then the objects themselves; then he will gaze upon the light of the moon and the stars and the spangled heaven; and he will see the sky and the stars by night better than the sun or the light of the sun by day?

Certainly.

At length they will see the sun and understand his nature.

Last of all he will be able to see the sun, and not mere 23 reflections of him in the water, but he will see him in his own proper place, and not in another; and he will contemplate him as he is.

Certainly.

24

He will then proceed to argue that this is he who 25 gives the season and the years, and is the guardian of all that is in the visible world, and in a certain way the cause of all things which he and his fellows have been accustomed to behold?

Clearly, he said, he would first see the sun and then 26 reason about him.

They would then pity their old companions of the den.

And when he remembered his old habitation, and the 27 wisdom of the den and his fellow prisoners, do you not suppose that he would felicitate himself on the change, and pity them?

Certainly, he would.

28

And if they were in the habit of conferring honors 29 among themselves on those who were quickest to observe the passing shadows and to remark which of them went before, and which followed after, and which were together; and who were therefore best able to draw conclusions as to the future, do you think that he would care for such honors and glories, or envy the possessors of them? Would he not say with Homer,

> Better to be the poor servant of a poor master,

and to endure anything, rather than think as they do and live after their manner?

Yes, he said, I think that he would rather suffer any- 30 thing than entertain these false notions and live in this miserable manner.

Imagine once more, I said, such an one coming sud- 31 denly out of the sun to be replaced in his old situation; would he not be certain to have his eyes full of darkness?

To be sure, he said. 32

And if there were a contest, and he had to compete 33 in measuring the shadows with the prisoners who had never moved out of the den, while his sight was still weak, and before his eyes had become steady (and the time which would be needed to acquire this new habit of sight might be very considerable), would he not be ridiculous? Men would say of him that up he went and down he came without his eyes; and that it was better not even to think of ascending; and if any one tried to loose another and lead him up to the light, let them only catch the offender, and they would put him to death.

No question, he said. 34

This entire allegory, I said, you may now append, dear 35 Glaucon, to the previous argument; the prison house is the world of sight, the light of the fire is the sun, and you will not misapprehend me if you interpret the journey upwards to be the ascent of the soul into the intellectual world according to my poor belief, which, at your desire, I have expressed—whether rightly or wrongly God knows. But, whether true or false, my opinion is that in the world of knowledge the idea of good appears last of all, and is seen only with an effort; and, when seen, is also inferred to be the universal author of all things beautiful and right, parent of light and of the lord of light in this visible world, and the immediate source of reason and truth in the intellectual; and that this is the power upon which he who would act rationally either in public or private life must have his eye fixed.

I agree, he said, as far as I am able to understand you. 36

Moreover, I said, you must not wonder that those 37 who attain to this beatific vision are unwilling to descend to human affairs; for their souls are ever hastening into the upper world where they desire to dwell; which desire of theirs is very natural, if our allegory may be trusted.

Yes, very natural. 38

And is there anything surprising in one who passes 39 from divine contemplations to the evil state of man, misbehaving himself in a ridiculous manner; if, while his eyes are blinking and before he has become accustomed

But when they returned to the den they would see much worse than those who had never left it.

The prison is the world of sight, the light of the fire is the sun.

Nothing extraordinary in the philosopher being unable to see in the dark.

to the surrounding darkness, he is compelled to fight in courts of law, or in other places, about the images or the shadows of images of justice, and is endeavoring to meet the conceptions of those who have never yet seen absolute justice?

Anything but surprising, he replied. 40

The eyes may be blinded in two ways, by excess or by defect of light.

Anyone who has common sense will remember that 41 the bewilderments of the eyes are of two kinds, and arise from two causes, either from coming out of the light or from going into the light, which is true of the mind's eye, quite as much as of the bodily eye; and he who remembers this when he sees anyone whose vision is perplexed and weak, will not be too ready to laugh; he will first ask whether that soul of man has come out of the brighter life, and is unable to see because unaccustomed to the dark, or having turned from darkness to the day is dazzled by excess of light. And he will count the one happy in his condition and state of being, and he will pity the other; or, if he have a mind to laugh at the soul which comes from below into the light, there will be more reason in this than in the laugh which greets him who returns from above out of the light into the den.

That, he said, is a very just distinction. 42

The conversion of the soul is the turning round the eye from darkness to light.

But then, if I am right, certain professors of education 43 must be wrong when they say that they can put a knowledge into the soul which was not there before, like sight into blind eyes.

They undoubtedly say this, he replied. 44

Whereas, our argument shows that the power and ca- 45 pacity of learning exists in the soul already; and that just as the eye was unable to turn from darkness to light without the whole body, so too the instrument of knowledge can only by the movement of the whole soul be turned from the world of becoming into that of being, and learn by degrees to endure the sight of being, and of the brightest and best of being, or in other words, of the good.

Very true. 46

And must there not be some art which will effect 47 conversion in the easiest and quickest manner; not implanting the faculty of sight, for that exists already, but has been turned in the wrong direction, and is looking away from the truth?

Yes, he said, such an art may be presumed. 48

The virtue of wisdom has a divine power which may be turned either towards good or towards evil.

And whereas the other so-called virtues of the soul 49 seem to be akin to bodily qualities, for even when they are not originally innate they can be implanted later by habit and exercise, the virtue of wisdom more than anything else contains a divine element which always remains, and by this conversion is rendered useful and profitable; or, on the other hand, hurtful and useless. Did you never observe the narrow intelligence flashing from the keen eye of a clever rogue—how eager he is, how clearly his paltry soul sees the way to his end; he is the reverse of blind, but his keen eyesight is forced into the service of evil, and he is mischievous in proportion to his cleverness?

Very true, he said. 50

But what if there had been a circumcision of such na- 51 tures in the days of their youth; and they had been severed from those sensual pleasures, such as eating and drinking, which, like leaden weights, were attached to them at their birth, and which drag them down and turn the vision of their souls upon the things that are below— if, I say, they had been released from these impediments and turned in the opposite direction, the very same faculty in them would have seen the truth as keenly as they see what their eyes are turned to now.

Very likely. 52

Neither the uneducated nor the overeducated will be good servants of the State.

Yes, I said; and there is another thing which is likely, 53 or rather a necessary inference from what has preceded, that neither the uneducated and uninformed of the truth, nor yet those who never make an end of their education, will be able ministers of State; not the former, because they have no single aim of duty which is the rule of all their actions, private as well as public; nor the latter, because they will not act at all except upon compulsion, fancying that they are already dwelling apart in the islands of the blessed.

Very true, he replied. 54

Then, I said, the business of us who are the founders 55 of the State will be to compel the best minds to attain that knowledge which we have already shown to be the greatest of all—they must continue to ascend until they arrive at the good; but when they have ascended and seen enough we must not allow them to do as they do now.

What do you mean? 56

Men should ascend to the upper world, but they should also return to the lower.

I mean that they remain in the upper world: but this 57 must not be allowed; they must be made to descend again among the prisoners in the den, and partake of their labors and honors, whether they are worth having or not.

But is not this unjust? he said; ought we to give them 58 a worse life, when they might have a better?

You have again forgotten, my friend, I said, the inten- 59 tion of the legislator, who did not aim at making any one class in the State happy above the rest; the happiness was to be in the whole State, and he held the citizens together by persuasion and necessity, making them bene-factors of the State, and therefore benefactors of one an-other; to this end he created them, not to please them-selves, but to be his instruments in binding up the State.

True, he said, I had forgotten. 60

The duties of philosophers.

Observe, Glaucon, that there will be no injustice in 61 compelling our philosophers to have a care and provi-dence of others; we shall explain to them that in other States, men of their class are not obliged to share in the toils of politics: and this is reasonable, for they grow up at their own sweet will, and the government would rather not have them. Being self-taught, they cannot be expected to show any gratitude for a culture which they have never received. But we have brought you into the world to be rulers of the hive, kings of yourselves and of the other citizens, and have educated you far better and more perfectly than they have been educated, and you

Their obligations to their country will induce them to take part in her government.

are better able to share in the double duty. Wherefore each of you, when his turn comes, must go down to the general underground abode, and get the habit of seeing in the dark. When you have acquired the habit, you will see ten thousand times better than the inhabitants of the den, and you will know what the several images are, and what they represent, because you have seen the beautiful and just and good in their truth. And thus our State, which is also yours, will be a reality, and not a dream

only, and will be administered in a spirit unlike that of
other States, in which men fight with one another about
shadows only and are distracted in the struggle for
power, which in their eyes is a great good. Whereas the
truth is that the State in which the rulers are most reluctant to govern is always the best and most quietly governed, and the State in which they are most eager, the
worst.

Quite true, he replied. 62

And will our pupils, when they hear this, refuse to 63
take their turn at the toils of State, when they are allowed to spend the greater part of their time with one
another in the heavenly light?

They will be
willing but not
anxious to
rule.

Impossible, he answered; for they are just men, and 64
the commands which we impose upon them are just;
there can be no doubt that every one of them will take
office as a stern necessity, and not after the fashion of
our present rulers of State.

The statesman
must be
provided with
a better life
than that of a
ruler; and then
he will not
covet office.

Yes, my friend, I said; and there lies the point. You 65
must contrive for your future rulers another and a better
life than that of a ruler, and then you may have a well-
ordered State; for only in the State which offers this, will
they rule who are truly rich, not in silver and gold, but
in virtue and wisdom, which are the true blessings of
life. Whereas if they go to the administration of public
affairs, poor and hungering after their own private advantage, thinking that hence they are to snatch the chief
good, order there can never be; for they will be fighting
about office, and the civil and domestic broils which
thus arise will be the ruin of the rulers themselves and
of the whole State.

Most true, he replied. 66

And the only life which looks down upon the life of 67
political ambition is that of true philosophy. Do you
know of any other?

Indeed, I do not, he said. 68

QUESTIONS

1. What does the situation seem to be in this dialogue? What would you say the relationship is between Socrates and Glaucon?
2. What is the allegory of the cave meant to represent?
3. Determine which of the following concepts seems most important in the dialogue: "truth," "justice," "happiness," "law." Is any of these concepts unimportant?
4. Socrates refers to "our philosophers" (para. 61 and elsewhere). What does he mean by that term?
5. How does the allegory relate to our concepts of sensory perception?
6. Are we made aware that Plato—rather than Socrates and Glaucon—is the author of this piece? What is the effect of Plato's presence (or lack of it)?

WRITING ASSIGNMENTS

1. Analyze the allegory of the cave for its strengths and weaknesses. Consider what it is meant to imply for people living in a world of the senses and what Plato implies lies behind that world. Consider the extent to which people are like (or unlike) the figures in the cave. Consider the extent to which the world we know is like the cave. Consider, too, the "revelations" implied in the allegory and its contemplation.
2. Socrates ends the dialogue by saying that after rulers of the state have served their term they must be able to look forward to a better life than that of being rulers. He and Glaucon agree that there is only one life that "looks down upon the life of political ambition"—"that of true philosophy." What is the life of true philosophy? Is it superior to that of being a ruler (or anything else)? How would you define its superiority? What would its qualities be? What would its concerns be? Would you be happy leading such a life?
3. In paragraph 43, Socrates refers to "professors of education." What do you think the nature of education was for Socrates and his pupils? Consider the questions of how education was conducted, who was educated, what the subjects of education must have been, and what the final purpose of education was. Inventory the passage for any references which might give some insight into the nature of education for Plato's contemporaries. If you wish, you may look up the subject of education in an encyclopedia or other resource, but be sure to relate your findings to this selection. Base your essay on the topic of definition.
4. In paragraph 61, Socrates outlines a program that would assure Athens of good rulers and good government. Clarify exactly what the program is, what its problems and benefits are, and how it would have to be put into action. Then decide whether or not the program would work. You may

consider whether or not it would work for our time, for Socrates' time, or both. If possible, use examples (hypothetical or real) to bolster your argument.

5. Socrates states unequivocally that Athens should compel the best and the most intelligent young men to be rulers of the state. Review his reasons for saying so; consider what his concept of the state is; then take a stand on the issue. Is it right to want to compel the best and most intelligent young people to become rulers? If so, would it be proper to compel those well suited for the professions of law, medicine, teaching, or religion to follow those respective callings? Would we not have an ideal society if everyone were forced to practice the calling for which they had the best aptitude?

JOHN LOCKE

On Ideas as the Materials
of All Our Knowledge

JOHN LOCKE *(1632–1704) was a prominent English philosopher whose political and religious beliefs often put him at odds with the established order. His father was a Puritan and an attorney who fought on the side of Parliament and against the king in the English civil wars of the 1640s. This meant that his family's tradition was republican and to some extent liberal (some said radical) in its attitude toward religion. The Puritans desired a purer form of church worship than the king's Anglicanism, which was too much like the religion of the Roman Catholics for the Locke's taste.*

These differences were more than religious. They involved decisions regarding the structure of the church and, to an extent, the structure of the government. Anglicanism, like Catholicism, operated in a hierarchical fashion: there was a single head of the church, the monarch, though the archbishop was directly in charge of church affairs; then there was an array of bishops who governed the church in the regions; and finally there were the priests and laymen. In the Anglican organization, the laymen took no part in the governance of the church, and thus they could not effect change in church matters.

From *Essay Concerning Human Understanding.*

The Puritans sought to break this pattern by eliminating bishops and by transferring authority to laymen—who according to the New Testament—made up the body of the church.

Political and religious affairs (which were often the same thing) during Locke's lifetime saw astonishing changes that affected his life in suprising ways. While he was young, the Puritan governance of England failed, and the Anglican church was restored by King Charles II in 1660, when Locke was a tutor (the equivalent of an instructor) at Christ Church, Oxford. There Locke lectured in Greek, rhetoric, and philosophy. He originally thought he would enter the clergy, but he felt that the restored Anglican church would not provide an atmosphere in which he could freely inquire into the truths of religion. Instead, he turned to medicine as a profession. For the next fifteen years he lived in London in the house of Lord Shaftesbury, an important political figure of the period. Locke continued his studies of philosophy during this time.

One of Locke's interests during this period is manifested in the title of his Essay Concerning Toleration (1666), which obviously reflected his desire to promote religious toleration as opposed to those who favored adherence to only one belief, which was the wish of the essentially conservative restored Anglican church. During the 1670s Locke began sketching his ideas for his most important work, Essay Concerning Human Understanding (1690), which began as a discussion among friends regarding important matters relating to what kinds of knowledge we have and how we have that knowledge. Long before he completed this work, however, he was forced out of England because of the fall into disfavor of his patron, Lord Shaftesbury. Locke went to France for several years, though he eventually returned to England and to Oxford. Later, however, he lived in Holland, and during the period when the Catholic king James II ruled England (1685–1688), Locke became acquainted with William of Orange, who was destined to become James's successor. This led to his returning in triumph to England when William was crowned king. Locke's last years were disappointing to him if only because the hoped-for toleration of religious beliefs did not take place; William was as narrow-minded as those who had preceded him.

In light of this background, one should keep in mind that the selection, which is from Essay Concerning Human Understanding, attempts to show that there is no knowledge that we are born with and no knowledge that we have other than through experience. This belief, which was not self-evident in Locke's time, led him to praise human reason as the most important tool by which the truth could be known. He therefore tended to deny the value of authority as the dispenser of truth. His treatise emphasized the individual's responsibility in clarifying the truth about the world. Instead of holding that certain moral codes were God-given and "imprinted" on the mind before birth, Locke held that everyone is born with a mind like a blank sheet of paper (tabula rasa in Latin) and that the individual's experiences are recorded on the mind.

This view is both a philosophical and a psychological one. It is directed at giving human understanding authority in human affairs because it makes the individual responsible for discovering the truth about the universe and God. It also makes the individual less a receiver of knowledge than a creator of knowledge. The excerpt presented here is Sterling P. Lamprecht's edited version of the first two books of the Essay Concerning Human Understanding. The purpose of these two books is to demonstrate that there is no such thing as innate knowledge and that all the knowledge we possess is a direct result of our daily experience and the operation of the mind.

In Locke's time, such a position was not widely accepted. In our time, it has been thought to be quite reasonable until very recently, when research in linguistics and biology began to constitute a challenge to Locke's theory. Linguist Noam Chomsky of the Massachusetts Institute of Technology has established that there are basic patterns for language acquisition that are in place in the mind at birth and that therefore all human language has certain predetermined patterns. Research in biology has discovered that some animals are born with "imprinted knowledge" in place. For example, even as a chick exits its shell, certain shapes of overhead shadows from other birds "mean" that a predator is overhead, whereas other shapes "mean" that the overhead bird is harmless. Locke may have taken that kind of thing into account when he admits that "there are natural tendencies imprinted on the minds of men" (para. 12). The interesting thing for us, however, is that the question is still quite a lively one.

LOCKE'S RHETORIC

Most of what Locke does in the selection is typical of philosophical writing: he presents an argument designed to establish the validity of a position. Locke sets forth his views, presents his reasons, gives examples which help prove his point, and takes into account contrary arguments and shows their weaknesses. He does this most clearly when he remarks that a statement such as "it is impossible *for the same thing to be, and not to be" (para. 5) is often thought to be among those truths imprinted upon the mind; yet, as he says in paragraphs 5 and 6, it is not imprinted on the minds of children or of idiots. This example alone refutes any argument against his view. It also demonstrates how very difficult it would be for anyone to attack his theory since the defender of the argument that humankind has innate ideas must come up with some ideas that both children and idiots hold in common with everyone else.*

The first book begins with a definition of the term "primary notions," which he derives from the Greek. (Many of his readers, who were learned doctors of theology, would have known Greek.) A loose definition of thinking also is given at the beginning of the second book: "that which his mind is applied about . . . being the ideas that are there" (para. 19). The concepts that are not defined are thought to be commonly intelligible, and no terms are used that are not readily understandable.

The second book is simpler to understand than the first, partly because it is less argumentative; it analyzes experience in a categorical way; that is, it establishes different kinds of ideas: those which result from perception (which he calls sensation) and those which result from reflection or analysis. Both, he says, are experiential, and thus neither is innate. In paragraphs 20–22, he calls these sources of knowledge two fountains, using a metaphor that represents change, purity, and nourishment. Locke is careful with his prose and rarely uses metaphoric language. He occasionally pauses to summarize his views (e.g. paras. 26 and 28). His purpose is to increase our understanding about human understanding, and therefore he does nothing to alienate his audience or to obscure his thinking.

On Ideas as the Materials
of All Our Knowledge

The Rejection of
Innate Ideas and Principles[1]

It is an established opinion among some men, that there are in the 1
understanding certain innate principles; some primary notions,
Κοιναὶ ἐννοιαι,[2] characters, as it were, stamped upon the mind of man,
which the soul receives in its very first being; and brings into the
world with it. It would be sufficient to convince unprejudiced readers
of the falseness of this supposition, if I should only show (as I hope I
shall in the following parts of this discourse) how men, barely by the
use of their natural faculties, may attain to all the knowledge they
have without the help of any innate impressions; and may arrive at
certainty without any such original notions or principles. For I imagine anyone will easily grant that it would be impertinent to suppose,
the ideas of colors innate in a creature, to whom God hath given sight,
and a power to receive them by the eyes, from external objects: and no
less unreasonable would it be to attribute several truths to the impressions of nature, and innate characters, when we may observe in ourselves faculties fit to attain as easy and certain knowledge of them as
if they were originally imprinted on the mind.

But because a man is not permitted without censure to follow his 2
own thoughts in the search of truth when they lead him ever so little
out of the common road, I shall set down the reasons that made me
doubt of the truth of that opinion as an excuse for my mistake, if I be
in one; which I leave to be considered by those who, with me, dispose
themselves to embrace truth wherever they find it.

There is nothing more commonly taken for granted, than that there 3
are certain principles both speculative and practical (for they speak of

---

[1]*Innate Ideas and Principles*   This is the title of Book I. The terms refer to primary
notions which are already a part of the individual at birth, not ideas the individual learns
through experience. The term innate ideas has become much more recognizable than the
more general term primary notions.

[2]**Κοιναὶ ἐννοιαι**   Primary notions.

both) universally agreed upon by all mankind: which therefore, they argue, must needs be constant impressions, which the souls of men receive in their first beings and which they bring into the world with them, as necessarily and really as they do any of their inherent faculties.[3]

This argument, drawn from universal consent, has this misfortune in it, that if it were true in matter of fact that there were certain truths wherein all mankind agreed, it would not prove them innate if there can be any other way shown, how men may come to that universal agreement in the things they do consent in; which I presume may be done.

But, which is worse, this argument of universal consent, which is made use of to prove innate principles, seems to me a demonstration that there are none such; because there are none to which all mankind give universal assent. I shall begin with the speculative, and instance in those magnified principles of demonstration; "whatsoever is, is;" and, "it is impossible for the same thing to be, and not to be;" which, of all others, I think have the most allowed title to innate. These have so settled a reputation of maxims universally received that it will, no doubt, be thought strange if anyone should seem to question it. But yet I take liberty to say that these propositions are so far from having a universal assent that there are a great part of mankind to whom they are not so much as known.

For, first, it is evident that all children and idiots have not the least apprehension or thought of them; and the want of that is enough to destroy that universal assent which must needs be the necessary concomitant of all innate truths: it seeming to me near a contradiction to say that there are truths imprinted on the soul which it perceives or understands not; imprinting if it signify anything, being nothing else but the making certain truths to be perceived. For to imprint anything on the mind without the mind's perceiving it seems to me hardly intelligible. If therefore children and idiots have souls, have minds, with those impressions upon them, they must unavoidably perceive them and necessarily know and assent to these truths: which since they do not, it is evident that there are no such impressions. For if they are not notions naturally imprinted, how can they be innate? and if they are notions imprinted, how can they be unknown? To say a notion is imprinted on the mind, and yet at the same time to say that the mind

4

5

6

---

[3]*inherent faculties* [In Locke's time a faculty was a specific aspect of mental function.] An inherent faculty of the kind that Locke refers to here might be that of reason or imagination, or more basically the faculty of perception.

is ignorant of it and never yet took notice of it, is to make this impression nothing. No proposition can be said to be in the mind which it never yet knew, which it was never yet conscious of. For if anyone may, then, by the same reason, all propositions that are true, and the mind is capable of ever assenting to, may be said to be in the mind, and to be imprinted: since, if any one can be said to be in the mind, which it never yet knew, it must be only because it is capable of knowing it, and so the mind is of all truths it ever shall know. Nay, thus truths may be imprinted on the mind which it never did nor ever shall know: for a man may live long and die at last in ignorance of many truths which his mind was capable of knowing, and that with certainty. So that if the capacity of knowing be the natural impression contended for, all the truths a man ever comes to know will, by this account, be every one of them innate; and this great point will amount to no more but only to a very improper way of speaking; which, while it pretends to assert the contrary, says nothing different from those who deny innate principles. For nobody, I think, ever denied that the mind was capable of knowing several truths. The capacity, they say, is innate, the knowledge acquired. But then to what end such contest for certain innate maxims? If truths can be imprinted on the understanding without being perceived, I can see no difference there can be between any truths the mind is capable of knowing in respect of their original: they must all be innate, or all adventitious:[4] in vain shall a man go about to distinguish them. He therefore that talks of innate notions in the understanding cannot (if he intend thereby any distinct sort of truths) mean such truths to be in the understanding, as it never perceived, and is yet wholly ignorant of. For if these words (to be in the understanding) have any propriety, they signify to be understood: so that, to be in the understanding, and not to be understood; to be in the mind, and never to be perceived; is all one, as to say, anything is, and is not, in the mind or understanding.

The senses at first let in particular ideas and furnish the yet empty cabinet; and the mind by degrees growing familiar with some of them, they are lodged in the memory, and names got to them. Afterwards the mind, proceeding farther, abstracts them, and by degrees learns the use of general names. In this manner the mind comes to be furnished with ideas and language, the materials about which to exercise its discursive faculty: and the use of reason becomes daily more visible as these materials, that give it employment, increase. But though the 7

---

[4]**adventitious** Added later, not innate.

having of general ideas, and the use of general words and reason, usually grow together; yet, I see not how this any way proves them innate. The knowledge of some truths, I confess, is very early in the mind; but in a way that shows them not to be innate. For, if we will observe, we shall find it still to be about ideas, not innate but acquired: it being about those first which are imprinted by external things, with which infants have earliest to do, which make the most frequent impressions on their senses. In ideas thus got, the mind discovers that some agree, and others differ, probably as soon as it has any use of memory; as soon as it is able to retain and perceive distinct ideas. But whether it be then or no, this is certain, it does so long before it has the use of words or comes to that which we commonly call "the use of reason." For a child knows as certainly, before it can speak, the difference between the ideas of sweet and bitter (i.e. that sweet is not bitter) as it knows afterwards (when it comes to speak) that wormwood and sugar-plums are not the same thing.

A child knows not that three and four are equal to seven till he comes to be able to count seven, and has got the name and idea of equality: and then, upon explaining those words, he presently assents to, or rather perceives the truth of that proposition. But neither does he then readily assent because it is an innate truth, nor was his assent wanting till then because he wanted the use of reason; but the truth of it appears to him as soon as he has settled in his mind the clear and distinct ideas that these names stand for: and then he knows the truth of that proposition, upon the same grounds, and by the same means, that he knew before, that a rod and a cherry are not the same thing; and upon the same grounds also, that he may come to know afterwards, "that it is impossible for the same thing to be, and not to be." So that the later it is before anyone comes to have those general ideas, about which those maxims are; or to know the signification of those general terms that stand for them; or to put together in his mind the ideas they stand for; the later also will it be before he comes to assent to those maxims, whose terms, with the ideas they stand for, being no more innate than those of a cat or a weasel, he must stay till time and observation have acquainted him with them; and then he will be in a capacity to know the truth of these maxims, upon the first occasion that shall make him put together those ideas in his mind, and observe whether they agree or disagree, according as is expressed in those propositions. And therefore it is that a man knows that eighteen and nineteen are equal to thirty-seven by the same self-evidence that he knows one and two to be equal to three: yet a child knows this not so soon as the other; not for want of the use of reason but because the ideas the words eighteen, nineteen, and thirty-seven stand for are not so soon got as those which are signified by one, two, and three.

Nor is this the prerogative of numbers alone, and propositions 9 made about several of them; but even natural philosophy, and all the other sciences,[5] afford propositions which are sure to meet with assent as soon as they are understood. That two bodies cannot be in the same place is a truth that nobody any more sticks at than at these maxims, "that it is impossible for the same thing to be, and not to be; that white is not black; that a square is not a circle; that yellowness is not sweetness": these and a million of such other propositions, as many at least as we have distinct ideas of, every man in his wits, at first hearing, and knowing what the names stand for, must necessarily assent to. If these men will be true to their own rule, and have assent at first hearing and understanding the terms, to be a mark of innate, they must allow, not only as many innate propositions as men have distinct ideas; but as many as men can make propositions wherein different ideas are denied one of another. Since every proposition wherein one different idea is denied of another will as certainly find assent at first hearing and understanding the terms, as general one "it is impossible for the same thing to be, and not to be"; or that which is the foundation of it, and is the easier understood of the two, "the same is not different": by which account they will have legions of innate propositions of this one sort without mentioning any other. But since no proposition can be innate unless the ideas about which it is be innate; this will be to suppose all our ideas of colors, sounds, tastes, figure, etc. innate; than which there cannot be anything more opposite to reason and experience. Universal and ready assent upon hearing and understanding the terms is (I grant) a mark of self-evidence: but self-evidence, depending not on innate impressions, but on something else (as we shall show hereafter) belongs to several propositions, which nobody was yet so extravagant as to pretend to be innate.

If those speculative maxims, whereof we discoursed in the forego- 10 ing chapter, have not an actual universal assent from all mankind, as we there proved, it is much more visible concerning practical principles, that they come short of a universal reception: and I think it will be hard to instance any one moral rule which can pretend to so general and ready an assent as, "what is, is"; or to be so manifest a truth as this, "that it is impossible for the same thing to be, and not to be."

---

[5]***natural philosophy, and all the other sciences*** Natural philosophy was equivalent in Locke's time to modern physics. The other sciences would have included botany, zoology, chemistry, and related subjects.

Whereby it is evident that they are farther removed from a title to be innate;[6] and the doubt of their being native impressions on the mind is stronger against those moral principles than the other. Not that it brings their truth at all in question: they are equally true, though not equally evident. Those speculative maxims carry their own evidence with them; but moral principles require reasoning and discourse, and some exercise of the mind, to discover the certainty of their truth. They lie not open as natural characters engraven on the mind; which, if any such were, they must needs be visible by themselves, and by their own light be certain and known to everybody. But this is no derogation[7] to their truth and certainty, no more than it is to the truth or certainty of the three angles of a triangle being equal to two right ones; because it is not so evident as "the whole is bigger than a part"; nor so apt to be assented to at first hearing. It may suffice that these moral rules are capable of demonstration; and therefore it is our own fault if we come not to a certain knowledge of them. But the ignorance wherein many men are of them, and the slowness of assent wherewith others receive them, are manifest proofs that they are not innate, and such as offer themselves to their view without searching.

Whether there be any such moral principles, wherein all men do   11 agree, I appeal to any who have been but moderately conversant in the history of mankind, and looked abroad beyond the smoke of their own chimneys. Where is that practical truth that is universally received without doubt or question, as it must be, if innate? Justice, and keeping of contracts, is that which most men seem to agree in. This is a principle which is thought to extend itself to the dens of thieves and the confederacies of the greatest villains; and they who have gone farthest towards the putting off of humanity itself keep faith and rules of justice one with another. I grant that outlaws themselves do this one among another; but it is without receiving these as the innate laws of nature. They practice them as rules of convenience within their own communities: but it is impossible to conceive that he embraces justice as a practical principle who acts fairly with his fellow highwayman and at the same time plunders or kills the next honest man he meets with. Justice and truth are the common ties of society; and therefore even outlaws and robbers, who break with all the world besides, must

---

[6]*a title to be innate*   Locke uses the word "title" in a legal sense meaning "possessing the qualities of." The speculative maxims he refers to are general wisdom as expressed in timeless sayings, and the crux of his argument is in the point that no one moral rule can be produced which is so universally accepted as to *entitle* it to be thought of as innate.

[7]*derogation*   Disparaging, detracting from.

keep faith and rules of equity among themselves, or else they cannot hold together. But will anyone say that those that live by fraud or rapine have innate principles of truth and justice which they allow and assent to?

Perhaps it will be urged that the tacit assent of their minds agrees 12 to what their practice contradicts. I answer, first, I have always thought the actions of men the best interpreters of their thoughts. But since it is certain that most men's practices, and some men's open professions, have either questioned or denied these principles, it is impossible to establish a universal consent (though we should look for it only among grown men) without which it is impossible to conclude them innate. Secondly, it is very strange and unreasonable to suppose innate practical principles that terminate only in contemplation. Practical principles derived from nature are there for operation, and must produce conformity of action, not barely speculative assent to their truth, or else they are in vain distinguished from speculative maxims. Nature, I confess, has put into man a desire of happiness and an aversion to misery: these indeed are innate practical principles, which (as practical principles ought) do continue constantly to operate and influence all our actions without ceasing: these may be observed in all persons and all ages, steady and universal; but these are inclinations of the appetite to good, not impressions of truth on the understanding. I deny not that there are natural tendencies imprinted on the minds of men; and that, from the very first instances of sense and perception, there are some things that are grateful, and others unwelcome to them; some things that they incline to, and others that they fly: but this makes nothing for innate characters on the mind, which are to be the principles of knowledge, regulating our practice. Such natural impressions on the understanding are so far from being confirmed hereby that this is an argument against them; since, if there were certain characters imprinted by nature on the understanding, as the principles of knowledge, we could not but perceive them constantly operate in us and influence our knowledge, as we do those others on the will and appetite; which never cease to be the constant springs and motives of all our actions, to which we perpetually feel them strongly impelling us.

Another reason that makes me doubt of any innate practical prin- 13 ciples is that I think there cannot any one moral rule be proposed whereof a man may not justly demand a reason: which would be perfectly ridiculous and absurd if they were innate, or so much as self-evident; which every innate principle must needs be, and not need any proof to ascertain its truth, nor want any reason to gain it approbation.

He would be thought void of common sense, who asked on the one side, or on the other side went to give, a reason why it is impossible for the same thing to be, and not to be. It carries its own light and evidence with it and needs no other proof: he that understands the terms assents to it for its own sake, or else nothing will ever be able to prevail with him to do it. But should that most unshaken rule of morality, and foundation of all social virtue, "that one should do as he would be done unto," be proposed to one who never heard it before, but yet is of capacity to understand its meaning, might he not without any absurdity ask a reason why? and were not he that proposed it bound to make out the truth and reasonableness of it to him? which plainly shows it not to be innate; for if it were, it could neither want nor receive any proof; but must needs (at least, as soon as heard and understood) be received and assented to as an unquestionable truth which a man can by no means doubt of. So that the truth of all these moral rules plainly depends upon some other antecedent to them, and from which they must be deduced; which could not be if either they were innate or so much as self-evident.

Principles of actions indeed there are lodged in men's appetites, but these are so far from being innate moral principles that if they were left to their full swing, they would carry men to the overturning of all morality. Moral laws are set as a curb and restraint to these exorbitant desires, which they cannot be but by rewards and punishments, that will overbalance the satisfaction anyone shall propose to himself in the breach of the law. If therefore anything be imprinted on the minds of all men as a law, all men must have a certain and unavoidable knowledge that certain and unavoidable punishment will attend the breach of it. For, if men can be ignorant or doubtful of what is innate, innate principles are insisted on, and urged to no purpose; truth and certainty (the things pretended) are not at all secured by them: but men are in the same uncertain, floating estate with, as without them. An evident indubitable knowledge of unavoidable punishment great enough to make the transgression very uneligible[8] must accompany an innate law; unless, with an innate law, they can suppose an innate gospel too. I would not here be mistaken, as if, because I deny an innate law, I thought there were none but positive laws. There is a great deal of difference between an innate law and a law of nature; between something imprinted on our minds in their very original and something that we being ignorant of may attain to the knowledge of by the

---

[8]**uneligible** Undesirable, unfitting. Locke's is the earliest recorded use of this now obsolete word.

use and due application of our natural faculties. And I think they equally forsake the truth who, running into the contrary extremes, either affirm an innate law or deny that there is a law knowable by the light of nature, i.e. without the help of positive revelation.

If any idea can be imagined innate, the idea of God may, of all others, for many reasons be thought so; since it is hard to conceive how there should be innate moral principles without an innate idea of a Deity: without a notion of a law-maker, it is impossible to have a notion of a law, and an obligation to observe it. Besides the atheists, taken notice of among the ancients, and left branded upon the records of history, hath not navigation discovered, in these later ages, whole nations at the bay of Soladania, in Brazil, in Boranday, and in the Caribbee islands, etc. among whom there was to be found no notion of a God, no religion? These are instances of nations where uncultivated nature has been left to itself, without the help of letters, and discipline, and the improvements of arts and sciences. But there are others to be found who have enjoyed these in a very great measure; who yet, for want of a due application of their thoughts this way, want the idea and knowledge of God. It will, I doubt not, be a surprise to others, as it was to me, to find the Siamites[9] of this number. But for this, let them consult the king of France's late envoy thither, who gives no better account of the Chinese themselves. And if we will not believe La Loubère,[10] the missionaries of China, even the Jesuits[11] themselves, the great encomiasts of the Chinese,[12] do all to a man agree, and will convince us that the sect of the literati, or learned, keeping to the old religion of China, and the ruling party there, are all of them atheists. And perhaps if we should, with attention, mind the lives and discourses of people not so far off, we should have too much reason to fear that many in more civilized countries have no very strong and clear impressions of a Deity upon their minds; and that the complaints of atheism, made from the pulpit, are not without reason. And though only some profligate wretches own it too bare-facedly now; yet per-

15

---

[9]*Siamites*   Residents of Siam, now Thailand.

[10]*Simon de La Loubère, (1642–1729)*   An envoy to Siam. He wrote *Du Royaume de Siam* (On the Royalty of Siam) (Paris, 1691). He participated in the government of Louis XIV.

[11]*Jesuits*   Roman Catholic order of priests founded in 1534 by St. Ignatius of Loyola. It was described as the Church Militant and often figured in missionary work among Indians in North and South America.

[12]*encomiasts of the Chinese*   An encomium is an essay in praise of something, and the Jesuits wrote numerous essays praising the Chinese.

haps we should hear more than we do of it from others, did not the fear of the magistrate's sword, or their neighbor's censure, tie up people's tongues: which, were the apprehensions of punishment or shame taken away, would as openly proclaim their atheism as their lives do.

But had all mankind, everywhere, a notion of a God (whereof yet 16 history tells us the contrary) it would not from thence follow that the idea of him was innate. For though no nation were to be found without a name, and some few dark notions of him: yet that would not prove them to be natural impressions on the mind, any more than the names of fire, or the sun, heat, or number do prove the ideas they stand for to be innate: because the names of those things, and the ideas of them, are so universally received and known among mankind. Nor, on the contrary, is the want of such a name, or the absence of such a notion out of men's minds, any argument against the being of a God; anymore than it would be a proof that there was no loadstone[13] in the world, because a great part of mankind had neither a notion of any such thing, nor a name for it; or be any show of argument to prove that there are no distinct and various species of angels, or intelligent beings above us, because we have no ideas of such distinct species, or names for them: for men being furnished with words, by the common language of their own countries, can scarce avoid having some kind of ideas of those things, whose names, those they converse with, have occasion frequently to mention to them. And if they carry with it the notion of excellency, greatness, or something extraordinary: if apprehension and concernment accompany it; if the fear of absolute and irresistible power set it on upon the mind, the idea is likely to sink the deeper and spread the farther; especially if it be such an idea as is agreeable to the common light of reason and naturally deducible from every part of our knowledge, as that of a God is. For the visible marks of extraordinary wisdom and power appear so plainly in all the works of the creation that a rational creature, who will but seriously reflect on them, cannot miss the discovery of a Deity. And the influence that the discovery of such a being must necessarily have on the minds of all, that have but once heard of it, is so great, and carries such a weight of thought and communication with it, that it seems stranger to me that a whole nation of men should be anywhere found so brutish as to want the notion of a God than that they should be without any notion of numbers or fire.

The name of God being once mentioned in any part of the world 17

---

[13]*loadstone* Magnet.

to express a superior, powerful, wise, invisible being, the suitableness of such a notion to the principles of common reason, and the interest men will always have to mention it often, must necessarily spread it far and wide, and continue it down to all generations; though yet the general reception of this name, and some imperfect and unsteady notions conveyed thereby to the unthinking part of mankind, prove not the idea to be innate; but only that they who made the discovery had made a right use of their reason, thought maturely of the causes of things, and traced them to their original; from whom other less considering people having once received so important a notion, it could not easily be lost again.

This is all could be inferred from the notion of a God, were it to be 18 found universally in all the tribes of mankind, and generally acknowledged by men grown to maturity in all countries.

The Origin of All
Our Ideas in Experience

Every man being conscious to himself that he thinks, and that 19 which his mind is applied about while thinking, being the ideas that are there, it is past doubt that men have in their minds several ideas, such as are those expressed by the words, Whiteness, Hardness, Sweetness, Thinking, Motion, Man, Elephant, Army, Drunkenness, and others. It is in the first place then to be inquired how he comes by them. I know it is a received doctrine that men have native ideas and original characters stamped upon their minds in their very first being. This opinion I have, at large, examined already; and, I suppose, what I have said, in the foregoing book, will be much more easily admitted when I have shown whence the understanding may get all the ideas it has, and by what ways and degrees they may come into the mind; for which I shall appeal to everyone's own observation and experience.

Let us then suppose the mind to be, as we say, white paper, void of 20 all characters, without any ideas; how comes it to be furnished? Whence comes it by that vast store which the busy and boundless fancy of man has painted on it, with an almost endless variety? Whence has it all the materials of reason and knowledge? To this I answer, in one word, from experience; in all that our knowledge is founded, and from that it ultimately derives itself. Our observation employed either about external sensible objects or about the internal operations of our minds, perceived and reflected on by ourselves, is that which supplies our understandings with all the materials of thinking. These two are the fountains of knowledge, from whence all the ideas we have, or can naturally have, do spring.

First, Our senses, conversant about particular sensible objects, do 21 convey into the mind several distinct perceptions of things, according to those various ways wherein those objects do affect them: and thus we come by those ideas we have, of Yellow, White, Heat, Cold, Soft, Hard, Bitter, Sweet, and all those which we call sensible qualities; which when I say the senses convey into the mind, I mean, they from external objects convey into the mind what produces there those perceptions. This great source of most of the ideas we have, depending wholly upon our senses, and derived by them to the understanding, I call SENSATION.

Secondly, The other fountain, from which experience furnished the 22 understanding with ideas, is the perception of the operations of our own mind within us, as it is employed about the ideas it has got; which operations, when the soul comes to reflect on and consider, do furnish the understanding with another set of ideas, which could not be had from things without; and such are Perception, Thinking, Doubting, Believing, Reasoning, Knowing, Willing, and all the different actings of our own minds; which we being conscious of and observing in ourselves, do from these receive into our understandings as distinct ideas, as we do from bodies affecting our senses. This source of ideas every man has wholly in himself; and though it be not sense, as having nothing to do with external objects, yet it is very like it, and might properly enough be called internal sense. But as I call the other sensation, so I call this REFLECTION, the ideas it affords being such only as the mind gets by reflecting on its own operations within itself. By reflection then, in the following part of this discourse, I would be understood to mean that notice which the mind takes of its own operations, and the manner of them; by reason whereof there come to be ideas of these operations in the understanding. These two, I say, *viz.* external material things, as the objects of sensation; and the operations of our own minds within, as the objects of reflection; are to me the only originals from whence all our ideas take their beginnings. The term operations here I use in a large sense, as comprehending not barely the actions of the mind about its ideas, but some sort of passions arising sometimes from them, such as is the satisfaction or uneasiness arising from any thought.

The understanding seems to me not to have the least glimmering 23 of any ideas which it doth not receive from one of these two. External objects furnish the mind with the ideas of sensible qualities, which are all those different perceptions they produce in us: and the mind furnishes the understanding with ideas of its own operations.

These, when we have taken a full survey of them and their several   24
modes, combinations,and relations, we shall find to contain all our
whole stock of ideas; and that we have nothing in our minds which
did not come in one of these two ways. Let anyone examine his own
thoughts, and thoroughly search into his understanding; and then let
him tell me whether all the original ideas he has there are any other
than of the objects of his senses, or of the operations of his mind,
considered as objects of his reflection; and how great a mass of knowledge soever he imagines to be lodged there he will, upon taking a strict
view, see that he has not any idea in his mind but what one of these
two have imprinted; though perhaps, with infinite variety com-
pounded and enlarged by the understanding, as we shall see hereafter.

To ask at what time a man has first any ideas is to ask when he   25
begins to perceive; having ideas and perception being the same thing.
I know it is an opinion that the soul always thinks and that it has the
actual perception of ideas in itself constantly as long as it exists; and
that actual thinking is as inseparable from the soul as actual extension
is from the body: which if true, to inquire after the beginning of a
man's ideas is the same as to inquire after the beginning of his soul.
For by this account soul and its ideas, as body and its extension, will
begin to exist both at the same time.

I see no reason therefore to believe that the soul thinks before the   26
senses have furnished it with ideas to think on; and as those are increased and retained, so it comes, by exercise, to improve its faculty
of thinking, in the several parts of it as well as afterwards, by compounding those ideas and reflecting on its own operations; it increases
its stock, as well as facility, in remembering, imagining, reasoning, and
other modes of thinking.

Follow a child from its birth and observe the alterations that time   27
makes, and you shall find, as the mind by the senses comes more and
more to be furnished with ideas, it comes to be more and more awake;
thinks more, the more it has matter to think on. After some time it
begins to know the objects, which, being most familiar with it, have
made lasting impressions. Thus it comes by degrees to know the persons it daily converses with, and distinguish them from strangers;
which are instances and effects of its coming to retain and distinguish
the ideas the senses convey to it. And so we may observe how the
mind, by degrees, improves in these and advances to the exercise of
those other faculties of enlarging, compounding, and abstracting its
ideas, and of reasoning about them, and reflecting upon all these; of
which I shall have occasion to speak more hereafter.

Thus the first capacity of human intellect is that the mind is fitted   28
to receive the impressions made on it; either through the senses by

outward objects; or by its own operations when it reflects on them. This is the first step a man makes towards the discovery of anything, and the ground-work whereon to build all those notions which ever he shall have naturally in this world. All those sublime thoughts which tower above the clouds and reach as high as heaven itself take their rise and footing here: in all that good extent wherein the mind wanders, in those remote speculations it may seem to be elevated with, it stirs not one jot beyond those ideas which sense or reflection have offered for its contemplation.

In this part the understanding is merely passive; and whether or no   29 it will have these beginnings, and as it were materials of knowledge, is not in its own power. For the objects of our senses do, many of them, obtrude their particular ideas upon our minds whether we will or no; and the operations of our minds will not let us be without at least some obscure notions of them. No man can be wholly ignorant of what he does when he thinks. These simple ideas, when offered to the mind, the understanding can no more refuse to have, nor alter, when they are imprinted, nor blot them out, and make new ones itself, than a mirror can refuse, alter, or obliterate the images or ideas which the objects set before it do therein produce. As the bodies that surround us do diversely affect our organs, the mind is forced to receive the impressions, and cannot avoid the perception of those ideas that are annexed to them.

QUESTIONS

1. What are some examples of the ideas that Locke thinks might be conceived of as innate?
2. What is the meaning of "innate idea"?
3. Have you ever felt that you were born with innate ideas? What kinds of ideas might people think of as innate?
4. How convincing is Locke's argument that there are no innate ideas?
5. Do you accept Locke's view that there is nothing that all people can agree on (para. 5)?
6. What moral ideas—which might be candidates for being thought of as innate ideas—could people be expected to agree on?

WRITING ASSIGNMENTS

1. Using Locke's method, establish whether the following statements could logically be considered as candidates for innate ideas: "Everything that

goes up must come down"; "You are not I"; "I think." Follow Locke's approach to ways of reviewing the statement; decide whether it is innate; and establish, in the manner he would use, the problems each statement presents that might restrict its likelihood for being innate.

2. Do you agree with Locke when he says that "No proposition can be said to be in the mind which it never yet knew, which it was never yet conscious of" (para. 6)? Consider this statement in light of what we know about the nature of the subconscious mind, as revealed in the essays by Freud and Jung in this book. Does their thinking substantially alter the truth of Locke's views? Take into account especially the argument that Jung makes in "The Concept of the Collective Unconscious," which proclaims that people are born with a collective unconscious. Is this concept a significant blow to Locke's theory?

3. In paragraph 6, Locke seems to be saying that the capacity to know the truth is innate, though the ideas that constitute the truth are acquired. Clarify his thinking on this idea and take a position on it: Do you agree or disagree? What are the reasons for your position?

4. In paragraph 12, Locke says, "Nature, I confess, has put into man a desire of happiness and an aversion to misery: these indeed are innate practical principles, which (as practical principles ought) do continue constantly to operate and influence all our actions without ceasing. . . . I deny not that there are natural tendencies imprinted on the minds of men." Would not these statements constitute an argument against his position? Concentrate on careful definition of terms as a means of establishing your own argument. Take a stand on this issue and argue it in the manner that you think Locke might have done.

5. Explain the distinction that Locke makes at the end of the essay, where he discusses sensation and reflection. Are there any other kinds of knowledge that, in this age, could be added to these two? How clear is Locke's distinction and how valid is it? Can you think of another distinction to add to these?

6. In the last few pages of the essay Locke talks extensively about the processes of the mind, and he says that one can observe the processes of one's own mind. Write an essay in which you discuss your observations of the workings of your mind. How does your mind work? Does your thinking change when you observe it? And, if you feel that you actually can observe your thinking, who then, is thinking? How can a person both think and observe his or her own thinking? Is that possible at all unless there are two "persons" in each of us?

7. Locke questions the possibility of the idea of God being innate. How convincing is his argument? What is the nature of his argument, and what are its strongest elements? He develops his view in paragraph 15, but the problem is also implied elsewhere in the essay. Is he correct in saying that the idea of God is not innate?

BERTRAND RUSSELL

A Free Man's Worship

BERTRAND RUSSELL (1872–1970) was one of England's most distinguished modern analytic philosophers. His early career was largely devoted to the study of mathematics, and The Principles of Mathematics (1900) was his first major work. The most important of his mathematical works was his collaboration with Alfred North Whitehead at Cambridge University on Principia Mathematica, published in three volumes (1910–1913). Both he and Whitehead had to contribute money to its publication. It attempted to show that mathematics derives from logic and that nothing but the principles of pure logic need to be understood for mathematics to be understood.

Russell's social conscience was aroused by the brutal bloodshed of World War I. Because of his pacifist views, he suffered imprisonment, libelous attack, and—worst of all—the loss of his lectureship in Philosophy at Cambridge in 1916. His interests from that time forth expanded from mathematics. Among the books that he wrote were Our Knowledge of the External World (1920), Analysis of Mind (1921), Marriage and Morals (1929), Education and the Social Order (1932), History of Western Philosophy (1945), and Why I Am Not a

From *Mysticism and Logic*.

Christian *(1957). He lectured frequently in England and America and was invited to be a faculty member at the City College of New York, but a New York judge denied him a visa because of imputed sexual immorality—in one of his books he had proposed a scheme of temporary marriage for undergraduates! Nonetheless, he remained in the United States, lecturing at the Barnes Foundation in Merion, Pennsylvania until in 1944 Cambridge reappointed him to its faculty. By then he was so widely known as a philosopher and social critic that he was honored by people of many nations. In 1950 he was awarded the Nobel Prize for Literature in recognition of the breadth of his writings.*

Russell's "A Free Man's Worship" is typical of him only to the extent that it celebrates the indomitableness of the human spirit and encourages us to respect the most human aspects of our being.

The opening portrays a bleak, meaningless cosmos in which we are caught and entangled. There is nothing to qualify any action as good or bad, nothing to energize the spirit, nothing to make us aware of the value of living. It is, Russell says clearly, the world that the atheist scientist might portray for us. Yet, Russell does not suggest rejecting Mephistopheles' view (after all, Mephistopheles is a demon and thus speaks from another world); rather, he asks that we accept Mephistopheles' view. He suggests we accept the meaninglessness, the senselessness, the blindness of creation, and move on from there. He urges us to respect what humans alone understand: goodness. Power, he tells us, is everywhere: in nature as storm and change, in time as fate, in death as finality. But this power is senseless; it is by nature bad. Were we to be simple materialists, he suggests, we would be yielding to the force of blind, senseless matter. Instead, he asks that we live with fate, with nature, with the thought of death, and that we worship goodness. In this Russell agrees with both Plato and Aristotle, whose concern for the soul is uppermost and who found materialists to be only slightly above the animals.

Russell pleads for humankind's emancipation from the worship of power. He pleads with us to lose our selfishness. "To abandon the struggle for private happiness, to expel all eagerness of temporary desire, to burn with passion for eternal things—this is emancipation, and this is the free man's worship" (para. 19).

RUSSELL'S RHETORIC

In reading this piece, we must keep in mind the fact that Russell's Nobel Prize was for literature, not for mathematics or philosophy.

Thus it is no surprise that all Russell's rhetorical achievements in the piece are the products of his style. He does not structure a persuasive argument; he does not divide the work neatly into beginning, middle, and end as a means of structuring the piece. Instead, he depends on summary and thorough analysis. He follows the implications of a thought almost casually, as if following a wandering stream.
as if following a wandering stream.

Impressive rhetorical qualities are exhibited in Russell's handling of image and metaphor and in his allusions to pertinent literature. The image is a literary device that appeals to our senses; it makes us see, hear, touch, smell, and feel what it refers to. Consider the images from Mephistopheles' speech: "from black masses of cloud hot sheets of rain deluged the barely solid crust" (para. 3). Consider his description of the imagination: "in the golden sunset magic of lyrics, where beauty shines and glows" (para. 14). And consider his description of fate: "doom falls pitiless and dark" (para. 21). Russell has the capacity to make us feel at the emotional level the seriousness of what he wishes to communicate intellectually.

Even more impressive are Russell's metaphors. The metaphor is a figure of speech that suggests a comparison, such as that of man's life to a march: "The life of Man is a long march through the night, surrounded by invisible foes" (para. 20). Before long, we suddenly find that life is not only like a march but also like a war (where marches are most common). Russell tells us in another metaphor that "Of all the arts, Tragedy is the proudest, the most triumphant; for it builds its shining citadel in the very centre of the enemy's country, on the very summit of his highest mountain; from its impregnable watchtowers" (para. 16). He asserts that we can "build a temple for the worship of our own ideals" (para. 14) and that "there is a cavern of darkness to be traversed before that temple can be entered" (para. 15). By this metaphor he suggests simply that we must be willing to grant Mephistopheles his vision of a meaningless world of matter as a prelude to understanding the true force of the spirit that lives in each of us.

A Free Man's Worship

To Dr. Faustus[1] in his study Mephistopheles told the history of the   1
Creation, saying:

"The endless praises of the choirs of angels had begun to grow   2
wearisome; for, after all, did he not deserve their praise? Had he not
given them endless joy? Would it not be more amusing to obtain un-
deserved praise, to be worshipped by beings whom he tortured? He
smiled inwardly, and resolved that the great drama should be performed.

"For countless ages the hot nebula whirled aimlessly through   3
space. At length it began to take shape, the central mass threw off
planets, the planets cooled, boiling seas and burning mountains heaved
and tossed, from black masses of cloud hot sheets of rain deluged the
barely solid crust. And now the first germ of life grew in the depths of
the ocean, and developed rapidly in the fructifying warmth into vast
forest trees, huge ferns springing from the damp mould, sea monsters
breeding, fighting, devouring, and passing away. And from the monsters, as the play unfolded itself, Man was born, with the power of
thought, the knowledge of good and evil, and the cruel thirst for worship. And Man saw that all is passing in this mad, monstrous world,
that all is struggling to snatch, at any cost, a few brief moments of life
before Death's inexorable decree. And Man said: 'There is a hidden
purpose, could we but fathom it, and the purpose is good; for we must
reverence something, and in the visible world there is nothing worthy
of reverence.' And Man stood aside from the struggle, resolving that
God intended harmony to come out of chaos by human efforts. And
when he followed the instincts which God had transmitted to him
from his ancestry of beasts of prey, he called it Sin, and asked God to
forgive him. But he doubted whether he could be justly forgiven, until
he invented a divine Plan by which God's wrath was to have been
appeased. And seeing the present was bad, he made it yet worse, that

---

[1]**Dr. Faustus**   In this sentence Russell is referring to *Doctor Faustus* (1588) by Christopher Marlowe (1564–1593). Johann Wolfgang von Goethe (1749–1832) also wrote on the
theme of Faustus's selling his soul to the Devil. Russell is offering, in what he calls
"outline," a summary of Mephistopheles' appeal.

thereby the future might be better. And he gave God thanks for the strength that enabled him to forgo even the joys that were possible. And God smiled; and when he saw that Man had become perfect in renunciation and worship, he sent another sun through the sky, which crashed into Man's sun; and all returned again to nebula.

" 'Yes,' he murmured, 'it was a good play; I will have it performed 4 again.' "

Such, in outline, but even more purposeless, more void of meaning, 5 is the world which Science presents for our belief. Amid such a world, if anywhere, our ideals henceforward must find a home. That Man is the product of causes which had no prevision of the end they were achieving; that his origin, his growth, his hopes and fears, his loves and beliefs, are but the outcome of accidental collocations of atoms;[2] that no fire, no heroism, no intensity of thought and feeling, can preserve an individual life beyond the grave; that all the labours of the ages, all the devotion, all the inspiration, all the noonday brightness of human genius, are destined to extinction in the vast death of the solar system, and that the whole temple of Man's achievement must inevitably be buried beneath the debris of a universe in ruins—all these things, if not quite beyond dispute, are yet so nearly certain, that no philosophy which rejects them can hope to stand. Only within the scaffolding of these truths, only on the firm foundation of unyielding despair, can the soul's habitation henceforth be safely built.

How, in such an alien and inhuman world, can so powerless a crea- 6 ture as Man preserve his aspirations untarnished? A strange mystery it is that Nature, omnipotent but blind, in the revolutions of her secular hurryings through the abysses of space, has brought forth at last a child, subject still to her power, but gifted with sight, with knowledge of good and evil, with the capacity of judging all the works of his unthinking Mother. In spite of Death, the mark and seal of the parental control, Man is yet free, during his brief years, to examine, to criticise, to know, and in imagination to create. To him alone, in the world with which he is acquainted, this freedom belongs; and in this lies his superiority to the resistless forces that control his outward life.

The savage, like ourselves, feels the oppression of his impotence 7 before the powers of Nature; but having in himself nothing that he respects more than Power, he is willing to prostrate himself before his gods, without inquiring whether they are worthy of his worship. Pathetic and very terrible is the long history of cruelty and torture, of

---

[2]***collocations of atoms*** groupings or arrangements of atoms.

degradation and human sacrifice, endured in the hope of placating the jealous gods: surely, the trembling believer thinks, when what is most precious has been freely given, their lust for blood must be appeased, and more will not be required. The religion of Moloch[3]—as such creeds may be generically called—is in essence the cringing submission of the slave, who dare not, even in his heart, allow the thought that his master deserves no adulation. Since the independence of ideals is not yet acknowledged, Power may be freely worshipped, and receive an unlimited respect, despite its wanton infliction of pain.

But gradually, as morality grows bolder, the claim of the ideal world begins to be felt; and worship, if it is not to cease, must be given to gods of another kind than those created by the savage. Some, though they feel the demands of the ideal, will still consciously reject them, still urging that naked Power is worthy of worship. Such is the attitude inculcated in God's answer to Job[4] out of the whirlwind: the divine power and knowledge are paraded, but of the divine goodness there is no hint. Such also is the attitude of those who, in our own day, base their morality upon the struggle for survival, maintaining that the survivors are necessarily the fittest. But others, not content with an answer so repugnant to the moral sense, will adopt the position which we have become accustomed to regard as specially religious, maintaining that, in some hidden manner, the world of fact is really harmonious with the world of ideals. Thus Man creates God, all-powerful and all-good, the mystic unity of what is and what should be. 8

But the world of fact, after all, is not good; and, in submitting our judgment to it, there is an element of slavishness from which our thoughts must be purged. For in all things it is well to exalt the dignity of Man, by freeing him as far as possible from the tyranny of nonhuman Power. When we have realised that Power is largely bad, that man, with his knowledge of good and evil, is but a helpless atom in a world which has no such knowledge, the choice is again presented to us: Shall we worship Force, or shall we worship Goodness? Shall our 9

---

[3]**Moloch** A pagan deity to which the sons of Judah sacrificed their children through a ritual of fire; see I Kings 11:7.

[4]**God's answer to Job** In the book of Job in the Bible, Satan asserts that he can tempt any of God's creatures to turn their backs on God. God insists that Job cannot be swayed. Satan tests Job, inflicting him with illness and destruction, but Job remains faithful. God explains to Job that he has suffered and come through the test. But Russell implies a criticism of the book of Job, in which suffering rather than love, and power rather than compassion, are stressed.

God exist and be evil, or shall he be recognised as the creation of our own conscience?

The answer to this question is very momentous, and affects pro- 10 foundly our whole morality. The worship of Force, to which Carlyle[5] and Nietzsche and the creed of Militarism have accustomed us, is the result of failure to maintain our own ideals against a hostile universe: it is itself a prostrate submission to evil, a sacrifice of our best to Moloch. If strength indeed is to be respected, let us respect rather the strength of those who refuse that false "recognition of facts" which fails to recognise that facts are often bad. Let us admit that, in the world we know, there are many things that would be better otherwise, and that the ideals to which we do and must adhere are not realised in the realm of matter. Let us preserve our respect for truth, for beauty, for the ideal of perfection which life does not permit us to attain, though none of these things meet with the approval of the unconscious universe. If Power is bad, as it seems to be, let us reject it from our hearts. In this lies Man's true freedom: in determination to worship only the God created by our own love of the good, to respect only the heaven which inspires the insight of our best moments. In action, in desire, we must submit perpetually to the tyranny of outside forces; but in thought, in aspiration, we are free, free from our fellowmen, free from the petty planet on which our bodies impotently crawl, free even, while we live, from the tyranny of death. Let us learn, then, that energy of faith which enables us to live constantly in the vision of the good; and let us descend, in action, into the world of fact, with that vision always before us.

When first the opposition of fact and ideal grows fully visible, a 11 spirit of fiery revolt, of fierce hatred of the gods, seems necessary to the assertion of freedom. To defy with Promethean constancy[6] a hos-

---

[5]**Thomas Carlyle (1795–1881)** Carlyle was an important historian, especially remembered for his studies of Frederick the Great, Oliver Cromwell, and the French Revolution. Russell is probably referring to his work on the French Revolution, which demonstrated the ways in which power could be used and misused. His *Sartor Resartus* (1832) inspired Friedrich Nietzsche (1844–1900) with its demonstration of the power of a strong personal will. Nietzsche's *The Will to Power* (1888) contains more than 1,000 aphorisms celebrating the independent will, the assertive and inspired person. Much of this philosophy of will power was misapplied to defend the actions of the Fascists in Europe before and during World War II.

[6]**Promethean constancy** Prometheus was a Titan of Greek mythology who gave fire to humankind. Zeus punished him by having him chained to a rock and having a giant bird constantly eat at his liver. Constancy is thus endurance, the will to prevail.

tile universe, to keep its evil always in view, always actively hated, to refuse no pain that the malice of Power can invent, appears to be the duty of all who will not bow before the inevitable. But indignation is still a bondage, for it compels our thoughts to be occupied with an evil world; and in the fierceness of desire from which rebellion springs there is a kind of self-assertion which it is necessary for the wise to overcome. Indignation is a submission of our thoughts, but not of our desires; the Stoic freedom[7] in which wisdom consists is found in the submission of our desires, but not of our thoughts. From the submission of our desires springs the virtue of resignation; from the freedom of our thoughts springs the whole world of art and philosophy, and the vision of beauty by which, at last, we half reconquer the reluctant world. But the vision of beauty is possible only to unfettered contemplation, to thoughts not weighted by the load of eager wishes; and thus Freedom comes only to those who no longer ask of life that it shall yield them any of those personal goods that are subject to the mutations of Time.

Although the necessity of renunciation is evidence of the existence 12 of evil, yet Christianity, in preaching it, has shown a wisdom exceeding that of the Promethean philosophy of rebellion. It must be admitted that, of the things we desire, some, though they prove impossible, are yet real goods; others, however, as ardently longed for, do not form part of a fully purified ideal. The belief that what must be renounced is bad, though sometimes false, is far less often false than untamed passion supposes; and the creed of religion, by providing a reason for proving that it is never false, has been the means of purifying our hopes by the discovery of many austere truths.

But there is in resignation a further good element: even real goods, 13 when they are unattainable, ought not to be fretfully desired. To every man comes, sooner or later, the great renunciation. For the young, there is nothing unattainable; a good thing desired with the whole force of a passionate will, and yet impossible, is to them not credible. Yet, by death, by illness, by poverty, or by the voice of duty, we must learn, each one of us, that the world was not made for us, and that, however beautiful may be the things we crave, Fate may nevertheless forbid them. It is the part of courage, when misfortune comes, to bear without repining the ruin of our hopes, to turn away our thoughts

---

[7]**Stoic freedom** This is a reference to the Stoic philosophy of acceptance of things as they come; it is also characterized by public service and good deeds. The Stoics flourished in the fourth and third centuries B.C. in Greece, but their influence also spread to Rome, where Seneca (4 B.C.–A.D. 65) wrote extensively on Stoicism.

from vain regrets. This degree of submission to Power is not only just and right: it is the very gate of wisdom.

But passive renunciation is not the whole of wisdom; for not by 14 renunciation alone can we build a temple for the worship of our own ideals. Haunting foreshadowings of the temple appear in the realm of imagination, in music, in architecture, in the untroubled kingdom of reason, and in the golden sunset magic of lyrics, where beauty shines and glows, remote from the touch of sorrow, remote from the fear of change, remote from the failures and disenchantments of the world of fact. In the contemplation of these things the vision of heaven will shape itself in our hearts, giving at once a touchstone to judge the world about us, and an inspiration by which to fashion to our needs whatever is not incapable of serving as a stone in the sacred temple.

Except for those rare spirits that are born without sin, there is a 15 cavern of darkness to be traversed before that temple can be entered. The gate of the cavern is despair, and its floor is paved with the grave-stones of abandoned hopes. There Self must die; there the eagerness, the greed of untamed desire must be slain, for only so can the soul be freed from the empire of Fate. But out of the cavern the Gate of Re-nunciation leads again to the daylight of wisdom, by whose radiance a new insight, a new joy, a new tenderness, shine forth to gladden the pilgrim's heart.

When, without the bitterness of impotent rebellion, we have learnt 16 both to resign ourselves to the outward rule of Fate and to recognise that the nonhuman world is unworthy of our worship, it becomes pos-sible at last so to transform and refashion the unconscious universe, so to transmute it in the crucible of imagination, that a new image of shining gold replaces the old idol of clay. In all the multiform facts of the world—in the visual shapes of trees and mountains and clouds, in the events of the life of man, even in the very omnipotence of Death— the insight of creative idealism can find the reflection of a beauty which its own thoughts first made. In this way mind asserts its subtle mastery over the thoughtless forces of Nature. The more evil the ma-terial with which it deals, the more thwarting to untrained desire, the greater is its achievement in inducing the reluctant rock to yield up its hidden treasures, the prouder its victory in compelling the opposing forces to swell the pageant of its triumph. Of all the arts, Tragedy is the proudest, the most triumphant; for it builds its shining citadel in the very centre of the enemy's country, on the very summit of his highest mountain; from its impregnable watchtowers, his camps and arsenals, his columns and forts, are all revealed; within its walls the free life continues, while the legions of Death and Pain and Despair, and all the servile captains of tyrant Fate, afford the burghers[8] of that dauntless city new spectacles of beauty. Happy those sacred ramparts, thrice happy the dwellers on that all-seeing eminence. Honour to those brave warriors who, through countless ages of warfare, have preserved for us the priceless heritage of liberty, and have kept undefiled by sacrilegious invaders the home of the unsubdued.

But the beauty of Tragedy does but make visible a quality which, in more or less obvious shapes, is present always and everywhere in life. In the spectacle of Death, in the endurance of intolerable pain, and in the irrevocableness of a vanished past, there is a sacredness, an overpowering awe, a feeling of the vastness, the depth, the inexhaustible mystery of existence, in which, as by some strange marriage of pain, the sufferer is bound to the world by bonds of sorrow. In these moments of insight, we lose all eagerness of temporary desire, all struggling and striving for petty ends, all care for the little trivial things that, to a superficial view, make up the common life of day by day; we see, surrounding the narrow raft illumined by the flickering light of human comradeship, the dark ocean on whose rolling waves we toss for a brief hour; from the great night without, a chill blast breaks in upon our refuge; all the loneliness of humanity amid hostile forces is concentrated upon the individual soul, which must struggle alone, with what of courage it can command, against the whole weight of a universe that cares nothing for its hopes and fears. Victory, in this struggle with the powers of darkness, is the true baptism into the glorious company of heroes, the true initiation into the overmastering beauty of human existence. From that awful encounter of the soul with the outer world, enunciation,[9] wisdom, and charity are born; and with their birth a new life begins. To take into the inmost shrine of the soul the irresistible forces whose puppets we seem to be—Death and change, the irrevocableness of the past, and the powerlessness of man before the blind hurry of the universe from vanity to vanity—to feel these things and know them is to conquer them. 17

This is the reason why the Past has such magical power. The beauty of its motionless and silent pictures is like the enchanted purity of late autumn, when the leaves, though one breath would make them fall, still glow against the sky in golden glory. The Past does not change or strive; like Duncan,[10] after life's fitful fever it sleeps well; 18

---

[8]*burghers*   The proper citizens of the town; the civic leaders.

[9]*enunciation*   A declaration or commitment to purpose.

[10]*Duncan*   A character in *Macbeth* (II.ii) by William Shakespeare (1564–1616), written about 1606. Duncan was the king murdered in his sleep by Macbeth.

what was eager and grasping, what was petty and transitory, has faded away, the things that were beautiful and eternal shine out of it like stars in the night. Its beauty, to a soul not worthy of it, is unendurable; but to a soul which has conquered Fate it is the key of religion.

The life of Man, viewed outwardly, is but a small thing in comparison with the forces of Nature. The slave is doomed to worship Time and Fate and Death, because they are greater than anything he finds in himself, and because all his thoughts are of things which they devour. But, great as they are, to think of them greatly, to feel their passionless splendour, is greater still. And such thought makes us free men; we no longer bow before the inevitable in Oriental subjection,[11] but we absorb it, and make it a part of ourselves. To abandon the struggle for private happiness, to expel all eagerness of temporary desire, to burn with passion for eternal things—this is emancipation, and this is the free man's worship. And this liberation is effected by a contemplation of Fate; for Fate itself is subdued by the mind which leaves nothing to be purged by the purifying fire of Time.

United with his fellow-men by the strongest of all ties, the tie of a common doom, the free man finds that a new vision is with him always, shedding over every daily task the light of love. The life of Man is a long march through the night, surrounded by invisible foes, tortured by weariness and pain, towards a goal that few can hope to reach, and where none may tarry long. One by one, as they march, our comrades vanish from our sight, seized by the silent orders of omnipotent Death. Very brief is the time in which we can help them, in which their happiness or misery is decided. Be it ours to shed sunshine on their path, to lighten their sorrows by the balm of sympathy, to give them the pure joy of a never-tiring affection, to strengthen failing courage, to instil faith in hours of despair. Let us not weigh in grudging scales their merits and demerits, but let us think only of their need— of the sorrows, the difficulties, perhaps the blindnesses, that make the misery of their lives; let us remember that they are fellow-sufferers in the same darkness, actors in the same tragedy with ourselves. And so, when their day is over, when their good and their evil have become eternal by the immortality of the past, be it ours to feel that, where they suffered, where they failed, no deed of ours was the cause; but wherever a spark of the divine fire kindled in their hearts, we were ready with encouragement, with sympathy, with brave words in which high courage glowed.

---

[11] *Oriental subjection*   The loss of self called for in many Eastern religions.

Brief and powerless is Man's life; on him and all his race the slow, 21
sure doom falls pitiless and dark. Blind to good and evil, reckless of
destruction, omnipotent matter rolls on its relentless way; for Man,
condemned today to lose his dearest, tomorrow himself to pass
through the gate of darkness, it remains only to cherish, ere yet the
blow falls, the lofty thoughts that ennoble his little day; disdaining
the coward terrors of the slave of Fate, to worship at the shrine that
his own hands have built; undismayed by the empire of chance, to
preserve a mind free from the wanton tyranny that rules his outward
life; proudly defiant of the irresistible forces that tolerate, for a moment, his knowledge and his condemnation, to sustain alone, a weary
but unyielding Atlas,[12] the world that his own ideals have fashioned
despite the trampling march of unconscious power.

---

[12]*Atlas*   A Greek mythic figure said to hold the pillars that separated heaven from the
earth.

QUESTIONS

1. What does Russell mean by power? What kinds of power can you find
   reference to?
2. Is it fair to say that Mephistopheles' description of creation agrees with
   science's description?
3. Why does Russell emphasize the fact that only humans understand the
   difference between good and evil?
4. Who did Russell expect to read this essay? What would their anxieties be?
   What would their attitudes toward belief be?
5. What does Russell seem to mean by the term "worship"? What does the
   savage's worship have in common with that of a "free man"?

WRITING ASSIGNMENTS

1. In the first five paragraphs, Russell paints a picture of the universe as a
   place of despair. On the one hand, it is the portrait of a demon; on the
   other, the portrait of modern science. Then he declares that "all these
   things, if not quite beyond dispute, are yet so nearly certain, that no philosophy which rejects them can hope to stand" (para. 5). Identify all the
   things Russell feels are nearly certain; then defend or attack this proposition that they are true beyond dispute.
2. In paragraph 10, Russell says, "If Power is bad, as it seems to be, let us
   reject it from our hearts. In this lies Man's true freedom: in determination

to worship only the God created by our own love of the good, to respect only the heaven which inspires the insight of our best moments." Establish exactly what is meant by these statements. Then establish your personal views on where true freedom lies. Point out what you can agree with Russell about and what you disagree on. Be sure to give your own arguments for your views. Decide for yourself what true freedom means for "Man."

3. Inventory the selection for the most interesting metaphors you can find. Find a dozen or so and list them. Establish exactly what they contribute to the power of this selection. What groupings do they fall into (military, natural, dramatic, etc.)? If there are a great many that are, say, military in nature, what does that fact mean for the force of Russell's argument? What moods are evoked by the metaphors? What emotions are meant to be aroused? Do you feel that any of the metaphors are overdone? Which metaphors are particularly effective? Do you think that the piece would be less interesting without them?

4. Assume that a group has declared that Russell is an atheist and that we should not read his work. Defend or attack the selection by siding with or against the "group." Is Russell being atheistic in this essay? What evidence will support or contradict such a view? If he were being atheistic, why would it be important not to read him? Or, why might it be very important to read him?

5. The title of this work is "A Free Man's Worship." What that actually is can be found in the definition in paragraph 19: "To abandon the struggle for private happiness, to expel all eagerness of temporary desire, to burn with passion for eternal things—this is emancipation, and this is the free man's worship." Begin your essay by clarifying each portion of this statement. Be sure to give examples where possible or to expand the statement enough so that someone who has not read this piece can understand what you mean. Then establish whether or not this really *is* a free man's worship. Why would it not be a slave's worship? What is freeing about it? Do you think that it represents emancipation in the same sense that Russell thinks it does?

SIMONE WEIL

Spiritual Autobiography

SIMONE WEIL (1909–1943) was born in Paris and died in Kent, England. Weil (pronounced Vay) is a highly controversial figure in modern thought, ranking in some people's estimation as among the most important thinkers of her generation. She has been praised by Jean-Paul Sartre, Albert Camus, and T. S. Eliot for the spiritual intensity of her life and her writing. She has been described in terms that are usually reserved for saints. She is, however, a remarkably contradictory person. Born a Jew yet feeling herself to be a Christian, she also resisted baptism into the Christian faith. Her struggles with Judaism parallel her struggles with the authoritative aspects of the Roman Catholic church. Always, her sympathies were with the weak. The tenents and practices of institutional religions were often at odds with her thinking.

She was an intellectual who demanded of herself that she bring her life into accord with her beliefs. She was influenced by Marxist thought when she was at the Sorbonne, and in 1931 she began teaching philosophy at a girls' school near Lyon. Her activities as a supporter of unemployed workers caused a scandal and cost her her job. It was not the last time such activism caused her to lose a teaching post. In 1934 she began to feel that physical labor is an essential part of the spiritual life, and thus she stopped teaching to become a worker. She eventually worked at the Renault plant. It was after she left her factory job she began to think of herself a Christian.

During the Spanish civil war in 1936 she took part on the side of the anti-Fascist Republicans, posing as a journalist. Her health, which had always been frail, was dealt a serious blow when, early in her stay in Spain, she spilled a pot of boiling oil on her leg. She was invalided out of the war and returned to France after only two months. During her convalescence, she traveled to Switzerland, then went to Italy where she found herself in the chapel of Santa Maria degli Angeli, where St. Francis of Assisi had often prayed. She found herself kneeling for the first time in her life—impressed, as she said, by a spiritual force that was greater than herself.

She was on extended sick leave from teaching in 1938 when the headaches that she had suffered from the age of twelve became almost unbearable. In the abbey of Solesmes that Easter she experienced a mystical revelation, as she informs us in her "Spiritual Autobiography." As she mentions, too, she became influenced by English metaphysical poetry of the seventeenth century, a spiritual, often mystical poetry that moved her deeply.

In 1939, at the beginning of World War II, she began writing extensively about religious matters and reading and studying Greek and Hindu philosophy. When France fell, she lived and worked on a farm in the unoccupied zone, called Vichy, and left some important writings with spiritual advisers. Among the most influential of the spiritual guides of this period was Father J.-M. Perrin, to whom the letter, "Spiritual Autobiography," is addressed.

In May 1942 Weil and her parents left France for Casablanca, then eventually worked their way to New York. While she was in New York, she attended mass daily. After only a short time she decided that she had to help the French Resistance in England, and she managed to find passage to Liverpool. However, both her earlier pacifist views and the fact that she had fought for the Spanish Republicans—essentially supported by Communists—made the authorities suspicious of her.

Eventually, she attached herself to a Free French ministry, but in response to the fact that some French were dying of starvation in the German-occupied area of France, she began to cut her food to match the rations of her compatriots on the Continent. During this period, she wrote extensively about politics and philosophy. Eventually, she fell ill and refused to eat. In her final illness she also refused baptism into the church, though she accepted the ministrations of a priest.

She died in 1943 of starvation and tuberculosis at the age of thirty-four.

"Spiritual Autobiography" tells Father Perrin a great deal about Weil's development as a Christian thinker. It also helps to explain why she felt herself to be Christian but refused to be baptized. She seems to have felt the need to remain an outsider, somewhat like Christ himself. Her religion was personal, mystical, outside the institutional church. Her writings are subtle and complex, and they constantly probe the spiritual meaning of life.

Her "Spiritual Autobiography" reads more like a memoir of a seventeenth-century mystic than it does of a twentieth-century philosopher. Yet, it is a document of a very unusual modern intellectual. It is unabashed, unashamed in describing events that are, to say the least, quite startling and, perhaps, difficult to believe. Yet, we cannot doubt that she believed what she said and that she expected Father Perrin to believe it too.

WEIL'S RHETORIC

This is a very straightforward work. Because it is a letter, it has a specific audience in mind, a priest who had been both her spiritual guide and her friend. Undoubtedly, Weil expected that the letter would be published, and therefore it is not typical of intimate correspondence. It is more like Martin Luther King, Jr.'s, "Letter from Birmingham Jail," and it, like King's is written in full awareness of the tradition of the epistles of the New Testament.

Interestingly, unlike King, she expected no reply, as she says immediately. She wrote the letter on May 15, and she left France forever on May 17. She implies that she and Father Perrin may have time for correspondence later, but her purposes are as explicit as are those stated in King's letter. She is trying to explain her indebtedness to Father Perrin and to convince him that she was not wrong to avoid baptism. Baptism would have brought her into the spiritual fold of Roman Catholicism—it would have made her officially a Christian.

Her letter is detailed, simple, and sometimes startling. She explains that, though she did not seek God, God found her. She tells us almost matter-of-factly that "Christ himself came down and took possession of me" (para. 21). Her reading had not prepared her for this event, and she is all the more grateful that this was so. It happened in a way that admitted no resistance; her experience was that of a *mystic, of a modern St. Teresa of Avila (1515–1582), who described her visions of Christ in her journals, which constitute her autobiography.*

When one reads this letter, it must be kept in mind that Weil was by no means an impressionable young woman. When she took a nationwide examination for college, she placed first in France; the great French intellectual Simone de Beauvoir was second. Weil's writings are deep, brilliant, and extensive in scope. They reveal a stunningly capacious mind. Thus, this record of a modern mystical experience cannot be simply dismissed. Rather, we must pay close attention to try to understand exactly what Weil experienced and to discover what that experience meant to her.

——————··⤜∞⤛··——————

Spiritual Autobiography

P.S. TO BE READ FIRST

This letter is fearfully long—but as there is no question of an an- 1
swer—especially as I shall doubtless have gone before it reaches you—
you have years ahead of you in which to read it if you care to. Read it
all the same, one day or another.

From Marseilles, about May 15

FATHER,

Before leaving I want to speak to you again, it may be the last time 2
perhaps, for over there I shall probably send you only my news from
time to time just so as to have yours.

I told you that I owed you an enormous debt. I want to try to tell 3
you exactly what it consists of. I think that if you could really understand what my spiritual state is you would not be at all sorry that you
did not lead me to baptism. But I do not know if it is possible for you
to understand this.

You neither brought me the Christian inspiration nor did you bring 4
me to Christ; for when I met you there was no longer any need; it had
been done without the intervention of any human being. If it had been
otherwise, if I had not already been won, not only implicitly but consciously, you would have given me nothing, because I should have

received nothing from you. My friendship for you would have been a reason for me to refuse your message, for I should have been afraid of the possibilities of error and illusion which human influence in the divine order is likely to involve.

I may say that never at any moment in my life have I "sought for 5 God." For this reason, which is probably too subjective, I do not like this expression and it strikes me as false. As soon as I reached adolescence, I saw the problem of God as a problem the data of which could not be obtained here below, and I decided that the only way of being sure not to reach a wrong solution, which seemed to me the greatest possible evil, was to leave it alone. So I left it alone. I neither affirmed nor denied anything. It seemed to me useless to solve the problem, for I thought that, being in this world, our business was to adopt the best attitude with regard to the problems of this world, and that such an attitude did not depend upon the solution of the problem of God.

This held good as far as I was concerned at any rate, for I never 6 hesitated in my choice of an attitude; I always adopted the Christian attitude as the only possible one. I might say that I was born, I grew up, and I always remained within the Christian inspiration. While the very name of God had no part in my thoughts, with regard to the problems of this world and this life I shared the Christian conception in an explicit and rigorous manner, with the most specific notions it involves. Some of these notions have been part of my outlook for as far back as I can remember. With others I know the time and manner of their coming and the form under which they imposed themselves upon me.

For instance I never allowed myself to think of a future state, but I 7 always believed that the instant of death is the center and object of life. I used to think that, for those who live as they should, it is the instant when, for an infinitesimal fraction of time, pure truth, naked, certain, and eternal, enters the soul. I may say that I never desired any other good for myself. I thought that the life leading to this good is not only defined by a code of morals common to all, but that for each one it consists of a succession of acts and events strictly personal to him, and so essential that he who leaves them on one side never reaches the goal. The notion of vocation was like this for me. I saw that the carrying out of a vocation differed from the actions dictated by reason or inclination in that it was due to an impulse of an essentially and manifestly different order; and not to follow such an impulse when it made itself felt, even if it demanded impossibilities, seemed to me the greatest of all ills. Hence my conception of obedience; and I put this conception to the test when I entered the factory and stayed on there, even when I was in that state of intense and uninterrupted misery about which I recently told you. The most beautiful life possible has always seemed to me to be one where everything is determined, either by the pressure of circumstances or by impulses such as I have just mentioned and where there is never any room for choice.

At fourteen I fell into one of those fits of bottomless despair that come with adolescence, and I seriously thought of dying because of the mediocrity of my natural faculties. The exceptional gifts of my brother, who had a childhood and youth comparable to those of Pascal,[1] brought my own inferiority home to me. I did not mind having no visible successes, but what did grieve me was the idea of being excluded from that transcendent kingdom to which only the truly great have access and wherein truth abides. I preferred to die rather than live without that truth. After months of inward darkness, I suddenly had the everlasting conviction that any human being, even though practically devoid of natural faculties, can penetrate to the kingdom of truth reserved for genius, if only he longs for truth and perpetually concentrates all his attention upon its attainment. He thus becomes a genius too, even though for lack of talent his genius cannot be visible from outside. Later on, when the strain of headaches caused the feeble faculties I possess to be invaded by a paralysis, which I was quick to imagine as probably incurable, the same conviction led me to persevere for ten years in an effort of concentrated attention that was practically unsupported by any hope of results. 8

Under the name of truth I also included beauty, virtue, and every kind of goodness, so that for me it was a question of a conception of the relationship between grace and desire. The conviction that had come to me was that when one hungers for bread one does not receive stones. But at that time I had not read the Gospel. 9

Just as I was certain that desire has in itself an efficacy in the realm of spiritual goodness whatever its form, I thought it was also possible that it might not be effective in any other realm. 10

As for the spirit of poverty, I do not remember any moment when it was not in me, although only to that unhappily small extent compatible with my imperfection. I fell in love with Saint Francis of 11

---

[1]***Blaise Pascal (1623–1662)*** French philosopher and mathematician whose most important work, *Pensées* (Thoughts), was published posthumously in 1670 in a version that was totally garbled. It was published again in 1844 in a restored version. He is famous for having pointed out that it is better to believe in God than not: there is everything to lose if God exists but nothing to lose if he does not exist. This has properly been condemned as a cynical and theologically useless argument.

Assisi[2] as soon as I came to know about him. I always believed and hoped that one day Fate would force upon me the condition of a vagabond and a Beggar which he embraced freely. Actually I felt the same way about prison.

From my earliest childhood I always had also the Christian idea of love for one's neighbor, to which I gave the name of justice—a name it bears in many passages of the gospel and which is so beautiful. You know that on this point I have failed seriously several times.

The duty of acceptance in all that concerns the will of God, whatever it may be, was impressed upon my mind as the first and most necessary of all duties from the time when I found it set down in Marcus Aurelius[3] under the form of the *amor fati* of the Stoics. I saw it as a duty we cannot fail in without dishonoring ourselves.

The idea of purity, with all that this word can imply for a Christian, took possession of me at the age of sixteen, after a period of several months during which I had been going through the emotional unrest natural in adolescence. This idea came to me when I was contemplating a mountain landscape and little by little it was imposed upon me in an irresistible manner.

Of course I knew quite well that my conception of life was Christian. That is why it never occurred to me that I could enter the Christian community. I had the idea that I was born inside. But to add dogma[4] to this conception of life, without being forced to do so by indisputable evidence, would have seemed to me like a lack of honesty. I should even have thought I was lacking in honesty had I considered the question of the truth of dogma as a problem for myself or even had I simply desired to reach a conclusion on this subject. I have an extremely severe standard for intellectual honesty, so severe that I never met anyone who did not seem to fall short of it in more than one respect; and I am always afraid of failing in it myself.

Keeping away from dogma in this way, I was prevented by a sort of shame from going into churches, though all the same I like being in

12

13

14

15

16

---

[2]***Saint Francis of Assisi (1182?–1226)*** Founder of the Franciscan order of Roman Catholic monks. He committed himself to poverty and a simple life and was a model of pious devotion. In 1224 he fasted on a mountaintop for forty days and nights and experienced the stigmata, an appearance on his body of the wounds of Christ on the cross.

[3]***Marcus Aurelius (121–180)*** Roman emperor and an important stoic philosopher. Stoicism praised self-sacrifice to the state and praised one who could suffer his fate with dignity and in silence. His *Meditations* is his most important work; *amor fati* means love of (one's) fate or contentment with one's lot.

[4]***dogma*** The tenets of the Roman Catholic faith.

them. Nevertheless, I had three contacts with Catholicism that really counted.

After my year in the factory, before going back to teaching, I had 17 been taken by my parents to Portugal, and while there I left them to go alone to a little village. I was, as it were, in pieces, soul and body. That contact with affliction had killed my youth. Until then I had not had any experience of affliction, unless we count my own, which, as it was my own, seemed to me, to have little importance, and which moreover was only a partial affliction, being biological and not social. I knew quite well that there was a great deal of affliction in the world, I was obsessed with the idea, but I had not had prolonged and first-hand experience of it. As I worked in the factory, indistinguishable to all eyes, including my own, from the anonymous mass, the affliction of others entered into my flesh and my soul. Nothing separated me from it, for I had really forgotten my past and I looked forward to no future, finding it difficult to imagine the possibility of surviving all the fatigue. What I went through there marked me in so lasting a manner that still today when any human being, whoever he may be and in whatever circumstances, speaks to me without brutality, I cannot help having the impression that there must be a mistake and that unfortunately the mistake will in all probability disappear. There I received forever the mark of a slave, like the branding of the red-hot iron the Romans put on the foreheads of their most despised slaves. Since then I have always regarded myself as a slave.

In this state of mind then, and in a wretched condition physically, 18 I entered the little Portuguese village, which, alas, was very wretched too, on the very day of the festival of its patron saint. I was alone. It was the evening and there was a full moon over the sea. The wives of the fishermen were, in procession, making a tour of all the ships, carrying candles and singing what must certainly be very ancient hymns of a heart-rending sadness. Nothing can give any idea of it. I have never heard anything so poignant unless it were the song of the boatmen on the Volga. There the conviction was suddenly borne in upon me that Christianity is pre-eminently the religion of slaves, that slaves cannot help belonging to it, and I among others.

In 1937 I had two marvelous days at Assisi. There, alone in the 19 little twelfth-century Romanesque chapel of Santa Maria degli Angeli,[5] an incomparable marvel of purity where Saint Francis often used to

---

[5]***Santa Maria degli Angeli*** Saint Mary of the Angels, a church in which St. Francis prayed and received enlightenment.

pray, something stronger than I was compelled me for the first time in my life to go down on my knees.

In 1938 I spent ten days at Solesmes, from Palm Sunday to Easter 20
Tuesday, following all the liturgical services. I was suffering from splitting headaches; each sound hurt me like a blow; by an extreme effort of concentration I was able to rise above this wretched flesh, to leave it to suffer by itself, heaped up in a corner, and to find a pure and perfect joy in the unimaginable beauty of the chanting and the words. This experience enabled me by analogy to get a better understanding of the possibility of loving divine love in the midst of affliction. It goes without saying that in the course of these services the thought of the Passion of Christ entered into my being once and for all.

There was a young English Catholic there from whom I gained my 21
first idea of the supernatural power of the sacraments because of the truly angelic radiance with which he seemed to be clothed after going to communion. Chance—for I always prefer saying chance rather than Providence—made of him a messenger to me. For he told me of the existence of those English poets of the seventeenth century who are named metaphysical. In reading them later on, I discovered the poem of which I read you what is unfortunately a very inadequate translation. It is called "Love".[6] I learned it by heart. Often, at the culminating point of a violent headache, I make myself say it over, concentrating all my attention upon it and clinging with all my soul to the tenderness it enshrines. I used to think I was merely reciting it as a beautiful poem, but without my knowing it the recitation had the virtue of a prayer. It was during one of these recitations that, as I told you, Christ himself came down and took possession of me.

In my arguments about the insolubility of the problem of God. I 22
had never forseen the possibility of that, of a real contact, person to person, here below, between a human being and God. I had vaguely heard tell of things of this kind, but I had never believed in them. In the *Fioretti*[7] the accounts of apparitions rather put me off if anything, like the miracles in the Gospel. Moreover, in this sudden possession of me by Christ, neither my senses nor my imagination had any part; I only felt in the midst of my suffering the presence of a love, like that which one can read in the smile on a beloved face.

I had never read any mystical works because I had never felt any 23

---

[6]***"Love"*** A poem by the English metaphysical poet George Herbert (1593–1633). He was a clergyman whose poems were often profoundly religious. His *The Temple* is a cycle of poems based on the architecture of the church.

[7]**Fioretti** Literally, little flowers. These were important writings of St. Francis.

call to read them. In reading as in other things I have always striven
to practice obedience. There is nothing more favorable to intellectual
progress, for as far as possible I only read what I am hungry for at the
moment when I have an appetite for it, and then I do not read, I *eat*.
God in his mercy had prevented me from reading the mystics, so that
it should be evident to me that I had not invented this absolutely unexpected contact.

Yet I still half refused, not my love but my intelligence. For it 24
seemed to me certain, and I still think so today, that one can never
wrestle enough with God if one does so out of pure regard for the
truth. Christ likes us to prefer truth to him because, before being
Christ, he is truth. If one turns aside from him to go toward the truth,
one will not go far before falling into his arms.

After this I came to feel that Plato was a mystic, that all the *Iliad* 25
is bathed in Christian light, and that Dionysus and Osiris[8] are in a
certain sense Christ himself; and my love was thereby redoubled.

I never wondered whether Jesus was or was not the Incarnation of 26
God; but in fact I was incapable of thinking of him without thinking
of him as God.

In the spring of 1940 I read the *Bhagavad-Gita*.[9] Strange to say it 27
was in reading those marvelous words, words with such a Christian
sound, put into the mouth of an incarnation of God, that I came to
feel strongly that we owe an allegiance to religious truth which is
quite different from the admiration we accord to a beautiful poem; it
is something far more categorical.

Yet I did not believe it to be possible for me to consider the ques- 28
tion of baptism. I felt that I could not honestly give up my opinions
concerning the non-Christian religions and concerning Israel—and as
a matter of fact time and meditation have only served to strengthen
them—and I thought that this constituted an absolute obstacle. I did
not imagine it as possible that a priest could even dream of granting
me baptism. If I had not met you, I should never have considered the
problem of baptism as a practical problem.

During all this time of spiritual progress I had never prayed. I was 29

---

[8]***the Iliad . . . Dionysus . . . Osiris*** Homer's epic *Iliad* tells the story of the
destruction of Troy and establishes the role of the Greek gods in human affairs. Dionysus
was, in ancient Greek religion, a god of fertility and was associated with ecstatic rites
and rituals. Osiris was the center of an important early cult originating in Egypt and was
associated with the god of the underworld.

[9]**Bhagavad-Gita** Song of the Blessed One; an Indian Sanskrit poem, part of the larger
Mahabarata. It is a sacred text explaining the relation of God to his loved one.

afraid of the power of suggestion that is in prayer—the very power for which Pascal recommends it. Pascal's method seems to me one of the worst for attaining faith.

Contact with you was not able to persuade me to pray. On the contrary I thought the danger was all the greater, since I also had to beware of the power of suggestion in my friendship with you. At the same time I found it very difficult not to pray and not to tell you so. Moreover I knew I could not tell you without completely misleading you about myself. At that time I should not have been able to make you understand. 30

Until last September I had never once prayed in all my life, at least not in the literal sense of the word. I had never said any words to God, either out loud or mentally. I had never pronounced a liturgical prayer. I had occasionally recited the *Salve Regina*,[10] but only as a beautiful poem. 31

Last summer, doing Greek with T——, I went through the Our Father word for word in Greek. We promised each other to learn it by heart. I do not think he ever did so, but some weeks later, as I was turning over the pages of the Gospel, I said to myself that since I had promised to do this thing and it was good, I ought to do it. I did it. The infinite sweetness of this Greek text so took hold of me that for several days I could not stop myself from saying it over all the time. A week afterward I began the vine harvest.[11] I recited the Our Father in Greek every day before work, and I repeated it very often in the vineyard. 32

Since that time I have made a practice of saying it through once each morning with absolute attention. If during the recitation my attention wanders or goes to sleep, in the minutest degree, I begin again until I have once succeeded in going through it with absolutely pure attention. Sometimes it comes about that I say it again out of sheer pleasure, but I only do it if I really feel the impulse. 33

The effect of this practice is extraordinary and surprises me every time, for, although I experience it each day, it exceeds my expectation at each repetition. 34

At times the very first words tear my thoughts from my body and transport it to a place outside space where there is neither perspective nor point of view. The infinity of the ordinary expanses of perception is replaced by an infinity to the second or sometimes the third degree. 35

---

[10]**Salve Regina**   Hail Mary, a prayer or hymn to the Virgin Mary.

[11]*vine harvest*   At the time, Weil was working in the fields as a farm laborer in an effort to simplify her life and to get in closer touch with the soil.

At the same time, filling every part of this infinity of infinity, there is silence, a silence which is not an absence of sound but which is the object of a positive sensation, more positive than that of sound. Noises, if there are any, only reach me after crossing this silence.

Sometimes, also during this recitation or at other moments, Christ 36 is present with me in person, but his presence is infinitely more real, more moving, more clear than on that first occasion when he took possession of me.

I should never have been able to take it upon myself to tell you all 37 this had it not been for the fact that I am going away. And as I am going more or less with the idea of probable death, I do not believe that I have the right to keep it to myself. For after all, the whole of this matter is not a question concerning me myself. It concerns God. I am really nothing in it all. If one could imagine any possibility of error in God, I should think that it had all happened to me by mistake. But perhaps God likes to use castaway objects, waste, rejects. After all, should the bread of the host be moldy, it would become the Body of Christ[12] just the same after the priest had consecrated it. Only it cannot refuse, while we can disobey. It sometimes seems to me that when I am treated in so merciful a way, every sin on my part must be a mortal sin. And I am constantly committing them.

I have told you that you are like a father and brother at the same 38 time to me. But these words only express an analogy. Perhaps at bottom they only correspond to a feeling of affection, of gratitude and admiration. For as to the spiritual direction of my soul, I think that God himself has taken it in hand from the start and still looks after it.

That does not prevent me from owing you the greatest debt of grat- 39 itude that I could ever have incurred toward any human being. This is exactly what it consists of.

First you once said to me at the beginning of our relationship some 40 words that went to the bottom of my soul. You said: "Be very careful, because if you should pass over something important through your own fault it would be a pity."

That made me see intellectual honesty in a new light. Till then I 41 had only thought of it as opposed to faith; your words made me think that perhaps, without my knowing it, there were in me obstacles to the faith, impure obstacles, such as prejudices, habits. I felt that after having said to myself for so many years simply: "Perhaps all that is

---

[12]***bread of the host . . . Body of Christ*** The doctrine of transubstantiation, part of the sacrament of the mass, establishes that when the priest consecrates the bread (the host) it becomes the body of Christ, which is then partaken by the communicant.

not true,"I ought, without ceasing to say it—I still take care to say it very often now—to join it to the opposite formula, namely: "Perhaps all that is true," and to make them alternate.

At the same time, in making the problem of baptism a practical 42 problem for me, you have forced me to face the whole question of the faith, dogma, and the sacraments, obliging me to consider them closely and at length with the fullest possible attention, making me see them as things toward which I have obligations that I have to discern and perform. I should never have done this otherwise and it is indispensible for me to do it.

But the greatest blessing you have brought me is of another order. 43 In gaining my friendship by your charity (which I have never met anything to equal), you have provided me with a source of the most compelling and pure inspiration that is to be found among human things. For nothing among human things has such power to keep our gaze fixed ever more intensely upon God, than friendship for the friends of God.

Nothing better enables me to measure the breadth of your charity 44 than the fact that you bore with me for so long and with such gentleness. I may seem to be joking, but that is not the case. It is true that you have not the same motives as I have myself (those about which I wrote to you the other day), for feeling hatred and repulsion toward me. But all the same I feel that your patience with me can only spring from a supernatural generosity.

I have not been able to avoid causing you the greatest disappoint- 45 ment it was in my power to cause you. But up to now, although I have often asked myself the question during prayer, during Mass, or in the light of the radiancy that remains in the soul after Mass, I have never once had, even for a moment, the feeling that God wants me to be in the Church. I have never even once had a feeling of uncertainty. I think that at the present time we can finally conclude that he does not want me in the Church. Do not have any regrets about it.

He does not want it so far at least. But unless I am mistaken I 46 should say that it is his will that I should stay outside for the future too, except perhaps at the moment of death. Yet I am always ready to obey an order, whatever it may be. I should joyfully obey the order to go to the very center of hell and to remain there eternally. I do not mean, of course, that I have a preference for orders of this nature. I am not perverse like that.

Christianity should contain all vocations without exception since 47 it is catholic. In consequence the Church should also. But in my eyes

Christianity is catholic by right but not in fact. So many things are outside it, so many things that I love and do not want to give up, so many things that God loves, otherwise they would not be in existence. All the immense stretches of past centuries, except the last twenty are among them; all the countries inhabited by colored races; all secular life in the white peoples' countries; in the history of these countries, all the traditions banned as heretical, those of the Manicheans and Albigenses[13] for instance; all those things resulting from the Renaissance, too often degraded but not quite without value.

Christianity being catholic by right but not in fact, I regard it as legitimate on my part to be a member of the Church by right but not in fact, not only for a time, but for my whole life if need be. 48

But it is not merely legitimate. So long as God does not give me the certainty that he is ordering me to do anything else, I think it is my duty. 49

I think, and so do you, that our obligation for the next two or three years, an obligation so strict that we can scarcely fail in it without treason, is to show the public the possibility of a truly incarnated Christianity. In all the history now known there has never been a period in which souls have been in such peril as they are today in every part of the globe. The bronze serpent must be lifted up again so that whoever raises his eyes to it may be saved. 50

But everything is so closely bound up together that Christianity cannot be really incarnated unless it is catholic in the sense that I have just defined. How could it circulate through the flesh of all the nations of Europe if it did not contain absolutely everything in itself? Except of course falsehood. But in everything that exists there is most of the time more truth than falsehood. 51

Having so intense and so painful a sense of this urgency, I should betray the truth, that is to say the aspect of truth that I see, if I left the point, where I have been since my birth, at the intersection of Christianity and everything that is not Christianity. 52

I have always remained at this exact point, on the threshold of the Church, without moving, quite still, ἐν ὑπομονῇ[14] (it is so much more 53

---

[13] ***Manicheans and Albigenses*** The Manicheans were a cult that developed before the time of Christ; they believed that good and evil were in a constant struggle for the possession of the world and that the fate of the world was in doubt. This belief was declared heretical because it did not demonstrate faith in the providence of God. Albigensians were a thirteenth-century sect of Christians in southern France; they were Manicheans who believed that all matter was evil, and they practiced a form of birth control in order to prevent the soul—the human spirit—from being entrapped in a material fleshly body.

[14] ἐν ὑπομονῇ In patient endurance.

beautiful a word than *patientia!*); only now my heart has been transported, forever, I hope, into the Blessed Sacrament exposed on the alter.

You see that I am very far from the thoughts that H——, with the 54 best of intentions, attributed to me. I am far also from being worried in any way.

If I am sad, it comes primarily from the permanent sadness that 55 destiny has imprinted forever upon my emotions, where the greatest and purest joys can only be superimposed and that at the price of a great effort of attention. It comes also from my miserable and continual sins; and from all the calamities of our time and of all those of all the past centuries.

I think that you should understand why I have always resisted you, 56 if in spite of being a priest you can admit that a genuine vocation might prevent anyone from entering the Church.

Otherwise a barrier of incomprehension will remain between us, 57 whether the error is on my part or on yours. This would grieve me from the point of view of my friendship for you, because in that case the result of all these efforts and desires, called forth by your charity toward me, would be a disappointment for you. Moreover, although it is not my fault, I should not be able to help feeling guilty of ingratitude. For, I repeat, my debt to you is beyond all measure.

I should like to draw your attention to one point. It is that there is 58 an absolutely insurmountable obstacle to the Incarnation of Christianity. It is the use of the two little words *anathema sit*.[15] It is not their existence, but the way they have been employed up till now. It is that also which prevents me from crossing the threshold of the Church. I remain beside all those things that cannot enter the Church, the universal repository, on account of those two little words. I remain beside them all the more because my own intelligence is numbered among them.

The Incarnation of Christianity implies a harmonious solution 59 of the problem of the relations between the individual and the collective. Harmony in the Pythagorean[16] sense; the just balance of

---

[15]**anathema sit** "It is evil"—the church's powerful curse; it is pronounced during excommunication. It was first pronounced during the excommunication of Martin Luther in 1520.

[16]***Pythagorean*** This refers to Pythagoras (6th century B.C.), a Greek philosopher who according to legend developed the tuned string and worked out the relationships between the notes of the musical scale.

contraries. This solution is precisely what men are thirsting for today.

The position of the intelligence is the key to this harmony, because 60 the intelligence is a specifically and rigorously individual thing. This harmony exists wherever the intelligence, remaining in its place, can be exercised without hindrance and can reach the complete fulfillment of its function. That is what Saint Thomas[17] says admirably of all the parts of the soul of Christ, with reference to his sensitiveness to pain during the crucifixion.

The special function of the intelligence requires total liberty, im- 61 plying the right to deny everything, and allowing of no domination. Wherever it usurps control there is an excess of individualism. Wherever it is hampered or uneasy there is an oppressive collectivism, or several of them.

The Church and the State should punish it, each one in its own 62 way, when it advocates actions of which they disapprove. When it remains in the region of purely theoretical speculation they still have the duty, should occasion arise, to put the public on their guard, by every effective means, against the danger of the practical influence certain speculations might have upon the conduct of life. But whatever these theoretical speculations may be, the Church and the State have no right either to try to stifle them or to inflict any penalty material or moral upon their authors. Notably, they should not be deprived of the sacraments if they desire them. For, whatever they may have said, even if they have publicly denied the existence of God, they may not have committed any sin. In such a case the Church should declare that they are in error, but it should not demand of them anything whatever in the way of a disavowal of what they have said, nor should it deprive them of the Bread of Life.

A collective body is the guardian of dogma; and dogma is an object 63 of contemplation for love, faith, and intelligence, three strictly individual faculties. Hence, almost since the beginning, the individual has been ill at ease in Christianity, and this uneasiness has been notably one of the intelligence. This cannot be denied.

Christ himself who is Truth itself, when he was speaking before an 64 assembly such as a council, did not address it in the same language as he used in an intimate conversation with his well-beloved friend, and

---

[17]**St. Thomas** St. Thomas Aquinas (1225?–1274) was among the most powerful philosophers of the Catholic Church. His *Summa Theologica* is still studied by modern theologians.

no doubt before the Pharisees[18] he might easily have been accused of contradiction and error. For by one of those laws of nature, which God himself respects, since he has willed them from all eternity, there are two languages that are quite distinct although made up of the same words; there is the collective language and there is the individual one. The Comforter whom Christ sends us, the Spirit of truth, speaks one or other of these languages, whichever circumstances demand, and by a necessity of their nature there is not agreement between them.

When genuine friends of God—such as was Eckhart[19] to my way of thinking—repeat words they have heard in secret amidst the silence of the union of love, and these words are in disagreement with the teaching of the Church, it is simply that the language of the market place is not that of the nuptial chamber.   65

Everybody knows that really intimate conversation is only possible between two or three. As soon as there are six or seven, collective language begins to dominate. That is why it is a complete misinterpretation to apply to the Church the words "Wheresoever two or three are gathered together in my name, there am I in the midst of them." Christ did not say two hundred, or fifty, or ten. He said two or three. He said precisely that he always forms the third in the intimacy of the tête-à-tête.[20]   65

Christ made promises to the Church, but none of these promises has the force of the expression "Thy Father who seeth in secret."[21] The word of God is the secret word. He who has not heard this word, even if he adheres to all the dogmas taught by the Church, has no contact with truth.   67

---

[18]**Pharisees**   Members of a Jewish group concerned with the law, both in its written and oral forms. Jesus spoke with them concerning the law and its interpretations. See Luke 7. Paul said, "After the most straitest sect of our religion I lived a Pharisee," Acts 26:5.

[19]**Meister Johannes Eckhart (1260?–1327)**   An important early German mystic and theologian. The church found it difficult to accept some of his teachings, and some things he said were condemned after his death. He believed that God was everything— that everything had its own essence but that its existence was only in God. His ideas have sometimes been thought to be pantheistic—seeing God in everything.

[20]**tête-à-tête**   Literally, "head to head;" an intimate conversation.

[21]**"Thy Father who seeth in secret."**   Matthew 6:1–4: "Take heed that ye do not your alms before men, to be seen of them: otherwise ye have no reward of your Father which is in heaven. Therefore when thou doest thine alms, do not sound a trumpet before thee, as the hypocrites do in the synagogues and in the streets, that they may have glory of men. Verily I say unto you, They have their reward. But when thou doest alms, let not thy left hand know what thy right hand doeth: that thine alms may be in secret: and thy Father which seeth in secret himself shall reward thee openly."

The function of the Church as the collective keeper of dogma is   68
indispensable. She has the right and the duty to punish those who
make a clear attack upon her within the specific range of this function,
by depriving them of the sacraments.

Thus, although I know practically nothing of this business, I in-   69
cline to think provisionally that she was right to punish Luther.[22]

But she is guilty of an abuse of power when she claims to force   70
love and intelligence to model their language upon her own. This
abuse of power is not of God. It comes from the natural tendency of
every form of collectivism, without exception, to abuse power.

The image of the Mystical Body of Christ is very attractive. But I   71
consider the importance given to this image today as one of the most
serious signs of our degeneration. For our true dignity is not to be parts
of a body, even though it be a mystical one, even though it be that of
Christ. It consists in this, that in the state of perfection, which is the
vocation of each one of us, we no longer live in ourselves, but Christ
lives in us; so that through our perfection Christ in his integrity and
in his indivisible unity, becomes in a sense each one of us, as he is
completely in each host. The hosts are not a *part* of his body.

This present-day importance of the image of the Mystical Body   72
shows how wretchedly susceptible Christians are to outside influences. Undoubtedly there is real intoxication in being a member of the
Mystical Body of Christ. But today a great many other mystical bodies,
which have not Christ for their head, produce an intoxication in their
members that to my way of thinking is of the same order.

As long as it is through obedience, I find sweetness in my depriva-   73
tion of the joy of membership in the Mystical Body of Christ. For if
God is willing to help me, I may thus bear witness that without this
joy one can nevertheless be faithful to Christ unto death. Social enthusiasms have such power today, they raise people so effectively to the
supreme degree of heroism in suffering and death, that I think it is as
well that a few sheep should remain outside the fold in order to bear
witness that the love of Christ is essentially something different.

The Church today defends the cause of the indefeasible rights[23] of   74

---

[22]**Martin Luther (1483–1546)** German theologian whose ninety-five theses in
1517 began the Protestant Reformation. He was excommunicated from the Roman Catholic church for refusing to change his stand on the question of whether good deeds contributed to salvation; he insisted that only faith mattered: doing good deeds was irrelevant to one's salvation.

[23]**indefeasible rights** Rights that cannot be made otherwise or cannot be repealed.
They are absolute rights.

the individual against collective oppression, of liberty of thought against tyranny. But these are causes readily embraced by those who find themselves momentarily to be the least strong. It is their only way of perhaps one day becoming the strongest. That is well known.

You may perhaps be offended by this idea. You are not the Church. 75 During the periods of the most atrocious abuse of power committed by the Church, there must have been some priests like you among the others. Your good faith is not a guarantee, even were it shared by all your Order. You cannot foresee what turn things may take.

In order that the present attitude of the Church should be effective 76 and that she should really penetrate like a wedge into social existence, she would have to say openly that she had changed or wished to change. Otherwise who could take her seriously when they remembered the Inquisition?[24] My friendship for you, which I extend through you to all your Order, makes it very painful for me to bring this up. But it existed. After the fall of the Roman Empire, which had been totalitarian, it was the Church that was the first to establish a rough sort of totalitarianism in Europe in the thirteenth century, after the war with the Albigenses. This tree bore much fruit.

And the motive power of this totalitarianism was the use of those 77 two little words: *anathema sit.*

It was moreover by a judicious transposition of this use that all the 78 parties which in our own day have founded totalitarian régimes were shaped. This is a point of history I have specially studied.

I must give you the impression of a Luciferian pride is speaking 79 thus of a great many matters that are too high for me and about which I have no right to understand anything. It is not my fault. Ideas come and settle in my mind by mistake, then, realizing their mistake, they absolutely insist on coming out. I do not know where they come from, or what they are worth, but, whatever the risk, I do not think I have the right to prevent this operation.

Good-by, I wish you all possible good things except the cross; for I 80 do not love my neighbor as myself, you particularly, as you have noticed. But Christ granted to his well-beloved disciple, and probably to all that disciple's spiritual lineage, to come to him not through degradation, defilement, and distress, but in uninterrupted joy, purity, and

---

[24]**the Inquisition** An organization founded by the church in the thirteenth century to root out heresy. It became a tyrannical court of inquiry which often tortured and executed its victims and expressed its power whimsically and viciously. It has become a symbol of the excesses that even benign powerful institutions such as the church sometimes can resort to.

sweetness. That is why I can allow myself to wish that even if one day you have the honor of dying a violent death for Our Lord, it may be with joy and without any anguish; also that only three of the beatitudes[25] (*mites, mundo corde, pacifici*) will apply to you. All the others involve more or less of suffering.

This wish is not due only to the frailty of human friendship. For, with any human being taken individually, I always find reasons for concluding that sorrow and misfortune do not suit him, either because he seems too mediocre for anything so great or, on the contrary, too precious to be destroyed. One cannot fail more seriously in the second of the two essential commandments. And as to the first, I fail to observe that, in a still more horrible manner, for every time I think of the crucifixion of Christ I commit the sin of envy.

Believe more than ever and forever in my filial and tenderly grateful friendship.

SIMONE WEIL

---

[25]***three of the beatitudes*** A reference to Christ's Sermon on the Mount, which begins, "Blessed are the poor in spirit." *Mites, mundo corde, pacifici* are the humble, the pure of heart, and the peacemakers.

QUESTIONS

1. What does Weil mean when she tells Father Perrin that she was not brought to Christianity by any human intervention?
2. What does the relationship between Father Perrin and Weil seem to have been like? What kind of an audience did she expect him to be for this letter?
3. Weil describes herself as an adolescent. What was she like?
4. The relationship of God to the truth is detailed in paragraph 24. What does Weil seem to mean in this paragraph? Do you agree with her?
5. What kind of religious experience is Weil describing? Is it what you think of when you think of religion and religious experience?

WRITING ASSIGNMENTS

1. Write a letter in response to Weil's. You needn't imagine yourself to be Father Perrin (although you may do so if you wish). In any case, simply respond to Simone Weil in your own voice and rely on your own attitudes toward religious experience. In the course of your letter, offer her your own "spiritual autobiography."

2. Relying on Weil's letter, describe her religious views. Remember that she avoided joining a specific religion; however, she felt herself to be genuinely religious. What does it mean to be religious but not be a member of a church? What does it mean to consider yourself a Christian but not permit yourself to be baptized into that faith? Remember that Weil addresses a man who is a priest—who has, in other words, the vocation that she says she lacks.

3. What is Weil's attitude toward God? Consider all that she says about God and try to imagine how she conceptualizes God. What would God want of her? What would God want of anyone? What does she feel she can give God? What, if anything, would she hold back?

4. Starting in paragraph 47, Weil expresses her reservations about the Catholic church. What are they? What is her attitude toward institutionalized religion? Does she include Father Perrin in the institution of the church?

5. What does Weil mean when she says that since her youth she has been "at the intersection of Christianity and everything that is not Christianity" (para. 52)? She says she feels that Christianity must include all that is not Christianity. What does she mean by this statement? What things would she consider as being part of Christianity today? What things would not be part of Christianity? Do you find yourself agreeing with her or not?

PAUL TILLICH

———◦∞◦———

Symbols of Faith

*P*AUL TILLICH *(1886–1965), the son of a Lutheran minister, was born in Starzeddel, Prussia, and studied at the universities of Berlin, Tübingen, and Halle. He received his doctorate from the University of Breslau. His reputation was established in philosophy and theology, and his published works in these areas is voluminous. In Germany he taught theology at Berlin, Marburg, and numerous other universities, but when Hitler was made chancellor in 1933, he was dismissed from the University of Frankfurt am Main. His religious views were totally opposed to the views of Hitler and his supporters.*

He came to the United States and accepted a post at Union Theological Seminary in New York City, where he taught for more than twenty years. When he left Union in 1955, he was made a university professor at Harvard. His last academic appointment was at the University of Chicago. During his last years, he taught to overflowing classrooms and was recognized as one of the most important, dynamic, and innovative theologians of the modern world.

His most important writings in theology are Systematic Theology *(3 vols. 1951–1963);* The Courage to Be *(1952);* Biblical Religion and the Search for Ultimate Reality *(1955);* Dynamics of Faith *(1957),*

From *Dynamics of Faith.*

from which the selection is taken; A History of Christian Thought
(1968); and What Is Religion? (1969), both the latter books being
among his many posthumous publications. One of the views most
central to the theology he constructed is expressed in "Symbols of
Faith." It concerns the nature of God.

Tillich developed his views regarding the "ultimate concern" as
early as 1932 in The Religious Situation, published while he was still
in Germany. The concept, which is developed in the selection, focuses
on the most significant of human concerns, "ultimate concerns,"
those we have regarding the essential nature of human life, the primary goals of living, and the most basic values we hold. Tillich says,
at least in one sense, that it is our capability of conceiving an ultimate concern that gives us such a strong sense of the value of faith.

Tillich refused to see God as an individual being with the limitations of all individual beings. He believed that God is infinite and
that any attempt to limit the concept of God to a single being is an
effort to make God a finite being, which he regarded as an impious
impossibility. Moreover, he discerned that the modern temptation toward materialism would spill over into matters of faith—which are
by definition spiritual—if Christians persisted in thinking of God as
a specific being. Rather, he conceived of God as Being itself.

He called this idea of God the "Protestant principle," a protesta-
tion against anything that attempts to reduce or confine the infinitude
of God in Christianity. Moreover, he became deeply interested in theories of modern psychology, seeing in the concept of the unconscious
a number of important religious expressions. For example, in "Symbols of Faith" he links religious symbols with the collective unconscious of Carl Jung (see pages 309–325), implying that the symbols of
faith are embedded deeply in the human psyche.

In his discussion of symbols, Tillich reminds us that all matters
of faith are expressed symbolically. He is quick to alert us to the fact
that symbols are essential to our understanding, that they are not
simple things that we construct for our own pleasure, but that they
are in essence an ingredient of human understanding that we inherit.
He also reminds us that nothing speaks to us more profoundly than
do symbols and that all faith is expressed in symbols.

TILLICH'S RHETORIC

Tillich's argument is very subtle. He establishes definitions and
categories for us to follow. He demonstrates that the question of athe-

ism may not even be tenable and that the concept of God is itself the most powerful symbol of faith we have. Further, he wants us to realize that faith is a complex matter; it is not limited to literal, materialistic symbols of religion such as statues or institutions. In fact, Tillich is critical of institutions such as the church and of the institutionalized interpretation of the Bible—a result, no doubt, of his experiences in Germany when the church acted to repress the individual in compliance with Hitler's programs. Tillich preserves one of the most important legacies of Protestantism: respect for the individual conscience.

He begins by defining the word "symbol." He enumerates six qualities of the symbol. He then explores these qualities in a succession of separate paragraphs at the beginning of the essay, devoting a single paragraph to each quality. Among the distinctions he establishes is the fact that symbols point beyond themselves to something else; they reveal levels of reality that otherwise remain hidden; they cannot be made arbitrarily but grow out of our unconscious and are accepted by the unconscious dimension of our being; finally, they appear when the situation is ready for them and die when the situation changes. He holds that the symbol expresses our deepest feelings and needs.

Tillich points to the fact that symbols are connected with many aspects of life: he mentions politics and the arts as well as matters of religion. As he says in paragraph 9, "Whatever we say about that which concerns us ultimately, whether or not we call it God, has a symbolic meaning. It points beyond itself while participating in that to which it points. In no other way can faith express itself adequately. The language of faith is the language of symbols."

Tillich constructs an argument that has several purposes. One is to convince us that the language of symbols is of great importance and that religion speaks in that language. Another is that the language of faith helps us to avoid the materialism that the modern world finds so easy to embrace. In addition, in discussing the nature of myth, Tillich attempts to convince us that all religious truths are embedded in myth and that the danger is not in accepting the concept of myth as part of religion but in "breaking the myth"—making the myth conscious by turning it into a literal interpretation that then ceases to be symbol and becomes a kind of quasi-scientific "fact." This he calls repression because it forces the individual to accept one interpretation and robs faith of its only natural language: symbol.

Such an argument as this is not likely to be acceptable to literalists or materialists. Moreover, it needs a very precise understanding of the concept of symbol and myth, which is why Tillich defines both terms with such great care. Thus, definition is one of his most important rhetorical devices. Thereafter, his rhetorical strategies involve examining his definitions, showing how they illuminate the concepts of faith that are at the center of his discussion, and then helping the reader follow through to the consequences of the preceding discussion. Those consequences involve accepting a rather revolutionary and expansive idea of religious faith. He asks us to somehow accept the concept of infinity when we approach the primary symbol of faith: God.

Symbols of Faith

The Meaning of Symbol

Man's ultimate concern must be expressed symbolically, because 1 symbolic language alone is able to express the ultimate. This statement demands explanation in several respects. In spite of the manifold research about the meaning and function of symbols which is going on in contemporary philosophy, every writer who uses the term "symbol" must explain his understanding of it.

Symbols have one characteristic in common with signs; they point 2 beyond themselves to something else. The red sign at the street corner points to the order to stop the movements of cars at certain intervals. A red light and the stopping of cars have essentially no relation to each other, but conventionally they are united as long as the convention lasts. The same is true of letters and numbers and partly even words. They point beyond themselves to sounds and meanings. They are given this special function by convention within a nation or by international conventions, as the mathematical signs. Sometimes such signs are called symbols; but this is unfortunate because it makes the distinction between signs and symbols more difficult. Decisive is the fact that signs do not participate in the reality of that to which they point, while symbols do. Therefore, signs can be replaced for reasons of expediency or convention, while symbols cannot.

This leads to the second characteristic of the symbol: It partici- 3
pates in that to which it points: the flag participates in the power and
dignity of the nation for which it stands. Therefore, it cannot be replaced except after an historic catastrophe that changes the reality of
the nation which it symbolizes. An attack on the flag is felt as an
attack on the majesty of the group in which it is acknowledged. Such
an attack is considered blasphemy.

The third characteristic of a symbol is that it opens up levels of 4
reality which otherwise are closed for us. All arts create symbols for a
level of reality which cannot be reached in any other way. A picture
and a poem reveal elements of reality which cannot be approached
scientifically. In the creative work of art we encounter reality in a dimension which is closed for us without such works. The symbol's
fourth characteristic not only opens up dimensions and elements of
reality which otherwise would remain unapproachable but also un-
locks dimensions and elements of our soul which correspond to the
dimensions and elements of reality. A great play gives us not only a
new vision of the human scene, but it opens up hidden depths of our
own being. Thus we are able to receive what the play reveals to us in
reality. There are within us dimensions of which we cannot become
aware except through symbols, as melodies and rhythms in music.

Symbols cannot be produced intentionally—this is the fifth char- 5
acteristic. They grow out of the individual or collective unconscious
and cannot function without being accepted by the unconscious dimension of our being. Symbols which have an especially social function, as political and religious symbols, are created or at least accepted
by the collective unconscious of the group in which they appear.

The sixth and last characteristic of the symbol is a consequence of 6
the fact that symbols cannot be invented. Like living beings, they grow
and they die. They grow when the situation is ripe for them, and they
die when the situation changes. The symbol of the "king" grew in a
special period of history, and it died in most parts of the world in our
period. Symbols do not grow because people are longing for them, and
they do not die because of scientific or practical criticism. They die
because they can no longer produce response in the group where they
originally found expression.

These are the main characteristics of every symbol. Genuine sym- 7
bols are created in several spheres of man's cultural creativity. We
have mentioned already the political and the artistic realm. We could
add history and, above all, religion, whose symbols will be our particular concern.

Religious Symbols

We have discussed the meaning of symbols generally because, as 8
we said, man's ultimate concern must be expressed symbolically! One
may ask: Why can it not be expressed directly and properly? If money,
success or the nation is someone's ultimate concern, can this not be
said in a direct way without symbolic language? Is it not only in those
cases in which the content of the ultimate concern is called "God"
that we are in the realm of symbols? The answer is that everything
which is a matter of unconditional concern is made into a god. If the
nation is someone's ultimate concern, the name of the nation becomes
a sacred name and the nation receives divine qualities which far sur-
pass the reality of the being and functioning of the nation. The nation
then stands for and symbolizes the true ultimate, but in an idolatrous
way. Success as ultimate concern is not the natural desire of actualiz-
ing potentialities, but is readiness to sacrifice all other values of life
for the sake of a position of power and social predominance. The anxiety about not being a success is an idolatrous form of the anxiety
about divine condemnation. Success is grace; lack of success, ultimate
judgment. In this way concepts designating ordinary realities become
idolatrous symbols of ultimate concern.

The reason for this transformation of concepts into symbols is the 9
character of ultimacy and the nature of faith. That which is the true
ultimate transcends the realm of finite reality infinitely. Therefore, no
finite reality can express it directly and properly. Religiously speaking,
God transcends his own name. This is why the use of his name easily
becomes an abuse or a blasphemy. Whatever we say about that which
concerns us ultimately, whether or not we call it God, has a symbolic
meaning. It points beyond itself while participating in that to which it
points. In no other way can faith express itself adequately. The language of faith is the language of symbols. If faith were what we have
shown that it is not, such an assertion could not be made. But faith,
understood as the state of being ultimately concerned, has no language
other than symbols. When saying this I always expect the question:
Only a symbol? He who asks this question shows that he has not understood the difference between signs and symbols nor the power of
symbolic language, which surpasses in quality and strength the power
of any nonsymbolic language. One should never say "only a symbol,"
but one should say "not less than a symbol." With this in mind we
can now describe the different kinds of symbols of faith.

The fundamental symbol of our ultimate concern is God. It is al- 10 ways present in any act of faith, even if the act of faith includes the denial of God. Where there is ultimate concern, God can be denied only in the name of God. One God can deny the other one. Ultimate concern cannot deny its own character as ultimate. Therefore, it affirms what is meant by the word "God." Atheism, consequently, can only mean the attempt to remove any ultimate concern—to remain unconcerned about the meaning of one's existence. Indifference toward the ultimate question is the only imaginable form of atheism. Whether it is possible is a problem which must remain unsolved at this point. In any case, he who denies God as a matter of ultimate concern affirms God, because he affirms ultimacy in his concern. God is the fundamental symbol for what concerns us ultimately. Again it would be completely wrong to ask: So God is nothing but a symbol? Because the next question has to be: A symbol for what? And then the answer would be: For God! God is symbol for God. This means that in the notion of God we must distinguish two elements: the element of ultimacy, which is a matter of immediate experience and not symbolic in itself, and the element of concreteness, which is taken from our ordinary experience and symbolically applied to God. The man whose ultimate concern is a sacred tree[1] has both the ultimacy of concern and the concreteness of the tree which symbolizes his relation to the ultimate. The man who adores Apollo[2] is ultimately concerned, but not in an abstract way. His ultimate concern is symbolized in the divine figure of Apollo. The man who glorifies Jahweh, the God of the Old Testament, has both an ultimate concern and a concrete image of what concerns him ultimately. This is the meaning of the seemingly cryptic statement that God is the symbol of God. In this qualified sense God is the fundamental and universal content of faith.

It is obvious that such an understanding of the meaning of God makes the discussions about the existence or nonexistence of God meaningless. It is meaningless to question the ultimacy of an ultimate concern. This element in the idea of God is in itself certain. The symbolic expression of this element varies endlessly through the whole history of mankind. Here again it would be meaningless to ask

11

---

[1] *a sacred tree* Many early religions, particularly in Greece, believed that certain trees were sacred, and they consecrated certain groves as holy places. The myths of the tree of life and the tree of knowledge may be holdovers from such belief. Some trees were associated with certain gods, such as the laurel, which was associated with Apollo.

[2] *Apollo* The most revered of all the gods in the Greek pantheon. He was associated with light, the arts, medicine, and prophecy.

whether one or another of the figures in which an ultimate concern is symbolized does "exist." If "existence" refers to something which can be found within the whole of reality, no divine being exists. The question is not this, but: which of the innumerable symbols of faith is most adequate to the meaning of faith? In other words, which symbol of ultimacy expresses the ultimate without idolatrous elements? This is the problem, and not the so-called "existence of God"—which is in itself an impossible combination of words. God as the ultimate in man's ultimate concern is more certain than any other certainty, even that of oneself. God as symbolized in a divine figure is a matter of daring faith, of courage and risk.

God is the basic symbol of faith, but not the only one. All the   12
qualities we attribute to him, power, love, justice, are taken from finite experiences and applied symbolically to that which is beyond finitude and infinity. If faith calls God "almighty," it uses the human experience of power in order to symbolize the content of its infinite concern, but it does not describe a highest being who can do as he pleases. So it is with all the other qualities and with all the actions, past, present and future, which men attribute to God. They are symbols taken from our daily experience, and not information about what God did once upon a time or will do sometime in the future. Faith is not the belief in such stories, but it is the acceptance of symbols that express our ultimate concern in terms of divine actions.

Another group of symbols of faith are manifestations of the divine   13
in things and events, in persons and communities, in words and documents. This whole realm of sacred objects is a treasure of symbols. Holy things are not holy in themselves, but they point beyond themselves to the source of all holiness, that which is of ultimate concern.

Symbols and Myths

The symbols of faith do not appear in isolation. They are united in   14
"stories of the gods," which is the meaning of the Greek word "mythos"—myth. The gods are individualized figures, analogous to human personalities, sexually differentiated, descending from each other, related to each other in love and struggle, producing world and man, acting in time and space. They participate in human greatness and misery, in creative and destructive works. They give to man cultural and religious traditions, and defend these sacred rites. They help and threaten the human race, especially some families, tribes or nations.

They appear in epiphanies and incarnations,[3] establish sacred places, rites and persons, and thus create a cult. But they themselves are under the command and threat of a fate which is beyond everything that is. This is mythology as developed most impressively in ancient Greece. But many of these characteristics can be found in every mythology. Usually the mythological gods are not equals. There is a hierarchy, at the top of which is a ruling god, as in Greece; or a trinity of them, as in India; or a duality of them, as in Persia. There are savior-gods who mediate between the highest gods and man, sometimes sharing the suffering and death of man in spite of their essential immortality. This is the world of the myth, great and strange, always changing but fundamentally the same: man's ultimate concern symbolized in divine figures and actions. Myths are symbols of faith combined in stories about divine-human encounters.

Myths are always present in every act of faith, because the language of faith is the symbol. They are also attacked, criticized and transcended in each of the great religions of mankind. The reason for this criticism is the very nature of the myth. It uses material from our ordinary experience. It puts the stories of the gods into the framework of time and space although it belongs to the nature of the ultimate to be beyond time and space. Above all, it divides the divine into several figures, removing ultimacy from each of them without removing their claim to ultimacy. This inescapably leads to conflicts of ultimate claims, able to destroy life, society, and consciousness. 15

The criticism of the myth first rejects the division of the divine and goes beyond it to one God, although in different ways according to the different types of religion. Even one God is an object of mythological language, and if spoken about is drawn into the framework of time and space. Even he loses his ultimacy if made to be the content of concrete concern. Consequently, the criticism of the myth does not end with the rejection of the polytheistic mythology.[4] 16

Monotheism also falls under the criticism of the myth. It needs, as one says today, "demythologization." This word has been used in connection with the elaboration of the mythical elements in stories and symbols of the Bible, both of the Old and the New Testaments—stories like those of the Paradise, of the fall of Adam, of the great Flood, 17

---

[3]***epiphanies and incarnations*** Epiphanies were revelations of the gods—the word means "a shining through of light." They took the form of signs or events that had apparent divine meaning. Incarnations were adoptions of human form by a god, something done frequently by Zeus and by Athena.

[4]***polytheistic mythology*** The Greek and Roman mythologies postulated many gods (polytheism), not a single god as the Jewish and Christian religions did.

of the Exodus from Egypt, of the virgin birth of the Messiah, of many of his miracles, of his resurrection and ascension, of his expected return as the judge of the universe. In short, all the stories in which divine-human interactions are told are considered as mythological in character, and objects of demythologization. What does this negative and artificial term mean? It must be accepted and supported if it points to the necessity of recognizing a symbol as a symbol and a myth as a myth. It must be attacked and rejected if it means the removal of symbols and myths altogether. Such an attempt is the third step in the criticism of the myth. It is an attempt which never can be successful, because symbol and myth are forms of the human consciousness which are always present. One can replace one myth by another, but one cannot remove the myth from man's spiritual life. For the myth is the combination of symbols of our ultimate concern.

A myth which is understood as a myth, but not removed or replaced, can be called a "broken myth." Christianity denies by its very nature any unbroken myth, because its presupposition is the first commandment: the affirmation of the ultimate as ultimate and the rejection of any kind of idolatry. All mythological elements in the Bible, and doctrine and liturgy should be recognized as mythological, but they should be maintained in their symbolic form and not be replaced by scientific substitutes. For there is no substitute for the use of symbols and myths: they are the language of faith. 18

The radical criticism of the myth is due to the fact that the primitive mythological consciousness resists the attempt to interpret the myth of myth. It is afraid of every act of demythologization. It believes that the broken myth is deprived of its truth and of its convincing power. Those who live in an unbroken mythological world feel safe and certain. They resist, often fanatically, any attempt to introduce an element of uncertainty by "breaking the myth," namely, by making conscious its symbolic character. Such resistance is supported by authoritarian systems, religious or political, in order to give security to the people under their control and unchallenged power to those who exercise the control. The resistance against demythologization expresses itself in "literalism." The symbols and myths are understood in their immediate meaning. The material, taken from nature and history, is used in its proper sense. The character of the symbol to point beyond itself to something else is disregarded. Creation is taken as a magic act which happened once upon a time. The fall of Adam is localized on a special geographical point and attributed to a human individual. The virgin birth of the Messiah is understood in biological 19 terms, resurrection and ascension as physical events, the second coming of the Christ as a telluric,[5] or cosmic, catastrophe. The presupposition of such literalism is that God is a being, acting in time and space, dwelling in a special place, affecting the course of events and being affected by them like any other being in the universe. Literalism deprives God of his ultimacy and, religiously speaking, of his majesty. It draws him down to the level of that which is not ultimate, the finite and conditional. In the last analysis it is not rational criticism of the myth which is decisive but the inner religious criticism. Faith, if it takes its symbols literally, becomes idolatrous! It calls something ultimate which is less than ultimate. Faith, conscious of the symbolic character of its symbols, gives God the honor which is due him.

One should distinguish two stages of literalism, the natural and the reactive. The natural stage of literalism is that in which the mythical and the literal are indistinguishable. The primitive period of individuals and groups consists in the inability to separate the creations of symbolic imagination from the facts which can be verified through observation and experiment. This stage has a full right of its own and should not be disturbed, either in individuals or in groups, up to the moment when man's questioning mind breaks the natural acceptance of the mythological visions as literal. If, however, this moment has come, two ways are possible. The one is to replace the unbroken by the broken myth. It is the objectively demanded way, although it is impossible for many people who prefer the repression of their questions to the uncertainty which appears with the breaking of the myth. They are forced into the second stage of literalism, the conscious one, which is aware of the questions but represses them, half consciously, half unconsciously. The tool of repression is usually an acknowledged authority with sacred qualities like the Church or the Bible, to which one owes unconditional surrender. This stage is still justifiable, if the questioning power is very weak and can easily be answered. It is unjustifiable if a mature mind is broken in its personal center by political or psychological methods, split in his unity, and hurt in his integrity. The enemy of a critical theology is not natural literalism but conscious literalism with repression of and aggression toward autonomous thought.

Symbols of faith cannot be replaced by other symbols, such as artistic ones, and they cannot be removed by scientific criticism. They

20

21

---

[5]*telluric* As rising from the earth; related to the earth itself, and, as Tillich uses the expression, to the planetary cosmos.

have a genuine standing in the human mind, just as science and art have. Their symbolic character is their truth and their power. Nothing less than symbols and myths can express our ultimate concern.

One more question arises, namely, whether myths are able to express every kind of ultimate concern. For example, Christian theologians argue that the word "myth" should be reserved for natural myths in which repetitive natural processes, such as the seasons, are understood in their ultimate meaning. They believe that if the world is seen as an historical process with beginning, end and center, as in Christianity and Judaism, the term "myth" should not be used. This would radically reduce the realm in which the term would be applicable. Myth could not be understood as the language of our ultimate concern, but only as a discarded idiom of this language. yet history proves that there are not only natural myths but also historical myths. If the earth is seen as the battleground of two divine powers, as in ancient Persia,[6] this is an historical myth. If the God of creation selects and guides a nation through history toward an end which transcends all history, this is an historical myth. If the Christ—a transcendent, divine being—appears in the fullness of time, lives, dies and is resurrected, this is an historical myth. Christianity is superior to those religions which are bound to a natural myth. But Christianity speaks the mythological language like every other religion. It is a broken myth, but it is a myth; otherwise Christianity would not be an expression of ultimate concern. 22

QUESTIONS

1. What does Tillich mean by the terms "sign" and "symbol"? Is your understanding similar to that of others who have read the selection?
2. Review the six characteristics of the symbol (paras. 1–6). Establish what each characteristic is.
3. What does Tillich mean by the term "ultimate concern"? He says that the concept of God is linked to this term.
4. One of the most subtle statements is that "the language of faith is the language of symbols" (para. 9). What does Tillich mean by this statement?

---

[6]*battleground . . . ancient Persia* One Persian belief was that the power of good, symbolized by light, was in eternal struggle with the power of evil, symbolized by darkness. Mazda, the power of light, had to be supported by mankind or else the powers of the dark might triumph.

Do you agree with him? Do you think that most religious people whom you know would agree with him?

5. Clarify what Tillich means by myth and how he links myth to religious faith.

WRITING ASSIGNMENTS

1. Do you agree with Tillich when he says, in paragraph 15, "Myths are always present in every act of faith, because the language of faith is the symbol"? Establish the way in which myth functions in the religions that you know about, and as you do so, be sure to use Tillich's technique of carefully defining myth. Remember that some people think a myth is something that is not true, but Tillich uses the term to signify that which is deeply true. If you have read Carl Jung's "The Concept of the Collective Unconscious," include your understanding of myth as a product of the collective unconscious in your discussion. Make it your purpose to convince an audience that Tillich's statement is correct or incorrect.

2. Among the tantalizing comments Tillich makes is: "In any case, he who denies God as a matter of ultimate concern affirms God, because he affirms ultimacy in his concern" (para. 10). This is an ingenious argument, but is it true? Take a stand on this question after you have reviewed Tillich's statement in context. He also says that atheism may not even be possible because all people understand that there are ultimate concerns in the universe, and he says that God is one with ultimate concern. Is this a reasonable argument? Is it true that, if one denies the existence of God, one somehow actually affirms God's existence?

3. In paragraph 12, Tillich raises an issue that had once plagued religious thinkers. The voluntarists in the seventeenth century maintained that God could do whatever he wished, including turning himself into the devil. For them it was impossible to limit the power of God. The antivoluntarists claimed that even God could not become the devil because the nature of God is goodness. When Tillich says that faith "does not describe a highest being who can do as he pleases," he is definitely siding with the antivoluntarists. Explain how Tillich's view of the nature of God makes it possible for him to take this position. What are the benefits—and what are the problems—of his view of the nature of God for modern religion? In what ways would you say Tillich's view of God is especially modern?

4. Tillich establishes a position on literalism in paragraphs 18–21. He argues that the parts of the Bible that are mythical should be interpreted accordingly; that is, they should not be interpreted literally. What does he mean by this argument? What parts of the Bible might he mean? Do you agree with him when he says that interpreting myth as if it were literal (what he calls "breaking the myth" or making the myth conscious) leads to

repression of individual beliefs? Offer your own interpretation of the conflict that Tillich seems to be discussing. Is it a conflict that is relevant to
today's views of religion?

5. A theology always postulates God and establishes the nature of God while
at the same time establishing the relationship between God and human
beings. Exactly what is the nature of Tillich's God, and what is the relationship of that God to human beings? To what extent does Tillich's view
seem religious to you? To what extent does it seem nonreligious? Establish
your own position as a religious person (practicing or nonpracticing) and
then express your sense of comfort or discomfort with Tillich's position.

6. If Tillich's argument has not convinced you regarding the way in which
symbols of faith function, explain why. Offer a counterargument, being
sure to take into account Tillich's chief points. Consider the question of
what kind of language the language of faith is if it is not symbolic and
indicate those parts of Tillich's argument which fail to convince you.

PART SIX

IDEAS IN THE
WORLD
OF THE ARTS

Aristotle
George Santayana ··· *Virginia Woolf*
Susanne K. Langer ··· *Susan Sontag*

INTRODUCTION

Aʀᴛ must be regarded as one of the major priorities of civilization. Yet its functions and its character have remained mysterious since the first stirrings of the aesthetic sensibilities in prehistoric times. People have meditated on the arts, confronted some of its complexities, and developed elaborate theories that revealed the fact that the arts—no matter how basic they are to our needs—are by no means simple to understand. The selections in this part range from ancient Greece to the present century. Three were written by philosophers, though two of the authors are known for their creative work. The range of the selections demonstrates only a part of the scope of subject matter and treatment that is possible in the arts: they represent only a fragment of the ideas that have been developed by thinkers who have realized the seriousness and significance of the arts.

The first essay, from the philosopher Aristotle's *Poetics,* stands as one of the most durable—perhaps the most durable—commentaries ever made on an art form. In this essay Aristotle focuses on the nature of tragedy, though he also touches on both comedy and epic. He is concerned with the conditions that are necessary for tragedy and with the elements that must be present in a tragic drama. Aristotle lived in one of the great ages of Greek drama, when Athens celebrated the feast of the god Dionysus and held the great competitions among the chief playwrights of the Greek city-states. The excitement generated by these competitions testifies to the fact that tragic drama was of immense importance to Greek society. Aristotle analyzes the relative importance of plot, character, setting, language, and other elements of the drama in order to attempt to develop an understanding of how tragedy functions as it does.

George Santayana, also a philosopher, wrote extensively on aesthetics, the philosophy of art. He is interested in the nature of beauty and in the relationship of art to the philosophical concerns of ethics and morals. Since both aesthetics and ethics depend on questions of choosing the good from the bad, they are related. Santayana interprets questions of choice interestingly: traditionally, ethics has been concerned with avoidance—with what not to do. Aesthetics has traditionally been concerned with preference—choosing that which is beautiful. Santayana believes that art and religion are products of the human imagination, and he thinks that they are to be especially valued as such. The connective between the contemplation of beauty and the contemplation of right action has special relevance for him in all his thinking about art.

Virginia Woolf is famous not as a thinker about the arts but as a literary artist. When she was questioned by a young poet about the nature and future of poetry, however, she responded with a "philosophical" meditation that attempts to clarify what poetry was doing in 1932. She believed that poets had turned inward and had limited themselves by writing only about themselves. Her reassurance to the young poet is based on her confidence in the continued growth and health of poetry, though she warns him to avoid too much introspection. Instead, she recommends that he do as Shakespeare did and write about other people. It is interesting advice, and it could certainly be given to young poets today.

On a more formal philosophical note, Susanne K. Langer calls our attention to the capacity of the arts to express and interpret emotions. In "Expressiveness," her contention is that there is a congruence between certain kinds of feelings and certain works of art. Furthermore, she holds that there is an important sense in which the arts can educate us emotionally. This insight has a special value for us, since education is ordinarily aimed primarily at the mind. Education of the emotions is rarely attempted in our schools—except, as Langer suggests, in our involvement with the arts. Her emphasis on expressiveness offers a fascinating insight into our relationship with the arts.

As a literary critic, novelist, and filmmaker, Susan Sontag brings both a practical and a theoretical understanding to the question of interpretation. In "Against Interpretation," a widely influential and very controversial essay, she takes a surprising stance. Instead of defending her own practice as a commentator and critic, she suggests that the act of interpretation should perhaps be suspended in favor of a close descriptive process which restores the sensuous immediacy of the work being discussed.

Her essay is characteristically brilliant and strikes at the heart of the act of interpretation as it has been practiced since the beginning. She reviews interpretation in the works of Plato and Aristotle, centering primarily on their theory of art as mimesis—as imitating life. Aristotle discusses this point in the *Poetics,* and Plato discusses it in "The Allegory of the Cave" from his *Republic.* Her approach to the problem of how interpretation affects our understanding of the arts has both a historical and a philosophical depth, and her command and review of the major ideas which have contributed to the way we think about interpretation is impressive.

All these writers are interesting for their reliance on the rhetorical device of establishing careful definitions on which to base their arguments. Since all of them are, in fact, constructing arguments in order to convince us that their ideas are not only relevant but correct, their definitions must be precise.

After the definition comes a logical structure. Arguments need premises—points of departure on which we can agree—and they require painstaking analysis in order to improve our understanding. It is no surprise, therefore, that all these writers are gifted analysts. Their subject—the arts—is an inherently complex one, so that it is nearly impossible to approach it head-on. Rather, the subject must be treated point by point, with a discussion of each of several significant ideas associated with key concepts. The nature of tragedy, beauty, poetry, expression, and interpretation can clarify only by the most careful and determined effort. Each writer brings special rhetorical skills to the task of thinking about art. These skills make an abstract and difficult subject more approachable.

ARISTOTLE

Poetics: Comedy and Epic and Tragedy

ARISTOTLE (384–322 B.C.) is one of a succession of impressive Greeks who changed the world of philosophy in ancient times. Socrates was Plato's teacher, and Plato was Aristotle's teacher, who in turn was Alexander the Great's teacher. Aristotle was a brilliant student in Plato's Academy; he remained there for twenty years and earned the nickname of the "Intellect" of the school. He later conducted his own school in Athens, called the Lyceum, in a spot sacred to Apollo. His views essentially differed from Plato's, although as long as Plato lived, Aristotle avoided direct conflict with his teacher.

Plato's views were based on idealistic principles. He held that ideas are more important than things that could be perceived; hence, perception is not of great worth. Conversely, Aristotle believed that perception was the starting point for all thought. Beginning with sense perception, the thinker could then proceed to abstract thought, which Aristotle, like Plato, held to be the most desirable and most distinctive kind of thought.

Aristotle's methods can be seen at work in the selection from the Poetics, *his treatise on Greek drama. The* Poetics *is a discussion of the principles of comedy and tragedy as they were commonly understood by the Greeks at that time, and it is well rooted both in observation and in an understanding of the history of drama and of the* traditions of the Greek festivals. Aristotle's theories about drama, in other words, are related to both his observation and his capacity to make comparisons and examine practices. Based on his observation, he is able to establish what the nature of comedy and tragedy is and to theorize about what things are most significant and most effective in the construction of drama.

The tradition in ancient Greece was for there to be an important series of contests between dramatists during the festival of Dionysus. The occasion was highly organized by the time Aristotle began to write about it; in fact, many of the greatest Greek dramatists had already done their work. Playwrights were chosen for the competition by experts. Prominent and wealthy citizens were awarded the honor of paying for the costs of the production of the plays, including the actors and the scaena (stage setting) and other equipment. The archons, or judges, would sit in a place of honor during the productions of the plays and, at the end, would award prizes. It was an immense honor to be awarded a prize, and all the greatest playwrights won several prizes during their lives.

The plays were public and popular events. The tragedies were usually produced in trilogies; afterward, very coarse comedies would be presented to change the mood. The tradition of social comedy—comedy that indirectly comments on society—was beginning to develop before Aristotle wrote, but it is clear that his chief focus is on the higher and nobler form of drama: tragedy. He tells us at the outset that comedy is drama about people who are low in estate. Naturally, he is speaking of his own time, and since he lived in an aristocratic world, in which some people were thought of as inherently noble and others as inherently common, he means that comedy is not about members of the nobility but about ordinary people.

Tragedy, on the other hand, is drama whose main characters are noble, and the chief point of tragedy is to show how a person's fortune can change because of circumstances that are—or may sometimes seem to be—beyond his or her control. It was essential for a tragic hero or heroine to be noble since he or she must fall from a great height (a commoner has no great height to fall from). The hero in a tragedy presents a model for all of us: if someone can fall from a great height, we can as well. Because the noble hero falls, his fate is inherently more moving and dramatic than the fall of an ordinary person; thus, it is naturally more suitable for tragedy.

Aristotle does not discuss fate, but the Greek view was that fate ruled the world and that the most noble thing a person could do was to face his or her fate with dignity, even when that fate might be grim. In this selection he talks at length about the requirements of tragedy and their relative importance. He notes important requirements for tragedy: plot, characters, verbal expression, thought, song-composition, and visual adornment (in order of importance). In part of his discussion, he takes each of these in turn and demonstrates its significance.

One of the most complex elements of Aristotle's thinking on drama is not readily apparent from this selection; it has to do with his theory of mimesis, or imitation. For him, art is "imitation of something else; in the case of plot, for example, it is the imitation of an action" (para. 12). This concept has been examined in detail in recent years, and it is important for us to understand that the matter of how a plot imitates an action is central to drama. Aristotle talks about the poet's job of representing "what is likely to happen" as opposed to the historian's job of representing "what has happened" (para. 20).

Among the more surprising aspects of his discussion may be the declaration that plot is more important than character (para. 8). He goes so far as to suggest that tragedy may exist without character but not without plot (para. 9). He also says that beginning dramatists are capable of creating characters but definitely not of creating plot. To us, this is surprising, because most modern theories of literature emphasize character. And when we think of great Shakespearian tragedies, we think of the characters whose names are the titles of the plays (e.g. Hamlet, King Lear, Macbeth, Othello, Julius Caesar, and Antony and Cleopatra).

Aristotle's concepts of peripety and recognition are central to any understanding of tragedy. Though he explains the terms in paragraph 26, they may well be discussed briefly here. "Peripety" derives from the Greek word meaning to walk; in other words, it means the progress of a character or action in a given direction—but with a sudden shift. For example, a character may appear to be heading toward a personal victory, only to have his efforts suddenly end in his unexpected defeat. Peripety—the sudden shift in the direction of events—is essential to tragedy. "Recognition" is the awareness of a significant truth that may, in fact, produce the peripety. As Aristotle says, the best recognition takes place at the same time as the peripety. Usually, the recognition in tragedy is the chief character's awareness of a truth which that character would rather suppress. Oedipus, in Sophocles' Oedipus Rex, discovers several things, but the worst thing is that the person whom he seeks as the one who has brought a curse *on the land is himself. He had long before heard the oracle tell him that he was fated to kill his father and marry his mother, and had left home as a result. But he did not know that he had been adopted and that when he was challenged at a crossroads by an older man— whom he fought with and killed—he had begun to carry out his fate. Only after he had married his mother and taken his father's place did he learn that he was the "criminal" he had set out to find. In* Oedipus Rex, *the recognition comes at the moment of the peripety, when Oedipus's fate "turned around."*

ARISTOTLE'S RHETORIC

One of the most interesting ironies about Aristotle is that the works he prepared for publication and by which he gained immense fame and influence were for the most part lost to the world by the end of the first century A.D. *At that time, another group of works surfaced that were edited in Rome and were produced in a scholarly edition. This group is peculiar for a clipped and notelike style that has led many modern Aristotle experts to conclude that these works were reconstructed from lectures.*

The Poetics *closely resembles a lecture that might have been given to students of drama. It has a number of the rhetorical "trademarks" of the lecture: it is on a single subject, along with related adjuncts, and it relies on a step-by-step procedure that always pauses to review what has already been said. In this selection Aristotle provides adequate definitions for all the key terms he introduces; he also takes care to refer his audience to elements that have been previously discussed (a number of these are referred to but are not included in this passage).*

Another Aristotelian trademark that may be a result of his writing for a student audience is his categorical structure. He constantly reminds us that things have a specific number of categories that will be discussed. Epic poetry has three qualities; tragedy has six elements; plot has two kinds—and so on. Whenever he can, Aristotle breaks things down into parts or categories and then examines each component separately on the assumption that such an examination will yield greater knowledge of the thing under discussion.

The Poetics *is a discussion of several categories of poetic performance, beginning with the comedy, then the epic, and proceeding to the tragedy. First each category is discussed; then its subcategories are discussed. Of course, the chief category is tragedy, and consid-*

ering the thought that Aristotle devoted to his treatment of it, he must have believed it to be the most noble, uplifting, serious, and important category of all.

Today, this essay is the starting point for all those who wish to talk and think about literature seriously. Aristotle's approach was so thorough that there are still people who think that no critical statement has since penetrated as deeply into the heart of dramatic literature. The principles presented in this essay are relevant to contemporary discussion of literature. All of us who wish to deepen our thinking about the art of literature must begin with an understanding of Aristotle.

Poetics: Comedy and Epic and Tragedy

Comedy

Comedy is as we said it was, an imitation of persons who are infe- 1
rior; not, however, going all the way to full villainy, but imitating the ugly, of which the ludicrous is one part. The ludicrous, that is, is a failing or a piece of ugliness which causes no pain or destruction; thus, to go no farther, the comic mask[1] is something ugly and distorted but painless.

Now the stages of development of tragedy, and the men who were 2
responsible for them, have not escaped notice but comedy did escape notice in the beginning because it was not taken seriously. (In fact it was late in its history that the presiding magistrate officially "granted a chorus" to the comic poets; until then they were volunteers.) Thus comedy already possessed certain defining characteristics when the first "comic poets," so-called, appear in the record. Who gave it masks, or prologues, or troupes of actors and all that sort of thing is not known. The composing of plots came originally from Sicily; of the

---

[1]**the comic mask** Actors in Greek drama wore masks behind which they spoke their lines. The comic mask showed a smiling face; the tragic mask, a weeping face.

Athenian poets, Crates[2] was the first to abandon the lampooning mode and compose arguments, that is, plots, of a general nature.

Epic and Tragedy

Well then, epic poetry followed in the wake of tragedy up to the 3 point of being a (1) good-sized (2) imitation (3) in verse (4) of people who are to be taken seriously; but in its having its verse unmixed with any other and being narrative in character, there they differ. Further, so far as its length is concerned tragedy tries as hard as it can to exist during a single daylight period, or to vary but little, while the epic is not limited in its time and so differs in that respect. Yet originally they used to do this in tragedies just as much as they did in epic poems.

The constituent elements are partly identical and partly limited to 4 tragedy. Hence anybody who knows about good and bad tragedy knows about epic also; for the elements that the epic possesses appertain to tragedy as well, but those of tragedy are not all found in the epic.

Tragedy and Its Six Constituent Elements. Our discussions of imita- 5 tive poetry in hexameters,[3] and of comedy, will come later; at present let us deal with tragedy, recovering from what has been said so far the definition of its essential nature, as it was in development. Tragedy, then, is a process of imitating an action which has serious implications, is complete, and possesses magnitude; by means of language which has been made sensuously attractive, with each of its varieties found separately in the parts; enacted by the persons themselves and not presented through narrative; through a course of pity and fear completing the purification of tragic acts which have those emotional characteristics. By "language made sensuously attractive" I mean language that has rhythm and melody, and by "its varieties found separately"

---

[2]*Crates (fl. 470 B.C.)* Greek actor and playwright, credited by Aristotle for developing Greek comedy into a fully plotted, credible form. Aristophanes (450–c.388 B.C.), another Greek comic playwright, says that Crates was the first to portray a drunk on stage.

[3]*hexameters* The first known metrical form for classical verse. Each line had six metrical feet, some of which were prescribed in advance. It is the meter used for epic poetry and for poetry designed to teach a lesson. The form has sometimes been used in comparatively modern poetry but rarely with success except in French.

I mean the fact that certain parts of the play are carried on through spoken verses alone and others the other way around, through song.

Now first of all, since they perform the imitation through action 6 (by acting it), the adornment of their visual appearance will perforce constitute some part of the making of tragedy; and song-composition and verbal expression also, for those are the media in which they perform the imitation. By "verbal expression" I mean the actual composition of the verses, and by "song-composition" something whose meaning is entirely clear.

Next, since it is an imitation of an action and is enacted by certain 7 people who are performing the action, and since those people must necessarily have certain traits both of character and thought (for it is thanks to these two factors that we speak of people's actions also as having a defined character, and it is in accordance with their actions that all either succeed or fail); and since the imitation of the action is the plot, for by "plot" I mean here the structuring of the events, and by the "characters" that in accordance with which we say that the persons who are acting have a defined moral character, and by "thought" all the passages in which they attempt to prove some thesis or set forth an opinion—it follows of necessity, then, that tragedy as a whole has just six constituent elements, in relation to the essence that makes it a distinct species; and they are plot, characters, verbal expression, thought, visual adornment, and song-composition. For the elements by which they imitate are two (i.e., verbal expression and song-composition), the manner in which they imitate is one (visual adornment), the things they imitate are three (plot, characters, thought), and there is nothing more beyond these. These then are the constituent forms they use.

The Relative Importance of the Six Elements. The greatest of these 8 elements is the structuring of the incidents. For tragedy is an imitation not of men but of a life, an action, and they have moral quality in accordance with their characters but are happy or unhappy in accordance with their actions; hence they are not active in order to imitate their characters, but they include the characters along with the actions for the sake of the latter. Thus the structure of events, the plot, is the goal of tragedy, and the goal is the greatest thing of all.

Again: a tragedy cannot exist without a plot, but it can without 9 characters: thus the tragedies of most of our modern poets are devoid of character, and in general many poets are like that; so also with the relationship between Zeuxis and Polygnotus,[4] among the painters: Polygnotus is a good portrayer of character, while Zeuxis' painting has no dimension of character at all.

Again: if one strings end to end speeches that are expressive of [10] character and carefully worked in thought and expression, he still will not achieve the result which we said was the aim of tragedy; the job will be done much better by a tragedy that is more deficient in these other respects but has a plot, a structure of events. It is much the same case as with painting: the most beautiful pigments smeared on at random will not give as much pleasure as a black-and-white outline picture. Besides, the most powerful means tragedy has for swaying our feelings, namely the peripeties and recognitions,[5] are elements of plot.

Again: an indicative sign is that those who are beginning a poetic [11] career manage to hit the mark in verbal expression and character portrayal sooner than they do in plot construction; and the same is true of practically all the earliest poets.

So plot is the basic principle, the heart and soul, as it were, of trag- [12] edy, and the characters come second: . . . it is the imitation of an action and imitates the persons primarily for the sake of their action.

Third in rank is thought. This is the ability to state the issues and [13] appropriate points pertaining to a given topic, an ability which springs from the arts of politics and rhetoric; in fact the earlier poets made their characters talk "politically," the present-day poets rhetorically. But "character" is that kind of utterance which clearly reveals the bent of a man's moral choice (hence there is no character in that class of utterances in which there is nothing at all that the speaker is choosing or rejecting), while "thought" is the passages in which they try to prove that something is so or not so, or state some general principle.

Fourth is the verbal expression of the speeches. I mean by this the [14] same thing that was said earlier, that the "verbal expression" is the conveyance of thought through language: a statement which has the same meaning whether one says "verses" or "speeches."

The song-composition of the remaining parts is the greatest of the [15]

---

[4]***Zeuxis (fl. 420–390 B.C.) and Polygnotus (c. 470–440 B.C.)*** Zeuxis developed a method of painting in which the figures were rounded and apparently three-dimensional. Thus, he was an illusionistic painter, imitating life in a realistic style. Polygnotus was famous as a painter, and his works were on the Acropolis as well as at Delphi. His draftsmanship was especially praised.

[5]***peripeties and recognitions*** The turning-about of fortune and the recognition on the part of the tragic hero of the truth. This is, for Aristotle, a critical moment in the drama, especially if both events happen simultaneously, as they do in *Oedipus Rex*. It is quite possible for these moments to happen apart from one another.

sensuous attractions, and the visual adornment of the dramatic persons can have a strong emotional effect but is the least artistic element, the least connected with the poetic art; in fact the force of tragedy can be felt even without benefit of public performance and actors, while for the production of the visual effect the property man's art is even more decisive than that of the poets.

General Principles of the Tragic Plot. With these distinctions out of the way, let us next discuss what the structuring of the events should be like, since this is both the basic and the most important element in the tragic art. We have established, then, that tragedy is an imitation of an action which is complete and whole and has some magnitude (for there is also such a thing as a whole that has no magnitude). "Whole" is that which has beginning, middle, and end. "Beginning" is that which does not necessarily follow on something else, but after it something else naturally is or happens; "end," the other way around, is that which naturally follows on something else, either necessarily or for the most part, but nothing else after it; and "middle" that which naturally follows on something else and something else on it. So, then, well constructed plots should neither begin nor end at any chance point but follow the guidelines just laid down.

Furthermore, since the beautiful, whether a living creature or anything that is composed of parts, should not only have these in a fixed order to one another but also possess a definite size which does not depend on chance—for beauty depends on size and order; hence neither can a very tiny creature turn out to be beautiful (since our perception of it grows blurred as it approaches the period of imperceptibility) nor an excessively huge one (for then it cannot all be perceived at once and so its unity and wholeness are lost), if for example there were a creature a thousand miles long—so, just as in the case of living creatures they must have some size, but one that can be taken in a single view, so with plots: they shoud have length, but such that they are easy to remember. As to a limit of the length, the one is determined by the tragic competitions and the ordinary span of attention. (If they had to compete with a hundred tragedies they would compete by the water clock, as they say used to be done [?].) But the limit fixed by the very nature of the case is: the longer the plot, up to the point of still being perspicuous as a whole, the finer it is so far as size is concerned; or to put it in general terms, the length in which, with things happening in unbroken sequence, a shift takes place either probably or necessarily from bad to good fortune or from good to bad—that is an acceptable norm of length.

But a plot is not unified, as some people think, simply because it 18
has to do with a single person. A large, indeed an indefinite number of
things can happen to a given individual, some of which go to constitute no unified event; and in the same way there can be many acts of
a given individual from which no single action emerges. Hence it
seems clear that those poets are wrong who have composed *Hera-
cleïds, Theseïds*, and the like. They think that since Heracles was a
single person it follows that the plot will be single too. But Homer,
superior as he is in all other respects, appears to have grasped this
point well also, thanks either to art or nature, for in composing an
Odyssey he did not incorporate into it everything that happened to the
hero, for example how he was wounded on Mt. Parnassus[6] or how he
feigned madness at the muster, neither of which events, by happening,
made it at all necessary or probable that the other should happen. Instead, he composed the *Odyssey*—and the *Iliad* similarly—around a
unified action of the kind we have been talking about.

A poetic imitation, then, ought to be unified in the same way as a 19
single imitation in any other mimetic field, by having a single object:
since the plot is an imitation of an action, the latter ought to be both
unified and complete, and the component events ought to be so firmly
compacted that if any one of them is shifted to another place, or removed, the whole is loosened up and dislocated; for an element whose
addition or subtraction makes no perceptible extra difference is not
really a part of the whole.

From what has been said it is also clear that the poet's job is not 20
to report what has happened but what is likely to happen: that is, what
is capable of happening according to the rule of probability or necessity. Thus the difference between the historian and the poet is not in
their utterances being in verse or prose (it would be quite possible for
Herodotus' work to be translated into verse, and it would not be any
the less a history with verse than it is without it); the difference lies
in the fact that the historian speaks of what has happened, the poet of
the kind of thing that *can* happen. Hence also poetry is a more philosophical and serious business than history; for poetry speaks more of
universals, history of particulars. "Universal" in this case is what kind

---

[6]*Mt. Parnassus* A mountain in central Greece traditionally sacred to Apollo. In legend,
Odysseus was wounded there, but the point Aristotle is making is that the writer of epics
need not include every detail of his hero's life in a given work. Homer, in writing the
Odyssey, was working with a hero, Odysseus, whose story had been legendary long before he began writing.

of person is likely to do or say certain kinds of things, according to probability or necessity; that is what poetry aims at, although it gives its persons particular names afterward; while the "particular" is what Alcibiades did or what happened to him.

In the field of comedy this point has been grasped: our comic poets 21 construct their plots on the basis of general probabilities and then assign names to the persons quite arbitrarily, instead of dealing with individuals as the old iambic poets[7] did. But in tragedy they still cling to the historically given names. The reason is that what is possible is persuasive; so what has not happened we are not yet ready to believe is possible, while what has happened is, we feel, obviously possible: for it would not have happened if it were impossible. Nevertheless, it is a fact that even in our tragedies, in some cases only one or two of the names are traditional, the rest being invented, and in some others none at all. It is so, for example, in Agathon's *Antheus*—the names in it are as fictional as the events—and it gives no less pleasure because of that. Hence the poets ought not to cling at all costs to the traditional plots, around which our tragedies are constructed. And in fact it is absurd to go searching for this kind of authentication, since even the familiar names are familiar to only a few in the audience and yet give the same kind of pleasure to all.

So from these considerations it is evident that the poet should be a 22 maker of his plots more than of his verses, insofar as he is a poet by virtue of his imitations and what he imitates is actions. Hence even if it happens that he puts something that has actually taken place into poetry, he is none the less a poet; for there is nothing to prevent some of the things that have happened from being the kind of things that can happen, and that is the sense in which he is their maker.

Simple and Complex Plots. Among simple plots and actions the epi- 23 sodic are the worst. By "episodic" plot I mean one in which there is no probability or necessity for the order in which the episodes follow one another. Such structures are composed by the bad poets because they are bad poets, but by the good poets because of the actors: in composing contest pieces for them, and stretching out the plot beyond its capacity, they are forced frequently to dislocate the sequence.

---

[7]**old iambic poets** Aristotle may be referring to Archilochus (fl. 650 B.C.) and the iambic style he developed. The iambic is a metrical foot of two syllables, a short and a long stress, and was the most popular metrical style before the time of Aristotle. "Dealing with individuals" implies using figures already known to the audience rather than figures whose names can be arbitrarily assigned because no one knows who they are.

Furthermore, since the tragic imitation is not only of a complete   24
action but also of events that are fearful and pathetic,[8] and these come
about best when they come about contrary to one's expectation yet
logically, one following from the other; that way they will be more
productive of wonder than if they happen merely at random, by
chance—because even among chance occurrences the ones people consider most marvelous are those that seem to have come about as if on
purpose: for example the way the statue of Mitys at Argos killed the
man who had been the cause of Mitys' death, by falling on him while
he was attending the festival; it stands to reason, people think, that
such things don't happen by chance—so plots of that sort cannot fail
to be artistically superior.

Some plots are simple, others are complex; indeed the actions of   25
which the plots are imitations already fall into these two categories.
By *"simple"* action I mean one the development of which being continuous and unified in the manner stated above, the reversal comes
without peripety or recognition, and by "complex" action one in
which the reversal is continuous but with recognition or peripety or
both. And these developments must grow out of the very structure of
the plot itself, in such a way that on the basis of what has happened
previously this particular outcome follows either by necessity or in
accordance with probability; for there is a great difference in whether
these events happen because of those or merely after them.

"Peripety" is a shift of what is being undertaken to the opposite in   26
the way previously stated, and that in accordance with probability or
necessity as we have just been saying; as for example in the *Oedipus*
the man who has come, thinking that he will reassure Oedipus, that
is, relieve him of his fear with respect to his mother, by revealing who
he once was, brings about the opposite; and in the *Lynceus*, as he
(Lynceus) is being led away with every prospect of being executed, and
Danaus pursuing him with every prospect of doing the executing, it
comes about as a result of the other things that have happened in the
play that *he* is executed and Lynceus is saved. And "recognition" is, as
indeed the name indicates, a shift from ignorance to awareness, point-

---

[8]*fearful and pathetic*   Aristotle said that tragedy should evoke two emotions: terror
and pity. The terror results from our realizing that what is happening to the hero might
just as easily happen to us; the pity results from our human sympathy with a fellow
sufferer. Therefore, the fearful and pathetic represent significant emotions appropriate to
our witnessing drama.

ing in the direction either of close blood ties or of hostility, of people who have previously been in a clearly marked state of happiness or unhappiness.

The finest recognition is one that happens at the same time as a 27 peripety, as is the case with the one in the *Oedipus*. Naturally, there are also other kinds of recognition: it is possible for one to take place in the prescribed manner in relation to inanimate objects and chance occurrences, and it is possible to recognize whether a person has acted or not acted. But the form that is most integrally a part of the plot, the action, is the one aforesaid; for that kind of recognition combined with peripety will excite either pity or fear (and these are the kinds of action of which tragedy is an imitation according to our definition), because both good and bad fortune will also be most likely to follow that kind of event. Since, further, the recognition is a recognition of persons, some are of one person by the other one only (when it is already known who the "other one" is), but sometimes it is necessary for both persons to go through a recognition, as for example Iphigenia is recognized by her brother through the sending of the letter, but of him by Iphigenia another recognition is required.

These then are two elements of plot: peripety and recognition; 28 third is the *pathos*. of these, peripety and recognition have been discussed; a *pathos* is a destructive or painful act, such as deaths on stage, paroxysms of pain, woundings, and all that sort of thing.

QUESTIONS

1. What is epic poetry?
2. What are the six elements of tragedy?
3. Which element do you feel is most important? Explain.
4. What do you think Aristotle's attitude is toward comedy? Why would he like or not like it? Is he influenced by his personal preferences?
5. What are the stages of development of the literature Aristotle describes?
6. What does Aristotle mean by "an imitation of an action"? What would be the relationship to actual life of a work that "imitates an action"?

WRITING ASSIGNMENTS

1. Using Aristotle's method of categorizing as well as his method of referring to a specific play (choose a Shakespearian or other "modern" tragedy), offer your own analysis of what tragedy is. Be sure to consider the purposes of

tragedy—what kinds of truths are revealed and what tragic seriousness is. Then establish the relationship of plot, character, verbal expression, and thought, as well as visual adornment (setting and production values) and music.

2. If you have recently read a tragedy, examine it for its peripety and recognition. When do such moments occur? Do they occur simultaneously? What brings them about, and what is their importance? Would the tragedy you read have retained its impact if the peripety had not occurred? If the recognition had not occurred? What is the emotional value of these moments? Would they have pleased Aristotle?

3. Do you agree with Aristotle that plot is more important than character in drama? You need not restrict yourself to tragedy. You may wish to analyze a film or a television production in your approach to this question. Do producers of television shows seem to be in accord with Aristotle's ideas? Do film producers? Do play producers take a different view? Do you think a good drama is possible without fully developed characters? Do you agree with Aristotle that there can be tragedy without characters but not without plot?

4. Aristotle ranks thought as less important than action and character (para. 13). By "thought" he seems to mean what we call the message of the drama. Do you agree that thought is third in importance? If possible, comment on this by reference to at least one play in a discussion of its thought. What happens to drama when thought is first in importance rather than third?

5. In paragraphs 20 and 21, Aristotle talks about the difference between poetry and history. Do you agree with what he says about the differences and with his evaluation of the two modes—that "poetry is a more philosophical and serious business than history; for poetry speaks more of universals, history of particulars" (para. 20)? Construct an argument that takes one side of this question and establish your position.

6. Based on your analysis of contemporary television situation comedies, how would you define comedy? Try to use the techniques Aristotle relies on: definitions, categorical analysis, summary of the discussion. Proceed as thoughtfully as possible toward a full discussion of the elements of comedy, the nature of the comic situations, the aims of comedy, the achievement of comedy, and the usefulness of comedy.

GEORGE SANTAYANA

---∞---

The Nature of Beauty

GEORGE SANTAYANA (1863–1952) spent much of his life feeling like a displaced person. He was born in Madrid and died in Rome. He spent much of his childhood in Boston and went to Harvard University, where he began teaching in 1889. He was on the faculty of Harvard as professor of philosophy at the same time William James was there. When he secured an inheritance in 1912, he left teaching and spent the rest of his life in Europe, settling in a convent in Rome to reflect and write. His major works are the five-volume The Life of Reason (1906), Scepticism and Animal Faith (1923), and the four-volume Realms of Being (1927–1940).

Santayana was a noted philosopher whose thought had a significant impact on his century. Yet he never developed any school or group of followers, and he never attached himself to any of the several schools that flourished in his time. In some ways he was a rather practical thinker, assuming that the material world was the source on which the world of thought depends. He believed, however, that all that was worthwhile in human experience had developed from the imagination. And for this reason he particularly valued art and reli-

---

From The Sense of Beauty.

gion, although he was never in any sense committed to a specific religious view. Of art, he said simply that it is the most splendid creation of man's reason.

As an aesthetician, he wrote extensively on art, emphasizing the fact that because it deals with human values, it is related to the field of ethics, which deals with moral values. Much of the selection presented here is devoted to the question of values and to the connection between aesthetics and ethics. Because Santayana is interested in making a series of fine distinctions in this piece, each section is carefully reasoned and argued. Some sections are difficult and require patient examination.

Santayana thought that art was of immense significance in the life of humankind. In this selection he is deeply concerned with the concept of beauty, which occupied most thinkers about art during the late nineteenth century, when he wrote this work (1896). He sees beauty as a value with certain qualities which are essential to isolate. For example, he says that "Beauty is pleasure regarded as the quality of a thing" (para. 48). But, in the process of reaching the point that enables him to say this, he reveals the ramifications of all the ideas that go into such an apparently straightforward statement.

SANTAYANA'S RHETORIC

Santayana was often regarded as a remarkably graceful writer. He published several volumes of poetry, and his novel, **The Last Puritan** *(1936), was exceptionally popular. Santayana's style is often remarkable. Sentences such as the following are noteworthy simply for their style: "The objects thus conceived and distinguished from our ideas of them, are at first compacted of all the impressions, feelings, and memories, which offer themselves for association and fall within the vortex of the amalgamating imagination" (para. 42). What this sentence says is that the imagination operates on our perception of things in order to give us our basic impression of them. The appropriateness of the image of the vortex is such that the concept becomes not only clearer but palpable and evident.*

There is another achievement which makes this essay rhetorically significant, the handling of the common topic of definition.

The entire work is a study of the nature of beauty, with its primary energy devoted to establishing a definition that satisfies the requirements set out in the opening paragraph: "A definition that should really define must be nothing less than the exposition of the origin, place, and elements of beauty as an object of human experience." Santayana attempts to provide such a definition.

Along with the task of definition comes the task of establishing the distinction between aesthetics and ethics, since both concern themselves with values. The fact that aesthetics does concern itself with values is the subject of paragraphs 1–8. Paragraphs 7–15 examine the rational aspects of preference, since beauty is that which is preferred. In establishing the distinction between the moral and the aesthetic, Santayana considers the difference between such things as work and play. He then takes a number of qualities—disinterestedness (being valued in itself, not for what it can do), objectivity, and universality—and examines them in turn. When he has completed his examination of these issues, he is in a position to entitle the last section of the work "The Definition of Beauty" (paras. 48–53).

As an extended definition, the work is remarkable. It demonstrates the fact that a full definition has to take into account many problems which at first glance do not appear to be a part of the original issue. But Santayana persists, moves patiently, and shows us—if not a satisfactory definition—at least what the materials of a definition must be.

The Nature of Beauty

The Philosophy of Beauty Is a Theory of Values

It would be easy to find a definition of beauty that should give in a few words a telling paraphrase of the word. We know on excellent authority that beauty is truth, that it is the expression of the ideal, the symbol of divine perfection, and the sensible manifestation of the good. A litany of these titles of honor might easily be compiled, and repeated in praise of our divinity. Such phrases stimulate thought and give us a momentary pleasure, but they hardly bring any permanent enlightenment. A definition that should really define must be nothing less than the exposition of the origin, place, and elements of beauty as an object of human experience. We must learn from it, as far as possible, why, when, and how beauty appears, what conditions an object must fulfill to be beautiful, what elements of our nature make us sensible of beauty, and what the relation is between the constitution of the object and the excitement of our susceptibility. Nothing less will really define beauty or make us understand what esthetic appreciation is. The definition of beauty in this sense will be the task of this whole book, a task that can be only very imperfectly accomplished within its limits.

The historical titles of our subject may give us a hint towards the 2 beginning of such a definition. Many writers of the last century called the philosophy of beauty *Criticism,* and the word is still retained as the title for the reasoned appreciation of works of art. We could hardly speak, however, of delight in nature as criticism. A sunset is not criticized; it is felt and enjoyed. The word "criticism," used on such an occasion, would emphasize too much the element of deliberate judgment and of comparison with standards. Beauty, although often so described, is seldom so perceived, and all the greatest excellences of nature and art are so far from being approved of by a rule that they themselves furnish the standard and ideal by which critics measure inferior effects.

This age of science and of nomenclature[1] has accordingly adopted 3 a more learned word, *Esthetics,* that is, the theory of perception or of susceptibility. If criticism is too narrow a word, pointing exclusively to our more artificial judgments, esthetics seems to be too broad and to include within its sphere all pleasures and pains, if not all perceptions whatsoever. Kant[2] used it, as we know, for his theory of time and space as forms of all perception; and it has at times been narrowed into an equivalent for the philosophy of art.

If we combine, however, the etymological meaning of criticism 4 with that of esthetics, we shall unite two essential qualities of the theory of beauty. Criticism implies judgment, and esthetics perception. To get the common ground, that of perceptions which are critical, or judgments which are perceptions, we must widen our notion of deliberate criticism so as to include those judgments of value which are instinctive and immediate, that is, to include pleasures and pains; and at the same time we must narrow our notion of esthetics so as to exclude all perceptions which are not appreciations, which do not find a value in their objects. We thus reach the sphere of critical or appre-

---

[1] *nomenclature* naming things; in this case, classification.
[2] *Immanuel Kant (1724–1804)* A German idealist philosopher who held that our perceptions of space and time are entirely limited by our senses.

ciative perception, which is, roughly speaking, what we mean to deal with. And retaining the word "esthetics," which is now current, we may therefore say that esthetics is concerned with the perception of values. The meaning and conditions of value are, then, what we must first consider.

Since the days of Descartes[3] it has been a conception familiar to philosophers that every visible event in nature might be explained by previous visible events, and that all the motions, for instance, of the tongue in speech, or of the hand in painting, might have merely physical causes. If consciousness is thus accessory to life and not essential to it, the race of man might have existed upon the earth and acquired all the arts necessary for its subsistence without possessing a single sensation, idea, or emotion. Natural selection might have secured the survival of those automata[4] which made useful reactions upon their environment. An instinct of self-preservation would have been developed, dangers would have been shunned without being feared, and injuries revenged without being felt.

In such a world there might have come to be the most perfect organization. There would have been what we should call the expression of the deepest interests and the apparent pursuit of conceived goods. For there would have been spontaneous and ingrained tendencies to avoid certain contingencies[5] and to produce others; all the dumb show[6] and evidence of thinking would have been patent to the observer. Yet there would surely have been no thinking, no expectation, and no conscious achievement in the whole process.

The onlooker might have feigned ends and objects of forethought, as we do in the case of the water that seeks its own level, or in that of the vacuum which nature abhors. But the particles of matter would have remained unconscious of their collocation,[7] and all nature would have been insensible of their changing arrangement. We only, the possible spectators of that process, by virtue of our own interests and habits, could see any progress or culmination in it. We should see culmination where the result attained satisfied our practical or esthetic demands, and progress wherever such a satisfaction was approached.

---

[3]***René Descartes (1596–1650)*** French philosopher famous for the expression "I think, therefore I am" *(cogito ergo sum)*, which he uses as a premise upon which to build his philosophy, tracing one cause-effect relationship after another.

[4]***automata*** robots, unfeeling beings.

[5]***contingencies*** developments.

[6]***dumb show*** pantomime, pretense.

[7]***collocation*** gathering, the nature of their organization.

But apart from ourselves, and our human bias, we can see in such a mechanical world no element of value whatever. In removing consciousness, we have removed the possibility of worth.

But it is not only in the absence of all consciousness that value   8
would be removed from the world; by a less violent abstraction from the totality of human experience, we might conceive beings of a purely intellectual cast, minds in which the transformations of nature were mirrored without any emotion. Every event would then be noted, its relations would be observed, its recurrence might even be expected; but all this would happen without a shadow of desire, of pleasure, or of regret. No event would be repulsive, no situation terrible. We might, in a word, have a world of idea without a world of will. In this case, as completely as if consciousness were absent altogether, all value and excellence would be gone. So that for the existence of good in any form it is not merely consciousness but emotional consciousness that is needed. Observation will not do, appreciation is required.

Preference Is Ultimately Irrational

We may therefore at once assert this axiom, important for all moral   9
philosophy and fatal to certain stubborn incoherences of thought, that there is no value apart from some appreciation of it, and no good apart from some preference of it before its absence or its opposite. In appreciation, in preference, lie the root and essence of all excellence. Or, as Spinoza[8] clearly expresses it, we desire nothing because it is good, but it is good only because we desire it.

It is true that in the absence of an instinctive reaction we can still   10
apply these epithets by an appeal to usage. We may agree that an action is bad or a building good, because we recognize in them a character which we have learned to designate by that adjective; but unless there is in us some trace of passionate reprobation or of sensible delight, there is no moral or esthetic judgment. It is all a question of propriety of speech, and of the empty titles of things. The verbal and mechanical proposition, that passes for judgment of worth, is the great cloak of ineptitude in these matters. Insensibility is very quick in the conventional use of words. If we appealed more often to actual feelings, our judgments would be more diverse, but they would be more

---

[8]***Baruch Spinoza (1632–1677)*** Dutch philosopher who wrote extensively on morals and on biblical criticism. His chief work is on ethics.

legitimate and instructive. Verbal judgments are often useful instruments of thought, but it is not by them that worth can ultimately be determined.

Values spring from the immediate and inexplicable reaction of vital 11 impulse, and from the irrational part of our nature. The rational part is by its essence relative; it leads us from data to conclusions, or from parts to wholes; it never furnishes the data with which it works. If any preference or precept were declared to be ultimate and primitive, it would thereby be declared to be irrational, since mediation, inference, and synthesis[9] are the essence of rationality. The idea of rationality is itself as arbitrary, as much dependent on the needs of a finite organization, as any other ideal. Only as ultimately securing tranquillity of mind, which the philosopher instinctively pursues, has it for him any necessity. In spite of the verbal propriety of saying that reason demands rationality, what really demands rationality, what makes it a good and indispensable thing and gives it all its authority, is not its own nature, but our need of it both in safe and economical action and in the pleasures of comprehension.

It is evident that beauty is a species of value, and what we have 12 said of value in general applies to this particular kind. A first approach to a definition of beauty has therefore been made by the exclusion of all intellectual judgments, all judgments of matter of fact or of relation. To substitute judgments of fact for judgments of value, is a sign of a pedantic and borrowed criticism. If we approach a work of art or nature scientifically, for the sake of its historical connections or proper classification, we do not approach it esthetically. The discovery of its date or of its author may be otherwise interesting; it only remotely affects our esthetic appreciation by adding to the direct effect certain associations. If the direct effect were absent, and the object in itself uninteresting, the circumstances would be immaterial. Molière's *Misanthrope*[10] says to the court poet who commends his sonnet as written in a quarter of an hour,

> *Voyons, monsieur, le temps ne fait rien à l'affaire,*

---

[9]*mediation, inference, and synthesis* The process of observing, drawing conclusions, and putting the conclusions to work.

[10]*Molière's* **Misanthrope** Molière was the stage name of Jean-Baptiste Poquelin (1622–1673), great French comic playwright and actor. In *The Misanthrope*, the puritanical title character despises and denounces the human weaknesses and vices of all the other characters, but is shown to be subject to them himself. The line means: "See here, sir, time has nothing to do with it." The point is that talent, not time, is what counts.

and so we might say to the critic that sinks into the archaeologist, show us the work, and let the date alone.

In an opposite direction the same substitution of facts for values 13 makes its appearance, whenever the reproduction of fact is made the sole standard of artistic excellence. Many half-trained observers condemn the work of some naïve or fanciful masters with a sneer, because, as they truly say, it is out of drawing. The implication is that to be correctly copied from a model is the prerequisite of all beauty. Correctness is, indeed, an element of effect and one which, in respect to familiar objects, is almost indispensable, because its absence would cause a disappointment and dissatisfaction incompatible with enjoyment. We learn to value truth more and more as our love and knowledge of nature increase. But fidelity is a merit only because it is in this way a factor in our pleasure. It stands on a level with all other ingredients of effect. When a man raises it to a solitary preeminence and becomes incapable of appreciating anything else, he betrays the decay of esthetic capacity. The scientific habit in him inhibits the artistic.

That facts have a value of their own, at once complicates and explains this question. We are naturally pleased by every perception, and recognition and surprise are particularly acute sensations. When we see a striking truth in any imitation we are therefore delighted, and this kind of pleasure is very legitimate, and enters into the best effects of all the representative arts. Truth and realism are therefore esthetically good, but they are not all sufficient, since the representation of everything is not equally pleasing and effective. The fact that resemblance is a source of satisfaction justifies the critic in demanding it, while the esthetic insufficiency of such veracity shows the different value of truth in science and in art. Science is the response to the demand for information, and in it we ask for the whole truth and nothing but the truth. Art is the response to the demand for entertainment, for the stimulation of our senses and imagination, and truth enters into it only as it subserves these ends.

Even the scientific value of truth is not, however, ultimate or absolute. It rests partly on practical, partly on esthetic interests. As our ideas are gradually brought into conformity with the facts by the painful process of selection—for intuition runs equally into truth and into error, and can settle nothing if not controlled by experience—we gain vastly in our command over our environment. This is the fundamental value of natural science, and the fruit it is yielding in our day. We have no better vision of nature and life than some of our predecessors, but we have greater material resources. To know the truth about the composition and history of things is good for this reason. It is also good because of the enlarged horizon it gives us, because the spectacle of nature is a marvelous and fascinating one, full of a serious sadness and large peace, which gives us back our birthright as children of the planet and naturalizes us upon the earth. This is the poetic value of the scientific *Weltanschauung.*[11] From these two benefits, the practical and the imaginative, all the value of truth is derived.

Esthetic and moral judgments are accordingly to be classed to- 16 gether in contrast to judgments intellectual; they are both judgments of value, while intellectual judgments are judgments of fact. If the latter have any value, it is only derivative, and our whole intellectual life has its only justification in its connection with our pleasures and pains.

Contrast between Moral and Esthetic Values

The relation between esthetic and moral judgments, between the 17 spheres of the beautiful and the good, is close, but the distinction between them is important. One factor of this distinction is that while esthetic judgments are mainly positive, that is, perceptions of good, moral judgments are mainly and fundamentally negative, or perceptions of evil. Another factor of the distinction is that whereas, in the perception of beauty, our judgment is necessarily intrinsic and based on the character of the immediate experience, and never consciously on the idea of an eventual utility in the object, judgments about moral worth, on the contrary, are always based, when they are positive, upon the consciousness of benefits probably involved. Both these distinctions need some elucidations.

Hedonistic ethics[12] have always had to struggle against the moral 18 sense of mankind. Earnest minds, that feel the weight and dignity of life, rebel against the assertion that the aim of right conduct is enjoyment. Pleasure usually appears to them as a temptation, and they sometimes go so far as to make avoidance of it a virtue. The truth is that morality is not mainly concerned with the attainment of pleasure; it is rather concerned, in all its deeper and more authoritative maxims, with the prevention of suffering. There is something artificial in the

---

[11]**Weltanschauung** A German term meaning a comprehensive world view, especially from a distinct intellectual position.

[12]***Hedonistic ethics*** A reference to the classical view of hedonists who predicated all their behavior on pleasurable sensations.

deliberate pursuit of pleasure; there is something absurd in the obligation to enjoy oneself. We feel no duty in that direction; we take to enjoyment naturally enough after the work of life is done, and the freedom and spontaneity of our pleasures are what is most essential to them.

The sad business of life is rather to escape certain dreadful evils to 19 which our nature exposes us—death, hunger, disease, weariness, isolation, and contempt. By the awful authority of these things which stand like specters behind every moral injunction, conscience in reality speaks, and a mind which they have duly impressed cannot but feel, by contrast, the hopeless triviality of the search for pleasure. It cannot but feel that a life abandoned to amusement and to changing impulses must run unawares into fatal dangers. The moment, however, that society emerges from the early pressure of the environment and is tolerably secure against primary evils, morality grows lax. The forms that life will further assume are not to be imposed by moral authority, but are determined by the genius of the race, the opportunities of the moment, and the tastes and resources of individual minds. The reign of duty gives place to the reign of freedom, and the law and the covenant to the dispensation of grace.[13]

The appreciation of beauty and its embodiment in the arts are activities which belong to our holiday life, when we are redeemed for the moment from the shadow of evil and the slavery to fear, and are following the bent of our nature where it chooses to lead us. The values, then, with which we here deal are positive; they were negative in the sphere of morality. The ugly is hardly an exception, because it is not the cause of any real pain. In itself it is rather a source of amusement. If its suggestions are vitally repulsive, its presence becomes a real evil towards which we assume a practical and moral attitude. And, correspondingly, the pleasant is never, as we have seen, the object of a truly moral injunction.

Work and Play

We have here, then, an important element of the distinction be- 21 tween esthetic and moral values. It is the same that has been pointed

---

[13]***dispensation of grace*** According to some Christian thinkers, the Old Testament stressed following the law as the means to salvation, and the New Testament stressed God's free granting of grace to replace the demands of the law.

to in the famous contrast between work and play. These terms may be used in different senses and their importance in moral classification differs with the meaning attached to them. We may call everything play which is useless activity, exercise that springs from the physiological impulse to discharge the energy which the exigencies of life have not called out. Work will then be all action that is necessary or useful for life. Evidently if work and play are thus objectively distinguished as useful and useless action, work is a eulogistic[14] term and play a disparaging one. It would be better for us that all our energy should be turned to account, that none of it should be wasted in aimless motion. Play, in this sense, is a sign of imperfect adaptation. It is proper to childhood, when the body and mind are not yet fit to cope with the environment, but it is unseemly in manhood and pitiable in old age, because it marks an atrophy[15] of human nature, and a failure to take hold of the opportunities of life.

Play is thus essentially frivolous. Some persons, understanding the 22 term in this sense, have felt an aversion, which every liberal mind will share, to classifying social pleasures, art, and religion under the head of play, and by that epithet condemning them, as a certain school seems to do, to gradual extinction as the race approaches maturity. But if all the useless ornaments of our life are to be cut off in the process of adaptation, evolution would impoverish instead of enriching our nature. Perhaps that is the tendency of evolution, and our barbarous ancestors amid their toils and wars, with their flaming passions and mythologies, lived better lives than are reserved to our well-adapted descendants.

We may be allowed to hope, however, that some imagination 23 may survive parasitically even in the most serviceable brain. Whatever course history may take—and we are not here concerned with prophecy—the question of what is desirable is not affected. To condemn spontaneous and delightful occupations because they are useless for self-preservation shows an uncritical prizing of life irrespective of its content. For such a system the worthiest function of the universe should be to establish perpetual motion. Uselessness is a fatal accusation to bring against any act which is done for its presumed utility, but those which are done for their own sake are their own justification.

At the same time there is an undeniable propriety in calling all the 24

---

[14]*eulogistic* Full of praise. Santayana says that work would be considered good, play bad.

[15]*atrophy* withering away.

liberal and imaginative activities of man play, because they are spontaneous, and not carried on under pressure of external necessity or danger. Their utility for self-preservation may be very indirect and accidental, but they are not worthless for that reason. On the contrary, we may measure the degree of happiness and civilization which any race has attained by the proportion of its energy which is devoted to free and generous pursuits, to the adornment of life and the culture of the imagination. For it is in the spontaneous play of his faculties that man finds himself and his happiness. Slavery is the most degrading condition of which he is capable, and he is as often a slave to the niggardliness of the earth and the inclemency of heaven, as to a master or an institution. He is a slave when all his energy is spent in avoiding suffering and death, when all his action is imposed from without, and no breath or strength is left him for free enjoyment.

Work and play here take on a different meaning, and become equivalent to servitude and freedom. The change consists in the subjective point of view from which the distinction is now made. We no longer mean by work all that is done usefully, but only what is done unwillingly and by the spur of necessity. By play we are designating, no longer what is done fruitlessly, but whatever is done spontaneously and for its own sake, whether it have or not an ulterior utility. Play, in this sense, may be our most useful occupation. So far would a gradual adaptation to the environment be from making this play obsolete, that it would tend to abolish work, and to make play universal. For with the elimination of all the conflicts and errors of instinct, the race would do spontaneously whatever conduced to its welfare and we should live safely and prosperously without external stimulus or restraint. . . . 25

In this second and subjective sense, then, work is the disparaging term and play the eulogistic one. All who feel the dignity and importance of the things of the imagination, need not hesitate to adopt the classification which designates them as play. We point out thereby, not that they have no value, but that their value is intrinsic, that in them is one of the sources of all worth. Evidently all values must be ultimately intrinsic. The useful is good because of the excellence of its consequences; but these must somewhere cease to be merely useful in their turn, or only excellent as means; somewhere we must reach the good that is good in itself and for its own sake, else the whole process is futile, and the utility of our first object illusory. We here reach the second factor in our distinction, between esthetic and moral values, which regards their immediacy. . . . 26

Esthetic and Physical Pleasure

We have now separated with some care intellectual and moral judg- 27
ments from the sphere of our subject, and found that we are to deal
only with perceptions of value, and with these only when they are
positive and immediate. But even with these distinctions the most remarkable characteristic of the sense of beauty remains undefined. All
pleasures are intrinsic and positive values, but all pleasures are not
perceptions of beauty. Pleasure is indeed the essence of that perception, but there is evidently in this particular pleasure a complication
which is not present in others and which is the basis of the distinction
made by consciousness and language between it and the rest. It will
be instructive to notice the degrees of this difference.

The bodily pleasures are those least resembling perceptions of 28
beauty. By bodily pleasures we mean, of course, more than pleasures
with a bodily seat; for that class would include them all, as well as all
forms and elements of consciousness. Esthetic pleasures have physical
conditions, they depend on the activity of the eye and the ear, of the
memory and the other ideational functions[16] of the brain. But we do
not connect those pleasures with their seats except in physiological
studies; the ideas with which esthetic pleasures are associated are not
the ideas of their bodily causes. The pleasures we call physical, and
regard as low, on the contrary, are those which call our attention to
some part of our own body, and which make no object so conspicuous
to us as the organ in which they arise.

There is here, then, a very marked distinction between physical 29
and esthetic pleasure; the organs of the latter must be transparent,
they must not intercept our attention, but carry it directly to some
external object. The greater dignity and range of esthetic pleasure is
thus made very intelligible. The soul is glad, as it were, to forget its
connection with the body and to fancy that it can travel over the world
with the liberty with which it changes the objects of its thought. The
mind passes from China to Peru without any conscious change in the
local tensions of the body. This illusion of disembodiment is very ex-
hilarating, while immersion in the flesh and confinement to some organ gives a tone of grossness and selfishness to our consciousness. The
generally meaner associations of physical pleasures also help to explain their comparative crudity.

---

[16]*ideational functions*   Capacities of the mind to imagine and to conceive ideas.

The Differentia of Esthetic Pleasure
Not Its Disinterestedness

The distinction between pleasure and the sense of beauty has [30] sometimes been said to consist in the unselfishness of esthetic satisfaction. In other pleasures, it is said, we gratify our senses and passion; in the contemplation of beauty we are raised above ourselves, the passions are silenced and we are happy in the recognition of a good that we do not seek to possess. The painter does not look at a spring of water with the eyes of a thirsty man, nor at a beautiful woman with those of a satyr.[17] The difference lies, it is urged, in the impersonality of the enjoyment. But this distinction is one of intensity and delicacy, not of nature, and it seems satisfactory only to the least esthetic minds.

In the second place, the supposed disinterestedness of esthetic de- [31] lights is not truly fundamental. Appreciation of a picture is not identical with the desire to buy it, but it is, or ought to be, closely related and preliminary to that desire. The beauties of nature and of the plastic arts are not consumed by being enjoyed; they retain all the efficacy to impress a second beholder. But this circumstance is accidental, and those esthetic objects which depend upon change and are exhausted in time, as are all performances, are things the enjoyment of which is an object of rivalry and is coveted as much as any other pleasure. And even plastic beauties can often not be enjoyed except by a few, on account of the necessity of travel or other difficulties of access, and then this esthetic enjoyment is as selfishly pursued as the rest.

The truth which the theory is trying to state seems rather to be [32] that when we seek esthetic pleasures we have no further pleasure in mind; that we do not mix up the satisfactions of vanity and proprietorship with the delight of contemplation. This is true, but it is true at bottom of all pursuits and enjoyments. Every real pleasure is in one sense disinterested. It is not sought with ulterior motives, and what fills the mind is no calculation, but the image of an object or event, suffused with emotion. A sophisticated consciousness may often take the idea of self as the touchstone of its inclinations; but this self, for the gratification and aggrandizement of which a man may live, is itself only a complex of aims and memories, which once had their direct objects, in which he had taken a spontaneous and unselfish interest. The gratifications which, merged together, make the selfishness are

---

[17]*satyr* Classical figure, half man, half goat; usually a symbol of lust.

each of them ingenuous,[18] and no more selfish than the most altruistic, impersonal emotion. The content of selfishness is a mass of unselfishness. There is no reference to the nominal essence called oneself either in one's appetites or in one's natural affections; yet a man absorbed in his meat and drink, in his houses and lands, in his children and dogs, is called selfish because these interests, although natural and instinctive in him, are not shared by others. The unselfish man is he whose nature has a more universal direction, whose interests are more widely diffused.

But as impersonal thoughts are such only in their object, not in 33 their subject or agent, since all thoughts are the thoughts of somebody: so also unselfish interests have to be somebody's interests. If we were not interested in beauty, if it were of no concern to our happiness whether things were beautiful or ugly, we should manifest not the maximum, but the total absence of esthetic faculty. The disinterestedness of this pleasure is, therefore, that of all primitive and intuitive satisfactions, which are in no way conditioned by a reference to an artificial general concept, like that of the self, all the potency of which must itself be derived from the independent energy of its component elements. I care about myself because "myself" is a name for the things I have at heart. To set up the verbal figment of personality and make it an object of concern apart from the interests which were its content and substance, turns the moralist, into a pedant, and ethics into a superstition. The self which is the object of *amour propre*[19] is an idol of the tribe, and needs to be disintegrated into the primitive objective interests that underlie it before the cultus of it can be justified by reason.

The Differentia of Esthetic Pleasure Not Its Universality

The supposed disinterestedness of our love of beauty passes into 34 another characteristic of it often regarded as essential—its universality. The pleasures of the senses have, it is said, no dogmatism in them; that anything gives me pleasure involves no assertion about its capac-

---

[18]*ingenuous* Innocent. *Altruistic* means unselfish.

[19]**amour propre** French term meaning self-esteem; self-conceit. The reference to "an idol of the tribe" is from Francis Bacon's "The Four Idols." The term means an intellectual prejudice common to all people. (See pages 327–343.) *Cultus* is a general acceptance or belief.

ity to give pleasure to another. But when I judge a thing to be beautiful, my judgment means that the thing is beautiful in itself, or (what is the same thing more critically expressed) that it should seem so to everybody. The claim to universality is, according to this doctrine, the essence of the esthetic; what makes the perception of beauty a judgment rather than a sensation. All esthetic precepts would be impossible, and all criticism arbitrary and subjective, unless we admit a paradoxical universality in our judgment, the philosophical implications of which we may then go on to develop. But we are fortunately not required to enter the labyrinth into which this method leads; there is a much simpler and clearer way of studying such questions, which is to challenge and analyze the assertion before us and seek its basis in human nature. Before this is done, we should run the risk of expanding a natural misconception or inaccuracy of thought into an inveterate and pernicious prejudice by making it the center of an elaborate construction.

That the claim of universality is such a natural inaccuracy will not 35 be hard to show. There is notoriously no great agreement upon esthetic matters; and such agreement as there is, is based upon similarity of origin, nature, and circumstance among men, a similarity which, where it exists, tends to bring about identity in all judgments and feelings. It is unmeaning to say that what is beautiful to one man *ought* to be beautiful to another. If their senses are the same, their associations and dispositions similar, then the same thing will certainly be beautiful to both. If their natures are different, the form which to one will be entrancing will be to another even invisible, because his classifications and discriminations in perception will be different, and he may see a hideous detached fragment or a shapeless aggregate of things, in what to another is a perfect whole—so entirely are the unities of objects unities of function and use. It is absurd to say that what is invisible to a given being *ought* to seem beautiful to him. Evidently this obligation of recognizing the same qualities is conditioned by the possession of the same faculties. But no two men have exactly the same faculties, nor can things have for any two exactly the same values.

What is loosely expressed by saying that anyone ought to see this 36 or that beauty is that he would see it if his disposition, training, or attention were what our ideal demands for him; and our ideal of what any one should be has complex but discoverable sources. We take, for instance, a certain pleasure in having our own judgments supported by those of others; we are intolerant, if not of the existence of a nature different from our own, at least of its expression in words and judgments. We are confirmed or made happy in our doubtful opinions by seeing them accepted universally. We are unable to find the basis of our taste in our own experience and therefore refuse to look for it there. If we were sure of our ground, we should be willing to acquiesce in the naturally different feelings and ways of others, as a man who is conscious of speaking his language with the accent of the capital confesses its arbitrariness with gaiety, and is pleased and interested in the variations of it he observes in provincials; but the provincial is always zealous to show that he has reason and ancient authority to justify his oddities. So people who have no sensations, and do not know why they judge, are always trying to show that they judge by universal reason.

Thus the frailty and superficiality of our own judgments cannot brook[20] contradiction. We abhor another man's doubt when we cannot tell him why we ourselves believe. Our ideal of other men tends therefore to include the agreement of their judgments with our own; and although we might acknowledge the fatuity of this demand in regard to natures very different from the human, we may be unreasonable enough to require that all races should admire the same style of architecture, and all ages the same poets. 37

The great actual unity of human taste within the range of conventional history helps the pretension. But in principle it is untenable. Nothing has less to do with the real merit of a work of imagination than the capacity of all men to appreciate it; the true test is the degree and kind of satisfaction it can give to him who appreciates it most. The symphony would lose nothing if half mankind had always been deaf, as nine-tenths of them actually are to the intricacies of its harmonies; but it would have lost much if no Beethoven[21] had existed. And more: incapacity to appreciate certain types of beauty may be the condition *sine qua non*[22] for the appreciation of another kind; the greatest capacity both for enjoyment and creation is highly specialized and exclusive, and hence the greatest ages of art have often been strangely intolerant. 38

The invectives of one school against another, perverse as they are philosophically, are artistically often signs of health, because they indicate a vital appreciation of certain kinds of beauty, a love of them that has grown into a jealous passion. The architects that have pieced 39

---

[20]***brook*** tolerate or permit.

[21]***Ludwig van Beethoven (1770–1827)*** Great German Romantic composer whose symphonies helped expand and define the form. He himself grew deaf in his late years.

[22]**sine qua non** A Latin term meaning the indispensable condition (lit., "without which nothing").

out the imperfections of ancient buildings with their own thoughts, like Charles V[23] when he raised his massive palace beside the Alhambra, may be condemned from a certain point of view. They marred much by their interference; but they showed a splendid confidence in their own intuitions, a proud assertion of their own taste, which is the greatest evidence of esthetic sincerity. On the contrary, our own gropings, eclecticism,[24] and archaeology are the symptoms of impotence. If we were less learned and less just, we might be more efficient. If our appreciation were less general, it might be more real, and if we trained our imagination into exclusiveness, it might attain to character.

The Differentia of Esthetic Pleasure: Its Objectification

There is, however, something more in the claim to universality in   40 esthetic judgments than the desire to generalize our own opinions. There is the expression of a curious but well-known psychological phenomenon, namely, the transformation of an element of sensation into the quality of a thing. If we say that other men should see the beauties we see, it is because we think those beauties *are in the object*, like its color, proportion, or size. Our judgment appears to us merely the perception and discovery of an external existence, of the real excellence that is without. But this notion is radically absurd and contradictory. Beauty, as we have seen, is a value; it cannot be conceived as an independent existence which affects our senses and which we consequently perceive. It exists in perception, and cannot exist otherwise. A beauty not perceived is a pleasure not felt, and a contradiction. But modern philosophy has taught us to say the same thing of every element of the perceived world; all are sensations; and their grouping into objects imagined to be permanent and external is the work of certain habits of our intelligence. We should be incapable of surveying or retaining the diffused experiences of life, unless we organized and classified them, and out of the chaos of impressions framed the world of conventional and recognizable objects.

How this is done is explained by the current theories of perception.   41

---

[23]*Charles V (1500–1558)* Holy Roman Emperor from 1519 to 1556, and also, as Charles I, king of Spain from 1516 to 1556. He defaced the Alhambra, an Islamic palace and fortress built in Granada, Spain, between 1248 and 1356, and built his own square palace next to it in a radically different style.

[24]*eclecticism* Habit of joining together many different styles.

External objects usually affect various senses at once, the impressions of which are thereby associated. Repeated experiences of one object are also associated on account of their similarity; hence a double tendency to merge and unify into a single percept, to which a name is attached, the group of those memories and reactions which in fact had one external thing for their cause. But this percept, once formed, is clearly different from those particular experiences out of which it grew. It is permanent, they are variable. They are but partial views and glimpses of it. The constituted notion therefore comes to be the reality, and the materials of it merely the appearance. The distinction between substance and quality, reality and appearance, matter and mind, has no other origin.

The objects thus conceived and distinguished from our ideas of 42 them, are at first compacted of all the impressions, feelings, and memories, which offer themselves for association and fall within the vortex[25] of the amalgamating imagination. Every sensation we get from a thing is originally treated as one of its qualities. Experiment, however, and the practical need of a simpler conception of the structure of objects lead us gradually to reduce the qualities of the object to a minimum, and to regard most perceptions as an effect of those few qualities upon us. These few primary qualities, like extension which we persist in treating as independently real and as the quality of a substance, are those which suffice to explain the order of our experiences. All the rest, like color, are relegated to the subjective sphere, as merely effects upon our minds, and apparent or secondary qualities of the object.

But this distinction has only a practical justification. Convenience 43 and economy of thought alone determine what combination of our sensations we shall continue to objectify and treat as the cause of the rest. The right and tendency to be objective is equal in all, since they are all prior to the artifice of thought by which we separate the concept from its materials, the thing from our experiences.

The qualities which we now conceive to belong to real objects are 44 for the most part images of sight and touch. One of the first classes of effects to be treated as secondary were naturally pleasures and pains, since it could commonly conduce very little to intelligent and successful action to conceive our pleasures and pains as resident in objects. But emotions are essentially capable of objectification, as well as impressions of sense; and one may well believe that a primitive and

---

[25]***vortex*** a rushing swirl, as is made by the water one lets out of a tub.

inexperienced consciousness would rather people the world with ghosts of its own terrors and passions than with projections of those luminous and mathematical concepts which as yet it could hardly have formed.

This animistic[26] and mythological habit of thought still holds its 45 own at the confines of knowledge, where mechanical explanations are not found. In ourselves, where nearness makes observation difficult, in the intricate chaos of animal and human life, we still appeal to the efficacy of will and ideas, as also in the remote night of cosmic and religious problems. But in all the intermediate realm of vulgar day, where mechanical science has made progress, the inclusion of emotional or passionate elements in the concept of the reality would be now an extravagance. Here our idea of things is composed exclusively of perceptual elements, of the ideas of form and of motion.

The beauty of objects, however, forms an exception to this rule. 46 Beauty is an emotional element, a pleasure of ours, which nevertheless we regard as a quality of things. But we are now prepared to understand the nature of this exception. It is the survival of a tendency originally universal to make every effect of a thing upon us a constituent of its conceived nature. The scientific idea of a thing is a great abstraction from the mass of perceptions and reactions which that thing produces; the esthetic idea is less abstract, since it retains the emotional reaction, the pleasure of the perception, as an integral part of the conceived thing.

Nor is it hard to find the ground of this survival in the sense of 47 beauty of an objectification of feeling elsewhere extinct. Most of the pleasures which objects cause are easily distinguished and separated from the perception of the object: the object has to be applied to a particular organ, like the palate, or swallowed like wine, or used and operated upon in some way before the pleasure arises. The cohesion is therefore slight between the pleasure and the other associated elements of sense; the pleasure is separated in time from the perception, or it is localized in a different organ, and consequently is at once recognized as an effect and not as a quality of the object. But when the process of perception itself is pleasant, as it may easily be, when the intellectual operation, by which the elements of sense are associated and projected, and the concept of the form and substance of the thing produced, is naturally delightful, then we have a pleasure intimately

---

[26]*animistic* Assuming that objects have souls or spirits. A characteristic of many religions, ancient and modern.

bound up in the thing, inseparable from its character and constitution, the seat of which in us is the same as the seat of the perception. We naturally fail, under these circumstances, to separate the pleasure from the other objectified feelings. It becomes, like them, a quality of the object, which we distinguish from pleasures not so incorporated in the perception of things, by giving it the name of beauty.

The Definition of Beauty

We have now reached our definition of beauty, which, in the terms 48 of our successive analysis and narrowing of the conception, is value positive, intrinsic, and objectified. Or, in less technical language, Beauty is pleasure regarded as the quality of a thing.

This definition is intended to sum up a variety of distinctions and 49 identifications which should perhaps be here more explicitly set down. Beauty is a value, that is, it is not a perception of a matter of fact or of a relation: it is an emotion, an affection of our volitional and appreciative nature. An object cannot be beautiful if it can give pleasure to nobody: a beauty to which all men were forever indifferent is a contradiction in terms.

In the second place, this value is positive, it is the sense of the 50 presence of something good, or (in the case of ugliness) of its absence. It is never the perception of a positive evil, it is never a negative value. That we are endowed with the sense of beauty is a pure gain which brings no evil with it. When the ugly ceases to be amusing or merely uninteresting and becomes disgusting, it becomes indeed a positive evil: but a moral and practical, not an esthetic, one. In esthetics that saying is true—often so disingenuous[27] in ethics—that evil is nothing but the absence of good: for even the tedium and vulgarity of an existence without beauty is not itself ugly so much as lamentable and degrading. The absence of esthetic goods is a moral evil: the esthetic evil is merely relative, and means less of esthetic good than was expected at the place and time. No form in itself gives pain, although some forms give pain by causing a shock of surprise even when they are really beautiful: as if a mother found a fine bull pup in her child's cradle, when her pain would not be esthetic in its nature.

Further, this pleasure must not be in the consequence of the utility 51 of the object or event, but in its immediate perception; in other words,

---

[27]***disingenuous*** insincere, not frank; willfully ignoring the truth.

beauty is an ultimate good, something that gives satisfaction to a natural function, to some fundamental need or capacity of our minds. Beauty is therefore a positive value that is intrinsic; it is a pleasure. These two circumstances sufficiently separate the sphere of esthetics from that of ethics. Moral values are generally negative, and always remote. Morality has to do with the avoidance of evil and the pursuit of good: esthetics only with enjoyment.

Finally, the pleasures of sense are distinguished from the perception of beauty, as sensation in general is distinguished from perception; by the objectification of the elements and their appearance as qualities rather of things than of consciousness. The passage from sensation to perception is gradual, and the path may be sometimes retraced: so it is with beauty and the pleasures of sensation. There is no sharp line between them, but it depends upon the degree of objectivity my feeling has attained at the moment whether I say "It pleases me," or "It is beautiful." If I am self-conscious and critical, I shall probably use one phrase; if I am impulsive and susceptible, the other. The more remote, interwoven, and inextricable the pleasure is, the more objective it will appear; and the union of two pleasures often makes one beauty. In Shakespeare's LIVth sonnet are these words: 52

> O how much more doth beauty beauteous seem
> By that sweet ornament which truth doth give!
> The rose looks fair, but fairer we it deem
> For that sweet odor which doth in it live.
> The canker-blooms have full as deep a dye
> As the perfumèd tincture of the roses,
> Hang on such thorns, and play as wantonly
> When summer's breath their maskèd buds discloses.
> But, for their beauty only is their show,
> They live unwooed and unrespected fade;
> Die to themselves. Sweet roses do not so:
> Of their sweet deaths are sweetest odors made.

One added ornament, we see, turns the deep dye, which was but show and mere sensation before, into an element of beauty and reality; and as truth is here the cooperation of perceptions, so beauty is the cooperation of pleasures. If color, form, and motion are hardly beautiful without the sweetness of the odor, how much more necessary would they be for the sweetness itself to become a beauty! If we had the perfume in a flask, no one would think of calling it beautiful: it would give us too detached and controllable a sensation. There would be no object in which it could be easily incorporated. But let it float from the garden, and it will add another sensuous charm to objects 53 simultaneously recognized, and help to make them beautiful. Thus beauty is constituted by the objectification of pleasure. It is pleasure objectified.

QUESTIONS

1. What does Santayana mean by the word "values"? What is a value in his terms?
2. What is the relationship of beauty to truth?
3. How are values perceived? Are values rational or emotional in nature?
4. Santayana says that "Beauty is a species of value" (para. 12). What does he seem to mean by this statement?
5. What is the scientific habit and what is its relation to truth?
6. What are the proper concerns of morality? Are they like or unlike the concerns of aesthetics?

WRITING ASSIGNMENTS

1. Santayana says that there is no value unless there is some appreciation of it (para. 9). Is this assertion true? Explain what leads Santayana to make this statement, then examine the strengths and weaknesses of his position. Consider the question of defining what a value is and what appreciation is.
2. Santayana has a great deal to say about the scientific attitude. Inventory the essay for his references to science, facts, and truth. What are his views on the usefulness of science? Refer to his comments on the "scientific habit" in paragraph 13 and to his comments on truth in subsequent paragraphs. How does the scientific attitude differ from the aesthetic attitude?
3. One comment Santayana makes is that "those [things] done for their own sake are their own justification" (para. 23). What do you do for its own sake? Is it its own justification? Is it related to the practice of science or of art? Do you think that your own experience supports Santayana's opinion or contradicts it? Make your essay support or oppose his views.
4. In paragraph 31, Santayana raises a touchy question: Should one dismiss all thoughts of ownership when appreciating a great painting? Is it really inappropriate to want to own a Picasso or a Rembrandt or any painting that one admires? Is, in fact, the admiration of beauty in general genuine only when questions of ownership or possession are dismissed from consideration? Or is it possible that the most intense and genuine appreciation of great art is almost always accompanied by desires of ownership and possession? If possible, answer these questions in an essay that refers to specific works of art, specific observations, and specific personal experiences.

5. In paragraph 37, Santayana talks about the fact that we like people to agree with our judgments: "Our ideal of other men tends therefore to include the agreement of their judgments with our own." Is this assertion generally true? Examine yourself and your friends in this regard. Do you find that most of your friends agree in judging the values of, say, popular or classical music, art, literature, and architecture? About which art form do you find the most heated disagreement? About which art form do you find the most intense agreement? You may choose a specific friend with whom to match your own interests and appreciation.

6. Beauty is one of the most difficult terms to define. You will notice that Santayana mentions few works of art, nor does he point to anything that is specifically beautiful (except for a sunset). As a result, his discussion is generally abstract. Offer your own definition of "the nature of beauty." In doing so, use any materials you find useful from Santayana's argument but try to make your definition clear, specific, concrete, and intelligible. Use the topic of definition as carefully as possible.

VIRGINIA WOOLF

A Letter to a Young Poet

VIRGINIA WOOLF (1882–1941), one of the most gifted of modern novelists, was part of a literary and artistic group that had formed when many of its members were at Cambridge University. When they graduated and took residence in London, they seemed to gravitate toward the area near Virginia Woolf's home in Tavistock Square, in Bloomsbury. Before long they were known as the Bloomsbury group and were often humorously referred to as "Bloomsberries." The fact that Virginia, her husband Leonard Woolf, her sister Vanessa Bell, with her husband Clive Bell, and their friends Lytton Strachey, Duncan Grant, David Garnett, John Maynard Keynes (see Part Two), and Roger Fry—as well as others less famous—all gathered together to talk about their work is significant. It meant that they had a forum for their thinking. And it meant, as well, that they were generous with their ideas.

"A Letter to a Young Poet" is symptomatic of the Bloomsbury ethic: it is strikingly generous when a highly successful and world-famous novelist takes time to write to an unknown poet to be encouraging. Woolf was like others in her group in that she felt that they were all part of an ongoing tradition of the arts. Anything she did to help those who were developing was an investment in the future of literature.

Woolf is best known for her adventurous and experimental novels, particularly Jacob's Room *(1922),* Mrs. Dalloway *(1925),* To the Lighthouse *(1927),* Orlando *(1928), and* The Waves *(1931). She also constantly wrote critical essays for papers and journals, and many of her essays, such as this letter, have been assembled in collections such as* The Common Reader, First Series *(1925), and* The Second Common Reader *(1932).*

Woolf was also noted for championing feminist causes. One of her most fascinating books, A Room of One's Own *(1929), treats the problems that women have when entering professional life, including the arts. There is a celebrated discussion in that book of what would have happened had Shakespeare had a sister who was as gifted as he. Her achievement as a novelist and a critic places her in the forefront of English writers, not only of her own time but of all time.*

"A Letter to a Young Poet" is fascinating not only for its general advice but also for its general assessment of the nature of poetry at the time. Woolf constantly excuses herself on the grounds that she is a prose writer and not a poet. At one point she mentions that she did not have a thorough university training and consequently knows none of the meters that are available to the poet. She refers to the fact that she had not gone to Cambridge, like the male members of the Bloomsbury group, but had been educated at home. Her father, Leslie Stephen, was a broadly educated man and a noted writer and editor, and his library was among the most impressive she could have had access to. Her mother died when she was twelve years old, and Woolf's life was unusually bookish. Yet, as she tells her correspondent in this letter, there is more to literature than "book-learning"; one must pay attention to the sensory experience of everyday life.

She tells her young poet that much of what she reads in contemporary poetry is centered on the poet. She bases this on a reading of three contemporary poets whose work she excerpts. None of the excerpts is especially impressive; from them, one could conclude that contemporary poetry is not in good shape. Yet she is optimistic rather than pessimistic—as is the imaginary old gentleman she opens the essay with—the fellow who condemns all modern verse, saying it is dead.

Her advice is extraordinary: she tells her poet to write about people who are unlike himself; in other words, not to focus on the poetic self but to use the poetic self to observe the world outside. She uses as her model William Shakespeare, whose characters, she insists, helped him create great poetry because they demanded that their lines be spoken as they had to be spoken—in their own voice rather than in Shakespeare's. She urges the young poet to observe other people and to observe them keenly.

WOOLF'S RHETORIC

Because this is a letter, it is relaxed in tone. Like many letters, however, this one has all earmarks of having been conceived as a document that could be published, and indeed it was the title essay in A Letter to a Young Poet *(1932). In this it resembles the letters of Martin Luther King, Jr., and Simone Weil in that it relates to a tradition of letters. Indeed, Woolf mentions that many letters are written for publication but that "authentic" letters are filled with the scraps and details of real life and therefore are burned. She knows her letter is not to be burned, and she adds the last, ironical lines saying that, in effect, the juicy parts are not included. She also refers to bits of gossip and scandal that were included in the letter to which she "responds," so that we have the feeling that this is part of an ongoing and lively correspondence between two people who know one another well. In a sense, we have the delightfully guilty feeling that we are eavesdropping.*

Among Woolf's rhetorical resources are allusion. She is able to allude to many literary greats because she is writing to a literary person. Those of us who are not "literary people" naturally need the footnotes, and Woolf knew that too; in a sense, she is taking this opportunity to introduce us to names of writers she has enjoyed, and because she is offhand about it, she does not seem to be an instructor but, rather, an interested friend. Remember that two of her most successful books are addressed to the "Common Reader," whom she always had in mind when she wrote. She is generous in that she wishes to share her enthusiasms and discoveries with everyone. Her declaration of ignorance about the intricacies of poetic meter remind us that she is not a know-it-all.

One of her most delightful rhetorical surprises is revealed in paragraph 4 where she decides to "be" the person she addresses. "Let me try to imagine . . . what it feels like to be a young poet in the autumn of 1931," she says, and then goes on to reveal her observations as if from that perspective. Her correspondent has told her that he is anxious, that he fears modern poetry is dead, that he does not know whether he can carry on. Her response respects his feelings but encourages him by commenting on poetry which is not altogether successful. She offers critical comments on the poetry she quotes, and as she does so she reminds the poet that she is simply giving him a personal reaction, a "hasty analysis" (para. 7). But it is one that leads her to encourage her friend to write about the world around him.

Poetry, she reminds him, has gone through many phases, and it is in a new and encouraging phase now. Therefore, he can break out in new directions, perhaps even write a poetry that would make people laugh. She wants to relieve the poet's "inner gloom" and "fixity" and encourage him to look outside himself. Ultimately she wants him to write about the "actual, the colloquial." In a sense, her conclusion to the letter is an amusing reminder that the parts that we do not get to see—"the intimate, the indiscreet, and indeed, the only really interesting parts of this letter . . ."—would be actual and colloquial.

———— ∞ ————

A Letter to a Young Poet

MY DEAR JOHN,

Did you ever meet, or was he before your day, that old gentleman— 1
I forget his name—who used to enliven conversation, especially at breakfast when the post came in, by saying that the art of letter-writing is dead? The penny post, the old gentleman used to say, has killed the art of letter-writing. Nobody, he continued, examining an envelope through his eyeglasses, has the time even to cross their t's. We rush, he went on, spreading his toast with marmalade, to the telephone. We commit our half-formed thoughts in ungrammatical phrases to the post card. Gray is dead, he continued; Horace Walpole is dead; Madame de Sévigné[1]—she is dead too, I suppose he was about to add, but a fit of choking cut him short, and he had to leave the room before he

---

[1]***Thomas Gray (1716–1771); Horace Walpole (1717–1797); Madame de Sévigné (1626–1696)*** Thomas Gray is famous for his "Elegy in a Country Churchyard" (1751) and is an important preromantic poet. Walpole, an intimate of Gray's at Eton, wrote *The Castle of Otranto* (1764), one of the first romantic novels. Like Gray and Walpole, Madame de Sévigné was well known for her vibrant letters and was part of one of the most dazzling intellectual circles in the history of France. She was a brilliant writer and a dashing woman.

had time to condemn all the arts, as his pleasure was, to the cemetery. But when the post came in this morning and I opened your letter stuffed with little blue sheets written all over in a cramped but not illegible hand—I regret to say, however, that several t's were uncrossed and the grammar of one sentence seems to be dubious—I replied after all these years to that elderly necrophilist[2]—Nonsense. The art of letter-writing has only just come into existence. It is the child of the penny post. And there is some truth in that remark, I think. Naturally when a letter cost half a crown to send, it had to prove itself a document of some importance; it was read aloud; it was tied up with green silk; after a certain number of years it was published for the infinite delectation of posterity. But your letter, on the contrary, will have to be burnt. It only cost three-halfpence to send. Therefore you could afford to be intimate, irreticent, indiscreet in the extreme. What you tell me about poor dear C. and his adventure on the Channel boat is deadly private; your ribald jests at the expense of M. would certainly ruin your friendship if they got about; I doubt, too, that posterity, unless it is much quicker in the wit than I expect, could follow the line of your thought from the roof which leaks ("splash, splash, splash into the soap dish") past Mrs. Gape, the charwoman, whose retort to the greengrocer gives me the keenest pleasure, via Miss Curtis and her odd confidence on the steps of the omnibus; to Siamese cats ("Wrap their noses in an old stocking my Aunt says if they howl"); so to the value of criticism to a writer; so to Donne; so to Gerard Hopkins;[3] so to tombstones; so to goldfish; and so with a sudden alarming swoop to "Do write and tell me where poetry's going, or if it's dead?" No, your letter, because it is a true letter—one that can neither be read aloud now, nor printed in time to come—will have to be burnt. Posterity must live upon Walpole and Madame de Sévigné. The great age of letter-writing, which is, of course, the present, will leave no letters behind it. And in making my reply there is only one question that I can answer or attempt to answer in public; about poetry and its death.

But before I begin, I must own up to those defects, both natural and acquired, which, as you will find, distort and invalidate all that I have to say about poetry. The lack of a sound university training has always made it impossible for me to distinguish between an iambic and a

---

[2]*necrophilist*   One who loves the dead (because the elderly gentleman believed that the arts were dead).
  [3]*John Donne (1572–1631); Gerard Manley Hopkins (1844–1889)*   Poets noted both for their intellectuality and for the complex wit of their poems. Both were clergymen: Donne was dean of St. Paul's, an Anglican cathedral; Hopkins was a Jesuit priest.

dactyl,[4] and if this were not enough to condemn one for ever, the practice of prose has bred in me, as in most prose writers, a foolish jealousy, a righteous indignation—anyhow, an emotion which the critic should be without. For how, we despised prose writers ask when we get together, could one say what one meant and observe the rules of poetry? Conceive dragging in "blade" because one had mentioned "maid"; and pairing "sorrow" with "borrow"? Rhyme is not only childish, but dishonest, we prose writers say. Then we go on to say, And look at their rules! How easy to be a poet! How strait the path is for them, and how strict! This you must do; this you must not. I would rather be a child and walk in a crocodile down a suburban path than write poetry, I have heard prose writers say. It must be like taking the veil and entering a religious order—observing the rites and rigors of meter. That explains why they repeat the same thing over and over again. Whereas we prose writers (I am only telling you the sort of nonsense prose writers talk when they are alone) are masters of language, not its slaves; nobody can teach us; nobody can coerce us; we say what we mean; we have the whole of life for our province. We are the creators, we are the explorers. . . . So we run on—nonsensically enough, I must admit.

Now that I have made a clean breast of these deficiencies, let us 3 proceed. From certain phrases in your letter I gather that you think that poetry is in a parlous way, and that your case as a poet in this particular autumn of 1931 is a great deal harder than Shakespeare's, Dryden's, Pope's or Tennyson's.[5] In fact it is the hardest case that has ever been known. Here you give me an opening, which I am prompt to seize, for a little lecture. Never think yourself singular, never think your own case much harder than other people's. I admit that the age we live in makes this difficult. For the first time in history there are readers—a large body of people, occupied in business, in sport, in nursing their grandfathers, in tying up parcels behind counters—they all read now; and they want to be told how to read and what to read; and their teachers—the reviewers, the lecturers, the broadcasters—must in all humanity make reading easy for them; assure them that literature

---

[4] ***an iamb and a dactyl*** Metrical feet: the iamb has an unaccented syllable followed by an accented syllable; the dactyl has an accented syllable followed by two unaccented syllables.

[5] ***William Shakespeare (1564–1616); John Dryden (1631–1700); Alexander Pope (1688–1744); Alfred, Lord Tennyson (1809–1892)*** Each of these poets was a giant in his own time. Shakespeare was the greatest Elizabethan poet, Dryden the most visible Restoration poet, Pope the most influential neoclassical poet, and Tennyson one of the greatest Victorian poets.

is violent and exciting, full of heroes and villains; of hostile forces perpetually in conflict; of fields strewn with bones; of solitary victors riding off on white horses wrapped in black cloaks to meet their death at the turn of the road. A pistol shot rings out. "The age of romance was over. The age of realism had begun"—you know the sort of thing. Now of course writers themselves know very well that there is not a word of truth in all this—there are no battles, and no murders and no defeats and no victories. But as it is of the utmost importance that readers should be amused, writers acquiesce. They dress themselves up. They act their parts. One leads; the other follows. One is romantic, the other realist. One is advanced, the other out of date. There is no harm in it, so long as you take it as a joke, but once you believe in it, once you begin to take yourself seriously as a leader or as a follower, as a modern or as a conservative, then you become a self-conscious, biting, and scratching little animal whose work is not of the slightest value or importance to anybody. Think of yourself rather as something much humbler and less spectacular, but to my mind far more interesting—a poet in whom live all the poets of the past, from whom all poets in time to come will spring. You have a touch of Chaucer[6] in you, and something of Shakespeare; Dryden, Pope, Tennyson—to mention only the respectable among your ancestors—stir in your blood and sometimes move your pen a little to the right or to the left. In short you are an immensely ancient, complex, and continuous character, for which reason please treat yourself with respect and think twice before you dress up as Guy Fawkes[7] and spring out upon timid old ladies at street corners, threatening death and demanding twopence-halfpenny.

However, as you say that you are in a fix ("it has never been so [4] hard to write poetry as it is today") and that poetry may be, you think, at its last gasp in England ("the novelists are doing all the interesting things now"), let me while away the time before the post goes in imagining your state and in hazarding one or two guesses which, since this is a letter, need not be taken too seriously or pressed too far. Let me try to put myself in your place; let me try to imagine, with your letter to help me, what it feels like to be a young poet in the autumn of 1931. (And taking my own advice, I shall treat you not as one poet in

---

[6]*Geoffrey Chaucer (1342–1400)* The most important English poet of the Middle Ages. He is best known for *The Canterbury Tales* (c. 1387–1400).

[7]*Guy Fawkes (1570–1606)* A would-be revolutionary English Catholic who plotted to blow up the assembled gathering of the king, his court, the law justices, and the House of Commons during King James I's coronation. He was discovered; the plot was revealed; and Fawkes and his fellow conspiraters were tried, convicted, and executed.

particular, but as several poets in one.) On the floor of your mind, then—is it not this that makes you a poet?—rhythm keeps up its perpetual beat. Sometimes it seems to die down to nothing; it lets you eat, sleep, talk like other people. Then again it swells and rises and attempts to sweep all the contents of your mind into one dominant dance. Tonight is such an occasion. Although you are alone, and have taken one boot off and are about to undo the other, you cannot go on with the process of undressing, but must instantly write at the bidding of the dance. You snatch pen and paper; you hardly trouble to hold the one or to straighten the other. And while you write, while the first stanzas of the dance are being fastened down, I will withdraw a little and look out of the window. A woman passes, then a man; a car glides to a stop and then—but there is no need to say what I see out of the window, nor indeed is there time, for I am suddenly recalled from my observations by a cry of rage or despair. your page is crumpled in a ball; your pen sticks upright by the nib in the carpet. If there were a cat to swing or a wife to murder now would be the time. So at least I infer from the ferocity of your expression. You are rasped, jarred, thoroughly out of temper. And if I am to guess the reason, it is, I should say, that the rhythm which was opening and shutting with a force that sent shocks of excitement from your head to your heels has encountered some hard and hostile object upon which it has smashed itself to pieces. Something has worked in which cannot be made into poetry; some foreign body, angular, sharp-edged, gritty, has refused to join in the dance. Obviously, suspicion attaches to Mrs. Gape; she has asked you to make a poem of her; then to Miss Curtis and her confidences on the omnibus; then to C., who has infected you with a wish to tell his story—and a very amusing one it was—in verse. But for some reason you cannot do their bidding. Chaucer could; Shakespeare could; so could Crabbe, Byron, and perhaps Robert Browning.[8] But it is October 1931, and for a long time now poetry has shirked contact with—what shall we call it?—Shall we shortly and no doubt inaccurately call it life? And will you come to my help by guessing what I mean? Well then, it has left all that to the novelist. Here you see how easy it would be for me to write two or three volumes in honor of prose and in mockery of verse; to say how wide and ample is the domain of the one, how starved and stunted the little grove of the other. But it would be simpler and perhaps fairer to check these theories by opening one

---

[8]*George Crabbe (1754–1832); George Gordon, Lord Byron (1788–1824); Robert Browning (1812–1889)* Crabbe and Byron were prominent romantic poets; Browning was one of the dominant poets of the later nineteenth century.

of the thin books of modern verse that lie on your table. I open and I find myself instantly confuted. Here are the common objects of daily prose—the bicycle and the omnibus. Obviously the poet is making his muse face facts. Listen:

> Which of you waking early and watching daybreak
> Will not hasten in heart, handsome, aware of wonder
> At light unleashed, advancing, a leader of movement,
> Breaking like surf on turf on road and roof,
> Or chasing shadow on downs like whippet racing,
> The stilled stone, halting at eyelash barrier,
> Enforcing in face a profile, marks of misuse,
> Beating impatient and importunate on boudoir shutters
> Where the old life is not up yet, with rays
> Exploring through rotting floor a dismantled mill—
> The old life never to be born again?

Yes, but how will he get through with it? I read on and find: 5

> Whistling as he shuts
> His door behind him, travelling to work by tube
> Or walking to the park to it to *ease the bowels,*

and read on and find again:

> As a boy lately come up from country to town
> Returns for the day to his village in *expensive shoes*—

and so on again to:

> Seeking a heaven on earth he chases his shadow,
> Loses his capital and his nerve in pursuing
> What yachtsmen, explorers, climbers and *buggers are after.*

These lines and the words I have emphasized are enough to con- 6 firm me in part of my guess at least. The poet is trying to include Mrs. Gape. He is honestly of opinion that she can be brought into poetry and will do very well there. Poetry, he feels, will be improved by the actual, the colloquial. But though I honor him for the attempt, I doubt that it is wholly successful. I feel a jar. I feel a shock. I feel as if I had stubbed my toe on the corner of the wardrobe.[9] Am I then, I go on to ask, shocked, prudishly and conventionally, by the words themselves? I think not. The shock is literally a shock. The poet as I guess has strained himself to include an emotion that is not domesticated and

---

[9]*wardrobe* In an English house of the time, the closet would have been a freestanding structure—a wardrobe—in a bedroom. Thus, it would be easy to stub a toe on it.

acclimatized to poetry; the effort has thrown him off his balance; he rights himself, as I am sure I shall find if I turn the page, by a violent recourse to the poetical—he invokes the moon or the nightingale. Anyhow, the transition is sharp. The poem is cracked in the middle. Look, it comes apart in my hands: here is reality on one side, here is beauty on the other; and instead of acquiring a whole object rounded and entire, I am left with broken parts in my hands which, since my reason has been roused and my imagination has not been allowed to take entire possession of me, I contemplate coldly, critically, and with distaste.

Such at least is the hasty analysis I make of my own sensations as a reader; but again I am interrupted. I see that you have overcome your difficulty, whatever it was; the pen is once more in action, and having torn up the first poem you are at work upon another. Now then if I want to understand your state of mind I must invent another explanation to account for this return of fluency. You have dismissed, as I suppose, all sorts of things that would come naturally to your pen if you had been writing prose—the charwoman, the omnibus, the incident on the Channel boat. Your range is restricted—I judge from your expression—concentrated and intensified. I hazard a guess that you are thinking now, not about things in general, but about yourself in particular. There is a fixity, a gloom, yet an inner glow that seem to hint that you are looking within and not without. But in order to consolidate these flimsy guesses about the meaning of an expression on a face, let me open another of the books on your table and check it by what I find there. Again I open at random and read this:

> To penetrate that room is my desire,
> The extreme attic of the mind, that lies
> Just beyond the last bend in the corridor.
> Writing I do it. Phrases, poems are keys.
> Loving's another way (but not so sure).
> A fire's in there, I think, there's truth at last
> Deep in a lumber chest. Sometimes I'm near
> But draughts puff out the matches, and I'm lost.
> Sometimes I'm lucky, find a key to turn,
> Open an inch or two—but always then
> A bell rings, someone calls, or cries of "fire"
> Arrest my hand when nothing's known or seen,
> And running down the stairs again I mourn.

and then this:

> There is a dark room,
> The locked and shuttered womb,

Where negative's made positive.
Another dark room,
The blind and bolted tomb,
Where positives change to negative.
We may not undo that or escape this, who
Have birth and death coiled in our bones,
Nothing we can do
Will sweeten the real rue,
That we begin, and end, with groans.

And then this:

Never being, but always at the edge of Being
My head, like Death mask, is brought into the Sun.
The shadow pointing finger across cheek,
I move lips for tasting, I move hands for touching,
But never am nearer than touching,
Though the spirit leans outward for seeing.
Observing rose, gold, eyes, an admired landscape,
My senses record the act of wishing
Wishing to be
Rose, gold, landscape or another—
Claiming fulfilment in the act of loving.

Since these quotations are chosen at random and I have yet found 8
three different poets writing about nothing, if not about the poet himself, I hold that the chances are that you too are engaged in the same
occupation. I conclude that self offers no impediment; self joins in the
dance; self lends itself to the rhythm; it is apparently easier to write a
poem about oneself than about any other subject. But what does one
mean by "oneself"? Not the self that Wordsworth, Keats, and Shelley[10]
have described—not the self that loves a woman, or that hates a tyrant, or that broods over the mystery of the world. No, the self that
you are engaged in describing is shut out from all that. It is a self that
sits alone in the room at night with the blinds drawn. In other words
the poet is much less interested in what we have in common than in
what he has apart. Hence I suppose the extreme difficulty of these
poems—and I have to confess that it would floor me completely to say
from one reading or even from two or three what these poems mean.
The poet is trying honestly and exactly to describe a world that has
perhaps no existence except for one particular person at one particular
moment. And the more sincere he is in keeping to the precise outline

---

[10]*William Wordsworth (1770–1850); John Keats (1795–1821); Percy Bysshe
Shelley (1792–1822)* All three are among the most important of the romantic poets.

of the roses and cabbages of his private universe, the more he puzzles us who have agreed in a lazy spirit of compromise to see roses and cabbages as they are seen, more or less, by the twenty-six passengers on the outside of an omnibus. He strains to describe; we strain to see; he flickers his torch; we catch a flying gleam. It is exciting; it is stimulating; but is that a tree, we ask, or is it perhaps an old woman tying up her shoe in the gutter?

Well, then, if there is any truth in what I am saying—if that is you 9 cannot write about the actual, the colloquial, Mrs. Gape or the Channel boat or Miss Curtis on the omnibus, without straining the machine of poetry, if, therefore, you are driven to contemplate landscapes and emotions within and must render visible to the world at large what you alone can see, then indeed yours is a hard case, and poetry, though still breathing—witness these little books—is drawing her breath in short, sharp gasps. Still, consider the symptoms. They are not the symptoms of death in the least. Death in literature, and I need not tell you how often literature has died in this country or in that, comes gracefully, smoothly, quietly. Lines slip easily down the accustomed grooves. The old designs are copied so glibly that we are half inclined to think them original, save for that very glibness. But here the very opposite is happening: here in my first quotation the poet breaks his machine because he will clog it with raw fact. In my second, he is unintelligible because of his desperate determination to tell the truth about himself. Thus I cannot help thinking that though you may be right in talking of the difficulty of the time, you are wrong to despair.

Is there not, alas, good reason to hope? I say "alas" because then I 10 must give my reasons, which are bound to be foolish and certain also to cause pain to the large and highly respectable society of necrophiles—Mr. Peabody, and his like—who much prefer death to life and are even now intoning the sacred and comfortable words, Keats is dead, Shelley is dead, Byron is dead. But it is late: necrophily induces slumber; the old gentlemen have fallen asleep over their classics, and if what I am about to say takes a sanguine tone—and for my part I do not believe in poets dying; Keats, Shelley, Byron are alive here in this room in you and you and you—I can take comfort from the thought that my hoping will not disturb their snoring. So to continue—why should not poetry, now that it has so honestly scraped itself free from certain falsities, the wreckage of the great Victorian age,[11] now that it

---

[11]**great Victorian age** A historical era, dating essentially from 1837, the accession of Queen Victoria to the throne of England, to 1901, the year of her death. It was an age

has so sincerely gone down into the mind of the poet and verified its outlines—a work of renovation that has to be done from time to time and was certainly needed, for bad poetry is almost always the result of forgetting oneself—all becomes distorted and impure if you lose sight of that central reality—now, I say, that poetry has done all this, why should it not once more open its eyes, look out of the window and write about other people? Two or three hundred years ago you were always writing about other people. Your pages were crammed with characters of the most opposite and various kinds—Hamlet, Cleopatra, Falstaff.[12] Not only did we go to you for drama, and for the subtleties of human character, but we also went to you, incredible though this now seems, for laughter. You made us roar with laughter. Then later, not more than a hundred years ago, you were lashing our follies, trouncing our hypocrisies, and dashing off the most brilliant of satires. You were Byron, remember; you wrote *Don Juan*.[13] You were Crabbe also; you took the most sordid details of the lives of peasants for your theme. Clearly therefore you have it in you to deal with a vast variety of subjects; it is only a temporary necessity that has shut you up in one room, alone, by yourself.

But how are you going to get out, into the world of other people? 11
That is your problem now, if I may hazard a guess—to find the right relationship, now that you know yourself, between the self that you know and the world outside. It is a difficult problem. No living poet has, I think, altogether solved it. And there are a thousand voices prophesying despair. Science, they say, has made poetry impossible; there is no poetry in motor cars and wireless. And we have no religion. All is tumultuous and transitional. Therefore, so people say, there can be no relation between the poet and the present age. But surely that is nonsense. These accidents are superficial; they do not go nearly deep enough to destroy the most profound and primitive of instincts, the instinct of rhythm. All you need now is to stand at the window and let your rhythmical sense open and shut, open and shut, boldly and freely, until one thing melts in another, until the taxis are dancing

---

of great industrial expansion, colonialization, and imperial design. It also was marked by a straitlaced social surface influenced by the manners of Victoria that produced "certain falsities" we now refer to as hypocrisies.

[12]***Hamlet, Cleopatra, Falstaff*** Characters in plays of Shakespeare. Falstaff appears in several plays, most notably *Henry IV, Part I* (1598), and *The Merry Wives of Windsor* (1602).

[13]**Don Juan** A long poem by Lord Byron centering on the romantic escapades of the legendary lover.

with the daffodils, until a whole has been made from all these separate fragments. I am talking nonsense, I know. What I mean is, summon all your courage, exert all your vigilance, invoke all the gifts that Nature has been induced to bestow. Then let your rhythmical sense wind itself in and out among men and women, omnibuses, sparrows—whatever comes along the street—until it has strung them together in one harmonious whole. That perhaps is your task—to find the relation between things that seem incompatible yet have a mysterious affinity, to absorb every experience that comes your way fearlessly and saturate it completely so that your poem is a whole, not a fragment; to rethink human life into poetry and so give us tragedy again and comedy by means of characters not spun out at length in the novelist's way, but condensed and synthesized in the poet's way—that is what we look to you to do now. But as I do not know what I mean by rhythm nor what I mean by life, and as most certainly I cannot tell you which objects can properly be combined together in a poem—that is entirely your affair—and as I cannot tell a dactyl from an iambic, and am therefore unable to say how you must modify and expand the rites and ceremonies of your ancient and mysterious art—I will move on to safer ground and turn again to these little books themselves.

When, then, I return to them I am, as I have admitted, filled, not   12 with forebodings of death, but with hopes for the future. But one does not always want to be thinking of the future, if, as sometimes happens, one is living in the present. When I read these poems, now, at the present moment, I find myself—reading, you know, is rather like opening the door to a horde of rebels who swarm out attacking one in twenty places at once—hit, roused, scraped, bared, swung through the air, so that life seems to flash by; then again blinded, knocked on the head—all of which are agreeable sensations for a reader (since nothing is more dismal than to open the door and get no response), and all I believe certain proof that this poet is alive and kicking. And yet mingling with these cries of delight, of jubilation, I record also, as I read, the repetition in the bass of one word intoned over and over again by some malcontent. At last then, silencing the others, I say to this malcontent, "Well, and what do *you* want?" Whereupon he bursts out, rather to my discomfort, "Beauty." Let me repeat, I take no responsibility for what my senses say when I read; I merely record the fact that there is a malcontent in me who complains that it seems to him odd, considering that English is a mixed language, a rich language; a language unmatched for its sound and color, for its power of imagery and suggestion—it seems to him odd that these modern poets should write as if they had neither ears nor eyes, neither soles to their feet nor palms to their hands, but only honest enterprising book-fed brains, unisexual bodies and—but here I interrupted him. For when it comes to saying that a poet should be bisexual, and that I think is what he was about to say, even I, who have had no scientific training whatsoever, draw the line and tell that voice to be silent.

But how far, if we discount these obvious absurdities, do you think   13 there is truth in this complaint? For my own part now that I have stopped reading, and can see the poems more or less as a whole, I think it is true that the eye and ear are starved of their rights. There is no sense of riches held in reserve behind the admirable exactitude of the lines I have quoted, as there is, for example, behind the exactitude of Mr. Yeats.[14] The poet clings to his one word, his only word, as a drowning man to a spar. And if this is so, I am ready to hazard a reason for it all the more readily because I think it bears out what I have just been saying. The art of writing, and that is perhaps what my malcontent means by "beauty," the art of having at one's beck and call every word in the language, of knowing their weights, colors, sounds, associations, and thus making them, as is so necessary in English, suggest more than they can state, can be learnt of course to some extent by reading—it is impossible to read too much; but much more drastically and effectively by imagining that one is not oneself but somebody different. How can you learn to write if you write only about one single person? To take the obvious example. Can you doubt that the reason why Shakespeare knew every sound and syllable in the language and could do precisely what he liked with grammar and syntax, was that Hamlet, Falstaff and Cleopatra rushed him into this knowledge; that the lords, officers, dependents, murderers and common soldiers of the plays insisted that he should say exactly what they felt in the words expressing their feelings? It was they who taught him to write, not the begetter of the Sonnets. So that if you want to satisfy all those senses that rise in a swarm whenever we drop a poem among them—the reason, the imagination, the eyes, the ears, the palms of the hands and the soles of the feet, not to mention a million more that the psychologists have yet to name, you will do well to embark upon a long poem in which people as unlike yourself as possible talk at the tops of their voices. And for heaven's sake, publish nothing before you are thirty.

That, I am sure, is of very great importance. Most of the faults in   14

---

[14]***William Butler Yeats (1865–1939)*** Yeats called himself the last romantic. He is considered one of the most influential modern poets writing in English.

the poems I have been reading can be explained, I think, by the fact that they have been exposed to the fierce light of publicity while they were still too young to stand the strain. It has shriveled them into a skeleton austerity, both emotional and verbal, which should not be characteristic of youth. The poet writes very well; he writes for the eye of a severe and intelligent public; but how much better he would have written if for ten years he had written for no eye but his own! After all, the years from twenty to thirty are years (let me refer to your letter again) of emotional excitement. The rain dripping, a wing flashing, someone passing—the commonest sounds and sights have power to fling one, as I seem to remember, from the heights of rapture to the depths of despair. And if the actual life is thus extreme, the visionary life should be free to follow. Write then, now that you are young, nonsense by the ream. Be silly, be sentimental, imitate Shelley, imitate Samuel Smiles;[15] give the rein to every impulse; commit every fault of style, grammar, taste, and syntax; pour out; tumble over; loose anger, love, satire, in whatever words you can catch, coerce or create, in whatever meter, prose, poetry, or gibberish that comes to hand. Thus you will learn to write. But if you publish, your freedom will be checked; you will be thinking what people will say; you will write for others when you ought only to be writing for yourself. And what point can there be in curbing the wild torrent of spontaneous nonsense which is now, for a few years only, your divine gift in order to publish prim little books of experimental verses? To make money? That, we both know, is out of the question. To get criticism? But your friends will pepper your manuscripts with far more serious and searching criticism than any you will get from the reviewers. As for fame, look I implore you at famous people; see how the waters of dullness spread around them as they enter; observe their pomposity, their prophetic airs; reflect that the greatest poets were anonymous; think how Shakespeare cared nothing for fame; how Donne tossed his poems into the wastepaper basket; write an essay giving a single instance of any modern English writer who has survived the disciples and the admirers, the autograph hunters and the interviewers, the dinners and the luncheons, the celebrations and the commemorations with which English society so effectively stops the mouths of its singers and silences their songs.

---

[15]*Samuel Smiles (1812–1904)* A Scots author and journalist, best known for numerous volumes of popular biography. He also wrote *Self-Help*, which was a widely read volume.

But enough. I, at any rate, refuse to be necrophilous. So long as you   15
and you and you, venerable and ancient representatives of Sappho,[16]
Shakespeare, and Shelley, are aged precisely twenty-three and propose—O enviable lot!—to spend the next fifty years of your lives in
writing poetry, I refuse to think that the art is dead. And if ever the
temptation to necrophilize comes over you, be warned by the fate of
that old gentleman whose name I forget, but I think that it was Peabody. In the very act of consigning all the arts to the grave he choked
over a large piece of hot buttered toast and the consolation then offered
him that he was about to join the elder Pliny in the shades gave him,
I am told, no sort of satisfaction whatsoever.

And now for the intimate, the indiscreet, and indeed, the only   16
really interesting parts of this letter. . . .

QUESTIONS

1. What state of mind was the young poet in when he wrote his letter to
   Woolf? What questions did he ask her?
2. Did Woolf feel that there were good reasons to be gloomy about the state
   of poetry at the time she began writing the letter?
3. What do the poetry excerpts tell you about the then current situation in
   poetry? Do you think these were good poems? What were their strengths?
   What were their weaknesses?
4. Does Woolf seem competent to talk about modern poetry? What seem to
   be her qualifications?
5. What does Woolf expect poetry to do? Does the young poet seem to expect
   the same things of poetry?
6. How useful do you think Woolf's advice might have been to this poet?

WRITING ASSIGNMENTS

1. Open a book of modern poetry or a current poetry magazine, or read some
   poetry from student publications and choose at random three selections
   from poems that can be considered contemporary. Offer your commentary
   on them in the same manner that Woolf comments on the poems she examines. She calls her examination a "hasty analysis," which alludes to its
   brevity. Aim to give your reader a sense of what your perception of contemporary poetry is based on the samples you choose. Do you find the

---

[16]*Sappho (fl. c. 610–580 B.C.)* A Greek lyric poet of the island of Lesbos. Her
work exists only in fragments, but she had a great reputation among the ancients.

same kinds of things to be true of poetry today as Woolf found in 1932?

2. Early in her essay, Woolf comments on the art of letter writing. She links the letter with the cost of sending it, referring at one point to the penny-post—a long-lost phenomenon. What is your assessment of the current state of the art of letter writing? Woolf says that her era is the great age of letter writing. Do you think she would say that today? Examine a variety of letters in the course of constructing your essay, including letters you have written and letters written to you (both personal and business). Then turn to the pages of the *New York Times,* your local or regional newspaper, a campus publication, *Time* magazine, the *Christian Science Monitor, TV Guide, Ebony,* and at least three other published sources. What is the state of the art of letter writing today?

3. Write a letter in response to Woolf's letter. Imagine yourself to be the person she addresses (though you need not think of yourself as "John") and respond with your own thoughts regarding her observations on poetry. Concern yourself with her main points and her attitudes toward the writing of poetry. Do not be afraid to take issue with her evaluations or her advice. Ask her questions that might elicit a further letter from her.

4. In paragraph 8, Woolf says, "it is apparently easier to write a poem about oneself than about any other subject." Determine whether this is true by writing a poem about yourself and by commenting on the ease or difficulty of the task. Give some thought to whether you felt it would be easy or difficult before you began, whether your expectations were fulfilled, and whether you think that other poets would be likely to have similar experiences.

5. In paragraph 12, Woolf gives the poet very detailed advice on what to do about his work. She urges him to listen to rhythms in language and to respond by observing life closely: "What I mean is, summon all your courage, exert all your vigilance, invoke all the gifts that Nature has been induced to bestow. Then let your rhythmical sense wind itself in and out among men and women, omnibuses, sparrows—whatever comes along the street—until it has strung them together in one harmonious whole. That perhaps is your task—to find the relation between things that seem incompatible yet have a mysterious affinity, to absorb every experience that comes your way fearlessly and saturate it completely so that your poem is a whole, not a fragment; to rethink human life into poetry and so give us tragedy again and comedy by means of characters not spun out at length in the novelist's way, but condensed and synthesized in the poet's way— that is what we look to you to do now." Try to take her advice by observing life around you. Write a poem that includes the speech patterns of people you know and of people you hear from any source at all (including radio and television), and create characters who make demands on you. Capture their speech and their attitudes toward life. Make your poem reflect the living experience that is yours each day.

SUSANNE K. LANGER

Expressiveness

SUSANNE K. LANGER (1895–1985) *developed a youthful interest in philosophy. She was born in New York and attended Radcliffe College of Harvard University, where she studied with Alfred North White-head and a number of other distinguished philosophers. She stayed on as a tutor at Harvard University from 1927 to 1942. Thereafter, she taught at the University of Delaware, Columbia University, and from 1954 to the end of her teaching career at Connecticut College. Her career as a teacher was distinguished, and her influence as a philosopher in the area of the arts has been widespread. Her* Philosophy in a New Key: A Study in the Symbolism of Reason, Rite, and Art *(1942) is probably her most widely read book. It deals carefully with certain implications of language and other kinds of symbols by which we shape our lives.*

In Problems of Art *(1957), from which the following selection is taken, she continues her interest in symbolism but concerns herself, too, with questions of creativity, abstraction, and the relation of emotion to the arts. "Expressiveness" is important because it at-*

From *Problems of Art*.

tempts to establish the ways in which a work of art will express emo-
tion. Her major assertion is, as it is in Philosophy in a New Key, *that*
the arts are somehow congruent with our emotions, that they express
those emotions. This view is extraordinarily complex, but it has also
been unusually influential. Her idea is that works of art are by nature
ineffable, that is, they cannot be reduced to language or discourse.
They simply are. Emotions are also not reducible to language: Who
can "translate" disappointment into words? In music, as Langer has
shown in another essay, we have become accustomed to a composer
using a specific musical passage to suggest a specific range of emo-
tions. Agitated strings and horns will suggest emotional agitation to
a listener. All that is rather oversimple, perhaps, but for many aes-
theticians, her view has the seeds of truth.

Essentially, Langer is interested in the ways in which the arts ex-
tend our capacities of understanding beyond language. She tells us
that "it is by virtue of language that we can think, remember, imag-
ine" (para. 19). But she also tells us that language has limits (para.
20) and that many human experiences are beyond the reach of lan-
guage to describe. The arts reach into these areas because they are
areas dominated by feeling.

One of the points she has made in her work in aesthetics is that
it is by virtue of studying and responding to works of art that we
educate our feelings. Most of us spend a good deal of time mastering
facts, learning processes, and performing rational exercises. But we
spend little time developing our emotional capacities. These are best
"educated" by the arts because the arts are products of emotional
understanding—they are, she says, congruent with feeling—and they
are therefore capable of extending our feelings. Thus, they can edu-
cate our emotions. The subject of "Expressiveness" is the issue of art's
capacity to express and interpret emotion.

LANGER'S RHETORIC

This work is, like most philosophical essays, a closely reasoned
one. Langer has an argument which takes a complex form. The pro-
cess of presenting the argument that the arts express emotion and that
we can learn from that expressiveness demands careful analysis of a
variety of implications. Analysis, taking the argument point by
point, is the principle that guides her rhetorical strategy.

Definition is the most important device she uses in her argument, since she must make clear precisely what she is talking about to enable us to grasp the importance of her position. The most difficult of all definitions in a work of this sort is the definition of art. But Langer aims directly at providing a definition that will work within her theory regarding expressiveness: "A work of art is an expressive form created for our perception through sense or imagination, and what it expresses is human feeling" (para. 5). This definition, like most definitions, presents problems.

Langer recognizes these problems and organizes the remainder of the work around the simplest approach to solving them. She tells us at the end of paragraph 5, "In stating what a work of art is, I have just used the words 'form,' 'expressive,' and 'created'; these are key words. One at a time, they will keep us engaged." The rest of this piece considers the implications of each of these terms in order. Paragraphs 6–17 treat of the questions relating to form, offering a complex definition of the term. Paragraphs 18–25 clarify the nature of expressiveness. The remainder of the piece examines the term "created," although this concept receives vastly less emphasis than do the first two.

In conducting her argument and in making the points she wishes to make about the relationship of the arts to expression, Langer's most reliable rhetorical strategy is that of attempting definitions. Once the terms of her definition of art are defined, we are in a position to accept or reject it. If we accept it, then we accept, too, her basic contention that the arts have in common one thing—the fact that they express emotions and feelings.

Expressiveness

When we talk about "Art" with a capital "A"—that is, about any 1
or all of the arts: painting, sculpture, architecture, the potter's and
goldsmith's and other designers' arts, music, dance, poetry, and prose
fiction, drama and film—it is a constant temptation to say things
about "Art" in this general sense that are true only in one special domain, or to assume that what holds for one art must hold for another.

For instance, the fact that music is made for performance, for presentation to the ear, and is simply not the same thing when it is given only to the tonal imagination of a reader silently perusing the score, has made some estheticians pass straight to the conclusion that literature, too, must be physically heard to be fully experienced, because words are originally spoken, not written; an obvious parallel, but a careless and, I think, invalid one. It is dangerous to set up principles by analogy, and generalize from a single consideration.

But it is natural, and safe enough, to ask analogous questions: 2 "What is the function of sound in music? What is the function of sound in poetry? What is the function of sound in prose composition? What is the function of sound in drama?" The answers may be quite heterogeneous; and that is itself an important fact, a guide to something more than a simple and sweeping theory. Such findings guide us to exact relations and abstract, variously exemplified basic principles.

At present, however, we are dealing with principles that have 3 proven to be the same in all the arts, when each kind of art—plastic, musical, balletic, poetic, and each major mode, such as literary and dramatic writing, or painting, sculpturing, building plastic shapes—has been studied in its own terms. Such candid study is more rewarding than the usual passionate declaration that all the arts are alike, only their materials differ, their principles are all the same, their techniques all analogous, etc. That is not only unsafe, but untrue. It is in pursuing the differences among them that one arrives, finally, at a point where no more differences appear; then one has found, not postulated, their unity. At that deep level there is only one concept exemplified in all the different arts, and that is the concept of Art.

The principles that obtain wholly and fundamentally in every kind 4 of art are few, but decisive; they determine what is art, and what is not. Expressiveness, in one definite and appropriate sense, is the same in all art works of any kind. What is created is not the same in any two distinct arts—this is, in fact, what makes them distinct—but the principle of creation is the same. And "living form" means the same in all of them.

A work of art is an expressive form created for our perception 5 through sense or imagination, and what it expresses is human feeling. The word "feeling" must be taken here in its broadest sense, meaning *everything that can be felt*, from physical sensation, pain and comfort, excitement and repose, to the most complex emotions, intellectual tensions, or the steady feeling-tones of a conscious human life. In stating what a work of art is, I have just used the words "form," "expressive," and "created"; these are key words. One at a time, they will keep us engaged.

Let us consider first what is meant, in this context, by a *form*. The 6 word has many meanings, all equally legitimate for various purposes; even in connection with art it has several. It may, for instance—and often does—denote the familiar, characteristic structures known as the sonnet form, the sestina, or the ballad form in poetry, the sonata form, the madrigal, or the symphony in music, the contre-dance[1] or the classical ballet in choreography, and so on. This is not what I mean; or rather, it is only a very small part of what I mean. There is another sense in which artists speak of "form" when they say, for instance, "form follows function," or declare that the one quality shared by all good works of art is "significant form," or entitle a book *The Problem of Form in Painting and Sculpture* or *The Life of Forms in Art,* or *Search for Form.* They are using "form" in a wider sense, which on the one hand is close to the commonest, popular meaning, namely just the *shape* of a thing, and on the other hand to the quite unpopular meaning it has in science and philosophy, where it designates something more abstract; "form" in its most abstract sense means structure, articulation, a whole resulting from the relation of mutually dependent factors, or more precisely, the way that whole is put together.

The abstract sense, which is sometimes called "logical form," is 7 involved in the notion of expression, at least the kind of expression that characterizes art. That is why artists, when they speak of achieving "form," use the word with something of an abstract connotation, even when they are talking about a visible and tangible art object in which that form is embodied.

The more recondite[2] concept of form is derived, of course, from the 8 naive one, that is, material shape. Perhaps the easiest way to grasp the idea of "logical form" is to trace its derivation.

Let us consider the most obvious sort of form, the shape of an object, say a lampshade. In any department store you will find a wide 9 choice of lampshades, mostly monstrosities, and what is monstrous is usually their shape. You select the least offensive one, maybe even a good one, but realize that the color, say violet, will not fit into your room; so you look about for another shade of the same shape but a

---

[1]*contre–dance* A formal, composed dance involving two lines of dancers; originally an English country dance.

[2]*recondite* learned and obscure.

different color, perhaps green. In recognizing this same shape in another object, possibly of another material as well as another color, you have quite naturally and easily abstracted the concept of this shape from your actual impression of the first lampshade. Presently it may occur to you that this shade is too big for your lamp; you ask whether they have *this same shade* (meaning another one of this shape) in a smaller size. The clerk understands you.

But what is *the same* in the big violet shade and the little green one? Nothing but the interrelations among their respective various dimensions. They are not "the same" even in their spatial properties, for none of their actual measures are alike; but their shapes are congruent. Their respective spatial factors are put together in the same way, so they exemplify the same form.

It is really astounding what complicated abstractions we make in our ordinary dealing with forms—that is to say, through what twists and transformations we recognize the same logical form. Consider the similarity of your two hands. Put one on the table, palm down, superimpose the other, palm down, as you may have superimposed cut-out geometric shapes in school—they are not alike at all. But their shapes are *exact opposites*. Their respective shapes fit the same description, provided that the description is modified by a principle of application whereby the measures are read one way for one hand and the other way for the other—like a timetable in which the list of stations is marked: "Eastbound, read down; Westbound, read up."

As the two hands exemplify the same form with a principle of reversal understood, so the list of stations describes two ways of moving, indicated by the advice to "read down" for one and "read up" for the other. We can all abstract the common element in these two respective trips, which is called the *route*. With a return ticket we may return only by the same route. The same principle relates a mold to the form of the thing that is cast in it, and establishes their formal correspondence, or common logical form.

So far we have considered only objects—lampshades, hands, or regions of the earth—as having forms. These have fixed shapes; their parts remain in fairly stable relations to each other. But there are also substances that have no definite shapes, such as gases, mists, and water, which take the shape of any bounded space that contains them. The interesting thing about such amorphous fluids[3] is that when they

---

[3]*amorphous fluids* Fluids without a shape of their own.

are put into violent motion they do exhibit visible forms, not bounded by any container. Think of the momentary efflorescence of a bursting rocket, the mushroom cloud of an atomic bomb, the funnel of water or dust screwing upward in a whirlwind. The instant the motion stops, or even slows beyond a certain degree, those shapes collapse and the apparent "thing" disappears. They are not shapes of things at all, but forms of motions, or dynamic forms.

Some dynamic forms, however, have more permanent manifesta- 14 tions, because the stuff that moves and makes them visible is constantly replenished. A waterfall seems to hang from the cliff, waving streamers of foam. Actually, of course, nothing stays there in midair; the water is always passing; but there is more and more water taking the same paths, so we have a lasting shape made and maintained by its passage—a permanent dynamic form. A quiet river, too, has dynamic form; if it stopped flowing it would either go dry or become a lake. Some twenty-five hundred years ago, Heracleitos[4] was struck by the fact that you cannot step twice into the same river at the same place—at least, if the river means the water, not its dynamic form, the flow.

When a river ceases to flow because the water is deflected or dried 15 up, there remains the river bed, sometimes cut deeply in solid stone. That bed is shaped by the flow, and records as graven lines the currents that have ceased to exist. Its shape is static, but it *expresses* the dynamic form of the river. Again, we have two congruent forms, like a cast and its mold, but this time the congruence is more remarkable because it holds between a dynamic form and a static one. That relation is important; we shall be dealing with it again when we come to consider the meaning of "living form" in art.

The congruence of two given perceptible forms is not always evi- 16 dent upon simple inspection. The common *logical* form they both exhibit may become apparent only when you know the principle whereby to relate them, as you compare the shapes of your hands not by direct correspondence, but by correspondence of opposite parts. Where the two exemplifications of the single logical form are unlike in most other respects one needs a rule for matching up the relevant factors of one with the relevant factors of the other; that is to say, a

---

[4]*Heracleitos (540?–475 B.C.)* A Greek philosopher who believed that the basis of all matter was fire. He also believed that everything was a result of the clash of opposite forces.

rule of translation, whereby one instance of the logical form is shown to correspond formally to the other.

The logical form itself is not another thing, but an abstract concept, or better an *abstractable* concept. We usually don't abstract it deliberately, but only use it, as we use our vocal cords in speech without first learning all about their operation and then applying our knowledge. Most people perceive intuitively the similarity of their two hands without thinking of them as conversely related; they can guess at the shape of the hollow inside a wooden shoe from the shape of a human foot, without any abstract study of topology.[5] But the first time they see a map in the Mercator projection[6]—with parallel lines of longitude, not meeting at the poles—they find it hard to believe that this corresponds logically to the circular map they used in school, where the meridians bulged apart toward the equator and met at both poles. The visible shapes of the continents are different on the two maps, and it takes abstract thinking to match up the two representations of the same earth. If, however, they have grown up with both maps, they will probably see the geographical relationships either way with equal ease, because these relationships are not *copied* by either map, but *expressed,* and expressed equally well by both; for the two maps are different *projections* of the same logical form, which the spherical earth exhibits in still another—that is, a spherical—projection.

17

An expressive form is any perceptible or imaginable whole that exhibits relationships of parts, or points, or even qualities or aspects within the whole, so that it may be taken to represent some other whole whose elements have analogous relations. The reason for using such a form as a symbol is usually that the thing it represents is not perceivable or readily imaginable. We cannot see the earth as an object. We let a map or a little globe express the relationships of places on the earth, and think about the earth by means of it. The understanding of one thing through another seems to be a deeply intuitive process in the human brain; it is so natural that we often have difficulty in distinguishing the symbolic expressive form from what it conveys. The symbol seems to be the thing itself, or contain it, or be contained in it. A child interested in a globe will not say, "This means the earth,"

18

---

[5]*topology*   The study or mapping of surfaces.

[6]*Mercator projection*   A flattened map of the earth. Gerardus Mercator (1512–1594), Flemish mapmaker, published his first Mercator projection in 1568, with longitudes and latitudes at right angles.

but "Look, this is the earth." A similar identification of symbol and meaning underlies the widespread conception of holy names, of the physical efficacy of rites, and many other primitive but culturally persistent phenomena. It has a bearing on our perception of artistic import; that is why I mention it here.

The most astounding and developed symbolic device humanity has   19
evolved is language. By means of language we can conceive the intangible, incorporeal things we call our *ideas*, and the equally inostensible[7] elements of our perceptual world that we call *facts*. It is by virtue of language that we can think, remember, imagine, and finally conceive a universe of facts. We can describe things and represent their relations, express rules of their interactions, speculate and predict and carry on a long symbolizing process known as reasoning. And above all, we can communicate, by producing a serried array of audible or visible words, in a pattern commonly known, and readily understood to reflect our multifarious concepts and percepts and their interconnections. This use of language is *discourse;* and the pattern of discourse is known as *discursive form*. It is a highly versatile, amazingly powerful pattern. It has impressed itself on our tacit thinking, so that we call all systematic reflection "discursive thought." It has made, far more than most people know, the very frame of our sensory experience—the frame of objective facts in which we carry on the practical business of life.

Yet even the discursive pattern has its limits of usefulness. An ex-   20
pressive form can express any complex of conceptions that, via some rule of projection, appears congruent with it, that is, appears to be of that form. Whatever there is in experience that will not take the impress—directly or indirectly—of discursive form, is not discursively communicable or, in the strictest sense, logically thinkable. It is unspeakable, ineffable;[8] according to practically all serious philosophical theories today, it is unknowable.

Yet there is a great deal of experience that is knowable, not only as   21
immediate, formless, meaningless impact, but as one aspect of the intricate web of life, yet defies discursive formulation, and therefore ver-

---

[7]*inostensible* Not apparent or evident. Langer implies here that the world of perceived "facts" is no more tangible than the world of ideas because all perceptions are filtered through the mind, which creates ideas of things.

[8]*ineffable* Literally, unspeakable; thus unknowable, because anything that cannot be expressed through language cannot be known.

bal expression: that is what we sometimes call the *subjective aspect* of experience, the direct feeling of it—what it is like to be waking and moving, to be drowsy, slowing down, or to be sociable, or to feel self-sufficient but alone; what it feels like to pursue an elusive thought or to have a big idea. All such directly felt experiences usually have no names—they are named, if at all, for the outward conditions that normally accompany their occurrence. Only the most striking ones have names like "anger," "hate," "love," "fear," and are collectively called "emotion." But we feel many things that never develop into any designable emotion. The ways we are moved are as various as the lights in a forest; and they may intersect, sometimes without cancelling each other, take shape and dissolve, conflict, explode into passion, or be transfigured. All these inseparable elements of subjective reality compose what we call the "inward life" of human beings. The usual factoring of that life-stream into mental, emotional, and sensory units is an arbitrary scheme of simplification that makes scientific treatment possible to a considerable extent; but we may already be close to the limit of its usefulness, that is, close to the point where its simplicity becomes an obstacle to further questioning and discovery instead of the revealing, ever-suitable logical projection it was expected to be.

Whatever resists projection into the discursive form of language is, indeed, hard to hold in conception, and perhaps impossible to communicate, in the proper and strict sense of the word "communicate." But fortunately our logical intuition, or form-perception, is really much more powerful than we commonly believe, and our knowledge—genuine knowledge, understanding—is considerably wider than our discourse. Even in the use of language, if we want to name something that is too new to have a name (for example, a newly invented gadget or a newly discovered creature), or want to express a relationship for which there is no verb or other connective word, we resort to metaphor; we mention it or describe it as something else, something analogous. The principle of metaphor is simply the principle of saying one thing and meaning another, and expecting to be understood to mean the other. A metaphor is not language, it is an idea expressed by language, an idea that in its turn functions as a symbol to express something. It is not discursive and therefore does not really make a statement of the idea it conveys; but it formulates a new conception for our direct imaginative grasp. 22

Sometimes our comprehension of a total experience is mediated by a metaphorical symbol because the experience is new, and language has words and phrases only for familiar notions. Then an extension of 23 language will gradually follow the wordless insight, and discursive expression will supersede the nondiscursive pristine symbol. This is, I think, the normal advance of human thought and language in that whole realm of knowledge where discourse is possible at all.

But the symbolic presentation of subjective reality for contempla- 24 tion is not only tentatively beyond the reach of language—that is, not merely beyond the words we have; it is impossible in the essential frame of language. That is why those semanticists[9] who recognize only discourse as a symbolic form must regard the whole life of feeling as formless, chaotic, capable only of symptomatic expression, typified in exclamations like "Ah!" "Ouch!" "My sainted aunt!" They usually do believe that art is an expression of feeling, but that "expression" in art is of this sort, indicating that the speaker has an emotion, a pain, or other personal experience, perhaps also giving us a clue to the general kind of experience it is—pleasant or unpleasant, violent or mild—but not setting that piece of inward life objectively before us so we may understand its intricacy, its rhythms and shifts of total appearance. The differences in feeling-tones or other elements of subjective experience are regarded as differences in quality, which must be felt to be appreciated. Furthermore, since we have no intellectual access to pure subjectivity, the only way to study it is to study the symptoms of the person who is having subjective experiences. This leads to physiological psychology—a very important and interesting field. But it tells us nothing about the phenomena of subjective life, and sometimes simplifies the problem by saying they don't exist.

Now, I believe the expression of feeling in a work of art—the func- 25 tion that makes the work an expressive form—is not symptomatic at all. An artist working on a tragedy need not be in personal despair or violent upheaval; nobody, indeed, could work in such a state of mind. His mind would be occupied with the causes of his emotional upset. Self-expression does not require composition and lucidity; a screaming baby gives his feeling far more release than any musician, but we don't go into a concert hall to hear a baby scream; in fact, if that baby is brought in we are likely to go out. We don't want self-expression.

A work of art presents feeling (in the broad sense I mentioned be- 26 fore, as everything that can be felt) for our contemplation, making it visible or audible or in some way perceivable through a symbol, not

---

[9]***semanticists*** Those concerned with the meaning of words; in this case, Langer refers to those who treat words as coherent symbols of meaning and think of feelings as simply reactions to (symptoms of) a stimulus.

inferable from[10] a symptom. Artistic form is congruent with the dynamic forms of our direct sensuous, mental, and emotional life; works of art are projections of "felt life," as Henry James[11] called it, into spatial, temporal, and poetic structures. They are images of feeling, that formulate it for our cognition. What is artistically good is whatever articulates and presents feeling to our understanding.

Artistic forms are more complex than any other symbolic forms we 27 know. They are, indeed, not abstractable from the works that exhibit them. We may abstract a shape from an object that has this shape, by disregarding color, weight and texture, even size; but to the total effect that is an artistic form, the color matters, the thickness of lines matters, and the appearance of texture and weight. A given triangle is the same in any position, but to an artistic form its location, balance, and surroundings are not indifferent. Form, in the sense in which we artists speak of "significant form" or "expressive form," is not an abstracted structure, but an apparition; and the vital processes of sense and emotion that a good work of art expresses seem to the beholder to be directly contained in it, not symbolized but really presented. The congruence is so striking that symbol and meaning appear as one reality. Actually, as one psychologist who is also a musician has written, "Music sounds as feelings feel." And likewise, in good painting, sculpture, or building, balanced shapes and colors, lines and masses look as emotions, vital tensions and their resolutions feel.

An artist, then, expresses feeling, but not in the way a politician 28 blows off steam or a baby laughs and cries. He formulates that elusive aspect of reality that is commonly taken to be amorphous and chaotic; that is, he objectifies the subjective realm. What he expresses is, therefore, not his own actual feelings, but what he knows about human feeling. Once he is in possession of a rich symbolism, that knowledge may actually exceed his entire personal experience. A work of art expresses a conception of life, emotion, inward reality. But it is neither a confessional nor a frozen tantrum; it is a developed metaphor, a nondiscursive symbol that articulates what is verbally ineffable—the logic of consciousness itself.

---

[10]*inferable from*   able to be rendered understandable from.

[11]*Henry James (1843–1916).*   One of America's greatest novelists; brother of the philosopher William James. "Felt life" was James's term for a deeply understood experience, particularly of the sort that developed into his own works.

QUESTIONS

1. What is Susanne Langer's definition of "art"?
2. Why does Langer tell us that it is "dangerous to set up principles by analogy" (para. 1)?
3. What does Langer mean by "feeling" (para. 5)?
4. Is Langer's use of the analogy of the lampshade "dangerous" (paras. 9–10)? Is it effective in her argument?
5. What does it mean to say that "Music sounds as feelings feel" (para. 27)?

WRITING ASSIGNMENTS

1. In paragraph 25, Langer says, "Now, I believe the expression of feeling in a work of art—the function that makes the work an expressive form—is not symptomatic at all." Clarify precisely what she means by this statement. Use her rhetorical method of relying on the topic of definition. The key terms to define are "expression of feeling," "expressive form," and "symptomatic." You may wish to quote from statements Langer makes on the question.
2. At one point Langer asserts that things which are not discursive, that is, not susceptible to discursive treatment, are not knowable. In essence, she is saying that language is essential for thinking and for knowing things. Is this assertion true? Is it possible for someone to know something that is not determined by language? If it is not possible, what are the implications for someone who is deficient in mastering language? To what extent is knowledge dependent on a mastery of language and discourse? Construct an essay that answers these questions.
3. One of the important points Langer makes at the end of this piece has to do with what feelings an artist expresses in a work of art. She discusses the question of whether a work of art is symptomatic; by that she means whether a given work expresses a feeling that the artist happens to have while he or she is creating. Her opinion is that the artist does not express feeling in this way. She says that the artist expresses what is serious about feelings, not his own feelings (para. 28). Do you feel that this assertion is true? Argue for this position using what you know about your own efforts to create works of art. But be sure, too, that you consult other people who make works of art for their views. It would help to ask anyone who is seriously interested in art what they think about this question. See paragraph 24.

4. In essence, this piece is an extended definition of art with separate definitions of several key terms. If possible, construct your own definition of art and use the technique Langer uses to develop a complete essay that clarifies the nature of that definition. If you find it impossible to construct your own definition, use someone else's definition. You may select one of the following definitions to work from:

> Art is the exercise of objectifying the depth of understanding of the human condition.

> A work of art is the most natural response the artist can give to the circumstances of his life.

> The work of art is by nature a symbolic interpretation of an artist's experience.

5. In paragraph 25, Langer asserts that we do not want self-expression in art. This statement may seem to be a contradiction in terms, since art is often represented to us as a useful means of self-expression. Is Langer's assertion correct? Analyze her statements on this subject, using her rhetorical strategies of definition. What exactly is self-expression, and how might it relate to art?

SUSAN SONTAG

Against Interpretation

SUSAN SONTAG *(b. 1933) is a probing critic whose commentaries on art, high and low, have earned her a place as a sharp, perceptive interpreter of aesthetic experience. But she is not an observer of art to the exclusion of other human concerns. Her political sensibilities were aroused, like those of many of her generation, because of the upheavals of the 1960s brought on by the Vietnam War and by civil disturbances at home. Much of her work has been published in intellectual journals aimed at an aware political audience.*

*Yet Sontag is a product of the academy, with degrees from the University of Chicago and Harvard University, and with experience as a faculty member at several colleges teaching both English and philosophy. She has been involved with film criticism and filmmaking since the late 1960s and has written and directed her own films, both feature films and documentaries. Some of her work has centered on the goals of feminism, but she has not always pleased feminists, who have often criticized her essay, "The Third World of Women" (*Partisan Review, 1973). *Her political activities were such that she journeyed to Hanoi, capital of North Vietnam, in 1968, during the worst period of the Vietnam War. Her book,* Trip to Hanoi *(1968), expresses her anguish at the nature of this painful war.*

Sontag is also a novelist and short-story writer, with several inter-

esting books to her credit—The Benefactor *(1963),* Death Kit *(1967), and* I, *etcetera (1978)—though her creative efforts has been somewhat slighted in contrast to the generally credited brilliance of her critical writings on the arts.* Against Interpretation and Other Essays *(1966) established her as among the most interesting and surprising of contemporary commentators on the arts. Her stance has always been surprising and provocative, as it is, for instance, in "Against Interpretation," which, in a book of criticism, seems to argue against the very process that makes criticism what it is.* Styles of Radical Will *(1969) continued a discussion of the modern sensibility and explored the issue of how we approach unusual and unexpected modern art forms.*

Two more recent books, Illness as Metaphor *(1977) and* On Photography *(1979), have had much impact. Her experience with cancer served as the impetus for the first book, which treated the ways in which society reacts to illness and the ways individuals sometimes exploit their illness. It is a book remarkable for its refusal to submit to the temptation to exploit the metaphor of illness in an autobiographical way. As a filmmaker and a relentless photographer, she wrote a book on photography that often condemned the way the camera appropriates everything visually without regard to the feelings or concerns of those who are photographed. Yet it is a book that stands as one of the most provocative and interesting statements on the art of photography.*

"Against Interpretation" is an essay that, in many ways, is a reaction to an age in which all art must submit to commentary and interpretation. Sontag makes an effort to assess exactly what interpretation is: "The task of interpretation is virtually one of translation. The interpreter says, Look, *don't you see that X is really—or, really means—A? That Y is really B? That Z is really C?" (para. 11). She believes that interpretation is not only an intermediary for works of art but that it substitutes for them and tames them. As she says, "one tames the work of art. Interpretation makes art manageable, comfortable" (para. 18). She is quick to admit that during some ages interpretation is a positive force, but she believes that in other ages—such as the present one—it is not.*

Early in the essay Sontag distinguishes between two aspects of the work of art: the form and the content. She focuses on literature and films, though she is obviously referring to all mimetic arts. As Aristotle tells us (see the first essay in this part), art imitates life and is therefore mimetic. Sontag explains that if art is mimetic it therefore has a content that relates it to life and that is interpretable. Her com-

plaint is not just that commentators separate the form of a work of art from its content but that the act of interpretation concentrates on content to the exclusion of form—or virtually so.

Content is meaning, and interpretation aims to explain the meaning of a work of art. As a result of an overemphasis on content, interpretation has helped to distort art: "Most American novelists and playwrights are really either journalists or gentlemen sociologists and psychologists. They are writing the literary equivalent of program music" (para. 30). The only art forms that escape this fate are those which are not mimetic: abstract and decorative arts. To these categories, she adds Pop Art, which is, like Andy Warhol's Campbell soup cans, uninterpretable as art because it is not only mimetic of life, it replicates life.

Ultimately, Sontag urges us to discontinue our emphasis on content and to restore attention to form. She believes that film is the most vital current art, and she reminds us that modern films—and she is thinking of those by artistic filmmakers, not those by commercial entertainers—are interesting largely by virtue of their visual form, by those elements which transcend content.

She ends her essay by making an appeal for a new approach to the arts, one that does not interpret but that examines and reports back on the facts, the perceptual elements of the work of art. She calls this "an erotics of art" because it emphasizes a growing awareness of sensory experience. She feels that sensory experience is important because the act of interpretation emphasizes intellectualization at the expense of experience. Thus, she says, "We must learn to see more, to hear more, to feel more" (para. 40).

SONTAG'S RHETORIC

Because this essay is an argument, Sontag depends on definition and on logical presentation. Ordinarily, she might have relied on sample interpretations or on concrete examples of works of art, but doing so is not possible in a general essay of this kind. Therefore, she depends upon establishing her definition of interpretation, commenting on how it affects works of art and their audience, and then making a recommendation based on her understanding. Naturally, she expects that we will share her understanding by the end of the essay.

Prominent in her rhetorical approach is a reliance on the historical survey. Since part of her argument is that interpretation can be good in some ages and not so good in other ages—and especially that it is not good in this age—the historical survey takes on significance. She begins with Plato and Aristotle, reminding us of Plato's view that everything we see on earth is an imitation of the ideal, which is in "heaven." As a result of that view, art is of little interest to Plato, since it can only be an imitation of an imitation. Aristotle developed the more acceptable view of art as mimetic—imitating life in order to reveal it more fully to us—and was, therefore, able to comment incisively on Greek drama in his Poetics.

Sontag goes on to discuss those who interpreted the Bible in the first centuries after Christ. She points out that the tradition of biblical hermeneutics—examining the Bible for its hidden meaning—derives from an era in which the text itself was unacceptable. She points out the example of the Song of Solomon, which is an explicit, elaborate love song. The Song of Solomon was interpreted to be a model of the wooing of the church by God—and therefore it was retained among the books of the Bible.

In more modern times, the doctrines of Karl Marx and Sigmund Freud demanded that we look behind art to their economic and psychological significance, respectively. Freud postulated that the dreams his patients discussed with him had a manifest content (what the dream seemed to be saying) and a more important latent content (what the dream was really saying). Psychoanalysis had among its tasks the job of determining the latent content and meaning of dreams, but it was not long before modern interpreters adopted the method and assumed that all art also had subtexts, hidden meanings that needed to be revealed through the process of interpretation.

Finally, in commenting on contemporary circumstances, Sontag reminds us that generations of commentary have begun to obscure the work of art and that commentary has become a substitute for it. If we accept this argument, we should agree with her that it is time to restore the work of art by putting intepretation aside so that we can approach the arts with a new, sensory freshness.

Against Interpretation

> Content is a glimpse of something, an encounter like a flash. It's very tiny—very tiny, content.
>
> WILLEM DE KOONING,
> *in an interview*

> It is only shallow people who do not judge by appearances. The mystery of the world is the visible, not the invisible.
>
> OSCAR WILDE,
> *in a letter*

The earliest experience of art must have been that it was incanta- 1
tory, magical; art was an instrument of ritual. (Cf. the paintings in the
caves at Lascaux, Altamira, Niaux, La Pasiega,[1] etc.) The earliest
theory of art, that of the Greek philosophers, proposed that art was
mimesis, imitation of reality.[2]

It is at this point that the peculiar question of the value of art 2
arose. For the mimetic theory, by its very terms, challenges art to justify itself.

Plato,[3] who proposed the theory, seems to have done so in order to 3
rule that the value of art is dubious. Since he considered ordinary material things as themselves mimetic objects, imitations of transcendent
forms or structures, even the best painting of a bed would be only an
"imitation of an imitation." For Plato, art is neither particularly useful
(the painting of a bed is no good to sleep on) nor, in the strict sense,
true. And Aristotle's arguments in defense of art do not really challenge Plato's view that all art is an elaborate *trompe l'oeil*,[4] and there-

---

[1]*Lascaux, Altamira, Niaux, La Pasiega* Limestone caves in France and Spain on the
walls of which are magnificent prehistoric paintings dating possibly to 15,000 B.C. The
subjects of the paintings are animals, and the paintings are thought to have been part of
magic rituals designed to gain control over the animals.

[2]*mimesis, imitation of reality* See Aristotle's *Poetics* (first selection, this
part): Aristotle suggests that art, whether painting or drama, imitates life.

[3]*Plato (c. 428–348 B.C.)* In "The Allegory of the Cave" (see Part Five), he demonstrates that reality is in "heaven" and that what we see on earth is only an imitation
of the divine ideal.

[4]*trompe l'oeil* French, "fool the eye"; an optical illusion; a style of painting that
gives the illusion of actual objects or a photograph.

fore a lie. But he does dispute Plato's idea that art is useless. Lie or no, art has a certain value according to Aristotle because it is a form of therapy. Art is useful, after all, Aristotle counters, medicinally useful in that it arouses and purges dangerous emotions.

In Plato and Aristotle, the mimetic theory of art goes hand in hand   4
with the assumption that art is always figurative. But advocates of the mimetic theory need not close their eyes to decorative and abstract art. The fallacy that art is necessarily a "realism" can be modified or scrapped without ever moving outside the problems delimited by the mimetic theory.

The fact is, all Western consciousness of and reflection upon art   5
have remained within the confines staked out by the Greek theory of art as mimesis or representation. It is through this theory that art as such—above and beyond given works of art—becomes problematic, in need of defense. And it is the defense of art which gives birth to the odd vision by which something we have learned to call "content," and to the well-intentioned move which makes content essential and form accessory.

Even in modern times, when most artists and critics have discarded   6
the theory of art as representation of an outer reality in favor of the theory of art as subjective expression, the main feature of the mimetic theory persists. Whether we conceive of the work of art on the model of a picture (art as a picture of reality) or on the model of a statement (art as the statement of the artist), content still comes first. The content may have changed. It may now be less figurative, less lucidly realistic. But it is still assumed that a work of art *is* its content. Or, as it's usually put today, that a work of art by definition says something. ("What X is saying is . . ." "What X is trying to say is . . ." "What X said is . . ." etc., etc.)

None of us can ever retrieve that innocence before all theory when   7
art knew no need to justify itself, when one did not ask of a work of art what it said because one knew (or thought one knew) what it did. From now to the end of consciousness, we are stuck with the task of defending art. We can only quarrel with one or another means of defense. Indeed, we have an obligation to overthrow any means of defending and justifying art which becomes particularly obtuse or onerous or insensitive to contemporary needs and practice.

This is the case, today, with the very idea of content itself. What-   8
ever it may have been in the past, the idea of content is today mainly a hindrance, a nuisance, a subtle or not so subtle philistinism.[5]

---

[5]*philistinism* A smugly uncultured or anticultural position.

Though the actual developments in many arts may seem to be 9
leading us away from the idea that a work of art is primarily its content, the idea still exerts an extraordinary hegemony. I want to suggest
that this is because the idea is now perpetuated in the guise of a certain way of encountering works of art thoroughly ingrained among
most people who take any of the arts seriously. What the overemphasis on the idea of content entails is the perennial, never-con-
summated project of *interpretation*. And, conversely, it is the habit
of approaching works of art in order to *interpret* them that sustains
the fancy that there really is such a thing as the content of a work
of art.

Of course, I don't mean interpretation in the broadest sense, the 10
sense in which Nietzsche[6] (rightly) says, "There are no facts, only
interpretations." By interpretation, I mean here a conscious act of the
mind which illustrates a certain code, certain "rules" of interpretation.

Directed to art, interpretation means plucking a set of elements 11
(the X, the Y, the Z, and so forth) from the whole work. The task of
interpretation is virtually one of translation. The interpreter says,
Look, don't you see that X is really—or, really means—A? That Y is
really B? That Z is really C?

What situation could prompt this curious project for transforming 12
a text? History gives us the materials for an answer. Interpretation first
appears in the culture of late classical antiquity, when the power and
credibility of myth had been broken by the "realistic" view of the
world introduced by scientific enlightenment. Once the question that
haunts post-mythic consciousness—that of the *seemliness* of religious
symbols—had been asked, the ancient texts were, in their pristine
form, no longer acceptable. Then interpretation was summoned, to
reconcile the ancient texts to "modern" demands. Thus, the Stoics,[7] to
accord with their view that the gods had to be moral, allegorized away
the rude features of Zeus and his boisterous clan in Homer's epics.
What Homer really designated by the adultery of Zeus with Leto, they
explained, was the union between power and wisdom. In the same

---

[6]*Friedrich Nietzsche (1844–1900)* One of the most important nineteenth-century German philosophers. His theory of the superman asserts that certain individuals
are above conventional wisdom and should be permitted to live and act as they wish.

[7]*the Stoics . . . Homer's epics* The Stoic philosophers in ancient Greece interpreted the Greek myths in accordance with their views of a morality of self-sacrifice and
public welfare. Homer (9th–8th centuries B.C.), who preceded the Stoics, could retell the
adulterous myths of Zeus without having to interpret them to fit a "higher" public morality.

vein, Philo of Alexandria[8] interpreted the literal historical narratives of the Hebrew Bible as spiritual paradigms. The story of the exodus from Egypt, the wandering in the desert for forty years, and the entry into the promised land, said Philo, was really an allegory of the individual soul's emancipation, tribulations, and final deliverance. Interpretation thus presupposes a discrepancy between the clear meaning of the text and the demands of (later) readers. It seeks to resolve that discrepancy. The situation is that for some reason a text has become unacceptable; yet it cannot be discarded. Interpretation is a radical strategy for conserving an old text, which is thought too precious to repudiate, by revamping it. The interpreter, without actually erasing or rewriting the text, *is* altering it. But he can't admit to doing this. He claims to be only making it intelligible, by disclosing its true meaning. However far the interpreters alter the text (another notorious example is the rabbinic and Christian "spiritual" interpretations of the clearly erotic Song of Songs[9]), they must claim to be reading off a sense that is already there.

Interpretation in our own time, however, is even more complex. 13 For the contemporary zeal for the project of interpretation is often prompted not by piety toward the troublesome text (which may conceal an aggression) but by an open aggressiveness, an overt contempt for appearances. The old style of interpretation was insistent, but respectful; it erected another meaning on top of the literal one. The modern style of interpretation excavates, and as it excavates, destroys; it digs "behind" the text, to find a sub-text which is the true one. The most celebrated and influential modern doctrines, those of Marx and Freud,[10] actually amount to elaborate systems of hermeneutics,[11] aggressive and impious theories of interpretation. All observable phenomena are bracketed, in Freud's phrase, as *manifest content*. This

---

[8]***Philo of Alexandria (30 B.C.–A.D. 45)*** A Jewish philosopher of importance to our knowledge of Jewish thought in the first century A.D. His theories were closely aligned with stoicism (see note 7). His most important work is a commentary on Genesis in which he sees all the characters as allegorical representations of states of the soul.

[9]***Song of Songs*** This is the Song of Solomon in the Bible, referred to in the headnote. The inclusion of the Song of Solomon in the Bible was marked by much dispute because it is an erotic, and very beautiful, piece of literature. The dispute was settled when agreement was reached in its interpretation: it was seen as a metaphor of the love of God for his creation.

[10]***Marx and Freud*** See the introductions for each of these authors in Parts One and Three, respectively.

[11]***hermeneutics*** A system of critical analysis that examines texts for their deeper meanings.

manifest content must be probed and pushed aside to find the true meaning—the *latent content*—beneath. For Marx, social events like revolutions and wars; for Freud, the events of individual lives (like neurotic symptoms and slips of the tongue) as well as texts (like a dream or a work of art)—all are treated as occasions for interpretation. According to Marx and Freud, these events only *seem* to be intelligible. Actually, they have no meaning without interpretation. To understand *is* to interpret. And to interpret is to restate the phenomenon, in effect to find an equivalent for it.

Thus, interpretation is not (as most people assume) an absolute   14
value, a gesture of mind situated in some timeless realm of capabilities. Interpretation must itself be evaluated, within a historical view of human consciousness. In some cultural contexts, interpretation is a liberating act. It is a means of revising, of transvaluing[12] of escaping the dead past. In other cultural contexts, it is reactionary, impertinent, cowardly, stifling.

Today is such a time, when the project of interpretation is largely   15
reactionary, stifling. Like the fumes of the automobile and of heavy industry which befoul the urban atmosphere, the effusion of interpretations of art today poisons our sensibilities. In a culture whose already classical dilemma is the hypertrophy[13] of the intellect at the expense of energy and sensual capability, interpretation is the revenge of the intellect upon art.

Even more. It is the revenge of the intellect upon the world. To   16
interpret is to impoverish, to deplete the world—in order to set up a shadow world of "meanings." It is to turn *the* world into *this* world. ("This world"! As if there were any other.)

The world, our world, is depleted, impoverished enough. Away   17
with all duplicates of it, until we again experience more immediately what we have.

In most modern instances, interpretation amounts to the philistine   18
refusal to leave the work of art alone. Real art has the capacity to make us nervous. By reducing the work of art to its content and then interpreting *that*, one tames the work of art. Interpretation makes art manageable, comfortable.

This philistinism of interpretation is more rife in literature than in   19

---

[12]***transvaluing*** The act of evaluating by a new principle, such as interpreting a sonnet of Shakespeare by means of Freudian principles.

[13]***hypertrophy*** overdevelopment.

any other art. For decades now, literary critics have understood it to be their task to translate the elements of the poem or play or novel or story into something else. Sometimes a writer will be so uneasy before the naked power of his art that he will install within the work itself—albeit with a little shyness, a touch of the good taste of irony—the clear and explicit interpretation of it. Thomas Mann[14] is an example of such an overcooperative author. In the case of more stubborn authors, the critic is only too happy to perform the job.

The work of Kafka,[15] for example, has been subjected to a mass 20
ravishment by no less than three armies of interpreters. Those who read Kafka as a social allegory see case studies of the frustrations and insanity of modern bureaucracy and its ultimate issuance in the totalitarian state. Those who read Kafka as a psychoanalytic allegory see desperate revelations of Kafka's fear of his father, his castration anxieties, his sense of his own impotence, his thralldom to his dreams. Those who read Kafka as a religious allegory explain that K. in *The Castle* is trying to gain access to heaven, that Joseph K. in *The Trial* is being judged by the inexorable and mysterious justice of God. . . . Another body of work that has attracted interpreters like leeches is that of Samuel Beckett,[16] Beckett's delicate dramas of the withdrawn consciousness—pared down to essentials, cut off, often represented as physically immobilized—are read as a statement about modern man's alienation from meaning or from God, or as an allegory of psychopathology.

Proust, Joyce, Faulkner, Rilke, Lawrence, Gide[17] . . . one could go 21
on citing author after author; the list is endless of those around whom thick encrustations of interpretation have taken hold. But it should be noted that interpretation is not simply the compliment that mediocrity pays to genius. It is, indeed, the modern way of understanding something, and is applied to works of every quality. Thus, in the notes

---

[14] **Thomas Mann (1875–1955)** The most significant modern German novelist. Sontag may be referring to his most important novel, *The Magic Mountain* (1924).

[15] **Franz Kafka (1883–1924)** A largely surreal writer whose dreamworlds are often close to the nightmare. The novels referred to, *The Castle* and *The Trial*, both published in 1937, concentrate on the struggles of the individual against institutions whose nature is baffling and intimidating.

[16] **Samuel Beckett (b. 1906)** Irish writer whose work is enigmatic. He is best known for his play *Waiting for Godot* (1956).

[17] **Marcel Proust (1871–1922); James Joyce (1882–1941); William Faulkner (1897–1962); Rainer Maria Rilke (1875–1926); D. H. Lawrence (1885–1930); André Gide (1869–1951)** Important modern writers whose work has attracted considerable interpretive attention.

that Elia Kazan[18] published on his production of *A Streetcar Named Desire*, it becomes clear that, in order to direct the play, Kazan had to discover that Stanley Kowalski represented the sensual and vengeful barbarism that was engulfing our culture, while Blanche DuBois was Western civilization, poetry, delicate apparel, dim lighting, refined feelings and all, though a little the worse for wear, to be sure. Tennessee Williams's forceful psychological melodrama now became intelligible: it was about something, about the decline of Western civilization. Apparently, were it to go on being a play about a handsome brute named Stanley Kowalski and a faded mangy belle named Blanche DuBois, it would not be manageable.

It doesn't matter whether artists intend, or don't intend, for their works to be interpreted. Perhaps Tennessee Williams thinks *Streetcar* 22 is about what Kazan thinks it to be about. It may be that Cocteau[19] in *The Blood of a Poet* and in *Orpheus* wanted the elaborate readings which have been given these films, in terms of Freudian symbolism and social critique. But the merit of these works certainly lies elsewhere than in their "meanings." Indeed, it is precisely to the extent that Williams's plays and Cocteau's films do suggest these portentous meanings[20] that they are defective, false, contrived, lacking in conviction.

From interviews, it appears that Resnais and Robbe-Grillet[21] con- 23 sciously designed *Last Year at Marienbad* to accommodate a multiplicity of equally plausible interpretations. But the temptation to interpret *Marienbad* should be resisted. What matters in *Marienbad* is the pure, untranslatable, sensuous immediacy of some of its images, and its rigorous if narrow solutions to certain problems of cinematic form.

Again, Ingmar Bergman[22] may have meant the tank rumbling down 24

---

[18]*Elia Kazan (b. 1909)* American theatrical director who championed the early productions of Tennessee Williams (1914–1984), particularly *A Streetcar Named Desire* (1947).

[19]*Jean Cocteau (1889–1963)* French writer, painter, filmmaker. His *Orpheus* (1924) reinterpreted the Greek myth for modern times.

[20]*portentous meanings* Meanings that imply great significance or seriousness and that may imply ominous developments. Sontag implies that the meanings suggested for the works are overblown and unlikely.

[21]*Alain Resnais (b. 1922) and Alain Robbe-Grillet (b. 1922)* The filmmaker and screenwriter, respectively, for a very "arty" and experimental film, *Last Year at Marienbad* (1961).

[22]*Ingmar Bergman (b. 1918)* The most important Swedish film director of the century; one of the most influential of modern directors.

the empty night street in *The Silence* as a phallic symbol. But if he did, it was a foolish thought. ("Never trust the teller, trust the tale," said Lawrence.) Taken as a brute object, as an immediate sensory equivalent for the mysterious abrupt armored happenings going on inside the hotel, that sequence with the tank is the most striking moment in the film. Those who reach for a Freudian interpretation of the tank are only expressing their lack of response to what is there on the screen.

It is always the case that interpretation of this type indicates a dissatisfaction (conscious or unconscious) with the work, a wish to replace it by something else.   25

Interpretation, based on the highly dubious theory that a work of art is composed of items of content, violates art. It makes art into an article for use, for arrangement into a mental scheme of categories.   26

Interpretation does not, of course, always prevail. In fact, a great deal of today's art may be understood as motivated by a flight from interpretation. To avoid interpretation, art may become parody. Or it may become abstract. Or it may become ("merely") decorative. Or it may become non-art.   27

The flight from interpretation seems particularly a feature of modern painting. Abstract painting is the attempt to have, in the ordinary sense, no content; since there is no content, there can be no interpretation. Pop Art[23] works by the opposite means to the same result; using a content so blatant, so "what it is," it, too, ends by being uninterpretable.   28

A great deal of modern poetry as well, starting from the great experiments of French poetry (including the movement that is misleadingly called Symbolism)[24] to put silence into poems and to reinstate the *magic* of the word, has escaped from the rough grip of interpretation. The most recent revolution in contemporary taste in poetry—the   29

---

[23]**Pop Art**   A form of art that in the later 1950s and the 1960s reacted against the high seriousness of abstract expressionism and other movements of the 1940s and 1950s. Instead of stressing deep content, it stressed no content; instead of profound meaning, no meaning other than what was observable.

[24]**Symbolism**   A movement in poetry begun in France in the later part of the nineteenth century and popularized in England by Arthur Symons. It sought expression through the symbol rather than through discursive language. By silencing the discourse, the symbolists hoped to put magic back into poetry—the magic representing what was inexpressible in words but could be felt in symbol.

revolution that has deposed Eliot and elevated Pound[25]—represents a turning away from content in poetry in the old sense, an impatience with what made modern poetry prey to the zeal of interpreters.

I am speaking mainly of the situation in America, of course. Inter- 30 pretation runs rampant here in those arts with a feeble and negligible avant-garde:[26] fiction and the drama. Most American novelists and playwrights are really either journalists or gentlemen sociologists and psychologists. They are writing the literary equivalent of program music. And so rudimentary, uninspired, and stagnant has been the sense of what might be done with form in fiction and drama that even when the content isn't simply information, news, it is still peculiarly visible, handier, more exposed. To the extent that novels and plays (in America), unlike poetry and painting and music, don't reflect any interesting concern with changes in their form, these arts remain prone to assault by interpretation.

But programmatic avant-gardism—which has meant, mostly, ex- 31 periments with form at the expense of content—is not the only defense against the infestation of art by interpretations. At least, I hope not. For this would be to commit art to being perpetually on the run. (It also perpetuates the very distinction between form and content which is, ultimately, an illusion.) Ideally, it is possible to elude the interpreters in another way, by making works of art whose surface is so unified and clean, whose momentum is so rapid, whose address is so direct that the work can be . . . just what it is. Is this possible now? It does happen in films, I believe. This is why cinema is the most alive, the most exciting, the most important of all art forms right now. Perhaps the way one tells how alive a particular art form is is by the latitude it gives for making mistakes in it and still being good. For example, a few of the films of Bergman—though crammed with lame messages about the modern spirit, thereby inviting interpretations— still triumph over the pretentious intentions of their director. In *Winter Light* and *The Silence*, the beauty and visual sophistication of the images subvert before our eyes the callow pseudo-intellectuality of the story and some of the dialogue. (The most remarkable instance of this sort of discrepancy is the work of D. W. Griffith).[27] In good films, there

---

[25]*T. S. Eliot (1888–1965) and Ezra Pound (1885–1972)* Two of America's most important modern poets.

[26]*avante-garde* Art that is ahead of its time; literally, in the advance guard of a movement forward.

[27]*D. W. Griffith (1875–1948)* The first world-class American film director.

is always a directness that entirely frees us from the itch to interpret. Many old Hollywood films, like those of Cukor, Walsh, Hawks,[28] and countless other directors, have this liberating antisymbolic quality, no less than the best work of the new European directors, like Truffaut's *Shoot the Piano Player* and *Jules and Jim*, Godard's *Breathless* and *Vivre sa Vie*, Antonioni's *L'Avventura*, and Olmi's[29] *The Fiancés*.

The fact that films have not been overrun by interpreters is in part   32 due simply to the newness of cinema as an art. It also owes to the happy accident that films for such a long time were just movies; in other words, that they were understood to be part of mass, as opposed to high, culture, and were left alone by most people with minds. Then, too, there is always something other than content in the cinema to grab hold of, for those who want to analyze. For the cinema, unlike the novel, possesses a vocabulary of forms—the explicit, complex, and discussable technology of camera movements, cutting, and composition of the frame that goes into the making of a film.

What kind of criticism, of commentary on the arts, is desirable to-   33 day? For I am not saying that works of art are ineffable, that they cannot be described or paraphrased. They can be. The question is how. What would criticism look like that would serve the work of art, not usurp its place?

What is needed, first, is more attention to form in art. If excessive   34 stress on *content* provokes the arrogance of interpretation, more extended and more thorough descriptions of *form* would silence. What is needed is a vocabulary—a descriptive, rather than prescriptive,[30] vocabulary—for forms.[31] The best criticism, and it is uncommon, is of

---

[28]*George Cukor (1899–1983); Raoul Walsh (1887–1980); Howard Hawks (1896–1977)* American filmmakers who were important before 1950.

[29]*François Truffaut (1931–1984); Jean-Luc Godard (b. 1930); Michelangelo Antonioni (b. 1912); Ermanno Olmi (b. 1931)* Important modern influences in the film.

[30]*descriptive, rather than prescriptive, vocabulary* A prescriptive vocabulary in criticism aims to establish what a work of art ought to be; a descriptive vocabulary concentrates on what is. Sontag encourages a criticism that tells us what has happened, not one that tells us what ought to happen.

[31]One of the difficulties is that our idea of form is spatial (the Greek metaphors for form are all derived from notions of space). This is why we have a more ready vocabulary of forms for the spatial than for the temporal arts. The exception among the temporal arts, of course, is the drama; perhaps this is because the drama is a narrative (i.e., temporal) form that extends itself visually and pictorially, upon a stage. What we don't have yet is a poetics of the novel, any clear notion of the forms of narration. Perhaps film criticism will be the occasion of a breakthrough here, since films are primarily a visual form yet they are also a subdivision of literature. [Sontag's note]

this sort that dissolves considerations of content into those of form. On film, drama, and painting respectively, I can think of Erwin Panofsky's essay "Style and Medium in the Motion Pictures," Northrop Frye's essay "A Conspectus of Dramatic Genres," Pierre Francastel's essay "The Destruction of a Plastic Space." Roland Barthes's book *On Racine* and his two essays on Robbe-Grillet are examples of formal analysis applied to the work of a single author. (The best essays in Erich Auerbach's *Mimesis,* like "The Scar of Odysseus," are also of this type.) An example of formal analysis applied simultaneously to genre and author is Walter Benjamin's essay "The Storyteller: Reflections on the Works of Nicolai Leskov."[32]

Equally valuable would be acts of criticism which would supply a   35 really accurate, sharp, loving description of the appearance of a work of art. This seems even harder to do than formal analysis. Some of Manny Farber's[33] film criticism, Dorothy Van Ghent's essay "The Dickens World: A View from Todgers'," Randall Jarrell's essay on Walt Whitman are among the rare examples of what I mean. These are essays which reveal the sensuous surface of art without mucking about in it.

Transparence is the highest, most liberating value in art—and in   36 criticism—today. Transparence means experiencing the luminousness of the thing in itself, of things being what they are. This is the greatness of, for example, the films of Bresson and Ozu and Renoir's[34] *The Rules of the Game.*

Once upon a time (say, for Dante),[35] it must have been a revolu-   37 tionary and creative move to design works of art so that they might be experienced on several levels. Now it is not. It reinforces the principle of redundancy that is the principal affliction of modern life.

Once upon a time (a time when high art was scarce), it must have   38 been a revolutionary and creative move to interpret works of art. Now it is not. What we decidedly do not need now is further to assimilate Art into Thought, or (worse yet) Art into Culture.

Interpretation takes the sensory experience of the work of art for   39

---

[32]***Panofsky and others*** These are all works by modern critics; they are the kind that Sontag feels will help to reinstate formal analysis.

[33]***Manny Farber and others*** These are examples of critics whose purpose is to describe accurately the surfaces of works of art.

[34]***Robert Bresson (b. 1907); Yasujiro Ozu (1903–1963); Alain Renoir (1894–1979)*** Directors who are or were significant influences on contemporary film-makers.

[35]***Dante Alighieri (1265–1321)*** Italian poet and scholar. His most important work was *The Divine Comedy.*

granted, and proceeds from there. This cannot be taken for granted now. Think of the sheer multiplication of works of art available to every one of us, super-added to the conflicting tastes and odors and sights of the urban environment that bombard our senses. Ours is a culture based on excess, on overproduction; the result is a steady loss of sharpness in our sensory experience. All the conditions of modern life—its material plenitude, its sheer crowdedness—conjoin to dull our sensory faculties. And it is in the light of the condition of our senses, our capacities (rather than those of another age), that the task of the critic must be assessed.

What is important now is to recover our senses. We must learn to *see* more, to *hear* more, to *feel* more.   40

Our task is not to find the maximum amount of content in a work   41
of art, much less to squeeze more content out of the work than is already there. Our task is to cut back content so that we can see the thing at all.

The aim of all commentary on art now should be to make works   42
of art—and, by analogy, our own experience—more, rather than less, real to us. The function of criticism should be to show *how it is what it is*, even *that it is what it is*, rather than to show *what it means*.

In place of a hermeneutics we need an erotics of art.   43

QUESTIONS

1. What does Sontag say about Plato's valuation of works of art? Does Plato's attitude toward art seem to derive naturally from his attitude toward mimesis? What is mimesis?
2. Sontag mentions two approaches to art: art as a statement of reality and art as a statement of the artist. Which of these is in agreement with your views of art?
3. What is Sontag's definition of interpretation? Is it satisfactory? Does her definition limit the nature of her argument?
4. Why would the Freudian idea of dreams having a manifest content and a latent content be of value to interpretation?
5. The term "hermeneutics" is used to describe a form of interpretation. What does Sontag seem to mean by this term?
6. What does Sontag mean by "an erotics of art"? Is it a useful term, or is it simply confusing?

WRITING ASSIGNMENTS

1. Sontag explains that works of art have a content and a form. She also explains that the terminology for formal elements in literary works is not as fully developed as it is for visual works. Therefore, it is difficult to talk about the form of a work of literature. If you were to comment on a work of literary art—of poetry, drama, or fiction—what formal elements would you have to discuss? Could you discuss them without performing an act of interpretation? Choose a specific work for your commentary. Root your discussion in an examination of one work.

2. Do you agree with Sontag about the artistic vitality of contemporary film? Using examples from films you have seen recently (whether on television or in a theater), defend or attack her judgment regarding the preeminence of the film among contemporary arts.

3. Establish what Sontag's views are on the form and content of a work of art. What does she think the problems are when making this distinction? Is she correct in assuming that this distinction may not be totally clear or totally tenable? How do you view this distinction? Is it reasonable? Is it difficult? Is it dangerous? Has your training in interpretation made this distinction more or less natural to you when approaching a work of art?

4. Sontag says in paragraph 6 that "most artists and critics have discarded the theory of art as representation of an outer reality in favor of the theory of art as subjective expression" and that "it is still assumed that a work of art *is* its content." To what extent do you think these statements are true? Refer to your experience in reading, in viewing paintings, or in experiencing other works of art. Is there any special problem in examining the form of a work of art if we assume that art is subjective expression—in other words, the expression of the artist's feelings or of his or her understanding of things? Would subjective expression be more likely to affect the content or the form of a work of art?

5. Take Sontag's advice and approach a favorite poem by doing as she says: create an erotics of art instead of a hermeneutics. In other words, follow up on what she says in her final words of advice in paragraph 42: "The aim of all commentary on art now should be to make the works of art—and, by analogy, our own experience—more, rather than less, real to us. The function of criticism should be to show *how it is what it is*, even *that it is what it is*, rather than to show *what it means*."

6. Offer a counterargument to Sontag's views. Write an essay called "In Defense of Interpretation" and try to establish clearly what interpretation is, how it functions, and why it is defensible. Why is it good? Why is it desirable? In the process, you may comment on any of Sontag's arguments and counter them in turn. Decide whether her distinction between form and content is acceptable and whether it is necessary to your argument. Use specific examples of your interpretation (or the interpretations of others) of works of art to defend your position.

SUGGESTIONS FOR FURTHER READING

———❧———

NICCOLÒ MACHIAVELLI

Anglo, Sydney. *Machiavelli: A Dissection.* New York: Harcourt, Brace, and World, 1970.

Bondanella, Peter. *Machiavelli and the Art of Renaissance History.* Detroit: Wayne State University Press, 1973.

Butterfield, Herbert. *The Structure of Machiavelli.* New York: Collins Books, 1962.

Jay, Anthony. *Management and Machiavelli: An Inquiry into the Politics of Corporate Life.* New York: Holt, Rinehart and Winston, 1968.

Jensen, De Lamar. *Machiavelli: Cynic, Patriot or Political Scientist?* Lexington, Mass.: D. C. Heath, 1960.

*Machiavelli, Niccolò. *The Viking Portable Machiavelli.* Edited and translated by Peter Bondanella and Mark Musa. New York: Viking Penguin, 1979.

---

*Starred entries throughout bibliographies indicate paperbacks or other inexpensive editions of the major works of these authors.

Olschki, Leonard. *Machiavelli the Scientist.* Berkeley, Calif.: Gallick Press, 1945.

Pocock, John. *The Machiavellian Moment.* Princeton, N.J.: Princeton University Press, 1974.

Parel, Anthony, ed. *The Political Calculus: Essays on Machiavelli's Philosophy.* Toronto: University of Toronto Press, 1972.

Ridofi, Roberto. *The Life of Machiavelli.* Translated by Cecil Grayson. Chicago: University of Chicago Press, 1963.

JEAN JACQUES ROUSSEAU

Blanchard, William. *Rousseau and the Spirit of Revolt.* Ann Arbor: University of Michigan Press, 1967.

Broome, Jack Howard. *Rousseau: A Study of His Thought.* New York: Barnes and Noble, 1963.

Cassirer, Ernst. *The Question of Jean Jacques Rousseau.* Translated and edited by Peter Gay. New York: Columbia University Press, 1954.

Chapman, John William. *Rousseau—Totalitarian or Liberal?* New York: Columbia University Press, 1956.

Dobinson, Charles Henry. *Jean Jacques Rousseau: His Thought and Its Relevance Today.* London: Methuen, 1969.

Huizinga, Jacob Herman. *Rousseau: The Self-Made Spirit.* New York: Grossman, 1976.

Masters, Roger. *The Political Philosophy of Rousseau.* Princeton, N.J.: Princeton University Press, 1968.

Murry, John Middleton. *Heroes of Thought.* New York: J. Messner, 1938.

Perkins, Merle. *Jean Jacques Rousseau on the Individual and Society.* Lexington: University Press of Kentucky, 1974.

*Rousseau, Jean Jacques. *The Annotated Social Contract.* Edited by Charles M. Sherover. New York: New American Library.

*Rousseau, Jean Jacques. *Confessions.* Translated by John M. Cohen. Baltimore: Penguin, 1953.

THOMAS JEFFERSON

Becker, Carl L. *The Declaration of Independence: A Study in the History of Political Ideas.* Rev. ed. New York: Knopf, 1966.

Brodie, Fawn M. *Thomas Jefferson: An Intimate History*. New York: Norton, 1974.

*Jefferson, Thomas. *The Life and Selected Writings of Thomas Jefferson*. Edited by Adrienne Koch and William Peden. New York: Modern Library, 1944.

*Jefferson, Thomas. *The Viking Portable Thomas Jefferson*. Edited by Merrill D. Peterson. New York: Viking Penguin, 1977.

Malone, Dumas. *Jefferson and His Time*. 6 vols. Boston: Little, Brown, 1948–1981.

Wills, Garry. *Inventing America: Jefferson's Declaration of Independence*. Garden City, N.Y.: Doubleday, 1978.

KARL MARX

Avineri, Schlomo. *The Social and Political Thought of Karl Marx*. London: Cambridge University Press, 1968.

Dupre, Louis. *The Philosophical Foundations of Marxism*. New York: Harcourt, Brace and World, 1966.

Fetscher, Irving. *Marx and Marxism*. New York: Herder and Herder, 1971.

Lichtheim, George. *Marxism: An Historical and Critical Study*. New York: Praeger, 1961.

Lukacs, Gyorgy. *History and Class Consciousness: Studies in Marxist Dialectics*. Cambridge, Mass.: MIT Press, 1971.

*Marx, Karl. *Capital*. 3 vols. New York: International Publishers, 1976.

*Marx, Karl. *The Communist Manifesto*. Edited by A. J. Taylor. Baltimore: Penguin, 1968.

Meszaros, Istvan. *Marx's Theory of Alienation*. New York: Harper and Row, 1972.

Ollman, Bertell. *Alienation: Marx's Conception of Man in Capitalist Society*. New York: Cambridge University Press, 1976.

Rubel, M., and M. Mamale. *Marx without Myth: A Chronological Study of His Life and Work*. New York: Harper and Row, 1975.

Tucker, Robert C. *The Marxian Revolutionary Idea*. New York: Norton, 1968.

FREDERICK DOUGLASS

Bontemps, Arna. *Free at Last: The Life of Frederick Douglass.* New York: Dodd, Mead, 1971.

Douglass, Frederick. *The Frederick Douglass Papers, Series One: Speeches, Debates, and Interviews, Volume I: 1841–1846.* Edited by John W. Blassingame, et al. New Haven, Conn.: Yale University Press, 1979.

Douglass, Frederick. *Frederick Douglass on Women's Rights.* Edited by Philip S. Foner. Westport, Conn.: Greenwood Press, 1976.

Douglass, Frederick. *The Life and Writings of Frederick Douglass.* Edited by Philip S. Foner. 5 vols. New York: International Publishers, 1950–1975.

*Douglass, Frederick. *Narrative of the Life of Frederick Douglass, an American Slave.* Edited by Benjamin Quarles. Cambridge, Mass.: Harvard University Press, 1960.

Foner, Philip S. *Frederick Douglass.* New York: Citadel, 1964.

Huggins, Nathan Irvin. *Slave and Citizen: The Life of Frederick Douglass.* Boston: Little, Brown, 1980.

Inge, Thomas, et al., eds. *Black American Writers: Bibliographical Essays,* Vol. 1. London: Macmillan, 1978.

Preston, Dickson J. *Young Frederick Douglass: The Maryland Years.* Baltimore: Johns Hopkins University Press, 1980.

Quarles, Benjamin. *Frederick Douglass.* Washington, D.C.: Associated Publishers, 1948.

Walker, Peter F. *Moral Choices: Memory, Desire, and Imagination in Nineteenth-Century American Abolition.* Baton Rouge: Louisiana State University Press, 1978.

Washington, Booker T. *Frederick Douglass.* Philadelphia: Jacobs, 1907.

HENRY DAVID THOREAU

Derleth, August William. *Concord Rebel: A Life of Henry David Thoreau.* Philadelphia: Cholton, 1962.

Hamilton, Franklin W. *Thoreau on the Art of Writing.* Flint, Mich.: Walden Press, 1967.

Harding, Walter Roy. *Henry David Thoreau: A Profile.* New York: Hill and Wang, 1971.

Gayet, Claude. *The Intellectual Development of Henry David Thoreau.* Stockholm: Almqvist and Wikseu International, 1981.

*Thoreau, Henry David. *The Best of Thoreau's Journal.* Edited by Carl Bode. Carbondale: Southern Illinois University Press, 1971.

*Thoreau, Henry David. *Collected Poems.* Edited by Carl Bode. Baltimore: Johns Hopkins University Press, 1964.

*Thoreau, Henry David. *Walden.* Edited by J. Lyndon Shanley. Princeton, N.J.: Princeton University Press, 1971.

*Thoreau, Henry David. *The Annotated Walden: Walden, or Life in the Woods.* New York: C. N. Potter, Crown, 1970.

*Thoreau, Henry David. *A Week on the Concord and Merrimack Rivers.* Edited by Carl Howde. Princeton N. J.: Princeton University Press, 1980.

ELIZABETH CADY STANTON

*Banner, Lois W. *Elizabeth Cady Stanton: A Radical for Woman's Rights.* Boston: Little, Brown, 1980.

DuBois, Ellen Carol. *Elizabeth Cady Stanton and Susan B. Anthony: Correspondence, Writings, and Speeches.* New York: Schocken, 1981.

Griffith, Elisabeth. *In Her Own Right: The Life of Elizabeth Cady Stanton.* New York: Oxford University Press, 1984.

Lutz, Alma. *Created Equal: A Biography of Elizabeth Cady Stanton.* New York: Octagon, 1974.

Oakly, Mary Anne B. *Elizabeth Cady Stanton.* Old Westbury, N.Y.: Feminist Press, 1972.

*Stanton, Elizabeth Cady. *Eighty Years and More: Reminiscences, (1815–1897).* New York: Schocken, 1971.

*Stanton, Elizabeth Cady. *History of Woman Suffrage.* New York: Arno Press, 1969.

*Stanton, Elizabeth Cady. *The Original Femininist Attack on the Bible.* New York: Arno Press, 1974.

Stanton, Elizabeth Cady. *The Woman's Bible.* New York: Arno Press, 1972.

MARTIN LUTHER KING, JR.

*King, Martin Luther, Jr. *Strength to Love.* Philadelphia: Fortress Press, 1981.

*King, Martin Luther, Jr. *Where Do We Go From Here: Chaos or Community?* Boston: Beacon Press, 1968.

*King, Martin Luther, Jr. *Why We Can't Wait.* New York: New American Library, 1965.

Lewis, David. *King: A Critical Biography.* New York: Praeger, 1970.

Lyght, Ernest Shaw. *The Religious and Philosophical Foundations in the Thought of Martin Luther King.* New York: Vantage Press, 1972.

Oates, Stephen B. *Let The Trumpet Sound: The Life of Martin Luther King, Jr.* New York: Harper and Row, 1982.

Ramachandram, G., and T. K. Mahadevan. *Nonviolence after Gandhi: A Study of Martin Luther King.* New Delhi: Gandhi Peace Foundation, 1968.

Walton, Hanes. *The Political Philosophy of Martin Luther King.* Westport, Conn.: Greenwich, 1971.

ADAM SMITH

Campbell, Thomas Douglas. *Adam Smith's Science of Morals.* London: Allen and Unwin, 1970.

Cropsey, Joseph. *Polity and Economy: An Interpretation of the Principle of Adam Smith.* The Hague: M. Nijhoff, 1957.

Dankert, Clyde Edward. *Adam Smith: Man of Letters and Economist.* Hicksville, New York: Exposition Press, 1974.

Foley, Vernard. *The Social Physics of Adam Smith.* West Lafayette, Ind.: Purdue University Press, 1976.

Macfie, Alec Lawrence. *The Individual in Society: Papers on Adam Smith.* London: Allen and Unwin, 1967.

Morrow, Clen Raymond. *The Ethical and Economic Theories of Adam Smith.* New York: A. M. Kelley, 1969.

*Smith, Adam. *Essays on Philosophical Subjects.* London: L. Richardson, 1822.

*Smith, Adam. *The Theory of Moral Sentiments.* Edinburgh: J. Ray, 1813.

Wilson, Thomas and Andrew S. Skinner. *The Market and the State: Essays in Honor of Adam Smith.* Oxford: Clarendon Press, 1976.

THOMAS ROBERT MALTHUS

Bonor, James. *Malthus and His Work.* New York: Macmillan, 1984.

Glass, David Victor. *Introduction to Malthus.* London: Watts, 1953.

James, Patricia D. *Population, Malthus, His Life and Times.* Boston: Routledge and Kegan Paul, 1977.

*Malthus, Thomas Robert. *Definitions in Political Economy.* New York: A. M. Kelley, 1963.

*Malthus, Thomas Robert. *An Essay on the Principles of Population.* London: Jay Murray, 1826.

*Malthus, Thomas Robert. *First Essays on Population, 1798.* London: Macmillan, 1966.

*Malthus, Thomas Robert. *The Pamphlets of Malthus.* New York: A. M. Kelley, 1970.

THORSTEIN VEBLEN

Diggins, John P. *The Bard of Savagery.* New York: Seabury Press, 1978.

Dorfman, Joseph. *Thorstein Veblen and His America.* New York: A. M. Kelley, 1966.

Riesman, David. *Thorstein Veblen: A Critical Reappraisal.* New York: Scribner's, 1953.

*Veblen, Thorstein. *The Portable Veblen.* Edited by Max Lerner. New York: Viking, 1950.

*Veblen, Thorstein. *The Theory of Business Enterprise.* New York: A. M. Kelley, 1965.

*Veblen, Thorstein. *The Theory of the Leisure Class.* Boston: Houghton Mifflin, 1973.

*Veblen, Thorstein. *The Higher Learning in America.* New York: B. W. Huebsch, 1918.

JOHN MAYNARD KEYNES

Harrod, Roy Forbes. *The Life of John Maynard Keynes.* New York: Harcourt, Brace, 1951.

Keynes, Milo, ed. *Essays on John Maynard Keynes.* London: Cambridge University Press, 1975.

*Keynes, John Maynard. *The Collected Writings.* London: Macmillan, 1971–1983.

*Keynes, John Maynard. *The Economic Consequences of the Peace.* New York: Harcourt, Brace, and Howe, 1920.

*Keynes, John Maynard. *The General Theory of Employment, Interest and Money.* New York: Harcourt, Brace, and World, 1965.

Minsky, Hyman P. *John Maynard Keynes.* New York: Columbia University Press, 1975.

Skidelsky, Robert. *John Maynard Keynes.* Vol. 1, *Hopes Betrayed, 1883–1920.* London: Macmillan, 1983.

Stein, Jerome L. *Monetarist, Keynesian, and New Classical Economics.* New York: New York University Press, 1983.

JOHN KENNETH GALBRAITH

*Galbraith, John Kenneth. *The Affluent Society.* Boston: Houghton Mifflin, 1978.

*Galbraith, John Kenneth. *The Age of Uncertainty.* Boston: Houghton Mifflin, 1977.

*Galbraith, John Kenneth. *Almost Everyone's Guide to Economics.* Boston: Houghton Mifflin, 1978.

*Galbraith, John Kenneth. *The Anatomy of Power.* Boston: Houghton Mifflin, 1983.

*Galbraith, John Kenneth. *A Contemporary Guide to Economics, Peace, and Laughter.* Boston: Houghton Mifflin, 1971.

*Galbraith, John Kenneth. *The Galbraith Reader.* Edited by the editors of Gambit. Ipswich, Mass.: Gambit, 1977.

*Galbraith, John Kenneth. *The Nature of Mass Poverty.* Cambridge, Mass.: Harvard University Press, 1979.

SIGMUND FREUD

Arlow, Jacob. *The Legacy of Sigmund Freud.* New York: International Universities Press, 1956.

Balogh, Penelope. *Freud: A Biographical Introduction.* New York: Scribner's 1972.

Clark, Ronald William. *Freud: The Man and the Cause.* London: Cape, 1980.

Fine, Reuben. *Freud: A Critical Reevaluation of His Theories.* New York: McKay, 1962.

Freeman, Lucy. *Freud Rediscovered.* New York: Arbor House, 1980.

*Freud, Sigmund. *General Selection from the Works of Sigmund Freud.* Garden City, N.Y.: Doubleday, 1957.

*Freud, Sigmund. *New Introductory Lectures in Psychoanalysis.* Edited by James Strachey. New York: Norton, 1965.

*Freud, Sigmund. *Outline of Psychoanalysis.* Edited by James Strachey. New York: Norton, 1970.

*Freud, Sigmund. *The Psychopathology of Everyday Life.* Edited by James Strachey. New York: Norton, 1971.

*Freud, Sigmund. *Three Contributions to the Theory of Sex.* Translated by A. A. Brill. New York: Dutton, 1962.

Fromm, Erich. *The Crisis of Psychoanalysis.* New York: Holt, Rinehart and Winston, 1970.

Jones, Ernest. *The Life and Work of Sigmund Freud.* Edited by Lionel Trilling and Steven Marcus. New York: Basic Books, 1961.

Masson, J. Moussaieff. *The Assault on Truth: Freud's Supression of the Seduction Theory.* New York: Farrar, Straus and Giroux, 1984.

Reiff, Philip. *Freud: The Mind of the Moralist.* Garden City, N.Y.: Doubleday, 1961.

Rosenfeld, Israel. *Freud: Character and Consciousness.* New York: University Books, 1970.

Stoodley, Bartlett. *The Concepts of Sigmund Freud.* Glencoe, Ill.: Free Press, 1959.

CARL JUNG

Fordheim, Frieda. *An Introduction to Jung's Psychology.* Baltimore: Penguin, 1954.

Hall, Calvin Springer. *A Primer of Jungian Psychology.* New York: New American Library, 1973.

Hannah, Barbara. *Jung: His Life and Work.* New York: Putnam, 1976.

*Jung, Carl. *Man and His Symbols.* New York: Dell, 1968.

*Jung, Carl. *Memories, Dreams, Reflections.* New York: Random House, 1965.

*Jung, Carl. *The Viking Portable Jung.* Edited by Joseph Campbell. New York: Viking Penguin, 1976.

Moreno, Artorio. *Jung, God, and Modern Man.* Notre Dame, Ind.: University of Notre Dame Press, 1970.

Prograff, Ira. *Jung's Psychology and Its Social Meaning.* New York: Julian Press, 1953.

Sanford, John. *The Invisible Partners: How the Male and Female in Each of Us Affects Our Relationships.* New York: Paulist Press, 1980.

Ulanov, Ann Bedford. *The Feminine in Jungian Psychology and in Christian Theology.* Evanston, Ill.: Northwestern University Press, 1971.

KAREN HORNEY

*Horney, Karen. *Feminine Psychology.* New York: Norton, 1967.

*Horney, Karen. *Neurosis and Human Growth.* New York: Norton, 1950.

*Horney, Karen. *The Neurotic Personality of Our Time.* New York: Norton, 1942.

*Horney, Karen. *Self-Analysis.* New York: Norton, 1937.

Rubin, Jack. *Karen Horney: Gentle Rebel of Psychoanalysis.* New York: Dial Press, 1978.

B. F. SKINNER

Hull, Clark Leonard. *Principles of Behavior: An Introduction to Behavior Theory.* New York: D. Appleton-Century, 1943.

McLeish, John. *The Science of Behavior.* London: Barrie and Rockliff, 1963.

*Skinner, B. F. *About Behaviorism.* New York: Random House, 1976.

*Skinner, B. F. *Beyond Freedom and Dignity.* New York: Bantam, 1972.

*Skinner, B. F. *Walden Two Revisited.* New York: Macmillan, 1976.

Staats, Arthur. *Social Behaviorism.* Homewood, Ill.: Dorsey, 1975.

Tilney, Frederick. *The Structural Basis of Behaviorism.* Philadelphia: J. B. Lippincott, 1930.

FRANCIS BACON

*Bacon, Francis. *Francis Bacon: A Selection of His Works.* Edited by Sidney Warhaft. Indianapolis: Odyssey Press, 1965.

*Bacon, Francis. *New Organon and Related Writings.* Edited by H. Fulton Anderson. Indianapolis: Bobbs-Merrill, 1960.

Eiseley, Loren. *Francis Bacon and the Modern Dilemma.* Lincoln: University of Nebraska Press, 1962.

Epstein, Joel. *Francis Bacon: A Political Biography.* Athens: Ohio University Press, 1977.

Farrington, Benjamin. *The Philosophy of Francis Bacon.* Liverpool: University Press, 1964.

Rossi, Paolo. *Francis Bacon: From Magic to Science.* Translated by Sacha Rabinovitch. Chicago: University of Chicago Press, 1968.

Stephens, James. *Francis Bacon and the Style of Science.* Chicago: University of Chicago Press, 1975.

Vickers, Brian. *Essential Articles for the Study of Francis Bacon.* Hamden, Conn.: Archon Books, 1968.

Wallace, Karl. *Francis Bacon on Communication and Rhetoric.* Chapel Hill: University of North Carolina Press, 1943.

CHARLES DARWIN

Appleman, Philip, ed. *Darwin.* New York: Norton, 1970.

Bannister, Robert. *Social Darwinism: Science and Myth in Anglo-American Social Thought.* Philadelphia: Temple University Press, 1979.

*Darwin, Charles. *The Autobiography of Charles Darwin.* Edited by Nora Barlow. New York: Norton, 1969.

*Darwin, Charles. *On the Origin of Species.* Edited by J. W. Burrow. Baltimore: Penguin, 1968.

*Darwin, Charles. *The Descent of Man and Selection in Relation to Sex.* Princeton, N.J.: Princeton University Press, 1981.

Eiseley, Loren. *Darwin's Century: Evolution and the Men Who Discovered It.* Garden City, N.Y.: Doubleday, 1958.

Himmelfarb, Gertrude. *Darwin and the Darwinian Revolution.* Garden City, N. Y.: Doubleday, 1962.

Irvine, William. *Apes, Angels, and Victorians.* New York: McGraw-Hill, 1955.

Miller, Jonathan. *Darwin for Beginners.* New York: Pantheon, 1982.

Russett, Cynthia. *Darwin in America.* San Francisco: Freeman, 1976.

C. P. SNOW

Greacen, Robert. *The World of C. P. Snow.* New York: London House and Maxwell, 1963.

Karl, Frederick Robert. *C. P. Snow: The Politics of Conscience.* Carbondale: S. Illinois University Press, 1963.

Leavis, F. R. *Nor Shall My Sword: Discourses on Pluralism, Compassion, and Social Hope.* New York: Barnes and Noble, 1972.

*Snow, C. P. *The Physicists.* Boston: Little, Brown, 1981.

*Snow, C. P. *The Conscience of the Rich.* London: Macmillan, 1958.

*Snow, C. P. *Corridors of Power.* New York: Scribner's, 1964.

*Snow, C. P. *Homecomings.* London: Macmillan, 1958.

*Snow, C. P. *The Two Cultures and the Scientific Revolution.* New York: Cambridge University Press, 1960.

GEORGE WALD

Abel, Ernest L. *Ancient Views on the Origins of Life.* Fairlawn, N. J.: Fairleigh Dickinson University Press, 1973.

Adler, Irving. *How Life Began.* New York: Harper and Row, 1977.

Anbar, Michael. *The Genesis of Life.* New York: Macmillan, 1985.

Day, William. *Genesis on Planet Earth.* New Haven: Yale University Press, 1984.

Hoyle, Fred. *Evolution from Space and Other Papers on the Origin of Life.* Hillside, N.J.: Enslow, 1982.

Oparin, Alexander. *Genesis and Evolutionary Development of Life.* Orlando, Fla.: Academic Press, 1969.

Thaxton, Charles B., et al. *The Mystery of Life's Origin: Reassessing Current Theories.* New York: Philosophical Library, 1984.

THOMAS KUHN

Gutting, Gary, ed. *Paradigms and Revolutions: Appraisals and Applications of Thomas Kuhn's Philosophy of Science.* Notre Dame, Ind.: University of Notre Dame Press, 1980.

*Kuhn, Thomas. *The Copernican Revolution: Planetary Astronomy in the Development of Western Thought.* Cambridge, Mass.: Harvard University Press, 1957.

*Kuhn, Thomas. *The Essential Tension: Selected Studies in Scientific Tradition.* Chicago: University of Chicago Press, 1979.

*Kuhn, Thomas. *The Structure of Scientific Revolutions.* 2nd ed. Chicago: University of Chicago Press, 1970.

STEPHEN JAY GOULD

*Gould, Stephen Jay. *Ever Since Darwin: Reflections in Natural History*. New York: Norton, 1977.

*Gould, Stephen Jay. *The Flamingo's Smile*. New York: Norton, 1985.

*Gould, Stephen Jay. *Hen's Teeth and Horse's Toes*. New York: Norton, 1983.

*Gould, Stephen Jay. *The Mismeasure of Man*. New York: Norton, 1981.

*Gould, Stephen Jay. *The Panda's Thumb: More Reflections in Natural History*. New York: Norton, 1980.

PLATO

Barrow, Robin. *Plato, Utilitarianism, and Education*. London: Routledge and Kegan Paul, 1975.

Brumbaugh, Robert Sherrick. *Plato for the Modern Age*. New York: Crowell-Collier, 1962.

Clegg, Jerry. *The Structure of Plato's Philosophy*. Lewisburg, Pa.: Bucknell University Press, 1976.

Cornford, Francis MacDonald. *Before and after Socrates*. Cambridge: Cambridge University Press, 1958.

Fox, Adam. *Plato for Pleasure*. London: Westhouse, 1945.

Grube, Georges. *Plato's Thought*. Boston: Beacon Press, 1958.

Gulley, Norman. *Plato's Theory of Knowledge*. New York: Barnes and Noble, 1962.

*Plato. *The Dialogues of Plato*. Edited by Justin D. Kaplan. New York: Washington Square Press, 1982.

*Plato. *The Viking Portable Plato*. Edited by Scott Buchanan. New York: Viking Penguin, 1977.

Rankin, H. D. *Plato and the Individual*. New York: Barnes and Noble, 1964.

Taylor, Alfred. *Plato: The Man and His Work*. London: Methuen, 1960.

Vlastos, Gregory. *Plato's Universe*. Seattle: University of Washington Press, 1975.

JOHN LOCKE

Aaron, Richard I. *John Locke.* 3rd ed. New York: Oxford University Press, 1971.

Jenkins, John H. *Understanding Locke: An Introduction to Philosophy Through John Locke's Essay.* Edinburgh: Edinburgh University Press, 1983.

Jolly, Nicholas. *Leibnitz and Locke.* New York: Oxford University Press, 1984.

*John Locke. *An Essay Concerning Human Understanding.* Edited by Peter H. Niddich. New York: Oxford University Press, 1979.

*John Locke. *Some Thoughts Concerning Education.* Edited by James L. Axtell. London: Cambridge University Press, 1968.

*John Locke. *Two Treatises of Government.* Edited by Peter Laslett. London: Cambridge University Press, 1967.

Maclean, Kenneth. *John Locke and English Literature of the Eighteenth Century.* New Haven: Yale University Press, 1936.

Richetti, John J. *Philosophical Writing: Locke, Berkeley, Hume.* Cambridge, Mass.: Harvard University Press, 1983.

Woodhouse, R. S. *Locke's Philosophy of Science and Knowledge.* Oxford: Basil Blackwell, 1971.

Yolton, John W. *Locke and the Compass of Human Understanding.* London: Cambridge University Press, 1970.

BERTRAND RUSSELL

Ayer, Alfred. *Bertrand Russell.* New York: Viking, 1972.

Booth, Wayne. *Modern Dogma and the Rhetoric of Assent.* Notre Dame, Ind.: University of Notre Dame Press, 1974.

Clark, Ronald William. *Bertrand Russell and His World.* New York: Thames and Hudson, 1981.

Dorward, Alan. *Bertrand Russell: A Short Guide to His Philosophy.* New York: Longmans, Green, 1951.

Gottschalk, Herbert. *Bertrand Russell: A Life.* New York: Roy, 1965.

Lewis, John. *Bertrand Russell: Philosopher and Humanist.* London: Laurence and Wishart, 1968.

Pears, David. *Bertrand Russell and the British Tradition in Philosophy.* London: Collins, 1967.

*Russell, Bertrand. *The Basic Writings of Bertrand Russell.* Edited by

Robert E. Egner and Lester E. Dennon. New York: Simon and Schuster, 1967.

*Russell, Bertrand. *Philosophical Essays.* New York: Simon and Schuster, 1968.

*Russell, Bertrand. *Problems of Philosophy.* New York: Oxford University Press, 1959.

*Russell, Bertrand. *Why I Am Not a Christian, and Other Essays on Religion and Related Subjects.* New York: Simon and Schuster, 1967.

Schoenman, Ralph, ed. *Bertrand Russell: Philosopher of the Century.* London: Allen and Unwin, 1967.

SIMONE WEIL

Cabaud, Jaques. *Simone Weil: A Fellowship in Love.* New York: Channel Press, 1965.

Davey, Marie Hagedleine. *The Mysticism of Simone Weil.* London: Rockcliff, 1951.

*Weil, Simone. *Gravity and Grace.* New York: Putnam, 1952.

*Weil, Simone. *Oppression and Liberty.* Amherst: University of Massachusetts Press, 1973.

*Weil, Simone. *Letter to a Priest.* New York: Putnam, 1954.

PAUL TILLICH

Armbrusker, Carl J. *The Vision of Paul Tillich.* New York: Sheed and Ward, 1967.

Pauck, Wilhelm. *Paul Tillich, His Life and Thought.* New York: Harper and Row, 1976.

Scharlemann, Robert P. *Reflection and Doubt in the Thought of Paul Tillich.* New Haven: Yale University Press, 1969.

*Tillich, Paul. *The Courage to Be.* New Haven: Yale University Press, 1952.

*Tillich, Paul. *Dynamics of Faith.* New York: Harper, 1958.

*Tillich, Paul. *My Search for Absolutes.* New York: Simon and Schuster, 1967.

*Tillich, Paul. *The New Being.* New York: Scribner's, 1955.

*Tillich, Paul. *On the Boundary: An Autobiographical Sketch.* New York: Scribner's, 1966.

*Tillich, Paul. *The Intellectual Legacy of Paul Tillich.* Edited by James R. Lyons. Detroit: Wayne State University Press, 1969.

ARISTOTLE

Adler, Mortimer. *Aristotle for Everybody: Difficult Thought Made Easy.* New York: Macmillan, 1978.

*Aristotle. *The Nichomachean Ethics.* Translated by Martin Ostwald. Indianapolis: Bobbs-Merrill, 1962.

*Aristotle. *The Pocket Aristotle.* Edited by Justin D. Kaplan. New York: Washington Square Press, 1982.

*Aristotle. *Poetics.* Edited by G. M. Kirkwood. New York: Norton, 1982.

*Aristotle. *Politics.* Rev. ed. New York: Viking Penguin, 1982.

Cherniss, Harold. *Aristotle's Criticism of Plato and the Academy.* Baltimore: Johns Hopkins University Press, 1944.

Davidson, Thomas. *Aristotle and Ancient Educational Ideals.* New York: Franklin, 1969.

Ferguson, John. *Aristotle.* New York: Twayne, 1972.

Hardie, William. *Aristotle's Ethical Theory.* New York: Oxford University Press, 1980.

Lloyd, Geoffrey. *Aristotle: The Growth and Structure of His Thought.* London: Cambridge University Press, 1968.

Lear, Jonathan. *Aristotle and Logical Theory.* London: Cambridge University Press, 1980.

Oates, Whitney. *Aristotle and the Problem of Value.* Princeton, N.J.: Princeton University Press, 1963.

Veatch, Henry. *Aristotle: A Contemporary Appreciation.* Bloomington: Indiana University Press, 1974.

GEORGE SANTAYANA

Arnett, Willard Eugene. *Santayana and the Sense of Beauty.* Bloomington: Indiana University Press, 1968.

Ashmore, Jerome. *Santayana, Art, and Aesthetics.* Cleveland: Press of Western Reserve University, 1966.

Butler, Richard. *The Life and Works of George Santayana.* Chicago: H. Regnery, 1960.

Kirkwood, Mossie May. *Santayana: Saint of the Imagination.* Toronto: University of Toronto Press, 1961.

Munitz, Milton Karl. *The Moral Philosophy of Santayana.* New York: Columbia University Press, 1939.

Munson, Thomas. *The Essential Wisdom of George Santayana.* New York: Columbia University Press, 1962.

*Santayana, George. *The Life of Reason.* 4 vols. New York: Dover, 1980–1982.

*Santayana, George. *Selected Critical Writings.* Edited by Norman Henfrey. New York: Cambridge University Press, 1968.

*Santayana, George. *The Sense of Beauty.* New York: Dover, 1955.

Schilpp, Paul Arthur, ed. *The Philosophy of George Santayana.* Evanston, Ill.: Northwestern University, 1940.

VIRGINIA WOOLF

Bell, Quentin. *Virginia Woolf: A Biography.* New York: Harcourt, Brace, Jovanovich, 1973.

Gordon, Lyndall. *Virginia Woolf: A Writer's Life.* London: Oxford University Press, 1984.

Rose, Phyllis. *A Woman of Letters: The Life of Virginia Woolf.* New York: Oxford University Press, 1981.

*Woolf, Virginia. *The Captain's Deathbed and Other Essays.* New York: Harcourt, Brace, 1950.

*Woolf, Virginia. *The Death of the Moth and Other Essays.* New York: Harcourt, Brace, 1942.

*Woolf, Virginia. *Moments of Being: Unpublished Autobiographical Works.* Edited by Jeanne Schulkind. New York: Harcourt, Brace, Jovanovich, 1973.

*Woolf, Virginia. *Night and Day.* New York: Harcourt, Brace, Jovanovich, 1973.

SUSANNE K. LANGER

*Langer, Susanne K. *Feeling and Form.* New York: Scribner's, 1953.

*Langer, Susanne K. *Mind: An Essay on Human Feeling.* 3 vols. Baltimore: Johns Hopkins University Press, 1967, 1973, 1982.

Langer, Susanne K. *Philosophical Sketches.* Baltimore: Johns Hopkins University Press, 1962.

*Langer, Susanne K. *Philosophy in a New Key.* 3rd ed. Cambridge, Mass.: Harvard University Press, 1957.

*Langer, Susanne K. *Problems of Art.* New York: Scribner's, 1957.

SUSAN SONTAG

*Sontag, Susan. *Against Interpretation and Other Essays.* New York: Farrar, Straus and Giroux, 1966.

*Sontag, Susan. *The Benefactor: A Novel.* New York: Farrar, Straus, 1963.

*Sontag, Susan. *Death Kit.* New York: Farrar, Straus and Giroux, 1970.

*Sontag, Susan. *I, Etcetera.* New York: Farrar, Straus and Giroux, 1970.

*Sontag, Susan. *Styles of Radical Will.* New York: Farrar, Straus and Giroux, 1969.

*Sontag, Susan. *Trip to Hanoi.* New York: Farrar, Straus, and Giroux, 1969.

Acknowledgments (continued from page iv)

Sigmund Freud. "Infantile Sexuality." From *The Basic Writings of Sigmund Freud,* translated and edited by Dr. A. A. Brill. Copyright 1938, copyright © renewed 1965 by Gioia B. Bernheim and Edmund R. Brill. Reprinted by permission. Originally from *Three Essays on the Theory of Sexuality* (1905).

John Kenneth Galbraith. "The Position of Poverty." From *The Affluent Society,* Second Edition, by John Kenneth Galbraith. Copyright © 1958, 1969 by John Kenneth Galbraith. Reprinted by permission of Houghton Mifflin Company.

Stephen Jay Gould. "Nonmoral Nature." With permission from *Natural History,* Vol. 91, No. 2. Copyright the American Museum of Natural History, 1982.

Karen Horney. "The Distrust Between the Sexes." Speech read before the Berlin-Brandenburg Branch of the German Women's Medical Association on November 20, 1930 as "Das Misstrauen zwischen den Geschlechtern." Die Ärztin, VII (1931), pp. 5–12. Reprinted in translation with the permission of the Karen Horney Estate.

Carl Jung. "The Concept of the Collective Unconscious." From *The Collected Works of C. G. Jung,* translated by R. F. C. Hull. Bollingen Series XX, Vol. 9, I: *The Archetypes and the Collective Unconscious.* Copyright © 1959, 1969 by Princeton University Press. Excerpt, pp. 42–53, reprinted by permission of Princeton University Press.

John Maynard Keynes. "Economic Possibilities for Our Grandchildren." Extract from Vol. 9, *Essays in Persuasion,* in *Collected Writings* by John Maynard Keynes. Reprinted by permission of Macmillan, London and Basingstoke.

Martin Luther King, Jr. "Letter from Birmingham Jail" (April 16, 1963). From *Why We Can't Wait* by Martin Luther King, Jr. Copyright © 1963 by Martin Luther King, Jr. Reprinted by permission of Harper & Row, Publishers, Inc.

Thomas S. Kuhn. "The Essential Tension: Tradition and Innovation in Scientific Research." From *The Third (1959) University of Utah Research Conference on the Identification of Scientific Talent (1959).* Permission granted by the University of Utah Press.

Susanne K. Langer. "Expressiveness." Originally titled "Expressiveness and Symbolism," © 1957 by Susanne K. Langer. Reprinted with permission of Charles Scribner's Sons.

John Locke. Sterling Lamprecht, "On Ideas as the Materials of All Our Knowledge" from *Locke Selections.* Copyright 1928 Charles Scribner's Sons; copyright renewed 1956. Reprinted with permission of Charles Scribner's Sons.

Niccolò Machiavelli. "The Qualities of the Prince." Excerpt from "The Prince" from *The Portable Machiavelli* translated by Peter Bondanella and Mark Musa. Copyright © 1979 by Viking Penguin Inc. Reprinted by permission of Viking Penguin Inc.

Jean Jacques Rousseau. "The Origin of Civil Society." From *Social Contract: Essays by Locke, Hume, and Rousseau*, edited by Sir Ernest Barker (1947). Reprinted by permission of Oxford University Press.

Bertrand Russell. "A Free Man's Worship." From *Mysticism and Logic* by Bertrand Russell. Reprinted by permission of George Allen & Unwin (Publishers) Ltd.

B. F. Skinner. "What Is Man?" From *Beyond Freedom and Dignity*, by B. F. Skinner. Copyright © 1971 by B. F. Skinner. Reprinted by permission of Alfred A. Knopf, Inc.

C. P. Snow. "The Moral Un-Neutrality of Science." © C. P. Snow, 1971. Reproduced by permission of Curtis Brown Ltd., London.

Susan Sontag. "Against Interpretation." From *Against Interpretation* by Susan Sontag. Copyright © 1964 by Susan Sontag. Reprinted by permission of Farrar, Straus, & Giroux, Inc.

Paul Tillich. "Symbols of Faith." From *Dynamics of Faith* by Paul Tillich, Volume X of the World Perspectives Series, planned and edited by Ruth Nanda Anshen. Copyright © 1957 by Paul Tillich.

Thorstein Veblen. "Pecuniary Emulation." From *The Theory of the Leisure Class*. Reprinted by permission of Houghton Mifflin Company.

George Wald. "The Origin of Life" by George Wald. Copyright © 1954 by Scientific American, Inc. All rights reserved.

Simone Weil. "Spiritual Autobiography." Reprinted with permission from *The Simone Weil Reader*, George Panichas, editor, copyright © 1976. Published by David McKay Company, Inc.

Virginia Woolf. "A Letter to a Young Poet." From *The Death of the Moth and Other Essays* by Virginia Woolf, copyright 1942 by Harcourt Brace Jovanovich, Inc.; renewed 1970 by Marjorie T. Parsons, Executrix. Reprinted by permission of Harcourt Brace Jovanovich, Inc., the Virginia Woolf Estate, and the Hogarth Press.

INDEX OF
RHETORICAL TERMS

To the Student

We regularly revise the books we publish in order to make them better. To do this well we need to know what instructors and students think of the previous edition. At some point your instructor will be asked to comment on *A World of Ideas*, Second Edition; now we would like to hear from you.

Please take a few minutes to rate the selections and complete this questionnaire. Send it to Bedford Books of St. Martin's Press, 29 Commonwealth Avenue, Boston, Massachusetts 02116. We promise to listen to what you have to say. Thanks.

School _____

School Location (city, state) _____

Course title _____

Instructor's name _____

	Definitely Keep	Probably Keep	Uncertain	Drop	Not Assigned
Part One					
Machiavelli	—	—	—	—	—
Rousseau	—	—	—	—	—
Jefferson	—	—	—	—	—
Marx	—	—	—	—	—
Douglass	—	—	—	—	—
Thoreau	—	—	—	—	—
Stanton	—	—	—	—	—
King	—	—	—	—	—
Part Two					
Smith	—	—	—	—	—
Malthus	—	—	—	—	—
Veblen	—	—	—	—	—
Keynes	—	—	—	—	—
Galbraith	—	—	—	—	—
Part Three					
Freud	—	—	—	—	—
Jung	—	—	—	—	—
Horney	—	—	—	—	—
Skinner	—	—	—	—	—

	Definitely Keep	Probably Keep	Uncertain	Drop	Not Assigned
Part Four					
Bacon	——	——	——	——	——
Darwin	——	——	——	——	——
Snow	——	——	——	——	——
Wald	——	——	——	——	——
Kuhn	——	——	——	——	——
Gould	——	——	——	——	——
Part Five					
Plato	——	——	——	——	——
Locke	——	——	——	——	——
Russell	——	——	——	——	——
Weil	——	——	——	——	——
Tillich	——	——	——	——	——
Part Six					
Aristotle	——	——	——	——	——
Santayana	——	——	——	——	——
Woolf	——	——	——	——	——
Langer	——	——	——	——	——
Sontag	——	——	——	——	——

Did you find the introductions to each selection helpful? How can we improve them? (Please use additional paper if necessary.)

_____

_____

Did your instructor assign the general introduction to the text? If so, did you find it useful?

_____

_____

Any general comments?

_____

_____

_____

Name _____ Date _____
Address _____